Praise for *The Romans*

"At last, a history of the Roman state as it has always been crying out to be told, and never has been! Not even Edward Gibbon, more than two hundred years ago, covered the full two-thousand-year span, as Edward J. Watts does here. And at last we learn the truth: that Rome's 'decline and fall' was brought about not by barbarian invaders from the east in the fifth and sixth centuries but by crusading Europeans from the Christian west in 1204. Watts tells this story with verve and aplomb, and a wealth of finely observed detail drawn from Roman historians' own accounts of their past."

—Roderick Beaton, author of *The Greeks*

"Here is the Roman story across two millennia, from the mists of the Iron Age to the medieval crusades. Sweeping and masterful, *The Romans* balances the themes of continuity and change, grand forces and individual characters. I'm often asked what one book on ancient Rome I would recommend—and now I have a new answer."

—Kyle Harper, author of *The Fate of Rome*

"Ed Watts tells the remarkable story of how Roman traditions of openness and flexibility allowed it to adjust and readjust to ever-changing circumstances over two millennia. Clearly written and well-informed, *The Romans* puts readers into direct contact with the voices of the Roman people over time and will become a classic in its own right."   —David Potter, author of *Constantine the Emperor*

"Watts's wonderfully readable and totally radical history asks us to see Rome as two millennia of Romans saw it—a highly flexible reference point, an argument for radical inclusion, and a set of enduring, if constantly reshaped, principles."

—Kimberly D. Bowes, University of Pennsylvania

"Lucid and accessible, *The Romans* is simply a splendid book that only Edward Watts could have written. He shows that Rome's march did not lead exclusively toward the Western Middle Ages. Rather, the book's magisterial sweep reveals Rome's immense resilience was thanks to its continuing embrace of foreigners, immigrants, the enslaved, and the poor, to whom it offered advancement and a future, and to its nimble administrative and economic structures. A fantastic, timely book."

—Susanna Elm, University of California, Berkeley

THE
ROMANS

ALSO BY EDWARD J. WATTS

The Eternal Decline and Fall of Rome:
The History of a Dangerous Idea

Mortal Republic: How Rome Fell into Tyranny

Hypatia: The Life and Legend of an Ancient Philosopher

The Final Pagan Generation:
Rome's Unexpected Path to Christianity

Riot in Alexandria: Tradition and Group Dynamics in
Late Antique Pagan and Christian Communities

City and School in Late Antique Athens and Alexandria

THE ROMANS

A 2,000-YEAR HISTORY

EDWARD J. WATTS

BASIC BOOKS
New York

Basic Books
Hachette Book Group
1290 Avenue of the Americas, New York, NY 10104
www.basicbooks.com

Printed in the United States of America

First Edition: October 2025

Published by Basic Books, an imprint of Hachette Book Group, Inc. The Basic Books name and logo is a registered trademark of the Hachette Book Group.

The Hachette Speakers Bureau provides a wide range of authors for speaking events. To find out more, go to www.hachettespeakersbureau.com or email HachetteSpeakers@hbgusa.com.

Basic Books may be purchased in bulk for business, educational, or promotional use. For more information, please contact your local bookseller or the Hachette Book Group Special Markets Department at special.markets@hbgusa.com.

The publisher is not responsible for websites (or their content) that are not owned by the publisher.

Print book interior design by Bart Dawson

Library of Congress Cataloging-in-Publication Data

Names: Watts, Edward J., 1975– author.
Title: The Romans : a 2,000-year history / Edward J. Watts.
Description: First edition. | New York : Basic Books, 2025. | Includes
  bibliographical references and index.
Identifiers: LCCN 2025003651 | ISBN 9781541619814 hardcover | ISBN
  9781541619821 ebook
Subjects: LCSH: Rome—History.
Classification: LCC DG209 .W37 2025 | DDC 937—dc23/eng/20250313
LC record available at https://lccn.loc.gov/2025003651

ISBNs: 9781541619814 (hardcover), 9781541619821 (ebook)

LSC-C

Printing 1, 2025

To Carol Vassiliadis

Note on Spelling of Roman Personal and Place Names

The language spoken by most citizens of the Roman state shifts from Latin to Greek during the events narrated in this book. I have found it impossible to use a standardized form of transliteration for Roman names without confusing readers. In general, I have chosen the spelling that I think is most familiar. I use English names for the people or places that are already well known and speak about "Rome" instead of "Roma" and "Constantine" instead of "Constantinus" or "Konstantinos." I use Latinized spellings of Greek or Latin names when these are well known to English speakers, as in the case of the emperor "Alexius Comnenus" instead of "Alexios Komnenos." When the name is unfamiliar to readers, however, I do not generally Latinize Greek names or render Latin names into English.

CONTENTS

Contents

Contents

PART 7
FROM ALEXIUS COMNENUS TO NICETAS CHONIATES

THE
ROMANS

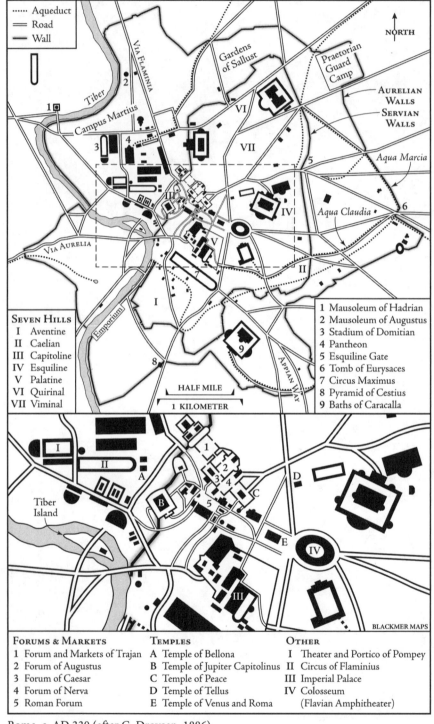

Legend (top left):

······ Aqueduct
═══ Road
━━━ Wall

NORTH

VIA FLAMINIA

Tiber

Gardens of Sallust

Praetorian Guard Camp

AURELIAN WALLS
SERVIAN WALLS

Campus Martius

VI

VII

Aqua Marcia

5

Aqua Claudia

6

III

IV

II

VIA AURELIA

V

Emporium

I

II

9

APPIAN WAY

8

SEVEN HILLS

I Aventine
II Caelian
III Capitoline
IV Esquiline
V Palatine
VI Quirinal
VII Viminal

HALF MILE

1 KILOMETER

1 Mausoleum of Hadrian
2 Mausoleum of Augustus
3 Stadium of Domitian
4 Pantheon
5 Esquiline Gate
6 Tomb of Eurysaces
7 Circus Maximus
8 Pyramid of Cestius
9 Baths of Caracalla

Inset (bottom):

I
II
A
Tiber Island
B
1
2
3 4
5
C
D
E
III
IV

BLACKMER MAPS

FORUMS & MARKETS
1 Forum and Markets of Trajan
2 Forum of Augustus
3 Forum of Caesar
4 Forum of Nerva
5 Roman Forum

TEMPLES
A Temple of Bellona
B Temple of Jupiter Capitolinus
C Temple of Peace
D Temple of Tellus
E Temple of Venus and Roma

OTHER
I Theater and Portico of Pompey
II Circus of Flaminius
III Imperial Palace
IV Colosseum
(Flavian Amphitheater)

Rome, c. AD 330 (after G. Droysen, 1886)

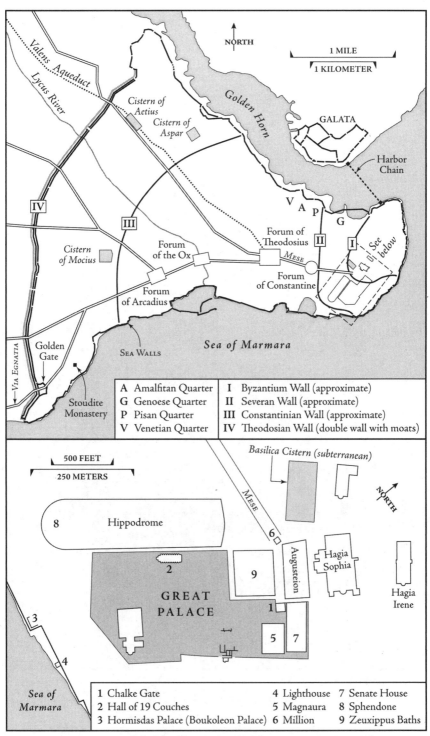

Constantinople, c. AD 1204 (above), with detail of the Great Palace area (below; after Müller-Wiener, 1977)

Republican Roman Italy

Introduction

The Two Millennia
of the Roman State

T HIS BOOK ANSWERS a simple question that is never asked. How did the Roman state survive for nearly 2,000 years?

The Roman polity began in the eighth century BC as a Latin-speaking, polytheistic monarchy set on seven hills above the Tiber River in Central Italy, and it ended in the early thirteenth century AD as a Greek-speaking, Christian empire centered on Constantinople just as the gunpowder age was dawning in Eurasia. In its two millennia, nearly everything changed about the Roman state and the world around it. And yet the state itself endured. Why?

We do not think to ask that question because the history of the Roman state is so long, the sources available to tell it so abundant, and the characters it features so diverse that historians tend to specialize in only certain periods of time. Scholars have traditionally divided Roman history into four periods: early Rome (from roughly the eighth century BC until about 300 BC), the middle and later phases of the Roman Republic (300 BC–31 BC), the high empire (31 BC–AD 180), and the late empire (AD 180–AD 395).

Until 395, Roman history is the unified study of a Roman state that, at its largest extent, stretched from Morocco to Mesopotamia and from Saudi Arabia to Scotland. In 395, this vast empire separated into an eastern Roman administration, centered on the city of

1

Constantinople, and a western Roman administration, based in Italy. This division was never intended to be permanent, and legally, both the eastern and western empires remained a single state. A law issued in Constantinople in AD 439, for example, applied to the entire empire, and bore two names: that of the eastern emperor, Theodosius II, and that of the western emperor, Valentinian III.

The fates of the two halves of the empire diverged in the fifth century AD as Rome lost territory in the west while retaining its land and people in the east. These divergent futures often invite scholars and students to focus on either the west or the east. Those working on the west attempt to explain how the Roman west transformed into the post-Roman world of early medieval Europe. Those working on the east continue looking at the Roman state, but, conventionally, they are no longer called Roman historians. Instead, most people now call them Byzantinists, and traditionally they define their period of study as one that begins with the dedication of Constantinople in AD 330.

The people that we now call "Byzantines," however, would not have understood that name.[1] They called themselves Romans. They called their state Romanía. And they called their language—which we now call Greek—Romeika.[2] Their history is Roman history, and, until 1204, the state they lived in was the same one that birthed Brutus, Julius Caesar, and Marcus Aurelius. Even though the Romans living at the end of that era had no doubts about their connection to the state that Romulus had supposedly founded some 2,000 years before their own time, their Roman polity is not studied today in a fashion that emphasizes this link.

On one level, this is completely understandable. The history of the Roman Empire in the thirteenth century AD is reconstructed using long narrative histories that are supplemented by personal letters, speeches, illustrated manuscripts, coins, jewelry, and personalized lead seals that once secured shipments of goods. We can worship in the same churches that Romans used in that period, see artworks Romans commissioned, and interact with objects bearing the names of the Romans who created them.

None of this is possible for the eighth century BC. There are no reliable texts for this period, because Romans did not yet have an alphabet. There are no buildings left, because the earliest Romans built flimsy structures out of perishable materials. And the precious few objects that survive cannot be tied to any individual people whose names we know. These immense differences in surviving sources mean that historians working at the beginning of Roman history and those working at its end ask different sorts of questions and tell different sorts of stories. It is easy to throw up one's hands and say that the vastness of Roman history makes a unified narrative impossible.

And yet there are important reasons why we should try to tell the entire Roman story without divisions. The different periods of Roman history that we have created are convenient for us, now, in the twenty-first century, but they do not reflect the experience of the Romans who lived through the events we describe. No Roman woke up in 300 BC and thanked the gods that she had made it out of early Roman history and entered the Middle Republic. And no one from the medieval Eastern Roman Empire would understand the modern decision to strip their recent ancestors of their Romanness and call them Byzantines on the day Constantinople was dedicated in AD 330. Most of the people we call Byzantines not only never lived in Constantinople, but never visited the city. To them, the use of that name as we apply it today would seem incomprehensible, at best, and insulting, at worst. It would be as if someone in a lunar colony in the thirty-sixth century decided that everyone who had lived in the western United States had stopped being Americans and started being Angelenos after Los Angeles became the second-largest city in the United States on April 7, 1984. If we remember that date at all, it is as the answer to an obscure trivia question, not an epoch-defining moment. If we would not accept that sort of distortion of our own identities by someone in the future, we should not do it to people in the past.

Telling the entire history of the Roman state, from beginning to end, allows us to get closer to the experiences and expectations of the Romans who lived in it, because in doing so, we do not artificially divide their lives into units they would not recognize. More importantly, when we acknowledge that the history of the Roman state spans two millennia, we can begin to see what features made it so enduring.

The Roman state survived for so long, in so many different conditions, because of the willingness of Romans to adapt to the world around them by incorporating new ideas and new approaches to every aspect of their personal and political lives. Romans did not invent representative democracy, or monotheism, or the concept of citizenship, but they did figure out how to make these ideas work on a larger scale than anyone in the ancient world had previously thought possible.

From the very beginning of their society, Romans "gladly received all strangers and made them citizens" while offering newcomers opportunities to succeed in ways that their own homelands did not.[3] Romans were unique among ancient and medieval societies in their willingness to grant large numbers of foreign-born people full membership in their political, religious, and economic life. This was true even of slaves, who received Roman citizenship when they were freed. While restrictive citizenship laws meant that other ancient societies, such as Athens or Sparta, could not easily grow their citizen bodies, Rome constantly expanded the ranks of its citizens, until, in AD 212, every free man, woman, and child in its vast empire received the rights and assumed the obligations of a Roman citizen. There were perhaps 60 million of them.

Romans did not just incorporate others by making them Roman. The Roman state also facilitated processes through which Roman life evolved to make use of the technology, ideas, and talents of these new Romans. It accepted new gods, adopted new ways of fighting, implemented new agricultural practices, and made use of new medical practices. New Romans continually infused their adopted polity with a vitality that older, less open societies in the ancient and medieval worlds never matched.

Although the long-term history of the Roman state reflects a national character defined by resilience, adaptability, and an

4

uncommon willingness to modify fundamental elements of Roman identity, Rome was also a profoundly conservative society, in which tradition moderated and calmed the pace of change. Romans welcomed the contributions of newcomers, but their state worked best when the push of the new was restrained somewhat by the pull of the old. Often, as this book will show, Roman reactionaries behaved in a fashion that seems ridiculous to us. It is hard not to laugh when senators in the early second century BC bemoaned the collapse in public morals that they believed had followed the introduction of pedestal tables from Greece. Surely all would be well with the world, they suggested, if only all Roman tables had four legs.[4] In other cases, however, Roman conservatives had a point. Rome certainly would have been better off if emperors like Nero had listened to some of the figures who tried to slow their efforts to remake the empire.

Rome's long-term success depended on its repeated ability to (mostly) strike an appropriate balance between change and tradition. Rome offered protection and a playing field with predictable rules on which talented newcomers could pursue their ambitions, but these attractive qualities merely catalyzed a long process through which Romans and non-Romans grew to trust and understand each other. Both Romans and non-Romans had to believe that the accommodations and sacrifices they made contributed to the long-term success of the community that they hoped to build together.

This point brings another essential ingredient of the Roman recipe for a long political life into focus: time. It took decades, and in some cases centuries, for this kind of trust to develop. When the process moved at its own pace, the state became stronger as its old and new members joined with each other. When Romans and non-Romans rushed to embrace each other too quickly, however, the relationship could seem insincere or transactional. In the worst cases, the two sides became wary of one another amid fears on the part of one that the other was simply using it to achieve its own short-term goals. These suspicions could even lead to bloodshed. Sometimes, as when the dictator Sulla massacred 6,000 Samnites whose recently granted Roman citizenship he refused to recognize, the deaths were caused by Romans unwilling to accept their new countrymen. In other cases, as when Goths were placed on the front lines of a bloody battle in 394, the new Romans turned against leaders they felt were using them as human cannon fodder. Fortunately, these disasters were strikingly rare. The state usually provided both old and new Romans with the time, security, and prosperity they needed to grow together.

There are two other elements of our story that I need to clarify before we start. The first is a seemingly simple question of definition. What is the Roman state? For the purposes of this book, I mean the political entity that took shape in the city of Rome, probably during the eighth century BC, and persisted without interruption until it was destroyed when the Fourth Crusade captured Constantinople and dissolved its government in AD 1204.

Both the beginning and the end points require some explanation. I chose to begin in the eighth century both because this roughly corresponds to the traditional date Romans used for the foundation of their city and because that date is consistent with some of the earliest archaeologically attested activity on the site of Rome. It is, of course, hard to say with any certainty what political life was like in Rome in the eighth or even most of the seventh century BC. That Rome was poor, lightly populated, and not terribly sophisticated. And yet, when the lights do begin to flicker on around the turn of the sixth century, we see robust political structures and institutions consistent with a monarchy that governed an aristocratically dominated society. I can't say for sure when these state structures first developed, but they were firmly in place when our sources begin to shift from mythological tales about wolves suckling foundlings to narratives of plausible historical events. If Romans say, and archaeology confirms, that some sort of political community existed on the Palatine then, I am willing to go along.

What can we say about the continuity of this state? Rome, after all, begins as a monarchy, becomes a republic, and then, for the last 60 percent of its history, is ruled by emperors. These changes in the Roman constitution do not, however, represent the end of the Roman state. There are a few good reasons for this. First, there is well-documented continuity in state institutions following these radical shifts in the nature of Roman government. So, for example, assemblies like the Comitia Centuriata, founded by the king Servius Tullius in the sixth century BC, continue meeting and performing roughly the same functions after the Republic replaces the monarchy. And after Augustus becomes emperor, in the first century BC, Rome retains the same legal system and many of the offices it did under the Republic.

Second, no Roman governing structure was so ossified that it resisted change. The Roman Republic repeatedly adapted and changed its constitution to such a degree that no one alive in 509 BC would have recognized the Republic as Cicero understood it 450 years later.[5] And yet no one would say that the Roman state ended at any point in this period. The empire also changed immensely between Augustus and its end in 1204. Even the monarchy, the most poorly attested of the Roman eras, evolved dramatically in the period of the final three kings, the only moments where we have anything like a semi-reliable narrative. Constitutional evolution, and even revolution, does not end a state.

But conquest does. And this is why I believe the Roman state ended in AD 1204 and not the conventionally recognized date of 1453. As you will see when we reach the Fourth Crusade, the Crusaders' capture of Constantinople represents a rupture that is quite different from the Roman-led revolutions that shifted the monarchy to a republic and then a republic to an empire. The Crusaders took Roman territory and, instead of respecting the legal and institutional systems in place, they imposed their own, foreign ways of doing things. They did not adapt the existing Roman state. They destroyed it and replaced it with something very different. Roman sources themselves say this explicitly. After Constantinople fell, free Romans remained—but they lived in a constellation of various Roman-run states that were set up in the Balkans and in Asia Minor to resist the Crusaders. All of them eventually developed into their own statelets, and ultimately, one of these Roman-run kingdoms, based in the city of Nicaea, managed to reconquer Constantinople in 1261. This was the political entity extinguished by the Ottomans in 1453. It was undeniably a Roman state, but it had no direct institutional link to the Roman state that had been founded on the Italian Peninsula in the eighth century BC. That connection had been severed by the Crusaders.

There is one other matter to address before we start our story. Because the narrator's perspective matters greatly in shaping a story's telling, I want to be explicit about the choices I have made. I firmly believe that individuals matter in history, and particularly, in Roman history, but so do the systems in which they operate. When Romans themselves spoke of their state, they usually agreed with Cicero that it was "the property of the people," who were "a multitude joined to one another by a consensus about law and the common good."[6] Romans never lost the sense that their polity needed to act in a fashion that reflected its citizens' consensus about what was lawful and what was good for all.

Strong political institutions, and, eventually, a durable and trust-worthy legal system, helped Rome remain connected to this citizen consensus. These structures often restrained the bad impulses of people and channeled their energies in appropriate directions, but Roman history is not just a history of its systems. It is instead dominated by a dynamic process through which these systems sometimes bent to the will and ideas of individuals. Roman systems fostered stability, but people, not systems, were the drivers of change in Rome. Individual Romans were the ones who pushed their fellow citizens to think in new ways about what should be lawful and good by changing outdated elements of their legal, political, religious, or military systems. They were also the ones who sometimes overreached and needed to be checked.

The history of the Roman state, then, is really a history of the Romans who shaped it as well as the institutions that guided and channeled their labor. By that measure, every person discussed in this book belonged to the Roman elite at some point in their lives. But the dynamism of the Roman state ensured that the people who belonged to the elite at any single moment came from both aristocratic and more humble backgrounds. Many of the men and women who ended their lives among the powerful and privileged began their lives as slaves, foreigners, peasants, internal migrants, and people forcibly displaced from their homes. While this is, in one way, a story focused on the elites who shaped the Roman state, it is just as much a story about the opportunities Rome presented to people born in poverty. This difference in perspective often derives simply from whether one is paying more attention to a figure's social standing at the time of death or to that same individual's social standing at birth.

This is as true of women as it is of men. While there were usually (but not always) limits on the sorts of public roles Roman women could play in their state, they understood what those limits were and how to regularly exercise the financial, symbolic, and political resources they possessed to change the direction of the state around them. Not only were these opportunities available to them, but women across Roman history understood how to use the real power they possessed to shift policy in the ways they wanted. Roman women were neither invisible nor powerless, nor were they without agency. And they certainly were not, as some male authors in the early empire assumed, waiting in the shadows until they could do something treacherous. Women were always active in the operation of the Roman political system, though in ways that were different from men and not always noticed or understood by the men writing histories. This means that I am not always able to speak at length about how Roman women influenced events in this narrative. But, even if the evidence for their activities is now sparse, we need to remember that they were there and their input mattered—even if it was not always documented.

Roman history, then, is the story of a very, very durable political entity that lasted for nearly twenty centuries, but it is also filled with charismatic, compelling, and inspiring people. This book will tell both stories—that of the state, and those of the eighty generations of Roman men and women who sustained, challenged, and changed it.

PART 1

FROM ROMULUS TO HANNIBAL

Chapter 1

Foundations

800–615 BC

A NY COMPREHENSIVE HISTORY of the Roman state must begin by acknowledging how unlikely Rome's achievement would have seemed to contemporaries at the time of its birth. The Mediterranean basin is filled with much older societies than that which emerged in Rome. Egypt urbanized, unified, and created a state more than 2,500 years before the site of Rome even had permanent buildings. Areas of Palestine, Syria, and Mesopotamia also urbanized and created sophisticated polities thousands of years before Rome. Even the Greek world was more than 1,000 years ahead of the Romans in developing political structures, systems of writing, and extensive trade networks.

As difficult as it may be for us to imagine, Central Italy remained an extremely backward land of pastoralists and itinerant herdsmen, without much evidence of fixed sites of habitation, through 1200 BC. The Italian Peninsula at that time was heavily forested and sparsely populated, with nothing more permanent than scattered hilltop settlements that probably housed less than 100 people each. These settlements slowly expanded until, by 900 BC, a few of them may have contained more than 1,000 people. Metal tools and signs of increasing agricultural production also point to the emergence of a more intensively farmed and thickly settled peninsula around that time.[1]

But Italy still had a long way to go. While finds of Mycenaean pottery in Southern Italy suggest there was trade linking the peninsula with the Greek world in the Bronze Age, there is little indication that the Italians had much to offer these Greek traders beyond raw materials.[2] Indeed, there is no evidence of any sort of finished Italian products making an impact in Greece. To whatever degree this exchange happened, it consisted of people from the economically and technologically advanced east trading with an underdeveloped Italy.

Rome was not even one of the first cities to develop on the relatively backward Italian Peninsula. The first signs of habitation in what is now the city of Rome are some graves dating to around 1000 BC.[3] By the late 800s BC, some small villages, of perhaps 100 or so people, had developed atop the Palatine, Capitoline, and Quirinal Hills. By the early 700s, population growth seems to have led the villages to blend into one another, with the settled area expanding down the hills to include the lowland area between the Palatine and Capitoline Hills—the area we know now as the Roman Forum.

The growth of these settlements should not blind us to their extremely primitive nature. They were villages filled with mud and clay huts erected around wooden posts stuck in holes drilled in the rock. In fact, we have an extremely good idea of what these huts would have looked like. Some eighth-century postholes have been found on the Palatine Hill, and contemporary burial practices in and around the site of Rome involved putting the ashes of the dead into hut-shaped clay vessels that are scale models of structures that match the layout of those Palatine postholes.[4] The inexpensive nature and poor quality of the grave goods enclosed in these burial urns reinforce our impression of an early Roman society in which everyone shared a similar level of poverty, at least relative to the larger and much more sophisticated urban centers of the eastern and southern Mediterranean.

The site that would become Rome had great potential, however. Its seven hills occupied defensible high ground above the spot where western Italy's main north-south coastal artery intersected with the Via Salaria, the ancient route joining the Italian interior to the sea.

The Isola Tiberina, an island in the middle of the Tiber River just west of the Capitoline Hill, offered a natural point for travelers to cross the river. Since the era's small seagoing ships could go no farther up the river, Rome served as a natural port where traders could offload their wares to Italian merchants and consumers who could in turn easily transport them east, north, and south. At the same time, as a port located upriver from the Mediterranean, Rome avoided the risk of naval attack.[5]

It is impossible to say when the settlements on the Palatine, Capitoline, and Quirinal Hills merged or when they began to call themselves Rome, but it is certain that Rome developed because these settlements expanded until they overlapped with one another. In the first century AD, the antiquarian Pliny described how Rome's "structures spread out so that they added many other cities to it," and he identifies two places, "Saturnia, on the site of the present city of Rome," and "Antipolis, now the Janiculum, forming part of Rome," as distinct polities that "have passed away" because Rome subsumed them.[6] The Capitoline, Aventine, Quirinal, and Viminal Hills, all of which would eventually be part of the canonical list of Rome's seven hills, do not appear on the list.[7]

The historical record also distinguishes between the community centered on the Palatine and another based around the Quirinal Hill. Romans had two distinct sets of priests, the Salii Palatini, associated with the Palatine, and the Salii Collini, connected to the Quirinal. Romans called themselves both Romani and Quirites, a term derived from the Quirinal Hill, and identified Castor and Pollux, the twin sons of Zeus, who are also called the Dioscuri, as the guardians of the state. Although the details about how the two hills joined one another are murky, their pairing echoed through Roman memory for centuries.[8]

The stories that Romans told about the foundation of their city also emphasize both territorial expansion and the incorporation of other groups. Unlike, say, Athenians, Romans never claimed to be a homogeneous people tied to one spot of land. They believed that they were a diverse, polyglot community founded by immigrants who came to the hills beside the Tiber and established a society that integrated people from surrounding areas.

Romans so prized their society's unique talent for incorporating others that their foundation myths grew into a nearly unintelligible tangle of overlapping and often contradictory events highlighting the roles played by multiple groups of people in the city's creation. Our fullest surviving Roman discussions of the foundation of the city come from the first century BC, more than seven centuries after the settlements in the Roman hills began to converge upon one another. These stories are not at all historical, but they reflect important truths about the innate characteristics Romans believed their society possessed.

Dionysius of Halicarnassus, a Greek speaker living in Rome at the end of the first century BC, wrote that Romans grew "from the smallest nation to the greatest ... by sharing the rights of citizenship with all who had been conquered by them in war," by "permitting all slaves who were freed by them to become citizens," and by including in their state all men "from whom [they] might gain an advantage."[9] Dionysius explained that Rome's capacity to get the best out of its heterogeneous population began when a Greek expedition led by Evander, a son of the god Hermes, established the first settlement on the Palatine more than sixty years before the Trojan War.[10] A few years later, Hercules pastured cattle on the future site of the Circus Maximus and gave some of his soldiers leave to settle on the Capitoline Hill.[11] Then, after the fall of Troy, the Trojan hero Aeneas, a son of Venus, led his people to Italy, settling not on the site of Rome itself, but in the nearby city of Lavinium. Aeneas's son Ascanius then founded the city of Alba Longa in the Alban Hills outside of Rome. The twins Romulus and Remus, the legendary founders of Rome, were descended from the ruling house of this city.[12]

The story of Romulus and Remus represents the best known of the Roman foundation myths.[13] They were the twin sons of Rhea Silva, a descendant of Aeneas and the daughter of Numitor, the deposed but rightful king of Alba Longa. When Numitor's brother Amulius seized the throne, he forced Rhea Silvia to become a Vestal Virgin, and as such she was forbidden from having any intercourse with men. One day, when she was gathering water from a spring sacred to the god Mars, the divinity seized and raped her before revealing his identity to her and promising that the twins he sired would be great warriors.[14] When the twins were born, Amulius ordered them to be left in the wilderness so that they would die of starvation or be adopted by someone who would not know their identities. They were discovered beside the Tiber River at the foot of the Palatine Hill and nursed by a Lupa, traditionally understood as a female wolf (though, as Dionysius and other authors note, this Latin word also means a prostitute).[15] A herdsman named Faustulus took the boys in, named them Romulus and Remus, and raised them as his own. After tending his flocks for some time, the twins learned their identity, returned to Alba Longa with armed followers, overthrew Amulius, and placed their grandfather back in power.[16] He tasked them with leading a group of people back to the site where the wolf had nursed them in order to colonize it, and the twins and their followers set off for the area that would become the city of Rome.

Tensions between the boys surfaced almost immediately. Romulus wanted to establish the city at the Palatine and name it after himself. Remus preferred a different site, a location that later bore the name Remoria. The twins first asked Numitor to decide who should lead the colony, but their grandfather instructed them to request guidance from the gods by observing the behavior of birds. The two brothers fell into deeper conflict when the auspices indicated that the gods favored Romulus, and eventually Romulus killed his brother. He then propitiated the gods and established his city, Rome, on the Palatine.[17]

Dionysius emphasizes that Romulus's Rome drew together the various peoples who had previously settled in the area. It included the people who had accompanied "Evander and the Arcadians, who settled round the Palatine hill"; the "Peloponnesians, who came along with Hercules and settled upon the Saturnian hill"; and "those who left Troy and were intermixed with the earlier settlers."[18] This framing allowed Dionysius to tie together multiple traditions about Rome's foundation into one relatively coherent story supporting his view that Rome represented a diverse community that drew upon the strengths of its various constituents to become greater than any of them could become alone. He hoped his reader would "forever renounce the views of those who make Rome a retreat of barbarians, fugitives and vagabonds, and let him confidently affirm it to be a Greek city."[19] Left unsaid was the fact that a reader who accepted this argument must also accept that Greeks in Dionysius's own time stood not as outsiders in Rome but as fundamental participants in the community of Romans from the very beginning of Roman history.

Few Romans would have agreed that Rome was a Greek city, but they shared Dionysius's belief that their community grew stronger through the incorporation of others. Livy, a first-century BC contemporary of Dionysius who wrote a massive history of Rome in Latin, describes how Romulus populated his new city by opening it up as a refuge for bandits, escaped slaves, and other "rabble."[20] This rabble was overwhelmingly made up of single men, but Romulus devised a plan to even out the population. He invited many of the city's neighbors to attend a festival for Neptune; they came, and, during the event, the unmarried Roman men seized the single women, most of whom were Sabines, and forced them into marriage.

It was common in the ancient world for conquering men to seize young female captives, but these acts of war usually resulted in the enslavement of the young women. Romulus instead reassured the women that they "would have the full rights of marriage, a share in the community's possessions, Roman citizenship," and natural-born children. Although they were captured, the Sabine women were not captives. They were now fully and completely Romans.[21]

Romulus's extension of citizenship "greatly mollified" the (entirely fictional) Sabine women, but their family members reacted as actual humans would, by persuading the Sabine ruler, Titus Tatius, to attack the Romans. Romulus defeated their forces, colonized two of their cities, and offered Roman citizenship to the families of the Sabine women whom the Romans had forcibly married. Then, as the war neared a bloody climax, the Sabine women themselves intervened and arranged a truce, through which Romulus and Titus Tatius agreed "not only to make peace but to make one state from two," in which they "shared the kingship but transferred all power to Rome."[22]

Historians like Dionysius and Livy needed to craft a narrative that joined the diverse traditions Romans knew about their early city and make them comprehensible. But ordinary Romans were often more concerned with the shrines and monuments that commemorated this history. Livy describes the establishment of a cult to Hercules on the site where Evander once encountered the demigod. Dionysius mentions a shrine at the site where the wolf suckled Romulus and Remus that included an ancient "statue . . . that represents a she-wolf suckling two infants," as well as a hut on the Palatine, "called the hut of Romulus," that was kept "as nearly as possible in its original condition."[23]

For Cicero, the tale of a Roman community that grew through agglomeration, conquest, and integration meant that Rome's success "was not based upon the genius of one man, but of many," and that many had ruled it collaboratively "over a long period of several centuries and many ages of men."[24] Cicero, too, believed that it all began with Romulus, who he said ruled alongside the Sabine king Titus Tatius. According to Cicero, Romulus "chose a royal council of the most eminent men" to advise him after Tatius's death, eventually formalizing their role by creating a body of elders called the Senate, a word derived from *senex* (Latin for "old men"). This body enabled him to build a consensus backing the "many wars he waged against his neighbors."[25]

Romans believed that this pattern of collaborative deliberation and incorporation of meritorious outsiders in Rome's ruling circles continued after Romulus's death. At that point, the Senate instituted the interregnum, "a new plan that had never before been heard about in all other nations," through which senators each took turns running the state for five days at a time until a new king was selected. This was done, Cicero claimed, because "our ancestors, rustics though they were, even then saw that royal virtue and wisdom, not ancestry, ought to be sought" when choosing a ruler, even if that meant "passing over their own citizens and choosing a foreigner as their king."[26]

Numa Pompilius, the Sabine whom later Romans identified as Rome's second king, balanced the warlike Roman character that Romulus had instilled with a concern for the political conditions that would allow Roman society to function without internal conflict. According to Cicero, he "implanted in them a love for peace and tranquility" by issuing laws and "establishing all branches of our religion . . . markets, games, and all sorts of festivals." These efforts "turned the minds of men who had become savage through their passion for war towards benevolence and kindness," and fostered "the stability of the state."[27] Romulus had given Rome the energy and drive to conquer an empire, but Numa instilled the virtues that Romans would need to rule it.

Cicero believed that the next three Roman kings had personalities that fostered the development of other key Roman national characteristics. Tullus Hostilius, the third of Rome's legendary kings, was as warlike as his name suggests, but he also continued to foster civic life by building infrastructure and instituting laws about the just conduct of war. Ancus Marcius, the fourth king, who also had Sabine roots, expanded Roman territory until it reached the sea, founding the port city of Ostia at the mouth of the Tiber. Ultimately, Cicero concludes, "it is quite clear that every king contributed many good and useful things" by introducing key elements of Rome's national character.[28]

The deliberately crafted stories of Rome's legendary origins retold by eloquent authors in the first century BC sensationalize the mundane history of a few small, poor communities perched on hillsides above the Tiber as they expanded and developed political and sacred institutions. This was not, as Cicero and his contemporaries believed, a process driven by heroic individuals who imparted their character on the new state. It instead grew out of the talents of the tens of thousands of men and women who lived in this expanding Roman community in the hundreds of years before history tracked it. Their names and deeds are lost, but they are Rome's true founders.

Chapter 2

The Roman Revolution
of Servius Tullius

615–535 BC

THE COLLECTIONS OF huts that made up earliest Rome began to look more like an established city at the end of the seventh century BC. Romans had started to accumulate wealth by farming cash crops such as olives and grapes, and had begun to manufacture higher-quality pottery using potters' wheels.[1] By 625 BC, Romans had paved the low-lying area between the Capitoline and Palatine Hills and turned it into the Roman Forum, which would serve as a marketplace and the center of Roman political and religious life.[2]

While parts of the city of Rome began to take a distinctive physical form, the people who lived in Rome remained a heterogeneous mixture of native-born Romans and immigrants from around Italy. There is little written evidence of any sort for this period, but the tiny fragments of writing we possess reveal a dynamic Roman community that readily adopted attributes of the multilingual, multicultural Italy in which it sat.

Romans proved particularly receptive to Greek influences. The first Greek settlers arrived in Southern Italy around 770 BC, and by the turn of the sixth century there were so many Greek settlements in the southern parts of the Italian Peninsula that the region came to be called Greater Greece. The Greek presence sparked significant changes in Rome. The Latin alphabet was rapidly derived from the Greek one, so that, as Rome grew, so, too, did a Roman culture of literacy.

Later Romans took pride in their ancestors' ability to adopt and perfect the *phalanx*, a military formation pioneered in the Greek world that consisted of multiple lines of heavily armed, tightly bunched soldiers, called *hoplites*, each carrying a large shield and a long spear. Each infantryman's shield protected half of his body and half of the body of the man standing next to him, and the long lines advanced slowly and in unison until they clashed with the enemy. As long as no soldier broke formation, the well-protected line was very difficult to defeat in a frontal engagement. The Romans, who had first encountered the phalanx when their enemies had used it against them, had immediately recognized its effectiveness. An anonymous later Roman historian wrote, "We then changed our armament and replaced it with theirs, [and] organized our forces in this way against theirs." The Roman soldiers, he said, were then "victorious when fighting in this fashion against men who had long been accustomed to phalanx battles."[3]

Not only did the phalanx make the Roman military more formidable, but it also revolutionized Roman society. Evidence from sixth-century Greece shows that the mutual trust ensuring that every infantryman in a phalanx remained in position also fostered a communal spirit that transformed political life. Before the development of the phalanx, battles had often been won by well-equipped, wealthy aristocratic warriors, like the heroes celebrated in Homeric poetry. But the long spears and tightly bunched infantry formations typical of a hoplite phalanx offered few opportunities for individual heroics. The wall of spears prevented even the bravest warrior from regularly engaging in single combat, and it so frightened horses that cavalry were reduced to trying to outflank the phalanx. Cohorts of well-trained infantry, not aristocrats, now won battles.

Most hoplites were middle-class or upper-middle-class people who had enough money to pay for their own military equipment, and their growing importance changed the political dynamics in Greek cities. Across the sixth century BC, angry hoplites toppled many of the hereditary aristocracies that governed Greek cities and installed men the Greeks called *tyrannoi,* or "tyrants." These rulers were often popular figures who "won the citizenry's confidence by slandering the elites," and they tended to bring political power to hoplite soldiers "by destroying . . . and banishing" the old ruling class.[4]

Many Greek tyrants operated from a similar playbook. Greek cities often separated their citizens into political or religious tribes ostensibly bound by some ancient kinship. Tyrants frequently reformed the tribal structure of the city in order to destroy the kinship and religious ties that had supported the aristocratic dominance of the previous regime. Tyrants also revised the citizen rolls, created new voting assemblies, and conducted censuses, to be sure the political power was distributed to those who could afford to serve in the phalanx. Many of them undertook large infrastructure projects that reflected the economically vibrant society their rule fostered. Ancient authors suggest that tyrants even shared tips with one another about how to manage their cities.[5]

The reigns of Tarquinius Priscus and Servius Tullius, two of Rome's last three kings, unfolded as Rome struggled to adapt to the changing military and political conditions unleashed by the hoplite revolution. Unlike the first legendary kings of Rome, both Tarquinius Priscus and Servius Tullius were historical figures. Roman tradition holds that Tarquinius Priscus, whose birth name was Lucumo, ruled from 615 to 579 BC, but it is far more likely that he lived in the middle of the sixth century.[6] The descendant of a Greek exile who had fled Corinth and settled in the Etruscan city of Tarquinii, Lucumo had inherited his father's estate and married a native of Tarquinii named Tanaquil. When he and Tanaquil became frustrated by the lack of opportunity in Tarquinii, Tanaquil "got the idea of leaving Tarquinii," and "Rome seemed to be the most promising place" for them. It was a city made up of "a new people where nobility could be quickly acquired and based on merit," and, as Dionysius of Halicarnassus puts it, "the Romans gladly received all strangers and made them citizens."[7]

When they arrived in Rome, Lucumo bought a large house and announced that his name was now Lucius Tarquinius Priscus, a Latin name combining a version of his old name, Lucumo, and a reference to his origins in Tarquinii. He "easily received citizenship" and became "an intimate associate of King Ancus Marcius." Then he campaigned for election to the kingship when Ancus died. After pointing out that "he was the third foreigner to aspire to the kingship," and emphasizing that he had lived in Rome "for the greatest part of the stage in one's life when men serve their city," Tarquin "was made king by the unanimous vote of the people."[8]

Tarquinius Priscus ruled Rome in a fashion that suggests his awareness of the revolutionary currents sweeping Mediterranean society. He immediately doubled the size of the Senate to include a host of new families and established the Roman equestrian order (often called the "Roman knights" by modern scholars).[9] Livy writes that Tarquinius Priscus chose to elevate the social status of these new elites "because he was thinking as much about strengthening his own position as he was about enlarging the state."[10] These moves solidified the king's authority at a time when he feared the political upheaval that had become endemic in sixth-century Italy and Greece.

Tarquinius Priscus also protected himself by building ties to a powerful warrior named Servius Tullius. Servius, who Roman authors claim was the son of a slave woman named Ocresia, was even more of an outsider than Tarquinius Priscus.[11] Roman tradition holds that Servius came to the attention of Tanaquil, Tarquinius Pricus's wife, when his head supposedly burst into flames while he slept and stopped burning when he woke.[12] According to Cicero, Tarquinius and his wife "regarded Servius as a son" and "took the greatest care to educate him."[13] They employed him as the top royal adviser and arranged for Servius to marry the king's own daughter. Servius demonstrated such military skill and "understanding of public affairs" that "the Roman people believed there was no difference whether Tarquinius or [Servius] Tullius looked after political life."[14]

These Roman stories work hard to explain why Rome's penultimate king began life as a slave. But the reality of Servius's rise in Rome was more historically interesting than the story about his burning head.[15] Rather than being like a demigod who grew up at the Roman royal court, Servius Tullius belongs to a group of militarily skilled sixth-century Italian adventurers who moved with their armies from place to place seeking power and wealth.

Our best evidence for Servius's career as a soldier of fortune comes from a cluster of stories preserved in both Roman and Etruscan sources, the most extensive of which survives in a speech delivered by the first-century AD Roman emperor Claudius. Before he unexpectedly became emperor, Claudius spent much of his time studying and writing about Etruscan history. In AD 48, he used his knowledge of Servius Tullius's past to defend the inclusion of Roman citizens from southern Gaul in the Senate. This was, Claudius claimed, consistent with the Roman pattern of including outsiders as "fellow citizens" that stretched back to Servius Tullius. Servius, Claudius claimed, was "born from the captive woman Ocresia, if we follow our sources," but, "if we follow the Etruscans," he was "the most faithful of all of the companions of Caelius Vivenna," the commander of a famous group of adventurers. When Caelius was defeated, Servius Tullius "left Etruria with what remained of Caelius's army," "occupied the Caelian Hill," "changed his own name because his name was Mastarna in Etruscan," and then "obtained royal power" in Rome.[16]

Other ancient sources confirm elements of Claudius's account. Dionysius of Halicarnassus agrees that the Caelian Hill was named for Caelius after it was occupied by his followers.[17] References to Caelius and his brother Aulus Vivenna show up on a host of artifacts from Etruria. The most notable of these, a painting in a tomb dating to the fourth century BC, depicts a battle scene featuring figures labeled Avle and Caile Vipinas, Macstarna, and Cneve Tarchnunies Rumarch—Etruscan spellings of names rendered in Latin as Aulus and Caelius Vivenna, Mastarna, and Gnaeus Tarquinius of Rome.[18] While the painting's details do not precisely match Claudius's speech, it does confirm the emperor's view that sixth-century Rome welcomed outsiders and integrated them into its ruling class when their talents and assets could benefit the state. Romans welcomed Tarquinius Priscus because of his great wealth, and they received Servius Tullius because he came with an army that he willingly deployed to help the city. In each case, these additions brought "the greatest advantage to the state."[19]

Whatever the circumstances that brought Servius Tullius to Rome, he quickly built a strong connection with Tarquinius Priscus and Tanaquil, probably by using the troops he commanded to support the king. This allowed him to eventually seize power after the sons of Ancus Marcius orchestrated the assassination of Tarquinius Priscus.

The assassins seriously wounded the king, but he was rushed into the royal palace by Tanaquil while barely alive. Tanaquil then took control of the situation. She closed the palace off, called Servius Tullius, and helped him secure power by giving a speech in which she exhorted Romans to obey Servius until Tarquin could heal. Tarquin in fact died and, once Servius had sufficiently "strengthened his position," he appeared with an armed guard and claimed the throne. He was the first king to take power with neither an interregnum nor an endorsement from the Roman aristocracy.[20] And, while Servius now ruled in Rome, he also understood that Tanaquil had made this possible.

Roman historians describe Servius taking a series of carefully calculated actions to reinforce Roman support for his regime while simultaneously rewarding Tanaquil for her help. He sponsored a public funeral for Tarquin and arranged for the two sons Tarquin had with Tanaquil to marry his own two daughters, an unmistakable move intended to lay the foundation for a royal dynasty. Servius also asked for and received a vote endorsing his assumption of royal power from an assembly of the Roman people, a crucial step toward building a coalition of soldiers and poorer citizens that could blunt any possible aristocratic challenges to his regime. He then rewarded his supporters with a program of populist economic reforms that forgave debts, distributed public land to the poor, and removed the administration of justice from Roman aristocrats.[21]

The new king further entrenched his power by overhauling the architecture of the Roman state. He remade the tribal structure, extended citizenship to all who lived in Roman territory (including freed slaves), coordinated the first census of the city, created a new assembly in which voting blocs were organized by economic class, and expanded the physical boundaries of the city of Rome.

Servius's tribal reform reflected a new way of thinking about what it meant to belong to the Roman political community. Many Greek tyrants replaced old, aristocratic-dominated tribes with new ones, but Servius's reform went further by redefining Roman tribes geographically. He separated the city of Rome into four regions, assigned one tribe to each region, and then divided the countryside into districts (*pagi*) that he attached to urban regions. At some point, either under Servius himself or under his successor, Tarquinius Superbus, these *pagi* began to break off into tribal districts themselves, until, by the end of the sixth century BC, the Roman polity included four urban and at least fifteen rural tribes.[22]

Servius's census systematically measured the property Rome's individual citizens owned in a fashion that was both more comprehensive and more complicated than the efforts undertaken by tyrants and political reformers in the Greek world. By the mid-sixth century, the citizens of most major Greek cities either held their wealth in coins with a defined value, minted by their cities, or had the capacity to calculate the approximate monetary value of their property. Servius Tullius's Rome, however, minted no coins. Romans instead stored their wealth in bronze nuggets that lacked a standard size, shape, or value. These items were weighed and valued for their bronze content alone. Thus Servius Tullius's census agents decided to use the *as*, the notional equivalent of one pound of bronze, as a standard assessment unit, and then defined the wealth of Rome's citizens in the pounds of bronze their property was worth.

The king used this count to identify the Romans who individually had the resources to pay for the military equipment required for service in the phalanx. While Romans would eventually be divided in a complicated system of 193 census classes, called centuries, Servius's initial division seems to have been much simpler.[23] The Romans who could equip themselves for infantry service belonged to one group, and those who could not formed another. All told, it seems that Rome could now field some 6,000 soldiers, grouped into a unit of 60 "centuries" that would eventually become the basis of the famed Roman legion.[24]

After Servius classified the Roman population by wealth, he created an assembly called the Comitia Centuriata that gave greater weight to the votes of the men who qualified for service in the Roman phalanx than to the votes of those who did not qualify because they had less wealth. The effect, Cicero later noted, was that, "while no one was prohibited by law from exercising their right to vote, [Servius] valued more the vote of those on whom the interests of the state depended the most." The Comitia Centuriata, which met in the Campus Martius (the field of the Roman war god, Mars), and voted on whether or not Rome would go to war, embodied the shift in power from kings who based their authority on the hereditary Roman aristocracy to Servius's new regime empowered by Rome's citizen infantry.[25]

Servius Tullius's reform of Roman social and political structures occurred at the same time that he was expanding Rome's physical dimensions. He absorbed the Quirinal and Viminal Hills north of the Forum, and he constructed an earthen berm and trench fortification system to block attackers from coming through the natural flatland northeast of the Quirinal, Viminal, and Esquiline Hills.[26] He then had the sacred boundary of the expanded city marked with consecrated boundary stones, an act that has led modern commentators to opine that he was "a second founder of Rome."[27] By the time of Servius's death in or around 535 BC, Rome was bigger, better organized, and more powerful than it ever had been before. It is no wonder that Romans associated Servius Tullius, the Roman king who had been born a slave, with Fortuna, the Roman goddess of good luck.[28]

Chapter 3

Counterrevolution and the Dawn of the Republic

535–494 BC

S ERVIUS TULLIUS REDEFINED nearly every aspect of Roman life following his illegal seizure of power in the mid-sixth century BC. The city grew in size and beauty, its citizenship expanded, and its political life became more inclusive. Under Servius's direction, Rome developed into the sacred and secular center of Latium, the Central Italian region in which it was located. Roman citizens now belonged to tribes defined by where they lived. The government had a record of how much property they owned, and it had a better idea of its citizens' capacity for infantry service. Perhaps most importantly, Servius empowered the Roman infantry to participate in decisions about whether and where Rome would fight. Prior to Servius's reforms, Roman kings had been chosen by the Roman aristocracy and checked by tribal structures that reinforced aristocratic predominance. No longer. Servius now ran Rome as a king whose power rested on the support of a wide group of citizen soldiers.

But Rome remained a small society, and Servius still needed to work closely with two influential groups that had reason to dislike his regime. The first group comprised the members of the old Roman aristocracy sidelined by Servius's political reforms. The second consisted of relatives of Tarquinius Priscus who felt that Servius had seized power that they might have claimed. While Tanaquil's support evidently remained firm for the rest of her life, other family members became impatient.

Servius did what he could to placate these figures, but it was not enough. Ancient authors describe his last days unfolding amid dramatic family intrigue. He fell victim to a plot supposedly hatched by his daughter Tullia, who was married to Tarquinius Priscus's son Arruns, and her brother-in-law Lucius Tarquin, Arruns's brother and the husband of Tullia's older sister. Tullia began conspiring with Lucius only after growing angry at Arruns's unwillingness to join with her in seizing power. She and Tarquin agreed to do away with their spouses—their own brother and sister—then marry each other and work together to overthrow Servius Tullius.[1]

The plot unfolded brutally. Tarquin understood that many of the members of the old Roman elite resented the reforms Servius Tullius had undertaken and appealed to them individually, with pitches tailored to their specific interests. He promised riches to ambitious young men looking to start their lives. He suggested to the older men that he would restore the kingship to the noble heights it had enjoyed under his father, Tarquinius Priscus. When he felt he had built enough aristocratic support, he led armed men into the Forum, summoned the Senate, and delivered a speech attacking Servius Tullius's lowly birth, illegal seizure of power, and his "promotion of the lowest sort of people to power."[2] Servius arrived to rebut the charges. But when it became clear that the king retained significant popular support, Tarquin had him murdered. Sources differ about whether assassins killed Servius in the street or Tarquin threw him down the stairs of the Senate House, but all agree that Tullia later ran over her father's body with her carriage on a street that came to be called the Street of Wickedness.[3]

This was, Livy wrote, "a crime worthy of a Greek tragedy," so heinous that it generated "hatred of the kings that would hasten the coming of liberty."[4] It is unclear how many details in Livy's story of betrayal, impiety, and patricide one can trust—especially when a scheming woman is made the central villain in the tale.[5] Livy's dramatic assessment of the coup and its soap-opera-like plot twists may simply reflect the misogyny of his time. However, Servius Tullius likely did lose his life in a coup, probably sparked by the combined grievances of Tarquin and the Roman hereditary aristocracy to whom Tarquin appealed. It is possible, perhaps even likely, that Tarquin really did claim that his overthrow of Servius (whose very name evinced his servile origins) would purge the state of the undesirable mob of new citizens that the deceased king had empowered. Such things were sometimes promised by those who overthrew Greek tyrannies—and it would not be surprising if Roman aristocrats nursed similar grievances.

If Tarquin made such promises, he did not deliver on them. The new citizens remained Roman, Servius's new tribes endured, and Tarquin retained Servius's Comitia Centuriata, the assembly of the Roman infantry that voted on issues of war and capital punishment. Tarquin quickly realized that, after his murder of their champion, he could not afford to anger the men serving in the Roman infantry. The Roman aristocrats soon became disappointed in Tarquin's failure to honor his promises to them.

As Roman aristocrats soured on Tarquin, his regime turned into a closed state that, Livy said, he "governed . . . by consulting only members of his own family," because he trusted few others. Cicero spoke of how Tarquin began his reign with "his hands stained with the blood of a most excellent king," and said he "feared that he might suffer that same highest penalty himself because of his crime." Dionysius of Halicarnassus described him "bringing charges against many of the most prominent men," accusing them of "conspiring against the king," and personally "condemning them to death" despite Servius's regulation that such cases must go before the Comitia Centuriata. Tarquin's regime then became "an avowed tyranny" in which he made himself "feared by others" so he could avoid punishment.[6]

Despite these claims, the early years of Tarquin's reign brought considerable successes to Rome. Tarquin moved aggressively to counter efforts by Rome's Latin allies to shake off Roman domination.

Not only did he restore their subordination to Rome, but he restructured the alliance so that Latin troops no longer had local commanders. They would instead serve under Roman leadership and would be answerable to Rome's king. Tarquin expanded Roman alliances beyond Latium by making overtures to the Hernici and Volsci, two groups based on the western slopes of the Apennines. The Hernici responded favorably, but, after the Volsci resisted, Tarquin captured and looted the wealthy Volscian city of Suessa Pometia. He then used the proceeds to begin work on a monumental temple of Jupiter atop the Capitoline Hill.[7]

Despite these accomplishments, some Romans became upset at what they perceived to be his arrogance. "Relying upon his victories and his wealth," Cicero would write, Tarquin "swelled with pride and became unable to control either his own conduct or that of his family."[8] He was now Tarquinius Superbus—Tarquin the Proud.

This name reflects Tarquin's broader failure to respond effectively to growing resentment at his apparent belief that royal power belonged to him as a sort of private patrimony. This conviction lay behind his prosecution of senators, his infliction of capital punishment without consulting the assembly, and his use of forced labor to complete infrastructure projects such as the Cloaca Maxima, a drainage channel that directed the city's wastewater into the Tiber.[9] Later Romans, however, were even more outraged that Tarquin's family members appear to have believed that the bodies of elite women also belonged to them.

The most notorious story told about how the royal family disregarded the basic rights of their subjects concerns Tarquinius Superbus's eldest son, Sextus. Tarquin had sent Sextus to the city of Collatia while he led the Roman army in an attack on the Italian city of Ardea, the main port in Latium. While in Collatia, Sextus stayed at the home of his cousin Lucius Tarquinius Collatinus, became infatuated with Lucretia, Collatinus's wife, and raped her when her husband was away. Lucretia, "grief stricken at this terrible disaster," summoned her father and her husband and asked them to pledge that "the adulterer will not go unpunished." She then stabbed herself in the heart with a dagger.[10] Tarquinius Superbus's nephew Lucius Junius Brutus, who had been traveling with Collatinus, then picked up Lucretia's dagger and swore an oath to her corpse: "I will pursue Lucius Tarquinius Superbus, together with his wicked wife and all his children . . . with whatever violence I can. Nor will I allow them or anyone else to be king at Rome."[11]

Brutus and Collatinus stationed loyal armed men in Collatia, journeyed the few miles to Rome alongside a levy of troops, and summoned an assembly, during which Brutus described what had happened to Lucretia. He "inflamed the people" by "recalling the shameful murder of Servius Tullius and how his daughter had driven over her father's body with her carriage," and then marshaled a force of young men to lead against Tarquinius Superbus. Tarquin and his family fled the city, and when Tarquin tried to return to retake the capital, he was turned away. He was now an exile. It was 509 BC, and he had reigned for a little more than twenty-five years.

This famous story about how the Roman monarchy ended and the Roman Republic began reads like a drama because later Roman authors structured their account as a sort of theatrical tragedy.[12] In Livy's telling, Tarquin and his family members lost sight of the lines that separated the needs of their family from those of the state. For Cicero, Tarquin's privileging of the narrow concerns of his family over the common good of the state caused Roman political life to revert to a more primitive condition.[13] His fall became a warning to later Romans about the dangers of allowing greed, pride, and private interests to supersede one's devotion to the state. This sort of degeneration violated the rights and threatened the lives of the citizens, who counted on the state and its laws to protect them.

These larger moral lessons infused later accounts of the Roman Republic's origins. According to Dionysius of Halicarnassus, the decision to establish a Roman representative democracy emerged from an assembly of the patrician order, the families who had made up Rome's hereditary aristocracy for as far back as records reached. In that assembly, patricians embarked on a detailed discussion of constitutional theory that Dionysius models on Plato's *Republic* (a work that would not appear until nearly 150 years after the Roman Republic's foundation). They debated the wisdom of continuing with a monarchy, shifting to a purely aristocratic form of government by the Senate, or setting the government up as a democracy, like the one in Athens (which, unfortunately for Dionysius, only became a democracy in 508 BC, the year after Rome's revolution). In the end, Brutus advocated for a mixed constitution in which two magistrates, called consuls, were elected each year to hold power.[14] All of the assembled patricians agreed with him and assented when Lucretia's father nominated Brutus and Collatinus to be the first consuls.

This revolution shifted the nature of power in the Roman state. Modern people tend to use ideas of economic class to mark social divisions, and it is common to see patricians referred to as the Roman ruling class. This is incorrect. The patricians were not an economic class but a social order, a difference one must understand to see how radical the government of the early Roman Republic was. Economic classes are determined by how much money a person possesses, and it is possible for someone to move to a higher economic class as their wealth increases. A social order is determined by the status of a person's family when they are born, and, in Rome, the patrician order was difficult to join unless one was born into it. In most cases, those who were born to non-patrician families spent their lives as plebeians, or plebs, the term for all those who were not patricians, even if they became very wealthy or important. Servius Tullius's reforms had created a class-based Roman government in which the most important Roman assembly was dominated by the plebeians wealthy enough to serve in the phalanx. The wealthiest of these plebeians were as rich as patricians, which meant that the Roman state of the last monarchs had a genuine ruling class made up of people belonging to both the patrician and plebeian orders. Someone of humble birth but considerable talent could, like Servius Tullius, elevate themselves into the center of that ruling class.

When Brutus inaugurated the Republic with a patrician-only meeting, he signaled that Rome was reverting to a system of government based on heredity. Patricians would now control the state, and plebeians, regardless of their wealth or military role, would become second-class citizens, reduced to voting only to approve or deny the policies and laws patricians crafted.

The full implications of the revolution remained unclear, however, when Brutus announced it to the plebeians who assembled in the Forum. He gave a rousing oration that described his own career, the persecution patricians had endured under Tarquin, and their resolution that "the Tarquinii and all their descendants shall be banished both from the city of Rome and from all the territory ruled by the Romans." He emphasized that anyone working to restore the Tarquins "shall be put to death," and then asked the plebeians to vote to replace the king with him and Collatinus, Rome's first consuls.[15]

Not long after the expulsion of Tarquin, Brutus's sons were caught conspiring to restore the king. They were brought before Brutus and, despite pleas from his fellow citizens that he spare his sons, the consul condemned them to death. "The most extraordinary and astonishing part of his behavior," Dionysius wrote, was that Brutus "was the only person . . . not to lament the fate of his sons, nor to pity himself for the desolation that was coming upon his house."[16] If Tarquin placed the interest of family above that of state, Brutus's decision to kill his own sons emphasized that, in the new Roman Republic, Romans would place the common good above the future of their own families.

Roman authors tell another, far less flattering, story about Brutus. Although Collatinus had been chosen as his consular colleague, Brutus contrived with the Senate to force Collatinus from office and into exile so that Rome could be "rid of the royal name" that he bore. This, Brutus said, would ensure that "kingship [would] depart from Rome together with the Tarquinian family."[17] And so Lucius Tarquinius Collatinus, Lucretia's widower and one of Rome's two first consuls, left the city as an exile soon after he took office simply because he shared the Tarquin family name. Brutus, who was Tarquin's nephew but was related to the king through his mother, could remain in office because he did not carry the name "Tarquin." Collatinus accepted the decision and withdrew from the city. Like Brutus's execution of his sons, Collatinus's exile established the principle of putting the demands of the state above one's own personal and familial needs.

Brutus's time as consul concluded heroically. Tarquin had fled to Etruria and gathered support from the Etruscan cities of Veii and his ancestral home of Tarquinii. He and his Etruscan allies met the forces of the new Republic at Silva Arsia, with Brutus commanding the cavalry, and Publius Valerius, the man who had replaced Collatinus as consul, leading the infantry. Brutus set out to scout the enemy when Tarquin's son Arruns recognized Brutus and charged at him. Both men fell dead, with Brutus the first consul to give his life for the Republic.[18] Publius Valerius and the infantry turned back the enemy assault and then carried Brutus's body back to Rome.

The next year saw another attack on Rome, this time with Tarquin working alongside Lars Porsenna, the king of the city of Clusium. Porsenna attacked Rome from the Janiculum, the hill that sits above the modern Roman neighborhood of Trastevere. As Roman citizens fled in panic, a Roman soldier named Horatius Cocles made a stand on the Pons Sublicius, a wooden bridge across the Tiber.[19] He and two companions prevented Porsenna's army from crossing until his compatriots on the eastern bank cut its span. Horatius's bravery so impressed Porsenna that he called off his attack and agreed to terms with the Romans.

Tarquin's final attempt to retake Rome resulted in more heroics. Working with his son-in-law, Tarquin orchestrated a revolt of the Latin League, the regional group of allies that Rome had dominated under the later kings. The Latin threat proved so serious that the young Republic appointed a patrician named Aulus Postumius to sole command over Roman forces, and he prevailed over the Latins in a hard-fought struggle near Lake Regillus in either 499 or 496 BC. Although the plebeians in the Roman infantry won the battle, Livy's story of Lake Regillus focused entirely on the patricians, who, he claims, inspired the lower-status infantry with acts of individual bravery.[20]

Livy's perspective on the fighting reflected the early Republic perfectly. It was a patrician-dominated representative democracy that gathered power around the aristocracy that Servius Tullius had side-lined. Under the Republic, patricians now held the highest magistracies in the state. They controlled the nomination process for those magistracies, and the wealthy plebeians in the infantry retained only the capacity to vote for which patrician they could tolerate in office. Most Romans had neither the opportunity to hold office nor the chance to nominate a candidate of their choosing.

This made the early Roman Republic even more reactionary than many of the regimes that toppled tyrants in the Greek world. In Athens, for example, the overthrow of the Athenian tyrant Peisistratus had led to the creation of a democracy in which the votes of all citizens would eventually be counted equally, regardless of their social status. The Roman Republic went in the opposite direction. Instead of expanding the power of ordinary citizens, it gave Roman patricians more power than they had enjoyed before Servius Tullius. Prior to Servius's reforms, patricians had nominated the Roman king, whose election would be certified by the vote of the plebeians. The Roman state prior to Servius had then represented a kind of collaborative enterprise in which patricians worked alongside plebeians under the supervision of a king that both sides collaboratively selected.

The new Republic lacked this balance, and there was now no king to mediate between patrician and plebeian demands. It remained stable for as long as Tarquin lived, and the threat of his restoration encouraged the patricians to cooperate with plebeians. His death in 495, however, meant that the "plebs, to whom the nobles had diligently attended up until that time, now began to be harmed by their superiors."[21]

Large numbers of plebeians rapidly fell into debt until they were "bound over to their creditors" as slaves. "These men," Livy wrote, came to the Forum and "grumbled that, although they fought abroad for freedom . . . at home they had been oppressed and enslaved by their fellow citizens." One old man then exposed his back and showed the scars from the lashings his master had inflicted on him. Pity for his plight turned to outrage when onlookers recognized that he was a decorated soldier who had been enslaved when he could not pay a war tax the patricians had assessed.[22] This prompted the plebeians to refuse to serve in the army until the consul who was trying to raise an army agreed to free any debtors who wished to serve and to safeguard their property while they fought. His pledge proved so hollow that, after the fighting ended, many of these men whose liberty he promised to safeguard fell right back into debt bondage when they returned home.

The same problem resurfaced in 494, when plebeians again refused to fight unless they secured debt relief. This time, the patricians and consuls charged Manius Valerius with resolving both the military situation and the problem with the striking soldiers. Valerius's forces won on the battlefield, but he angrily resigned his command when Roman lenders again refused to observe the guarantees he gave to indebted soldiers.[23] Valerius's plebeian soldiers mutinied not long after he stormed out of the Senate House.

The rebellious army initially debated killing the consuls and staging an armed revolt. Although they had the manpower to do this, a plebeian named Gaius Sicinius Bellutus persuaded them to negotiate with the patricians in a fashion that emphasized the strength plebeians possessed but refused to use against their city. The plebeian soldiers marched out of the city limits, built a fortified camp, and negotiated until, Livy wrote, "an agreement was reached on the following terms: The plebeians should have their own magistrates, who would be sacrosanct. These officials should have the right to give help to plebeians in actions against the [patrician] consuls, but no [patrician] could hold this office. And so two tribunes of the plebs were elected and they chose three others to be their colleagues."[24] Sicinius was one of the five.

So concluded the first secession of the plebs in 493 BC. By the time it ended, the basic political architecture of the Roman Republic had taken shape. The creation of the tribune of the plebs and the patrician recognition of institutions that gave plebs a meaningful voice in the direction of the state recalibrated the Republic. What had been a patrician-dominated state with minimal non-patrician input became again a collaborative enterprise in which both patricians and non-patricians played a role in decision-making. Just as importantly, the secession of the plebs also established a precedent that Romans would not resort to violence to resolve political conflicts. The rebellious soldiers could have seized the city and changed the constitution by force. They chose not to do so. They struck peacefully and began a fruitful negotiation with their political opponents that resolved the problem without violence.

Or so we are told. The secession of the plebs, like so much else in our historical accounts of the first generation of the Roman Republic, is heavy on moralizing but short on details that one could independently verify. This story, like those involving the rape of Lucretia and Brutus's killing of his sons, has invited a great deal of skepticism. Patrician heroes had played their part in shaping the political and moral character of the new Republic across the first fifteen years. Now Sicinius and his plebeian associates could model similar exemplary conduct as they peacefully pushed the Roman Republic to become more inclusive and responsive to their needs.

But we should not so easily discard these stories because some details seem to resonate too neatly with Roman ideals. They actually paint a compelling picture of the widespread and long-standing disorder that Rome's republican revolution caused. The broad outlines of this disorder are consistent with other pieces of evidence we can assemble. Even before Tarquin fell, a set of distinct tensions threatened the integrity of his regime and Rome's control over the region around the city. The divisions within Tarquin's family may not have erupted into exactly the sort of dramatic conflicts described earlier, but it is difficult to ignore the serious sense of infighting within the sprawling clan of the Tarquinii, centered on which family members should be influential in Rome and how they could exercise their power. It is, then, plausible that Tarquinius Superbus would assert a family claim to the kingship against Servius Tullius because he was the biological heir of Tarquinius Priscus. It is equally plausible that figures such as Brutus and Collatinus feared that Tarquin's increasingly absolutist conception of the kingship would sideline peripheral members of the family (like themselves) as power became more concentrated among his sons. Brutus and Collatinus could act on these concerns because their overlapping positions as members of the ruling family and the wider Roman nobility positioned them to build a coalition of disgruntled family members and disenchanted aristocrats.

The revolution that overthrew the Roman monarchy also destabilized the region that Tarquin's army had recently dominated. Perhaps the best evidence for this comes from the text of a treaty executed between Rome and the North African city of Carthage in the year that the Roman monarchy fell. The treaty recognizes Roman and Carthaginian spheres of influence and regulates the activity that each power can undertake in the other's lands. It defines the Roman sphere of influence as "Ardea, Antium, Laurentium, Circei, Tarracina . . . [and] any other people of the Latins that are subject to Rome," as well as areas "which are not subject to Rome" in Latium. The Carthaginians should "keep their hands off their cities, and, if they take one, they shall deliver it unharmed to the Romans."[25]

The Carthaginian agreement granted the new Roman Republic a few important benefits. First, it offered international recognition to the new regime—a key point, given Tarquin's efforts to regain his throne with the support of Rome's neighbors. Second, by committing to turn over any territory it conquered within the Roman sphere of influence, Carthage offered an implicit assurance that any Carthaginian military intervention in Italy would benefit Rome. This probably mattered very little to cities in Latium, but it could have prevented Greek cities in Campania or Southern Italy from offering support to Tarquin. Finally, the Carthaginian treaty allows us to see the difference between the sphere of influence Rome claimed and what the new Republic really controlled. Ardea, for example, is listed as a Roman subject city—but this was the city Tarquin was besieging when Romans revolted against him. The Latin revolts our sources describe similarly suggest that the Republic sustained allied defections and territorial losses in its early years that shrunk the land Rome controlled.

This upheaval had internal implications for the patrician order. In 504 BC, just five years after the Republic took shape, the Sabine leader

Attus Clausus left Sabine territory, changed his name to Appius Claudius, and defected to Rome rather than directing his family, clients, and loyal soldiers to fight against the Romans. His followers were given land and Roman citizenship. They formed a new voting tribe, and Appius Claudius received patrician status. He was then "enrolled in the Senate and, before too long, was regarded as one of its leading members."[26] He was made consul in 495. In that position, he advocated for aggressive actions against the seceding plebeians with a vigor that certainly came from his desire to protect the patrician prerogatives he had recently secured.

Appius Claudius's rapid integration into the Roman ruling structure resembles how the Roman kings Tarquinius Priscus and Servius Tullius had leveraged their financial and military resources to negotiate positions of power in exchange for joining the Roman state. In Appius's case, however, it was the new political structures and status hierarchy of the Republic, rather than the customs of the Roman monarchy, that set the parameters dictating what he could gain by joining Rome. His reward—patrician status, Senate membership, a voting tribe made up of his own clients, and eventually the consulship—was significant, but it was now framed in the political and social currency of the Republic.

In the hectic first years of the Republic, Romans could ignore the inherent tension between the old Roman way of welcoming new people and new leaders into the state's highest ranks and the Republic's fundamentally reactionary political structure. But, as the fifth century progressed, there came a time when the Republic was no longer fighting for survival. The patrician order then became less responsive to the needs of the Roman citizens and soldiers who served the state, and Rome's wealthy and powerful non-patricians began to resist patrician domination. Rather than resolving this tension, the secession of the plebs in 494 BC started more than a century of tense negotiations over non-patrician access to the Republic's most important offices and lawmaking activities.

Chapter 4

The Heroes of the Early Republic

494–431 BC

WHEN LATER ROMANS wrote about the history of the early Roman Republic, they told a story in which the state won wars, expanded its territory, and moved toward a constitution that granted equal status to patricians and plebeians. None of these things happened in any sustained fashion for much of the fifth century BC. During these years, the dynamic, growing city-state that Rome had been under the later kings stagnated as the revolutionary energy that propelled the first generation of Roman Republicans faded. Expansion stalled as Rome shifted from taking territory to defending what it had. The loss of income from conquests, and the costs of enemy attacks on Roman farmland, led to food shortages and significant tensions in Roman political life that efforts to restructure the offices of the Republic failed to calm.

With few collective victories to celebrate, later Roman historians shifted the stories they told to focus on leaders such as Servilius Ahala and Cincinnatus, men who placed service to the Republic over their own ambitions as they led Rome's confrontations with external adversaries and domestic villains. While no actual person could embody Roman virtue as purely as these men supposedly did, the stories told about these fifth-century Roman heroes do allow us to see the genuine problems Rome struggled to reveal and the significant challenges Roman leaders struggled to overcome during the turbulent first half of the fifth century BC.

The problems began when the Volsci and Aequi began raiding Roman territory on a nearly annual basis in 494. These regular attacks, which lasted for decades, arose from the declaration of a *ver sacrum* (Sacred Spring). This was an ancient Italic custom in which communities responded to "moments of great danger" by vowing to the god Mars that, if they survived, they would "burn alive all the living beings that were born the following spring." Human children were not burned, but "once they reached adulthood, [community leaders] blindfolded them and chased them away to live outside of their borders."[1] We do not know what particular danger prompted the declaration of a *ver sacrum* or when exactly this crisis hit the mountain communities in the Apennines. It is clear, though, that the young Volcsian, Aequian, Samnite, and Sabine children who were dedicated to Mars in that *ver sacrum* came of age in the early 490s. Once they did, these surplus young men and women exerted unremitting pressure on the urban communities in the Italian foothills and along the western Italian coast as they pushed to conquer and settle new areas.

Attacks by these Italic peoples wore down many Italian polities. The Greek cities on the west coast of Italy suffered such sustained attacks that only Velia and Naples remained in Greek hands by the end of the fifth century. Etruscan communities south of Rome also lost their independence, either through conquest or, in the case of Capua, following a coup in which the Samnites who were being incorporated into the citizen body of the city-state overthrew the city's government.[2] The Volsci even tried to join the Latin revolt against the new Roman Republic in the 490s, but the Roman victory at Lake Regillus eliminated that possible source of support.[3] Despite this initial reverse, the Volsci, the Aequi, and the Sabines continued attacking Rome and the cities of Latium regularly.

Ultimately, pressure from these less developed communities in the Apennines forced the settled, urban areas of Latium into an alliance that reconstituted the Roman-led, pan-Latin arrangements built by Tarquinius Superbus.[4] In 486 BC, the neighboring Hernici cities allied with Rome under similar terms so that, like the Latins, they could collectively resist the Volsci. They also organized their own forces in a separate contingent that served under a commander sent by Rome.[5]

These were not alliances of convenience that the Romans quickly discarded. They lasted for decades and resulted not just in joint military operations, but also in the creation of colonies settled by members of each of the three allied communities and placed on the frontiers between Latin or Hernician territory and that were dominated by the Italic invaders.[6] Because most of the colonies bordered Latin lands, they were enrolled in the Latin League, and the colonists received a sort of mutually transferable citizenship, through which a Latin citizen moving to another Latin city could secure citizenship there.[7]

The foundation of these colonies should not mislead us into imagining that Rome and its allies enjoyed a great deal of success in these wars. They did not. At the beginning of their raiding, the Volsci, the Aequi, and the Sabines seem to have overrun as much as 50 percent of the territory in Latium. Rome itself seems to have mostly escaped direct attack, but our sources speak of only occasional Roman victories. Even some of the ones that are celebrated seem not to have checked the invaders for long.

These victories may have had limited military effects, but they helped define the career of Lucius Quinctius Cincinnatus, one of the greatest heroes in Roman history. On December 1, 460, Cincinnatus was chosen to finish out the consular term of Publius Valerius Publicola, who had died fighting to liberate the Capitoline Hill from a force of Roman exiles serving alongside a Sabine commander. Livy reports that Cincinnatus immediately gave an oration haranguing all Romans for making Rome "a disorderly household rather than the Republic of the Roman people." He so "impressed the plebs and the senators" that they "believed that the Republic had been restored to its old self." Cincinnatus then withdrew to private life.[8]

Cincinnatus returned in 458 when the Senate appointed him dictator and tasked him with rescuing a consular army besieged by the Aequi. A dictator held power for up to six months, had powers unchecked by other Roman magistrates, and was the only Roman official against whose decisions citizens could not appeal. This sort of power could have inspired fear among Romans, but Cincinnatus's actions during his dictatorship in 458 helped calm these fears. Cincinnatus summoned the Roman men of fighting age to assemble in the Campus Martius, led the hastily organized army out to fight the Aequi, and forced their quick surrender. He then distributed all of the booty seized from the Aequi to his own soldiers and "resigned his dictatorship on its sixteenth day even though his term was for six months."[9] Although Cincinnatus owned only four acres of farmland, Dionysius of Halicarnassus reports that Cincinnatus refused a senatorial offer to "accept as much of the conquered land as he wished" and "retired to his small farm and resumed his life of a farmer working his own land . . . glorying more in his poverty than others in their riches."[10]

This was just the sort of image Romans wanted to have about the principles that animated their leaders. Cincinnatus emphasized that service to the Republic was worth more than money, reassured Romans that virtue could restrain the exercise of absolute power, and showed Romans that noble poverty conferred its own sorts of rewards. But Cincinnatus was unique in choosing his poverty. Most Romans in the mid-fifth century had no option but to endure far greater deprivations than Cincinnatus ever faced.

The Italic raiding that Romans and their allies endured badly disrupted life in the small, poor, rural regions where most of the fighting took place and caused periodic food shortages in the cities of Latium. Ancient sources record fourteen food crises between 508 and 384 BC, with most of them concentrated in the decades of the fifth century when the worst raiding occurred.[11] This means that, on average, Romans encountered famines once a decade for more than a century.

Even when food remained available, Rome's small farmers regularly went into debt to buy seeds in the spring or rent equipment during harvests. If the Volsci raided the farm, or a family member was called to serve on a campaign, the family would not have enough grain in the fall to pay back what they had borrowed at the beginning of the year. The borrowers who failed to provide the grain they had promised fell into a form of bondage that required them (or their sons) to work for the lender as a dependent laborer. Sometimes, if a lender chose to do so, the debtor could even be stripped of his Roman citizenship and sold abroad as a slave—or killed.[12]

Rome had few easy solutions to the growing discontent these conditions produced. If the Republic had continued to expand militarily, it could have sent these poorer Romans out as colonists. But Rome's few fifth-century conquests meant that this release valve was mostly closed. Instead, tensions within the city mounted as ambitious plebeian leaders and Roman elites worked to gain political advantage from the city's acute food shortages. In 456, a tribune of the plebs named Lucius Icilius pushed a law through the plebeian assembly that distributed public lands on the Aventine to plebeians. This was done without direct approval or involvement from the consuls, but little could be done to oppose the measure once plebeians began enthusiastically building homes on the land.[13]

Other Romans sought to capitalize on the food problems in even more disruptive ways. In 439, the wealthy young plebeian Spurius Maelius bought up a large quantity of grain from Etruria and began to give it away for free during the second year of a punishing famine. Maelius was not yet old enough to stand for elected office, but he saw the grain distributions as a path for him "to become king" before he was even old enough to stand for the consulship.[14] Maelius began giving speeches about the crisis, offering advice to those who asked him about grain distributions, and attacking patricians who, unlike him, refused to sacrifice their fortunes to "import provisions into the city."[15] In the meantime, Maelius's private efforts to supply Rome meant that "the city lacked none of the previous abundance" of food. "The whole populace," Dionysius of Halicarnassus claimed, "was ready to grant him whatever reward he wanted as soon as it was able to vote for magistrates."[16]

A group of patricians then approached the Senate and claimed to have "incontrovertible proof" that Maelius was "forming a plot against the Republic." Cincinnatus was again appointed dictator and charged with resolving the crisis. That same evening, Cincinnatus ordered the consuls and the troops under their command to occupy the Capitol. When Maelius began to hold court in the Forum the following morning, Cincinnatus's deputy, Servilius, led an armed group of equites (Roman knights) down from the Capitoline Hill and into the Forum. He informed Maelius that Cincinnatus had summoned him to answer charges of fomenting rebellion. Maelius called out, "Plebeians, help me! I am being snatched away by the men in power because of my goodwill to you." As a mob of his supporters swarmed toward Servilius, Maelius ran from the Forum. He was caught by Servilius's knights and killed when he tried to resist.[17]

This is the story that Dionysius of Halicarnassus believed to be "the most credible account of Maelius's death," but some of the earliest Roman historians told another, much more evocative, story about the incident.[18] They said that Servilius had concealed a dagger under his arm, approached Maelius as if he wished to speak to him, and then "bared his sword and plunged it into [Maelius's] throat." Following this deed, they said, he "ran to the Senate house . . . brandishing his sword that dripped with blood and shouting . . . that he had destroyed the tyrant at the command of the Senate." He was given the nickname Ahala, an honorific that derived from the Roman word for "armpit," because that was where he had concealed the dagger. He became such a symbol of the principled defense of Roman freedom that Cicero referenced him to show that "there was once such virtue in this republic, that brave men would repress wicked citizens."[19]

The stories of patriotic fifth-century Romans like Cincinnatus and Ahala reassured future generations that a hero could be counted on to step forward and rescue Rome from internal or external threats. Fifth-century Romans, however, did not simply sit back and wait for a savior when they were attacked or starving. Instead, they looked for ways in which the Republican constitution could be improved to eliminate these tensions.

The most notable attempt came in the later 450s, when Rome decided to choose a set of magistrates who would run the state while crafting a written code of laws for the city and its citizens. The story began in 462 when a tribune of the plebs demanded the production of a written law code. In 454, Rome supposedly sent an embassy to Athens to examine the Athenian law code of Solon.[20] Then, in 451, all of the patrician and plebeian magistrates in the state stepped down from their offices simultaneously and agreed to the election of "a board of ten men" who would "exercise the supreme executive power and draw up a code of law."[21] These men were called the *decemvirs* (literally "ten men").

Livy describes the *decemvirate* as a fundamental shift in "the form of the Roman government," just as "when power had passed from kings to consuls."[22] The decemvirs enjoyed lawmaking powers; took turns "dispensing justice to the people in rotation, one day in ten"; and formed a leadership college that united both the plebeian and non-plebeian magistracies and assemblies into one integrated state apparatus. The repeated tensions of the 460s and 450s had revealed the destabilizing effects of a political system in which plebeian leaders could exploit the tribunate and the plebeian assembly to build a political following for themselves by picking fights with patrician consuls. For Rome to function well amid the crises of the fifth century, it needed to "reintegrate the plebs into the state by doing away with the tribunes," even if that also meant the elimination of the consulship.[23]

While it seems that perhaps only one plebeian belonged to the initial group of decemvirs, the patrician Appius Claudius played a key role in convincing plebeians to accept this arrangement.[24] The son of the Appius Claudius who had joined the Republic in 504 BC, he had once been a "fierce and savage persecutor of the plebs" but, Livy says, he "suddenly emerged as their supporter in order to seize every breath of popularity."[25] Although Appius Claudius did this for self-serving reasons, his outreach built a popular consensus around the legislative actions of this first group of decemvirs. By the end of the year, they had put together ten bronze tablets inscribed with the text of Roman laws.

Cicero and many other later Romans praised the work of this first group of decemvirs. "When these men had composed, with the greatest justice and wisdom, ten tables of laws," they agreed to step down and "caused another board of ten men to be elected in the following year." But, Cicero continued, "the honor and justice of the second group was not similarly lauded."[26] Appius Claudius managed the election for the second group of decemvirs and manipulated the process so that he was reelected for a second term even though he stood against Cincinnatus.[27] When Appius Claudius won that second term, Livy wrote, "that was the end of Appius' wearing an alien mask." He worked with his new colleagues to frame what Livy calls "a perpetual decemvirate" in which they would "not hold elections" but "continue to exercise power" indefinitely. "They looked like ten kings," and many "thought [they] were looking for a pretext to initiate a bloodbath."[28]

Not only did the new decemvirs behave tyrannically, but they pursued the legislative codification for which they were ostensibly appointed with far less energy than their predecessors. Only two new tables of laws appeared in 450 BC. These were, Cicero wrote, "two tables of unjust laws" that included one that "most cruelly prevented intermarriage between plebeians and patricians even though this privilege is usually permitted even between citizens of different states."[29] As the year progressed, the decemvirs behaved with increasing impunity as "their squads" took advantage of the absence of plebeian tribunes to "bully and rob the plebeians of their property and possessions." Physical attacks soon followed. Some plebeians were "beheaded," and their "execution [was] followed by the awarding of the victim's property to his executioner."[30] Not surprisingly, there was no election to replace this group of decemvirs after their terms ended in 450.

Roman sources maintain that the decemvirs fell from power in 449 after an ally of Appius Claudius asserted that a plebeian girl named Verginia was his slave so that Appius could rape her. A crowd of plebeians in the Forum tried to prevent Verginia from being seized, but she was brought before Appius Claudius's court so he could decide about her legal status. Appius ruled against Verginia, and her father killed her so she would not be illegally enslaved and ravaged. Outrage at Appius's actions prompted a revolt by the army, a secession of the plebs, and the dissolution of the decemvirate. Appius killed himself before he could be put on trial.[31]

The Roman Republic prior to the decemvirate often operated as two competing patrician- and plebeian-dominated states that existed within one polity, and their fall brought back the Republic's old magistracies. Romans seem to have choreographed this restoration in such a way that patrician-dominated entities catalyzed the elections for the plebeian magistracies and then the plebeians initiated the restoration of the consulship. This process began with a senatorial decree that the pontifex maximus, a patrician who served as Rome's chief religious official, should conduct an election for ten new tribunes of the plebs, because the state had no serving magistrates who could do so. Once the tribunes were elected, they immediately "carried a resolution [in the plebeian assembly] to elect consuls." The new consuls were Lucius Valerius and Marcus Horatius, the two men who had worked with plebeian leaders to overthrow the decemvirs.[32]

Valerius and Horatius made three legislative changes to ensure that the institutions that had once belonged to the parallel patrician and plebeian Roman states could work together productively. First, they offered full legal recognition of the sacrosanctity of the plebeian tribunes, the plebeian aediles in charge of temple maintenance and marketplace supervision, and judges who plebeians claimed should protect the lives of these plebeian champions. Second, they affirmed that Rome would no longer create magistracies like the decemvirate that prevented other Roman citizens from exercising the right to appeal a magistrate's actions or decisions. Finally, they had the Comitia Centuriata approve a law that "what the plebs should pass when voting by tribes should be binding on the people." With that law, patricians legally recognized the legitimacy of the plebeian magistrates and the laws passed by the plebeian assembly. The parallel Roman states were now unified.[33]

The Valerio-Horatian laws resolved some of the structural inconsistencies that grew out of the aristocratic Republican revolution and the plebeian reaction to it, but a better constitutional framework could not stabilize the Republic by itself. Rome needed to also address the military and economic conditions that had made life in the fifth-century Republic so tense. Fortunately for the Romans, their military fortunes turned not long after the consulship of Valerius and Horatius. Samnite attacks disappear from our sources around 450 BC, and in 431, Rome won the Battle of Algidus against the Aequi and Volsci.[34] After this battle, the Aequi and Volsci no longer had the capacity to regularly attack Rome. And, as the terrors of the first two-thirds of the fifth century receded, Rome soon began to expand again.

Chapter 5

Rome Becomes Rome

431–338 BC

T HE VICTORY OVER Aequian and Volscian forces at the Battle of
Algidus in 431 ended their persistent attacks on Roman territory and set up two events that would long define Rome's approach to
the world. The first of these, the Roman conquest of the Etruscan city
of Veii in 396 BC, represented the early Republic's greatest triumph
and pointed Rome toward a strategy for incorporating large new territories and populations into the state. The second, the sack of Rome
in 386 BC by a group of Gallic barbarians from the north, inflicted
its greatest trauma and pushed Romans to imagine that security
could truly arrive only when the state's borders extended far beyond
the capital's walls. Together, these two moments forced the Republic
to deepen the political integration of plebeians and patricians so it
could create a more uniform ruling class capable of administering
the rapidly growing state.

Rome's conflict with Veii catalyzed all these developments.
Veii was a large, wealthy, and well-defended city that sat on a plateau perched above the fertile farmland it governed. Veii controlled
around half as much territory as the Republic itself and shared a
contested border with Rome that sparked repeated conflicts in the
later fifth century. The two city-states initially battled over the town

of Fidenae, a site located about six miles north of Rome. Fidenae was a natural bridgehead over the Tiber: Whoever controlled it would be able to determine which merchants and armies reached the Tiber's mouth.[1] Rome seized the town in 435 and held it despite Veientine attacks across the 420s. The two cities eventually agreed to a truce that lasted until 407. At that time, as the delegations from both cities met to discuss an extension, news reached Rome that a Volscian force had massacred the Roman garrison in the town of Verrugo. A Roman army had quickly arrived and defeated the Volscians, but the initial defeat emboldened the Veientines, and they threatened to murder the Roman envoys unless they revised the terms of the treaty significantly.[2]

The patrician-dominated Senate asked Roman magistrates to put a motion before the people (probably in the Comitia Centuriata) authorizing war with Veii. Remembering the hardships plebeian soldiers had endured in earlier wars, some tribunes objected to a major war with a powerful Etruscan state to Rome's northwest. They attacked it as a "war against the plebeians" that was designed to expose them "to the hardships of military service and slaughter by the enemy," while their families struggled to survive the economic impact of their service "far away from the city."[3]

Roman elites responded by agreeing to pay soldiers out of the public coffers. This concession represented a crucial step in unlocking the full military potential of the Roman state. In the past, Roman soldiers had provided their own equipment, covered their own expenses, and had often gone into debt to cover the losses their families sustained when the head of the household could not work on the farm. Now Roman soldiers would be paid to serve and would all have the same standard gear.[4] Rome covered these new costs by imposing a tax on all citizens that the wealthiest Romans paid by bringing wagons of bronze ingots to the treasury, because Rome did not yet use coins. Plebeians of military age who had been skeptical of the declaration of war against Veii responded enthusiastically to the opportunity to get paid to fight for their Republic. "Nothing," Livy would write, "was ever received by the plebs with such joy," and "no one, as long as he had any strength, would spare his life's blood in service of such a generous state."[5]

Despite these reforms, Rome's third war with Veii would become one of the longest and most symbolically important conflicts in early Roman history. Roman tradition held that it dragged on for ten years, the same length of time as the Greek siege of Troy, and that it involved year-round campaigning, a new feature of Roman military life.[6] And the narrative later historians told became embroidered with more and more fabulous stories as their accounts of the conflict progressed. This did not bother later Romans. Even Livy, who preserved many of the most impressively implausible tales, put aside his skepticism and remarked, "I am satisfied if things which resemble the truth are accepted as true in such ancient affairs."[7]

These tales that "resemble the truth" fill much of the fifth book of Livy's history and enabled him to show how the tangible, material fate of the Roman state connected to the religious and political behaviors of its citizens. Livy overlays details of the war with discussions of political tensions in Rome, divine signs the Romans misunderstood, and portents whose significance Romans belatedly grasped.[8] Patrician and plebeian bickering features prominently. They fought about how to interpret shifts in the weather, the credibility of prophecies, and even what to do with the plunder Rome planned to take from Veii—before Rome even won the war.[9] What emerges is a portrait of a society on the brink of dramatic changes that lacked the cohesion or social sophistication to manage them.[10]

As is so typical of our accounts of early Republican history, a Roman hero emerged to resolve the internal and external conflicts. In 396 BC, the Romans appointed the dictator Camillus to conclude the war. Livy describes Camillus restoring order by punishing deserters from the army besieging Veii, enrolling a new army in which "no one refused to serve," and drawing troops from Rome's Latin and Hernician allies. As soon as Camillus reached Veii, he commanded the army to work in shifts, so they could tunnel underneath the city's formidable walls. Those not digging were ordered to work on aboveground siege works, to give the impression that the Romans intended to climb over Veii's walls or batter down its gates.[11]

Camillus disguised work on the tunnel so expertly that, when Romans erupted into the temple of the goddess Juno, the shocked defenders panicked. Romans emerging from the ground fanned out to attack the soldiers on the walls from behind, broke the bolts that held the gates shut, and set fires to scatter the population. The main forces then looted the city and enslaved the survivors.[12]

Livy makes clear that the next phase in the conflict, after "the fall of Veii, the wealthiest city of the Etruscan people," involved the incorporation of its people, territory, and gods into the Roman state. Before his final assault, Camillus, invoking "Juno Regina, you who now dwell in Veii," prayed that the goddess would "follow us in our victory into the city that is ours," and promised to build her "a temple worthy of [her] greatness" in Rome should the attack succeed. After all resistance in Veii ceased, selected members of the army were ritually cleansed and sent to approach the statue of Juno. "One of them," Livy writes, asked the goddess, "'Juno, do you want to go to Rome?'" And "at this, all the others cried out that the goddess had nodded her assent." She was then carried to the Aventine, "where," he says, "Camillus later dedicated the temple that he had vowed." Juno's arrival on the Aventine solidified the incorporation of Veii into an expanded Roman state.[13]

Camillus's great victory did not calm the tensions between patricians and plebeians that the war with Veii had exposed. Almost immediately after Camillus celebrated his triumph, plebeians began to complain about having to pay to fulfill a vow that Camillus made to grant 10 percent of the plunder from Veii to the cult of Apollo based in the Greek city of Delphi.[14] In 395 BC, disturbances again roiled Rome after plebeians proposed that half of the Roman population should move to Veii and live under plebeian leadership, so that "the Roman people could inhabit the two cities under a common government." Livy says that the patricians prevented a vote that would "force [Romans] to abandon their native land and citizens" and allow "Veii to enjoy greater fortune after her capture than when she was unharmed."[15] Ultimately, the patricians agreed to distribute a little more than four acres of land taken from the territory of Veii to each plebeian on the condition that "Rome would not be abandoned."[16] Finally, as the 390s concluded, Camillus himself was exiled, just after a plebeian had reported hearing an inhuman voice call out that Romans should expect Gallic barbarians in Rome.[17] For Livy, these events showed that Roman society had learned nothing from the war with Veii. "Not only did men reject the warnings of the gods as Fate began her assault," Livy wrote, "but they even removed Marcus Furius [Camillus], Rome's only human help, from the city" as a crisis approached.[18]

Like the war with Veii, the coming of the Gauls to Rome so deeply impacted later Roman literature that the details of what happened are exceedingly difficult to reconstruct. Even the year in which it happened is disputed, though 386 BC seems the most likely choice.[19] Generally, though, the Gallic attack on Rome was part of a larger movement of Gauls into Northern Italy that began in the sixth century BC and saw Gallic settlers gradually push south across the Po River Valley and probe the defenses of established Italian communities.[20] The powerful Etruscan cities of Central Italy usually checked the Gauls before they reached Rome, but the Senones, the Gallic force that attacked Rome, were something of a different case. Led by a man named Brennus, the Senones entered Etruria as mercenaries hired to intervene in an internal political conflict in the city of Clusium.[21] The leaders of Clusium requested Roman help in dealing with these mercenaries, but the ambassadors that Rome sent became involved in the fighting when the Gauls ignored their order to withdraw.[22] This violation of the long-established convention stipulating that emissaries were to remain neutral prompted Brennus to advance on Rome.[23]

Neither patricians nor plebeians grasped the seriousness of Brennus's approach. They instead fell back into the plebeian and patrician divisions that had plagued the city during and after the war with Veii. Patricians wanted to sanction Quintus Fabius, the emissary who played the most prominent part in the fighting at Clusium. Plebeians, though, not only refused to endorse this recommendation but chose Fabius as one of the military commanders who would confront the Gauls. In the meantime, an enraged Brennus and his followers marched toward Roman territory, defeated a Roman force near the Allia River, and then made for the city itself.[24]

The Senones entered the nearly abandoned capital through the Colline Gate. Some survivors from the Battle of the Allia fortified the Capitoline Hill, but most of the Roman army and civilian population had fled to Veii, while the Vestal Virgins went in a different direction so they could hide the "sacred objects of the Roman state" in the Etruscan city of Caere.[25] The Gauls occupied the Forum, set a guard to watch the defenders on the Capitoline Hill, and then began looting.

Livy describes a scene in which the plebeian homes were all locked and abandoned but elderly patricians who had held consulships remained in their homes with the doors open, seated on ivory chairs and waiting to die. "After the slaughter of the leading men," he reports, "no mortal was spared. Houses were plundered and, when empty, torched," in a holocaust that "leveled everything."[26] The Gauls then tried a series of failed assaults on the Capitoline, one of which was supposedly foiled by the honking of the sacred geese associated with Juno, formerly the goddess of Veii.[27]

In the meantime, Camillus and the Roman refugees in Veii organized an army that marched to Rome and defeated the Gauls in two battles. Camillus argued forcefully that, despite the destruction in Rome, Romans should not succumb to the temptation of moving to Veii. Instead, they should remain true to their city and the gods that protected it. Livy ends Book Five of his history with the Roman decision to stay and rebuild.[28] The same decision to stay at Rome and rebuild it "from a state of utter destruction" concludes the episode in Plutarch's *Life of Camillus.*

Plutarch and Livy were not alone in focusing significant attention on the Gallic sack of Rome and Rome's recovery from it. In fact, this was the first Roman historical event noted by contemporary Greek authors, and a host of later Latin authors also spoke either directly or indirectly about the Gallic sack.[29] The event so profoundly shook the Romans that Augustan-era calendars marked July 18, the date of the Roman battlefield rout, as the Day of the Allia, one of only two Roman defeats so commemorated.[30] The mere threat of a future Gallic attack allowed Rome to draft priests and old men who normally would be exempt from military service. Some have even suggested that the Romans later engaged in a sort of defensive imperialism designed to push the Roman frontiers back from the capital to prevent a repeat of Brennus's destruction.[31]

The reality of the Gallic sack is far more complicated than the legends told by ancient historians suggest. Archaeological excavations show little trace of a massive layer of burned structures that would accompany the sort of absolute destruction the ancient historians describe. It seems much more likely that the Romans deliberately evacuated the city. The Gauls then plundered the empty space and withdrew, perhaps after receiving some payment from the Roman state.[32] Even the successful defense of the Capitoline Hill now seems dubious.[33] So too do Livy's claims that the Romans debated abandoning the devastated city, that Camillus persuaded them to stay, and that the chaotic and unplanned layout of Rome in his day reflected the haphazard nature of the city's rapid reconstruction.[34]

In truth, later Roman tradition seems to have almost entirely fabricated Camillus's role. A more likely narrative can be culled from a range of less dramatic but more reliable sources that describe the Gauls moving south to serve in an army of the Sicilian city of Syracuse that fought in Southern Italy after their sack of Rome. The Gallic forces were then intercepted on their way back north later in the year by an army from the Roman-allied Etruscan city of Caere, the city to which the Vestal Virgins had fled. The Caeretans defeated Brennus's band and recovered much of the plunder the Gauls had taken in Rome as well as the ransom they were paid to leave the city. Rome's alliance system, rather than the innate heroism of a great Roman, led to the defeat of this wandering band of Gallic warriors.[35]

The Gallic sack of Rome then highlights a particular point of inflection for how Rome exercised power in Central Italy. In a way, Rome survived the Gallic sack because of the military alliances with other independent Italian city-states that had dominated Roman policy in the fifth century, and because of the embryonic Roman imperial structure that the capture of Veii had begun to create. Rome's civilians survived, and its army regrouped, because the Republic directly controlled Veii. But the Gauls were defeated by Rome's Caeretan allies.

DESPITE THE EFFORTS of Caere, the aftermath of the Gallic sack saw Rome begin to pivot away from its fifth-century alliances and toward a territorial expansion that directly integrated newly conquered people into the Roman state. In the year after the Gallic sack, Rome extended citizenship to the surviving residents of Veii as well as to the inhabitants of some smaller communities Rome had recently conquered.[36] The nature of Rome's alliances also began to change as Rome favored more important cities like Caere and Massalia (the modern French city of Marseilles) over its older Latin and Hernician friends.[37] Those older relationships deteriorated to such a degree that some Latin cities and colonies eventually joined an anti-Roman alliance with the Volscians. This included two Latin colonies that Rome had established in Volscian territory in the fifth century as well as the cities of Praeneste and Tusculum.

Rome had defeated all the defectors by 380, and its treatment of Tusculum created a template for how it would handle similar behavior for the rest of the fourth century. Although it had broken its alliance with Rome, Tusculum surrendered without a fight after the ever-present Camillus led an army to the city. Its leaders traveled to Rome, spoke before the Senate, and acknowledged that they had "wronged" their allies. The Senate granted them "peace at that time and, not long after, full citizenship," at which point "the legions were marched back from Tusculum."[38] The Senate did not extend citizenship out of generosity. This was instead an effort to use the presence of a Roman army to irrevocably bind Tusculum to Rome by making its residents Roman.

Rome continued to fight former allies in Central Italy for much of the mid-fourth century in conflicts that transformed polities once joined to Rome by voluntary alliances into Roman territory. This process accelerated greatly in 343 when Rome intervened in a complicated conflict in Campania, the coastal region of western Italy centered around the Bay of Naples. Rome entered the war by allying with the city of Capua against the Samnites, a group of tribes inhabiting the mountains to Campania's east with which Rome had once been allied. Less than two years after the fighting began, Rome switched sides and resumed its alliance with the Samnites. This Roman reversal prompted a widespread revolt by many of Rome's Latin allies, several Campanian cities, and the Volscians. By 338, Rome had defeated all of them.

Rome used its new military dominance to redefine the political relationships that governed life across much of Latium and Campania. Rome directly absorbed some captured cities into the Roman state and extended Roman citizenship to their residents. Other defeated cities retained control over their local political life, but lost any capacity to conduct foreign affairs, and were often compelled to cede so much territory that they existed as islands in a Roman sea. A final category of states received a special sort of Roman citizenship called *civitas sine suffragio*, literally "citizenship without voting rights," that made them "liable for all the burdens and obligations of full citizens" but gave them "no political rights."[39] These cities had to provide troops to the Roman army, but they had no say in whether Rome fought or where the fighting might take place. The only tangible benefits they received were the rights to marry Roman citizens and to conduct business in Rome.

Romans could not have known it at the time, but this nuanced approach to defeated adversaries would allow them to build the most formidable military machine the Mediterranean world had ever known. One of the biggest challenges that ancient states faced was balancing expansion with effective government. A state that grew too large, too quickly, often struggled to maintain control over its diverse subject populations, who chafed at the loss of their independence. But a state that granted full political rights to a subject population could also find itself struggling to function effectively, as political institutions built for a citizen body of a certain size failed to meet the needs of a larger group of citizens.

Rome had stumbled upon a partial solution to both problems by creating what the historian Tim Cornell has called a "Roman commonwealth." This structure maximized the military resources Rome could draw from its defeated adversaries and minimized its need to manage the domestic affairs of cities used to functioning independently.[40] Because Rome could determine the status accorded to a defeated enemy, it could scale up this approach as it expanded into new territories.

These foreign successes came as a few leading plebeians sought to fashion a unified ruling class by breaking down the divisions between the patrician and plebeian magistracies. From 445 until 367 BC, the chief magistrates in the Roman state had alternated irregularly between consuls and consular tribunes, a military command with powers like that of a consul.[41] Only patricians served as consuls in this period, and although the consular tribune position was open to plebeians, few were ever elected.[42] Some wealthy plebeians had become frustrated at the limitations this system placed on their political careers and wanted a return to annual consulships that could be held by both patricians and plebeians.[43]

Few plebeians cared very much about expanding the career prospects of their order's richest and most powerful members, and their leaders understood that no change to rules governing consular eligibility could pass unless it was packaged with other, more popular ideas. In 376 BC, two ambitious tribunes, Caius Licinius Stolo and Lucius Sextius Lateranus, linked the unpopular consular reform to measures that would lift the threat of debt bondage from plebeians and reform the way that public land seized from defeated enemies was distributed.[44] Livy describes Licinius and Sextius effectively shutting down the operation of much of the Roman state for most of the next decade as they fought to get these three laws approved. Not only did they block elections to patrician magistracies (between 375 and 371), but they stopped a vote in the plebeian assembly when it looked like the debt relief and land reforms would pass but the consular reform would not.[45]

Finally, in 367, the three measures passed together in a reform package historians call the Licinio-Sextian laws after the two tribunes who fought for them. The first law reworked the loans that Romans had taken out, by deducting all interest payments a debtor had made from the loan principal and then allowing for the balance of the loan to be paid off in three annual installments. This law was a good start, but it took a series of subsequent reforms before the institution of debt bondage finally disappeared. The second law established that no one could lease more than 500 *iugera* (about 300 acres) of public land per family, but, although this limit was codified, it proved difficult to enforce. Eventually, it was not enforced at all.[46]

Unsurprisingly, the tribunes most wanted to implement the law opening the consulship to plebeians. Although this reform seems to us to shift the structures of Roman political life, the consulship combined military, political, and religious duties, and Romans themselves were most concerned about whether the gods would accept religious ceremonies led by plebeians. Licinius and Sextius alleviated this concern by reconstituting the board of men who interpreted the sacred Sibylline books so that it included an equal number of patricians and plebeians. This was, Livy wrote, "regarded as a further step to opening up the path to the consulship" for plebeians, because it allowed other Romans to see that the gods had not been troubled by plebeians participating in elements of Roman religious life from which they had previously been excluded. It was only after the gods indicated their approval that the plebeian assembly agreed to support a full-time restoration of the consulship.[47]

The other highest offices of the Roman state quickly opened up to plebeians after the barrier to their consular service crumbled. In little more than a decade, Romans selected their first plebeian dictator and censor (the magistrate responsible for conducting the census, among other duties). Within a generation, Romans had become so comfortable with plebeian higher magistrates that they passed laws requiring that at least one consul each year and one censor each census must be a plebeian.[48] Plebeian service in all magistracies, once taboo, was now deemed essential to the state's health. Rome had finally developed a single ruling class made up of wealthy and well-connected patricians and plebeians.

The law mandating at least one plebeian censor was passed just one year before Rome completed its victory over the Samnites, the Latins, and their allies. The year 338 BC then saw Rome stabilize its domestic affairs, finalize the creation of a genuine patrician and plebeian ruling nobility, and arrive at a strategy for integrating conquered peoples into the growing state. Rome was ready to dominate Italy.

Chapter 6

Roman Domination of Italy

338–272 BC

THE REMARKABLE SETTLEMENTS of 338 BC created the internal and external infrastructure that enabled Rome to absorb much of the Italian Peninsula over the next six decades. Rome's system of strategically incorporating the territory and people of a defeated adversary, either by allowing that state to remain an independent ally of Rome or by making its population Roman citizens with or without voting rights, allowed it to build larger armies that could fight far from the capital. In 338, Rome was the leading power in Central Italy. By 280, it dominated the peninsula through a patchwork of territorial annexations, colonial establishments, citizenship extensions, and compulsory alliances.

This expansion occurred in the context of two long wars that are now called the Second and Third Samnite Wars. Although the fighting began in Samnium, these conflicts grew to include most of the major powers in the peninsula. The Etruscans, Umbrians, Samnites, Greek cities, and even Gauls entered the conflicts at various points. As the wars progressed and Roman power grew, these diverse peoples formed grand coalitions in which they combined forces to confront Rome. But Rome eventually prevailed, in large part because each successful engagement increased the size of Rome's territory, enlarged its citizen body, and added to the number of recruits it could compel its allies to provide.

The Second Samnite War began as a regional conflict in which the Samnites tried to block further Roman expansion into Central Italy. In 321, the Samnites trapped an invading Roman army led by both consuls in a valley called the Caudine Forks.

The account we have of the Battle at Caudine Forks has transformed what certainly was a major, bloody Roman defeat into a bloodless morality tale remembered as one of the defining events of fourth-century BC Roman history.[1] As Livy describes it, the Samnite commander Gaius Pontius ensnared the full Roman army and sent a letter to his father asking what to do with them. His father advised him to pardon the Romans and bind Rome in friendship to the Samnites. This confused Pontius and he sent a second messenger to ask for clarification. His father replied that if Pontius did not want to pardon the Romans, he should kill them all so that Rome could not easily rearm. The old man warned, however, that a middle course of humiliation without destroying the Roman army would entrench Roman anger but not diminish their capacity to avenge the indignity. Disregarding his father's advice, Pontius forced the Romans to swear to observe a truce with the Samnites and embarrassed them by compelling them to march unarmed between the ranks of the Samnite troops. He then took hostages as security that the truce would be observed. The consuls returned to Rome, told the Senate to refuse to endorse the treaty, and volunteered to be returned to the Samnites so that the state could resume hostilities without violating the religious pledge the consuls had made personally.

Whatever happened at the Caudine Forks checked Roman expansion against the Samnites for five years. But Livy's fictional warning delivered by Pontius's father foreshadowed the actions of an angry military power that returned to the war with greater capacity when fighting resumed. Rome had used the ceasefire to absorb more of the regions near Samnium. In 318, it established new voting tribes, the Ufentina and Falerina, so that Roman citizens in Campania could vote. This paved the way for Roman armies to campaign in the Southern Italian regions of Apulia and Lucania, and they soon had much of Samnium surrounded.

Rome returned to action with a larger military that fought more effectively. By 311, the Republic had increased the size of its army to four legions, so that Rome could campaign in more places at once. The allied contingents who joined these legions gave Rome the largest pool of fighting men in Italy. Roman capabilities were also enhanced through the creation of a new, more flexible system of fighting based on the *maniple*, a tactical unit involving four differently equipped rows of troops that could strike rapidly and then withdraw through the lines of the next batch of Romans to take the field. The youngest soldiers began the battle by bombarding the enemy with waves of missiles. They withdrew through the lines of the *hastati*, inexperienced infantrymen who were equipped with javelins and short swords. After the *hastati* exhausted themselves, they retreated through the approaching lines of the more experienced *principes*. Then, if the *principes* needed to do so, they could withdraw and be replaced by the *triarii*, the most heavily armed and experienced soldiers in the Roman army.[2]

Rome's superior manpower and tactics wore down its regional adversaries over the last two decades of the third century. By the time the war ended with a Roman-Samnite peace treaty in 304, Rome had absorbed most of Etruria. Meanwhile, the Aequi, Hernici, and Italic peoples along the Adriatic had also come under Roman domination. The Aequi fared particularly badly after Romans responded to their refusal to become Roman citizens with a lightning invasion that massacred civilians, burned towns, and then implanted Roman colonists on Aequian lands.[3]

Other Italians proved more compliant than the Aequi. Many of the peoples of the eastern Italian region of Abruzzi joined Rome as permanent allies between 304 and 302. Some towns came under Roman control through the extension of citizenship without voting rights. In cases where a significant city resisted Rome too actively, the Romans captured it and sent colonists to hold the area. Such was the case with the colony of Narnia, founded in Umbria following the

Roman capture of the city of Nequinum. But Rome also incorporated some cities more deeply into the state by granting their residents full citizenship, creating two new voting tribes to enable them to vote in Rome.[4]

By this time, Roman expansion had taken on such momentum that a number of Italian cities and peoples realized they faced a choice: They could either become a part of Rome's commonwealth of allies and citizens, and share in the rewards of its victories, or they could band together and resist. Enough of them chose to resist that the Third Samnite War soon erupted. The spark came in 298, when Rome, which was still fighting in Etruria and Umbria, provoked the Samnites by forging an alliance with the Lucanians, a group living in the coastal region south of Samnium.

Fighting simultaneously on two fronts stretched the Republic's military resources and its political institutions. Rome's most accomplished and experienced commanders were charged with leading armies for much longer than the usual one-year terms that Roman magistrates served. After three years of fighting, five such "promagistrates" were commanding in the war's various theaters. Meanwhile, the Samnites had joined with Etruscans, Umbrians, and Gallic forces based on the other side of Etruria.[5]

The Roman and anti-Roman coalitions met in a decisive battle near the Umbrian town of Sentinum in 295 that turned when the consul Publius Decius Mus decided to lead a series of cavalry charges into the Gallic army. His first charge pushed the Gallic cavalry back from the fray, but the second drew the consul and his companions far beyond the front lines. Gallic soldiers and wagons quickly surrounded them, panicking both the men and their horses. The chaos in the Roman ranks prompted the Gallic infantry to charge so that they could rout their Roman adversaries.

At that moment Decius Mus decided to perform a *devotio*, a ritual vow in which a general audibly pledges to sacrifice his life for the Republic so the gods may guarantee that his army wins a battle. His father, Publius Decius Mus the Elder, had done this at the Battle of Vesuvius in 340 BC; forty-five years later, his son elected to do the same thing at Sentinum. According to Livy, he declared, upon announcing his decision, "It is the privilege of our family that we should be sacrificed to avert the nation's perils." Then he said the ritual prayers and "spurred his charger against the Gallic lines, where he saw that they were thickest, and, hurling himself against the weapons of the enemy, he met his death."[6]

The *devotio* had the desired effect. The enemy army broke as Decius Mus's consular colleague Quintus Fabius Maximus Rullianus sent a squad of cavalry to attack the Gauls from behind, and they were followed by a group of Roman *principes*. The Romans and their allies then cut through the disordered enemy and slaughtered so many Gauls that, as Livy put it, "the consul's body could not be found that day, because it was buried under heaps of slain Gauls."[7]

Decius Mus's self-sacrifice helped decide the war. By 290, Rome had overrun all of Samnium. Ten years later, Roman territory extended all the way to the Adriatic. Strings of Roman colonies and populations living as Roman citizens both with and without the right to vote spread across the center of the Italian Peninsula. Decius Mus's sacrifice was rightly remembered as a key event in catalyzing this growth.

Another aspect of Decius Mus's action explains why the Republic functioned so well internally amid such dramatic territorial expansion and extensions of citizenship. Both Publius Decius Mus the Elder and his son were plebeian consuls who belonged to the joint patrician-plebeian Roman nobility birthed by the Licinio-Sextian laws of 367. When Decius Mus the Elder died during his consulship in 340, he had done so as just the second plebeian consul to hold office following passage of the law requiring one consul a year to be a plebeian. His sacrifice resonated with both patricians and plebeians among the Roman ruling class. But that of his son was commemorated even more impressively. When Fabius, Decius Mus the Younger's surviving senatorial colleague, returned to Rome in triumph, Livy described how the soldiers marching in the procession and the crowd witnessing it "celebrated no less the glorious death of Publius Decius than the victory of Fabius, reviving by their praise of the son the memory of the father, whose death (and its service to the

Republic) had now been matched."⁸ Fabius was a patrician, but he, his soldiers, and the Roman public saw no problem in commemorating Fabius's plebeian colleague alongside him.

While Decius Mus the Younger's *devotio* had an immense effect on the fortunes of the Roman state, it was only in death that he managed to surpass his father's legacy. Although he had been elected consul four times, Livy suggests that he had spent his entire political career struggling to measure up to his revered father. This was not unusual among Romans. They spent much of their lives in spaces that forced them to regularly reflect upon the achievements of their ancestors.⁹ The main public atrium in an elite Roman family house contained images of ancestors that stared down at the current residents. The head of the family would speak about all of their achievements each year during the Roman Parentalia, a festival that involved activities showing respect for ancestors, such as traveling to a family tomb filled with sarcophagi bearing epitaphs that detailed the achievements of the deceased.¹⁰

The young patrician and plebeian notables who regularly interacted with these ancestral relics likely felt a unique intergenerational obligation to maintain the family's status. A man could feel proud to have exceeded the rank and public honors of his father and grandfather. He would be satisfied to match them. But falling short of their achievements represented a real failure, something that all subsequent generations would note as they looked at the images of their ancestors and spoke about their lives. These future Romans would note with pride the men who had risen to higher office than any family member before them, but would think very little of the men under whom the family's fortunes declined.

Young, ambitious Romans felt even more intense pressure to measure up to their ancestors because Roman voters and other elites controlled their access to the offices and honors they craved. Elite families accepted this because, as the cabal that controlled the Republic, they collectively decided how to distribute the rewards for service to Rome among themselves. At the same time, talented Romans looking to either revive their families' fortunes or become the first in their families to hold high magistracies looked for ways to break the stranglehold that fourth-century patricians and plebeians held on these offices.

No FOURTH-CENTURY FIGURE did this more aggressively than the patrician Appius Claudius Caecus. He made for an interesting populist champion. His family had entered the patrician order in 504 BC when his ancestor (also named Appius Claudius) arrived in Rome with an army of attendants and offered to join the Republic. Livy describes this early Appius Claudius as a reactionary figure who strongly opposed the earliest moves to establish plebeian magistracies and the Concilium Plebis (Plebeian Assembly) in the 490s. Another ancestor, also named Appius Claudius, had been the archvillain among the second group of decemvirs who had refused to step down in 449 BC. It was his attempted rape of Verginia that had precipitated the secessions of the plebs that brought the decemvirate down.

Appius Claudius Caecus has a much more complicated historical legacy. He, too, is a villain in Livy's telling, but fortunately, some of his own words survive to add more nuance to the historian's narrative. Sometimes seen as the father of Latin prose writing, Caecus wrote a work on Roman law and a series of famous sayings. Only fragments of these works and of some of his political speeches now survive, but they show a figure deeply attached to the idea of facilitating the continued expansion of Roman democracy beyond the core of noble patrician and plebeian families that the reforms of the 340s had empowered.[11]

Caecus did not pursue these reforms simply because he thought they would make Rome better. He advanced them because doing so helped his own career as well. Although the Claudii were a historically important family, their fortunes had declined following the fall of the decemvirate. Between 444 and 367 BC, only two members of the family held one of the top magistracies in Rome. Caecus's grandfather held a consulship in 349, but he died in office without doing anything of consequence. His father's career peaked when he was selected for a dictatorship in 337 from which he was immediately forced to abdicate. When Caecus began his career, the Claudii seemed to be a fading patrician family.

Caecus's early political career showed little promise until, perhaps out of desperation, he chose to run for election as censor. Fourth-century censors enjoyed considerable prestige, but they lacked the lawmaking capacities of tribunes and the military authority of consuls. Elected every five years, they performed duties that took too long for holders of annual magistracies to complete. Censors assumed responsibility for monitoring and awarding public works contracts, but their most important task was to supervise the count of Rome's citizens. They assessed the wealth of all citizens and made sure they were appropriately registered in the correct voting tribes and centuries. The process ordinarily took around a year and a half to complete and concluded with a sacred ritual of purification to mark the Roman population's transition from one era to another.

The power of the censors expanded dramatically at some point between 338 and 318 BC when a tribune of the plebs named Ovinius introduced a law that radically changed the nature of the Senate. Up to this point, the consuls had chosen the senators every year as they began serving their term in the consulship. The senators had then served as an advisory body during their term of office. When the consuls stepped down, a new Senate would be chosen by the new consuls. Ovinius wanted to require the censors to choose the senators instead of the consuls. Under his proposal, the censors would "enroll in the Senate the best men," so that the composition of the Senate would remain relatively stable. In other words, the law took the decision about senatorial membership away from annual magistrates and turned it over to the censors, who took office every five years. They were bound to "enroll the best men for all orders," a requirement that mandated the creation of a permanent body of important patricians and plebeians with a standard (albeit somewhat ambiguous) criterion for membership.[12]

The proposal, called the Lex Ovinia, was passed by the Plebeian Assembly. Ovinius may have intended only a minor shift to ensure that the new generation of plebeian magistrates could never be removed from the Senate by a patrician consul. But the law had major long-term implications. Before the Lex Ovinia, magistrates tended to work primarily with citizen assemblies when crafting and implementing policies, but the growth of Roman power had made this process inefficient. The new, more permanent Senate stepped forward to decide on issues such as military mobilizations that had once been the preserve of citizen assemblies.

In Republican Rome, it often took a bit of time for ambitious politicians to recognize how a change in the workings of the constitution could be exploited for their personal benefit. So it was with the Lex Ovinia. It was not until 312 BC that Appius Claudius Caecus won election to the censorship with a revolutionary understanding of what that office could do.[13] Unlike many of his peers, Caecus grasped that Roman censors who could combine the disparate powers and responsibilities of the office could now remake much of the political and economic life of the city. Once he entered office, he almost immediately began to use the office as a platform to build his own personal political machine.

Senatorial reform was a key part of his agenda. Caecus included the sons of freed slaves among its members, a step that Livy says allowed him to "gain influence in the Senate house" by bringing in people of low birth beholden to Caecus. It did not work initially. "Because of their hatred for him and their desire to please the most distinguished men," whenever the consuls called the Senate they only summoned the members listed by Caecus's predecessors. These supporters did not make a significant difference in Caecus's prospects.[14]

The low-born Romans were, however, not the real focus of his senatorial outreach. Caecus understood that the censorship also gave him an opportunity to build a much stronger, more enduring coalition of political clients. Censors could order, pay for, and attach their names to construction projects without receiving senatorial approval. Caecus realized that building monumental infrastructure could draw the attention of all Rome to his efforts, while offering Caecus a powerful tool for delivering lucrative contracts to new Roman citizens who owned land through which public works might pass. When Appius Claudius Caecus built Rome's first aqueduct, the ten-mile-long Aqua Appia (Appian Aqueduct), he "spent a large sum of public money for this construction without a decree of the Senate."[15] He also used the censor's position to pay for the building of the Appian Way, the first great Roman road, which stretched from the southern side of the city of Rome down to Capua in Campania. The first-century historian Diodorus Siculus called the road, named after the censor who built it, "a deathless monument" to a man who "was ambitious in the public interest."[16]

These projects served a host of political and military purposes. The Appian Way offered Roman and allied troops a fast and efficient route by which to travel to the southern theaters of the Samnite War. It ran through old Roman territory at first, then cut through areas that had recently been integrated into the Roman state, but whose elites had not yet become affiliated with any Roman political leader. As the road construction progressed toward Capua, Caecus bound to himself a network of these new Romans by purchasing their land, renting laborers they found, and connecting their farms to the bustling markets of the capital. He also may have enrolled some of these new clients in the Senate. At any rate, his new connections helped Caecus to rebuild the power and reputation of his family. Unlike some of the senators he chose, these new men had the wealth and power to remain enrolled in the future.[17]

Caecus also used censorial control over the distribution of Roman citizens into voting blocks to advance his immediate political prospects. Romans could only vote in person, in the city of Rome, and elections were decided not by whether a candidate received a majority of votes but by whether they carried the support of a majority of Rome's 31 voting tribes (or 193 voting centuries, if the election was held in the Comitia Centuriata). Not all tribes had an equal number of voters turn up, however. The four urban tribes based in Rome had the greatest number of voters, by far. Distance and travel expenses meant that the twenty-seven rural tribes usually had far fewer voters present than the four urban tribes, and those rural voters who did participate tended to be wealthier men who could afford to leave their homes to travel to the city to vote. This meant that a ballot cast by an individual member of a rural tribe counted for more than that of an individual from an urban tribe, even though it was likely less representative of the sensibilities of average citizens. It also meant that candidates could win elections despite losing the overall popular vote.

Appius Claudius Caecus used his new power as censor to allow all citizens to declare which voting class and which tribes they wanted to join, so that the voters once concentrated in the four urban tribes could now spread out among the twenty-seven rural ones. The maneuver offered a way to address the problem of unrepresentative electoral outcomes, but the redistribution did not last long. Diodorus describes how it incited the "hostility of the nobles," who saw it as a ploy by Caecus to gain "the goodwill of the many" by increasing the voting power of Roman citizens who owed him a debt of gratitude.[18] The next censors returned Romans to the geographically defined tribes. The voters, "in opposition to the nobles and in support of Appius," responded by electing Gnaeus Flavius as the aedile in charge of Roman markets. Flavius was "the first Roman whose father had been a slave to gain that office," and, perhaps just as importantly, he was also a client of Appius Claudius Caecus.[19]

Caecus's nakedly ambitious approach to the censor's essential and sacred public duty contrasted strongly with the behavior of his censorial colleague Lucius Plautius. Plautius, who imagined the job in very traditional terms, stepped down when the count of citizens had been completed a little more than a year after his term began. Caecus refused to do this. He stayed in office until the reforms he sponsored and the construction projects he began were all completed. Caecus even survived efforts by the Senate and a group of tribunes of the plebs to compel him to leave office or face arrest.[20]

Even if his reforms largely failed, his actions as censor defined a political brand that propelled him to heights not matched by his most recent ancestors. He twice won election to the consulship, served as dictator, and was one of the military commanders who led Roman armies in the Third Samnite War. But the moment that has forever defined Appius Claudius Caecus's legacy came in 280 BC.

By that time, the Roman victory in the Samnite Wars and subsequent expansion meant that the Roman commonwealth extended to the Po River in the north and deep into Magna Graecia in the south. Rome first entered that southern region in 285, when it allied with the city of Thurii, but subsequent alliances with other Greek cities led to the isolation of Tarentum, Southern Italy's most powerful city-state. Although Rome had agreed not to sail into Tarentine waters, Roman warships appeared near Tarentum in 282 BC in a clear provocation. The Tarentines responded by marching on Thurii, expelling the Roman garrison, and replacing the pro-Roman aristocracy with a democracy like their own.

Rome beat back the Tarentine forces from Thurii and put Tarentum itself under siege, but the Tarentine assembly invited the Greek king Pyrrhus of Epirus to come to Southern Italy and fight on their behalf. A cousin of Alexander the Great, Pyrrhus brought a powerful army of professional infantry, skilled cavalrymen, and elephant-mounted shock troops that he believed would overwhelm the citizen levies of the Romans. Pyrrhus had designs on seizing the Macedonian throne that had once belonged to Alexander and looked to this Italian campaign to build a base from which to recruit allies to help him mount more expansive campaigns in Sicily and ultimately Greece.[21]

Pyrrhus assumed that the quality of his troops would enable him to easily defeat the Romans and then impose a peace treaty on Rome and its allies that bound them to himself as he campaigned elsewhere. When the Romans took the field to fight, however, Pyrrhus was astonished at how well the Roman maniples fought. Although he attacked the Romans as they were crossing a river, they held their ground until a charge by Pyrrhus's elephants broke the lines of Roman soldiers who had never fought the animals.[22]

The elephants had terrified the Romans, and the defeat caused the defection of some Samnite and Lucanian communities that the Romans had recently absorbed. But the victory had also been costly for Pyrrhus. Although the king had won, he had lost large numbers of professionally trained troops. These soldiers had a lot of experience fighting together and could not easily be replaced.[23]

The Romans, on the other hand, "lost no time in filling up their depleted legions and raising others." Pyrrhus, soon realizing that he lacked the manpower to achieve military domination in Italy, sent his trusted adviser Cineas of Thessaly to Rome bearing an offer of peace and a military alliance to the Romans. Pyrrhus asked only that the Romans agree to an alliance with "himself, immunity for the Tarentines, and nothing else."[24]

"Most of the senators," Plutarch wrote, "were plainly inclined towards peace, since they had been defeated in one great battle, and expected another with a larger army, now that the Italian Greeks had joined Pyrrhus." It was at this moment, we are told, that Appius Claudius Caecus reemerged. The years had been hard on him. He remained "a man of distinction, but one whom old age and blindness had forced to give up all public activities." He was so infirm that he needed "his attendants to lift him up and had himself carried on a litter through the forum to the Senate-house. When he had reached the door, his sons and sons-in-law took him up in their arms and brought him inside." The spectacle quieted the senators.[25]

The speech that Appius Claudius Caecus gave changed Roman history.[26] He began by telling his younger colleagues, "Up to this time, O Romans, I have regarded the misfortune to my eyes as an affliction, but it now distresses me that I am not deaf as well as blind, that I might not hear these shameful resolutions and decrees of yours." In his younger days, Caecus continued, Romans had spoken about how they would have defeated Alexander the Great if he had turned west instead of east. Pyrrhus was a mere shadow of Alexander. The thought of bowing to him, Caecus continued, "diminishes the glory of Rome," and any peace treaty with him would cause others to "despise" Rome and allow "the Tarentines and Samnites to mock the Romans."[27]

It is often lost on a modern audience that many Roman senators were relatively young men. In the imperial period, their average age would have been around forty.[28] The senators who heard Caecus's speech were not old enough to remember a time before Rome dominated Italy. Many of them had not even been adults when Decius Mus sacrificed himself so that Rome could win the Battle of Sentinum. It was left to Appius Claudius Caecus, one of the last publicly active members of the generation that had won Italy for Rome, to remind his countrymen that what his generation had won, theirs could lose. Roman humiliation lurked beneath Pyrrhus's generous terms, and as the Samnite and Lucanian defections to Pyrrhus showed, humiliation was dangerous. Roman domination of Italy depended upon the magical combination of Italian eagerness to share in Rome's victories and fear of the consequences of betraying Rome. It took Appius Claudius Caecus to remind the Romans that the commonwealth on which their power and security depended could rapidly fall apart if Rome refused to fight to maintain it.[29]

This speech was Appius Claudius Caecus's final and most impactful public act. His epitaph in the Forum of Augustus concisely summarizes its effect: "He prohibited the establishment of peace with king Pyrrhus." Rome instead agreed to fight on. Pyrrhus advanced toward Rome, turned back to the south, and tried and failed to convince Naples and Capua to defect. In 279, Pyrrhus met and defeated a second Roman army, but Rome again inflicted serious losses on Pyrrhus and his allies. This event convinced Pyrrhus that Southern Italy would never serve as a secure base for his planned conquests. As he left the region, Pyrrhus supposedly commented, "If we should win one more battle against the Romans, we will be totally destroyed."[30] He returned once more to the Italian mainland and suffered a defeat at the hands of the Romans in 275 that prompted him to abandon Tarentum to its fate. The Republic placed colonies on the lands taken from the rebels who had joined Pyrrhus, and with the fall of Tarentum in 272, it finally, and fully, answered Appius Claudius Caecus's call for vengeance. Rome was now ready to expand beyond Italy and across the Mediterranean.

Chapter 7

Rome and Carthage

272–220 BC

R OME'S ULTIMATE VICTORY over Pyrrhus, its violent punishment of Italians who defected to the Greek king, and the surrender of Tarentum in 272 BC made the Roman Republic one the five largest states in the Mediterranean. Its only real rivals were three kingdoms carved out of the fragments of Alexander the Great's empire and the North African city of Carthage.

Each of these rivals controlled substantial territories. The Antigonid kingdom was centered on Macedon and exercised authority over much of Greece. The Seleucid Empire governed lands stretching from Asia Minor to Pakistan from its imperial centers in Mesopotamia, and, later, from the Syrian city of Antioch. The Ptolemaic kingdom controlled the Nile Valley and the Mediterranean coast from the Levant to modern Libya from its capital at the Egyptian city of Alexandria. Carthaginian territory extended across the Western Mediterranean and included much of coastal North Africa, southern Spain, Central Mediterranean islands such as Sardinia, and the western part of Sicily.

None of these powers had sufficient strength to destroy one another in 270 BC, but they all engaged in fighting over border territories. The Seleucids and Ptolemies battled over the area that is now Israel and Lebanon. The Antigonids fought the Seleucids and

Ptolemies in and around the Aegean and tried to prevent the remaining independent city-states in Greece from organizing sufficiently to liberate themselves from Macedonian hegemony. Carthage feared that the powerful eastern Sicilian Greek city-state of Syracuse might join with the Greek cities on the Italian mainland to threaten the Carthaginian presence on the island's west.

Rome would eventually eclipse all of these other powers, but Carthage was both the nearest and the one whose interests most closely conflicted with those of the expanding Republic. It had not always been so. Rome and Carthage had worked with one another for centuries. Their cooperation dated back at least to the treaty Carthage signed with Rome following the fall of Tarquinis Superbus, but Rome and Carthage had cooperated as recently as the 270s, when a Carthaginian fleet attacked Pyrrhus's ships as he tried to ferry troops from Sicily to fight Rome on the Italian mainland.[1]

The collaborative relationship between Rome and Carthage collapsed in 264 BC because of a conflict sparked by a Campanian mercenary group called the Mamertini. The Mamertini seized the Sicilian city of Messana and begun using it as a base to raid and "levy tribute" throughout Sicily.[2] When the Syracusan leader Hiero responded by sending out an army that placed Messana under siege, the Mamertini appealed to Syracuse's Sicilian rival Carthage and to Rome, which had come to control the Italian city of Rhegium, which lay on the other side of the narrow body of water separating the mainland from Sicily. The Mamertini offered "to entrust themselves and their citadel to the Carthaginians," if Carthage helped, but also said they would "turn the city over" to Rome if it came to their aid. They claimed that Rome, in particular, was obligated to help because the Mamertini were "members of the same race" as the Romans.[3]

Both Rome and Carthage wanted to stop Hiero from seizing control of the Sicilian side of the Strait of Messana, but Carthage moved faster, dispatching a commander named Hanno, who garrisoned Messana's citadel and forced Hiero to withdraw. This action changed Roman calculations. Rome had only recently taken control of Rhegium, and the Senate feared that either a Syracusan or Carthaginian presence in Messana might affect Roman control of Southern Italy.

A divided Senate then took the extraordinary step of making no recommendation about whether to send aid to the Mamertini, forcing the consuls to place the question of going to war before the Comitia Centuriata. They then convinced the centuries to vote in favor of a Roman intervention in Sicily that, they promised, would bring "great gains . . . to every individual from the spoils of war."[4] After the vote, the consul Appius Claudius Caudex, a relative of Appius Claudius Caecus, received the command and proceeded with "a strong force" to Rhegium.[5]

Once the Mamertini knew that Roman troops were coming, they asked Hanno, the Carthaginian commander, to leave Messana. Hanno did as he was told, but instead of withdrawing from the area, he camped his army outside the city and deployed his fleet to prevent the Romans from crossing the strait. The Syracusan army also remained in the field near Messana, so Hiero, the Syracusan leader, sent envoys to Hanno "to discuss their common interest" in preventing Rome from establishing a presence on Sicily. Carthage and Syracuse then "formed an alliance to make war on the Romans unless they should depart from Sicily with all speed."[6]

When Appius Claudius Caudex reached Rhegium, he first tried to negotiate the withdrawal of the Syracusan and Carthaginian forces by asserting that Messana was now under Roman protection. The embassy failed, but he managed to evade the Carthaginian blockade and sneak his army across the straits at night using ships provided by Roman allies. Once he reached Sicily, Caudex again tried to negotiate an end to the standoff—and again failed to do so. Only at that point did he attack his rivals. He first took the field against Hiero, "drove the enemy back to their camp, stripped the enemy dead," and compelled the Syracusans to retreat. He then attacked the Carthaginians, "killed large numbers of their troops, and forced them to retreat in disorder" to Carthaginian territory in western Sicily.[7]

The following year, the newly appointed consuls continued the war Appius Claudius Caudex had begun. Rome sent perhaps as many as 40,000 troops to the island. The size and strength of the army prompted many "Sicilian cities to rise against the Carthaginians and Syracusans and come over to the Romans." Hiero, too, broke with Carthage, "placed himself under Roman protection, and kept them provided with essential supplies at all times," while they campaigned on Sicily. He also agreed to pay a large war indemnity of 150,000 silver drachmas to Rome.[8] With the conflict seemingly winding down, one of the consuls led his army back across the straits while his colleague attacked some towns under Carthaginian control, in order to induce Carthage to come to terms with Rome as well.

Carthage was not done fighting. It had learned from Rome's pattern of expansion in Italy, and it understood that Rome had the manpower and the military capacity to expand its holdings in Sicily now that it had secured a presence on the island. The danger that Rome might attack seemed particularly acute because of the way Sicilian cities had so quickly accepted Roman control. Carthage then "recruited mercenaries[,] . . . dispatched them all to Sicily," and concentrated the army in the strategic city of Agrigentum. Seeing this as a sign that Carthage planned to intensify the conflict, Rome sent both consuls back to Sicily so they could attack Agrigentum before all the mercenary reinforcements could arrive.[9] The consuls put it under siege, defeated a large relief force sent from Africa, and captured the city when the Carthaginian mercenaries abandoned it.

These operations began a war unlike any Rome had fought before. The victory at Agrigentum prompted Rome to imagine that a conquest of Sicily would resemble its rapid absorption of the Greek cities in Southern Italy. Carthage, however, controlled more territory than Rome. It had more money and administrative sophistication than Rome and had the best navy in the Western Mediterranean. Its capital lay on the other side of the Mediterranean from Italy. And Carthage was much better equipped to fight on the island of Sicily than Rome was, as Rome's greatest strengths lay in the size and skill of its armies, and it in fact had no navy.

Rome, however, soon challenged Carthaginian naval superiority by building its own fleet. The initial landing of Roman troops in

Sicily took place using ships borrowed from the Greek cities subject to Roman authority in Southern Italy. These small vessels were far less powerful than the Carthaginian quinqueremes, fast and powerful warships with five decks of oars. Because ancient naval warfare consisted primarily of tactical struggles in which combatants maneuvered to puncture their opponent's hulls with bronze rams, the larger and faster Carthaginian ships commanded the sea.

Rome tried to quickly rectify this situation. During the Roman crossing to Sicily, a Carthaginian quinquereme ran aground on the Italian side of the straits. The Romans captured the ship and reverse-engineered a fleet of 120 quinqueremes by "using it as a model."[10] It was one thing to have a fleet of quinqueremes, but it was quite another to know how to sail and fight with such complicated vessels. The Greek historian Polybius describes the Romans placing their rowers "on benches on dry land" for training. They learned how to synchronize their strokes while the shipwrights finished building the ships. But the sailors had less than three weeks of actual practice on the sea before they saw their first action against the mighty Carthaginian quinqueremes, the best ships in the region.[11]

The fight was a disaster. One of the consuls engaged a Carthaginian fleet of twenty ships with seventeen of the new Roman vessels outside of Lipara. The Carthaginian admiral executed a nighttime maneuver and trapped the Roman vessels in the harbor as the terrified Roman sailors scurried back to land. The Carthaginians then captured all seventeen ships and sailed them back to join their own fleet.

The Roman response showed tremendous ingenuity. Roman armies fought on land with a confidence that the raw sailors had lacked when they confronted the much more experienced Carthaginians on the sea. The Romans then decided to refashion naval warfare so it involved the hand-to-hand combat at which Roman soldiers excelled. They attached a round pole with a pulley to their ships and attached it to a gangplank with a spike on its ends. This device, called a *corvus* (from the Latin word for a raven), would be "dropped on the deck of an enemy vessel when a ship charged an opponent," wrote

Polybius. "As soon as the raven was embedded in the planks of the deck and fastened the two ships together, soldiers would leap into the enemy vessel." The *corvus* rendered the strange and disorienting experience of fighting at sea into something close to a land battle.[12]

The Romans first deployed the *corvus* in 260 during a naval battle outside of Mylae, along Sicily's northeastern tip. The overeager Carthaginians had put 130 ships to sea and charged the Romans, but they then "found that their vessels were invariably held fast by the 'ravens' as Roman troops swarmed aboard . . . and fought them hand-to-hand," as if in "a battle on dry land." "Unnerved by these tactics," Polybius wrote, the Carthaginians "turned and fled . . . and, in all, lost fifty ships."[13]

Carthage soon adapted to the *corvus*, but the device had given Roman sailors time to become comfortable enough with conventional naval warfare that the war became a stalemate. After eight years of fighting, primarily in and around Sicily, the Senate authorized an invasion of North Africa in 256 so that "the Carthaginians would feel that the war no longer threatened Sicily but their own territory."[14] It began with a Roman naval victory off the coast of Libya that allowed the Republic to land 20,000 troops. The Roman consul Marcus Atilius Regulus spent much of the next year advancing on Carthage, pillaging the countryside, and setting up camp on the outskirts of the capital.

The war could have ended then, but Atilius overreached. When a Carthaginian delegation was sent to discuss peace terms, he treated them with such harshness that, Diodorus reports, they felt "peace framed by him was no better than slavery."[15] They resolved to fight on, and in 255, they routed Atilius's forces with the help of a Spartan mercenary commander named Xanthippus. Xanthippus had arranged a sophisticated attack in which Carthaginian elephants scattered the legions and allowed cavalry to envelop the Roman lines. This victory "reversed the course of the whole war."[16] It forced a Roman evacuation of North Africa, and, by the time a storm wrecked much of the Roman fleet, neither side had gained a clear advantage over the other.[17]

The war then became what Polybius evocatively called "a boxing match in which two champions, both in perfect training and both distinguished for their courage . . . exchange blow after blow," but lacked the ability to knock the other out.[18] This type of fighting cost Rome dearly. "The Romans and their allies," Diodorus wrote, "lost thousands of ships and no fewer than one hundred thousand men, including those who perished by shipwreck." This included both the fleet lost during the retreat from North Africa in 254 and another destroyed by the Carthaginians in a battle near the Sicilian port of Drepana in 249.[19]

Rome persevered through twenty-two years of bitter, ruinously expensive conflict until, in 242, Polybius reports, "the Romans braced themselves for a final life or death effort" by building a third great fleet. As "there were no funds in the treasury to finance the enterprise," individual Romans granted the state money "to build and outfit a quinquereme, with the understanding that they would be repaid" if Rome won the war.[20] This crowdsourced Roman fleet seized the harbor at Drepana, cut off the Carthaginian defenders of the Sicilian city of Lilybaeum, and then defeated a Carthaginian fleet sent to relieve the city. The Carthaginians, Polybius wrote, had "the resolution and the will" to keep fighting, but "they found themselves at an impasse when they counted their resources." They sued for peace, evacuated what remained of their Sicilian territory, and agreed to pay the Romans an indemnity of more than four tons of silver a year for the next twenty years.[21]

This peace treaty concluded the war, but it did not end Carthage's problems. Carthage had entrusted most of its land operations to mercenaries who rebelled once the state could no longer pay them. Tribes in Libya to the east of Carthage and Numidia to its west soon joined the rebellion, as did major African cities such as Utica, an ally located about twenty-eight miles west of Carthage.[22] Utica even appealed to Rome for help in 239 BC, although Rome elected not to intervene in what would be called the Libyan War.

Rome proved more receptive when rebellious mercenaries on the Carthaginian-controlled island of Sardinia appealed for help the following year. Before the Carthaginians could land a force to retake the island, Rome informed them that it had taken control. "The Carthaginians," Polybius wrote, "had no choice but to yield to circumstances. . . . So they evacuated Sardinia and agreed to pay 1200 talents [of silver] in addition to the sum already demanded."[23] For good measure, Rome also absorbed the island of Corsica.

The conflict that Romans called the First Punic War fundamentally changed both combatants. For the first time, Rome had confronted the challenge of absorbing large amounts of overseas territory. Roman expansion in Italy had slowly patched together a geographically contiguous Roman commonwealth across the peninsula. The large and diverse islands of Sicily, Corsica, and Sardinia did not adjoin any existing Roman territory, and were absorbed by Rome very quickly. This left the Romans with two rather uncomfortable choices for how they would govern the people living in this new territory. They could either extend their system of citizenship and alliance to include residents of territory outside of Italy, or they could treat those people as subjects who did not participate politically in the Roman state. The former ran the risk of diluting Roman citizenship. The latter meant that Rome's representative democracy would also become an imperial power.

The Republic chose to become an imperial power. In 227, it created the provinces of Sicily and Sardinia, placed Corsica in the Sardinian province, and assigned praetors to govern each of the two provinces.[24] Sicily stood out as a particularly important administrative post. A militarized, Roman-controlled, midway point between Rome and Carthage, Sicily also provided vast amounts of grain to feed the Republic and its armies. Because Rome had no model for how to govern such a place, its governors appear to have adapted existing administrative structures. They extended to the whole island a taxation model through which the western region's old Carthaginian overlords took one-tenth of the agricultural production of their Sicilian subjects. Much of this grain fed the Roman troops who garrisoned the island, Roman forces abroad, and Roman citizens in Italy rather than Sicilians themselves.[25] This sort of exploitative behavior changed what it meant to be a Roman magistrate. While officials in Rome implemented the will of the Roman citizens who elected them, provincial governors instead exercised dominion over the lives and property of Roman subjects who had no say in who would serve in the post. Moreover, they had limited ability to appeal his actions.

Roman domestic political behavior also changed in the aftermath of the First Punic War. The problems grew out of Roman actions in a strip of land in Northern Italy that the Republic had conquered (and ethnically cleansed of Gauls) in the 280s and 270s BC. Rome had left this land largely empty, so that it could serve as a buffer zone, and as a result, "the Gauls [had] remained quiet and at peace with Rome for forty-five years."[26]

The balance changed in the 230s as the Roman population and economy were recovering from the long conflict with Carthage. In 232, an ambitious tribune of the plebs, Gaius Flaminius (who would later become the first Roman praetor to govern Sicily), proposed dividing "among [Roman] citizens" the formerly "Gallic territory" that had been left vacant. This "demagogic measure" prompted the strong opposition of Fabius Maximus, the scion of one of the most accomplished Roman aristocratic clans, and much of the Senate, but Flaminius was able to push the law through with plebeian support. His success sparked a rivalry with Fabius that colored Roman political life for much of the next decade and a half.[27]

Flaminius's land distributions had overcome domestic opposition, but, if Polybius is to be believed, they "convinced" the Gauls "that the Romans" were fighting "to expel and exterminate them altogether." The Gallic tribes south of the Alps summoned Gallic soldiers from beyond the Alps to join an anti-Roman alliance, eventually assembling as many as 50,000 soldiers and 20,000 cavalry. Rome responded with a massive mobilization of its own that divided soldiers from across Italy into a main army, positioned at the Gallic frontier; a reserve, based in Rome itself; and a field army under one of the consuls. The Gallic army won an initial battle near Faesulae (the modern Florentine suburb of

Fiesole), but a Roman victory outside of the Etrurian town of Telamon in 225, followed by three years of campaigns in Gallic territory, turned the war into an overwhelming Roman victory.[28]

The power of Roman arms could not obscure increasing dysfunction in the capital as the personal rivalry between Flaminius and Fabius began to pollute political life. Despite strong opposition from Fabius and his allies, Flaminius was elected consul as the Gallic War drew toward its close. When he set out to campaign against the Gauls in 223, stories began circulating about "portents," such as the Tuscan sky appearing to be on fire, a river in Northern Italy running the color of blood, and a vulture perching in the Roman Forum for a few days. "On account of these portents" and "because some people said that the consuls had been chosen illegally," the Senate sent Flaminius a message ordering him to return home and stand down from the consulship. Flaminius knew what had prompted the message. His rival Fabius Maximus was one of the augurs responsible for determining whether the gods had approved of the election. As Cicero would later write, Fabius was prone to saying that whatever he believed "was done for the safety of the Republic happened under the best auspices, and that whatever was inimical to the Republic was against the auspices." Flaminius "received the letter but did not open it" and instead continued his campaign.[29]

After defeating the Gauls in a battle, Flaminius opened the letter and replied that his victory showed that the gods approved of his election. He also "insisted that, in their jealousy of him," the senators were deliberately "misrepresenting the will of the gods." Flaminius "laid waste to the countryside" and distributed the plunder to his soldiers "as a way to win their favor." When he and his consular colleague finally returned to Rome, the Senate "charged them with disobedience," but they were saved by an enthusiastic majority of ordinary Romans who protected them from senatorial sanction and voted them a triumph.[30]

Flaminius's victory had helped secure Rome's victory in the Gallic War, but that success should not obscure the risks he took with his behavior or the problems posed by the actions of his rival Fabius Maximus. Senatorial decrees mattered, and Flaminius's willingness to ignore them encouraged a division between the elites in the Senate and the ordinary Romans who supported him. Honest readings of divine communications also mattered, and the cynical use of them by Fabius and his allies undercut Romans' faith in the integrity of the systems established to ensure that the state did not anger its gods. After two decades of tremendous military successes, Romans could perhaps be forgiven if they imagined that antics like those of Flaminius and Fabius might not matter much in the long run. But Roman fortunes were about to change dramatically.

Chapter 8

Fabius, Scipio, and Hannibal

220–200 BC

CARTHAGE COMPENSATED FOR the loss of Sicily, Sardinia, and Corsica in the First Punic War by expanding its holdings in Spain. In the early 230s BC, it dispatched Hamilcar Barca, the general who had defeated its rebellious mercenaries in Africa, to conquer Spain, "so that its resources could be used to prepare for a war against Rome."[1] Hamilcar was "accompanied by his son Hannibal, who was then nine years old," and who, Polybius reports, would later claim that, before they left, his father had forced him "to swear that he would never become a friend to the Romans."[2] Over the next decade, Hamilcar used a combination of force and diplomacy to place much of Spain under Carthaginian control. Upon his death the command passed to his son-in-law Hasdrubal.[3]

Rome showed only desultory interest in this Carthaginian expansion. It twice sent envoys to Spain to ascertain the extent of Carthaginian ambitions. When one embassy arrived in 231, Hamilcar "embarrassed the envoys" by telling them that "he was obliged to fight against the Spaniards in order to pay the Romans the money still owed to them."[4] Another Roman embassy arrived a few years later and agreed with Hasdrubal that the Ebro River, a boundary that lay far to the north of the current Carthaginian lands, would be the geographical limit of Carthaginian influence in Spain.[5] Rome inserted a poison pill into the Ebro River agreement, however. Sometime before they signed, Rome committed to protect Saguntum (modern Sagunto), a Spanish city located about ninety miles south of the Ebro.[6] This alliance offered Rome a pretext to intervene in Spanish affairs if Carthaginian power grew too great. But the Romans had no inkling that they would need to defend this distant Spanish ally only six years later.

The Saguntum attack came so soon because Hasdrubal was assassinated in 221 and replaced by Hannibal.[7] Hannibal quickly pushed the boundary of Carthaginian territory to the Ebro River and then persuaded the Carthaginian government to sanction an attack on Saguntum by sparking a conflict between Saguntum and the Turbuletes, a tribe whose lands bordered the city. Under Hannibal's direction, the Turbuletes sent envoys to Carthage explaining that Rome was using the Saguntines to destabilize Carthaginian Spain.[8] At that point, Hannibal was prepared not just to capture Saguntum but also to wage a larger war against Rome.

The Romans, who had no idea what Hannibal intended, responded cautiously when Saguntum requested Roman help. The Senate dispatched envoys to Hannibal asking him to break off the siege. When he refused, the messengers set off for Carthage to "demand the surrender of the general so he would answer for his breach of the treaty."[9] Hannibal could not have cared less. "While the Romans were wasting time sending envoys," Livy wrote, Hannibal captured Saguntum. News of the city's fall in 218 reached Rome at almost the same time that the ambassadors returned from Carthage.[10]

Rome still dithered. Instead of mobilizing, the Senate sent one final mission to Carthage to try to avoid the war that Hannibal was already fighting. Fabius Maximus led the delegation of three senators who were to determine whether Hannibal's attack had been the act of a rogue commander. The historian Appian describes a dramatic scene in the Carthaginian Senate where Fabius "pointed to the fold of his toga and, smiling, said: 'Carthaginians, I bring before you here either peace or war. Take whichever you choose.'" The Carthaginians replied, "Give us whichever you like," and, when the envoys "offered them war, all of them cried out 'We accept.'"[11]

Realizing that war could not be avoided, Fabius and his emissaries went to Spain to try to foment rebellion among the Spanish subjects of Carthage. They were struck by the Spanish disinterest. Livy reported that one tribe even rebuffed them with the curt reply: "Look for allies where the fall of Saguntum has not been heard about."[12] The envoys heard the same story when they moved on to Gaul, where they were told it was "a most stupid and impudent thing" to ask Gauls to die to protect Rome when all "had heard that men of their race were being expelled from Italy, made to pay tribute to Rome, and subjected to every other humiliation." Only the Greek colony of Massalia (modern Marseilles) was willing to consider Rome's appeal.[13] Fabius was beginning to understand how far the impacts of Rome's dithering and political opportunism now reached.

Spirits remained high within the capital. "The whole city," Livy wrote, was "in a state of excitement . . . and everyone was looking forward to a war" that the Roman populace believed would be fought on Carthaginian territory.[14] So Rome settled on a strategy in which 64,000 Roman and allied infantry, 6,200 cavalry, and 240 ships would be dispatched under consular command to fight Carthage on two different fronts. One group, led by Publius Cornelius Scipio, was to move toward Spain, while another, led by Tiberius Sempronius Longus, was to invade Africa.[15]

No one expected that Hannibal would bring the war to them.

Early in the spring of 218, however, Hannibal set out for Italy with around 50,000 infantry, 9,000 cavalry, and 37 elephants.[16] He had much better luck building alliances with Spanish and Gallic groups than Fabius had, and Hannibal secured passage all the way to the Rhône River. As he approached Italy, the Gallic population "revolted to join the Carthaginians" and began attacking the Roman "colonists who were being settled in Gallic territory in the Po valley."[17] The farmers and land surveyors that Rome had sent out to distribute and cultivate the land fled to the city of Mutina, which the Gauls then blockaded. When the Senate sent a praetor to relieve Mutina, Livy reports that he needed to be rescued after he stupidly "advanced without sending scouting parties and fell into an ambush."[18] The war was off to a very inauspicious start.

In the meantime, the consul Scipio moved leisurely toward Spain without realizing that Hannibal had already reached the Rhône. When he heard this news upon landing in Massalia, Scipio sent a detachment of cavalry that skirmished with the Carthaginians, but they could not stop their crossing of the river.[19] Scipio arrived at Hannibal's abandoned camp along the Rhône three days after Hannibal had left it, and realized that "he would not catch his opponent after he had gotten such a long head start." Scipio then divided his army, sent some troops to Spain, and sailed the rest back to Italy so they could confront Hannibal.[20]

Scipio landed in Pisa as Hannibal was coming down from the Alps and reinforced his troops with "an army of raw recruits." Then he pressed "with all speed to the Po so that he might engage with the enemy before [Hannibal] had recovered his strength."[21] Hannibal expected and welcomed the challenge. Although he had lost more than half his infantry and a third of his cavalry during the Rhône and Alpine crossings, he believed that his tactical skill would allow his troops to defeat any Roman armies that confronted them.[22] His victories in battle were part of a larger strategy to erode the Roman manpower advantage by inducing allies tired of losing men for Rome to defect to Carthage. Hannibal understood, said Polybius, that, "when a general leads his army into a foreign country, . . . his only chance lies in sustaining the hopes of his allies by continually striking a fresh blow," and in maintaining the invasion's momentum.[23] His success depended on the Romans fighting him regularly until a string of Carthaginian victories caused Rome's Italian allies to abandon the commonwealth.

The two armies met for the first time close to the River Ticinus, north of the Po. The Romans lost the battle, and Scipio, who had sustained a serious injury, retreated south of the Po, so that Hannibal's powerful cavalry would no longer be able to operate in the riparian plain.[24] Validating Hannibal's strategy, a group of Celtic soldiers serving under Scipio then defected to Hannibal.[25] The Romans offered "pretexts to persuade themselves that this was not really a defeat," but Hannibal's victory concerned the Senate enough that it recalled the other consul, Sempronius, from Sicily and combined his forces with what was left of Scipio's army.[26]

With his consular term nearing an end that December, Sempronius decided to risk a great battle with Hannibal so that he might get credit for a decisive victory. He could not have made a more foolish decision. Hannibal "made it a principle not to be drawn into a decisive engagement . . . on a casual impulse."[27] Sempronius, who did not possess such restraint, chose to fight on a "raw, sleety morning" during which the Romans had to "wade across water up to their breasts" as they crossed the icy Trebia River.[28] When they emerged from the water, "they had hardly strength to hold their weapons and they began to grow faint from fatigue."[29] Hannibal lured them forward until the tired Roman infantry found itself attacked on its sides by Carthaginian cavalry and elephants; meanwhile, 2,200 troops that Hannibal had concealed in the brush along the riverbank pressed on them from the rear. Only 10,000 of the perhaps 50,000 Romans and allies Sempronius led into battle survived.[30] Scipio then led the wounded and the other survivors to winter quarters in the colonies of Placentia and Cremona.

The failures of the war's aristocratic leaders then propelled the populist Flaminius to the consulship and control over the Roman war against Hannibal. Remembering how Fabius and his allies in the Senate had declared his previous consulship illegal, Flaminius began his term not in Rome but in the northern colony of Ariminum, since he "suspected that they would endeavor to detain him in the City."[31] He had good reason to suspect senatorial malfeasance. Livy records that "it was unanimously decided that he should be recalled [and] brought back by force if necessary . . . before he returned to his army and province."[32] Flaminius understood that he needed to move quickly if he wanted to defeat Hannibal before having to fight the Senate to maintain his command.[33] Hannibal knew this too.

Flaminius and his co-consul initially decided to search for Hannibal's army separately, bottle the Carthaginian up in Northern Italy without offering a decisive battle, and then combine forces before attacking.[34] Hannibal's entry into Etruria, however, changed Flaminius's approach. Hannibal "calculated that, if he marched past his opponent's army and advanced into the region in front of him, Flaminius would be sensitive to the jeers of the rank and file" and tricked into giving battle at a site Hannibal chose.[35]

Hannibal calculated correctly. Plutarch describes Flaminius as "a man of a fiery and ambitious nature" who "was elated by great victories," and easily excited when he thought one was at hand. Flaminius spotted Hannibal's army along the shores of Lake Trasimeno (on the modern border between the Italian provinces of Umbria and Tuscany). Taking advantage of a thick morning fog, Hannibal hid his infantry and cavalry in the hills above a narrow path that led to a wider plain along the lakeshore. "Eager that he alone should have credit for the expected victory," Flaminius ordered his forces to advance right past the hidden Carthaginians.[36]

When the Romans entered the battlefield, some Carthaginian units descended in front of the narrow Roman column to prevent it from leaving the lakeshore, and others blocked the Roman retreat. Hannibal's hidden infantry and cavalry then flowed down from their positions on hills that the fog had obscured. The stunned Romans could not form up lines and had no way to defend themselves against the Carthaginians charging downhill. The lake prevented them from moving backward, and the road out of the killing field was blocked by the Carthaginian line. Perhaps as many as 15,000 Romans and their allies were slaughtered, including Flaminius himself. His body was never found.[37]

Roman citizens responded to news of Flaminius's defeat by acclaiming Fabius Maximus as dictator, a dramatic action that side-stepped the usual process through which a consul appointed a dictator.[38] Fabius radically shifted Roman strategy by shadowing Hannibal but avoiding any battles on terms or locations set by the Carthaginian. Instead, the Romans "followed and kept him in view in the hope that a favorable opportunity for battle might arise." If it did not, Fabius remained unworried. He believed that it was more important to restore the morale of his men through small but steady victories than to try to defeat Hannibal's much more experienced army in one great battle.[39]

Fabius also recognized that Hannibal's caution prevented him from attacking the Roman armies that shadowed him. He understood how this deliberate approach frustrated a commander who believed that he could win a war with Rome only by defeating its armies in large battles. But Fabius's tactics soon began to frustrate the Romans nearly as much as they frustrated Hannibal. A steady flow of reports about Hannibal burning and plundering Italian farms reached Rome, prompting "constant denunciation" from tribunes of the plebs allied with Fabius's opponents. Fabius also attracted senatorial anger over a botched prisoner exchange that he negotiated with Hannibal.[40] He was summoned to Rome and attacked by a tribune as "not just a weakling, nor even a coward, but an actual traitor."[41]

Fabius's troubles in Rome hinted at a larger struggle over who would assume the populist mantle that Flaminius had once worn. Soon after Fabius's six-month term ended, Rome held elections for the consulship, and Terentius Varro, who promised that "he would conquer the enemy the very day he saw them," was elected. After the election, Varro "assembled and enrolled a larger force than the Romans had ever employed against any enemy."[42] Plutarch counted 88,000 troops. Livy estimated the army's size at around 55,000. But, for "Fabius and all sensible Romans," Plutarch said, there was only "terror," because they "thought their city could not recover if she lost so many men."[43] When Fabius tried to convince Varro's consular colleague Lucius Aemilius Paullus to block any actions by Varro that put the entire army at risk, Paullus responded bluntly, "If I consider my own interests, it is better for me to face the spears of the enemy than the votes of my fellow citizens."[44] Roman political dissension then marched alongside the tens of thousands of soldiers Varro led toward Hannibal.

Hannibal gave Varro his battle outside of the Southern Italian town of Cannae on August 2, 216 BC. The Carthaginian had carefully positioned his army on an open plain with the wind to his back so that his superior cavalry could maneuver. As dust blew into the Romans' eyes, Hannibal allowed the center of his line to slowly fall back, until the Roman forces converged on one another in the middle of a great crescent. This restricted the movement of the Roman infantry, negated the Romans' superior numbers, and allowed them to be enveloped by Hannibal's forces.[45]

The Roman losses were overwhelming. Livy wrote, "The total number of casualties was 45,500 infantry and 2,700 cavalrymen killed—equally divided between citizens and allies. Among the dead were . . . eighty distinguished men who were either members of the Senate or held offices that qualified them for membership."[46] Polybius counted 70,000 dead; modern scholars lower the number to perhaps 30,000.[47] However one counts, though, Cannae was the worst military defeat Rome had ever suffered—and the Senate, which had only 300 members, felt the losses particularly acutely.

"In their two years of war with Hannibal in Italy," Appian would later write, "the Romans had lost more than 100,000 of their own and allied soldiers."[48] This is a sum greater than the number of Americans who have died in battle since the end of World War II—and this is despite the fact that the American population is exponentially larger than Rome's in the third century BC. In less than two years, Hannibal had killed as much as 35 percent of the entire population of fighting-age men in the Republic. As news of the disaster at Cannae spread to the city, people "crowded into the streets, wailing and calling out for their relatives."[49]

Fabius Maximus took charge. Plutarch reports that Fabius "persuaded the Senate to convene," "put guards at the city gates in order to keep the frightened crowds from abandoning the city," and "set time limits for the mourning of the dead."[50] When the initial panic subsided, the Senate began rebuilding the Roman army, establishing four new legions and a cavalry of 1,000 out of a mix of very young citizens, slaves purchased from their masters, convicts, and defaulted debtors. It also sent a message to Rome's allies to marshal more troops to support a war effort guided by Fabius's deliberate approach.[51]

Rome began rebuilding its army under Fabius's leadership, but the largest group of Roman soldiers remained the survivors of Cannae. Some of these men thought the Republic's prospects were so bleak that "it should be given up for lost," until a young military tribune named Publius Cornelius Scipio, the son of the consul Hannibal had defeated in 218 BC, held his sword over one of the men contemplating desertion. Scipio swore that he would "not abandon the Republic of Rome, nor . . . suffer any other Roman citizen to do so," before warning that his "sword [was] drawn against" anyone refusing to pledge renewed allegiance to Rome. Scipio's performance kept the veterans of Cannae together long enough that 4,500 more troops, who had been scattered around Southern Italy, joined them in the city of Canusium. There was "now something like a consular army" that could attend to the defense of Rome while Fabius built a new army that could again execute his strategy of shadowing Hannibal.[52]

The situation elsewhere in Italy remained dire. Hannibal resisted the urge to attack Rome itself, a large city with strong walls that would ensure a long siege, and focused on peeling off Roman allies in Campania, Apulia, Bruttium, and Samnium.[53] Most of these, like the city of Tarentum, were among the last cities in Italy to fall under Roman domination. But the defection of Capua was different. The second-largest city in Italy and the key to controlling the fertile region of Campania, Capua was populated by Roman citizens who joined Hannibal so they could lead the future Italy that Rome's seemingly imminent defeat would create.[54] The victory at Cannae also persuaded King Philip V of Macedon to enter the war against Rome, and induced the Sicilian city of Syracuse to break its alliance with Rome.[55]

Rome retained some significant advantages. While cities like Tarentum and Capua looked forward to dominating their neighbors now that Roman control over Italy was teetering, many of those neighboring cities preferred the distant, somewhat disinterested authority of Rome to the meddling of hated regional rivals. Allies like these stuck with Rome because they believed it could win and, when it did, they relished the chance to take booty, territory, and privileges from their uppity Italian rivals who had turned to Hannibal. Rome's long-standing relationships with elites in the cities that had defected also compelled Hannibal to guard against aristocratic coups that might throw out pro-Carthaginian regimes.[56]

These local and regional dynamics forced Hannibal to defend Italian allied territory just as the Fabian strategy slowed his momentum. At the same time that Fabius frustrated Hannibal in Italy, Rome decided to dramatically expand its armies and fight aggressively on all the other fronts in this sprawling conflict. Romans broke the tradition of rotating annual commands so that their best generals could remain in place. Fabius Maximus held three consulships in the six years after Cannae, while other capable commanders also were elected to multiple consulships or made proconsuls and propraetors so they could command armies operating outside of Italy for years at a time. In addition, they were given many more soldiers. In the later third century BC, Rome had usually fielded about four legions a year, but the Republic kept increasing its troop numbers after Cannae. At one point, in 211, the Republic had twenty-five legions divided between theaters in Italy, Spain, Sicily, and Greece, as well as two fleets positioned to guard against crossings of troops from Africa and Greece. Perhaps 70 percent of the entire male citizen population between the ages of seventeen and thirty were fighting in the war.[57]

Rome's embrace of total war took a severe toll on civilians, who endured shortages of food and basic necessities as Hannibal strangled the trade networks that supplied the Republic. By the end of the 210s, however, Rome's counterattacks had begun to limit the economic damage. Syracuse fell in 212, after an epic siege that saw the Syracusan mathematician Archimedes devise "artillery and military devices of various kinds" to frustrate the Roman attackers.[58] The tons of precious metal that Rome took from Syracuse enabled the Senate to create a new Roman monetary system based on a silver coin called the denarius.[59] The denarius would remain the most important coin in the Roman monetary system for nearly five hundred years.

Despite these successes, Roman commanders still hesitated to fight a large battle against Hannibal. They instead eroded his Italian support by attacking multiple cities at the same time and forcing the Carthaginian general to choose either to divide his forces or to abandon some of his allies. When Rome retook the cities that Hannibal could not defend, it often retaliated ferociously. After capturing Capua, Rome executed its leaders, enslaved most of the rest of its population, and forced those who remained to leave the city and its territory. Capua ceased to exist as a polity; its lands instead became the property of the Roman people. The sale or lease of land confiscated from disloyal Italian allies gave the Senate a new source of funds to help destitute Romans, as well as a new stream of plunder to remind Rome's loyal allies why they found the Roman commonwealth so appealing.[60]

Roman armies were also successful abroad. The Macedonian war proved far less frightening to Romans than it might have seemed at first, because Rome outsourced most of the fighting to its allies in mainland Greece. The Senate then followed along when these allies signed a peace treaty with Philip in 205. In Spain, Publius Cornelius Scipio, the man who had rallied the Roman survivors after Cannae, transformed a Roman campaign intended to prevent reinforcements from reaching Hannibal into a war of conquest that eliminated the Carthaginian presence by 206.

Scipio's successes in Spain grew out of his tactical genius. Hannibal had mastered a two-dimensional battlefield that he prepared by arraying lines of soldiers in a certain formation—to a large degree, his planning dictated how the two armies would advance. Scipio developed a much more dynamic approach, in which Roman forces engaged in multiple maneuvers across the course of a single attack. Not only were Scipio's plans of attack less obvious to the enemy than more conventional methods, but he also could confuse the enemy during the battle and split components of its army off from the main body of troops. This allowed Scipio to neutralize Carthaginian numerical superiority while also counteracting some of the advantages his opponents could gain by arraying their armies on favorable terrain. He was, in short, the Roman tactician who could answer Hannibal.[61]

The thirty-year-old Scipio was a new Roman generation's answer to the politics and strategies of Fabius and the other old generals whose leadership shepherded Rome through the terrible years after Cannae but whose cautious approach seemed to be growing stale.[62] Recognizing that Rome's capture of Tarentum, Hannibal's last major Italian port, had isolated the Carthaginians and freed Rome to fight even more aggressively abroad, Scipio ran for the consulship in 206. He generated enthusiasm for his approach to the war by displaying "14,342 pounds of silver and a great quantity of silver coins" that he had seized from Carthaginian Spain and then won the unanimous support of all the voting blocs in the consular election.[63] Scipio began "telling people that he had been returned as consul . . . to bring [the war] to an end, and the only way of doing that was for him to take an army over to Africa."[64]

When the Senate debated Scipio's proposal, Fabius Maximus accused him of "regarding glory as more important than the welfare of the commonwealth."[65] Fabius probably hoped this language would remind Romans of the catastrophes caused by the rashness of Flaminius and Varro, but, Livy writes, most believed the attack derived from his "jealousy of Scipio's successes." With Fabius's reservations noted, the Senate granted Scipio "permission to sail to Africa."[66] However, at the same time, the senators also tried to dissuade him from doing this, by giving him an army made up of the discredited survivors of Cannae—who had not been allowed to leave active service for the past eleven years—and the remnants of any other legions that had been defeated. He was given permission to sail only thirty ships, which he had to arrange to be built himself using supplies donated by allies. He had them all built within forty-five days.[67] Scipio then sailed to Sicily and began training his army of misfits.

The training went so well that Scipio landed his forces in Africa within two years. They proceeded to inflict a series of defeats on the Carthaginians and their Numidian allies, prompting Carthage to recall Hannibal from Italy. Scipio's invasion of Africa then did what Fabius's patience could not. It had freed Italy of Hannibal, and it had given a new generation of Roman leaders the freedom to end the conflict in their own way. Perhaps fittingly, Fabius Maximus died before the war concluded.

The battle that decided the war took place in October 202 at Zama, southwest of Carthage. Hannibal enjoyed superior numbers, commanding more than 10,000 battle-hardened veterans who had served under him in Italy. He planned to use his eighty war elephants to charge Scipio's lines and then deploy his veterans when the Romans were either exhausted or disordered. But Scipio's tactical mastery blunted Hannibal's initial assault. Scipio positioned his troops so that there were wide gaps between the lines of his infantry through which the charging elephants could be directed. He also placed lightly armed troops in front of the main force, so that they could throw javelins and other projectiles at the elephants. Some elephants rampaged back toward Hannibal's lines under this barrage of missiles, and others fell before reaching the Romans. Most of the rest charged harmlessly through the gaps in the Roman lines.

Scipio also countered Hannibal's plan to use his veterans as a reserve force that could pounce on Roman disorganization. After the Roman troops defeated the first two, less experienced waves of Carthaginian troops, Scipio reformed his lines so that the principes and his formidable triarii—the most experienced soldiers—could join up to form a single line. Then, as the Romans advanced across what Livy called "slippery, bloodstained ground" that "had become blocked with heaps of bodies," Scipio's cavalry attacked Hannibal's troops from behind. The resulting slaughter saw perhaps 20,000 Carthaginian troops killed, nearly as many captured, and the Carthaginian army destroyed. Scipio had given Hannibal his own Cannae.[68]

Hannibal escaped the battlefield, but the war was lost. Scipio negotiated a peace treaty that allowed Rome to keep the territory it had taken from Carthage in Spain. Carthage retained its independence, but it agreed to become a Roman ally, with severe restrictions on the size of its military and its freedom to use force. Perhaps most importantly, Carthage agreed to pay an immense annual tribute in precious metals to Rome for the next fifty years. This was a mild treaty, but it was one that Scipio himself wanted to conclude before the consuls for the next year could be sent to Africa to take over his command. Even so, one of them refused to let the Senate vote on Scipio's peace treaty or any other business "until Africa was decreed his province" and he was allowed to lead an army there.[69] That refusal forced the tribunes to end the war through a vote in the plebeian assembly.[70] With Hannibal now defeated, the politics of personal ambition had returned to Rome.

LIVY UNDERSTOOD WHAT the war's end meant for both Scipio and Hannibal. In a speech that he put in the mouth of Hannibal, Livy wrote that "no great State can remain quiet. If it has no enemy abroad, it finds one at home" and takes particular delight in undermining its own most accomplished citizens.[71] This is why neither Scipio nor Hannibal would ever truly escape from the legacy of the great Battle of Zama. Scipio returned to Italy a hero. As he marched to Rome, "multitudes poured out from the cities to do him honor," and "crowds of peasants blocked the roads in the country districts." When he celebrated his Carthaginian triumph, the "procession in which he rode into the City was the most brilliant that had ever been seen."[72] In honor of his great victory, he was thereafter known as Scipio Africanus.

It was all too much. Now the richest man in Roman history, Scipio rewarded his 35,000 soldiers with plunder equal to four months of military pay and an acre and a quarter of land in Italy.[73] He paid for lavish games and a series of public monuments commemorating his military victories, including an arch with seven gilded statues that he erected on the Capitoline Hill in Rome.[74] This display of pride incited a backlash that eventually led to Scipio's prosecution for bribery in 185 BC. He was acquitted, but the trial so scarred Scipio that he left public life and retired to an estate in Campania. He died there two years later, after ordering that his remains should never be returned to Rome.

Hannibal fared even worse. Scipio's peace treaty permitted Hannibal to return to public life in Carthage. He was elected as the chief magistrate of the Carthaginian state and soon undertook a reform of a notoriously corrupt court of 104 judges.[75] While this earned him significant popular approval, the displaced oligarchs who had previously dominated the court began working with Roman enemies of Hannibal to undermine him. Livy reports that "Scipio Africanus opposed this policy for a long time," because he felt that Rome had no business working with "factions at Carthage" to discredit Hannibal "after having defeated him in war."[76] But Scipio lost the argument, and the Senate sent a delegation to Carthage accusing Hannibal of working alongside the Syrian king Antiochus III, a monarch against whom Rome would soon go to war.

Hannibal fled first to Tyre, the ancient city that had been the birthplace of the first Carthaginian colonists, and then traveled to Antiochus's court in the Anatolian city of Ephesus. Hannibal joined the Syrian king's military staff and advised him when war with Rome started, but he was forced to flee after Rome defeated Antiochus. Hannibal spent the next few years fighting for smaller states that opposed Rome before the Romans threatened one of his protectors with war if he did not give Hannibal up. He agreed, but Hannibal died before the Romans got their hands on him. It is possible, though not entirely certain, that his life ended in 183 BC, the same year that Scipio died.

Twenty years after the fighting ended, the Second Punic War had finally consumed the last of its biggest heroes. The inscription on Scipio's tomb read, "Ungrateful fatherland, you shall not even have my bones."[77]

PART 2

FROM THE GRACCHI
TO NERO

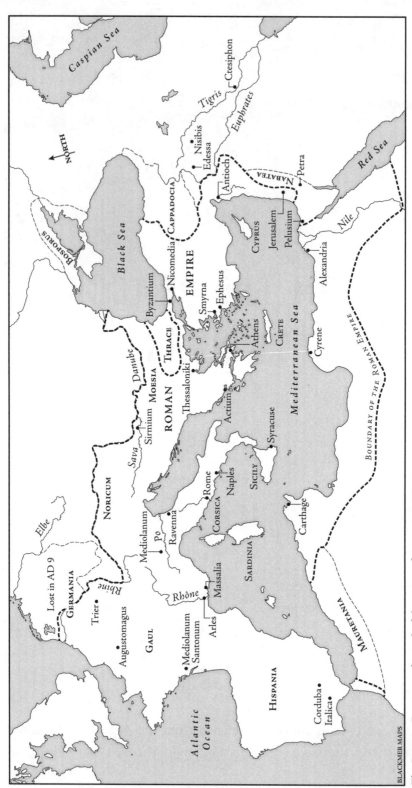

The Roman Empire at the end of the reign of Augustus, AD 14

Chapter 9

Economic Inequality, Political Opportunism, and Gaius Gracchus

---
200–120 BC

T HE DECADES FOLLOWING Rome's victory in the Second Punic War brought neither peace abroad nor calm within the Republic. While the defeat of Carthage greatly reduced any threat coming from Africa, Rome had fought less effectively in other arenas of the sprawling conflict. In Northern Italy, it took another decade for Rome to resume full control of the areas Hannibal had helped the Gauls take. The capture of Carthaginian Spain led the Senate to create two Spanish provinces, but it took sixty years to pacify them.

The biggest military challenges Rome faced in the first half of the second century BC came not from the west or south but from the Eastern Mediterranean remnants of Alexander the Great's empire. Rome had already fought a war with one of them, the kingdom of Macedon, but most of that fighting was done by Rome's Greek allies. This gave the Macedonian king, Philip V, the mistaken impression that Rome feared the formidable Macedonian phalanx. Rome didn't. And when Philip V formed an alliance with the Seleucid king, Antiochus III (whose domains stretched from the Aegean to Afghanistan), and they agreed to dismantle Rome's ally, the Ptolemaic kingdom of Egypt, Rome sent an embassy telling the Macedonian that any such action would prompt Roman intervention. Philip did not listen, and in 197 BC the Roman maniples showed themselves superior to the Macedonian phalanx when they won the Battle of Cynoscephalae.[1]

After that Macedonian defeat, Rome forced Philip to evacuate Central Greece, disband his fleet, and pay Rome a massive war indemnity, but it did not seize any of his Greek territory. Instead, the Roman commander Titus Quinctius Flamininus, while presiding over a magnificently staged event at the Isthmian Games in Corinth in 194, proclaimed the freedom of Greece from any foreign garrisons or tribute payments.[2] He separately indicated to the Seleucids that Greek cities in Asia Minor were also to be left alone, and then withdrew to Italy.[3]

Two years later, the Seleucid king, Antiochus, taking advantage of the vacuum Flamininus had left behind, crossed into Greece with an army of 10,000 infantry, 500 cavalry, and six elephants. He was being advised by none other than Hannibal. It is hard to imagine what more Antiochus could have done to enrage the Romans. They immediately declared war and defeated him at the pass of Thermopylae. Then they forced him to withdraw from Europe, pursuing him as he retreated from the Aegean until Lucius Cornelius Scipio, the brother of Scipio Africanus, defeated Antiochus, Hannibal, and their army at Magnesia in late 190 or 189 BC. This victory led to Scipio receiving the name Scipio Asiaticus.

The treaty with Antiochus resembled the one made with Philip V. It compelled Antiochus to leave the Greek cities he controlled along the Aegean and pay Rome another massive indemnity. Rome again did not take control of the vacated land, instead gifting it to Roman allies in Greece, Pergamum, Rhodes, and, in a twist, Macedon, because it had allowed Scipio's army to cross its territory during the war. Yet again, the arrangement did not work. Rome was forced to fight two more wars in Greece over the next forty years as various powers in the peninsula tried to fill the void Rome left each time it withdrew. Finally, and perhaps inevitably, Rome gave up on allowing Greeks to manage their own affairs. In 146, it responded to yet another Greek war by destroying Corinth and making Macedonia a province garrisoned with Roman troops. The Romans had learned that conquest was the only way they could ensure that no hostile power would challenge their hegemony in distant regions.

While this lesson seems to have made sense in Greece, Roman leaders also applied it to Carthage. This was completely unfair. Rome's relations with Carthage had been cooperative since the end of the Second Punic War. By the 150s, however, the prominent Roman senator Cato (now known as Cato the Elder) began to fear that an independent Carthage would eventually emerge as a more formidable threat than anything Rome saw in the east. He made it his mission to goad Rome into a conflict, going so far as to end all the speeches he gave in the Senate, on any topic, with the phrase "And Carthage must be destroyed."

The Carthaginians refused to be baited into a war, but Roman provocations grew increasingly hard to ignore. The most egregious came in 149 BC, when a group of Roman commissioners arrived in Carthage to investigate why the Carthaginians had used their armed forces to respond to a Numidian attack without receiving Roman approval. Carthage agreed to submit to any conditions the emissaries set and was shocked when they ordered the seafaring Carthaginians to abandon their city and move inland. This sparked a war that ended in 146 with Carthage suffering the same fate as Corinth. The city was stormed and razed, its population enslaved, and the territory that had belonged to it became the Roman province of Africa.

ROME'S RAPID EXPANSION in the fifty-six years separating the Battle of Zama and the destructions of Corinth and Carthage sparked the most remarkable economic evolution seen in any ancient state. Rome had entered the First Punic War with a barely monetized economy that had only just begun minting its own coins. It was, charitably speaking, not much more sophisticated than the economies of

Greek city-states of the late sixth century BC. The First Punic War began in 264 BC, and the Battle of Zama was in 202. By 146, Rome had developed a mature financial sector with a complexity and wealth-generating capacity that surpassed anything the Mediterranean world had ever seen.

Two features marked this shift. The first was the rapid rebound of the Roman population following the devastation of Hannibal's invasion. The census numbers, although incomplete, show that the Roman male citizen population collapsed from 270,713 to 137,108 between 234 and 209, a period that includes the years when Hannibal inflicted the heaviest casualties on the Roman army. This left the Republic with large plots of land left vacant because their owners had died. Elsewhere in Italy, Romans had either killed or dispossessed tens or even hundreds of thousands whose cities had joined with Hannibal and whose lands needed to be farmed again, quickly, so that they did not revert to wilderness. Wealthy Italians in allied cities began renting tracts of land owned by the Roman state, and the Roman government decided to overlook the law prohibiting people from cultivating more than 500 *iugera* (about 300 acres) of public land.[4] Italians also began marrying younger, so that they could have more children.[5] The city of Rome grew from perhaps 200,000 people at the end of the war with Hannibal to 500,000 or more by the mid-130s BC. This led to a prolonged period of per capita income growth that helped both rich and poor Italians.

The second change in Roman economic life sparked much faster wealth accumulation among a subgroup of Roman elites. The massive amount of treasure brought in by the war indemnities paid by Macedon, Carthage, and the Seleucids initially caused an economic bubble to form that flooded Rome with money in a fashion that seemed unsustainable. Once the indemnities stopped, however, the Republic figured out how to create stable revenue streams. It did so by using contractors to rapidly develop revenue sources in the new provinces. Taxes provided the most immediate source of funds, but Romans also began the large-scale extraction of precious metals in Spain, Macedonia, and Northern Italy. By the mid-150s, these operations were annually generating more than twice the revenue plundered from Carthage by Scipio fifty years earlier.[6]

The Republic did not, however, believe in building a large bureaucracy to handle tax collection, mining, or infrastructure work in the provinces. Instead, it entrusted these revenue-generating activities to contractors, who in turn paid the Republic for their (often) multiyear contracts in advance. This system effectively guaranteed the state an immediate fixed amount of revenue, while the contractor and his agents profited by bringing home more money than they paid the Roman state.

Particularly savvy Romans came to understand that the profitability of these public contracts was so reliable that one could effectively gauge their potential value in advance. Since most bidders lacked the cash on hand to pay up front for the contracts, they had to take out loans to cover their costs. Lenders quickly realized that these loans themselves had a value that could be calculated based on the likelihood of repayment and the amount of additional income it would generate. The Roman innovation was to see that a price could be set for the resale of large loans that had a calculable value. Reselling a loan would recapitalize the lender. He could then make another loan—which he could again sell to generate more investment capital. These innovative financial instruments vastly increased the amount of "money" in circulation in Rome, but much of that new money concentrated around a few of Italy's wealthiest individuals.[7]

The Roman nouveau riche garishly flaunted the wealth their financial savvy produced. As early as the 180s BC, Romans shook their heads at the triumphal procession of Gnaeus Manlius Vulso, a commander who defeated the Seleucids in battle and "brought into Rome for the first time, bronze couches, costly coverlets, tapestry, other fabrics, and . . . pedestal tables." As Rome's conquests spread to Greece and Carthage, the regular infusion of plunder and slaves changed aspects of elite domestic life as well. Roman banquets became flashy events centered around elaborate meals prepared by skilled chefs and served by attractive waiters. Beautiful "girls" at these events "played on the harp and sang and danced."[8]

All of this occurred at the same time that the economic prospects of young Italians born in rural areas were beginning to constrict. By the 160s, much of the once-vacant public land was again under cultivation, and more children were remaining on the family farms. Italian custom dictated that all living sons generally received an equal share of the family property when a father died. This meant that, within a few generations, these family farms would be divided into plots too small to support a family. Crucially for the Roman state, many of these farms also became too small for their owners to meet the property qualification for military service.[9]

The Republic struggled to respond. In 167, the Senate stopped collecting taxes on Italian lands held by its citizens, but this tax cut did not result in the renewed prosperity trickling down to other Romans. Instead, unlike a modern state, the Republic had no ability to use taxes on the rich to redistribute resources to the poor, or to prevent the economic separation of the small class of superwealthy Romans from everyone else.

The pulling away of Rome's wealthiest citizens from everyone else catalyzed a unique alliance between ambitious, elite Roman politicians who could not keep up with their financially savvy colleagues and poorer Romans who resented the constriction of their economic opportunities. Reformers talked about sending some Romans out to colonize Northern Italy, and proposed tweaks to the laws allowing people to rent public land to farm. But popular discontent was rising too quickly for the Republic's slow, deliberate, consensus-based political process to keep up.

Writing nearly a century later, Cicero hinted at the basic conflict the Republic was struggling to address. "A Republic," he wrote, "is an entity of the people. But a people is not just a collection of humans assembled arbitrarily. It is a collection of a multitude joined to one another by a consensus about law and the common good."[10] The Republic of the late 140s struggled to uphold both law and its commitment to the common good. The Roman super rich had become rich lawfully, and the just exercise of law should protect what they had legally acquired. But, regardless of its legality, most Romans did not feel that this level of wealth inequality was good for the Republic. Addressing inequality by taking the property of the rich would undermine the rule of law unless the rich agreed to it, but steps to protect the property of the wealthy would seem just only if there was broad acceptance of them. Consensus could lead Rome out of this moment of tension, but consensus takes time to develop in a representative democracy. And Roman patience ran out as the 140s ended.

As THE 130s dawned, popular anger and elite political opportunism spawned a new, more malignant type of politician who saw a way to capitalize on the rising frustration Romans felt about their government's inaction. These populists began by championing a series of laws that made it possible for Romans to vote by secret ballot.[11] Then, with secret voting possible, they advanced economic reforms that the elites would likely have blocked in the past by intimidating the voters. The most prominent of the populists was Tiberius Gracchus.

Tiberius was descended from two of Rome's leading families. He was the son of Tiberius Sempronius Gracchus, a senator who had held two consulships, and Cornelia, the daughter of Scipio Africanus, the man who had defeated Hannibal. Tiberius's early political career reflected the priorities of his ancestors, but his ascent stalled when he negotiated an agreement to save the lives of a Roman army that had surrendered in Spain. Some senators had denounced the pact "as a disaster and disgrace" to Rome, comparing it to the surrender at Caudine Forks and arguing that it should be renounced. Ordinary Romans, however, were happy that Tiberius had "saved the lives of so many citizens."[12]

Tiberius saw an opportunity to use this popular support to revive his political fortunes. In 134 BC, when he stood for election as one of the ten tribunes of the plebs, he raged against the "gangs of foreign slaves, by whose aid the rich cultivated their estates" and "drove away the free citizens" who once fought for Rome.[13] We now know that large estates like this were rare in the Italian countryside at this time, but Tiberius was a powerful speaker, and he told a tale that resonated with the people.[14] Even if the story was not true, it felt true. And this was enough to get him elected.

Once in office, Tiberius thundered about radical inequality but proposed only a modest reform to address it. He would enforce the limit on how much public land could be rented for farming, take back any land above that threshold, and compensate the farmers who relinquished it. The excess land taken from these renters would then be distributed to landless citizens. In reality, the restrictions would mean that at most 15,000 families would receive grants of land—out of an Italian population then numbering several million.[15]

The Roman Republic was built around the idea of achieving political consensus before action was taken, and none yet existed around this sort of land reform. In fact, something similar to what Tiberius was proposing had been blocked in 140 BC by Roman politicians allied with the elite Italians who held leases on most of the land Tiberius wanted to redistribute.[16] It likely did not surprise Roman political observers that Tiberius's law was quickly vetoed by Octavius, one of his fellow tribunes, because wealthy Italians who did not have a vote in Rome depended on revenues generated by the public lands that Tiberius was targeting.

Plutarch writes that Tiberius then "withdrew his conciliatory law, and introduced one which was more gratifying to the people." The new proposal would force "the illegal holders of the land . . . [to] vacate" it without compensation.[17] Tiberius suggested that Octavius was corruptly blocking the law because he himself held leases on large tracts of public land; he even offered to pay Octavius for the property he would lose out of his own pocket.[18] When Octavius still refused to lift his veto, Tiberius asked the plebeian assembly to vote to remove Octavius from office. They did as requested, and the deposed tribune barely escaped being injured by a mob of Gracchan supporters when he fled the meeting.[19]

The threats and intimidation that Octavius experienced prefigured a wider campaign that saw Tiberius Gracchus push supporters to embrace ever more radical measures to implement the land reform law. When the Senate refused to provide the funds necessary to pay for the surveyors and equipment Tiberius's land distributions required, the tribune had the plebeian assembly seize legal authority over the treasury of Pergamum from the Senate on the grounds that its recently deceased king had willed that money to "the Roman people" and only the assembly spoke with the people's genuine voice.[20]

The tensions increased when Tiberius announced that he would run for a second term as tribune, an action that tribunes had rarely taken in the centuries since the higher magistracies had been opened up to plebeians. Tiberius told supporters that he was running for reelection so that he could remain protected from the physical attacks of senators and others who were angry at him for his land reforms. Plutarch reports that Tiberius even said he feared that "his enemies would break into his house at night and kill him," and induced his followers to spend "the night on guard" outside of his home.[21]

Tiberius's dramatic appeals made conflict inevitable. As plebeians gathered to cast their votes for tribune, a scuffle broke out on the margins of the crowd between his supporters and opponents. When word of the fighting reached the Senate, Tiberius's cousin Scipio Nasica led a group of senators and attendants out to confront Tiberius. The mob seized the tribune and clubbed him to death.

This was the first political murder in Rome in almost three centuries and it horrified Romans.[22] Cicero believed that Tiberius's threats and extraconstitutional measures had pushed Rome toward a political abyss. He even set his fictional dialogue *De re publica* (*On the Republic*) in the year 129 BC, because he retrospectively believed that had been the last moment when the Republic could have been stabilized after "the death of Tiberius Gracchus had divided one people into two factions."[23] Cicero emphasized that Tiberius's tactics of intimidation and willingness to disregard the law had set Rome on a very dangerous course. "If this habit of lawlessness begins to spread," he wrote, it "changes our rule from one of justice to one of force." This made him "anxious for our descendants and for the permanence of our Republic."

Other Roman authors would later judge that Rome was "no longer a Republic" after Tiberius's death but a state dominated by "the rule of force and violence."[24] Most Romans at the time hoped to find a way to move forward by punishing those who they felt had caused the violence, but they disagreed vehemently about how to do this. Tiberius's opponents in the Senate compelled the consuls who took office the following year to convene a special court to investigate the disturbance. Some associates of Tiberius were executed at the direction of Publius Popillius Laenas, the consul who presided over the court "with utmost severity."[25] One supporter, named Caius Villius, was even supposedly killed by being shut up in a cage with vipers.[26] The plebeian assembly never approved the investigation, and the executed were all denied the right of appeal to the people that Roman citizens had long taken for granted. Both of these factors were clear problems that invited some to see the executed as martyrs.[27] This was, the historian Sallust would later write, a moment when "bloodshed was ended not by law but by the pleasure of the victors."[28]

Surprisingly, everyone agreed that the land commission should now work without senatorial obstruction. "The Senate," Plutarch would later write, "tried to conciliate the people now that matters had gone too far." It "no longer opposed the distribution of public land," but allowed the commission to continue working for more than a decade, and even appointed a new member to take the spot vacated by Tiberius's death.[29]

THESE LAND DISTRIBUTIONS may have decreased popular anger in Rome, but they incensed the wealthy non-Roman Italians who had no say in whether the state would seize and give away the land they were farming. This controversy was particularly unwelcome given the increasingly tense relations between Rome and its Italian allies. One of the features of Rome's emerging Mediterranean empire in the middle decades of the second century was a growing set of legal distinctions between Romans, Italians, and the conquered peoples of

Spain, North Africa, and Greece. Italian soldiers had shared in the plunder from these conquests, Italian merchants had profited from business activities in Rome's new provinces, and savvy Italian investors had gained significant wealth from their participation in Rome's midcentury financial revolution. Even the young Italian poor struggling to make a living on the small farms left to them by their parents often traveled to Rome to work.

The political integration of Italians had stagnated while the economic ties between Rome and its Italian allies deepened. Although Roman policy and the booming economy of the city had deeply affected Italians of all social statuses, those Italians lacked the ability to vote on laws and, in some cases, even lacked the legal right to work in Rome, as Roman citizenship extensions slowed.[30] Romans, too, appreciated that their citizenship status now placed them well above noncitizen Italians in the peninsula's social hierarchy.

This distinction mattered particularly within the city of Rome, the place where the largest communities of Roman citizens and noncitizens lived and worked side by side. Rome had for years taken sporadic measures against people illegally claiming Roman citizenship, but the first politician known to have campaigned for an openly anti-Italian-immigrant policy was a tribune of the plebs named Marcus Junius Pennus. In 126 BC, he passed a law "barring foreigners from enjoying the advantages of their city and excluding them from its borders."[31] Roundups of migrants ensued. These actions, which Cicero later called "altogether contrary to the laws of humanity," were worsened by the fact that, unlike Roman citizens, Italians in Rome had no right to appeal any mistreatment they suffered from a magistrate.[32]

The following year, the consul Marcus Fulvius Flaccus responded to Pennus's xenophobic populism by introducing a law to extend citizenship to allies so that they would be, as Appian put it, "partners in the empire rather than subjects."[33] The reform failed, and when Flaccus refused to answer pointed questions about the law in a Senate meeting, he was ordered to leave Rome and lead an army to fight in Gaul.[34] Probably not coincidentally, the Latin city of Fregellae rebelled against Rome following the failure of Flaccus's proposal. The revolt was put down so violently that the city was destroyed.[35]

The loudest voice raised in opposition to Pennus in 126 BC belonged to Tiberius Gracchus's younger brother Gaius, a man as powerfully motivated by his principles as Tiberius was by opportunism.[36] In 124, Gaius Gracchus chose to run for the tribunate on an ambitious platform of reforms he felt would improve the economic and political lives of all Romans and Italians. Universally recognized as the best speaker of his generation, he possessed "an amazing genius" that, Cicero wrote, combined "noble language" with a "judicious . . . great and striking manner of speaking," so that he expressed "his sentiments virtuously." But Gaius also spoke with such emotion that he could seem almost unhinged.[37] A Gracchus behaving that way sparked concern that he, too, might incite violence.

Alarmed senators took steps to prevent Gaius from even standing for election by charging that his conduct made him ineligible to run. Gaius, though, spoke so effectively in his own defense that "he left court with the reputation of having been most grossly wronged," wrote Plutarch. When some senators next charged him with being behind the rebellion in Fregellae, Gaius "completely established his innocence and then began to canvass immediately for the tribuneship."[38]

The election that made Gaius tribune was one of the most remarkable in Roman history. According to Plutarch, "all men of note, without exception, opposed him"—and, in an ordinary election, "men of note" made up a significant portion of the rural tribe members who voted. If the vote had been ordinary, Gaius would have easily lost most of the thirty-one rural voting tribes. He counteracted this elite opposition by inspiring "so great a throng from the country to pour into the city" that the "Campus Martius could not accommodate the crowds."[39] This influx of ordinary men and infrequent voters did not completely overcome the structural advantages elites enjoyed, but it was enough for Gaius to come in fourth among the ten tribunes elected for the year.

Gaius then deployed his oratorical gifts to "bring the people around to his side" in support of a far-reaching political program.[40]

It began with a law requiring any magistrate who had banished a citizen without a trial to himself stand trial. Popillius Laenas, the harsh judge who had condemned many of Tiberius's associates, fled Italy to avoid prosecution. Gaius next sponsored laws "constructing roads and establishing granaries," and placed "himself as director and manager of these projects," so that, as Appius Claudius Caecus had done 200 years earlier, he might build relationships with the contractors and landowners who benefited from the work.[41] Gaius created a publicly funded grain distribution program that sold grain at below-market rates to any Roman citizens who wanted it.[42] He combatted corruption by placing equestrians (Roman knights, the second most important social group in the late Republic) on the juries deciding civil and criminal cases and extending Roman citizenship to any citizen of an allied city who successfully prosecuted a Roman magistrate for misconduct.[43] This not only gave Italians a tool to fight administrative misconduct, but also offered a path for those wronged by Romans to be compensated by becoming full members of the Roman political community.

The most ambitious element of his program was revitalizing the colonization program that the Republic had once used to provide land to settlers. While most previous colonies had been in Italy, Gaius proposed placing a colony on the site once occupied by the city of Carthage. He later proposed establishing two more colonies on the sites once occupied by Capua and Tarentum, all of them defeated Roman enemies situated in economically advantageous locations.[44]

Gaius's reforms and his planned new colonies earned him reelection to the tribunate for 122, a feat that his brother had failed to achieve, but he spent two months of his time in office in Africa supervising preparations for the colony in Carthage.[45] This was an eternity in the one-year term that tribunes usually served, and it gave senators the chance to outflank him. While Gaius was away, Livius Drusus, one of Gaius's fellow tribunes, proposed twelve new colonies in Italy, a more attractive location than Carthage for Romans. If they were established, the twelve colonies would house perhaps 36,000 Roman families.[46] But Drusus had no intention of actually founding these colonies. His actions, Plutarch would write, were "neither honorable nor advantageous," because their sole purpose was "to surpass Gaius in pleasing and gratifying the people."[47] The gambit worked, however. "The people became more amicably disposed towards the Senate" and particularly appreciated that, unlike Gaius, Drusus "never appeared to propose anything for himself or in his own interests."[48] They failed to appreciate that he had no incentive to include himself in projects because he knew they would never come to fruition.

Gaius soon undercut his popularity with Roman voters even further. Wanting to ensure that any reforms designed to benefit Roman citizens did not also adversely impact noncitizen Italians, he had exempted some land farmed by Italian allies from redistribution by the land commission. In 122, he went even further and proposed a law that would extend Roman citizenship to all the citizens of Rome's Latin allies and grant Latin rights (which gave people rights of marriage and commerce with Roman citizens) to all other Italian allies.[49] This new citizenship expansion would help offset Italian concerns about the direction of Roman politics by making many Italians full members of the Roman political community.

Gaius possessed a remarkably prescient vision of what a more stable and integrated Roman state would look like. It would be a political community that joined all Italians and used the resources drawn from Rome's Mediterranean empire to materially support them through food distributions and infrastructure projects. Italians would spread across the Mediterranean in colonies planted on the most strategic and economically important sites once occupied by Roman adversaries. Indeed, this is much like the vision that Julius Caesar would implement in the next century. Gaius had seen the Roman future and had done a great deal to begin building it.

But other Romans were not yet ready to embrace that future. Extending citizenship proved to be even more of a political disaster than personally supervising the Carthaginian colony. The consul Gaius Fannius, a man elected to the consulship with Gracchus's help, dramatically turned against his ally and argued against "the admission of the Latin and Italian allies to the freedom of Rome."[50] The tribune Livius Drusus then vetoed Gaius's law and proposed an alternative that exempted allies from scourging.[51] When crowds of Gaius's Italian supporters began thronging the city, "the Senate prevailed upon the consul Fannius to drive out of the city all who were not Romans." Gaius promised to support his allies if they remained in the city, but there was little he could do without giving "his enemies the opportunity they sought" to charge him with fomenting violence, "just as they had done to his brother."[52]

These blows to Gaius's public standing denied him a third term as tribune. With Gaius out of office, the new consuls took a series of provocative actions, including the defunding of his Carthaginian colony. Gaius showed restraint, but he "set out to gather a fresh body of partisans for opposition to the consul," in case things turned violent. His mother, Cornelia, even collaborated with him to hire foreign fighters who might work on his behalf.[53]

Violence broke out on the day scheduled for a vote to annul Gaius's laws. Before voting began, however, his supporters attacked and killed one of the servants of the consul Lucius Opimius. Gaius "was distressed and upbraided his followers," Plutarch wrote, but "Opimius was elated as if he had gotten something for which he was waiting." He dissolved the assembly, convened the senators the next morning, and was enjoined by them "to save the city as best he could, and to put down the tyrants."[54] This formulation, called the Senatus Consultum Ultimum (SCU), suspended a Roman citizen's legal right to a trial, his right to appeal, and the tribune's ability to put his person between a Roman citizen and a magistrate who was abusing him.[55] The decree also effectively created an emergency condition that negated Gaius's own law penalizing a magistrate who harmed a citizen without holding a trial.

A massacre followed. Led by Opimius, armed senators, equites, and their attendants killed Gaius Gracchus, who, according to Plutarch, "was unwilling to arm himself, but went forth in his toga" as if he were going to address the people in the Forum.[56] One of Opimius's associates then carried Gaius's head around the city as a trophy until a senator bought it from him after agreeing to pay as much gold as the head weighed.[57] The mob also slaughtered 3,000 of Gaius's supporters, all of whom had been "put to death without trial" by a Roman consul theoretically bound to protect the rights of citizens.[58]

Opimius then had the gall to pay for a Temple of Concord to be built in the Roman Forum just across from the Senate House as a way to symbolize the peace he claimed to have restored. This angered the citizens even more, because he seemed to be "celebrating a triumph in view of all this slaughter of citizens." One night, a brave vandal added a line to the temple's dedicatory inscription: "A work of insane discord produces a temple of Concord."[59]

The vandal understood the Roman and Italian reality of the era far better than Opimius ever did. If Gaius had shown a promising Roman future, Opimius underlined a horrible Roman present. He and his allies had done immense damage both to Rome's relationships with its closest Italian allies and to the social compact that bound the Republic to its citizens. Neither group ever again really trusted that the leaders of the Republic would respect their rights. They also no longer believed that the structures of the Republic remained robust enough to restrain the excesses of men like Opimius. With legal protections eroding, Romans and their allies would now begin to look for extralegal ways to protect themselves from violence and injustice. Their search would lead to the end of the Republic.

Chapter 10

Marius and Sulla

120–80 BC

THE KILLINGS OF Gaius Gracchus and 3,000 of his supporters so horrified Romans that many surviving reform-minded politicians retreated from political life. While Gaius and Tiberius's mother, Cornelia, kept their legacies alive by hosting meetings of supporters and publishing their writings, most male reformers adopted a low profile. A few leading families dominated the consulship, and those consuls preserved a fragile peace. They permitted the Gracchan land commission and the grain dole to continue operating and kept Gaius's judicial reforms in place. Romans who did not want to dwell on the trauma of the 120s were willing to cede a measure of control over their political lives in exchange for stability. As the 110s progressed, however, the consolidation of power in a narrow oligarchy generated "unlimited and unrestrained greed that invaded, violated, and devastated everything," the historian Sallust later wrote.[1] Romans came to realize that when an oligarchy went unchallenged by reformers, it was capable of producing only a temporary, superficial stability while concealing the deep social rot that was slowly undermining the Republic.

The scale of elite corruption burst into the open as Roman venality caused the Republic to badly mismanage a conflict with the Numidian king Jugurtha. The conflict now called the Jugurthine War began in 118 BC when Jugurtha, one of three successors appointed by the Numidian king Micipsa, killed one of his corulers and forced the other, Adherbal, to seek Roman protection. Jugurtha was a gifted military commander who had fought alongside Roman commanders in Spain, and he had proved to be an astute observer of changing Roman mores. Sallust wrote that Jugurtha had learned how Roman "nobles" saw "riches as more powerful motivators than honor and virtue," and believed that he could use bribery to blunt any Roman action taken to support Adherbal. Jugurtha thus sent "large gifts to . . . those who held the most influence in the Senate," so that he could "transform the extreme hostility of the Roman nobles" about the way he took power "into gratitude and support."[2]

The Senate ultimately decided to divide the kingdom between Jurgurtha and Adherbal, but when fighting resumed in 112, Jugurtha's forces trapped Adherbal in his capital, Cirta. They then stormed the capital and murdered groups of Roman and Italian merchants who were present. Rome sent a general to punish Jugurtha, but he again bribed his way out of trouble and purchased a peace treaty. When he was summoned to Rome to explain the suspiciously mild agreement, Jugurtha's charisma (and money) convinced one of the tribunes of the plebs to block the tribunal from hearing testimony.[3]

Outraged Romans demanded that the war be restarted, but as hostilities recommenced, four former consuls and one sitting priest were convicted of corruption in trials that Sallust characterized as dripping with "bitterness and violence based upon rumor and irrational passion of the people." Part of the hostility grew out of frustration with the poor performance of an army infected by the twin plagues of oligarchic corruption and military incompetence. The course of the war began to change when the command of Roman forces passed to Quintus Caecilius Metellus, the consul of 109. Metellus managed to rebuild the confidence of the Roman army, but before he could defeat Jugurtha, he was replaced by Gaius Marius, a new commander from outside the "arrogant cabal" of elites that had dominated Roman politics since Gaius Gracchus's murder.[4]

Marius, in fact, was a political client of Metellus and had served on the staff of his African army. When Marius mentioned that he wanted to run for consul, Metellus, his own patron, scoffed that he should not "entertain thoughts above his station," but "instead . . . be satisfied with what [was his]."[5] Far from being discouraged by this condescending attitude, Marius recognized that his patron's words were a gift. Roman knights, businessmen, and ordinary voters were fed up with Rome's arrogant and corrupt aristocracy, and he could generate support by using this story to amplify their outrage. He easily won the election.

Marius called his consulship "the spoils" that the people "seized" from the "nobles" they "had conquered." Marius worked with allied tribunes of the plebs to get the Numidian command shifted from Metellus to himself. After he won this vote, Marius asked the Senate to approve his request to recruit new soldiers to take to Numidia. The Senate quickly agreed, probably because they suspected that Marius would fail to rally a war-weary population to join up at a time when Rome already had forces in Numidia and another large army fighting in Gaul.

Marius surprised the senators by abandoning the Roman custom that only recruits who met a minimum property qualification could serve in the Roman military.[6] Marius's most eager volunteers came from the Roman poor, who saw him as a military genius who would lead them to easy victory and substantial plunder.[7] Marius understood that his reputation depended upon the success of his land-poor, untrained recruits and carefully deployed these eager, untested soldiers in minor engagements to acclimate them to fighting together before they confronted Jugurtha's best troops. Although this strategy extended the fighting for several years, Marius ultimately defeated Jugurtha, forced him to flee, and then captured the fugitive king after he was betrayed by his father-in-law, the Mauretanian king Bocchus.[8]

Bocchus actually handed Jugurtha over to Lucius Cornelius Sulla, a man on Marius's staff who, with Bocchus's support, would eventually develop into Marius's most significant political antagonist. But this slowly developing rivalry did not hinder Marius's cooperation with Sulla as he led a series of campaigns in Gaul designed to avenge a devastating defeat Rome had suffered in 105 BC at Arausio (outside of the modern French city of Orange) in which more than 80,000 soldiers died.[9] The defeat was caused in part by the patrician Quintus Servilius Caepio's refusal to cooperate with his superior, the plebeian consul Gnaeus Mallius Maximus. Marius again looked to be the perfect savior at a moment when elite arrogance and incompetence had led to the death of tens of thousands of Romans and allowed barbarian troops to threaten Northern Italy.

Marius's consulship in 104 BC was the first of five consecutive terms he would serve. As his electoral victories continued, he gravitated toward disreputable allies who promised to reward his landless troops in ways that more conventional politicians would not. When Marius entered the third of these five consulships, he linked up with Lucius Appuleius Saturninus, a tribune of the plebs willing to use violence and intimidation to push through laws granting land to the Roman citizens and noncitizen Italians who had served under Marius during the campaign with Jugurtha.[10]

Marius's alliance with Saturninus coincided with a breakdown in his relationship with Sulla. Sulla served as Marius's legate in 104 and then as a military tribune in 103, but he responded to Marius's collaboration with Saturninus by backing Marius's rival Quintus Lutatius Catulus in the consular election of 103, and then defecting to serve on Catulus's staff.[11] When Marius's and Catulus's armies were fighting together and both began to run out of supplies, Sulla "made the provisions for Catulus's army so abundant that they lived in plenty," a situation that "greatly distressed" Marius because it meant that Sulla had shown himself to be more capable of meeting soldiers' needs than Marius.[12]

Despite these tensions, the two armies continued to fight together, defeating a confederation of Germans and Gauls in July 101. They killed tens of thousands, captured as many as 60,000 slaves, and celebrated a spectacular joint triumph in Rome. Marius capitalized on this good feeling by announcing that he would run for his fifth consecutive consular term. But the Roman public was beginning to tire of this onetime insurgent who had come to embody the political establishment.[13] Marius won only after paying substantial bribes to his voters while Saturninus intimidated the supporters of his rivals.

Marius's tenure was a disaster. Near the beginning of his term, he collaborated with Saturninus and the praetor Gaius Servilius Glaucia to distribute the land left vacant by the mass slaughter and enslavement of the vanquished Gauls among Marius's soldiers.[14] Marius's veterans and Saturninus's armed partisans ensured passage of the land redistribution law by flooding Rome's streets, brawling with their opponents, and driving hostile tribunes from the Rostra when they tried to impose their veto on the law.[15]

Saturninus's behavior got worse as the year progressed until, in December of 100, he and Glaucia violently disrupted the consular election. Marius had finally decided to step away from the office and Glaucia stood instead. Glaucia and Saturninus understood that an electoral victory might again depend upon violence and intimidation, so Glaucia's supporters armed themselves before they came to the polling place. They hoped he would win, but they stood ready to fight if that would prevent his loss.

Roman elections for consul were decided when candidates won a majority of the 193 voting centuries. Each century announced its vote separately, one at a time, until the votes of 97 agreed. As the votes were cast, it became clear that Glaucia would lose the consulship to a man named Gaius Memmius. Rather than accept this outcome, Glaucia and his supporters disrupted the vote counting and beat Memmius to death. The assembled voters fled in terror before the election could conclude.

The Roman historian Appian wrote that "neither laws nor any sense of shame" remained among the Romans after the bloodshed began. Supporters of both sides battled in the streets before Glaucia and Saturninus retreated with their supporters to the Capitoline Hill and barricaded it. The Senate then declared a Senatus Consultum Ultimum, the same drastic step that empowered the consul to use any means at his disposal to save the state that had led to the death of Gaius Gracchus, and directed Marius to suppress the insurrection.

The Senatus Consultum Ultimum meant that Marius could no longer pretend not to see Glaucia's abuses. He had to act, but Marius "was vexed" about whether to defend his old ally or protect the Republic. Marius ultimately chose the latter. He "armed some of his men reluctantly" and surrounded the Capitol until Glaucia and his supporters evacuated. Marius granted them safe passage down to the building where the Roman Senate often met, but once they reached it, an angry mob set upon the insurrectionists and killed them with a barrage of clay tiles broken off from the chamber's roof.[16]

The murders of Memmius, Glaucia, Saturninus, and their followers shattered the guarantee that the Republic could protect the lives of its citizens, the stakeholders in Rome's collaborative political enterprise. "No one," Appian writes, "had any more hope of protection" from a political system whose leaders had sanctioned the killing of others and been killed in response.[17] They also could not look to Marius, the dominant political figure of the previous decade, for any guidance or protection, because he had helped to create the climate that had permitted these violent excesses. He ended his term a diminished man and soon left Rome for a tour of Asia Minor, a journey commonly undertaken by disgraced Roman politicians who feared retaliation from their enemies.

Marius's fall came as Sulla leveraged "the reputation he had won in war" to run for office.[18] Sallust wrote that Sulla was "eloquent, resourceful, and able to make friends easily," but also ruthlessly calculating when deciding how to act toward others in both his public and private lives.[19] He overcame his father's relative poverty by securing a significant inheritance from his stepmother and another from a rich older woman to whom he had attached himself romantically.[20] As these successes mounted, Sulla came to trust a series of visions, oracles, and other divine messages that foretold his good fortune and personal achievements. He became so convinced that Fortune favored him that he styled himself Sulla Felix (Sulla the Lucky).[21]

Sulla campaigned for praetor in 99 BC but lost because the voters wanted him to serve instead as aedile, which would make him responsible, among other things, for public festivals and games. According to

Plutarch, they hoped "he would treat them to splendid hunting scenes and combats of Libyan wild beasts" provided by his friend Bocchus of Mauretania.[22] Sulla ran again for praetor in 98, however, and won election by bribing voters. He then assumed a command in Asia Minor that required him to stabilize a tense situation between the kingdom of Cappadocia and Mithridates, the king of Pontus.

Sulla returned to Rome in 93 BC so he could run for consul.[23] Bocchus again supported Sulla's campaign by dedicating "some images bearing trophies on the Capitol, and beside them gilded figures representing Jugurtha being surrendered by Bocchus to Sulla," but Marius believed that this monument diminished his own achievement in winning the Jugurthine War.[24] This prompted a Marian ally to sue Sulla for extorting money from one of the Asian kings with whom he had recently worked. The baseless accusation never went to trial, but it sufficiently dented Sulla's reputation that failed to secure the consulship.[25]

Sulla would have become an extremely obscure historical footnote had Rome's Italian allies not revolted after decades of frustration about Roman political programs that harmed their economic interests.[26] The situation exploded in 91 BC because of the careless actions of the tribune Livius Drusus. Drusus wanted to build support for an unpopular judicial reform by bundling it with another law that would found colonies of Roman citizens on public land in Italy and Sicily. These colonies would be on property largely farmed by Italian allies who were not eligible for settlement in the new colonies.[27] When rumors reached Rome of Italian plots to violently resist the redistribution of these farms, Drusus tried to salvage his program by expanding Roman citizenship to include all Italian allies.[28] Not long after he made this nakedly opportunistic proposal, an assassin killed him in the atrium of his house.[29]

Italy exploded after Drusus's death. The violence in what Romans would come to call the Social War began when a crowd of *socii*, or noncitizen Italian allies, in the city of Asculum murdered two Roman officials and all the other Roman citizens who were present.[30] Soon rebellious cities across Central and Southern Italy formed a political and military union against Rome. Many communities, particularly in Umbria and Etruria, remained loyal to Rome even though the Romans initially focused more on punishing Roman supporters of Drusus than on mobilizing against the Italian rebels.[31] As the year 90 progressed, though, the seriousness of the situation became clear, and the Senate summoned some of Rome's most experienced commanders out of retirement.

Marius was the most famous of the old lions to return to the battlefield. He largely calmed the war's northern front after helping Rome recover from a series of disastrous military reverses. Rome, however, struggled in the south, as the Samnites captured communities along the Bay of Naples. These losses prompted the Republic to free and arm slaves so that it could protect the coast between Cumae and Rome.[32] That October, the Republic finally addressed the cause of the revolt when the consul Lucius Julius Caesar passed a law granting Roman citizenship to the Latin, Etruscan, and Umbrian communities that did not rebel.[33] This was followed, probably in 89 BC, by another law extending citizenship to all individual Italians who presented themselves before a praetor.[34] Later that year, one of the consuls sponsored a law extending Latin rights, a political status just below that of full Roman citizenship, to the non-Italian inhabitants of Cisalpine Gaul, the area that now comprises much of modern Italy north of the Po River.[35]

These political changes combined with Roman military successes to drain much of the energy out of the Italian rebellion, but Sulla emerged as the hero of the last phase of the fighting. Plutarch described his ability to undertake "successful actions . . . on the spur of the moment," and his astute sense of how to manipulate the emotions of his soldiers by balancing the discipline needed to win a war with a generosity that richly rewarded his victorious soldiers.[36] This unique combination of qualities made Sulla's soldiers intensely loyal to him.

Sulla would soon need to call upon the loyalty of his troops. He returned to Rome at the end of 89, was elected consul for the year 88, and was chosen to lead a campaign against his old adversary

Mithridates of Pontus as soon as his term in office ended. This promised to be an important command. Mithridates had capitalized on Rome's preoccupation with Italy to invade Roman Asia, plunder its cities, and massacre their people, including as many as 80,000 Romans and Italian businessmen living on the mainland and on neighboring islands such as Rhodes.[37]

These murders reverberated across the Mediterranean. Not only did the loss of tax revenue from Asia imperil the public grain dole on which so many poor Romans depended, but it also proved devastating for the Roman financial system. Cicero described how "very many people lost large fortunes in Asia," which led to "a collapse in credit at Rome, because repayments were interrupted."[38] The rapidly deteriorating economic conditions even erupted into political violence when a mob of debtors murdered a praetor who tried to force them to use legal channels to mediate disputes with their creditors.

Sulla and his men saw the Mithridatic War as a chance to restore Roman pride and exact vengeance on Rome's most hated villain while also plundering some of the richest cities on earth. They were not the only ones. Marius saw it this way, too, and began working with a tribune named Publius Sulpicius Rufus to usurp Sulla's command. Plutarch describes how an old, overweight Marius tried to build enthusiasm for his bid by "going down every day to engage in athletic exercises" with young men training in the Campus Martius, a sight that "moved people to pity."[39] But Marius's daily shows of his nearly septuagenarian physique in the Campus Martius mattered much less than the private army of 3,000 armed men that Sulpicius had recruited to sway elections.[40]

Sulpicius brought 600 core supporters that he called his anti-Senate with him on the day that he proposed that the plebeians should vote to take the command against Mithridates away from Sulla and give it to Marius.[41] When Sulpicius's goons began fighting with Sulla's supporters, Sulla felt compelled to declare a suspension of all public business due to the unrest. Sulpicius then ordered his anti-Senate "to come into the Forum with concealed daggers and to do whatever was necessary, including killing the consuls, if that was required."[42] Fearing assassination, Sulla fled to the house of his old colleague Marius. Sulpicius then used the consul's flight to secure the votes needed to give the Mithridates command to Marius.[43]

Although Marius had protected Sulla from an attack that might have killed him, Sulla was not willing to accept the legality of Marius's elevation. He left Marius's house, traveled to the army he had commanded during the Social War, and called an assembly of the troops in which, Appian reports, he "urged [his men] to be ready to obey his orders." The soldiers "understood what he meant" and "ordered him to lead them to Rome," so that they could forcibly seize the command Sulpicius had taken from Sulla.[44] All but one of Sulla's officers left the army, "because they could not accept leading an army against their homeland," but the rank and file remained loyal as Sulla led them against the capital.[45]

Sulla attacked the low-lying area between the Esquiline and Oppian Hills, the weak point in the city's defense that Roman rulers since Servius Tullius had tried to fortify.[46] Other detachments also broke through weak points near the Colline Gate and at the spot where a wooden bridge crossed the Tiber. Once Sulla entered the city, angry Roman civilians took up positions on the rooftops of apartment blocks and bombarded his army with projectiles. Sulla "erupted in a passion" and ordered his archers to fire burning arrows at the assailants.[47]

Sulla's response once he secured Rome suggests that he wanted people to think he had merely asserted his right as consul to use force against a faction that had illegally deprived him of his consular power. On the next day, Appian reports, Sulla and his co-consul "summoned the people to an assembly" in which they "lamented that the Republic had been given over to demagogues for so long and that it had been necessary for them [i.e., the consuls] to do what they had done."[48] In order to avoid a fall back into dysfunction, the consuls proposed three reforms. First, no question should be brought before the popular assembly without first being approved by the Senate. Second, all voting should be done by the old, property-based centuries first created by Servius Tullius, rather than in the tribe-based voting done in the plebeian assembly. Third, all acts of Sulpicius voted upon after the violence started in the assembly should be proclaimed illegal.

If Sulla had continued to exercise restraint, one could almost imagine that his military attack on Rome was a return to normalcy after yet another moment of civil strife. But Sulla's next actions laid bare that this was actually "the first time an army of her own citizens had invaded Rome as an enemy force."[49] Acting as a victorious general rather than an elected Roman magistrate, Sulla condemned Marius, Sulpicius, and ten others to death, without a trial and without the right of appeal. This order violated two basic rights that the Republic had guaranteed its citizens.

After this point, Appian wrote, "there was no restraint upon violence either from a sense of shame or regard for laws, the Republic, or the fatherland." Sulpicius was killed, Marius fled to North Africa, and Sulla authorized the confiscation of their properties. Sulla then superintended the consular election for the year 87 and forced Lucius Cornelius Cinna, "a man of the opposite faction" who won election, to swear that he would "be favorable to his policies." Sulla ignored a call by one of the tribunes to stand trial for misconduct during his consular term, and then set off to fight Mithridates.[50]

Cinna abandoned his "solemn oath" soon after Sulla departed. He instead allied himself with Marius, who had returned to Italy and recruited an army of Etruscans "ready to do what Sulla had done and use force to take over their homeland."[51] Cinna took control of a Roman army based in Campania and augmented it with Samnite forces, to whom he offered Roman citizenship as well as the right to retain any plunder they had seized in the Social War.[52] Marius, Cinna, and their Etruscan and Samnite armies then marched to Rome, placed the city under siege, and, after starvation encouraged the mass defection of people and soldiers, took control of the capital.[53]

They showed even less restraint than Sulla had. After annulling all the laws Sulla had issued after his capture of Rome, Marius and Cinna ordered the execution of a host of Sullan loyalists and the mounting of their heads on the Rostra.[54] The two generals also arranged their own appointment as consuls for 86, but Marius died not long after taking office. His demise freed Cinna from the vindictiveness of his colleague and enabled him to reconcile with the many people who wanted to put the recent violence behind them. Cinna built a coalition of Roman elites who accepted the legitimacy of his regime and participated in its administration of Italy.[55] One of the most ancient Roman noble families, the Caesares, even married their son Julius Caesar to Cinna's daughter.

Sulla recognized that he could not fight both the government in Rome and Mithridates, so he played along with Cinna's idea that concord had been restored to the Republic until he accomplished enough to declare victory in the east.[56] After a siege stretching into 86, Sulla defeated the pro-Mithridates forces that controlled Athens, sacked the city, and robbed temples across Greece so that he could get enough plunder to "corrupt and win over to himself the soldiers of other generals."[57] Not only did these rewards keep Sulla's soldiers happy, but they also induced others to defect to his cause. In 85, Cinna's regime in Rome sent an army east to relieve Sulla of his command, after the Senate assigned the province of Asia to the consul Flaccus.[58] Instead of accepting his replacement, Sulla negotiated a peace agreement with Mithridates's agents in Greece and assessed a massive fine on the Greek and Asian cities that had defected to the king. Then Sulla returned to Italy "to take vengeance on all of those in the city" who had wronged him and his supporters.[59]

News of Sulla's imminent return prompted Cinna to raise an army to confront him, but when Cinna ordered the troops to sail from Italy to what is now coastal Croatia, they mutinied and killed him. Sulla was then able to land in Italy unopposed. As he moved through the peninsula, people flocked to join what seemed to be the winning campaign of a generous commander. The new Roman citizens of Samnite Southern Italy, however, feared "destruction, death, confiscation, and wholesale extermination" if Sulla prevailed in the civil war.[60] They fought on until Sulla defeated them decisively at the

Battle of the Colline Gate in 82 BC, as they tried to defend the capital.[61] Thousands were captured in the final phases of fighting.

Sulla had no more reason to pretend to be conciliatory after their final defeat. He had won control of Rome and could implement whatever victor's justice he wished. "Sulla," Plutarch would later write, "now so busied himself with slaughter that murders without number or limit filled the city."[62] Sulla first published a list of 40 senators and 1,600 Roman knights who were to be executed and whose property was to be confiscated. More people across Italy soon were added to the list, as were people suspected of helping or being kind to those who had been proscribed. Others were included by Sulla simply "so that he could gratify his supporters."[63]

Sulla saved the worst violence for the Senate meeting when he announced the form his restored Republic would take. Plutarch describes how he brought 6,000 captives to the Circus of Flaminius in Rome and then "summoned the Senate to meet in the Temple of Bellona," a space just above the circus dedicated to a goddess known for bloodthirsty madness in battle. "At the same moment Sulla began to speak in the Senate . . . those assigned to the task began to cut to pieces the six thousand in the circus." The "cries of the crowd being massacred . . . filled the air" and terrified the senators, "but Sulla . . . ordered them to listen to his words and not concern themselves with what was going on outside."[64]

Sulla knew they could not avoid listening. The tortures and executions of these thousands of Romans undermined the basic promise at the core of Rome's Republic. Cicero's words, quoted earlier, are worth recalling: "A Republic," he would later write, "is an entity of the people. But a people is not a collection of humans assembled in any old way. It is a collection of a multitude joined to one another by a consensus about law and the common good."[65] Citizens were stakeholders in the Roman Republic, and when Rome extended citizenship to new communities or people, their voices were supposed to matter in any conversations about law and the common good. This principle had been upheld until Sulla. The voices of the Samnites in the circus were those of Roman citizens, and Sulla was not only dismissing these protections and nullifying their legal status, but taking their very lives. The same was true for the hundreds of other Romans whose lives and property he took.

Appian records why Sulla felt this was justified. After what Sulpicius, Marius, and Cinna had done, Sulla believed that the Republic no longer had the capacity to "provide permanent security to himself and those exiles who had fled to him." "With this single sentence," Appian concludes, Sulla "made it clear that he . . . was contemplating seizing power" so he could avoid falling victim to violence the laws could no longer prevent.[66]

Sulla revived for himself the old office of dictator that the Republic had not used since the time of Hannibal. He then arranged to receive a full amnesty for his actions during the war and was granted "power of life and death, of confiscation, of colonization, of founding or demolishing cities, and of taking away or bestowing kingdoms at his pleasure."[67] Sulla first used these powers to grant his most loyal officers large shares of the land and property that had been seized from his enemies in Etruria, Campania, and Southern Italy. These veterans would now garrison Italy.[68]

Sulla then set about redesigning the structures of the Republic. He took control of elections and allowed only his personally approved candidates to stand for office.[69] He expanded the Senate to include the wealthiest Roman knights, so that no figures could follow Marius's path and build a powerful political coalition around equestrian anger at the Senate. To prevent tribunes from using their office as a political stepping stone, he prohibited any tribune from ever pursuing higher office, restricted their ability to propose new laws, and limited the circumstances in which they could exercise their vetoes. Other people seeking magistracies were also constrained. Sulla specified a minimum age that a candidate must reach before becoming eligible to run for each office, and he required that all offices must be held in a specific order so that one could not, for example, become a consul unless he had previously served as an aedile, quaestor, and praetor.

And then it was over. Sulla resigned the dictatorship in 80 BC and returned to private life, naively believing that he had restored a functional Republic to Rome. It is remarkable that a man who had such a clear-eyed view of how to maneuver advantageously in the collapsing Republic of the 80s could be so optimistic about its revival.

Sulla retired to the countryside, married a new wife, consorted with beautiful actresses, and wrote terrible poems. He died, Plutarch records with some relish, of "a disease that was insignificant in its beginnings," but which his philandering allowed to turn into an illness "that corrupted his whole flesh and converted it into worms." Sulla bathed, purged, and cleansed his body, but "it was of no use ... [T]he swarm of vermin defied all purification." By the end of the illness, the worms "came swarming out in such numbers that all his clothing, bath, washbasins, and food became infected with the corruption."[70] Sulla lived on as a stinking and vile creature who now putrefied all he touched.

Plutarch's description of Sulla's final illness offers a thinly veiled metaphor for the condition in which Sulla left the Republic. Sulla had entered political life in the 110s when the Republic was ill, but not fatally so. His actions then pushed Rome into an orgy of ambition, greed, and violence that caused an incurable affliction. The Republic remained just barely alive after Sulla's purification of the state, but, like the ineffective treatments Sulla received for his body, his new constitution could not stop Rome from rotting from within. Thanks to Sulla, the Republic now corrupted all who interacted with it. It would outlive Sulla, but it would die no less horrifically.

Chapter 11

Sulla's Children

80–44 BC

T HE THIRTY YEARS following the death of Sulla saw his reformed Republic slowly collapse as an entire generation traumatized by his dictatorship struggled to repair the damage he had done. This generation included some of the most famous men in Roman history—among them Pompey the Great, Cicero, Julius Caesar, and Cato the Younger, all born between 106 and 95. Together with their older contemporary Crassus (born in 115), they tried to advance their own careers in a fashion that avoided the political violence that had tipped Rome into civil war. All of these men desperately wanted to preserve the Republic they loved, but their patriotic affection could not prevent the violent destruction of a political system that none of them ultimately trusted to protect their lives.

Complicated systems like the Roman Republic control the stakes surrounding individual political competition. When the structures of the state are strong, they provide for nonviolent political competition in which the rewards of victory and the costs of defeat are relatively predictable. Rome offered this guarantee to officeholders and failed candidates alike for three centuries, until the slaying of Tiberius Gracchus introduced murder as a political tool. But Sulla was the first Roman leader to believe that the Republic was so sick that he could only "be safe" if, as Sallust put it, "he was worse and more detestable than [the people's] dread of him."[1] Sulla saw politics as a fight in which the loser would die and the winner would hold unchecked power for as long as he wished, with subordinates submitting to him "in exchange for dominance" over other Romans.[2] This lesson appalled the generation of Roman politicians who came of age during Sulla's career and saw the horrors that arose when one combined unlimited ambition with a willingness to embrace political violence.

Pompey was the first of these men to become prominent. He was the son of Gnaeus Pompeius Strabo, an influential general who rose from the Central Italian region of Picenum to the consulship at the end of the Social War. Strabo held that office in 89 BC, took control of an army as a proconsul in 88, and then managed to retain his army despite the efforts of both Sulla and Cinna to remove him. He died in 87 after spending years using his soldiers as a tool to bargain for a second consulship while also profiting from the fighting.[3]

Pompey was only twenty when his father died, but he understood how his father exploited the chaos of the Social War to get control of an army and why Strabo retained that army even after the legal basis for his command expired. The army kept him alive, and powerful, but Strabo's willingness to allow his troops to plunder Roman communities made him so hated that, soon after his father's death, political opponents initiated a prosecution of Pompey. They claimed Pompey had taken plunder from the capture of the city of Ausculum that rightfully belonged to the Republic, but the litigants misjudged the young man. Pompey not only beat the case, but he ended up marrying Antistia, the daughter of the judge presiding over the trial, four days after his acquittal.[4] Pompey then began working tentatively with the regime of Cinna, although he returned to Picenum shortly before Cinna was killed.[5]

His father's example inspired Pompey to take advantage of Sulla's landing in Italy. Using his family connections and the residual fear they inspired in his home region, Pompey recruited a personal army of three legions from the major cities in Picenum, which he then led to Sulla's camp. His initiative impressed Sulla enough that he tasked Pompey with securing the province of Cisalpine Gaul and then defeating the consul Carbo in Sicily.[6] Pompey fought well, captured Carbo, and executed the consul in such brutal fashion that a shocked Roman populace began to call him *adulescentulus carnifex,* or "the teenaged butcher." But Pompey also had the foresight to pardon many people who knew he could have killed them. This gave him a network of grateful clients in Sicily and North Africa who might support him in the future.[7]

Pompey's relationship with Sulla soured after he refused an order from the dictator to return two of his personally recruited legions to Italy. Pompey manufactured a mutiny and had his soldiers claim that "they would never forsake their general," while they implored that Pompey "never trust himself to the tyrant."[8] Pompey's public demonstrations of his growing independence from Sulla culminated in an exchange where Pompey told Sulla that "more people worship the rising sun than the setting sun."[9] The gulf between them grew so large that Sulla left Pompey out of his will, a step that reinforced Pompey's independence and gave him more freedom of action in a post-Sullan world.

Pompey spent much of the rest of the 70s commanding armies while avoiding election to any office to which military commands were normally attached. He instead became a permanent commander of an army loyal to himself that served under senatorial sanction. Because he held no office, Pompey had no colleague with equal powers. He never faced voters, and he was bound by none of the formal limits that constrained magistrates. He instead fought for the Republic on his own terms.

Romans tolerated this because Pompey won a string of important victories for the Republic under difficult conditions. In 78, he suppressed a rebellion by the consul Marcus Aemilius Lepidus. He then went to Spain to destroy the regime of Quintus Sertorius, an old Marian general who had escaped even Sulla.[10] After Sertorius was assassinated and his forces defeated, Pompey pardoned as many influential people in Spain as he could so that they, too, would be his future supporters.[11] On his way back from Spain, Pompey's army cut apart what remained of the slaves who had rebelled under the leadership of Spartacus.

Pompey then surprised everyone. Instead of using his army and his clients in Spain, Sicily, and North Africa to seize power in Rome, he announced that he would run for the consulship. Pompey was too young to serve as consul under Sulla's constitution, and he had held none of the requisite lower offices, but Romans were grateful that he chose to pursue power peacefully rather than seizing it forcefully.[12] He won election easily.

Marcus Licinius Crassus was his colleague when Pompey's term began in 70. Although nearly a decade older than Pompey and the richest man Rome had ever known, Crassus seemed to most Romans like Pompey's junior partner, and he seemed to nurse a "jealous rivalry" with his colleague that made cooperation difficult.[13] Their relationship became even more fraught when Pompey, who had never before held an elected Roman magistracy, proposed restoring the powers of the tribunate and the chance for tribunes to again hold higher office that Sulla had taken away. He was rewarded for this by a grateful tribune who proposed giving land to the veterans of Pompey's Spanish campaign.[14] Crassus worried that this use of an allied tribune to secure state resources for Pompey's soldiers strongly resembled how Marius and Sulla had rewarded soldiers in the past, but no one wanted a civil war.[15] Near the end of their term, a figure who claimed divine inspiration informed Pompey and Crassus that Jupiter demanded that they reconcile before the year ended.[16] After crowds of citizens took up this call, Crassus extended his hand to Pompey, and "they shook hands amid universal acclamations" from Romans who believed they had "avoided a massive civil conflict."[17]

Pompey and Crassus then returned to the sorts of activities that made them so influential. Crassus pursued lucrative business ventures that enhanced his political influence, while ambitious tribunes granted Pompey a series of military commands through which he brought much of what is now coastal Turkey, Syria, Lebanon, and Israel under direct or indirect Roman control. By the time Pompey returned to Rome in 62, he had conquered more territory than any Roman general had ever conquered before.

NEW PLAYERS FROM the post-Sullan generation emerged in Rome while Pompey was away. Marcus Tullius Cicero, the oldest of this group, was the most impressive and accomplished Latin orator and prose stylist of all time, but Cassius Dio echoes the feelings of many when he says that Cicero was also "wearisome, burdensome, disliked," and "the greatest boaster alive."[18] People mostly tolerated Cicero because his skill as a courtroom advocate made him a useful ally in a Roman Republic where lawsuits had become a political weapon.[19] His ability to blend philosophical principle, rhetorical forcefulness, and eloquence with a talent for devastatingly witty insults propelled his political career through a rapid succession of elected offices, which he always obtained at the youngest age Sulla's laws permitted, until he won the consulship for 63 BC.

Cicero's younger contemporary Marcus Porcius Cato (known to us as Cato the Younger) offered a different sort of ethically inspired political leadership. Whereas Cicero was the first of his family to join the Roman Senate, Cato was the great-grandson of the stern and calculating Marcus Porcius Cato (Cato the Elder), whose loud, public proclamations of his fidelity to tradition had shaped so much of Roman conservatism in the first half of the second century BC. Although he bore his ancestor's famous name, his father and nearly all the other male members of the Porcii Catones family died before Cato the Younger reached the age of four. This meant that he had lived first with his maternal uncle Livius Drusus, the tribune whose murder had sparked the Social War, and later with other maternal relatives. Benefiting from his family's ties to Sulla, Cato entered public life while Sulla was dictator by joining the board of fifteen priests who controlled rituals within the city of Rome. At roughly the same time, he enrolled as a student of the Stoic philosopher Antipater of Tyre and began advertising his virtue by walking around the city without shoes or a tunic, just as, he claimed, Romulus had done. By the time Cato joined the Senate in 64 BC, he was known as an austere traditionalist eager to push the post-Sullan Roman world back to what he claimed were its virtuous foundations.[20]

Julius Caesar entered the Senate with a very different profile. He came from a Roman patrician family that claimed descent from the goddess Venus and Aeneas, but the Caesares had embraced populism in more recent years. Marius married Caesar's aunt Julia, and as a young man Julius Caesar married Cinna's daughter Cornelia. He escaped proscription when Sulla entered Rome because he was only seventeen, but Sulla confiscated his father's property and Cornelia's dowry while stripping the young man of the priesthood of Jupiter that he had assumed following his father's death. Sulla also ordered Caesar to divorce Cornelia, but Caesar chose to go into exile instead. He returned to Rome only after his mother and the Vestal Virgins intervened with Sulla on his behalf.[21]

Caesar understood that Sulla belonged to Rome's past rather than its future, but he differed from his contemporaries not just in disavowing Sulla but in embracing Marius. This distinction mattered greatly. Pompey, Crassus, and Cato all had connections to Sulla before they demonstratively distanced themselves from him in public and calculated ways. They all became anti-Sullans looking to a new Roman future, men who had effectively unmoored themselves from the recent Roman past. Caesar, however, believed that untapped political potential lay in connecting himself to the legacy of Sulla's great adversary Marius.[22] Caesar saw that his status as Marius's nephew uniquely positioned him to reintroduce Marius to the Roman public.

At the funeral of his aunt Julia in 69 BC, Caesar "made a brilliant public speech in her honor in the Forum and was bold enough to display images of Marius himself in the funeral procession." Such images, Plutarch wrote, "had not been seen since Sulla came into power." Some Sullan partisans objected to the sight of Marius, but they "were shouted down by the crowd," which "welcomed Caesar with loud applause . . . for having brought back to Rome . . . the honors due to Marius."[23] Caesar had anticipated the outcry, but he had wagered that any anger about his decision to display images of a dead woman's husband at her own funeral would only remind Romans of the cruelty shown by Sulla and his backers.

Caesar's claim on Marius's legacy—and his willingness to chase popularity through "lavish expenditures on theatrical performances, processions, and public banquets"—catalyzed a rapid progression through the lower rungs of senatorial offices. And then, in 63 BC, his growing popularity led to him winning election as pontifex maximus, the city's chief religious official. Caesar was only thirty-seven at the time, and his unexpected victory astonished many of the senators, who had convinced themselves that Caesar's "influence would wane once he stopped spending money." They now feared that he might mobilize the people and violently seize power.[24]

THAT YEAR DID indeed see an outbreak of political violence, but Caesar was not to blame. The problem instead grew out of the unsustainable debts incurred by Lucius Sergius Catilina (now often called simply Catiline) when he waged two consecutive unsuccessful consular campaigns in 64 and 63 BC.[25] Believing he could escape debt only if he imitated Sulla's capture of the Roman state, Catiline crafted an audacious plan to murder Cicero, seize Rome, and redistribute property among his supporters. He recruited an army of perhaps 10,000 troops in Etruria, appealed to a Gallic tribe called the Allobroges for auxiliary support, and plotted a series of assassinations and arson attacks in the capital designed to incapacitate the Roman government.

But Catiline had misunderstood the moment. While many Romans did certainly feel a sense of desperation about economic inequality, the leading members of the post-Sullan generation did not yet share Catiline's cynicism about the state of the Republic. They remembered what Sulla's violence had produced and did not want a repeat of it. In late October of 63, Crassus and some other senators informed Cicero that a massacre was planned in Rome. The Senate declared a public emergency, and Catiline fled the city after a failed attempt to kill Cicero on November 7.

When envoys carrying letters from Catiline to the Allobroges were arrested on December 2, Roman leaders who had lived through Sulla's massacres sought to suppress Catiline's revolt without contravening the laws and mores of the Republic.[26] The following day, Cicero reassured the general public with a speech describing the discovery of the conspirators' plans.[27] Things began to spin out of control on December 4, however, when one of the accused conspirators, without evidence, implicated Crassus, and two others tried to bribe Cicero to lodge a false accusation against Caesar.[28] Both efforts failed, but rumors about Caesar's treachery meant that he encountered men with drawn swords as he left the Senate meeting. In just one day, senators had moved from praising Cicero's detection of Catiline's plot to using it as a pretext to attack their political rivals.

On December 5, the Senate discussed the conspirators' fate. The first man to speak was Decimus Junius Silanus, one of the incoming consuls, who had defeated Catiline in the most recent election. He advocated executing the men under arrest as well as any plotters still at large. Julius Caesar, one of the incoming praetors, spoke soon afterward. Sallust reports that Caesar emphasized how Roman law dictated that "Roman citizens, even when convicted" of a crime, "shall not lose their lives but shall instead be permitted to go into exile." Sulla had shown the dangers of disregarding this legal principle. Everyone in Rome, Caesar continued, "commended" Sulla when he ordered the execution of one murderous official, but "that act was the beginning of great bloodshed" because it freed the dictator to do what he wished to his fellow citizens without legal restraints. After that, there was "no end to the killing until Sulla glutted all of his followers with riches."[29]

Then Cato, one of the tribunes just elected, rose to speak in equally powerful terms about why Rome should nevertheless execute the conspirators. Laws, Cato explained, do not apply to citizens willing to attack their own country and threaten "the lives and liberty" of all Romans. Catiline had endangered Rome in so terrible a fashion that "punishment after the manner of our forefathers," like Brutus, who killed even their own sons when they were disloyal to Rome "ought to be inflicted" on the Catilinarian traitors. Rome's tenuous peace, in Cato's view, could be saved only through sternness and brutality, even if this breached legal norms.[30]

These were, Sallust wrote, "two men of towering merit, though of opposite character." Caesar was generous, forgiving, and known for "relieving difficulties," while Cato was "as severe as one could be," especially when confronting the failures of others.[31] Both men, however, had spoken honestly about how they felt the Republic could be salvaged. And the senators responded not with the rationality Caesar advocated but with the vindictiveness and fear that Cato channeled. Not only did they vote for immediate execution, but some senators even considered punishing Caesar for advocating a more moderate punishment for the conspirators that was consistent with the law. By "placing anger above [their] reputations" and "allowing villainy . . . to outweigh [the senators'] dignity," Sallust felt that the Senate had eliminated Catiline's immediate political threat but furthered Rome's fall away from justice and reason.[32]

THE EXECUTION OF the conspirators without trial created an ethical rootlessness that deeply complicated Rome's response to Pompey as he concluded his extraordinary campaign of conquest in the Eastern Mediterranean. Pompey's mandate to campaign in the east ended when Mithridates committed suicide in 63 BC, but fears about his intentions descended on the capital even before the ten-day celebration of his victory concluded.[33] Cato, Crassus, and even Cicero assumed that Pompey would follow Sulla, return from the east, and use his loyal and powerful army to seize control of the Roman state.[34] But Pompey proved them wrong. Although he "could have taken Italy and gained for himself all that Rome controlled," wrote Cassius Dio, he instead dismissed his army "without waiting for any vote to be passed by the Senate or the people" to reward him or his soldiers.[35] This proved to be a catastrophic miscalculation.

Pompey believed that this dramatic gesture would peacefully reintegrate him into Roman political life, but his rivals took advantage of his sudden weakness by humiliating him and delaying the public celebration of his triumphs.[36] Cato also froze measures to legalize the status of the eastern provinces Pompey had conquered and to provide land to his veterans. Pompey privately "repented of having let his legions go so soon," since by doing so he had "placed himself under the power of his enemies."[37]

Cato and his allies also targeted Crassus and Cicero, but their most consequential obstruction involved Caesar.[38] Caesar's political career continued to flourish in the years after the Catilinarian conspiracy, but his popularity was sustained by such extensive borrowing that Crassus had to bail him out so that he could be permitted to leave Rome to serve as governor of Lusitania in Spain in 62 BC.[39] Only a successful campaign for consul and a lucrative command after his term ended would enable Caesar to pay off the money he owed.

Because of his service in Spain, the Senate had voted Caesar a triumph that he hoped to use to launch his campaign for the consulship.[40] There was one problem with Caesar's plan. An honored general could not enter the city of Rome before his triumph, but a consular candidate needed to present himself in the city to begin his campaign. Caesar asked for permission to register his candidacy in absentia, but Cato filibustered the entire Senate meeting during which the measure could come to a vote. When Caesar reacted by forgoing the triumph, Cato backed a measure assigning the consuls for 59 BC the "woods and pastures" of Italy as their province, so that, if Caesar won election, he would have neither an army nor a way to get out of debt. Then, as the electoral campaign began, Cato showed how shallow his commitment to democratic integrity was by buying votes for Marcus Calpurnius Bibulus, Cato's son-in-law and Caesar's main rival in the election.[41]

Caesar responded by reaching out to Pompey and Crassus, the most powerful of the many victims of Cato's obstruction. Pompey and Crassus had fallen out again following their joint consulship, but Caesar had friendly relationships with both men and explained to them that their rivalry only "increased the power of . . . Cato, whose influence would be nothing if Crassus and Pompey united."[42]

Crassus and Pompey helped Caesar win one of the consulships, but Bibulus was chosen as his colleague. Faced with the prospect of a year of obstruction by Cato and Bibulus, Caesar proposed an informal agreement in which he, Pompey, and Crassus would "do things in common on behalf of each other."[43] This arrangement, which we now call the First Triumvirate, meant nothing more than that each man would use his resources to back the policies and ambitions of the other two. Crassus's wealth, Caesar's charisma, and Pompey's military reputation meant that this team could now overwhelm any roadblocks that Cato and Bibulus threw up against them. Although none of the three wanted the Republic to end, they no longer believed that it could limit the power of ambitious politicians while addressing the real needs of its citizens and subjects. As a result, Caesar's consulship in 59 saw these committed Republicans repeatedly take destructive actions that they believed were necessary to keep the Republic functional but that, paradoxically, hastened its end.

Soon after Caesar and Bibulus entered office, Caesar proposed meticulously drafted legislation to move some of the population from the crowded capital, settle Pompey's veterans, and return vacant Italian farms to cultivation. He had the text read aloud in the Senate and asked each senator individually whether he had any criticism of the law. Not even Cato found specific text to which he could object. "Even though he could find no fault with the measure," reports Cassius Dio, "Cato nevertheless urged on general principles" that the law be rejected.[44]

Caesar then decided to remove Cato from the discussion by putting the measure before the plebeian assembly, a move he justified by saying that no senator had found any provisions in the law objectionable. Pompey and Crassus spoke in favor of the law, with Pompey indicating that he would use force if opponents tried to violently block a vote, but Bibulus declared the entire rest of the year a sacred period in which no assemblies could be held or votes taken.[45] Caesar simply ignored him and scheduled a vote. When the day came, Bibulus forced his way through the crowds and began speaking against the law before Caesar's supporters swarmed him, assaulted the lictors who accompanied him, and beat the tribunes allied with him. Bibulus fled the scene, and Caesar's law was approved.

Bibulus subsequently withdrew from public life, and Caesar spent the rest of his consular term securing legislative victories for his allies. He backed Crassus's bailout of equestrian tax farmers in Asia, ratified Pompey's eastern conquests, and settled Roman farmers on public land in Campania. Caesar's own reward came when he received military command over four legions that he could take to the provinces of Cisalpine Gaul, Illyricum, and Transalpine Gaul. He departed at the end of his term and spent the rest of the decade expanding Roman control deeper into Gaul. By 50 BC, he had conquered much of what is now modern France, Belgium, and the Netherlands as well as pieces of modern Germany and Switzerland. As his victories mounted, Caesar developed a sophisticated public relations operation in which he informed Romans about his many military successes and the bravery of his troops through regular commentaries distributed in the capital.[46]

In the meantime, political violence returned to Rome. By the middle of the 50s, the growing unrest so troubled Cicero that he began work on a dialogue called *De re publica* (*On the Republic*), his most consequential work of political philosophy. Cicero wrote that Rome possessed a republic designed and perfected by generations of practical men who, unlike Greek philosophers, learned by doing. Now it looked "like a beautiful painting whose colors were beginning to fade." "[We may] retain the name Republic," he wrote, "but we have long since lost the actual thing." "Lawlessness" and violence were changing their system of government "from one of justice to one of force."[47]

Cicero's basic rule for the functioning of a Republic was that "nothing is done through violence," but, during the three years it took him to finish *De re publica*, Rome degenerated into something that looked a lot like the republic of violence the work warned against.[48] "Murders happened every day," Cassius Dio later wrote, "and they could not even hold elections."[49] Regular street fighting between factions paralyzed political life. When Cato's brother-in-law ran for consul against Crassus and Pompey in 56, the campaign was marred by such regular violence that the vote was postponed until after the consular term was scheduled to begin the following January. The election only happened then because Caesar threatened to deploy his forces in Rome if violence persisted.

These sorts of delays soon became common. The elections to choose the consuls of 53 did not happen until the summer of that year, at which point the consuls looking to take office in 52 had already begun campaigning. Then the election for 52 did not take place at all, following a murderous brawl between supporters of the political rivals Publius Clodius Pulcher and Titus Annius Milo on the Appian Way.[50] Peace returned only when the Senate decided to appoint Pompey as sole consul for the year 52 and give him an army with which to pacify the city.[51]

Cicero perceptively analyzed the illusion of calm that Pompey's domination created. A state dominated by one citizen's overwhelming power might "seem as if it was at peace," he said, because "men feared each other," but it would fall back into violence as soon as someone felt strong enough or desperate enough to challenge that leader.[52] All it took to shatter Rome's delicate balance of fear was someone with the confidence to challenge Pompey. And, as the 50s came to a close, Cato, Pompey, and their allies pushed Caesar to that point of desperation.

Caesar's Gallic conquests had made him a popular, wealthy man and transformed his soldiers into a cohesive, intensely loyal corps as skilled as any Rome had ever sent into battle. But Caesar's authority to campaign in Gaul was due to expire at the end of 50 BC, and he feared returning to Rome without some assurances that he could protect himself from violence. He also very much wanted to avoid the politically motivated prosecutions that figures allied with Cato and Bibulus were rumored to be ready to launch as soon as Caesar found himself without an army or an office to shield him.[53]

Opportunistic politicians in Rome encouraged Pompey's rivalry with Caesar, which intensified after Crassus died while fighting in Mesopotamia in 53. Cato understood intuitively what Cicero had explained philosophically. The façade of a Republic continued to exist only because the strong hand of Pompey prevented the kind of routine political violence that had paralyzed the state earlier in the 50s. Cato feared that Caesar's return would upset this tenuous balance, but men like the tribune Gaius Curio welcomed that disruption. An ambitious figure with limited prospects in the Pompey-dominated Republic, Curio looked to a future where a grateful Caesar might offer him greater rewards.[54]

The question of how Caesar might return to Rome peacefully and without fear of prosecution dominated Roman politics for much of the year 51 and all of 50. Eventually, Curio managed to shift the question from when Caesar should dismiss his forces to a broader discussion of why Caesar should do so while Pompey kept control of his own army. Infuriated, Pompey responded that Caesar's command should end after the consular elections scheduled to be held in November of 50, an arbitrary date that alarmed Caesar.

The façade of genuine representative government fell away when the final Senate meeting of the year saw the senators vote on three resolutions. The first, Appian recounts, asked "whether successors should be sent to Caesar" so they could relieve him of command over his armies. This was approved. The second asked, "Should Pompey be deprived of his command?" This motion was defeated. Curio then asked the senators to vote on "whether both"—meaning both Caesar and Pompey—"should lay down their commands." At this, "22 senators voted in the negative while 370 approved the opinion of Curio in order to avoid civil discord."[55] The clearest proof that the will of the people and their representatives no longer mattered came from the fact that Pompey and Caesar both ignored this vote.

One of the consuls then ordered a Roman army at Capua to be turned against Caesar in response to a false rumor that Caesar had moved into Italy. When Curio protested that this step was based on a lie, the consul went to Pompey and ordered him "to march against Caesar on behalf of your country."[56] Curio and his fellow tribunes then fled Rome to seek refuge with Caesar's army, while the Senate, which Caesar wrote felt "compelled by its terror at the presence of

Pompey's army," declared Caesar an enemy of the state.[57] In response, Caesar went before his troops and told them that legal political activities "were now branded as a crime and suppressed by violence." The soldiers responded that "they were ready to defend their commander and the tribunes of the plebs from all injuries."[58]

So began the civil wars that ended the Republic.

THE FIRST ACTION came on January 10, 49 BC, when Caesar crossed the Rubicon, a river that separated Italy from Gaul. Under a law passed by Sulla, it was treason for a provincial governor to order soldiers under arms into Italy. When Caesar brought his forces across the Rubicon, he ended any possibility that a legal settlement could be reached. His political conflict with Pompey and his allies now would end violently.

Three of Caesar's ten powerful legions quickly took control of Italy, forcing Pompey and much of the Senate to decamp to Greece.[59] Caesar wrested control of Sardinia, Corsica, Sicily, and ultimately Spain from forces loyal to Pompey in lightning-fast campaigns so that, by December, he held all Roman territory in Europe west of the Adriatic. Then, after ensuring his own election as consul for the following year, Caesar evaded a blockade and confronted Pompey in the Balkans.

Pompey had used the time since his flight from Italy to assemble a much larger, but less capable, army than that commanded by Caesar. More than 200 senators, 10 former consuls, and at least 10 different men who held the right to command an army all relentlessly pressured Pompey to resolve the war with one large, pitched battle.[60] Pompey knew this was unnecessarily risky because Caesar's experienced but undersupplied troops seemed on the verge of mutiny. The politics of the moment and the pressures of his allies, however, eventually compelled him to attack.[61]

Pompey should have trusted his instincts. When the two armies met on August 9 near Pharsalus in Thessaly, Caesar's experience commanding his well-trained troops allowed him to neutralize Pompey's cavalry (a force that was seven times larger than Caesar's own), and then to overwhelm Pompey's more numerous but less experienced infantry.[62] Pompey fled to Alexandria in Egypt and was beheaded not long after he stepped off the boat.[63]

The next few years saw Caesar fight wars around the Mediterranean against both the remnants of the grand army Pompey had once commanded and the outside powers looking to take advantage of Roman political dysfunction. Caesar defeated external foes like the Pontic king Pharnaces, whose loss in August 47 prompted Caesar's famous line "Veni, Vidi, Vici" (I came, I saw, I conquered).[64] His Roman foes fared no better. Cato committed suicide in April 46 after Caesar defeated forces under his control outside of Thapsus in North Africa. One of Pompey's sons died in 45 after leading resistance to Caesar in Spain. Only Sextus Pompey, another of the commander's sons, who controlled a fleet in the Central Mediterranean, was still actively opposing Caesar by 44. But he was more of a nuisance than a genuine threat to Caesar's power.

Caesar now stood alone, but, unlike Pompey, he realized that the normal political institutions of the state were no longer functioning. Caesar then set about trying to reorganize Roman political life under the notion that a strongman could restore the security of Republican political processes. Here again, the shadow of Sulla loomed. Caesar's own victimization by the dictator made him unwilling to unleash a reign of terror like that through which Sulla had birthed his reformed Republic. Caesar instead offered liberal grants of clemency to the people who had fought against him in the civil war. Not only did they keep their lives and properties, but many former adversaries even found themselves considered for magistracies. He also refused to emulate Sulla by confiscating properties to distribute to his soldiers. Instead, he gave his veterans plots of public land and used his own money to pay for the agricultural implements they needed to work that land.[65]

Caesar nevertheless struggled to define the dominant position he held over Rome. In 46, he assumed the office of dictator for a ten-year term. He also began the year as consul, took personal control over all Roman armies and public funds, and acquired the power of the censors.[66] He continued to fill these roles in 45, though he resigned the consulship soon after the year began so that he could handpick his successor. By 44, Caesar took to screening candidates for lower offices and only allowing those he approved to stand for election.[67] He even prepared a list of all the magistrates who would take office in 43, as well as the consuls and tribunes for 42. His dictatorship became permanent in early 44, and he marked this step by breaking with a Roman precedent by placing his own face on denarii, an honor not previously granted living people. The coins identified him as Caesar, Dictator in Perpetuity.[68] In February, Caesar even tested public opinion by having Marc Antony, one of the year's consuls, offer him a crown during the Lupercalia. The public did not take kindly to this, and Caesar feigned anger as he refused Antony's offer.

Caesar's actions discomforted more than just the crowd on hand for the Lupercalia. Graffiti began appearing on statues of Brutus, the man Romans credited with expelling the kings and founding the Republic, in which people bemoaned the fact that he was no longer alive. Some even called on his descendants to show that they were worthy of his name.[69] They were thinking of one man in particular: Marcus Junius Brutus, a young senator whose entire public career had been built around his principled defense of the Republic and the liberty it supposedly represented. In 54 BC, Brutus had introduced himself to Romans by serving as moneyer and issuing two types of denarii. The first featured the portrait and name of the goddess Libertas on the front and a back showing his ancestor, the Brutus who had founded the Republic, walking with lictors above the legend "BRUTUS." The second showed a portrait of that Brutus with an identifying legend on the front and Ahala, the assassin of Maelius and another of the moneyer's supposed ancestors, on the back.[70]

These two coins identified the modern Brutus with the heroic narrative of the early Republic that Romans liked to believe in which great figures like Ahala rose up to defend the Republic against the political domination of one man. They did so with their words, if possible, or with their swords, if necessary. In the 50s, Brutus's invocations of his tyrannicide ancestors offered a powerful statement that he stood for liberty under the law against the attacks of men like Catiline and Clodius. By 44 BC, however, ideas of liberty, legality, and even Republicanism had all become much more complicated than they had been before. Caesar effectively controlled Rome, but he did so under the legal framework of the Republic. He was, then, not a tyrant but a legal ruler—and yet his regime seemed to distort the liberty that the Republic protected.

Gaius Cassius Longinus forced Brutus to stand up for the liberty he once claimed to defend in 44 BC.[71] Both Brutus and Cassius had fought for Pompey during the most recent civil war before accepting clemency from Caesar and agreeing to serve in government positions under his new regime. Cassius, however, had become uneasy with the direction of Caesar's regime and convinced Brutus that Caesar needed to fall from power. They recruited a group of senators who felt similarly, and a conspiracy, led by Cassius and Brutus, soon took shape against the dictator.[72] On March 15, Brutus, Cassius, and the assailants they had recruited set upon the dictator as he was entering a Senate meeting in the Theater of Pompey. Unveiling hidden daggers, they stabbed Caesar twenty-three times, killing him as he fell to the floor beneath a statue of Pompey.

The conspirators believed sincerely that their actions had saved the Republic. Brutus had even written a speech that he planned to give to the Senate to commemorate liberty's return. But the speech went undelivered as panicked senators scattered to protect their homes and families. Brutus, Cassius, and their fellow conspirators did not yet appreciate that their ideal Republic had already perished. All they had done was remove the man who maintained order, and they offered no one who could take his place. Brutus and his colleagues expected freedom. Instead, they unleashed anarchy.

Chapter 12

Rome's First Emperor

44–19 BC

T HE ROMAN REPUBLIC usually changed slowly as its leaders negotiated with one another to adapt its systems to new realities, but Rome could evolve rapidly at times of profound crisis. Few months in Roman history saw things change as quickly as the four weeks following the murder of Julius Caesar. These were the days that decided whether Caesar would be cast in the Tiber as a tyrant or honored as a god. These were the days that decided whether Caesar's acts would be annulled or remain law. And, perhaps most importantly, these were the days that decided whether Rome would remain a Republic or open itself to a new form of government.

With so much at stake, it is astonishing that, on March 15, 44—the Ides of March—no one knew what Caesar's murder meant. Nothing went as planned. Everyone panicked. After Caesar breathed his last, no one had any clear idea what would come next. The world's largest city at the heart of the greatest empire the Mediterranean has ever known nearly imploded.

None of this was remotely imaginable that morning. The city was calm, with some scheduled gladiatorial combats and a routine Senate meeting the most exciting things on the day's calendar. Caesar was planning to leave in three days for a major military campaign against the Parthian Empire in Iraq. In fact, the conspirators who stabbed

Caesar chose the March 15 Senate meeting because they anticipated that the Parthian War would keep him away from Rome for such a long time that they might not get another chance to strike. They also believed that, if Caesar died in front of the assembled senators, enthusiasm about Rome's liberation would flow from the Senate to less prominent citizens.[1]

Precisely the opposite happened. Instead of inspiring the Senate to embrace liberty, Brutus and his colleagues sparked chaos. Caesar's co-consul Marcus Antonius (whose name has been anglicized as Marc Antony) fled to his house near the Temple of Tellus, just north of the Roman Forum, because he feared that the assassins might target him next. His fellow senators also scampered home, and their flight caused armed gladiators, preparing nearby for the day's combats, to scatter as well. Caesar had once warned the Senate that the rest of Rome's citizens looked to it for leadership, and he would not have been surprised to see other Romans follow their Senate's cowardly example that day.[2]

Brutus and Cassius also panicked. Fearing Caesar's ally Marcus Aemilius Lepidus, who commanded the only military force in the capital, they rushed up the Capitoline Hill, which they had hired gladiators to defend, and began bribing people to support them. In just a few hours, the self-proclaimed aristocratic liberators of Rome had nearly reenacted the failed coup mounted by the populists Saturninus and Glaucia five decades before.[3]

Brutus and Cassius were not Saturninus and Glaucia, however. They still enjoyed strong support from some senators who hoped to profit from this sudden regime change. Cicero, for example, appeared on the Capitoline and urged the conspirators to summon the Senate and order Antony killed as well.[4] Some men appointed to magistracies by Caesar made a show of casting aside the trappings of their offices. The conspirators had not yet won the argument about whether Caesar was to be praised or condemned, but they did have enough powerful allies that they could avoid the sort of sudden condemnation by the Senate that Saturninus and Glaucia had faced.

The assassins did not, however, have the brute force to counter the Caesarians. As the next day dawned, Brutus and his associates looked down from the Capitoline to see that Lepidus's army had occupied the Forum. Brutus then emerged to give a speech, but it was far different from the one he had planned to give the previous morning. He now confirmed the legality of the rewards Caesar had granted to soldiers and veterans who had served in his wars.[5] This was legally inconsistent with his claims about Caesar's tyranny. In theory, the acts of a tyrant had no legal validity, but Brutus now understood that insisting on such legalities would likely lead to his own quick death.

On the other side of the Forum, Antony, too, had recovered his bearings. He organized an afternoon meeting with Caesar's supporters during which they collectively talked Lepidus out of taking immediate military action.[6] They decided to have Antony use his powers as consul to summon the Senate and offer to reconcile, at least temporarily, with the assassins.

This approach particularly benefited Antony. Time was his best ally because it allowed him to undercut the purity of Brutus's claim to have liberated the Republic from tyranny. Time would also weaken Lepidus, as it dulled the raw emotions propelling calls for immediate, violent vengeance coming from some radical Caesarians.[7] Antony was ready when the senators gathered on the 17th in the Temple of Tellus, near the side of the Forum closest to Antony's home and most distant from the Capitoline Hill. Brutus and Cassius refused to leave their Capitoline redoubt and risk a journey through Lepidus's legion. The other senators showed only slightly more courage, while Cicero unctuously advocated reconciliation with Antony, a man whose murder he had sought two days previously.[8]

This Senate meeting began a three-day period in which Antony exercised a mastery over the Roman public mood that no Roman ever surpassed. After allowing the senators to fumble around anxiously as they sought to figure out what their colleagues thought about the events of the past two days, Antony reminded the senators that they, too, had benefited from Caesar's actions when they accepted the offices and honors he had offered. If they declared him a tyrant, most of them would invalidate key moments of their own careers.[9] He then proposed a compromise. The Senate should affirm the legality of Caesar's acts, extend an amnesty to Caesar's assassins, grant Caesar a public funeral, and allow for the public reading of his will. Antony, Brutus, Cassius, and Lepidus then had dinner together to show to all Romans that they had reconciled.

This dinner party represented the beginning rather than the end of Antony's efforts to shape public perceptions about Caesar. The public reading of Caesar's will gave Antony the chance to channel the voice of the dictator to large crowds of Caesarian partisans and curious Romans. When the document was read aloud, the Roman people learned that the assassins had killed a man who planned to leave money to every Roman living in the city. When they also heard that Caesar had named some of the men who killed him as beneficiaries of his estate, they recognized how these murderers had personally betrayed someone who considered them dear friends.[10] The assassination now looked much less like a high-minded act of liberation and more like a sacrilege.[11]

Caesar's masterfully staged funeral gave Antony a chance to transform these public sentiments into action.[12] Caesar's uncleaned body was brought to the Forum with his "gaping wounds" and dried blood visible to much of the crowd.[13] Antony also arranged for a wax model of the corpse to be placed on a high pole that spun around so that those in the crowd who were too far away to see it could still appreciate the violence done to it. "The people," Appian wrote, "could no longer bear the most pitiful sight displayed for them."[14]

Angry crowds surged through the Forum and out into the city. They burned the Senate House, attacked houses belonging to Caesar's murderers, and killed those they thought had been involved in the conspiracy. Other supporters built a funeral pyre for Caesar and constructed an impromptu altar for him in the Forum near the Rostra, where flowers are still left today.

Antony positioned himself as the only person who could calm the city. He convinced Lepidus to leave Rome for a scheduled military command and, with senatorial approval, recruited 6,000 former centurions to serve as his bodyguards.[15] By the middle of April, savvy Romans recognized that Antony was positioning himself to become like Caesar himself or Pompey in the 50s. He hoped to emerge as the indispensable leading man in the sort of broken Republic that Cicero described as "seeming as if it was at peace" because "men feared each other."[16]

It was at this moment that a most unlikely challenger appeared in Rome. Caesar's will provided for the posthumous adoption of Octavian, the eighteen-year-old grandson of Caesar's sister, and named the youth as his primary heir. If he accepted the terms of the will, Octavian would legally take the name Julius Caesar, with all the associated opportunities and risks. Everyone from Antony to Octavian's mother, Atia, hoped that Octavian would remain safe by renouncing the adoption and inheritance that Caesar had provided to him.[17]

Octavian was unpersuaded. He had been in Apollonia, a city in modern Albania, waiting with a Roman army for Caesar to cross the Adriatic and begin his Parthian campaign. He knew how devoted Caesar's troops were to their commander, and he saw firsthand how deeply his murder affected them. He also understood their sincerity when they offered to protect him if he went to Italy to accept his inheritance.

Octavian arrived in Rome around April 11, accompanied by his soldiers and other Italians who had "flocked to him" on his journey, but unencumbered by the baggage of political compromise that tainted Antony.[18] Octavian understood that he needed to be careful to demonstrate a unique fidelity to Caesar's memory without appearing so dangerous that Antony or the Senate might move to violently suppress his actions. So first he legally accepted Caesar's inheritance along with responsibility for administering the distributions of money the will required. Next he requested that the pontifex maximus sanction Caesar's posthumous adoption and his name change, a necessary legality that accompanied all adoptions in Rome.[19]

Antony, however, channeled his inner Cato. The consul used procedural delays to prevent the approval of Octavian's adoption and permitted legal challenges to Octavian's ownership of Caesar's property, so that he would be unable to pay Romans the money Caesar's will granted them.[20] Octavian made sure that regular Romans and soldiers knew that Antony was holding up their payments through bureaucratic chicanery and frivolous lawsuits.[21] He then made a show of paying the promised amounts anyway by tapping into his own personal funds.[22] Antony's obstruction had only allowed Octavian to demonstrate more clearly that he, not Antony, truly championed Caesar's legacy.

Struggling to adjust to this abrupt loss of goodwill in Rome, Antony rearranged the provincial assignments for the year 43 so he would become the new governor of two of Caesar's old Gallic provinces. Because this action would displace one of Caesar's murderers, the power grab prompted Brutus and Cassius to go east and recruit an army to confront Antony.[23] Cicero began delivering speeches that included aggressive attacks on Antony's character that autumn, describing him as "a brute beast" who had begun his public career "as a public prostitute."[24] Antony had lost the Senate.

Antony tried to pivot back to regain the trust of Caesar's supporters, but he fared no better there. He first claimed that Octavian had tried to assassinate him, but this obvious slander simply prompted Octavian to offer bonuses to any Caesarian veteran who would protect him from Antony. Antony next went to Brundisium on the Adriatic coast to take command of the army that Caesar had hoped to lead to Parthia, but most of the troops there knew Octavian and refused to follow Antony. He was forced to randomly execute disobedient soldiers before the army agreed to go to Gaul with him. Finally, in late November, Antony twice summoned the Senate to ask it to declare Octavian a public enemy. Each time he did this, a legion under Antony's nominal control publicly declared its allegiance to Octavian.[25] Antony had now also lost Caesar's legionaries.

In December 44, the Senate and Octavian both saw the chance to eliminate a greatly weakened Antony as he led his unenthusiastic army into Cisalpine Gaul to dislodge Decimus Brutus, the assassin of Caesar who held the province. Octavian quickly pledged to deploy the legions loyal to him against Antony if the Senate should need them.

This was a trap, but the Senate did not think enough of Octavian to understand it at the time. His army was made up of veteran Roman soldiers, but until that point, they were an illegal private army serving under a teenager with no legal right to command them. When the senators agreed to his offer, they retroactively recognized the legitimacy of his command. Octavian's soldiers then immediately flanked him with lictors, the ceremonial officials who always accompanied a man empowered by the Roman state to command an army.

Octavian's army joined with troops commanded by Aulus Hirtius and Gaius Vibius Pansa Caetronianus, the two consuls who took office in January 43, and defeated Antony in two battles outside of Mutina (modern Modena) between April 14 and April 21. Antony led the remnants of his army to join up with Lepidus in northern Gaul to regroup under his protection. The senatorial victory had been costly, however. Pansa was fatally wounded in the first battle, and Hirtius died in the second. Octavian, the sole commander to survive, then returned to Rome with the victorious armies.[26] It was now clear to him that the power of experienced, professional, well-trained Roman soldiers far surpassed that of raw recruits, and that he needed to retain such men for as long as he could.

This made the Senate's next move particularly dangerous. Antony's retreat convinced the Senate that it had neutralized the power of Caesar's followers and it could now safely dispose of Octavian. The senators granted honors to just about every commander imaginable. Decimus Brutus received a triumph simply for watching the fight from behind the walls of Mutina. Cassius, who was in Syria, also received a senatorial command. Octavian got little of substance. Even worse, the Senate had decided to take away the powerful, loyal, veteran soldiers under Octavian's command and assign them to Decimus Brutus.

Octavian then began talking with Lepidus about switching sides, while his armies made clear that they refused to leave his service.[27]

The senators' position further eroded when messengers from Lepidus arrived on May 30, 43, and informed them that Lepidus had joined forces with Antony.[28] The senators sent an embassy to mend relations with Octavian's army, but they refused to include Octavian in the discussions. His troops responded by sending their own delegation to Rome demanding that their commander be made consul. When the Senate rejected this demand, Octavian marched his army to Rome. He captured the city that August, augmenting his forces with three more legions that defected from the Senate to him.[29]

Octavian then undertook a rapid sequence of administrative actions to secure his power and status as Caesar's heir. He and one of his relatives were elected to fill the consular vacancies left by the deaths of Hirtius and Pansa. They distributed bonuses to his soldiers, arranged for the long-delayed legalization of Octavian's adoption by Caesar, passed a law that made Caesar's assassination a crime, and held a trial for those who had participated in the murder.[30] In the early autumn, Octavian traveled to Bononia (modern Bologna) to meet with Antony and Lepidus in order to plan the new shape of the Roman state.

The three men agreed on a radical new way of organizing power. Under the terms of a law passed by Octavian's co-consul, Octavian resigned the consulship and joined with Antony and Lepidus on a board of three men assigned the task of "reconstituting the Republic." This triumvirate would rule Rome for the next five years, holding imperium over armies, appointing magistrates, and making laws. They collectively presided over a public meeting in Rome on November 27 that rubber-stamped the power they arrogated to themselves. Then, on November 28, an order was posted that proscribed 130 men and ordered the confiscation of their property.[31] Antony apparently insisted that Cicero be placed on the list because of his public attacks, though it is hard to imagine that Octavian or Lepidus argued vehemently against this. The orator was seized and killed on December 7.

Appian claims to preserve the decree announcing the proscriptions. It offers a chilling account of a dead Republic in which neither laws nor customs nor the goodwill of fellow Romans could guarantee the rights citizens once took for granted. The decree "ordered that the heads of the victims should be brought to the triumvirs for a fixed reward . . . and all persons were required to provide the opportunity for searching their homes." The triumvirs explained that they felt that only such terrifying brutality could prevent them from suffering the same fate as Caesar, killed by "perfidious traitors who . . . conspired against their benefactors after they received clemency." Since the conspirators could not "be mollified by kindness," the triumvirs "prefer[red] to anticipate [their] enemies rather than suffer at their hands."[32]

The first round of November proscriptions eliminated adversaries and enabled the triumvirs to seize the resources they needed to fight Brutus and Cassius. The self-proclaimed "liberators" had assembled a large army in the Eastern Mediterranean that they paid for by extorting silver from Roman allies, selling entire municipalities into slavery, and sacking towns that resisted their demands.[33] None of these actions were legal, but Brutus and Cassius rationalized them, believing that their violations of the rights of Roman subjects served the larger goal of protecting the liberty of Roman citizens. Few in the provinces followed their logic.

With Lepidus staying in the west, Antony and Octavian led the triumviral forces east to confront Brutus and Cassius. Both sides commanded massive armies that may have each included more than 100,000 men. When their armies clashed in October of 42 outside the Greek city of Philippi, the battle lines extended so far that Brutus and Cassius, who each commanded one wing, could not see how their colleague fared. This proved extremely consequential. Antony's forces routed those of Cassius, but Cassius, who did not know that Brutus's forces had triumphed over those of Octavian on the other side of the battlefield, committed suicide rather than be taken captive. A few weeks later, Brutus foolishly joined battle a second time, was defeated, and then committed suicide along with much of his officer corps. Most of the surviving troops then joined the triumvirs.[34]

The victory at Philippi brought Rome's Eastern Mediterranean territories under triumviral control and prompted a renegotiation of the lands each man controlled. Antony, who now looked like the most powerful of the three men, received authority over both Gaul and the east. Octavian was forced to run Italy amid the social and economic chaos unleashed by the discharge and settlement of waves of veterans from the triumviral armies. And Lepidus, now clearly in third place, was given control of Africa. This was not a sustainable arrangement—and everyone knew it.

The first fracture came when Octavian confiscated the territories of eighteen Italian cities so that he could acquire enough land to settle Caesar's veterans. Antony capitalized on the anger this caused by entrusting his wife, Fulvia, and his brother, Lucius, with organizing an armed resistance by displaced Italians disgruntled by the confiscations. In early 40, Octavian blockaded them in the city of Perusia, stormed its walls, massacred the defenders, and sent Lucius and Fulvia into exile.[35] Antony responded later that summer by besieging five legions loyal to Octavian in Brundisium, but his troops refused to kill men they still saw as their comrades. Although Antony and Octavian now disliked each other intensely, their troops forced them to compromise rather than fight.

Instead of destroying one another, the two triumvirs negotiated a more equitable division of territory. Octavian gained Gaul, Illyricum, and the rest of the west so he could better support the needs of Italy. Lepidus, who was not present at the meeting, or apparently even consulted, retained Africa. Antony got the eastern provinces as well as the right to recruit forces in Italy. And, because Fulvia had just died, the reconciliation was sealed by Antony's marriage to Octavian's sister Octavia.

This renegotiation kept the peace between the triumvirs until their five-year term expired in 38. Antony and Octavian then met in Tarentum the following year to negotiate and organize a popular vote granting an extension of the triumvirate until 33. Lepidus again went uninvited. By the end of 36, however, the triumvirate had begun to break down. In the east, Antony's deepening romantic relationship with the Egyptian queen Cleopatra humiliated Octavia, strained his ties to Octavian, and led to speculation that

Antony was neglecting Rome's military objectives. It was said that he preferred to luxuriate in Egypt with Cleopatra rather than serving Rome alongside his soldiers. In the west, Lepidus foolishly decided to challenge Octavian's authority when they were campaigning jointly in Sicily. When Octavian arrived, however, Lepidus's legions abandoned him. Lepidus was forced to return to private life, though he sporadically appeared at public events whenever Octavian wanted him to show his subservience. Lepidus had become so unthreatening that he was permitted to live on until he died of natural causes in 13 BC.[36]

OCTAVIAN NOW CONTROLLED the west, had forty-five legions at his disposal, and began to position himself for a final conflict with Antony. He burnished his reputation by fighting a successful war in Illyricum. Then he embarked on an extensive campaign to repair the infrastructure in the city of Rome, expanding the city's water supply.[37] The water works alone included "700 cisterns, 500 fountains, and 130 distribution tanks" that his right-hand man Marcus Agrippa built "in the space of a single year," astounding numbers for a city long unable to effectively provide its growing population with a supply of clean water.[38] In the meantime, Octavian's propagandists contrasted his energy and competence with Antony's love-struck sloth, an impression compounded by Antony's decision to celebrate a military victory alongside Cleopatra in the Egyptian city of Alexandria rather than in Rome.[39]

Despite Octavian's propaganda, Antony retained considerable advantages as the triumvirate's second five-year term neared its expiration on the final day of 33. With Lepidus sidelined and Antony blending Roman power with the military resources of Cleopatra's Egyptian kingdom, a further extension of the triumvirate was impossible. But Octavian needed something to replace the legal authority the triumvirate gave him. Without it, the new consuls who were to take office would technically replace him as the legal authorities running affairs in Italy. Both men were allies of Antony and, on the first day of 32, one of them introduced a motion in the Senate to sanction Octavian for clinging to power after his triumviral position expired. It is not clear how Antony and his allies expected Octavian to respond, but they were utterly unprepared when he marched into Rome with troops, summoned the Senate, sat on an ivory throne between the consuls, and promised to deliver evidence of Antony's treason before a future Senate meeting.

Octavian's unsubtle threat to unleash his army against the city prompted the consuls and a number of senators to flee to Antony before the measure stripping Octavian of his power could be approved, but the sense of impending war also pushed some of Antony's associates to return to Italy. After two of them told Octavian "what was written in [Antony's] will," Octavian seized the document, "carried it into the Senate and, later, the popular assembly and read it out." Romans were shocked at the "enormous presents" Antony "gave to his children by the Egyptian queen," and came to "believe that, if Antony should prevail, he would bestow their city on Cleopatra and transfer the seat of power to Egypt."[40]

Octavian could now reframe his imminent fight with Antony as a foreign war against Cleopatra, a queen who held such power over Antony that he and the armies he commanded were no longer acting in the best interests of the Roman people. Later that year, Octavian orchestrated events across Italy where, he later wrote, individual Roman citizens "swore allegiance to me and demanded me as leader in a war" in which Octavian's enemies were their enemies as well.[41] This oath, which came to be called the Oath of All Italy, replaced Octavian's lapsed triumviral powers with new legal authority to lead armies on behalf of his fellow citizens.[42]

Octavian masterfully framed Antony's relationship with Cleopatra as a disqualifying feature of his character. In doing so, he changed Italian views of Antony and implanted doubts in the minds of Antony's troops that helped decide the outcome of the civil war. When Octavian's navy defeated that of Antony and Cleopatra at the Battle of Actium in the summer of 31, Antony abandoned his soldiers and fled to Egypt with Cleopatra. The troops that he left behind, who were based on land, could not help but believe that Octavian had spoken the truth about their general. Even Antony's Roman forces in eastern Africa believed the propaganda. They defected to Octavian when he landed in Egypt the following year. Like Brutus and Cassius before them, Antony and Cleopatra chose to commit suicide rather than fall captive to Octavian. Egypt then became a Roman province, but Octavian assumed private ownership of the royal lands that had belonged to Cleopatra and her ancestors.[43]

OCTAVIAN WAS NOW the richest individual in Roman history, and he understood that this wealth could be used as a political war chest. It could help him install a system that made him both Rome's most powerful man and an indispensable citizen without whom the state could not function. His private fortune would now supplement the public expenditures of the Republic, but only in ways that served his own interest. He had the money to personally reward his soldiers, provide for Roman citizens, and support friends, especially those who could help him build a more stable Roman political order around himself. He also preserved for himself every right to refuse to spend money on people or causes he did not like or want to underwrite.

This type of transactional patronage could not, by itself, restructure Roman political life, and Octavian had no good model for how to do this. Sulla had been an older man when he had taken power as dictator, and he had retired after he felt he had restored the Republic. He was dead long before his reforms failed. Caesar had tried to float above the rest of Rome as a perpetual dictator, someone who kept the peace and addressed the problems faced by a zombie Republic, but his model failed spectacularly on the Ides of March.

Octavian was a young man of thirty-three when he conquered Egypt. He could neither reform Rome and retire like Sulla nor expect to survive for long if he ruled like Caesar. He needed to create a new form of Roman government that preserved the prerogatives of the Republic without giving senators and other elites the illusion that they might succeed in replacing him. He knew he would die if he failed.

Unlike Republican absolutists such as Brutus or Cato, Octavian did not believe that states existed as either free or not free. Freedom exists on a spectrum, and Octavian understood that whatever system he created would succeed only if it gave Rome the security of an autocracy while preserving as many of the symbolic freedoms of the Republic as possible. This ambiguity was more easily maintained than one might imagine. The Roman Republic had always been a political system in which all Roman citizens expected equal protection under the law while accepting an unequal say in making policy. Poorer and less socially prominent Romans voted, but their votes often represented a sort of symbolic assent to the outcome of a political process dominated by the wealthy and aristocratic.

The new Roman autocrat moved slowly and deliberately. Octavian did not return to Rome for nearly a year after Antony's defeat in August of 30 BC. In August of the year 29, he entered the city to celebrate the most spectacular triumph the city had ever seen, a three-day-long procession from August 13 to 15 marking his victories in Dalmatia, at Actium, and in Egypt. On August 18, he sponsored a magnificent set of games in which Romans saw rhinos and hippos for the first time. Then, using his private account filled with the riches of Egypt, he "paid all of the debts that he himself owed to others . . . and did not insist on payment of others' debts to him." Romans, Cassius Dio later wrote, "forgot all of their unpleasant experiences and viewed his triumph with pleasure, as if the vanquished had all been foreigners."[44]

Over the next two years, Octavian built toward a style of government that retained as many of the trappings of the Republic as possible while giving him unique autonomy to change things as he wished. At first, this consisted of Octavian and his ally Agrippa assuming both the consulship and the censorship for 28 BC to rebuild the membership of the Senate following the deaths of so many senators during the civil wars. Only men friendly to Octavian were considered. Then, in January of 27 BC, Octavian gave a speech in which he claimed that he was returning the Republic to the control of the Senate. The senators played their part well, refusing to take the Republic back unless Octavian agreed to a new system in which he retained control of all Roman armies, appointed governors of his choice to supervise the provinces containing Roman troops, and paid the pensions of all soldiers from his private accounts. The soldiers would take loyalty oaths to him personally, an action that regularly affirmed their willingness to defend the man who would fund their pensions. The senators took responsibility for appointing governors of the provinces that did not have armies and resumed managing many of the functions of the Roman state.

Octavian's settlement in January of 27 BC included two other important components. First, the formal powers he exercised to direct legislative and political activities in Rome would derive from the consulship, an office that he apparently intended to hold indefinitely.[45] Second, on January 16, he "was called Augustus by decree of the Senate."[46] The title Augustus, Cassius Dio explained, "signified that he was more than human" and "clearly [showed] the splendor of [his] position" even while it "[conferred] no particular power."[47]

This arrangement proved unstable. As Augustus served his eleventh consulship in 23 BC, either an illness or an assassination attempt prompted him to resign the office midyear and renegotiate the constitutional basis of his power.[48] Beginning that July, Augustus's authority derived not from the prerogatives of a consul but from a collection of powers that equated to the individual capacities of many other magistrates. Like a consul, he received the right to summon the Senate, make the first motion in its meetings, and propose laws without holding the office. Like a proconsul, he received a form of *imperium* that enabled his orders to supersede those of any commander in a province in the event of a conflict. This effectively made Augustus a proconsul with military authority over the entire Roman world, but, again, he did not actually hold a proconsulship. And, like a tribune of the plebs, Augustus received political power in the plebeian assembly and personal sacrosanctity without assuming that office either.

This new structure worked much better. Roman senators were not angry that Augustus had monopolized power in the state when he was holding consulships each year. They were, however, anxious about how his perpetual consulship decreased the number of consulships available to others, increasing the likelihood that senators would fall short of the consular status their ancestors had enjoyed. Most of these senators simply wanted to be able to say they had held the consulship, even if they did very little of consequence while in office. Augustus was betting that they would accept a restricted political role that was mostly symbolic but still reaffirmed their status as leading citizens. Senators were now not that different from the ordinary Romans who, for centuries, had turned up for assemblies and voted for magistrates even though their individual votes counted for very little.

Augustus then made an extremely astute decision. Intuiting that Romans needed to be reminded that he ensured peace, prosperity, and legal protections, he left Rome soon after his new powers took effect. He stayed away for nearly three years and starved the capital of both the stabilizing force his presence provided and the regular influx of resources from his personal fortune that residents had come to expect. The results were predictably disastrous. Floods, political violence, food shortages, and divine portents of disaster regularly afflicted the capital while Augustus was away. "The Romans," Cassius Dio would write, "believed that these woes had come upon them for no other reason than that they did not have Augustus."[49]

When Augustus finally came back to Rome in 19 BC, Cassius Dio wrote that "there was no similarity between the conduct of the people during his absence, when they quarreled, and when he was present."[50] This made Romans more confident in the sustainability of Augustus's new political and social order. In 13 BC, the poet Horace put this notion into verse: "While Caesar rules, no civil strife / Shall break our rest, nor violence rude, / Nor rage, that whets the slaughtering knife / And plunges wretched towns in feud."[51]

And yet Augustus himself emphasized that his real achievement was not creating a personal form of rule, but "restoring the Republic to liberty."[52] He adamantly maintained that Rome remained a Republic during the more than forty years he ran its political life, and he claimed that he had "received no magistracy offered contrary to the customs of the ancestors."[53] This was technically correct. Augustus enjoyed no powers that went against Republican custom, and, in his telling, this meant the Republic lived on as he served dutifully as "curator of the laws and customs" of the Romans.[54]

Augustus admitted he "exceeded all in influence," but he still maintained the pretense that he was just a capable aristocrat who served Rome in the way the state asked and gave benevolently from his private resources to causes he felt made Rome better. Augustus emphatically did not own Rome, and he never asserted that his descendants had a hereditary right to rule it. He governed as the custodian of the state appointed by the Roman people. This Roman state was not the idealized Republic of Brutus or Cato, but it was also not the monarchical tyranny of Tarquinius Superbus. Romans now understood that elements of their Republic could coexist with an autocrat. The next 1,200 years would show how Romans maintained their ownership of this modified *res publica* while entrusting its management to one man or woman.

Chapter 13

The Terrors of Tiberius

19 BC–AD 37

ONE OF THE most dangerous challenges an autocrat faces is identifying a viable successor. That person must be capable, but not too ambitious, and must not be politically potent enough to overthrow his patron. Augustus first confronted this problem when he was temporarily incapacitated by a serious illness at age forty. He gave his trusted general Marcus Agrippa his ring, a symbol of the passing of imperial authority, and soon after his recovery formally marked Agrippa as his deputy. In 21 BC, he sealed the arrangement by marrying Agrippa to Julia, his only biological child.[1]

Agrippa was a perfect choice. He "was exceedingly beloved" by the Roman people, but came from a modest family, and was unlikely to try to overthrow the emperor to whom he owed his prominence.[2] Instead, the two men developed an effective partnership: Agrippa managed affairs in Rome during the periods when Augustus traveled the empire, and Augustus did the same when Agrippa was dispatched to the provinces. Over time Agrippa became Augustus's equal in power and authority, although Augustus remained the senior figure.

Agrippa's death in March of 12 BC upset Augustus's immediate succession plans. It forced him to look to two other potential successors, his grandsons Gaius and Lucius, Agrippa's sons with Julia. Augustus also leaned on his stepsons Tiberius and Drusus, the children born of his wife Livia's first marriage, to lead major combat operations in his name along Rome's northern frontiers. Tiberius, in particular, stood out for his military success in campaigns in the Balkans and was rewarded with a consulship when he was just twenty-eight years old.

"Because his grandsons were still boys" at the time of Agrippa's death, Cassius Dio wrote, Augustus "reluctantly chose Tiberius" to be his "assistant in public affairs" and to "surpass all others in rank and in influence."[3] The emperor felt that this promotion also entitled him to demand that Tiberius divorce his wife Vipsania, a woman whom Tiberius adored and with whom he had a son named Drusus, so he could marry Julia, Agrippa's widow and Tiberius's stepsister.[4] Although Julia may once have been attracted to Tiberius, Augustus did not keep Tiberius in Rome long enough for him to develop affection for her.[5] He sent Tiberius to fight in Illyricum between 11 and 8 BC and then dispatched him to Germany in 8 BC. By 6 BC, the marriage was collapsing amid Tiberius's prolonged absences, his indifference toward Julia, and her infidelities.[6]

Tiberius wanted no more of the drama and asked Augustus's permission to retire to the island of Rhodes. A restful retreat from public life was a familiar part of elite political careers in the Republic—and under Augustus—but Augustus and Tiberius's mother, Livia, tried to prevent the imperial heir from taking this step. Finally, Tiberius "refused to take food for four days" until his parents relented. He left Julia and his son in Rome, hastened to the port of Ostia, and sailed away.[7] In 2 BC, Tiberius finally divorced Julia. Augustus eventually sent her into exile because of her repeated adulteries.[8]

Tiberius's departure forced Augustus to prematurely designate his grandsons Gaius and Lucius as successors, but Lucius died in AD 2 and Gaius did the same two years later. The early deaths of two young, prominent imperial heirs so close together troubled many Romans. Cassius Dio wrote that Gaius's death "was due to a sudden illness," but "suspicion attached to Livia, particularly because it was at this time that Tiberius returned to Rome" with her assistance.[9] People wondered if Livia had perhaps cleared the way for Tiberius to become emperor because the deaths of Augustus's two grandsons meant that "[her child] alone remained." Now, "everything centered on him."[10]

It is extremely unlikely that Livia had anything to do with the fate of Gaius and Lucius. Both young men had traveled extensively, under stressful conditions, during a time when sanitation was poor. Every new destination opened the possibility of encountering unknown microbes. Later centuries would show that it was not at all uncommon for emperors or imperial officials to contract infections on such trips but, in these centuries before germ theory appeared, these illnesses often were attributed to poison or magic.

The implausible charges against Livia highlight another novel aspect of the Roman autocracy Augustus had created. In the past, Roman women had usually stood apart from politics, with little direct involvement in affairs of state. Even when they did speak openly about public affairs, women emphasized that they were motivated by principle rather than ambition. During the terrors of the Second Triumvirate, for example, Hortensia, the daughter of the orator Hortensius, gave an exceptional speech before the Senate in which she attacked the taxes that Octavian and his allies had levied on 1,400 elite women. She emphasized to the triumvirs that her opposition must be seen as principled because women had "no part in the honors, commands, and offices for which you contend against each other." This meant that she had nothing to gain by making a dramatic public gesture other than changing a policy she believed to be unjust.[11]

But the personalized nature of Augustan autocracy allowed Livia to exercise real power without being subject to the direct scrutiny of officeholding. This terrified Roman men, who imagined that the politics that really mattered in Rome were playing out behind closed doors. They feared that Livia was manipulating the weak or besotted men who ran Rome, killing those who stood in the way of her designs, and using her official position to avoid accountability for her actions. None of these things were true, but Augustan-era elites had become prone to believing conspiracy theories about the empress. Many no longer believed the truths they were told about Roman political life.

In the last decade of his life Augustus continued to tinker with the hierarchy of the family members serving below him through a series of adoptions and forced marriages. In addition to his decision to adopt Tiberius in AD 4, Augustus adopted his third grandson, a teenager named Marcus Agrippa Postumus, who had been born to Julia shortly after Agrippa's death. Augustus also forced Tiberius to adopt his nephew Germanicus, and compelled Germanicus to marry Augustus's granddaughter Agrippina, so he could deepen his connection to Augustus himself. In AD 7, Augustus cleared the path for Tiberius and Germanicus by sending Agrippa Postumus into exile, and then, in AD 13, he arranged for Tiberius to share all of the powers of the emperor.[12]

Augustus left one final vicious surprise for his family. When he died in Nola on August 19, AD 14, assassins were sent to kill Agrippa Postumus before he could consider contesting Tiberius's succession. Although some whispered that this was yet another murderous plot by Livia, it is instead much more likely that, even from the grave, Augustus remained dedicated to the idea that no action was too brutal if it enhanced the stability of his Roman Empire.[13]

When the new emperor first came before the Senate in early September, Tiberius only asked the senators to discuss Augustus's funeral. Then, when the meeting began, the consuls swore allegiance "to Tiberius Caesar," and "soon the senators, the soldiers and the people followed."[14] Romans had been collectively vowing their support for a sovereign since they had sworn the Oath of All Italy to Augustus four decades previously, but Tiberius inserted uncertainty into what could have been a formal ceremony recognizing his authority. He made sure the senators understood that the troops that protected him "do not belong to me, but to the Republic," and proposed dividing responsibility for the empire among three men.[15] After long deliberation, Tiberius reluctantly agreed to assume full control, but he also promised that he would one day lay down his power and retire.[16] According to the historian Tacitus, Tiberius wanted Romans to understand that he was "the person chosen and called by the state," rather than a man who had inherited the empire through "the plotting of an old woman and the adoption of a senile old man."[17]

Tiberius did not just use the language of Republicanism; he tried to govern as if the Roman Republic of Augustan propaganda really existed. He initially refused to accept the title Augustus from the Senate, regularly denied permission for the construction of temples to himself, reminded those wanting to see him as a god that he was "only mortal," and mocked the Senate when it tried to rename the month of November in his honor.[18] These steps were supposed to encourage the Senate to again serve as the primary decision-making body in the state. Tiberius further empowered it by allowing senators to directly select some Roman magistrates. This reform ended the centuries-old process of ordinary Romans coming together in voting tribes and electing candidates, but, as Tacitus wrote, "the withdrawal of the right to vote brought no protest beyond idle murmurs from the people."[19]

Once the Senate chose the magistrates, Tiberius deferred to the traditional prerogatives of their offices "as if it were still the old Republic." Cassius Dio described how "he did little or nothing on his own authority," but "brought all matters, even the slightest thing, before the Senate."[20] During these discussions, he gave "his own opinion" but allowed "everyone complete freedom to speak against it," and he respected the majority view if "others voted in opposition to him."[21] This was a matter of principle to Tiberius, who "often asserted that in a free country there should be free speech and free thought."[22]

Tiberius genuinely wanted the Senate to take political initiative, but elite Romans no longer knew how to accept the liberty he offered them. Tacitus explained that Augustus had neutered independent thought and action by first killing "his most ferocious opponents." He had then "conciliated" everyone else with money or grain or circuses while he "slowly took for himself the roles of the Senate, the magistrates, and the laws, without any opposition." By the time of Augustus's death, the Roman aristocracy had become accustomed to the "cheerful acceptance of slavery as the smoothest road to wealth and office." Members of the elite craved the "new order and safety" of the empire Augustus had established "in preference to the old ways and adventure." The "groveling" acquiescence of the senators so bothered Tiberius that he frequently left Senate meetings muttering to himself in Greek, "These men!—how ready they are for slavery!"[23]

Although the Senate groveled when Tiberius wanted to hear independent voices, some legions, by contrast, showed an unwelcome level of independence. Augustus had used Roman military power much more strategically than his Republican predecessors, whose wars had left Rome controlling a patchwork of territories across Europe. Some regions, such as Spain, were not fully pacified despite a long Roman presence. Others, including the Roman territories in the Balkans, were difficult to defend, and presented challenges for maintaining efficient lines of communication with the capital. Many of these problems grew out of the tendency for Republican commanders to seek relatively quick victories that promised large amounts of plunder from settled and urbanized people. Those same commanders disliked fighting in the less densely populated and economically unsophisticated lands along the Rhine and Danube Rivers. Augustus, however, understood that these major rivers formed natural boundaries that could be easily defended while also facilitating communication and supply routes for the forces that protected the Roman frontiers. He then embarked on a series of wars of expansion designed to push Roman territory north and east until it reached those rivers.

The Rhine would become the limit of Roman territory in northwestern Europe, but Augustus originally envisioned Rome expanding even farther east until it reached the Elbe.[24] His initial forays across the Rhine, led by Tiberius and his brother Drusus in the teens and aughts of the first century BC, gave Rome tentative control over German territory stretching to the Elbe. But, in AD 9, Publius Quintilius Varus, the governor of Germany and commander of three full Roman legions, suffered an overwhelming defeat in the Battle of the Teutoburg Forest. The emperor, who had assumed that Germany east of the Rhine had been pacified, had sent Varus to serve as a civilian administrator of a new Roman province. After the devastating loss, he decided to abandon the lands east of the Rhine rather than try to recapture them. Most of his successors respected this sensible decision.[25]

The rout at Teutoburg had also forced Augustus to quickly rebuild the professional armies that Varus had lost without diminishing the quality and loyalty of the troops. He filled the reconstituted northwestern defenses with "a levy held in the city" of Rome that, according to Tacitus, brought a "crowd prone to recklessness and intolerant of hard work" to a frontier they lacked the discipline to defend obediently.[26]

When this crowd of soldiers heard of Augustus's death, they rose up to demand better wages for the new recruits and early retirement for the veterans who had been redeployed from other places. The demands quickly turned violent. Legionaries attacked their commanding officers, beat some of them to death, and then threw their bodies into the Rhine.[27] A similar eruption happened in Pannonia, the region encompassing parts of modern Austria, Hungary, Serbia, and Croatia that Augustus had joined to the empire in the last years of the first century BC.[28]

Tiberius responded deftly. He believed that the rules-based political system Augustus had built could stop the civil war the soldiers hoped to unleash, and he understood that the system needed to be seen to have stopped the revolts successfully.[29] Despite considerable pressure for Tiberius to "go in person," he knew his presence would reinforce the idea that the emperor alone brought stability to Rome. He instead delegated the response to his adopted son Germanicus and his natural son Drusus, who both had the constitutional power to command the rebellious armies. This strategy made sense, Tacitus insightfully wrote, because, "in the persons of his sons," Tiberius could handle both mutinous armies "at once, without hazarding the emperor's reputation." Tiberius also could use Germanicus and Drusus as agents with whom the mutineers could negotiate, since "it was excusable for the young princes to refer certain questions to their father," but, if "the emperor is rebuffed, what resource was left?"[30]

Germanicus and Drusus demonstrated the loyalty and skill their emperor needed. In Pannonia, Drusus bluffed his way through public meetings with the mutineers before dividing their ranks and killing their leaders.[31] In Germany, Germanicus flatly denied the rebellious soldiers' call that he rise in rebellion against Tiberius. His charisma enabled him to turn the majority of his soldiers against the mutineers, a task made easier by the affection the legions had for his young son Gaius (whom they had nicknamed Caligula, "Little Boots," because of the cute miniature soldier costume he wore). Ultimately, troops loyal to the emperor attacked the camp of the mutineers. Germanicus then launched a large offensive across the Rhine that simultaneously avenged the defeat of Varus and distracted the remaining German legionaries from the causes of their discontent.[32]

Tiberius soon settled into a pattern of working with the Senate to choose qualified officeholders, whom he empowered to actually accomplish things.[33] He took particular care to ensure the proper, unbiased functioning of the legal system. Tiberius sat in on court cases to be sure they were judged fairly and reminded jurors that the laws were to be applied regardless of any perception of imperial favor.[34] Charges against senators were referred to the judgment of the Senate, and Tiberius personally presided over these cases "with such self-control as to avoid the appearance of either softening or sharpening the charges."[35]

Tiberius had learned from Augustus how powerful the selective use of his personal funds could be. Unlike Augustus's tendency to spend liberally on public gifts and flashy construction projects, Tiberius preferred to use his personal funds as a stabilizer to protect Romans from the full effects of crises.[36] He sought sustainable solutions to economic problems. Following a spike in grain prices in AD 19, for example, Tiberius designed a scheme fixing the price of grain in Rome and subsidizing the grain merchants to make up for their lost income.[37] He also used his personal funds to pay for recovery efforts following an earthquake in Asia Minor, and to rebuild structures on Aventine Hill after a large fire.[38] Then, in AD 33, Tiberius infused Roman banks with 25 million denarii of his own money to stabilize the economy amid a financial crisis.[39]

Germanicus's death in 19 forced Tiberius to change the way he ruled. In part, this was because Tiberius had meant what he said when he told the Senate that he aimed to retire from imperial power. Augustus had envisioned the position of emperor as a lifetime appointment in part because he could imagine no other life. Tiberius saw the job as a life sentence from which he hoped to be paroled, and he believed as a general principle that old, exhausted, or no longer competent emperors should abdicate. And Tiberius, who was about to turn sixty-one when Germanicus died, was indeed getting old. His eyesight was terrible. His energy and motivation to rule had dissipated. His son Drusus, who was then in his mid-thirties, had served Rome capably, and he understood the job. Tiberius believed that Rome would fare better if he handed imperial power to a younger, more energetic successor. So in the year 22, he arranged for the Senate to confer tribunician power on Drusus, a step that officially marked him as sharing his father's status as emperor and positioned him to assume greater responsibilities as Tiberius faded into retirement.

It was not to be. Drusus died the following year. While rumors of poison again circulated around the capital, Tiberius responded as any shocked and grieving parent might. Tacitus described how he evinced little overt emotion while he "embraced work in the place of comfort."[40] This behavior seemed bewildering to senators, who feared punishment if they misread the intentions of an emperor saddened by the death of his child and burned out by imperial responsibilities he loathed. The next generation of male family members consisted of Germanicus's eleven-year-old son Caligula, Drusus's four-year-old son Tiberius Gemellus, and Tiberius's thirty-three-year-old nephew Claudius, an odd scholar of Etruscan lore that few thought emperor material.[41] Tiberius now realized he must serve in an office he did not want for the rest of his life.

Later Romans used the deaths of Germanicus and Drusus to demarcate a profound shift in Tiberius's administration. Cassius Dio wrote that "up to this time, Tiberius had done a great many excellent things and had made but few errors; but now . . . he changed to precisely the reverse of his previous conduct."[42] The dearth of mature and capable members of the imperial family forced this shift because Tiberius could no longer delegate governing tasks to relatives. He turned instead to Lucius Aelius Sejanus, a trusted subordinate from an equestrian family. When Tiberius departed from Rome for good in AD 26 to settle in Campania, he left Sejanus in charge. Crowds of petitioners disrupted his peace in Campania, however, so Tiberius withdrew to the island of Capri, a more remote location that lacked even a proper harbor.[43]

This self-imposed exile was a terrible thing for both Tiberius and the empire he led. Sejanus preyed on Tiberius's isolation by feeding him information about plots and intrigues, pushing the old emperor into paranoia. Sejanus took particular advantage of the *lex maiestas*, a law designed to punish anyone who "diminished the 'majesty of the Roman people' by betrayal of an army, seditious incitement of the populace, or any acts that wronged the Republic."[44] This legal concept extended back at least to Saturninus in the 100s BC, but Augustus had expanded *maiestas* to also include attacks on the reputation of the emperor. Early in his reign, Tiberius had deferred to a long-standing idea among Romans that "actions could be indicted but words were immune" from such challenges and expressed outrage that *maiestas* cases might lead to executions.[45]

The emperor's opinion changed as Sejanus's influence increased. In the year 25, when Tiberius was still in Rome, a senator named Cremutius Cordus joked that a statue of Sejanus placed at the Theater of Pompey meant that "now the Theater is really ruined." Sejanus responded by arranging a *maiestas* indictment against Cordus because, in the reign of Augustus, the senator had "published a history eulogizing Brutus, and styling Cassius the last of the Romans." Augustus himself had read the work and found nothing objectionable in it, but this was a different moment. In his defense, Cordus proclaimed, "My words are indicted, for I am entirely innocent with respect to my actions." Cordus spoke the truth, but, sensing the mood of the emperor and his associates, he elected to starve himself to death rather than wait for a verdict. Sejanus then pressured the Senate to order all copies of Cordus's history to be burned.[46]

After Tiberius retreated to Capri, Sejanus used *maiestas* accusations with increasing frequency against senators he disliked. As Sejanus "grew more formidable," wrote Cassius Dio, "senators and others looked to him as if he were emperor."[47] He seeded much of the administration with loyalists, his birthday became a public holiday, statues of him appeared around the city, and petitioners sent envoys to him alongside (or even instead of) those they sent to Tiberius.[48] In AD 31, Sejanus arranged to wed Livilla, Tiberius's niece and the sister of Germanicus, at which point, Dio reports, "it was said that [Sejanus] was emperor and Tiberius the island potentate" of Capri.[49]

These sorts of sentiments finally induced Tiberius to counteract Sejanus's power grab. In order to learn the attitudes people held toward Sejanus, the emperor dispatched a series of contradictory messages to Rome that both praised and criticized Sejanus while teasing a possible return to the city by the emperor himself.[50] Tiberius communicated that he intended for Caligula to succeed him, began omitting some of the ceremonial titles that Sejanus used, and forbade Sejanus from leaving the capital.[51] Finally, on October 18 of 31, Tiberius struck directly. Naevius Sertorius Macro, a trusted member of the Roman city watch and fire brigade, escorted Sejanus into the Senate and dismissed his bodyguards. Macro then surrounded the building with members of the city watch and delivered a letter from Tiberius to the consuls. The letter, Dio writes, began with other business but ended by ordering the detention of Sejanus and two of his closet senatorial allies.[52]

Cassius Dio dislikes Tiberius intensely, but he writes about this letter with a macabre admiration for the emperor's ability to execute such a complicated plan. The letter, he says, first had senators lauding Sejanus because they believed he was about to receive a share of Tiberius's tribunician power. As the reading progressed, though, the senators began to understand that Tiberius was telling them "the opposite of what they expected." Some senators "who were seated near [Sejanus] actually rose up and left him because they no longer wished to share a seat with the man whom they previously had prized as their friend." Sejanus remained in his seat, quietly listening to the charges, until he was summoned to go forward by the consul. Sejanus, who "was unaccustomed to having orders addressed to him," had to be reminded that he had to obey the consul's commands. The consul then asked one senator whether Sejanus should be imprisoned. When that senator said yes, Sejanus was led away.[53]

The Senate then convicted Sejanus of treason. He was executed, and his body was thrown down the Scalae Gemoniae, a set of stairs descending from the Capitoline Hill to the Forum. Dio reports that the "rabble abused [the body] for three days and afterwards cast it into the river," as a sort of ritual cleansing of the city from the pollution Sejanus had brought.[54] Brutal attacks on Sejanus's family followed Tiberius's sudden, precise strike on the man himself. Sejanus's children were put to death, with the executioner first raping his daughter because it was illegal to put a virgin girl to death. His first wife committed suicide after writing a letter to Tiberius implicating Livilla, Sejanus's betrothed, in the death of Tiberius's son Drusus. Although the charges were unlikely to be true, Livilla's supposed associates were executed and, Dio reports, she was starved to death by her own mother after Tiberius entrusted Livilla's fate to her.[55]

Later Roman historians described the last years of Tiberius's life as a reign of terror in which informants brought the paranoid and isolated emperor ever more implausible charges against suspected allies of Sejanus. Tacitus tells about an old woman named Vitia who "was put to death because she wept at the killing of her son."[56] Agrippina, the widow of Germanicus and granddaughter of Augustus, was first imprisoned at the urging of Sejanus and then starved to death after his fall. Her son was treated even worse: He died in prison after eating his mattress.[57]

Behind these gruesome stories about the fates of the real and imagined allies of Sejanus lurked the shadow of the old Tiberius and his commitment to due process. Tiberius "caused all accusations to be lodged with the Senate," because he believed strongly that "the Senate should pass sentence" rather than the emperor.[58] This deference to the Senate was completely consistent with how Tiberius had reigned since taking power, but it terrified the senators who had witnessed the sudden fall of Sejanus, and who wondered what would happen if they voted incorrectly, or said the wrong thing during the trials the emperor forced them to conduct.

These sensible fears were probably misplaced. Modern historians have counted the number of people ancient authors describe being charged with *maiestas* or other forms of treason under Tiberius. The numbers are surprisingly small—most count fewer than a hundred charges lodged across the twenty-three years of Tiberius's reign. The majority of the charges did not result in conviction, and even fewer resulted in execution. The trials of Tiberius's last years constituted a reign of terror for senators not because many died but because all feared they might. This is a crucial difference. The anxieties produced by Tiberius's behavior undercut the Republican values of free speech and senatorial autonomy the emperor believed ought to guide Rome. Tiberius's refusal to return to the capital meant he had no idea that he had forced Romans to speak and vote "publicly as if they had been freed from a tyranny" while privately they lived in fear of an autocrat.[59]

Tacitus and Dio both recount a story of Tiberius's final moments that encapsulates the dread his behavior could inspire. In the late winter of 37, Tiberius settled into a villa in the city of Misenum to die. "On March 16," Tacitus wrote, "Tiberius's breathing stopped while Caligula, Macro, and their associates were in the villa." People began congratulating Caligula on his accession when, suddenly, they received word that Tiberius had woken up and was asking for food. "General panic ensued," until either Caligula or Macro grabbed a pile of bedclothes, went into the emperor's room, and smothered him.[60] He was seventy-seven years old.

The story almost certainly is not true, but it was repeated frequently because it highlighted the reactions that Tiberius had inadvertently produced. The emperor had been hampered by his own inability to convince people that they could trust the freedoms he said they possessed. Eventually, his frustration at senatorial subservience eroded any trust he once enjoyed with the Senate. This led a man who

Tacitus described as "a great official under Augustus" to plunge into "crime and ignominy" by the end of his life.[61] But, in reality, Tiberius was a good man and capable emperor who simply lived too long. His reputation and his empire would have been better off if he had been able to retire as he had planned. Instead, Rome found itself adrift for more than a decade until the old emperor died—and entrusted the empire to Caligula.

Chapter 14

Caligula and Claudius
Stumble Toward a New Rome

AD 37–54

T HE ORDERLY TRANSITION between the elderly Tiberius and the young Caligula in March of 37 occurred amid widespread excitement.[1] Rome was used to being run by old men. No one younger than fifty had ruled since Augustus's fiftieth birthday in 13 BC, a half century before Caligula took power, and Caligula offered a vitality that few Romans could remember their emperors possessing. They saw no sign of the violent, capricious ruler he would become.

Caligula changed Rome's political tenor almost immediately through a series of mostly symbolic breaks with the recent past. He displayed an ostentatious generosity that contrasted with Tiberius's parsimoniousness by cutting taxes; paying compensation to fire victims; granting money to gladiators, actors, soldiers, and regular Romans; and sponsoring lavish games and races.[2] He demonstrated a commitment to liberty by restoring the voting assemblies through which regular Roman citizens elected magistrates, and he "promised to share his power" with the Senate. He suspended investigations of *maiestas*, freed prisoners being held on that charge, and claimed (falsely) to have burned all documents connected to their cases. He even reversed Tiberius's ban on Cordus's history of Brutus and Cassius.[3] When Caligula assumed the consulship in July of 37, alongside his uncle Claudius, he gave a speech "denouncing [the emperor] Tiberius for each and every one of the crimes of which he was commonly accused" that so impressed the Senate that Cassius Dio claims it was "decreed that this speech should be read every year."[4]

Caligula also quickly took steps to emphasize a familial piety that Tiberius had lacked. He dedicated a shrine to his maternal great-grandfather Augustus; had his paternal grandmother, Antonia, declared Augusta; and brought the ashes of his brother and his mother, Agrippina, to Rome so they could be interred in the Mausoleum of Augustus on the Campus Martius.[5] He asked the Senate to divinize Tiberius, though he decided not to press the issue when the Senate demurred.[6] Caligula adopted Tiberius Gemellus, Drusus's son, as his own and arranged for him to receive the title *princeps iuventutis*, a clear marker that designated Gemellus as his successor.[7]

And then, seven months into his reign, Caligula became very sick.

IN ALEXANDRIA, THE Jewish philosopher Philo recalled that his home city, the empire's second most populous, froze in suspense when the news of the emperor's illness arrived. Like residents of all the other major cities in the Eastern Mediterranean, Alexandrians feared that the sudden death of the emperor might lead to a period of political violence. When news arrived that Caligula had recovered, "no one could recall so great and general a joy affecting any one country or people" or "the whole of the habitable world."[8]

Philo's comments reveal both how serious Caligula's illness was and, perhaps more importantly, how the distinct regions and peoples living under Roman control saw their place in the empire. Philo uses very precise Greek terms to describe the empire, marking it as a political system that encompassed nearly the entire habitable world and that joined diverse regions and peoples in a common enterprise. Most of the residents of the empire outside of Italy remained subjects without the benefits of Roman citizenship, but many of them had come to identify with the Roman state in the seventy years since Augustus had become emperor. Increasing numbers of people in the provinces had also become full Roman citizens. This was especially true of local elites like Philo.

The early emperors understood that their empire became stronger when it incorporated new citizens from the provinces in a fashion that allowed these people to identify as Roman while also retaining "their native traditions."[9] Speaking specifically of Jewish migrants, Philo explains that Augustus "neither ejected them from Rome nor deprived them of their Roman citizenship because they observed Judaism." Tiberius ordered provincial governors to "speak respectfully to members of our nation [i.e., Jews] in different cities" around the empire.[10] Jews who were Roman citizens enjoyed the same rights and protections as all other Romans even while they retained their historical Jewish practices and customs. This achievement, Philo felt, made the Roman Empire the only vessel that could hold together many different nations and regions in a common political project.

Other places around the Roman world show the physical, administrative, and cultural infrastructure that brought the empire together. In Gaul, a series of local and imperial initiatives transformed elites from the diverse Gallic tribes that fought Caesar into a Romanized aristocracy under Augustus and Tiberius. The modern French city of Saintes offers a glimpse of how this worked. Located at a natural crossing point in the Charente River about twenty miles from the Atlantic, Saintes was the chief settlement of the Santones, a Gallic tribe that cooperated with Julius Caesar during his conquest of Gaul in the mid-50s BC.[11] The Romans renamed the settlement Mediolanum Santonum, rebuilt its center along a grid plan, connected it to the wider empire by a road network built by Agrippa, and made it the provincial capital of Aquitania.[12] By the time of Caligula's accession, the city had a population of perhaps 15,000 people, a spectacular amphitheater, a bridge across the Charente, a river port, an aqueduct, and a monumental arch that welcomed travelers coming to the city from Lyon.

This arch, which celebrated the joint consulship of Tiberius and Caligula's father Germanicus in 18 or 19, belongs to an explosion of monuments built in the first century AD by the Roman citizen descendants of Gallic elites. Gaius Julius Rufus, a Roman citizen, a priest of the cult of Rome and Augustus in Lyon, and the holder of a local magistracy, paid for its erection. On the arch's inscription, Gaius Julius Rufus describes himself as the son of another Gaius Julius, but his father also bore the Gallic name Catuaneunius. His grandfather, who received citizenship from Caesar, is Gaius Julius Agedomonis, and his great-grandfather is simply known by his Gallic name Epotsoviridi.[13] Romans like Rufus remembered their Celtic past and honored their independent Celtic ancestors, but they also bore Roman names, advertised their Roman citizenship, served as leaders of Roman cults, and enjoyed themselves at Roman games. They were Roman, but, to borrow from Philo, they lived in the country of the Santones and also remained a part of the Santonic nation.

The first-century amphitheater built in the small city of Senlis (ancient Augustomagus) suggests that large Roman construction projects appealed to more than the narrow, Romanized Gallic elite. Augustomagus sat where the road Agrippa built from Lyon to the English Channel intersected with the road running from Rouen to Reims, and its amphitheater held as many as 10,000 people, far larger than the town's population. The amphitheater, then, was not built to serve locals alone. It instead drew travelers, performers, vendors, and others from around the region who would descend upon the town to attend the Roman games and performances it hosted.

This was the Roman world that held its breath as news of Caligula's illness spread. Although most people in it were not yet Roman citizens, Caligula was their emperor, and when he recovered, Philo said, people were full of gratitude for "the good health and prosperity of their ruler."[14] They did not yet know that Caligula had emerged from his illness a changed, vicious man.[15]

THE EMPEROR'S NEW volatility surfaced almost immediately. Without any evidence at all, Caligula charged his adopted son and heir,
Tiberius Gemellus, with poisoning him, then forced the prince to
kill himself. Gemellus was so young and naïve that he had to ask his
guards where one stabbed oneself when trying to commit suicide.[16]
Caligula next ordered the death of Macro, the counselor of Tiberius
who had masterminded Caligula's succession, because the emperor
believed some people thought he depended too heavily on Macro's
counsel.[17] Soon after this he forced his own father-in-law, and his primary liaison with the Senate, to commit suicide after he took a sea-
sickness medication that Caligula wrongly assumed was an antidote
to poison.[18] He even ordered a man to kill himself after learning that
the man had sworn an oath to give up his own life if Caligula recovered from his illness.[19]

Caligula encountered more serious problems as his first year in
office neared its end. Tiberius had left him an inheritance worth 27
million gold pieces in the imperial private account, but "in less than
a year," Suetonius reports, Caligula had "squandered [the] entire fortune." Stories began circulating that Caligula "drank valuable pearls
dissolved in vinegar, and provided his guests with golden bread and
golden meat" when they dined with him.[20] Authors tell sensation-
alized stories about his orgies, his incestuous relationship with his
sister, and his intention to name his horse, Incitatus, as consul. He
once even caused a food shortage in Rome by sending the boats of
the grain fleet to Puteoli, so they could be tied together to form a
three-mile-long bridge. Caligula rode across the bridge in a chariot
two times and then ordered it dismantled.[21]

The next three years brought greater financial problems as
Caligula's spending and cruelty grew.[22] He restarted *maiestas* trials,
convicted people on the basis of the incriminating documents that
he supposedly had burned at the outset of his reign, and confiscated
their property.[23] He secured funds by fining road commissioners
when the roads they managed fell into disrepair, and he ordered that
any new laws related to taxes should be written in tiny letters that

people could not read.[24] Anyone violating these new laws would pay significant financial penalties. When people began protesting that these measures were unfair, Caligula commanded soldiers to kill them.[25]

Caligula's instability affected people in the provinces as well. Caligula collected large amounts of money from Gaul under the pretext that he would campaign in Germany or lead a war of conquest against Britain. Nothing ever came of the German campaign, and when the British invasion force marshaled on the shore of the English Channel, Caligula just ordered them to gather seashells.[26] Romans assumed that the money collected for the British campaign in fact funded the emperor's luxurious lifestyle.

As Caligula's behavior became increasingly irrational, he began intimating that he was a god. He built a sacred precinct for himself in the city of Miletus and arranged for a lodge to be created on the Capitoline Hill where he could dwell with Jupiter. Styling himself Jupiter Latiaris, he appointed his wife, Caesonia, and his uncle Claudius to be his priests.[27] Romans had come to accept that emperors could ascend to the level of gods after their deaths, but living emperors were still viewed as people who had been chosen to lead the state by their fellow citizens. They were men, not gods.

Caligula's desire to be publicly recognized as a god also soured his relationship with Jews, whose belief in a single God made it impossible for them to accept the notion of the emperor being divine.[28] Popular awareness of Caligula's bad feelings toward the Jews ultimately sparked an anti-Jewish riot in Alexandria. Mobs of Alexandrian Greeks attacked Jewish homes, plundered their property, and erected statues of Caligula in synagogues.[29] When the Alexandrian Jewish community sent Philo to speak with Caligula, Philo learned that the emperor had ordered Publius Petronius, the military commander of Syria, to use the army to erect a golden statue of Zeus in the Jewish temple of Jerusalem. Petronius wisely fabricated all sorts of delays that prevented him from doing what was ordered.[30] Eventually Philo and Agrippa, the Jewish client king ruling what is now the

Golan Heights and southwestern Syria on Rome's behalf, convinced Caligula to keep the statue out of the temple.[31]

Ultimately it was a petty private dispute rather than senatorial discontent or provincial dissatisfaction that doomed Caligula. Augustus had established an elite military unit called the praetorian guard and entrusted it with protecting the emperor. The praetorians needed to work closely with the emperor and trust him, but Caligula regularly mocked one of their officers, Cassius Chaerea, as a "sissy."[32] Eventually Chaerea snapped. On January 24 of the year 41, he and a group of co-conspirators attacked Caligula while he was on his way to watch a performance. "When [Caligula] had fallen," Cassius Dio recorded, "all continued to stab him savagely, even though he was dead; and some even tasted of his flesh. His wife and daughter were also promptly slain."[33]

Caligula's madness and sudden death highlighted a problem with the Roman imperial system that the competence of Augustus and Tiberius had obscured. Sometimes the people receiving a lifetime appointment as emperor would either not be up to the job or, like Caligula, would lose the capacity to do it while in office. Rome lacked a mechanism to remove such a sovereign. But perhaps the greatest indictment of the system came from the fact that the Senate, the army, and the provincial governors all understood Caligula's manifest unfitness for office—and yet the fate of Rome turned on the personal grievance of a prickly soldier. It set an extremely poor precedent that such a consequential action could arise from so insignificant a cause.

THE FOLLOWING DAYS did little to calm Roman concerns about their political system. Caligula's uncle Claudius had been with the emperor when he was attacked and fled to the imperial apartments in terror. A group of praetorians plundering the palace found Claudius trembling behind the drapes lining a balcony. One of them recognized Claudius as a member of the imperial family, pulled him to his feet, and hailed him as emperor. Claudius was then carried in a litter into the praetorian camp. In the meantime, the Senate and the consuls had "taken possession of the Forum and the Capitol" and, Suetonius wrote, "resolved to maintain the public liberty" that Caligula's murder had unexpectedly seemed to restore.[34]

The next day saw a face-off between the senators considering some sort of renewed Republican system and the praetorians who, as imperial protectors, had the most to lose from such a radical change. The Senate moved slowly and, as it bickered, regular Romans assembled and began calling for Claudius to be recognized as ruler. Claudius had the good sense to "allow the armed assembly of soldiers to swear allegiance to him and then promised each of them 15,000 sesterces" in exchange for their support.[35] Once the troops protecting the senators deserted to Claudius, the Senate "yielded and voted him all the remaining prerogatives of power."[36]

Claudius was the grandson of Livia, the brother of Germanicus, and the nephew of Tiberius, but he was a most unlikely choice for emperor. He had been a sickly child and had moved and spoken so awkwardly that Augustus had banned him from attending public events.[37] Claudius was almost fifty when he held his first truly significant public office, the consulship that he shared with Caligula, and he had then begun to take Caligula's place occasionally during public events. Despite this new prominence, Claudius remained a subject of mockery. He had a habit of falling into a deep sleep at dinner parties. Other attendees would throw olive pits at him and place shoes on his hands, so that when he woke up he would rub his eyes with them.[38] Instead of enjoying court life, Claudius seems to have spent most of his time studying Etruscan history.

Claudius performed well for an emperor who was believed to have such limited capacities. He understood that he had effectively seized power from senators who had hoped to restore some version of public liberty, and he symbolically acknowledged their feelings by posting images on his coins of Libertas holding a *pileus*, the kind of hat given to freed slaves that Brutus had once put on coins celebrating the murder of Julius Caesar.[39] Claudius waited for thirty days to go to the Senate, and when he did appear, he "gave honors" to those "who had openly shown their eagerness for democracy" and "promised them immunity" from prosecution.[40] He again banned prosecutions for *maiestas*, a symbolic act that senators surely did not trust to remain in place for long. And yet Claudius neither prosecuted anyone for *maiestas* nor took any vengeance on those "who had wronged or insulted him when he was a private citizen."[41] He also actually burned the incriminating papers that Caligula claimed to have destroyed but never really did—and then returned the property that Caligula had confiscated to the families of his victims.[42]

Claudius took similar care in resolving problems in the provinces. He addressed the recent anti-Jewish actions in Egypt by issuing an edict to all the cities of the empire that affirmed the rights of Jews to "maintain their ancestral customs without hindrance."[43] As his reign progressed, Claudius's interaction with provincials showed even greater astuteness. He conquered much of southeastern Britain with an army that he commanded and that included the last known use of Roman war elephants.[44] As the conquest progressed under his subordinates, Claudius encouraged Britons to adopt Roman manners by granting large sums of money to important local figures and extending Roman citizenship to them in much the same way that Julius Caesar's campaigns in Gaul had enfranchised Gallic aristocrats.[45]

The citizenship extensions in Britain were not exceptional. An inscription from the Moroccan town of Volubilis in the very southwestern corner of the empire honors a local man named Marcus Valerius Severus, the son of Bostar, who "obtained for his people Roman citizenship, the right to marry non-Roman wives, and a tax exemption" directly from the emperor. Like Gaius Julius Rufus in Gaul, this prominent Mauretanian-Roman treasured both his new status and his family roots in his African homeland.[46] Severus was but one of the very "many people [who] sought Roman franchise by personal application to the emperor."[47]

Claudius also believed that some citizens born outside of Italy should be permitted to hold the same Roman offices as Italians. As censor in 48, he received a request from a group of citizens of Gallic descent asking to serve in the Senate. Claudius embraced the opportunity to refashion the membership of a Senate that did not particularly respect him by including new, wealthier, friendlier members drawn from Gaul. This move provoked a heated discussion in the Senate that Claudius quieted with a speech now preserved on a bronze tablet called the Tablet of Lyon that was also later adapted by Tacitus.

Throughout all Roman history, Claudius argued, the Roman government had always opened itself up to the participation of Romans who were not born citizens. It had begun with the kings passing power to "foreigners" like Tarquinius Priscus and continued when Claudius's "great-uncle Augustus and [his] uncle Tiberius decided to admit into this Senate" the elites of Italy and southern Gaul, "all of them good and wealthy men, of course." Now Claudius wished to do the same for the rest of the Gallic provinces. Although some might claim, Claudius continued, that Italians were better than provincial senators, no one should reject a potential provincial senator as long as the man was a good choice.

The current Senate objected strongly to this reasoning for two reasons. The most obvious one was that they knew that Claudius wanted new senators who would be grateful to him for their elevation because he needed their political support. But a second, less obvious reason seems to have animated their anger even more. The current senators, Tacitus explained, feared a reduction in their own standing when "every place is crowded by these rich men" from Gaul while no "distinctions will be left for the remnants of our nobility or for any impoverished senators from Latium."[48]

These older senators feared that Claudius's new elite of wealthy Gauls—like Gaius Julius Rufus—would supplant the more established, but less wealthy, aristocracy that currently populated the Senate. This was, of course, the very thing that Claudius wanted. Among the senators made most uncomfortable by Claudius's proposal were the remnants of the old Republican aristocracy. Some of these men would have been the leading voices in the senatorial discussions about restoring a Republic following Caligula's death. Their attempt to end the empire had been pardoned, of course, but it could not be forgotten. It was in Claudius's interests to dilute their influence by adding powerful new voices that strongly supported him.

Claudius also had a subtle, but potent, response to another group of senators who harbored these doubts. Many of the Italo-Romans now fearing the influx of Gallic senators were themselves part of an effort by Augustus and Tiberius to rebuild the post–civil war Senate with the wealthy elites of Italy whose families had received citizenship during and immediately following the Social War. This was why the emperor reminded the Senate of Augustus's and Tiberius's expansions, alongside the backhanded comment that all the new senators of that time were "good and wealthy men, of course." Of course. They were the ancestors of some of the very men who now argued against including new senators.

Claudius did not leave the old Roman senatorial families totally disappointed. There were new honors that he could offer them, too. "Given the fewness of the families now remaining" from the times of Romulus and Brutus, said Tacitus, Claudius "enrolled all the senators of the longest standing or those who had brilliant parents among the ranks of the patricians."[49] His promotion of plebeian Roman senators to the ranks of the patricians gave the current aristocracy a reward that offset some of the fear that their descendants might be displaced by wealthier newcomers. Claudius now presided over a system where he enhanced the status of those he selected so that "they were in debt to him."[50]

Claudius proved much less adept at preventing his tumultuous romantic life from intruding politically. He was married four times. The first two marriages ended in divorce amid charges of adultery and emotional abuse by his wives before he took power. He married his third wife, Messalina, during the reign of Caligula. She was the mother of his son, a boy renamed Britannicus after the conquest of Britain, but Messalina was also habitually unfaithful to him. She plotted a coup with a senator named Gaius Silius during the year of Claudius's censorship, and Tacitus suggests that she even tried to cement her position in a post-coup order by marrying Silius while

Claudius was away from the city.[51] The coup was soon suppressed, and both plotters were killed.[52]

In 49, Claudius married his niece Agrippina, the ambitious daughter of his brother Germanicus who already had a son from a previous marriage. Unlike Claudius, Agrippina was directly descended from Augustus, and this made her young son, the future emperor Nero, a plausible figurehead around which a challenge to Claudius's power could coalesce. The marriage then made strategic sense, but Claudius's troubles navigating complicated personal situations doomed it. In 53, Agrippina arranged for Nero to marry Claudius's young daughter Octavia. When Claudius died the following year, Agrippina was said to have poisoned him with a mushroom, because she feared that Claudius's natural son Britannicus might supplant Nero as imperial heir.[53] The tale of his poisoning may or may not be true, but Agrippina was prepared to quickly arrange affairs so that Nero, rather than Britannicus, would succeed her late husband. If she did not murder Claudius, the events to come suggest that she already knew what she wanted to happen when he died—even if it did not correspond to the emperor's own wishes.

The deaths of Caligula and Claudius then show the fragility of a political system that depended on the life and capacity of one man to function. Caligula governed poorly, and Claudius capably, but both men were ultimately done in by the actions of ambitious or disgruntled individuals. Their sudden deaths taught Romans about the deeply personal nature of imperial rule as well as the precarity of its long-term stability. These lessons proved difficult to unlearn.

Chapter 15

Nero

54–69

NERO, ONE OF the most notorious and misunderstood of all Roman emperors, came to the throne at the age of sixteen after his stepfather, Claudius, died in October 54. Although Claudius's will prescribed that his natural son Britannicus would share power with Nero, imperial power did not belong to an emperor. He was entrusted with it by the Roman state, and unlike a house or piece of jewelry, he had no legal right to dictate who would hold power after his death. Agrippina—Augustus's great-granddaughter, Claudius's wife, and Nero's mother by her first marriage—knew this, and she ensured that Claudius's will was never read. When Britannicus died under mysterious circumstances within a year of his father's death, he did so as a private citizen who had never tasted the imperial power his father hoped he would enjoy.[1]

Agrippina had been working to position Nero for power since her wedding to Claudius in 49. When Nero was a teenager, she had arranged for Seneca, a wealthy senator known for his embrace of Stoic philosophy, to serve as his tutor and occasional speechwriter. Seneca had a keen sense of what other senators might like to hear from the young prince and coached Nero about what he ought to say to curry their favor.[2]

Nero's first five years as emperor generally unfolded in a fashion that senators supported, in large part because Agrippina worked with Seneca and the praetorian prefect Sextus Afranius Burrus to set the young emperor's domestic and military priorities. Soon after taking power, Nero gave a speech to the Senate (that Seneca had written) emphasizing that he would end the grudges that some senators felt typified the reign of Claudius.[3] He agreed to assume the costs of the increasingly expensive games that quaestors were expected to sponsor, and, during the census of 58, he added his own funds to those belonging to three senators who looked likely to be demoted because they no longer met the property qualification for senatorial service.[4]

Nero soon tired of Agrippina's condescension and arrogance, but their relationship really soured when, despite his marriage to Claudius's daughter Claudia Octavia, Nero fell in love with a freedwoman named Acte in 55.[5] Agrippina tried to end the relationship, and Nero took revenge by removing one of her courtiers. According to Tacitus, Agrippina then told Nero that he owed his power to her, and as the daughter of Germanicus, she would not accept being sidelined by "the crippled Burrus" and Seneca.[6]

Agrippina wasn't wrong about the source of Nero's power, but this impolitic truth led to her being forced from the palace, denied bodyguards, and held in a villa in the countryside. Eventually, after he failed to convince those around him that Acte came from an exotic royal bloodline, Nero recognized that he could not marry a woman of her social status.[7] He then began an affair with Poppaea Sabina, the wife of his friend Marcus Otho. Nero sent Otho to govern Lusitania (the province that comprised much of what is now southwestern Spain and Portugal) while his affair with Sabina deepened. Unlike Acte, she was a potential marriage match for Nero, but the emperor and Sabina both saw Agrippina as the main roadblock to that marriage occurring.[8]

Nero understood that Agrippina's support among the praetorians and her supposed expertise in poisoning demanded that he design a creative accident to end her life.[9] Cassius Dio describes a specially designed ship that could separate, drop its passengers into the sea, and then become seaworthy again, while Tacitus says it was rigged to tip its passengers into the water and then bounce back so it again stood upright.[10] Whatever the actual nature of the vessel, Agrippina boarded it on a clear, calm night and was soon dumped into the sea.[11] She was rescued, but Nero later sent soldiers from the fleet to kill her.[12] "Thus it was," Dio wrote, "that Agrippina, the daughter of Germanicus, granddaughter of Agrippa, and descendant of Augustus, was slain by the very son to whom she had given the sovereignty" of Rome.[13]

AGRIPPINA'S MURDER IN 59 abruptly ended what the future emperor Trajan would later call the Five Good Years of Nero.[14] Terrified advisers ceased speaking honestly to the emperor, most senators stopped protesting his actions, and Nero "came to believe that anything in his power to do was right."[15] The death of Burrus and the retirement of Seneca in 62 further deprived Nero of the input of the experienced officials most familiar with his disposition.[16] Any constructive feedback they might have given was now replaced by either sycophancy or attention-grabbing displays of defiance. Most senators went along with whatever the emperor asked, but the philosopher Thrasea Paetus refused to vote on many of them, because, as Paetus once remarked, "Nero can kill me, but he cannot harm me."[17] Suetonius reports that within the city of Rome a wave of anonymous graffiti appeared saying, "Orestes, Nero, Alcmeon, all matricides."[18] Ominously, people who were caught expressing such thoughts were not prosecuted, because, it was rumored, Nero was afraid to have to defend himself against a charge all knew to be true.[19]

All was not well outside of the capital, either. In 60 or 61, Britain erupted in rebellion. Boudica, the queen of the Iceni tribe based around modern Norfolk, capitalized upon British disaffection with a Roman regime that many felt had lied to its new subjects. Claudius had granted British elites significant sums of money, but Neronian officials declared that what had seemed like grants were in fact loans—and demanded immediate repayment. When this happened, private Roman lenders also called in the loans they had made to the island. Seneca alone supposedly owned 10 million denarii in British debt.[20] British anger at these conditions swelled Boudica's army until it was large enough to overwhelm cities such as London and Colchester before Roman forces regrouped and snuffed out the rebellion in 61.

Boudica's revolt was the first of a series of crises that hit Nero's regime across the 60s. The most serious of these was a massive fire that incinerated much of the city of Rome in July 64. The blaze first broke out on July 19 near the Circus Maximus and waxed and waned for nine days before it was finally extinguished. Tacitus wrote that only four of Rome's fourteen districts "remained uninjured, three were levelled to the ground, while in the other seven, there were left only a few shattered, half-burnt relics of houses." The elite districts on the Palatine Hill and the imperial palace sustained some of the worst damage.[21]

Nero was not in the city at the time, but rumors circulated that he bore responsibility for the conflagration. Part of the problem was the way the fire developed. The sparking up and dying down of the flames as they spread across the city led Romans to suspect (quite falsely) that Nero had ordered people to randomly set fires across the city over several days. These suspicions were amplified by the charges that some members of the city watch looted homes instead of fighting the fires.[22]

Once Nero arrived in the capital, he did what he could to alleviate the immediate misery. He opened the Campus Martius, public buildings, and his own gardens to those who had lost their homes, while also building temporary housing for them. He sent for food from neighboring towns and subsidized the price of grain in Rome. All of this could not stifle the rumor that, "when the city was in flames, the emperor appeared on a private stage and sang of the destruction of Troy, comparing present misfortunes with the calamities of antiquity."[23] This is the origin of the famous story that Nero fiddled while Rome burned.

Nero did not fiddle while watching the flames, but he did handle the fire's aftermath poorly. While many thousands of Romans struggled to find shelter and secure materials to rebuild their homes, Nero "erected a mansion" called the Domus Aurea, or Golden House. He decorated it with "jewels and gold" and placed it in a park-like setting constructed around an artificial lake excavated from what had been the densely populated land stretching from the Palatine to the Oppian and Caelian Hills.[24] According to Suetonius, Nero's palace contained "dining-rooms with fretted ceilings of ivory, whose panels could turn and shower down flowers and were fitted with pipes for sprinkling the guests with perfumes," as well as a "main banquet hall that was circular and constantly revolved day and night, like the heavens."[25]

Nero's palace did not go over well with the Roman public. It was not that the Roman public did not believe he should have a palace. The imperial residence had become a Roman version of the White House that served as both the emperor's home and a secure site where he could govern and hold audiences with senators and foreign dignitaries. Nero, however, went far beyond what other Romans thought necessary in an official residence at a time when many others were suffering.

The emperor soon settled on a scapegoat when he recognized the depth of public anger. In antiquity, massive disasters were often seen as evidence of divine displeasure. Nero ordered priests to consult the sacred *Sibylline Books* and pray to many different traditional Roman gods, so that the divine anger that had caused the fire of 64 might be assuaged. But, Tacitus reported, most people still could not "banish the sinister belief that Nero ordered the conflagration." In order to "get rid of the report," he continued, "Nero fastened the guilt and inflicted the most exquisite tortures on a class hated for their abominations, called Christians." Nero ordered the mass arrest of "all who pleaded guilty" to being a Christian and had many of them "nailed to crosses . . . and burnt, to serve as a nightly illumination." The emperor even "offered his gardens for the spectacle" of watching these human beings become torches each night, a disgusting level of brutality that "inspired a feeling of compassion" for people who were "destroyed not for the public good but to satiate one man's cruelty."[26]

Nero's mass arrest of Christians, which occurred roughly a generation after Jesus's death, marks the first time that a non-Christian author mentions the religion. It also testifies to both the capital's religious diversity and the pace of Christian expansion. For non-Christians like Tacitus, the presence of Christians showed that Rome had become the city "where all things hideous and shameful from every part of the world find their center and become popular."[27] Nero was exploiting the prejudice that non-Roman influences harmed Rome by diluting its true nature, but his severe persecution against a "class of men given to a new and mischievous superstition" neither rid the city of Christians nor calmed anyone's anger.[28]

In 65, a group of senators, knights, and praetorians revolted by "the emperor's crimes" ineptly conspired to overthrow Nero and replace him with the ex-consul Gaius Calpurnius Piso. Unfortunately, the plotters deliberated for too long and had too many household attendants who could hear what was in the works. They were betrayed when a slave of one of the conspirators reported the plot to Nero.[29]

Nero's vengeance was swift, severe, and wide-ranging. Shocked by the breadth of the conspiracy, he locked the city down with soldiers— including German auxiliaries, whom he seems to have trusted more than his praetorians. The known conspirators were quickly rounded up and executed, but the emperor ordered a broader investigation that soon ensnared people who had not been involved with Piso's plot. Even Seneca, who had retired from Nero's service in 62, was arrested based on a general conversation that he had with another person about Piso, but he committed suicide before he could be tried.[30]

Nero murdered others simply because he disliked them. In 66, he ordered the execution of Thrasea Paetus after a series of public actions that emphasized the senator's loathing of the emperor. Paetus walked out of the Senate during a discussion of how to congratulate Nero on the death of Agrippina. He did the same when the senators were considering whether to give divine honors to the pregnant Poppaea

Sabina, after Nero killed her in 65 by kicking her in the stomach.[31] Paetus also refused to take the customary oaths of loyalty to the emperor, offered no sacrifices for his welfare, and had boycotted Senate meetings for most of the past three years.[32] Once Paetus learned that he was going to be arrested, he stayed in his gardens to await his death. The last surviving passages of Tacitus's *Annals* describe Paetus's final moments in a way that mirrors Plato's account of Socrates's execution. Tacitus wanted Romans to understand that Paetus's death tarnished their state just as that of Socrates had stained Athens.[33]

Nero's problems were not just confined to the capital. In 66, the province of Judaea revolted after a local dispute about sacrificing to Nero led to the murder of Roman soldiers. When the governor of Syria failed to solve the problem, Nero appointed Vespasian, an outstanding commander with experience dating back to the conquest of Britain, to deal with what had become a province-wide uprising. Vespasian and his son Titus did this brutally. The Jewish revolt ended with the capture of Jerusalem, the enslavement of tens of thousands of Jews, the destruction of the magnificent Jewish temple that Herod had built, and the plundering of sacred objects, including the temple menorah.

Nero responded to these misfortunes by leaving Rome for Greece in September 66. In the years since Agrippina's death, he had embraced poetry writing, singing, acting, and chariot racing in increasingly public ways. Roman aristocrats tended to see these activities as unbecoming to a gentleman, but the Greek world was different.[34] Greek kings, including Cleopatra's father, performed music publicly, and Alexander the Great's father had won multiple victories in the Olympics.[35] Nero decided to prove that his skills exceeded those famous Greek predecessors by entering all four of the major Greek sporting competitions: the Olympic, Isthmian, Nemean, and Pythian Games. As in the modern world, the Olympics were held every four years, a cycle called an Olympiad. Under normal circumstances, the Olympics and Isthmian Games were held in the first year of the Olympiad, the Nemean Games in the second and fourth years, and the Pythian and Isthmian Games in the third year.

Nero, however, ordered that all four games be held during his time in Greece so he could win them all. The Olympics alone saw Nero win six events, including the newly added competitions in lyre playing and tragedy.

Nero showed his gratitude by spending lots of money on the region. He had an imperial residence built in Olympia for his stay in the city and gave money to the oracular shrine at Delphi. He began work on a canal at Corinth that would allow ships to avoid sailing around the Peloponnese. And he granted Roman citizenship to any judges who awarded him prizes when he performed at a Greek festival. Then, on November 29, 67, he summoned "as many people as possible" to Corinth so that they could see him "reward most noble Greece for its goodwill and piety towards me."[36] When they arrived, Nero announced to the assembled Greeks that they would "receive freedom and immunity from taxation." Other emperors had "conferred freedom on individual cities," Nero said, "but only Nero has done so for an entire province."[37]

The site, occasion, and substance of Nero's speech granting Greece its freedom evoked the moment in 196 BC when the Roman general Titus Quinctius Flamininus had used the Isthmian Games to grant Greece its political freedom, but Nero's grant differed significantly from that of his Republican predecessor. Flamininus had given Greece the freedom to exist outside of the control of any outside party—including Rome. Nero was not liberating Greece from Roman rule. He was instead personally granting Greeks a privileged status within the Roman Empire that liberated them from Roman tax burdens. Only a small fraction of Greeks witnessed Nero's speech at Corinth and his participation in Greek games, but Nero's agents issued propaganda that advertised Nero's generosity to Greeks and portrayed him as a liberator.[38] Nero had then carefully positioned himself as a political patron for the whole region.

A considered policy lay behind Nero's Greek journey. The great fire, Piso's coup attempt, and the executions of real and suspected conspirators had destroyed the political powerbase that Burrus and Seneca had built for Nero. Just as Claudius had sought to reinforce his weak political hand by bringing Gallic figures into the Senate, Nero now turned to Greece.

This move made a great deal of sense. The Greek-speaking elites of the Eastern Mediterranean represented a large, rich group of people who had not yet been well integrated into the offices of the Roman state. They were not senators, they did not aspire to Roman magistracies, and they spent most of their time and money serving their home cities. But Nero was young and desperate. Greece offered him a chance to build a robust political foundation that drew upon the strongest, wealthiest, and most dynamic parts of an increasingly integrated Roman world. He would not see results immediately, however, and Nero frequently struggled to prevent his idiosyncratic ideas and behaviors from sabotaging the practical policy benefits of his actions. Just as his interest in a richly decorated masterpiece of architectural and landscape design sabotaged support for a new imperial palace, so, too, did his affinity for the Greek world prevent him from recognizing problems in Italy that had boiled up while he was playing hero across the Adriatic Sea.

BEFORE HE LEFT for Greece, Nero decided to delegate "complete authority" to a freedman, Helius, and granted him the power to "banish . . . or put to death" any Roman of any rank without even "notifying" the emperor.[39] Italians quickly tired of him. Although Helius sent repeated messages to Nero about the growing discontent in Rome, he could never convince the emperor to return to the capital. Finally, Helius himself showed up in Greece to inform Nero that "a great conspiracy against him was emerging in Rome." He eventually persuaded Nero to come back to Italy.[40]

Nero still failed to appreciate the seriousness of the situation after he landed. He stopped in Naples, Antium, and Alba so that citizens of those cities could fete his athletic and artistic brilliance.[41] When he finally reached Rome, he had "a portion of the city wall . . . and a section of the gates taken down" because he had heard that doing so "was customary upon the return of victors from the games."[42] He then staged a triumphal procession in a chariot once used by Augustus to celebrate military victories. After processing through the city, he entered the grounds of the Domus Aurea as the Roman masses and "the senators most of all" acclaimed him.[43]

Nero soon traveled to Naples. He refused to give speeches or communicate with the senators and generals in any way other than by letter, so that he could rest his singing voice. Then, on March 20 or 21 of 68, Nero received word of the rebellion of Gaius Julius Vindex, the governor of Gallia Lugdunensis.[44] Vindex, who resented the supplemental taxes Nero had imposed on Gallic communities to pay for the rebuilding of the capital, had called an assembly of Gallic notables and spoken about his own disenchantment with Nero. He convinced the tribal leaders to summon Gallic troops to overthrow the emperor.[45] Vindex did not imagine this as an anti-Roman revolt, like the one Boudica had led in Britain, or the Jewish revolt in Judaea. Vindex was a Roman senator, and many of the tribal leaders he worked with were probably Roman citizens. They did not want to leave the empire; they simply wanted a new, better emperor.

Vindex "was not working to get the imperial office for himself," Dio explained, but instead sent messengers to other governors with armies in the hope that one of them would serve as the figure around which a wider revolt against Nero could coalesce. When it became clear that some governors had informed Nero about the plot instead of joining it, Vindex "selected Servius Sulpicius Galba," the impeccably credentialed governor of Spain.[46] As Galba consulted with Otho and Aulus Caecina Alienus, the other two governors of provinces in the Iberian Peninsula, Vindex issued coins without an imperial face on them and sent anti-Neronian pamphlets into Italy.[47]

Galba's armies proclaimed him emperor on April 6, 68, a little more than two weeks after Nero learned about Vindex's revolt. Before Vindex could join up with Galba, however, his Gallic troops were badly beaten by legions commanded by Lucius Verginius Rufus, the governor of Germany. Perhaps as many as 20,000 Gauls died in the fighting, and, as Dio recorded, Vindex killed himself after despairing that he had failed to secure "the overthrow of Nero and the liberation of the Romans."[48] The worst part about Vindex's death is that it may have been unnecessary. It is possible that Rufus had already agreed to support Galba, and his troops may have gone to battle anyway out of a desire to plunder.[49] Whatever their motivation for fighting, Rufus's troops had so little loyalty to Nero that, after the battle, they tried to get Rufus to accept the imperial title. He refused.[50]

Nero still occupied an extremely strong position in the early spring of 68—and Galba knew it. Plutarch says that Galba "spent his time in repenting of what he had done . . . rather than in taking any of the steps necessary" to win a civil war.[51] But the threat to the regime paralyzed Nero until he squandered every advantage he possessed. Instead of rallying his supporters when he learned of Galba's acclamation, Nero "fainted and lay for a long time as if catatonic," before "declaring that it was all over for him."[52] He continued to lack any real perspective as the conflict with Galba developed. Nero hosted luxurious feasts whenever he received good news, but fell into deep depressions whenever he learned of reverses. When he finally was persuaded that he needed to lead an army to confront the usurper, he spent more time planning how his water organ and other musical instruments could be carried to war than he did developing a military strategy.[53]

Nero's inability to figure out how to fund the civil war proved to be his fatal failing. When he instituted a massive new tax that transferred what should have been public revenue directly to his own private accounts, he lost all support in Rome.[54] In early June, with Galba's armies still far away, the Senate voted to condemn Nero and accept Galba as the new emperor. The praetorian guards defected after one of Galba's agents promised them a bounty of 7,500 denarii apiece.[55] With the palace empty and his person unprotected, Nero fled the city and committed suicide at the villa of his freedman Phaon, one of his few friends who stayed loyal to the end. Nero's childhood nurses, and Acte, his first love, arranged for his burial in the tomb of his father's family.[56]

"The death of Nero," Tacitus wrote, "had been welcomed initially by a surge of relief . . . but a well-hidden secret of the principate had been revealed: it was possible for an emperor to be chosen outside of Rome."[57] Augustus and Tiberius had known how dangerous this secret would be if it ever came to light, and they had done their best to bury it beneath a system that checked the power and limited the knowledge of every figure who could reasonably aspire to be emperor. No one, however, could have imagined the danger that Galba faced when that system broke, allowing every governor with an army to nurture imperial dreams.

GALBA ARRIVED IN Rome with neither the knowledge nor the practical flexibility to govern an empire that was technically at peace but in which every governor could aspire to be emperor himself. He also failed to understand that important aspects of the Roman system were broken. Nero had levied a special tax not because he needed a new water organ but because he needed a new army—and Galba was stuck paying Nero's bills. He did his best to increase revenue by "revoking all of the grants made by Nero," taking back gifts Nero had given to friends, and forcing Greek cities to return funds the emperor had disbursed to them.[58] When the praetorian soldiers asked for the bonus money Galba had promised, Cassius Dio reported, he replied, "I am accustomed to levy soldiers, not to buy them."[59]

Galba soon earned a reputation for vindictiveness as well as miserliness. He ordered his cavalrymen to slaughter 7,000 rowers whom Nero had transferred from the imperial fleet to the army when they declined to return to their ships.[60] He condemned the Neronian governors of Africa and Lower Germany to death, and he removed Lucius Verginius Rufus from his post in Upper Germany because he had been too slow to renounce Nero.[61] He also decreed the execution of the woman rumored to have provided the poison that killed Claudius.

All of this meant that Galba quickly "incurred the hatred of almost all men of every class and became especially detested by the soldiers."[62] In early January of 69, Galba received a report that the legions in Upper Germany "had broken their oath of loyalty and were calling for a change of emperor" from Galba to any other candidate decided by the Senate.[63] Galba responded by deciding to appoint an imperial deputy who could serve as his designated heir.

Two candidates stood out. Marcus Otho, the ex-husband of Nero's second wife, Poppaea, who governed Lusitania when Galba rebelled, had quickly joined the revolt. He traveled with Galba's army and was favored by one of Galba's main advisers. Galba's other advisers preferred Lucius Calpurnius Piso Frugi Licinianus, a thirty-one-year-old descendant of both Crassus and Pompey the Great.[64] On January 10, Galba announced the choice of Piso to the praetorian guards. Although the officers cheered, Tacitus reported that "gloom and silence predominated throughout the rest" of the troops when Galba again refused to give them "some token of generosity" to commemorate Piso's elevation.[65]

When Otho learned that Galba had chosen Piso, he began working with disgruntled praetorians to overthrow the emperor. On January 15, Otho joined Galba and some others to participate in a sacrifice. Otho excused himself before the sacrifice could be completed and was greeted by twenty-three praetorians, the only ones who were loyal to him at that moment. He was shocked that so few had come, but the anger at Galba was so great that the rest of the praetorians joined the rebellion when they learned what was happening. So, too, did the men who were left in Nero's old naval legion, as well as a group of auxiliaries from the Balkans that Galba had also alienated. Otho's praetorians secured strategic points in the city and induced Galba to leave the palace, by spreading a false rumor that Otho had been killed. Then they decapitated Galba. Otho, as the new emperor, traveled through the carnage in the Forum and listened as the Senate legitimized his seizure of imperial power.[66]

Galba's death accelerated Rome's descent into a full civil war for the first time in a century. The year 69 became known as the "Year of Four Emperors" because of the speed with which imperial claimants rose and fell. In fact, when Otho overthrew Galba in Rome, news was already on its way to the capital that the legions of Upper and Lower Germany had acclaimed Aulus Vitellius, the new governor Galba had sent to replace Rufus, as emperor on January 2.[67]

After Vitellius rebuffed Otho's proposal to negotiate a way to share imperial power, Otho led the soldiers he had in Italy north to confront Vitellius.[68] The two Roman armies met outside of Cremona, where Vitellius's German legions prevailed after a bloody battle. Otho could have pulled back to defend the Po, but on April 16 he elected to commit suicide rather than persisting in a conflict that would cause the loss of more Roman lives.[69] Suetonius, whose father served under Otho in the war, confirms that these were Otho's final sentiments. "My father," Suetonius wrote, said "that Otho, even when he was a private citizen, so loathed civil strife . . . that he would no longer endanger the lives of such brave men."[70]

Unfortunately, Vitellius was only the third of the four men to rule in 69. In May, Vespasian, the commander of the Roman forces fighting the Jewish war, mounted a powerful challenge backed by the legions of Syria, the best and most experienced troops Rome had at that time. By July, Vespasian had seized Egypt, the source of much of the capital's grain, and he soon gained the loyalty of Roman armies in the Balkans. As winter began, Vitellius realized that his cause was lost. On December 18, Tacitus recounts, he "walked down from the palace dressed in black" and "gave a short speech saying that he was abdicating in the interests of peace and of his country." He tried to leave "the insignia of Empire in the Temple of Concord."[71]

The praetorians, who had too much to lose if a new regime took power, forced Vitellius to return to the palace and mounted a defense of Rome against Vespasian's forces. Tens of thousands were killed, the capital looted, the Temple of Jupiter burned, and Vitellius was slaughtered.[72] When the fighting was over, an exhausted Roman world welcomed Vespasian as their new emperor, and his son, the formidable general Titus, as Caesar and heir apparent. A new dynasty was ready to begin.

PART 3

FROM THE FLAVIANS TO AURELIAN

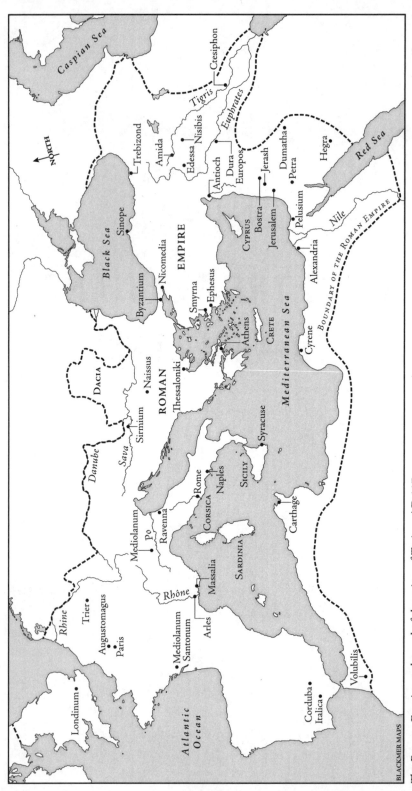

The Roman Empire at the end of the reign of Trajan, AD 117

Chapter 16

The Flavian Empire of
the New Roman Elite

69–96

IT WOULD HAVE seemed inconceivable that someone like Vespasian could become emperor when Vindex revolted in early 68. Vindex himself seems not to have considered the possibility that someone like him, a Gallic aristocrat from Aquitaine, could aspire to imperial power, but Vespasian, born Titus Flavius Vespasianus, had an even more modest family background. Vespasian's grandfather had been the first family member to leave the Sabine town of Reate when he had joined Pompey's army in the civil war against Caesar. Vespasian's father, Titus Flavius Sabinus, had become wealthy investing in tax contracts in the province of Asia during the stable years when Augustus ruled. Vespasian's brother, also named Sabinus, had been the first member of the family to join the Senate. He rose to the office of urban prefect before dying in the fighting just before Vespasian's forces captured Rome.[1]

While his brother rose through the ranks of the Senate, Vespasian distinguished himself as a military officer, culminating in his command in the Judaean War (a position he owed to Nero's tendency to place capable men from undistinguished families in charge of his most powerful armies).[2] In an empire that had only been ruled by men drawn from an inner circle of elite Roman families, an emperor who was the son of an Italian banker from a small Sabine territory did not inspire much reverence.

When Vespasian arrived in the middle of 70, he found a capital deeply in need of rebuilding. The city had not really recovered from the great fire of 64, and Vespasian's own forces had ravaged some of the few areas that had escaped damage during that conflagration. Rome also remained politically damaged. Vespasian's armies had "hunted the vanquished down with relentless hate," until "the streets were choked with bodies, the squares and temples stained with blood." Slaves and clients denounced their senatorial masters and patrons who had repeatedly contorted themselves to cater to the whims of each of the four emperors who had died in the previous year and a half. Unlucky civilians were killed in the chaos caused by "generals who had been keen enough to start the civil war, but [were] incapable of controlling the strife on the day it was won." A spirit of vengeance also had led to the reprisal killings of many figures who were associated with Vitellius's regime or were thought to pose a threat to Vespasian's.[3] Mucianus, the ally that Vespasian had sent ahead to liase with his son Domitian, also confiscated large sums of money from real and imagined opponents so that the new emperor would have full coffers with which to pay bonuses to the soldiers when he arrived.[4] They clearly wanted to avoid the sort of mistakes that had doomed Galba.

Vespasian kept his own hands clean. Instead of a call for retaliation, he sent a large load of grain from Alexandria and a dispatch revoking the "disfranchisement of those who had been condemned by Nero . . . and an immediate end to any ongoing investigations."[5] The new emperor then set to work creating a sense of order amid the destruction, in part by stressing that his authority derived from the same sources as that exercised by the venerated emperors of the past. The text of the legal document through which the Senate defined Vespasian's powers emphasizes that they matched those of "the deified Augustus and Tiberius Julius Caesar Augustus and Tiberius Claudius Caesar Augustus Germanicus."[6] Caligula, Nero, Galba, Otho, and Vitellius were all missing. This would be a regime based on the best of the Julio-Claudian emperors, not the failed sovereigns of the past few years.

Vespasian soon took up the powers of a censor, remade the Senate, and "expelled those who least deserved the honor and enrolled the most distinguished of the Italians and provincials."[7] This move relied on some of the same logic as Claudius's extension of senatorial eligibility to Gallic elites, but the scope of Vespasian's actions far exceeded what Claudius had done a generation earlier. Vespasian needed to replace more senators than Claudius, and, as the victor in a civil war, he needed more loyalists in the body as well. Some of the new senators could come from Italy, but the provinces had many more powerful men eager to trade loyalty for the honor of senatorial membership.

For those older Italians and provincial senators who remained, Vespasian permitted them to engage in a sort of collective amnesia in which the actions of those who had been close to his immediate predecessors were allowed to be forgotten. At one of the first Senate meetings held under the new regime, Helvidius Priscus, the son-in-law of Thrasea Paetus, called for punishment of one of the senators who had accused Paetus. Tacitus says that two senators promptly walked out after telling Priscus that "he was playing king in the presence of the emperor's son," Domitian. Domitian then opened the next Senate meeting with a speech emphasizing "the need to let bygones be bygones and [to] forget the measures forced upon men by the previous regime."[8]

Many senators eagerly embraced Domitian's invitation. Marcus Cluvius Rufus, for example, had traveled to Greece with Nero, governed Spain under Galba, backed Otho after Galba's death, and then transformed into a supporter of Vitellius. Under Vespasian, he wrote an influential history that detailed Neronian vices in a way that allowed him to refashion his public profile to suit the new age.[9] Many other authors writing in the years following Vespasian's victory became similarly obsequious, explaining how the new Flavian dynasty offered a return to sobriety and stability after more than a decade of vicious leadership and military indiscipline. They usually ignored their own part in these past events.

Vespasian also set about reconstructing damaged public spaces in Rome. The most crucial work centered on the ruined Capitoline Temple to Jupiter. Even before Vespasian arrived in Rome, Helvidius Priscus had "proposed that the restoration of the Capitol be shouldered by the state" and run by the Senate.[10] The new emperor was not foolish enough to fall into his trap. Instead of delegating such a symbolically important task to the Senate, Vespasian personally took it on. Vespasian, Cassius Dio wrote, "was himself the first to carry out a load of soil" in order to ensure that he, and not the senators, would receive credit for the rebuilding.[11]

Vespasian repaired other damaged or deteriorated structures in a fashion that made them more beautiful or more functional than they originally had been. When he restored the flow of the Aqua Claudia in the areas of the city where it crossed major roadways, Vespasian erected beautiful marble gateways that replaced the utilitarian brickwork of Claudius's original. Travelers were greeted with a magnificent inscription specifying both the original builder and the problems with his work that Vespasian repaired.[12] In areas where "the city was unsightly from former fires and fallen buildings," Vespasian "allowed anyone to take possession of vacant sites and build upon them, in cases where the owners failed to do so."[13]

Vespasian also embarked on impressive new construction projects appropriate for a new imperial dynasty. The centerpiece was the massive Temple of Peace that sat northeast of the Roman Forum, on land abutting the Forum of Augustus and just below the grounds of Nero's Domus Aurea.[14] This location was perfect, because Vespasian hoped that people visiting the monument would think of how the new emperor compared to those two predecessors. Vespasian's emphasis on peace reminded Romans that he had concluded the civil war, but it also linked him with Augustus's identity as a peacemaker following his own victory in a civil conflict.[15] The contrast with Nero was equally clear. Vespasian paid for the temple's construction with plunder taken from the Jewish War, a conflict that started because of Neronian neglect and concluded with a Vespasianic total victory. Vespasian, said the Jewish historian Josephus, "had the temple adorned with pictures and statues," including the temple treasures from Jerusalem.[16] Whereas Nero kept his artistic treasures hidden away in the imperial palace, Vespasian displayed them openly in a space that the public could visit.

The Domus Aurea presented Vespasian with another challenge. Unlike Galba, Otho, and Vitellius, Vespasian refused to use the palace, knowing this decision would play well with senators and ordinary Romans who believed that Nero had capitalized on their losses to build it.[17] Vespasian, Tacitus wrote, instead "spent most of his time in the Gardens of Sallust," the estate that once belonged to the historian Sallust but became a public park under Claudius, and it was there that he "would receive anyone who desired to see him, not only senators but also ordinary people."[18] Vespasian not only made himself accessible, but he soon decided to transform the underutilized Domus Aurea into a space that all Romans could enjoy. Nero had constructed a vast artificial lake in the valley between the Oppian and Caelian Hills, intending for it to serve as a focal point for the vistas from residential buildings and reception spaces within the complex. Again using funds from his victory in Judaea, Vespasian filled in the lake and began building a massive, centrally located amphitheater there that all Romans could use—the structure that would be called the Flavian Amphitheater when it was finished and that we now call the Colosseum.[19]

A Roman amphitheater represented a more politically palatable way to use Nero's old pleasure grounds than a public park would have. In a park, Romans of all social statures could mingle freely, whereas Roman amphitheaters organized entry and seating in ways that corresponded to social standing in the community. The emperor and empress had a box at the center of the arena. The most important priests and magistrates sat in another box across the arena from the emperor, and members of the Roman Senate sat in a section called the podium that abutted the boxes and enclosed the rest of the arena floor. Roman knights, the next most prestigious social group, took their places in the seats above the senators. Ordinary Roman citizens filled out a large middle section of seating, which in turn was subdivided into blocks reserved for soldiers, married men, and other distinct groups. Noncitizens sat in the upper deck. When it was completed, the Colosseum had eighty numbered entryways, and each spectator got a token indicating which one they were to use to get to their seats. Senators used different gates from regular citizens, walked through different arcades to their seats, and may even have accessed different toilets and drinking fountains.

Despite these rigid divisions, the Roman amphitheater was also a place that spoke to the promise of social mobility. This was a key point for the new empire of Vespasian. The Colosseum created a world in which Vespasian, the man who built it, was the grandson of a man whose seats would have been far away from the action. Many of the new senators sitting on the podium also descended from people who would, at best, have been able to sit in the upper deck. Romans could look at the tiers of seating and picture their own and their descendants' movement across social classes. The Colosseum's open, spatially segregated environment reinforced the rules and opportunities of Rome's intensely stratified society.

While generally popular, Vespasian confronted resistance from two very different quarters. First, he struggled to deal effectively with the challenges posed by outspoken and philosophically inclined senators in Rome. Helvidius Priscus was the most notorious of these, and he became increasingly confrontational and disrespectful as the reign progressed. Helvidius, who "bore a grudge against Vespasian and would not let him alone," insulted the emperor in public, refused to call him by his proper name, and failed to acknowledge that Vespasian was emperor in the edicts he issued while serving as praetor.[20] Although Helvidius claimed to be taking a principled, philosophical stand by "denouncing royalty and praising democracy," Cassius Dio writes that Helvidius was instead engaged in a political performance designed "to bring about a revolution."[21] Vespasian ultimately felt compelled to exile Helvidius from Rome and order his execution. Even the same authors who attacked Tiberius and Nero for actions like this generally accepted that Vespasian had no choice but to do away with the politically toxic senator.[22]

Helvidius Priscus was irritating but easily neutralized. A more vexing problem arose from the popularity that Nero still enjoyed in wide swaths of the Roman world. Around the year 100, the Greek philosopher and sophist Dio Chrysostom commented that "even now everybody wishes he were still alive," because of the late emperor's successes in finding meaningful ways for people outside of Italy to participate in the life of the empire. Greeks so desperately wanted Nero to be their emperor that many who "had been firmly convinced that he was still alive" were tricked by imposters claiming to be Nero.[23]

The first such case happened in 69 during the reign of Otho when a talented singer and harpist who looked like Nero appeared in Greece and collected a small army that he wanted to lead to Rome. The governor of Galatia in Asia Minor captured and executed him. His body was then sent to Rome to prove that Nero was, in fact, dead.[24] Even so, a second fake Nero appeared in the year 80, again in the Greek world. He attracted the support of a member of the Parthian royal family but was blocked before he could cross the frontier.[25] A third Neronian imposter showed up in 88 and attracted both Parthian royal support and the backing of some Roman governors in the east before he, too, was stopped.[26]

This odd affection for phantom Neros pointed to a Greek yearning for substantial and meaningful relationships with emperors that Nero had tried to cultivate. Vespasian's son Domitian seized this opportunity, in large part because, like Claudius two generations earlier, Domitian needed to build a rich, loyal base of support in the Senate to overcome a group of incumbents disenchanted with his leadership.

WHEN DOMITIAN BECAME emperor on September 14 in the year 81, he inherited a massive fiscal mess. The mess had been caused by his predecessor and older brother Titus, who had succeeded their father in the summer of 79 but died of a fever after less than two years in power. The fiscal problem had stemmed from the fact that Titus had made it "his fixed rule not to let anyone go away without hope" of a gift or monetary grant when they petitioned him.[27] This included everyone from humble individuals to the survivors of the volcanic eruption that buried Pompeii.[28] "Most of what Titus did," Cassius Dio wrote, "was not characterized by anything noteworthy," but he did "produce remarkable spectacles in dedicating the Colosseum."[29] These extremely costly games lasted for 100 days and involved gladiatorial combat, mock naval battles (after flooding the arena), and the slaughter of over 9,000 animals.[30] He also distributed gifts to the members of the audience by throwing "little wooden balls inscribed" with the names of prizes that people could receive when they returned the ball.[31] The luckiest recipients went home with objects made of gold, horses, or cattle. Titus wept when the festivities ended—and then he died of a fever the very next day.[32]

Domitian divinized his generous brother, erected an arch in his honor on the Via Sacra, and then set to work trying to pay for his brother's lavish party while fixing an empire that few at the time recognized needed repairs. Whatever he did, however, seemed to pale in comparison to what his brother had achieved. Domitian reigned for more than fifteen years, a term in office that only Augustus and Tiberius had exceeded at that point, but he never managed to endear himself to senators from old Roman noble families. Part of this was generational. Domitian was only twenty-nine when he took power, and despite the efforts of his father, he presided over a Senate filled with men whose careers had begun in the reigns of Nero and Claudius. Many senators whose ancestors had been senators under Augustus or the old Republican nobility thought that their lineage alone made them more worthy of imperial power than a young man born into what had, until very recently, been a middling family.[33]

These sorts of men neither respected Domitian nor understood the goals of many of his policies. Cassius Dio, Tacitus, and Suetonius all claim that Domitian initiated wars when they need not have occurred, and that he celebrated sham triumphs for minor or incomplete victories.[34] In reality, Domitian managed Rome's northern frontier through a system of alliances that maintained a balance of power rather than by engaging in outright conquest. His strategy required a series of grinding wars along the northern frontiers through which a string of modest Roman victories gradually grew into a sustained peace.[35] By the time of his death in 96, Domitian's persistence had worn down many of Rome's German adversaries to such a degree that he was able to withdraw two legions from the Rhine.[36] He was also preparing to embark on a campaign against the three tribes near the Danube that remained hostile to Rome in an attempt to bring similar calm to the empire's Eastern European frontier.

Rather than offering a nuanced appraisal of these sorts of complicated policies, our sources echo the criticism of Domitian's senatorial opponents. Tacitus, Suetonius, Cassius Dio, and others complained that Domitian held games, but they were not as lavish as those given by Titus. Dio even whines that Domitian once put on an overcoat when it was raining and still expected people to stay with him at the games.[37] These same authors note that Domitian regularly distributed money to the populace and paid for banquets for them. They say that he once left 500 tickets for prizes on the seats of senators who attended the games, but that he also illegally confiscated money from senators and raised taxes to offset his spending.[38] In reality, Domitian maintained a healthy budget surplus and was the only Roman emperor ever to increase both the weight and the purity of the denarius.

Most damningly, the authors writing after his death framed Domitian as a tyrant, although some of the evidence they adduce is utterly bizarre. Suetonius, for example, indicts Domitian for reading "nothing except the memoirs and transactions of Tiberius Caesar," and asserts that when Titus died, Domitian "granted him no recognition at all beyond approving his deification."[39] Suetonius not only fails to tell us what honor beyond deification one might wish for, but also does not acknowledge that Domitian erected a large arch to Titus's memory in the Roman Forum. It still stands nearly 2,000 years later as an obvious indictment of Suetonius's credibility.

The portrait of Domitian's supposed tyranny rests most heavily on the contrast between his willingness to execute senators and the refusal of his sainted brother Titus to kill any during his short time in power.[40] While this is true, it is a claim without context. Titus appears not to have killed any senators during his time as emperor, but he killed so many senators during his father's principate that people spoke openly of him being a new Nero at the time of his accession.[41] Suetonius excuses these murders, which included an ex-consul that Titus invited to dinner and then led to execution by walking behind him with a knife pressed into his back, as "conduct through which [Titus] provided for his safety in the future."[42]

Unlike Titus, Domitian faced genuine and sustained opposition from senators. In some cases, he overreacted. There was no great danger that compelled him to execute the son of Helvidius Priscus for writing a play that mocked the emperor's marriage troubles. Nor was there any good reason to kill a senator for writing a biography of Priscus, or to expel philosophers from Rome.[43] Domitian deserves the criticism he received here—though, of course, many of those who criticize Domitian's conduct against these men excuse similar actions by Vespasian.

Other senators posed threats that were both real and deadly. In 87 or 88, the governor of Asia cooperated with one of the false Neros to try to topple Domitian's regime. Domitian had him executed for "plotting revolution"—which he undoubtedly was guilty of doing.[44] Then, in January of 89, the ex-consul Lucius Antonius Saturninus and the two legions under his control collaborated with the German Chatti tribe to try to overthrow Domitian.[45] This was an actual civil war, though one that concluded quickly because of the intervention of troops commanded by the future emperor Trajan. Cassius Dio, however, asserts that Domitian used the revolt as a pretext "to commit a series of murders . . . and it would be impossible to say how many he killed."[46] Despite Dio's exaggerated claim, it is possible to count the number of senators Domitian executed. There were sixteen, in more than fifteen years in power. This was less than the number killed by the Divine Claudius, who reigned for fewer years.[47]

Domitian resembled Claudius in another way too. Like his divinized predecessor, Domitian addressed his problems with the Senate by using his powers as censor to remake its composition. In

85, Domitian assumed the role of perpetual censor and set about steadily diversifying both the Senate and the ranks of officeholders so that people from a much wider range of places could participate in the state at its highest levels.[48] And, not coincidentally, these men, like Claudius's Gallic senators half a century earlier, were more likely to be loyal to the emperor to whom they owed their appointments.

Domitian's actions pushed the Senate to better reflect some of the diversity in the city around it. Rome in the 90s was a fast-changing, disorienting metropolis of 1 million people flooded by immigrants from the provinces who, some Romans felt, had overrun the capital with their strange languages, religions, and cultural practices. Grumpy Romans complained about the groves of old temples becoming marketplaces where Jewish merchants operated, mocked the capital as a Rome of Greeks, and shook their heads at the Syrians who played odd instruments while entertaining crowds at the circus. The most skilled of these immigrants were, however, becoming fixtures of elite society as teachers, artists, and friends to the established Roman elite.[49]

Domitian hoped to catalyze a process through which Rome would become the home city not just of Greek teachers or Syrian musicians but the elite from those regions as well. The massive Roman conquests of the first century BC had sparked immigration from those provinces to the capital, but they had also enabled Roman colonists and carpetbaggers to spread steadily across the empire's new territories. These Romans often intermarried with the local elite and had children who were born into both Roman citizenship and immense inherited wealth in their home regions. As in Gaul, local elites were often the third- or fourth-generation descendants of people who had received Roman citizenship from a general or patron in the second or first century BC.

By the time of Domitian's reign, aristocrats in areas as diverse as Gaul, Spain, Africa, Greece, and Asia Minor had built powerful social and economic networks linking their home regions to the imperial center. This meant that the almost exclusively Italian Roman Senate presided over by Augustus had, by Domitian's accession, become perhaps 15 to 20 percent provincial. The first of these non-Italian senators came from nearby areas in Europe, but, by the 80s, senators from North Africa and the Eastern Mediterranean had emerged too. These provincials were newcomers to the senatorial stage, but as they became accustomed to the political dynamics of the capital, they came to realize that their wealth exceeded that of many of the old Italian elites. They now wanted their influence to rise accordingly.

Domitian recognized these changes as they unfolded and adapted subtly but consciously to take advantage of them. In the first years of his regime, he followed the pattern established by his father and brother of restricting the ordinary consulship—the empire's highest elite honor, whose holders gave their names to the year—primarily to family members.[50] After the year 84, however, the pool of consuls steadily expanded. Domitian appeared roughly every other year as an ordinary consul, but other consuls (both ordinary and otherwise) included imperial counselors such as the future emperor Nerva, establishment senators from historically accomplished families, and, notably, prominent aristocrats from the east.[51]

Domitian's outreach to these non-Italian senatorial elites worked well. They were, in fact, more loyal to him than some Italian governors had been. When the Parthian Empire threatened to invade in support of the false Nero in 88, the eastern-born governors of the frontier provinces of Cappadocia and Syria that Domitian had appointed remained loyal, while the Italian Gaius Vettulenus Civica Cerealis did not. The loyal governors received higher offices (including consulships). Vettulenus was executed. Similarly, the Spaniard Trajan was given an ordinary consulship in 91 after he helped Domitian put down the revolt of Saturninus. This shows that Domitian had in fact arrived at a way to create a more geographically diverse Senate that was both more likely to be loyal to him and more receptive to the sorts of rewards he could provide to them. This seemed to bode well both for his survival and for the long-term stability of his dynasty. But things in imperial Rome sometimes did not turn out as an emperor planned.

Chapter 17

Nerva, Trajan, Hadrian, and the Adoptive Dynasty

96–138

T HE GREATEST STRENGTH and the biggest weakness of the Roman imperial system was its dependence upon the life of a single man. This served the state well at some crucial moments in its history. Caligula's unstable reign had ended without warning when a single individual decided to end the emperor's life. In other cases, though, the sudden murder of an emperor upset a carefully designed and well-planned effort to reform and improve the empire. This is what happened on September 18, 96, when the emperor Domitian was killed.

Domitian's death shocked Rome. He was killed in the middle of the day, four days after marking his sixteenth year in office and a few days before he was to depart for a campaign along the Danube. The city was in the middle of a fourteen-day festival that brought crowds to Rome from the countryside. Domitian had spent the morning adjudicating legal disputes in the new imperial palace atop the Palatine Hill that overlooked the Colosseum before retreating to his private quarters for an afternoon nap. As he entered his chamber, he was set upon by an assassin who knew to remove the emperor's emergency dagger. The defenseless Domitian was killed before his guards could reach him.[1] The man behind the plot, the senator Marcus Cocceius

Nerva, was lurking in the palace waiting for word of the emperor's death. When it came, Nerva worked with allies in the command of the praetorian guards to secure their acquiescence, and then, on the morning of September 19, he summoned the Senate so it could vote to give imperial power to him.

Nerva and his supporters wanted Romans to believe that his coup had brought about the liberation of the empire from Domitian's tyranny, but, outside of a relatively small group of senators, most people did not see things that way.[2] The shocked crowds of people still in the city for the festival, the stunned praetorian guards, and the armies had all liked—or perhaps even loved—Domitian.[3] None of them wanted to trade the capable sovereign of the past fifteen years for an old, sickly, disloyal senatorial placeholder.

Nerva was all these things. At nearly sixty-six, he was the second-oldest man to assume imperial power thus far (trailing only Galba). While Domitian had spent the most time on active military campaigns of any emperor since Augustus, Nerva was so feeble that, we are told by Cassius Dio, "he had to vomit up his food" to eat.[4] Even worse, Nerva made for an odd champion of liberty. A relative of Otho, Nerva had also been a favorite of the emperor Nero, and he may have been responsible for tipping Nero off about the conspiracy to make Piso emperor. He had also served as a close adviser of Domitian for many years. Now he had betrayed his friend and emperor. It would have been hard for many in Rome to imagine a more disreputable new sovereign.

Nerva did what he could to appeal to the traditionalist Roman senators, the one constituency that overwhelmingly welcomed the new regime. In return for a senatorial decree ordering the overthrow of all monuments of Domitian, Nerva canceled the sentences of exile that Domitian had passed on senators, released those awaiting punishment for treason, executed slaves who had informed on their masters, and prohibited anyone from lodging accusations of treason or religious deviance.[5] Then, within the month, Nerva expanded the consular lists that Domitian had already prepared for the next year to include a group of Italian senatorial lions in winter, such as the eighty-four-year-old Lucius Verginius Rufus, the governor of Germany whose soldiers had defeated Vindex nearly thirty years before.[6]

The next few months demonstrated how quickly a poor emperor could spoil the work of a capable predecessor. Nerva squandered the budget surplus that Domitian had amassed by giving cash to soldiers and tax remissions to the wealthy. Then he was compelled to raise funds by melting down gold and silver statues and selling things from the imperial palace.[7] By January 97, Nerva had so little money that he convened a senatorial commission to investigate possible places where expenditures could be cut.[8] Ultimately, the emperor's legal permissiveness and financial extravagance grew so troubling that the consul Fronto told him that, while it was bad to have an emperor who permitted no one to do anything, it was worse to have one who permitted everyone to do everything.[9] The liberty that Nerva claimed to have restored quickly degenerated into an exceedingly expensive near anarchy.[10]

Nerva's hold on power began slipping in the middle of 97. First, there was a comically inept coup attempt by a descendant of Crassus, Caesar and Pompey's colleague in the First Triumvirate. Nerva, having learned about the coup, invited its leader to the imperial box during a public spectacle. Then he handed him a sword and dared him to use it.[11] Crassus shrunk away, and Nerva chose not to punish him. It is unclear, however, whether Nerva hoped this story would signal his mercifulness or Crassus's ineptitude.

Soldiers read it as weakness. Later that year, the new commander of the praetorian guard, who remained loyal to Domitian's memory, incited his men to surround the imperial palace. The guardsmen could have overthrown Nerva just as they had Galba three decades before, but they asked only that Nerva execute the figures responsible for the murder of Domitian, an emperor to whom many of the praetorians remained devoted. Nerva tried to defuse the situation by offering the guards his own neck to cut, but the guards persisted in their demands. Nerva was then compelled to agree to the punishment of the men whose treachery enabled him to take the throne.[12]

Another echo of the chaos following the fall of Rome's first dynasty in 68 came that autumn, when Nerva decided to adopt Trajan, the commander of the legions in Germany, and name him as his successor. This followed a set of secret negotiations to forestall a revolt from the same provinces that had propelled Vitellius to power.[13] "Finding himself held in such contempt" by both senators and soldiers, Nerva "ascended the Capitol" and announced the adoption to the Roman public.[14] Soon afterward, the Senate named Trajan Caesar and designated him as Nerva's successor. Trajan would become the first Roman emperor born outside of Italy.

Nerva's choice represented a careful calculation about how to stabilize a regime that was beginning to look like a less successful version of Galba's. The forty-five-year-old Trajan guaranteed the loyalty of the powerful armies in Germany, but he was also the perfect antidote to the Italy-first approach that Nerva had charted for most of the past year. He had been born in Italica, a Spanish city founded by Scipio Africanus as a place to settle wounded Roman veterans of the Second Punic War. Trajan's own family tree had both Roman and Iberian branches, but by the time of Trajan's birth, the family had sent at least two generations to the Roman Senate. Trajan's father had been consul in 72, and had entered the ranks of Roman patricians following his service under Vespasian in the Jewish War.[15] Trajan himself sat at the center of a network of elites in Spain and Gaul that had produced important senators during the Flavian period. These figures lacked the pedigree of old Italian families like those of Nerva or Crassus, but they were often much wealthier.[16] If Nerva's regime initially pointed to the Italian Roman past, Trajan's offered a chance to reorient the empire toward a Mediterranean future.

Trajan's impact could be seen immediately in the number of Hispano- and Gallo-Romans who served short terms alongside him as consul during the first half of 98, a group quite distinct from the "Italian non-entities" that Nerva preferred.[17] In the first list of consuls appointed by Trajan alone, one sees a return to the regional diversity of the early 90s as Gallic and Spanish senators were joined by prominent colleagues from the Greek East. The more integrated empire Domitian had envisioned was again taking shape.

Nerva died on January 27, 98, a few months after naming Trajan his successor. Trajan was spending the winter in Cologne and learned of Nerva's death from the future emperor Hadrian.[18] Intriguingly, Trajan did not go immediately to Rome. He instead elected to remain along the northern frontier, continuing a tour of Rome's military defenses that would take him from Germany down the Rhine and along the path of the Danube.[19] He did not return to Rome for nearly two years, a period that enabled him to solidify support among the troops while building a distinctive profile for himself outside the bubble of the capital.

Trajan nevertheless made sure that the capital knew he was firmly in command of the empire. He requested that the Senate recognize Nerva as a god and perform the same public rites to commemorate his ascension to heaven that had once been accorded to the emperor Augustus.[20] He also summoned the leaders of the praetorian guard who had rioted under Nerva—and had them executed once they arrived.[21] This made clear to all of the restless figures in the capital that the chaos of Nerva's early reign had ended now that Trajan was in charge.

When Trajan came to Rome for the first time as emperor in the autumn of 99, the event contrasted greatly with the lavish spectacles that had often accompanied Domitian's returns to the capital. As crowds filled the city streets to greet him, Trajan entered on foot, forgoing the triumphal chariots of many of his predecessors. He embraced many of the senators he met, greeted leading equestrians by name without any reminders from his staff, gave the traditional sacrifice at the Palatine, and entered the palace Domitian had built.[22] His staff made sure to spread the word that, when she arrived at the palace, Trajan's wife, Plotina, turned and said to those assembled that she hoped to leave the palace the same sort of woman she was when she first entered it.[23]

Trajan's behavior in 98 and 99 previewed an approach to running the empire that would, broadly speaking, typify the remainder of his nineteen-year reign. This was a new type of imperial regime that included more provincials and permitted Trajan to be away from Rome, in the provinces, for longer than any emperor had been before. Nerva had apparently never left Italy, but Trajan spent long periods of time on campaign beyond the empire's frontiers. Although he was in the capital only intermittently, Trajan did more than any preceding Roman emperor to remake the physical space of the capital. His massive building projects included major improvements to Rome's water infrastructure. He had a new hexagonal basin built in the harbor of Portus, north of Ostia, and constructed a massive Forum and market complex that required extensive excavations of the edges of the Quirinal and Capitoline Hills. The effect of Trajan's markets was so dramatic that, more than 250 years later, the emperor Constantius II could only gape in amazement at "the gigantic complex around him" that "never again would be imitated by mortal men."[24] And Trajan was not shy about advertising his building program on coins, so that Romans who never visited the capital could see images of Trajan's Forum and Trajan's Column, the monumental sculpted column at its center that rose to the height once reached by the hillsides he had removed.[25]

Trajan also initiated programs that benefited Italians outside of Rome. One of the most dramatic steps he took was to forbid the collection of public debts that had been incurred before the beginning of his reign.[26] Trajan also implemented a public welfare program called the Institutio Alimentaria, originally designed by Nerva. Under Trajan, the Alimentaria became an elegant scheme to sustainably stimulate the economies of Italian cities. Once enough people in a city indicated their interest in the program, Trajan issued low-interest loans to the wealthiest figures in the city. They, in turn, invested the money, generating profits that could be used in part to benefit their home city. Meanwhile, their annual interest payments provided funds to support poor local parents and children.[27]

Trajan initially relied upon many of the senators that Nerva and Domitian had favored, but the personnel around him quickly became much more diverse and dynamic. The Spaniard Lucius Licinius Sura, who had helped secure Trajan's adoption by Nerva, remained a close ally of the new emperor, but Trajan also worked closely with Greek elites from the east. He followed Domitian by incorporating some of the wealthiest and most important eastern elites into the Roman senatorial order. Many of them were descended from old Hellenistic royal families. In addition, he arranged consular selections for descendants of the Judaean king Herod the Great and the Seleucid royal family.[28]

The Senate's increasing geographical diversity prompted Trajan to bind these provincial senators closely to Rome's Italian heartland. Sometime around 106, he required all candidates standing for election to senatorial offices to invest one-third of their fortunes in Italian real estate. This law prompted many provincials with interest in a senatorial career to buy Italian property at very high prices. It also meant that many of those who sold Italian properties (at those same inflated prices) could take their profits and invest them in the discounted provincial estates that the new senators had been compelled to sell. The effect, of course, was to accelerate the development of an empire-wide aristocracy that, as Trajan explained, would treat "Rome and Italy as their homeland" while also strengthening the ties that bound the provinces to Rome.[29]

Trajan managed these changing internal dynamics while initiating the conquest of the kingdom of Dacia, a state that occupied what is now roughly the territorial core of modern Romania. Trajan's policy toward Dacia dramatically recalibrated Domitian's approach, which had made it a Roman client kingdom that received an annual subsidy, and had welcomed Roman engineers to improve the kingdom's infrastructure.[30] Although later historians framed this as an unprecedented Roman concession to an enemy, Domitian had seen it as a strategic victory, because it incorporated Dacia into an alliance system that would pacify Rome's Danube frontier. The new roads and bridges that Domitian's engineers had built across Dacian territory were strategic assets, constructed for Roman troops to use during the German campaign that Domitian planned to join before his assassination. These were not signs of Roman weakness. They were a projection of strength.[31]

Trajan saw things very differently. Domitian's conciliation of the Dacian king Decebalus may have made strategic sense, but it did not inspire much pride among Romans. When Domitian's German war reached its conclusion in 99, the Dacian alliance he had forged became effectively useless.[32] But a large, battle-tested Roman army remained based near the Danube, and, in March of 101, Trajan ordered it to cross the Dacian frontier so he could win for himself the glory of sub-jugating the kingdom. Thus began the first of two Dacian wars. The first war ended the following year with a treaty reaffirming Dacia's status as a client kingdom but eliminating the Roman payments and technical exchanges. A second Dacian war, which erupted in 105, fol-lowing a Dacian invasion of Roman territory, ended with the death of the Dacian king Decebalus in 106 and the Roman absorption of most of his territory.

That same year saw Trajan annex the Nabataean kingdom, a desert realm centered on the city of Petra that stretched from Syria to the Red Sea coast of Saudi Arabia and from the Jordanian desert in the east across the Negev and Sinai Peninsula to the Mediterranean Sea.[33] This annexation seems to have been largely peaceful, with the emperor sending legionaries from Syria and Egypt to occupy Petra following the death of the Nabataean king Rabbel II.[34]

The conquests of Arabia and Dacia required the emperor to incorporate people living in two very different polities into the Roman Empire. In Dacia, the warfare effectively destroyed the cit-ies and ruling elites around which political life centered. A Roman governor for Dacia was appointed within a month of the war's con-clusion, and he set about working with Roman forces to fortify the Dacian provincial frontier and improve the roads in the new prov-ince.[35] Roman colonists flooded the new province, populating new Roman towns that, unlike in Gaul or Britain, did not spring up in places that had been prominent in the area's pre-Roman past. Many of the old spaces were abandoned, and Roman Dacia developed around planned cities in new locations. Their leading citizens tended to be Roman transplants.[36]

The situation in Arabia was different. The Roman absorption of the Nabataean kingdom involved very little violence and unfolded in a way that allowed the members of the old Nabataean elite to retain their social positions and property rights. As in Dacia, the assumption of Roman control over Arabia sparked a great deal of new construction, but the new Roman administration worked to preserve Arabia's existing cities. Trajan and Gaius Claudius Severus, the province's first long-term governor, superintended the construction of the Via Nova Traiana linking the Gulf of Aqaba to Syria, as well as an expansion of the northern city of Bostra, the province's new administrative center. The old Nabataean capital of Petra, however, was not ignored. Trajan named it the "metropolis of Arabia" and gave it a higher notional status than Bostra. A triumphal arch to Trajan was erected in the city and dedicated in 114. The arch's Greek inscription celebrated both the emperor and the city's status as a metropolis.[37]

The rules governing life in the new province did change significantly, however. Trajan "compelled [Arabia] to obey [Roman] laws" and shift to the Roman legal system, reports the fourth-century historian Ammianus Marcellinus.[38] His account is confirmed by a remarkable set of thirty-six documents archived in 132 by a Jewish woman named Babatha. They show that she conducted her business affairs according to Nabataean law until the conquest, and then, by the 110s, had started operating in accordance with Roman law.[39] This made the province of Arabia exceptional. Most Roman subjects who did not have Roman citizenship continued to conduct their economic and civic affairs under either the local law of their home region or according to the terms of a legal settlement made at the time of Rome's absorption of their territory.[40] But Trajan imagined a future where Roman law would bind everyone in the empire, not just Roman citizens, and found it more efficient to just make the transition immediately in Arabia.

The first decade of Trajan's reign was a glorious time of Roman economic, political, and territorial expansion. However, in the last few years of his life, the ambitious emperor undertook an extensive, expensive, and flawed military campaign against the Parthians in Mesopotamia. The war began when Trajan ordered 80,000 troops across the Armenian frontier in 114. They quickly took over the Armenian kingdom and absorbed many of the smaller kingdoms occupying the highlands of what is now eastern Turkey and northern Iraq. In 116, Trajan advanced into the cities and farmlands situated between the Tigris and Euphrates Rivers, occupying the famous city of Babylon and the Parthian capital of Ctesiphon. Trajan was even able to erect a statue of himself beside the Persian Gulf. The Roman Empire would never extend any farther east and, to commemorate this, the Roman Senate voted to give Trajan the honorary title Parthicus. Trajan himself celebrated the capture of Ctesiphon by issuing a gold coin that displayed two Parthian captives seated beneath a victory trophy. It carried the legend "PARTHIA CAPTA."[41]

Trajan's celebration proved extremely premature. Roman forces had swiftly occupied a great deal of territory, but the Parthians had not been defeated. They had instead withdrawn from the lowlands of Mesopotamia into the Zagros Mountains, where they began to organize an insurgency that would make Trajan's new conquests ungovernable. Soon, Parthian-sponsored rebellions erupted in cities all along the Tigris and Euphrates. Although Roman armies had recaptured nearly all of the rebellious cities by early 117, the revolts persuaded Trajan to return authority in Armenia to a pro-Roman Armenian king and to place a Roman-backed Parthian pretender on the throne in Ctesiphon. Trajan planned to return to campaign more in Mesopotamia, but he suffered a stroke and died in August 117.

TRAJAN HAD NO son, and, unlike Nerva, he had designated no successor. His wife, Plotina, therefore arranged for Hadrian, another native of Italica in Spain, whose father was Trajan's first cousin, to take power. Hadrian, whose full name was Publius Aelius Hadrianus, was at that moment governing Syria and commanding a large army tasked with stamping out a Jewish revolt that had begun in Libya, and had briefly seized Alexandria. In an account that echoes the accession of Servius Tullius and Tiberius, Cassius Dio wrote that "the death of Trajan was concealed for several days in order that Hadrian's adoption might be announced first." The proof, Dio continued, was in the fact that the letters to the Senate about the adoption and succession "were signed, not by [Trajan], but by Plotina—although she had not done this in any previous instance."[42]

Maybe so, but Hadrian's adoption and succession highlighted a fundamental shift in how imperial power was conveyed. Both Nerva and Trajan had adopted mature, accomplished successors who had proven themselves to be capable of handling imperial power. Neither emperor had done this completely of their own free will, but Rome had now arrived at a way to avoid the catastrophes that an adolescent, incompetent, or ill-prepared emperor could cause.

Hadrian began making difficult and controversial decisions almost immediately. The Mesopotamian war was his first challenge. Roman forces had won nearly every major engagement in the campaign, but Rome's large and capable army found it difficult to respond to local insurrections and attacks by a Parthian adversary able to melt back into mountainous regions where the Romans dared not follow them. Hadrian then "relinquished all of the conquests across the Euphrates and Tigris Rivers," according to a later account, "because . . . those areas that [could not] be defended, should be declared liberated." He then gave the territory to the allied governments Rome had just installed.[43]

The Roman withdrawal happened very quickly. Hadrian officially took power on August 11, and Roman forces vacated Dura Europos, one of the bases on the Euphrates farthest to the west, on September 30. Once Roman troops departed, the ally that Trajan installed as Parthian king in Ctesiphon saw his regime collapse. "Thus it was," Cassius Dio wrote, "that the Romans, in conquering Armenia, most of Mesopotamia, and the Parthians, had undergone severe hardships and dangers for nothing."[44]

Hadrian did not apologize for withdrawing from the lands across the Euphrates. He instead claimed to be "reinstituting the approach of the earlier emperors" before Trajan and "devoting himself to actions that maintained peace across the empire."[45] He even considered retreating from Dacia, but ultimately he decided not to, because "many Roman citizens would be betrayed to barbarians." These were citizens whom "Trajan had transferred . . . to populate the country and its cities after his Dacian victory."[46] Without saying it openly, Hadrian wanted Rome to return to the policies of Domitian, in which it no longer fought wars of expansion but instead focused on maintaining a robust defense of the imperial core and improving conditions within the empire.

Hadrian spent much of his reign traveling across the empire to personally inspect Rome's lands and soldiers. When he visited the armies, he took credit for rebuilding Roman military discipline. When he visited cities, he repaired decrepit buildings, modernized infrastructure and expanded cities across three continents, including a huge extension of Italica, his Spanish hometown.[47]

Hadrian's interactions with the Greek world were particularly notable. If his foreign policy silently followed a model set up by Domitian, his attitude toward Greek cities and culture offered a more mature and nuanced version of the outreach Nero had tried more than half a century before. Hadrian showed much more skill, patience, and genuine understanding of the Greek world than Nero ever did. Whereas Nero wanted to appeal to Greeks by doing historically Greek things in large public settings like the Olympic Games, Hadrian focused on building ties to contemporary Greek cultural leaders. The early second century AD saw the increasing public prominence of a form of competitive Greek rhetorical performance that would later be called the Second Sophistic.[48] Hadrian was the first Roman emperor to involve himself deeply in the unique personal and political dynamics the movement created.

Although the empire's main sophistic centers were the old Greek cities along the Aegean coast, sophists who led this movement came from around the Roman Empire. The best ones filled large venues with thousands of paying customers eager to hear them declaim about moral or historical themes. Like a modern rapper, a famous sophist distinguished himself with a unique cadence and diction that made him instantly recognizable to an aficionado. Not only did they sound like rappers, but they were the equivalent of high-brow rock stars. In fact, the Odeon of Herodes Atticus in Athens, which was built for sophistic performances at around this time, has more recently hosted acts like Sting, Elton John, and the Foo Fighters.

The best sophists knew how to develop a public image that transcended their speaking talents. The third-century sophist Philostratus describes his intellectual ancestor Favorinus, who came from the Gallic city of Arles, as someone "born two gendered and a hermaphrodite." "When he grew older," Philostratus continued, "he had no beard and his voice was high pitched, thin, and shrill."[49] Favorinus, however, understood that this distinctive identity could be lucrative for a performer who embraced it. During his colorful career, he escaped a lawsuit that charged him with adultery as well as a conflict with Hadrian, turning these controversies into things that enhanced his personal brand. He often repeated the claim that he was utterly unique, because, "although he was a Gaul, he lived as a Greek; although a eunuch, he was tried as an adulterer; although he quarreled with an emperor, he was still alive." Favorinus's "learned and pleasing speaking style," his distinctive persona, and his unique reputation for escaping punishment for outlandish misdeeds made him such a sensation that "interest in his speeches in Rome was so universal that people in the audience who did not understand Greek still shared in the pleasure he gave."[50]

The story of Favorinus's quarrel with Hadrian served both parties. While Favorinus could boast about escaping punishment from an emperor, Philostratus wrote that the argument "must really be seen as a credit to Hadrian because, although he was emperor, he disagreed as an equal with one whom it was in his power to put to death." This showed Hadrian to be "a ruler who . . . controls his anger" and "kept it in check by reason."[51] It also telegraphed to Greeks that Hadrian understood how to model his own behavior toward Greeks on the values that Greeks felt a just sovereign should embody. Both emperor and subject benefited.

Sophists offered Hadrian another sort of valuable link to his Greek subjects. Unlike Nero's chariot drivers and actors, the sophists with whom Hadrian interacted were high-status individuals who enjoyed Roman citizenship as well as citizenship in their home cities. Hadrian saw in these rich and powerful sophists a wonderful way to build a multifaceted partnership with their communities that deepened the links between the Roman imperial enterprise and the cultural and political leaders of the Greek world. One beneficiary was Marcus Antonius Polemo, the grandson of a Roman client king of Pontus and a descendant of Marc Antony, to whom Hadrian granted membership in the famous Alexandrian Museum and a grant of 250,000 denarii.[52]

Athens, the intellectual and cultural epicenter of the Second Sophistic, stood out as the jewel of Hadrian's Hellenic outreach. The emperor was an honorary Athenian citizen and even served as an Athenian archon, the chief magistrate in the city, in 112. He was later initiated into the Eleusinian Mysteries and rebuilt and modernized much of the city infrastructure. This included the construction of a large library with halls for sophistic performances near the foot of the Acropolis, the extension of modern water lines and other infrastructure east of the old city's core, and the construction of a large Roman bath. The ceremonial centerpiece of his work came when he completed the Temple of Olympian Zeus, a massive construction project that had been initiated by the Athenian tyrant Peisistratus in the sixth century BC. Polemo was invited to give a speech at the dedication.[53] Hadrian then built a monumental arch that set off his new and improved Athens from the old city.

These actions endeared Hadrian to Greeks in a fashion unlike anything previous emperors had achieved, but Athens was not the only city in the Eastern Mediterranean that Hadrian refurbished. He spent substantial sums on Jerusalem and the Jordanian city of Jerash as well. The city restorations that Hadrian undertook had something of a uniform plan. Just like Athens, Jerash and Jerusalem both were given new, Hadrianic quarters marked off by a sort of triumphal arch. In Jerash and Jerusalem, the arch even seems to have had the same dimensions and basic architectural plans.

This sort of attention seems to have been fine for Jerash, but it was a real problem in Jerusalem. The latter had not recovered from its brutal sack by Titus in 70, and a significant portion of what had been its southwestern core was now occupied by the 10th Legion's permanent military camp. Although Jerusalem could benefit from Hadrian's largess, Jews in the city and surrounding province did not appreciate the conditions that the emperor attached to his rebuilding program. Hadrian reconstructed the northern parts of the city along a Roman plan and renamed it Aelia Capitolina, a designation that blended his family name, Aelius, with the title of the god Jupiter. There are also suggestions of a Temple to Jupiter built near the site of the old, destroyed Jewish Temple.[54]

These provocations proved too much. Judaea revolted in 132 and Hadrian was forced to reassign Sextus Julius Severus, one of his best generals, from campaigning in Britain to deal with the situation in Judaea. His armies put the revolt down with such brutality that the historian Cassius Dio records 580,000 Jews dying, as well as the destruction of 985 Jewish villages, by the time the war ended in 135. Jews were then barred from entering Aelia Capitolina. "Nearly the whole of Judaea," Dio wrote, "was left desolate . . . and many Romans also perished in this war," a tragedy that Hadrian acknowledged in his message to the Senate at the war's conclusion.[55]

Many others also paid for their resistance to Hadrian's attempt to catalyze a deeper connection between Rome and its diverse subjects. The energetic emperor had little patience for senators, generals, or provincials who tried to slow or block his plans. Even his own advisers sometimes faced punishment when they stood in his way. Not only did the Mesopotamian withdrawal cause Hadrian to execute some of Trajan's most trusted advisers shortly after taking power, but he also purged some of his own associates during the last years of his life. Hadrian was even rumored to have ordered the murder of a famous architect who once mocked the pumpkin-shaped architectural domes that the emperor liked to include in his construction projects. By the end of his life, Romans had become so tired of the emperor that, according to Dio, "the people hated him despite the excellent things he had accomplished."[56]

This is remarkable because, to a modern eye, Hadrian's efforts look like things we would imagine to be popular and relatively painless. Hadrian withdrew from a war that Rome could not win by claiming he was returning to an established Roman policy of stable frontiers. He promised to redirect the resources that came from fighting foreign wars to improving conditions within imperial boundaries for everyone—and he largely delivered on these promises.

Hadrian, however, did not grasp that radical changes can be disorienting to people. This was especially true of Roman senators who thrived under an older system where Italy extracted wealth from its provinces and oppressed their residents. Hadrian was pursuing a different sort of Roman Empire where the emperor acknowledged the power, status, and culture of both his Italian and his non-Italian subjects. The city of Rome already functioned like this in the second century. Hadrian correctly understood that the empire again needed to follow the path of its capital.

Chapter 18

Pius and Marcus

138–180

HADRIAN SPENT HIS last years unable to travel, miserable, and stuck in Italy as his health declined. His wife, Sabina, died in 136. Their marriage had been childless, and Hadrian, who had begun to suffer from bleeding problems that caused extremely painful swelling in his body, feared leaving the empire without a recognized successor. His first choice, Lucius Ceionius Commodus Verus, was one of the consuls for 136 and had previously served effectively as a governor in Pannonia. When Hadrian announced his adoption, the emperor in waiting changed his name to Lucius Aelius Verus Caesar.[1] He was then awarded a consulship for 137, and coins were issued celebrating him as Hadrian's successor.[2]

The choice of a relatively inexperienced imperial successor prompted the usual griping from senators who felt they should have been selected instead. Hadrian handled the matter poorly and ordered the execution of his brother-in-law when he complained.[3] The situation deteriorated further as it became clear that Aelius's health was even more precarious than Hadrian's. Aelius "could not even make a speech in the Senate thanking Hadrian for his adoption," said one account, and he died in January 138 of a hemorrhage.[4]

Hadrian was himself very ill and needed to name another successor who "was noble, mild, tractable, prudent, [and] neither young enough to do anything reckless nor old enough to neglect anything." He gathered several leading middle-aged senators together and told them he was now choosing Titus Aurelius Fulvus Boionius Arrius Antoninus as his new successor, a senator from a family that originated in southern Gaul who would come to be known as Antoninus Pius. This choice prompted another round of senatorial discontent. As a result, Hadrian had to deprive the urban prefect in Rome of his position in order to prevent a coup attempt.[5]

Hadrian added an intriguing condition to Antoninus's adoption. Because Antoninus had no sons, Hadrian required him to agree to designate two successors of his own: Lucius Verus, the son of the recently deceased Aelius, and Marcus Annius Verus, Antoninus's nephew, whom we now know as Marcus Aurelius.[6] Conditions like this were routinely ignored in the Julio-Claudian period, but Antoninus upheld his promise to Hadrian and married his daughter Faustina to Marcus Aurelius to secure the young man's place in the imperial succession. In due time, Marcus would then betroth Lucilla, one of the daughters he had with Faustina, to Lucius Verus.

This was all in the future, however. Hadrian's final illness became a brutal and painful ordeal that slowly killed the emperor over the first few months of 138. He "often would ask for poison or a sword," according to Cassius Dio, but his terrified associates refused to help him, even when he "drew a colored line around a spot beneath his nipple . . . in order that he might there be struck by a fatal blow and die painlessly."[7] When Antoninus learned of this, according to another chronicler, he and the leading civic and military officials in Rome went to Hadrian and told him to "endure with fortitude the hard necessity of illness," because, if he did not, it would imperil both Antoninus's succession and his life. The emperor-in-waiting would be "no better than a parricide if he, an adopted son, allowed Hadrian to be killed."[8]

Although Antoninus's words may seem insensitive, he was right to be concerned about the implications if people believed Hadrian had died of anything other than natural causes. Augustus, Tiberius, and Titus had died of illnesses, but rumors still circulated that their

successors had sped their demise. Hadrian remained wildly popular in many parts of the empire and with the army, segments of
the Roman world that Antoninus had no interest in irritating. His
very public statement that Hadrian must endure until the end was a
clear-eyed assessment of what was necessary for the political stability
of the Roman state. It was also a powerful inoculation against any
suspicion that he had conspired against his adopted father.

As his condition worsened, Hadrian left Rome for the seaside
town of Baiae and entrusted the daily government of the empire to
Antoninus. He died on July 10. Antoninus then set to work doing
what he believed was required of a dutiful son and successor.

Convincing a reluctant Senate to divinize Hadrian proved his
most challenging initial task. Many senators were angry over the
executions that had tainted Hadrian's last years. But the fight over
Hadrian's legacy also suggested how Antoninus would interact with
the Senate. Antoninus did not come to power in an exceptionally
strong position, yet he brilliantly navigated the situation. Unlike
Caligula, who had let the matter of Tiberius's divinization drop when
the senators complained, Antoninus refused to budge when senators
balked at his advocacy for Hadrian. According to the account of Cassius Dio, he instead told the Senate, "Well, then, I will not govern you
either, if Hadrian has been repudiated and made a public enemy. If
that is the case, you will of course have to annul all his acts, of which
my adoption was one." No senator was willing to plunge the empire
into chaos over the issue. "Through respect for [Antoninus] and a fear
of the soldiers, the Senate then bestowed honors on Hadrian."[9]

Antoninus also understood that he needed to give the Senate something in exchange for this victory. When the senators and
others who had been accused of conspiring against his succession
were brought before him, Antoninus "punished no one but said:
'I must not begin my career as your leader with such actions," and
released the accused. It was at this time that grateful senators voted
to grant Antoninus the title "Pius." The name, which meant "dutiful"
or "pious," was in recognition of both his filial devotion to Hadrian
and his pardoning of those accused of conspiring against him.[10]

Sophists and provincials shared the senators' affection for the new emperor. In AD 144, around the time that Antoninus Pius dedicated the massive Temple of Venus and Rome that overlooked the Colosseum, a twenty-seven-year-old rhetorician named Aelius Aristides, the rising star of the sophistic generation after Favorinus and Polemo, delivered a remarkable oration in Rome.[11] Aristides began his speech with praise of the wonders of the city of Rome itself. It was massive, had tall and beautiful buildings, and lots of commerce from around the world passing through its port.[12] But Aristides's oration soon took a surprising turn as the praise he offered to the city of Rome transformed into a celebration of the empire the city had built.

Rome, Aristides proclaimed, had created a state that, "alone of all who have ever gained an empire, rules over men who are free." It did not simply tie the world together with improved infrastructure and military power, but "made citizenship expansion a worthy goal and caused the label 'Roman' to mark . . . a common nationality." This meant that Rome had established "a free Republic for the community of the whole world" in which all people prosper "like members of a single family."[13]

But Aristides did not believe that all who lived in the empire should share this prosperity equally. Rome wisely had "divided all . . . into two groups" and "added to [its] citizen body . . . the better part of the world's talent, courage, and leadership." Those who were less talented, courageous, or dynamic, however, Rome had "recognized as a group under [its] power." The best people were citizens, the rest were subjects, with "each man given the post appropriate to him based . . . on his deeds" and qualifications. As a result, Aristides claimed, "the present regime suits and serves both rich and poor" in the fashion most appropriate to their talents.[14]

Antoninus Pius himself encouraged Romans to see his empire as a place that drew upon the talents of its best and worthiest citizens, regardless of their origins. Part of his genius grew out of his unique ability to serve as a mirror that reflected the ideals of others. He shunned the spotlight and sought to be known for his upright character rather than ostentatious displays of wealth and power.[15] Unlike

Hadrian, who relished traveling around the empire, Pius never left Italy as emperor. Within Italy, "he reduced imperial pomp to the utmost simplicity and gained the greatest respect because of this." He was also intensely devoted to his administrators. "He removed none of the men he had inherited from Hadrian" and was "so loyal and steadfast that he retained good men in government" for far longer than was customary.[16]

Pius took particular care to maintain infrastructure. He organized repairs to the Colosseum and paid for the construction of new port facilities, lighthouses, aqueducts, and city gates in towns across the empire. One of the most common coins he issued advertised his restoration of the Temple of Augustus in Rome. Infrastructure work particularly appealed to this modest emperor because it was collaborative. Pius "helped many communities to erect new buildings and restore the old ones" by partnering with their leading citizens. He even "gave financial aid to magistrates and senators" so that they could "perform public works" in their hometowns. His "contempt for the bubble of fame" meant that he readily shared credit for these projects with as many people as would collaborate with him on them.[17]

The reign was not without problems. The emperor faced at least two attempted usurpations, as well as a war that disrupted Red Sea trade, but his calm response to these issues made most Romans even more enthusiastic about the direction of the empire. Aristides concluded his *Roman Oration* by saying that Pius was a "great governor who, like a champion in the games, clearly excels his own ancestors. . . . One would say that justice and law are, in truth, whatever he decrees."[18] Marcus Aurelius later modeled his own reign on Antoninus Pius, telling himself continually to "Do all things as a disciple of Pius."[19]

For Marcus, as he wrote in his *Meditations*, this meant being "always ready to hear suggestions for the common good" and "having a strong determination to give everyone the attention he was due," even if that meant "patiently enduring their criticism." When someone made a particularly good argument in his presence, Pius had "always [been] ready to acknowledge their eloquence or knowledge without any jealousy." He remained, until the end of his life, "a man who looked to what needed to be done and not to the credit he could gain by doing it."[20]

MARCUS THOUGHT MUCH more deeply and systematically than Pius had about how to rule. While he found his predecessor's leadership inspiring, he also sought a deeper, more refined set of principles through which to govern his people and his own life. This search led the emperor to Greek intellectual traditions. Hadrian and Pius had recognized the cultural authority of Greek sophists and philosophers and cooperated with them. Marcus personally joined their world.

Marcus figures prominently in sources discussing the sophists of the late second century as a person whose interactions with these Greek intellectuals and performers conferred a sort of unmatched prestige. Philostratus, the chronicler of so much of what we know about the sophists' careers, recorded how Marcus enrolled as a student under one teacher, attended the lectures of another, and proposed themes for a rhetorical competition won by a third.[21] He appointed a sophist named Alexander (who had the delightful nickname "the Clay Plato," because of his "godlike appearance") as a secretary, and Alexander helped him draft eloquent Greek-language official communications.[22] He endowed a set of five professorships in Athens—one each in rhetoric, Epicurean philosophy, Platonism, Aristotelianism, and Stoicism. He personally selected the sophist Theodotus to serve as the inaugural holder of the chair in rhetoric, and he entrusted the selection of the chairs in philosophy to Herodes Atticus, an Athenian sophist who had also served as Roman consul.[23]

Like Pius, Marcus made occasional displays of deference to prominent sophists that telegraphed his respect for them and the cultural traditions they transmitted. One of the most celebrated such incidents came when Aelius Aristides used an innovative literary piece, called the *Monody on the Destruction of Smyrna*, to beg Marcus to pay for Smyrna to be rebuilt after a catastrophic earthquake. Before Aristides's speech, monodies were poetic laments offered publicly following the death of either a prominent figure or someone who died too young. Aristides took the power of a poetic lament, channeled it into an emotionally striking piece of prose, and used it to persuade Marcus Aurelius to help Smyrna rise from its ruins.[24] Marcus was so moved by the work that he immediately released funds for the city's rebuilding.[25]

Not all cases involving Greek sophists could be resolved so easily. In 171, Marcus was forced to step in and judge a conflict involving three of the empire's wealthiest and most prominent senators. The dispute centered on Athenian complaints about the conduct of Herodes Atticus. Herodes was Athens's biggest civic benefactor, but many Athenians disliked him intensely after he deducted debts they owed him from a monetary bequest his father had made to all Athenian citizens.[26] No Roman official was sufficiently powerful or motivated to respond to Athenian anger at Herodes until the two brothers Sextus Quintilius Condianus and Sextus Quintilius Valerius Maximus came into office.[27]

The Quintilii were formidable adversaries. They had a history of animosity toward Herodes, who had once mocked them in front of Marcus Aurelius. The emperor was not surprised when the brothers forwarded a complaint about the "tyranny" of Herodes that they had received from the Athenian city assembly. When Herodes was summoned to defend himself, he uncharacteristically "launched into invectives against the emperor." Marcus responded masterfully. He decided to overlook the breach in decorum, but agreed to an Athenian proposal that banned Herodes from entering the city limits. Herodes was punished, but the punishment displayed both Marcus's forgiveness of personal slights and his deference to decisions made locally by civic and imperial magistrates. "Thus," Philostratus said, "did Marcus conduct this affair in the manner of a philosopher."[28]

Marcus's embrace of Greek philosophy was no pose. Stoic philosophy guided his approach to ruling the empire and managing his own life to such a degree that he wrote about its effect in his *Meditations*. This remarkable text blends philosophical contemplation with musings about how a ruler could apply Greek philosophy to make his state better and his own life bearable. In a remarkable testament to the second-century historical moment, the Roman emperor wrote the *Meditations* in Greek. Rome had come a long way since the time of Cato the Elder, who had sought to expel Greek philosophers from the city because he believed they would corrupt proper Roman virtues.

The *Meditations* are such a compelling read because they allude to the profound personal and emotional toll that ruling the empire took on Marcus. From 161 until 169, Marcus ruled alongside his co-emperor Lucius Verus, the son of Aelius. The two men did not get along particularly well, but they gave the impression that they ruled together harmoniously until Verus died of an illness early in 169. It is not entirely clear what felled the thirty-three-year-old emperor, but that year roughly coincided with the peak of the first-ever smallpox epidemic in the Roman world. The disease emerged in 166 and probably traveled westward from Parthia along with Verus's returning army. The Roman world was full of infectious diseases, but smallpox was something different. It produced horrible black poxes that covered a victim's skin as well as the internal surfaces of the body. The afflicted person endured fevers, excruciating pain, and other ghastly symptoms, including week-long diarrhea that turned from red to black as the blood oozing from the poxes of the digestive tract clotted.[29]

The scale of the epidemic shocked Romans even more than the symptoms. As many as 7.5 million of the 75 million people living in the empire died during that first outbreak.[30] This caused severe disruptions to nearly everything Romans did. The army could not fight, city councils could not meet, community organizations collapsed, local services stopped working as the magistrates responsible for them died, and the deaths of farmers left fields fallow. Even the people who survived the plague emerged physically and emotionally scarred. Aelius Aristides believed that he survived the plague only because a young boy in his city died instead.[31] As cities filled with plague victims and traumatized survivors, they sent increasingly desperate embassies to shrines of Apollo, who was thought to be the god of plagues and cures, among his other roles. They erected statues to the god and posted oracular verses above their doorways to attempt to ward off the pestilence.[32] Most of the advice they received failed. Instead, "like some beast," a contemporary wrote, the plague "destroyed not just a few people but rampaged across whole cities and destroyed them."[33]

Marcus Aurelius responded to these losses with the calm deliberation of a Stoic philosopher. He could not control the plague, but he did have the capacity to guide the Roman state and its people through the many overlapping crises the pandemic caused. Smallpox had devastated the legions, so Marcus repopulated them with slaves and gladiators who could be freed and trained to fight.[34] He invited German immigrants to cross the border and settle in Roman territory, so that they could work the farms that smallpox had emptied. Cities were permitted to rebuild their city councils by including anyone able to serve, even the sons of freed slaves.[35]

Marcus firmly believed that Romans ought to respond to the crisis by mobilizing everyone who could help in whatever capacity they could be most helpful. Not only did he encourage Romans to work together to help the empire survive, but he also recognized the need to acknowledge the positive contributions his fellow citizens had made. "So long as a person did anything good," Cassius Dio wrote, Marcus "would praise him and use him for the service in which he excelled, but to his other conduct he paid no attention." If someone failed to do something Marcus asked, he did not attack them. This was true even if, like Herodes Atticus, they acted aggressively toward the emperor: "He himself refrained from doing anything offensive . . . and he tolerated the offences of the others, neither investigating nor punishing them." This kind of leadership created a common esprit de corps among Romans that made Dio "admire [Marcus] all the more": "Amid unusual and extraordinary difficulties, he both survived himself and preserved the empire."[36]

Dio believed that Marcus "ruled better than any others who had ever been in any position of power."[37] But his successes as a ruler took an immense personal toll. Rome's most philosophical emperor spent the majority of his reign on campaign, fighting wars along Rome's northern frontiers. His mind remained sharp, but his body deteriorated, until the emperor became dependent on an opium-infused tonic that dulled his physical pain. Tragedy also stalked his family. Faustina gave birth to at least fourteen children, nine boys and five girls, but most of them died before reaching adulthood. This included eight of the nine sons; among the boys, only the future emperor Commodus lived past the age of nine.

Personal betrayal compounded these family tragedies. In 175, Marcus's friend Gaius Avidius Cassius, who was serving as governor of his native Syria, rebelled following a rumor that Marcus was near death.[38] The revolt was suppressed in a few months, but Marcus "did not exult and was not elated. He grieved."[39] Then Marcus's wife, Faustina, died while accompanying him on a trip to the east intended to mend relationships with people who may have supported the revolt.

The last few years of Marcus's reign saw Rome run by a physically exhausted, prematurely aged emperor. He was determined to serve Rome for as long as his body held out, but he also understood the danger of leaving the state in the hands of a frail sovereign who had not appointed a successor. He decided to break with the pattern established by his four most recent predecessors. Unlike Nerva, Trajan, Hadrian, and Pius, Marcus did have a son of his own. Commodus had been born in 161 while Marcus was serving as emperor. He had outlived all his male siblings, and he had grown up in the public eye. As the child of Marcus and Faustina, Commodus was the son of one emperor and the grandson of that emperor's predecessor, Antoninus Pius.[40] No Roman had ever been more clearly marked for imperial power from birth.

Marcus spent the last years of his life preparing Commodus to take power. In 177, he had Commodus appointed co-emperor. He then arranged for Commodus to accompany him on campaign and celebrated a joint triumph with his son.[41] Imperial propaganda marked the bond between father and son by crafting official images that made them appear almost identical.[42] It was no surprise that the eighteen-year-old succeeded Marcus when he died in March of

180 at the age of fifty-eight. Few in Rome would have been alarmed by this at the time, but the replacement of the philosophical Marcus with Commodus would later be seen as a huge shift in the fortunes of the empire. Cassius Dio was serving in the Roman Senate in 180, and he understood that the loss of the steady and stable leadership that second-century Romans had taken for granted made Rome's challenges even more difficult to bear. When Marcus passed, Dio wrote, "our history now descends from a kingdom of gold to one of iron and rust, as did the affairs of the Romans."[43]

Chapter 19

Commodus, Septimius Severus, and the Age of Rust

180–211

THE FORTY-TWO YEARS separating the accession of Antoninus Pius and the death of Marcus Aurelius represented one of the most stable periods in Roman imperial history. Not since the reigns of Augustus and Tiberius had Rome experienced a longer period of time with so few changes in who held power over the empire. But the Age of Rust that Cassius Dio said dawned after Marcus's death proved to be as politically unsettled as the mid-second century was calm.

No one imagined such an outcome when Marcus died in 180. His successor, Commodus, was the first male child born to a ruling emperor who lived to adulthood.[1] This made him a beloved and, to some degree, even cherished figure as the news of so many deaths of children born to Marcus and Faustina regularly hit Romans. It was rare for natural-born sons to succeed their fathers. The only one to do so to that point, the emperor Titus in 79, was already grown when his father Vespasian took power. Marcus did his best to prepare his son for office, so that Commodus's awareness of how to rule might offset some of the errors immaturity might otherwise cause. He closely supervised his son's education and brought him along on a campaign against the Germans in 172. Although Commodus fell ill and had to leave that campaign early, he still received the title Germanicus.[2]

All of this training set the stage for Marcus to appoint Commodus co-emperor in November 176, when the boy was sixteen years old, but Marcus did not live long enough to fully prepare his son for the job.[3] He died when Commodus was only nineteen, leaving him partially trained for a position that many emperors had come to see as a sort of life sentence of inescapable public labor. In the midst of his final illness, the contemporary historian Herodian wrote, Marcus urged his friends to "serve as guides [for Commodus] in the tempest and storm of life" so that they could be "many fathers" to him in his absence. If they continued providing the sort of guidance Marcus had offered, he believed they would "provide [them]selves and everyone else with an excellent emperor."[4]

This sounded wonderful, but clear danger signs emerged as Commodus's reign began. Cassius Dio writes that Commodus was "as guileless as any man who ever lived," trusting people completely without suspecting their motivations.[5] This was fine when he was surrounded by the able advisers his father left him, but, even then, there were hints of problems to come. Dio was in the Senate on the day that Commodus gave his first speech to the body as emperor. It was, Dio reports, a mediocre performance in which "he uttered a lot of trivialities and, among the various stories he told in his own praise, was one where he had saved the life of his father who had fallen into a swamp."[6]

The Senate's lukewarm response to the new emperor foreshadowed a more serious issue. Commodus's older sister Lucilla, the widow of Lucius Verus, resented her younger brother's power. After Verus's death, Marcus had compelled her to marry a prominent Syrian senator, who was much older than her, named Tiberius Claudius Pompeianus. Marcus had desperately wanted to cement his ties to the senator, though Lucilla and her mother had both objected that the match would diminish Lucilla's status as a former empress.[7]

Marcus and Commodus had tried to placate Lucilla by ensuring that she "retained all of the privileges of an Augusta," including "occupying the empress's seat in the imperial box at theaters and having the sacred flame carried before her" when she moved around the city.[8] Lucilla, however, seems to have hoped that Marcus might elevate her again, perhaps by naming her new husband as his successor, or as a senior emperor who could guide Commodus.

When Commodus assumed the purple alone and married Crispina, the daughter of one of the largest landholders in the Italian region of Lucania, Lucilla assembled a team of plotters to kill Commodus outside the Colosseum. Unfortunately, Quintianus, the young senator who volunteered to stab the emperor, had the competence of a second-rate comic book villain. When Commodus was entering the Colosseum, Quintianus "drew his dagger and shouted at Commodus that he had been sent by the Senate to kill him." While he was "making his little speech and waving his dagger, he was seized by the emperor's bodyguards before he could strike, and died for his stupidity in revealing the plot prematurely."[9]

This "disastrous stroke of ill fortune completely altered [Commodus's] previously mild, moderate disposition," for completely understandable reasons.[10] Commodus was only twenty-one and had just learned that his sister had tried to kill him. Although very few senators knew about the plot, Commodus "took Quintianus's words to heart and . . . now considered the entire Senate his collective enemy."[11] His suspicion also extended to members of the imperial household and the sober advisers Marcus had entrusted with the continued training of his son. Many of them lost their lives as Commodus began to suspect their loyalty.[12]

Commodus turned toward less reputable advisers, who took advantage of his inexperience, exploited his fears, and encouraged, as Cassius Dio put it, "a bad pattern of behaviors, which in turn led him to lustfulness and cruelty."[13] While Commodus drifted away from the associates of his father, the men who remained around him used his disinterest in politics to displace their rivals and enrich themselves.

The first of these attendants to rise and fall was Sextus Tigidius Perennis, whom Commodus installed as praetorian prefect.[14] Perennis "was always advising the emperor to eliminate and destroy the prominent men," so that he could enrich himself "by confiscating their property."[15] Among his victims were the Quintilii, the brothers whose feud with Herodes Atticus had led to the rhetorician's infamous audience with Marcus Aurelius. They were executed in the aftermath of Lucilla's plot, and Commodus took possession of their villa on the Appian Way.[16]

Perennis soon fell victim to the sorts of intrigues that doom the courtiers of disinterested emperors. "The soldiers," Dio wrote, "blamed Perennis whenever anything happened." Their anger bubbled over in different ways across the empire in the mid-180s. In one notable case, a deserter named Maternus induced enough soldiers to join him that they were able to besiege an entire legion before they were suppressed.[17] Perennis tried to restore order, but, in 185, the armies in Britain objected to Perennis replacing their commander. They sent a delegation to Commodus to claim that Perennis was plotting to overthrow the emperor. "Commodus believed them" and "delivered [Perennis] to the very soldiers he commanded" so they could execute him.[18]

Commodus then allowed Marcus Aurelius Cleander, the freedman in charge of the imperial bedchamber, to move into the role Perennis had played. Cleander proved even more corruptible than Perennis, selling offices, consulships, and positions in the Senate to anyone able to pay.[19] But Cleander also took the blame when conditions in Rome became more difficult. In 189, Rome was hit by a new wave of smallpox, and at one point it was killing upward of 2,000 people a day in the capital.[20] The following year brought a severe food shortage in Rome. Cassius Dio describes an incident where "a crowd of children ran into the Circus Maximus" during a horse race, causing a disturbance that induced a mass of spectators to go to "find Commodus," who was staying a little more than six miles away at the villa he had seized from the Quintilii. Although there were many praetorian troops onsite, the emperor "was so terrified" of the approaching mob and the "curses on Cleander" that the people were chanting that he "ordered Cleander to be slain."[21]

Cleander's fall left Commodus without an effective buffer between himself and popular discontent. This posed a real problem for an emperor who was breaking dramatically with the old rules governing what an emperor did and how he portrayed his relationship to his subjects. Commodus now spent most of this time at estates away from Rome because he had effectively "given up his judicial and administrative duties."[22] He instead fixated on learning to defend himself. Commodus sent for instructors from around the world so that he could learn to shoot like a Parthian bowman, use javelins like fighters in Morocco, and fight in hand-to-hand combat like gladiators.

Initially all this training was done in private, but by the early 190s Commodus had begun to show off his skills in public. He fought both as a gladiator and as a participant in the hunts of wild beasts put on in the amphitheaters around the Roman world. In one memorable display in the Colosseum that Herodian describes, he arranged for "a hundred lions to appear in one group as if from beneath the earth, and he killed the entire hundred with exactly one hundred javelins. All the bodies lay stretched out in a straight line for some distance; they could thus be counted with no difficulty, and no one saw a single extra javelin."[23]

Senators were appalled that the emperor was performing these sorts of feats in public, however impressive they were. Cassius Dio found them both disgusting and ridiculous. He and the other senators were forced to turn up and sit in the front rows of the Colosseum wearing cloaks that usually were donned only at a time when an emperor had died. This evidently served as a symbolic recognition of the risks that Commodus was assuming when he fought.[24] And although the emperor took these events seriously, the senators struggled to do so. During one such event, Commodus killed an ostrich, and as he twirled its severed head before a group of senators, Dio was forced to chew one of the leaves of his laurel crown to avoid laughing audibly.[25]

By 192, Commodus had tipped into what many saw as madness. Styling himself the "Roman Hercules," he issued coins and official portraits that depicted him draped in the hero's traditional lion skin.[26] He had months of the year and legions of the army renamed in his honor. After a fire devastated the Forum and the Palatine, he even ordered that Rome be called Colonia Commodiana to commemorate his refounding of the city.[27] Soon after the fire, Commodus decamped to the Vectilian Villa, a location on the Caelian Hill that Herodian derided as a "gladiatorial barracks."[28] He was murdered there on New Year's Eve of 192.

WHEN ROMANS WOKE up on January 1, 193, they heard the unbelievable news that Commodus, the thirty-two-year-old who had been the strongest, most robust emperor Rome had ever known, had died of a stroke in the night.[29] Even more curious news followed. Although the Vectilian Villa, only about a block southeast of the main complex of gladiatorial facilities adjoining the Colosseum that included a hospital, Commodus had not been taken there for treatment or examination.[30] Instead, said Herodian, his servants had "wrapped the emperor's body in bed linen, tied it securely . . . and sent it out of the palace as if it were no more than laundry, somewhat bulkier than usual."[31] When dawn broke, Commodus's body was already in the imperial tomb in the Mausoleum of Hadrian, more than three miles away. It was no longer possible to examine the body or conduct an autopsy.

Although no one really believed the official story that the emperor had died a natural death, this did not particularly worry Publius Helvius Pertinax, the new emperor. Pertinax, the official story went, had been aroused from sleep by the praetorian commander Laetus, the bedroom attendant Eclectus, and Marcia, Commodus's concubine, who together had asked him to assume imperial power. He had agreed to do this and had gone with Laetus to the praetorian camp to address the soldiers. After pledging 3,000 denarii to each praetorian, "finally, Pertinax was hailed as emperor, if only by a few at first."[32] He had effectively bought the throne.

Pertinax then summoned the Senate to approve the soldiers' choice.[33] The midnight meeting became a logistical nightmare. No one could find the night watchman to open the Senate chamber on New Year's Eve, so the senators crowded into the nearby Temple of Concord. Cassius Dio, who attended that night, described the bleary-eyed senators trying to make sense of this set of events. Though everyone knew it to be a coup, few dared to openly call it one.[34] Pertinax, Dio said, came before the senators and claimed, "I have been named emperor by the soldiers; however, I do not want the office and shall resign it at once, this very day, because of my age and feeble health, and because of the distressing state of affairs."[35] Dio pretended to be reassured by this, but the new consul Falco (whose term began while the Senate was meeting that night) approached the new emperor and whispered, "We know what sort of an emperor you will be from this, because we see behind you Laetus and Marcia, the instruments of Commodus' crimes." Pertinax responded with a chilling warning: "You are young, Consul, and do not know the necessity of obedience."[36]

Pertinax could have been a good, perhaps even great, emperor had he taken power under different conditions. Not only was he one of the few advisers of Marcus Aurelius who had survived Commodus's purges, but he also brought the mutinous British armies under control following their role in the overthrow of Perennis.[37] According to Cassius Dio, he was "a noble and good man" who "conducted himself in a democratic fashion" toward the senators by "making himself available and listening readily" to any issue senators raised with him.[38] Pertinax had both the qualifications and the personality to succeed. But he lacked the timing. Romans at that moment did not understand that Commodus had been, in a sense, a loose lid keeping tensions across many different parts of the empire from boiling over. Only his unquestioned legitimacy as the son of Marcus Aurelius and grandson of Antoninus Pius had kept the state from falling into civil war.

Pertinax fell from power before some parts of the empire even knew that Commodus had died. He ran out of money by the middle of March and, in desperation, organized an auction of Commodus's possessions, so he could pay the praetorians what he had promised.[39] The financial situation so alarmed Laetus, the praetorian commander, that he enlisted Falco, the consul, in another coup attempt. It was quickly detected, but Pertinax, who understood the weakness of his position, pardoned Falco and lied to the Senate about how much money he had given the praetorians.[40] Fearing what his own fate might be if the emperor fell, and aiming to control events himself, Laetus encouraged the praetorians to storm the imperial palace on March 28. They seized Pertinax and killed him along with the bedroom attendant Eclectus, who had been Laetus's partner in the coup that had brought Pertinax to power.[41]

LAETUS HAD PRE-POSITIONED Pertinax' father-in-law, Titus Flavius Claudius Sulpicianus, in the praetorian camp so that he would be on hand to claim the throne Pertinax was about to vacate. Unfortunately for Sulpicianus and Laetus, another Roman learned of the assassination before Sulpicianus could agree on a price to pay the praetorians in exchange for their support of his imperial claim. The senator Marcus Didius Julianus "hastily made his way to the praetorian guard camp and, standing at the gates of the enclosure, . . . began to offer money to the soldiers in exchange for the right to rule over Rome." This was, Dio said, "as if both the city and its entire Empire were [being] auctioned off" by the praetorians who had just killed their emperor. "Sulpicianus would have won," because he "was inside the camp and was the prefect of the city," but Julianus raised his bid by 5,000 denarii per soldier and began "shouting it in a loud voice and also indicating the amount on his fingers" from outside the wall. This was high enough. The soldiers accepted his offer, welcomed Julianus into their encampment, and proclaimed him emperor.[42] Julianus then let Sulpicianus walk away without penalty.

That evening, a large contingent of armed praetorian troops marched with Julianus to the Senate House. Senators were summoned individually, and when they received the news, Dio wrote, "we were seized with fear of Julianus and the soldiers, especially those of us who had received favor from Pertinax." Terrified that the night might be his last, Dio bathed and had dinner before heading to the Senate to await his fate. Julianus, however, was much more interested in delivering a pompous speech than in punishing senators.

He told the senators, "I see that you need a ruler, and I myself am more worthy to rule you than anyone else." Moved more by the ranks of armed praetorians ringing the Senate House than the argument Julianus made, the senators approved his appointment as emperor. Julianus then climbed the ramp leading from the Forum to the imperial palace, sat down at the palace dinner table, and mocked the simple food Pertinax had expected to eat that evening.[43]

The next morning, Dio and the other senators came to the palace to pay their individual respects to the new emperor. They knew enough to hide their feelings, but Dio says that "the ordinary people went about openly with sullen looks, speaking openly about their discontent" from the Rostra. When Julianus descended from the Palatine to meet with the Senate later that day, the crowds in the Forum "began shouting, as if by some prearranged signal, calling him the thief of the empire."[44] The increasingly angry mob blocked his way and some of them even began throwing stones at him.[45] Julianus responded by ordering the soldiers to kill the people in the crowd nearest to him. The protesters eventually withdrew, but many people armed themselves with homemade weapons and encamped in the Circus Maximus just below the imperial palace. They spent the night chanting for Gaius Pescennius Niger, the general commanding the armies in Syria, to march to Italy and get rid of Julianus. Julianus, who was spending his first full night in the imperial palace, must have slept very little as these thousands of voices calling for his overthrow echoed through his vast new home.

The legionary commanders along the frontiers reacted with the same fury that the Roman populace did to the news that Julianus had purchased the throne. Unlike the poorly armed residents of the capital, however, they commanded armies that would let them respond. As soon as Niger heard about the chants calling on him to rebel, he informed "his soldiers and the rest of the inhabitants of the East" that he planned to do what the Roman crowd had asked of him.[46]

This was not, Niger would later say, an action motivated by personal ambition, but a defense of the principle that the Roman people alone had the right to choose their rulers. He marched against Julianus because he felt he must heed a call "from the Roman people."[47] Niger was fighting for the Republic in its most traditional sense because he believed that the Roman state, the *res publica*, was a public trust that belonged to its citizens. It was not, and should never be, the personal property of a sovereign who purchased it.

There was a problem though. News in the Roman world traveled only as quickly as the person carrying it could move, and Niger, in Syria, was a long way from Rome. In fact, news took so long to travel there that, on March 17, soldiers in the Syrian frontier town of Dura Europus erected an altar praying for the safety of Commodus, the emperor who had died more than two months before. Niger apparently did not hear about Pertinax's death until mid-April. In the meantime, two other governors had also rebelled and begun moving their forces toward Rome. On April 9, Lucius Septimius Severus, the governor of Pannonia, directed his troops to march quickly into Italy. A few days later, the British governor, Decimus Clodius Albinus, also saw an opportunity to seize power.[48]

A weak, unpopular emperor in the center and angry soldiers on the periphery presented the perfect recipe for a sprawling civil war that could tear the unity of the state apart. Severus seems to have understood the danger best. Cassius Dio writes that Severus "was the shrewdest of the three" rebellious generals because he understood that Julianus's zombie regime would endure only until one of them reached Rome. Severus's province was closest to the capital, so he had an advantage. He quickly gained the support of the other governors who had troops in the provinces lining the Rhine and Danube frontiers, but he feared having to fight through Italy as both Niger and Albinus moved their forces toward him.[49] He needed to make an alliance with one of the other imperial claimants. Because he knew that Niger was claiming a popular mandate to rule that made him an unlikely partner, Severus "sent a letter with one of his trusted friends to Albinus, appointing him Caesar."[50] Albinus then supported Severus's claim.

Severus's speed shocked Julianus. He moved so quickly that his armies arrived at the Italian frontier before news of his invasion reached the capital. Italy had not seen significant fighting for more than a century and lacked defensive structures that could deter Severus's large army. Julianus responded by fortifying the palace and drilling the praetorians, who were not a field army, in strange battle tactics that included the use of elephants. As Severus advanced and the forces sent against him defected, a panicked Julianus asked the Senate to vote a share of imperial power to Severus. But Severus had already communicated to the leadership of the praetorians that he intended no harm to them if they surrendered and handed over the people who had killed Pertinax. Dio, who attended the Senate meeting in which this information was presented, explains that, when the Senate heard Severus's offer, it "sentenced Julianus to death, named Severus emperor, and bestowed divine honors on Pertinax." Julianus was then killed in the palace while crying out, "What evil have I done? Whom have I killed?" He had reigned for sixty-six days.[51]

Severus's first action when he approached Rome was to deal with the praetorian guards. He summoned them out of the city to meet with him and surrounded them with troops from his legions. The new emperor kept to his word not to harm them, but only in the most literal sense. According to Dio, Severus "inflicted the death penalty on the praetorians who had taken part in the killing of Pertinax," and then dismissed the other praetorians from service. He ordered them to give up their weapons and horses and leave the city. We don't know what he did with Julianus's elephant corps. Since the time of Augustus, the praetorians had been largely recruited from Italy, but Severus replaced these unreliable Italians with men from his own legions. From that point forward, praetorian service would represent a reward for "whoever proved brave in war," rather than being the exclusive preserve of men from Rome's historic core.[52]

Conservative opinion recoiled at this change. Dio claimed that diversification of the praetorian ranks "ruined the youth of Italy, who turned to brigandage and gladiatorial fighting in place of service in the army." The praetorian guards changed from a body of "men of respectable appearance" into "a throng of motley soldiers most savage in appearance, most terrifying in speech, and most boorish in conversation." In essence, Dio objected to this reform because, for the first time, the praetorians would now reflect the wider ethnic, linguistic, and cultural makeup of the entire Roman world. This was a remarkable statement for a Greek-speaking senator born in Asia Minor to make, but it reveals how the Greek immigrants and new senators who were outsiders a century before had now become fixtures of the elite Roman establishment.[53]

But Severus was not at all a fixture of the establishment. He had been born in North Africa, and he spoke Latin with a heavy, distinctive accent. He was also dark-skinned, a detail we know from the "Severan Tondo," a color portrait of the emperor and his family painted on a circular wooden panel from around AD 200. Severus had been the first senator in his family, and he had not married into an old Roman noble family. His Syrian wife, Julia Domna, was descended from the royal family of Emesa (modern Homs). This regime then provided Rome with its first African emperor and its first empress born on the Asian continent.

Because of the threat from Niger, Severus needed to counteract the resistance to change that Dio's complaints voiced. He did this in a few ways. First, he linked himself to Pertinax, a figure whose brief reign that winter now appeared idyllic to Romans living through a summer of violent turmoil. Severus ensured that the Senate voted to approve divine honors to Pertinax at the same time that they recognized his own authority over the empire. Severus asked the Senate to grant him permission to add the name "Pertinax" to his own, and he presided over an elaborate funeral in which he gave a eulogy from the Rostra. During the funeral, Dio says, "We [the senators] cried aloud frequently . . . now praising Pertinax and then lamenting him."[54]

Severus further telegraphed his desire to build trust with the Senate during his first address to the body, in which he promised that, "like the good emperors in the past . . . he would not put any senator to death." His outreach worked well initially. Even the cynical Dio embraced Severus to the point that he composed a short book explaining the divine portents that prefigured his rise to power. Severus sent him a long thank-you note that persuaded Dio to expand the project into a monumental history of Rome from its origins until his own time.[55]

Senatorial backing was important, but Severus still had a civil war to fight against Niger, and his soldiers demanded attention. One source reports that, "while he was in the Senate, the soldiers, in a state of mutiny, demanded ten thousand *sesterces* [i.e., 2,500 denarii] a man." While Severus wanted to resist them, he realized he could not calm the mutiny without giving in to their demand.[56] This was an inauspicious beginning to his reign, but Severus understood that issues with military compensation and the quality of life of Roman soldiers had been causing profound discontent in the armies for at least a decade. He would need to address these problems if he wanted to die a natural death.

After a month in Rome, Severus set off to fight Niger. He moved much more aggressively than his adversary. Niger, who had been consolidating control over Roman Asia, had established a European beachhead in the city of Byzantium (the site that would later become Constantinople), but he was only able to advance another sixty miles into Thrace before Severus's forces defeated him and pushed him out of Europe, except for Byzantium.[57] Severus's army forced Niger out of northwestern Asia Minor that autumn, then expelled him from Asia Minor altogether in May 194, following a victory at Issus, around 60 miles from the Syrian capital of Antioch. Niger pulled back to Antioch but was captured and killed as he tried to flee to Parthia.[58]

The city of Byzantium, however, still resisted Severus. Located on a peninsula surrounded by fast-moving and treacherous currents, it was perhaps the most defensible major settlement in the entire Roman world. Capturing it proved such a daunting prospect that the emperor's generals tried to induce its surrender by displaying Niger's severed head outside the walls rather than risking an assault. It didn't work. Byzantium held out against Severus for another year and was taken only after widespread starvation induced many Byzantines to either sail away or resort to cannibalism. When Byzantium finally did fall, Severus executed all the magistrates and soldiers in the city and demolished the city walls.[59]

Around the time that Byzantium fell, Severus broke with Albinus, his former adversary-turned-successor-designate. Severus removed Albinus from his position as Caesar and elevated his own son, born Lucius Septimius Bassianus—whom we now know as Caracalla—in his place. At the same time, Severus went to the Senate and claimed that he had been adopted by Marcus Aurelius. This was a lie that, Dio says, "caused us extensive dismay."[60] Severus compelled the Senate to deify Commodus and began to call himself the "son of the divine Marcus Antoninus." He changed Caracalla's legal name to Marcus Aurelius Antoninus.[61] By 199, Severus had removed the name Pertinax from the titulature he used on his coins and began calling himself Severus Pius in order to evoke the legacy of his notional grandfather Antoninus Pius.[62]

The war with Albinus, the elevation of Caracalla, and the embrace of the Antonine legacy were all precipitated by reports that "the more distinguished senators were sending [Albinus] personal, private letters urging him to come to Rome."[63] The Senate thus greeted news of the breach between Severus and Albinus with studied quiet—as Cassius Dio put it, "not inclining toward one or the other so as not to share their risks and hopes." Regular people, however, so strongly disapproved of what they saw as Severus choosing to fight his former ally that they organized an antiwar demonstration in the Circus Maximus. Dio, who was there, describes a packed space in which the crowds chanted in unison, "Until what time will we continue to suffer these things? Until when will we wage war on ourselves?"[64] This did nothing to persuade Severus to stop the attack on Albinus, whom he defeated in 197.

THE YEARS THAT followed saw Severus skillfully rehabilitate the physical, military, and political infrastructure of the state. The physical infrastructure repairs were so massive that a visitor wandering the ancient ruins in Rome today will walk by many buildings constructed or repaired by Severus. Much of this involved redeveloping areas of Rome's monumental center damaged in the great fire of 192. On the Palatine, he expanded the imperial palace, built a bath complex adjacent to it, and constructed the Septizodium, a spectacular multistory fountain at the corner where the palace grounds met the Circus Maximus. He restored the Pantheon and the Theater of Pompey in the Campus Martius, and he redeveloped a large swath of devastated land stretching almost from the Colosseum to the Tiber that included much of the Roman Forum.[65] Among the structures he repaired were Vespasian's Forum of Peace, Trajan's Forum, the Temple of Saturn, the Temple of Vespasian, and the Portico of Octavia, a walkway and library complex a block away from the banks of the Tiber. A 2,000-square-foot marble map of the city of Rome that labeled and showed the floor plans of all the structures in the city was then hung in the rebuilt Temple of Peace, so that Romans could view the fully rebuilt city in all its overwhelming magnificence. He commemorated all of this work with a coin series naming him the "Restorer of the City," as well as a celebration of the Saecular Games to mark the purification and renewal of Rome following a period of turmoil.[66]

Severus's rebuilt Roman military reinforced the sense that the empire had righted itself. Roman forces fought much more effectively under him than they had under even his most esteemed Antonine predecessors. Severus captured and held territory in Mesopotamia that Trajan had not been able to secure. His Mesopotamian campaign even saw him plunder the Parthian capital of Ctesiphon, where he seized the royal treasury and took over 100,000 captives. His troops were much happier after he increased their pay, and after he permitted soldiers to marry women from the regions in which they were serving.[67]

This marriage reform mattered greatly to the many soldiers garrisoning the frontiers who had been cohabiting with local women and fathering children. Under the former regulations, they had not been able to marry until the soldier's discharge. The prohibition dated back to a time when most legionaries were Italians serving far from home, but Severan legions included people from across the empire, including contingents who lived in the regions they defended. Soldiers with local ties were much more likely to stay with the women to whom they were now connected and the children they fathered. Marriage offered immediate legal recognition of these children and a sense of family stability in the frontier regions housing large numbers of Roman soldiers. This was a real step toward addressing the angry legions of the frontiers. And it had cost the emperor nothing.

Politically, Severus's regime brought a cohort of new, often North African, elites to Rome to assist in the running of the empire. The most powerful of these, Gaius Fulvius Plautianus, had been born in Severus's hometown of Leptis Magna. He served as Severus's most trusted lieutenant, first as the commander of the city watch and then as the prefect of Severus's reconstituted praetorian guard.[68] Over time, Cassius Dio remarked caustically, "Severus yielded to Plautianus to such a degree that the latter occupied the position of emperor and Severus that of prefect."[69] Severus even arranged for Caracalla to marry Plautilla, Plautianus's daughter, in an effort to solidify the regime's next generation by joining the two families.[70]

Caracalla, however, hated Plautilla and her father.[71] Severus's wife, Julia Domna, also turned against Plautianus, when he ordered agents to have her followed. Finally, in 205, Plautianus decided to try to overthrow Severus and take power himself, but the plot was discovered. Plautianus was brought before Severus to be interrogated. With Severus slow to respond, Caracalla gave the order for Plautianus's execution on January 22, 205, and commanded that his public portraits be destroyed.[72]

Plautianus's fall reflected Caracalla's growing assertiveness and impatience with his father. Severus had hoped that Caracalla and his younger brother, Publius Septimius Geta, could reign together following his death, but the two brothers loathed each other. In 208, Severus arranged for his sons to accompany him on campaign in Britain so he might foster a reconciliation. Severus left Geta in the part of the province that remained firmly under Roman control while

Caracalla went with his father as they "marched out against the barbarians." Caracalla used this time to build support among the troops "in every possible way, including slanderous attacks on his brother," so that "the soldiers would look to him alone for orders" when his father died.[73]

Severus knew what Caracalla was doing and did his best to curtail its effects. But by 211, he had become so weak that he lacked the capacity to respond. Instead, as he lay dying in Britain that February, he told both of his sons, "You two must get along, enrich the soldiers, and disregard everyone else."[74] They could manage only two of the three things he asked.

Caracalla and Geta argued constantly about how to divide the empire during the trip back to Rome from Britain after their father's death. Finally, on December 26, 211, Julia Domna summoned both sons to her quarters in Rome after Caracalla had asked her to facilitate a reconciliation. Instead, members of the praetorian guard rushed at Geta, who, "at the sight of them," wrote Dio, "ran to his mother and clung to her chest and breasts." He was stabbed while she held him in her arms. The empress then "saw her son perishing in the most impious fashion": "Covered in his blood, she received him back into the very womb from which he had been born."[75]

Caracalla now reigned alone. His reaction to the murder of his brother would forever change the Roman state.

Chapter 20

Caracalla's Empire of Romans

211–244

A s Geta lay dying in his mother's arms, Caracalla "rushed out from the chambers at a sprint, and cried out, as he went through the entire palace, that he had escaped a great danger and barely been saved." He commanded the guards on duty at the palace to take him to the praetorian camp, because he would be safe if he stayed there, but "if he remained in the hall of the palace, he would be killed." These soldiers, Herodian says, "trusted him because they did not know what had been done."[1]

The praetorian camp lay approximately two miles away from the palace, and the most direct route took Caracalla and the soldiers through the crowded Roman Forum and by the Senate House. "Ordinary people," Herodian wrote, "were alarmed to see the emperor being borne in a rush through the middle of the city at nightfall." The praetorians were no more comfortable when Caracalla burst into their barracks. He immediately "rushed to the camp's temple, bowed down before the soldiers' standards and images of their gods, and, throwing himself on the ground, . . . made a vow of thanks and offered a sacrifice for his salvation."[2]

The soldiers sleeping in preparation for overnight duty awoke with a jolt, while others began running to him from their baths, and all the praetorians quickly assembled in formation. Caracalla told them he had barely escaped a plot against his life hatched by a "very dangerous enemy," and that the gods had elected to preserve him to rule the empire alone. He informed the soldiers that he would give them 2,500 denarii each "as a reward for his safety and securing sole rule," and that he would raise the regular military pay by 50 percent.[3]

Caracalla spent the night in the praetorian camp before summoning the Senate the next morning. Flanked by soldiers, he entered wearing a cuirass under his toga and told the senators that he was "not ignorant that everyone immediately hates the murder of a family member," and that the "victim always appears to be in the right and the victor in the wrong."[4] This was a different situation, though, because Geta had "attacked him with a sword," and had died as Caracalla was defending himself. Caracalla asked the Senate to declare Geta a public enemy, which triggered public condemnation of Geta's memory. Caracalla's agents erased Geta's name and face from monuments, ceremonial arches, and even individual coins.[5] The senators were told to "thank the gods for saving at least one of your emperors," and to "cease the dissension" in their "souls and minds." Caracalla delivered this last admonition "at the top of his lungs, full of anger, and giving a piercing stare at the friends of Geta" in the chamber.[6]

A majority of the Senate and a faction of courtiers and praetorians had quietly hoped that Geta would prevail over his brother in the sectarian struggle they had all expected to break out. Caracalla moved quickly against them.[7] He sent his aunt, Julia Maesa, home to Emesa and forced his mother to "rejoice and laugh as though some most fortunate thing had happened," while guards watched so that she did not "even shed tears in private" over Geta.[8] So many servants, palace attendants, freedmen, and soldiers presumed loyal to Geta were murdered that "their corpses [were] put on wagons, carried out of the city, and cremated in a heap."[9] "Senators distinguished by birth and wealth were executed as Geta's friends" along with Pertinax's son, the son of Lucilla and Lucius Verus, and "anyone connected to any emperor by birth."[10] The great jurist Papinian, who had been serving as a praetorian prefect, was killed with an axe after the praetorians accused him of being close to Geta. Even Caracalla's elderly tutor Clio was drawn into the fray in the aftermath of Geta's death when he was dragged through the Forum in his bath slippers and tunic until popular outcry forced the soldiers to release him.[11]

IT WAS OFTEN the case that the experiences of a few hundred senators meant very little to the tens of millions of people living elsewhere in the Roman Empire, but the difference between senatorial complaints and popular enthusiasm was never greater among Romans than in the months following Geta's death. In 212, Caracalla reacted to his "salvation" by issuing a law of monumental importance to the entire empire. In this law, Caracalla wrote, "I wish to thank the immortal gods because they preserved me," and that he would show his appreciation by "doing something in accordance with their greatness." For this reason, he said, "I give Roman citizenship to all of those who dwell in the empire, with their rights in their local communities remaining intact."[12]

With this proclamation, which scholars call the Antonine Constitution after Caracalla's official name, Antoninus, the great Roman experiment in extending citizenship to conquered peoples reached its natural endpoint. Now every free person in the empire was a full member of the Roman political community. The distinction between subject and citizen that Aelius Aristides had explored in the 140s no longer existed. But Caracalla also added an important qualifier that made his view of an empire full of Romans perfectly consistent with that described by Philo under Claudius and praised by Aristides in the age of Antoninus Pius. The local customs of these new Romans remained intact. Universal Roman citizenship made everyone in the empire Roman, but it did not destroy whatever other identity they possessed. This was an addition to their identity, not a replacement.

The effect was dramatic and intensely personal. A full Roman name usually had three components—a praenomen, a nomen, and a cognomen. Julius Caesar's name, for example, was Gaius (the praenomen) Julius (the nomen) Caesar (the cognomen), and Caracalla's legal name in 212 was Marcus (praenomen) Aurelius (nomen) Antoninus (cognomen). When someone received citizenship, it was customary for them to assume the nomen of the patron who sponsored their citizenship. After 212, there was an explosion of Romans who suddenly bore Caracalla's nomen, Aurelius, in recognition of his role in awarding them citizenship. By 213, many of the non-Roman names in official documents, such as military rosters, had been replaced by flocks of new Aurelii who had gained citizenship from the Antonine Constitution.[13]

The communities, regions, and local notables of the empire suddenly confronted the unexpected challenges posed by uniform Roman citizenship status in communities that had long been accustomed to seeing Roman citizenship as the prerogative of a narrow elite. The papyrus that preserves our text of the Antonine Constitution also records some of the unanticipated problems the law caused in Egypt.[14] Prior to 212, native Egyptians who wanted Roman citizenship would first need to possess citizenship in the provincial capital of Alexandria, a status that also gave them the right to live and work in the wealthy city. After Caracalla's extension of universal citizenship, Egyptians began flocking to Alexandria for greater economic opportunities, because they believed that Roman citizenship also conferred the right to work in the Egyptian metropolis.

This internal migration so overwhelmed Alexandria with people and denuded the Egyptian towns of young, physically able workers that Caracalla quickly issued a second law, also preserved on the papyrus, clarifying that native Egyptians still do not have the right to be in Alexandria. He expelled "all of the Egyptians who are in Alexandria" illegally and "are disturbing the city because of their number and their uselessness." He also asserted that it was easy to tell who these "rustic Egyptians" were because they spoke differently, "[had] different appearances and characteristics," and "their daily customs [were] different from civilized behavior."[15] Universal Roman citizenship then did not mean that the cultural distinctions between various ethnic populations had dissolved or that the legal limits on who could be where had ended. What had changed was their relationship to

Rome. All were now participants rather than subjects in the Roman polity.

The Jewish community faced a different sort of challenge. Rabbis had developed a robust and comprehensive legal structure that, at least in theory, governed all aspects of Jewish life. In Philo's first-century conception, these were the laws of the Jewish nation that existed under Roman rulers who did not interfere with the rules governing Jewish life. After Caracalla's extension of citizenship, ordinary Jews began to use Roman civil law with increasing frequency, a tendency that threatened the claims of some rabbis that rabbinic teaching must govern Jewish civil interactions.[16] Rabbis responded by emphasizing the overlap between Jewish and Roman civil law, in one case telling a story in which a Roman official visited a rabbinic academy and praised the laws of the Torah.[17] There was even a growing interest in charting how non-Jews might convert to Judaism now that Jews and Gentiles shared an identical and equal citizenship status in the empire.[18]

Dio was much less optimistic than the rabbis about the implications of Caracalla's edict. He could not understand the Antonine Constitution as anything but a money grab through which Caracalla "made everyone in his empire Roman in order to increase his income from them."[19] His avarice, Dio believed, had grown out of "the craftiness of his mother and the Syrian race to which she belonged," and had inspired Caracalla to elevate rich people to positions of influence they did not deserve. This included the first-ever consul of Egyptian origin, a man named Publius Aelius Coeranus, whom Caracalla had named as a senator and consul despite the fact that he had held no prior offices. Dio's complaints, though, reflected his own bitterness as a senator whose career had stagnated as newcomers from some of the empire's underrepresented provinces surpassed him. Dio was an older senator living in a different, disorienting world—and it troubled him.[20]

It is unlikely that Caracalla thought very hard about any of these effects before he issued his universal citizenship law. According to the Antonine Constitution, he simply wished to augment the greatness of "the immortal gods that saved [him]" by increasing the number of Roman subjects who came to the temples, brought offerings, and shared in his victory.

The emperor needed the support. The murder of Geta tormented him to such a degree that "he suffered from distressing visions in which he often believed he was pursued by his father and his brother armed with swords." He couldn't sleep, and he "made use of every oracle and summoned seers from every land" to try to get some relief from the pain. He was said to have even summoned the spirit of Commodus to ask for help. When Commodus told him that a divine judgment drew near, Caracalla appealed to all the gods he could identify. Eventually Caracalla left Rome in January 213 for a tour of the empire before embarking on a Mesopotamian campaign. Everywhere he traveled, he "went to the gods himself, hoping to prevail upon them by appearing in person and doing all that devotees ought to do, but he received nothing in return that healed him."[21]

As time passed, Caracalla became increasingly close to his soldiers, marching and eating with them, and refusing to bathe or change clothes unless they were able to do the same. Herodian says that he would even "take on his shoulders the legionary standards, great long things, heavily ornamented with gold and difficult for even the strongest soldiers to carry." Although he shared their spartan conditions on campaign, Caracalla lavished large bonuses on both the praetorians and enlisted men.[22]

Caracalla's close interactions with common soldiers coexisted uneasily with his growing propensity to erupt at regular citizens. At one point, he visited Alexandria to pay his respects at the tomb of Alexander the Great. Emperors rarely visited Alexandria, and the city was packed with people wishing to catch a glimpse of their ruler. Despite the welcome he received, something—our sources do not say what—happened that angered the emperor.[23] Cassius Dio says that Caracalla responded by ordering his soldiers to "slaughter so many people that he did not even venture to say anything about their number, but instead wrote to the Senate that he did not care who or how many had died because they all deserved this fate." While the killing unfolded, Caracalla spent his time in the Temple of Serapis, a massive sacred complex shrine perched atop the highest hill in the city.[24]

Caracalla's reign ended abruptly on April 8, 217. The previous few years had seen the Romans embark on a dizzying series of military campaigns in both Germany and along the eastern frontier. In the east, Caracalla eyed a war of conquest in Mesopotamia. It began with his absorption of the Parthian client kingdom of Osrohene that formed a buffer between Roman and Parthian territory. Caracalla then provoked war with Parthia by proposing to marry the daughter of the Parthian king, and then using the king's refusal as a pretext to launch an invasion. Roman forces raided much of northern Mesopotamia during the campaigning season of 216. As Caracalla prepared for a second year of fighting, he ordered a small cavalry detachment to accompany him while he offered a sacrifice at the Temple of the Moon God in the city of Harran. But the emperor became sick to his stomach as they traveled and "went off with one person to relieve his troubles," while "all the rest turned their backs and went a distance away," to give the emperor privacy. Caracalla was then stabbed from behind by a lone assailant as he was pulling down his underclothes. He died almost instantly.[25] It would take three days for his successor, the praetorian commander Macrinus, to be proclaimed emperor by the army. A Moor from North Africa who had a pierced ear, Macrinus was the first non-senator to rule Rome.[26]

He did not last long. Caracalla's aunt Julia Maesa orchestrated a coup by telling the army in Syria that her grandchildren, the future emperors Elagabalus and Alexander Severus, were the illegitimate sons of Caracalla.[27] The rumor was obviously false, but the army disliked Macrinus, liked the Severan family, and wanted an excuse to overthrow their emperor. Troops around Emesa decided to back the usurpation, and as it became clear that Macrinus was losing his grip, the Senate followed the army in rescinding its support for him. Macrinus was declared a public enemy, and Elagabalus, whom the senators had never met, was accepted as emperor. Cassius Dio thought Macrinus a capable administrator and a good man who nevertheless deserved his death "because he grasped at supreme power before he had the title of senator."[28] In other words, he would have been a good emperor, except that the army did not like him and senators thought him too lowly to hold the office. The old senator still stubbornly refused to understand the new world in which he lived.

ELAGABALUS FORCED ROMANS to confront, in a very visible way, what it meant to live in a state where the dress, worship, and customs of millions of new Roman citizens could suddenly occupy the very core of public life. The Antonine Constitution had obliterated the old hierarchies that separated elite and cultured Roman citizens and the noncitizen masses who hailed from distant provinces. When the fourteen-year-old Elagabalus arrived in the capital, he believed he was living in a new, more inclusive world.

The new emperor held the hereditary priesthood of Elagabal, the sun god of Emesa. Unlike Greek and Roman gods, who were represented by anthropomorphic statues, Elagabal was a large conical asteroid. Not only was his favorite god strange, but Elagabalus refused to adapt his dress, behavior, interests, or religious practices to senatorial expectations. Herodian said that the first official portrait he sent to the Senate and people of Rome depicted him "as he appeared in public, performing as a priest alongside an image of the Emesene god to whom he was making a sacrifice."[29] This was the first step in a religious program through which Elagabalus sought to place the god to whom he was devoted atop the Roman pantheon.

The next stages were even more controversial. Elagabalus welcomed the god's large rock to Rome with a procession in which, Herodian writes, "he placed the sun god in a chariot adorned with gold and jewels." He had six horses lead it into the city "as if the god itself were the charioteer." The emperor "ran backwards in front of the chariot, facing the god" on a path dusted with gold. The people ran with him, "carrying torches and tossing wreaths and flowers," while the praetorians "carried statues of all the gods" alongside them.[30] Once the rock arrived in the city, Elagabalus installed it in a magnificent new temple perched on the edge of the Palatine Hill overlooking the Colosseum, across the Via Sacra from the Temple of Venus and Rome.

Elagabalus then "sought a wife for the god" by auditioning various female deities for the role while he himself divorced his first wife, a girl from the aristocratic Cornelii family, so he could wed a Vestal Virgin named Julia Aquilia Severa. This was a deep breach in religious custom, but the emperor justified it by asserting that "the marriage of a priest and priestess was both proper and sanctioned" as a human parallel for the divine marriage he was arranging for his god. Sensing a public outcry, Elagabalus soon divorced Severa, married a third wife, and declared that his god would wed Urania, the Carthaginian moon goddess. He required the city of Carthage to pay a large sum for the goddess's dowry and "ordered all men in Rome and Italy to celebrate with lavish feasts and festivals . . . the marriage of the two deities." Once the marriage of the gods took place, Elagabalus then divorced his third wife and began living with Severa again.[31]

Elagabalus reigned for less than four years and was married and divorced three times in that span, a remarkable turnover of wives no Roman emperor ever matched. This was, however, one of the less stunning features of the young man's biography. Cassius Dio criticized the emperor's tendency to "dance not only in the orchestra but also while walking, performing sacrifices, receiving salutations, or giving a speech," and the fact that "he was frequently seen in public clad in the barbaric dress which Syrian priests use."[32] Dio evoked the ancient stereotype of effeminate Syrians when he criticized the emperor for looking and behaving "like a woman," because he "sometimes wore a hair net, painted his eyes with white lead," and was a passive recipient of sexual penetration by men.[33] Dio recounted a series of sexual acts that he believed had debased the emperor, including a marriage to another man, a fetish for being "punished," a fascination with a well-endowed athlete named Zoticus, and a request that a doctor surgically create a vagina for Elagabalus.[34]

It is unclear how many of Dio's more extreme charges we can take seriously.[35] He certainly believed that Elagabalus's practices pertaining to dress, dance, and love could destabilize a Roman state whose own cultural traditions the emperor chose to ignore. Nothing shows this better than the story of Elagabalus's quest for a vagina, a physical act that would permanently blur the bodily distinction between male and female genders on the emperor's body. Dio's criticism of this quest, in particular, can be read as a metaphor for his larger concern that Elagabalus's reign would weaken the state by blurring the distinction between a powerful, masculine Roman Italy and the effete, feminine Roman East.

Dio was even more explicit about the threat he felt Elagabalus posed to native Roman customs and traditions when he wrote about his religious actions. These were objectionable "not because he introduced a foreign god into Rome or in his exalting the god in very strange ways, but in placing him even above Jupiter himself."[36] Religious diversity was not an issue, even for an old, grumpy senator like Dio. He was instead concerned that Elagabalus was trying to supplant rather than supplement Rome's native traditions.

Dio was not alone in feeling this way. Being "hated by the populace and by the soldiers," as well as by many in the Senate, represented a potentially fatal problem, not just for the emperor but for the women who were the actual power behind the throne. In June 221, Maesa, sensing that popular and military discontent might degenerate into a rebellion, compelled Elagabalus to adopt his cousin, the thirteen-year-old Alexander Severus, and make him Caesar.[37]

Alexander proved much more compliant than his older cousin Elagabalus. Maesa made sure Romans knew that, rather than practicing dancing, "not a single day passed in which [Alexander] did not train himself in literature and military drills."[38] When Elagabalus tried to teach his cousin "dancing and prancing," Alexander's mother, Julia Mamaea, told everyone who would listen that she "kept him from taking part in disgraceful activities unworthy of an emperor."[39] Alexander worked from dawn to dusk, and when his workday ended, he unwound by reading either Plato's *Republic* (in Greek) or Cicero's *On the Republic* (in Latin). Even his dinner parties were notoriously boring. Elagabalus had staged elaborate feasts with lots of wine, and he would let his pet leopard wander across the couches on which his drunken guests had passed out. Alexander, by contrast, refused to use fine tableware, forced his guests to drink from modest-sized goblets, and treated attendees to lectures by famous legal scholars. When Alexander really wanted to cut loose, he would let his guests watch puppies and piglets play with each other on the floor.[40]

Alexander's boring persona endeared him to the praetorian guards, who were tiring of Elagabalus's drama. On March 11, 222, when Alexander temporarily disappeared from public view, rumors spread that Elagabalus was trying to strip him of his position as Caesar and execute him. Elagabalus and his mother went to the praetorian camp to try to calm the soldiers, but they were seized, stripped naked, and beheaded. Their bodies were then dragged down to the Tiber in a ritual cleansing of the divine pollution they had supposedly brought to the city. Alexander was then proclaimed emperor by the praetorians and carried into the palace.[41]

THE SENATE DID not object to the elevation of Alexander, the purging of Elagabalan loyalists that followed, or the decision to ship Elagabalus's meteor back to Syria. Although they had been sidelined yet again in an imperial transition executed by the military, senators welcomed the fall of the odd emperor and gleefully accepted Maesa's creation of a council of senators to help her manage the state on behalf of the adolescent sovereign. The jurist Ulpian, one of the best legal minds in all of Roman history, headed this advisory group. Alexander bowed to the Senate in other ways, too. Older senators, including Cassius Dio and the biographer Marius Maximus, had a career renaissance under Alexander. Dio would proudly write that he "found it impossible to give an accurate account of events in Rome" after Alexander took power because he was too busy holding governorships in the provinces.[42]

Although Alexander's grandmother, Maesa; his mother, Mamaea; and his mentor, Ulpian, created an illusion of constitutional normality around the young emperor, tensions between senators, the urban population in the capital, and soldiers festered. Ulpian cut the amount of money given to the praetorian guards and was then assassinated by them despite taking refuge in the palace alongside the emperor and his mother. This happened amid a "great quarrel between the populace and praetorians" in Rome in which they "fought one another for three days, with much loss of life on both sides." It ended only when the praetorians began burning the city to force its residents to agree to terms.[43]

Dio ends his history in 229, just early enough that he could comment on, but not fully appreciate, the significance of an external development that would shape Roman history for the next four centuries. In 224, the Parthian Empire fell to a new Persian dynasty called the Sassanians. Rome's recent history of successes in Mesopotamia under Septimius Severus and Caracalla had led Romans to underestimate the potential threat from an energized Persian state reaching from the Indus to the Euphrates. Dio wrote that Ardashir, the new Persian shah, had "boasted that he would take back all that had come to him from his forefathers, which is to say everything that the ancient Persians had once held, as far as the Greek [i.e., Aegean] Sea." Dio was not particularly worried though. He wrote that "[Ardashir] himself does not seem to be of any particular consequence."[44]

It did not take long to see that Dio had badly underestimated the new Persian shah. In 230, Ardashir initiated attacks across the Roman frontier and confronted defenses that were not designed to repel such a strong and aggressive force.[45] Alexander Severus responded by setting out from Rome and gathering troops from the provinces along his way until he built a large enough field army to counterattack. Crucially, he also brought his mother with him.

Alexander's generals planned a large, extremely complicated invasion of western Persian territory. Three different Roman armies were to cross the frontier and meet at a prearranged point near the capital of Ctesiphon, but fissures appeared before the armies even crossed the border.[46] Mutinies broke out among Egyptian troops, while a group of Syrian soldiers tried to elevate another emperor.[47]

The armies also had mixed success once they crossed the frontier. The northern force accomplished little in Armenia, and the southern force was destroyed in a devastating battle. But the central force reconquered some of the territories that had been seized by Severus and Caracalla but that Ardashir had then captured.[48] Alexander, who commanded the largest group, failed to advance personally into Persian territory and was blamed for not preventing the "staggering disaster" suffered by the southern army. Herodian records that whispered rumors began to circulate among the soldiers that Mamaea had "blocked [Alexander's] efforts at courage by persuading him that he should let others risk their lives for him."[49]

As the Persian campaign wrapped up, Alexander led some of the remnants of his invasion force to Germany to deal with an incursion across the Rhine by the Alamanni, but instead of retaliating, he negotiated a settlement that included a payment in gold to the Germans.[50] The soldiers, some of whom had marched more than 2,000 miles with the emperor, were incensed that Alexander was still "doing nothing courageous or energetic" on the battlefield. They rallied around an officer named Maximinus, a massive and vigorous man who had trained many of them. Praising "the courage of Maximinus and despising Alexander as a momma's boy," Herodian wrote, the troops assembled on the parade grounds, placed a purple robe on Maximinus, and marched on Alexander's headquarters.[51]

Alexander begged the troops at headquarters to protect him, but they refused to fight and instead voiced grievances about their commanders, about Mamaea's greed, and about Alexander's stingy gifts. Alexander and his mother were given up to Maximinus and killed. The twenty-six-year-old was the first emperor to be killed by his own army while on campaign. "He had," Herodian wrote, "ruled fourteen years without blame or bloodshed." It would be many decades before Romans could say anything like that again about one of their rulers.[52]

THE FIELD ARMIES had now proven that they had the same capacity as the praetorian guards to destroy an emperor and raise his replacement. They were, however, not yet strong enough to ensure that an emperor they put in place could retain power if the Senate objected—and the Senate found a lot to object to in Maximinus, a Thracian by birth (and thus called "Maximinus Thrax"). Like Macrinus, he was not a senator when he took power. Like Elagabalus, he came from a strange part of the empire and was rumored to behave in odd ways. Over time, rumors circulated about his semi-barbaric, almost animalistic predilections. He was said to be eight and a half feet tall and the son of "a barbarian father and mother" who had "barely mastered Latin speech and spoke almost pure Thracian."[53] His daily diet consisted of drinking "a Capitoline amphora of wine [almost seven gallons] and eating forty pounds of meat." He would also "often catch his sweat and put it in cups or a small jar, and he could exhibit by this means two or three pints of it."[54]

None of this is likely to be true—or, in most cases, even possible—but intense suspicion of Maximinus made senators eager to back any rival who might emerge. Maximinus's difficulties finding the money to pay his soldiers what he had promised them exacerbated the situation. The recent wars had depleted the Roman treasury to such a degree that Maximinus felt compelled to cut the size of the grain dole in the city of Rome. He reduced other public expenditures in the capital as well, and he sliced the budget for the public holidays celebrating divinized emperors.[55]

In 238, the senators got their chance to act against the unpopular Maximinus. When the emperor's onerous taxes prompted a revolt in the province of Africa, the Senate rushed to condemn him as a tyrant and recognized the legitimacy of Gordian I and II, the father and son pair whom Africans had proclaimed co-emperors. Thus began the chaotic Year of the Six Emperors.

The two Gordians, the younger of whom was descended from Herodes Atticus on his mother's side, should have known better than to launch a revolt from a province with no army. They fell from power twenty-two days later when the governor of Numidia led the only legion in the area against them.[56] Fearing how Maximinus might punish them, the senators in Rome quickly elevated Balbinus and Pupienus, two older senators, to act as co-emperors and lead a defense against Maximinus.[57] The people of Rome, however, would not accept the Senate arrogating the selection of new emperors to itself. A faction rioted and compelled the Senate to agree to accept Gordian III, the thirteen-year-old grandson of Gordian I and nephew of Gordian II, as a third partner in leading the empire. By the end of the summer, Maximinus's soldiers had revolted and killed him outside of Aquileia, and the praetorian guards had killed the senatorial emperors Balbinus and Pupienus.[58] The child Gordian III was now sole emperor.

Herodian's history ends here, with the author unable to hide his deflation at "the undeserved and impious fate suffered by [Balbinus and Pupienus]." He concludes simply by saying that "Gordian, at the age of about thirteen, was designated emperor and assumed the burden of the Roman empire."[59] Herodian knew that Gordian's position was secure only because he was too young for any Roman faction to give up hope that he might be influenced to support them.

The Year of Six Emperors had revealed how much the institutions at the center of the empire had weakened. Armies, urban mobs, praetorian guards, and senators could now all proclaim emperors, but none of these segments of Roman society were strong enough to maintain the power of the emperors they proclaimed. The Roman state's next great political crisis had just begun.

Chapter 21

The Third-Century Crisis

244–284

I N 248, THE emperor Philip I celebrated the 1,000th anniversary of Rome's foundation with what he intended to be a magnificent set of games. Philip had come to power in 244 following the mysterious death of the young emperor Gordian III while he led his army back from Persian territory. The soldiers had chosen Philip, an Arab who was serving as Gordian's praetorian prefect, as his successor, and, like Macrinus and Maximinus Thrax, the previous two military emperors, he came from a remote part of the empire that had provided Rome with few senators and no previous emperors.[1] Their failures emphasized to Philip that he needed to get to Rome quickly so he could build ties with senators before they became restless. This led him to negotiate a peace treaty with the Persians in which he paid a war indemnity and signed off on Persian domination of Armenia. He then issued a coin bragging that "Peace has been established with the Persians," lavished gifts on his soldiers, seduced the senators with pledges of moderation, and arranged the divinization of Gordian III.[2]

Philip wanted Rome's 1,000th anniversary festival to illustrate the dawning of a new golden age of peace and good fortune.[3] He filled the Colosseum with spectacles featuring "32 elephants . . . 10 elk, 10 tigers, 60 tame lions, 30 tame leopards, 10 hyenas, 1,000 pairs of gladiators, 6 hippos, a rhino, 10 wild lions, 10 giraffes, 20 wild asses, and 40 wild horses."[4] This roster of beasts would have scarcely merited mention in previous centuries. Titus, for example, had displayed 9,000 animals in the games that opened the Colosseum; Trajan had celebrated the conquest of Dacia with games featuring 11,000 animals; and Augustus claimed to have organized hunts that killed over 3,500 "African wild beasts" across his reign.[5] Philip had managed to produce less than 100 "African wild beasts," and most of them were more like tame circus animals than fearsome killers. And even this crop of animals had taken years to assemble. Many had been procured by Gordian in the expectation that they could take part in a Persian triumph in 244, but the elephants were even older. The first 10 had been purchased by Alexander Severus. Gordian had procured the next 12. Philip could find only 10 more.[6]

Overhunting certainly contributed to the emperor's inability to procure large numbers of exotic animals, but the changing dynamics of Rome's relationship to the rest of the empire played at least as great a role. The empire no longer existed simply to supply Rome's needs. The needs of each province and the millions of Roman citizens living in them now mattered in a way that had not previously been the case. Many of these newer Roman citizens had adopted Roman tastes in entertainment. By the 240s, for example, more than 30 cities in the province of Africa had their own amphitheaters that demanded their own supply of African animals.

Not only had local demand for African animals increased dramatically, but second-century imperial policies encouraging the development of marginal land in North Africa squeezed wildlife populations.[7] Early third-century improvements in frontier defenses along the desert fringes of the Sahara and the foothills of the Atlas Mountains allowed farmers to push farther inland, destroying wide expanses of natural habitat in the process. The ecological damage done to the megafauna in North Africa happened in large part because of the Roman government's successful efforts to encourage economic opportunity for Africans.

In the middle decades of the third century the rest of the empire began to expect the same sort of imperial concern for economic prosperity and security that North Africans received from the Severans. Philip understood this desire and grasped that an empire centered on one emperor in Rome would struggle to respond effectively to the challenges his fellow citizens faced across the state's vast territory. As a result, when he traveled west to the capital in 244, he left his brother, Priscus, as the top military and civilian official in the east, and appointed his brother-in-law, Severianus, to command Roman forces along the lower Danube.[8] The power of each man thus extended across multiple provinces, superseding that of any individual provincial governor. Priscus and Severianus each served in their respective regions as "the man who gave judgement in place of the emperor" whenever regional problems and concerns arose.[9]

Philip created this new, regional administrative superstructure to make the empire more responsive to the local problems of its citizens. The plan, however, did not work. Priscus became the object of hatred in the east because of his "exactions of exorbitant taxes," and Severianus so angered people in the north that his administration prompted a rebellion, spearheaded by a rival emperor of Gallic descent named Pacatianus. Gaius Messius Quintus Decius, the senator Philip sent in response, crushed the rebellion only to have the defeated soldiers proclaim him emperor. He led his troops into Italy, defeated Philip outside of Verona, and killed the emperor and his son.[10]

The conservative Decius proved to be the opposite of the forward-thinking Philip. Instead of administrative reform, Decius believed the empire needed a jolt back to its military, cultural, and religious traditions.[11] He changed his name to Trajan Decius and issued a coin series featuring most of the divinized emperors of the past two and a half centuries in order to emphasize that he was bringing back Roman greatness, but Trajan Decius struggled to distinguish performative traditionalism from meaningful policies. A few months after taking power in 249, he attempted to reinvigorate the traditional religious practices that, in his view, had made the state strong. He instead caused the first empire-wide persecution of Christians.

Roman religion operated on a loose consensus that people would participate in the rituals that meant something to them and regularly express their gratitude to the gods they worshipped for the success of the state. But the empire was large, its gods diverse, and attendance was never taken at any single religious event. Trajan Decius, however, decided to require all Romans to appear individually before a public official, offer some incense, pour some wine on the ground, and receive a receipt from the public official saying they had done so.[12] He did not realize that, after the extension of universal citizenship across the entire empire, every Christian in the Roman Empire would be unable to comply with this law, because it meant breaking Christianity's total prohibition on participating in sacrifices.

Mid-third-century Christianity was a rapidly growing faith that had many more adherents in the large cities of the Eastern Mediterranean than it did in the west or in the Balkans, the areas of the empire that Trajan Decius knew best. Christian persecutions had occurred sporadically for nearly 200 years, but they were localized affairs that grew out of tensions within communities rather than policies pushed down from the imperial center. No previous emperor had wanted to target all Christians, nor had they spent much time thinking about individual Christians living in their midst. The faith was illegal insofar as some (but not all) of its practitioners refused to worship Roman gods, but anti-Christian actions were extremely low in priority for Roman governors.[13] Most Christians with only local citizenships would have been able to escape such an edict if it had been issued in 209. Now, as Roman citizens, they all were subject to its penalties.

The law hit hardest in places where local tensions between Christians and non-Christians were already high. In Alexandria, a city with one of the largest Christian populations in the world at the time, some Christians fled while others died after refusing to abide by the emperor's decree. But most Christians, even in Alexandria, ultimately did what the emperor asked. Some of them approached the altars "pale and trembling," according to the Christian historian Eusebius, because "they were afraid either to die or sacrifice." Others "declared boldly that they had never been Christians" and "advanced more readily to the altars." Still more Christians "remained faithful" until they were arrested or brought to trial, while a small minority of

Christians "endured great tortures until they finally retracted."[14] In the end, Trajan Decius had inadvertently used state power on a massive scale against a group that bothered few of their fellow citizens. The suffering he caused was altogether pointless.

Trajan Decius's military grandstanding proved even more disastrous than his religious initiatives. He provoked a Gothic invasion by stopping payments that Philip had agreed to make, and then prohibited his subjects from taking measures to defend themselves when attacked.[15] When the emperor decided to attack the Goths as they withdrew from Roman territory with their plunder, he blundered into a battle on swampy land near the city of Abritus (modern Razgrad in Bulgaria), and died along with his son and much of his army when they became bogged down in the muck.[16]

Trajan Decius's defeat by the Goths ushered in the most difficult decade the Roman state had endured in at least two centuries. Four emperors rose and fell between 251 and 253 amid barbarian raids that crossed the northern frontiers, rebellions in the provinces, and a plague that caused a disease similar to Ebola.[17] The army particularly suffered during these years. Trajan Decius's death, civil wars, and the casualties due to plague depleted the well-trained Roman forces—the ones that won battles because they were better drilled and more experienced than their adversaries. The less experienced soldiers who replaced them often suffered devastating losses when they fought. No defeat was worse than the one in 252 when a Persian attack destroyed the Roman army protecting Syria, killing perhaps as many as 60,000 soldiers. Persian troops then overran the province, plundered its cities, and sacked Antioch, the third-largest urban area in the empire.[18] The Persians took so many captives from Antioch that Roman sources say it was "no longer called a city," because it was left "entirely ruined and naked, houseless, uninhabited."[19]

THE REELING EMPIRE seemed to fall into capable hands when the old, accomplished senator Valerian took power in September 253. Valerian had held the position of president of the Senate for more than a decade. He had served as censor under Decius and had commanded armies in the recent civil wars.[20] His extensive experience as both a senator and a military leader made him acceptable to both the Senate and the armies, the two centers of Roman power that had eyed each other distrustfully since the time of Alexander Severus. Despite his advanced age, Valerian spent much of his reign crisscrossing the empire so he could reassure Roman citizens in the provinces that he cared about their needs. At one point, he journeyed from Syria to Cologne and back to Rome in a little more than a year and a half.[21]

These efforts, however, did not improve Roman life very much. As Valerian became increasingly desperate to reverse the empire's fortunes, his coins show an increased emphasis on piety, public sacrifice, health, and the healing power of Apollo.[22] Eusebius wrote that the emperor had once "been mild and friendly toward" Christians, but, by 257, he had heard from pagan priests that Christians were hindering the effectiveness of some religious ceremonies. Valerian responded with two edicts that, unlike Trajan Decius's measures, deliberately targeted the church and its members. His first edict appeared in August 257 and ordered that Christian leaders must either perform sacrifices or be sent into exile. In the summer of 258, he issued a second edict mandating the execution of all male Christians who refused to take part in the sacrifices, the confiscation of property belonging to female Christians, and the enslavement of Christians in imperial service.[23]

Valerian's persecutions neither destroyed the church nor helped the empire. Bishop Cyprian of Carthage wrote that the persecutions in fact strengthened the church, because Christians who remained faithful despite imperial pressure formed the nucleus of a more pious and robust community.[24] At the same time, the empire was growing weaker. Between late 258 and mid-260, German raiders crossed both the Rhine and the Alps to enter Italy, the first barbarian armies to penetrate the peninsula since the time of Marius. They sacked cities and captured a large number of Roman citizens before turning back and heading for home in 260. Herulian ships from the Black Sea entered the Aegean and raided as far as the Mediterranean coast of what is now southern Turkey.

The Persians represented an even greater threat. As Valerian led his army east to counter a Persian invasion of Mesopotamia, plague descended on the soldiers. The ill and tired army was defeated in the field and then besieged near the Anatolian city of Edessa. Valerian left to meet with the Persian shah to negotiate an armistice, but instead he was captured, taken off to Persia, and imprisoned there for the rest of his life. One tradition says that he was flayed alive.[25]

The emperor's capture ended the persecution of Christians and led to the collapse of his army. Persian forces flowed out into Syria and eastern Asia Minor, their eagerness to plunder destroying their discipline and leaving them utterly unprepared for the Roman counterattack. Valerian's son and co-emperor Gallienus had been left in charge of the western territories of the empire, but he did not lead the Roman reaction. It was improvised by Romans living in the area, who reinforced the imperial military forces with whatever local, armed resistance could be organized. The motley troops then served under the command of the most senior regional Roman official they could find. In Asia Minor, forces led by a treasury secretary named Macrianus pushed the Persians back after fighting in Cilicia and then proclaimed his sons Macrianus and Quietus emperors.[26] Along the Danube, two governors named Regalianus and Ingenuus also rebelled after mobilizing armies.[27]

These usurpations in Asia Minor and the Balkans were snuffed out by 261, but in other parts of the Roman world the reaction to the collapse of central authority in 260 had more lasting effects. Along the Rhine frontier, Postumus, a Roman commander who came from what is now the Netherlands, led a revolt of Roman troops and local civilian levies against Gallienus.[28] Unlike the rebels in Anatolia and along the Danube, Postumus did not try to advance on Rome or overthrow Gallienus. Rather than using his resources to try to seize control over all Romans, he turned his attention to improving the security of Romans living in European territories north of the Alps and along the Atlantic coast. When Postumus and a local German levy destroyed a group of barbarians who had raided Italy and "freed many thousands of Italian captives" that Gallienus's central government could not, his regime emphasized to everyone that the Roman state could function much more effectively if the people living in the imperial center were willing to cede some authority to their eager and capable fellow citizens living closer to the frontiers.[29]

Something similar happened in Syria. After Valerian's capture, a man named Odaenathus, who was the leader of the oasis city of Palmyra and a Roman client king, combined his own formidable troops with the remnants of Valerian's army. Acting under the nominal authority of Gallienus, Odaenathus led a devastating counterattack on the Persian troops that had retreated following their defeat in Cilicia.[30] Gallienus played along and appointed Odaenathus the "commander of the East," a position that officially must have resembled what Philip the Arab had given his brother Priscus in the late 240s.[31] Odaenathus then invaded Persian Mesopotamia twice in the next seven years. The first attack, in 262 or 263, penetrated as far as the Persian capital of Ctesiphon. The second, which he launched in 267, may again have reached the vicinity of Ctesiphon.[32]

If the disasters of the 250s had ruined the ability of the central government to effectively marshal and utilize the resources of Rome's immense empire, the successes of the early 260s showed how powerful these regional resources remained. This meant that the Roman internal power struggles reignited after Postumus and Odaenathus removed the immediate danger of imperial collapse by stabilizing the frontiers using the wealth and personnel of the provinces. Odaenathus was the first to fall. He was assassinated in late 267 or early 268, following a plot likely orchestrated by Gallienus and executed by local Palmyrene rivals. Gallienus was assassinated in September 268, and Postumus was killed by his troops in early 269 after he resisted their calls to invade Italy and sack the city of Mainz.[33]

THESE MEN HAD all either assented to or failed to effectively challenge the informal but stable regional divisions of the empire in the 260s, and their deaths only brought more Roman infighting. After the general Marius overthrew Postumus, civil strife in Gaul quickly eliminated the Gallic regime's ability to do anything more than protect its territorial core. Claudius II Gothicus, the new emperor in Rome, took advantage of the chaos to retake Spain and the Rhône River Valley for the central empire.

In Syria, Odaenathus's widow, Zenobia, arranged for their young son Vabalathus to take power in Palmyra, an oddity in a city with scant tradition of hereditary monarchy. Zenobia also claimed that Odaenathus's Roman title of "commander of the East" had passed down to her son. When Claudius II refused to assent to this, Zenobia ordered Palmyrene forces to invade Egypt and remove it from central governmental control. Even so, the three Roman statelets centered in Gaul, Rome, and Palmyra could only challenge the division of Roman territory that emerged in the early 260s. Neither the central government in Rome nor the Roman principalities centered in Gaul and Palmyra had the power to seize control of all Roman territory for themselves.

At the same time, Gaul, the central empire, and the Palmyrene-controlled lands all remained Roman territory, governed by Roman law and populated by Roman citizens.[34] They could not be anything else. The people living in them were Romans who valued that identity and had no desire to live in a non-Roman state. Their sovereigns knew this. Every ruler of the Gallic Empire issued coins bearing the Roman imperial title they claimed. Until the final moments of Vabalathus's reign, he affirmed his theoretical loyalty to the emperor based in Rome by placing that emperor's picture on the front of his coins. Vabalathus's portrait adorned the reverse, however, with text marking the youth as king of Palmyra and a man of Roman consular status who held a legitimate Roman military command.[35]

Rome's internal rivalries coexisted with a string of foreign military successes. The stabilization of the frontiers in the mid-260s gave Rome time to recruit and train new, professional soldiers, including a powerful cavalry corps that Claudius II deployed with great effectiveness. Although he reigned for less than two years, Claudius's forces won impressive victories over two separate invasions by Allemanic and Gothic armies, earning him the titles Germanicus Maximus and Gothicus. The Gothic victory was particularly impressive. Claudius defeated and destroyed a force said to number more than 300,000 men that was carried across the Black Sea on 2,000 ships— both impossibly large numbers that convey the incalculable number of Goths Claudius killed.[36]

When Claudius II Gothicus died from plague in early 270, his most accomplished commander, Aurelian, quickly displaced the emperor's brother Quintillus, who had briefly seized power.[37] Aurelian immediately faced two separate barbarian incursions, by the Juthungi and the Vandals, that he beat back in the autumn and early winter of 270.[38] Then, in a particularly poorly understood event in 271, Aurelian "fell upon the rich [in the city of Rome] like a tsunami," killing senators and seizing their property following a revolt in the capital led by mint workers. As he reconstituted the Senate with members loyal to himself, Aurelian asserted his dominance over the city by constructing a massive brick and concrete wall around Rome, the first systematic attempt to fortify the capital against attack since the much smaller, militarily obsolete Servian walls of the early Republic.[39] He wanted no Roman to again question his strength.

Aurelian next embarked on a series of military campaigns designed to establish his dominance over the rest of the Roman world by reunifying all the territory ruled by Romans under his sole control. The Palmyrene-controlled Roman East was his first target. In 272, he arranged for the defection of Egypt, and then marched his army through Palmyrene lands in Asia Minor before entering Syria.[40] In a decisive battle outside of Emesa, Aurelian's formidable cavalry "were on the point of breaking their ranks" before "a divine form spread encouragement throughout the soldiers and horsemen." Rallying, they forced Zenobia to retreat. When Aurelian entered Emesa, he "at once made his way to the Temple of Elagabal," the god his predecessor Elagabalus had worshipped, and "there saw the same divine form which he had seen supporting his cause in the battle."[41] Aurelian would remain a devotee of this solar cult for the rest of his life.

Zenobia's defeat at Emesa left the road to Palmyra open, and Aurelian soon captured the city and its king. Zenobia was apprehended a bit later, reportedly as she fled toward the Euphrates in the hope of convincing the Persian shah to enter the war on her behalf.[42] Then, in 274, Aurelian reabsorbed Roman Gaul and seized Tetricus I and Tetricus II, the last two Gallic emperors, following a victory at Châlons in 274.[43] A fourth-century historian wrote, evocatively but most incorrectly, that, at this moment, Aurelian "was not unlike Alexander the Great or Caesar the Dictator; for in the space of three years he retook the Roman world from invaders."[44]

At the end of 274, Aurelian staged one of the most impressive triumphal processions in Roman history, displaying the vast plunder he had taken from Gaul and Syria. Zenobia, Tetricus I, and Tetricus II were its stars. Both of the Gallic emperors wore scarlet cloaks, yellow tunics, and Gallic trousers, while Zenobia "was decked with jewels and in gold chains so heavy that their weight was borne by others."[45] They were followed by people carrying the crowns of victory sent by all the major cities in the empire, the residents of Rome marching in their guilds, Roman troops, and senators. Aurelian's intended message was clear: He had reunited all Romans into a single state.

Aurelian understood that reunification of the empire could not be done through military victories alone. A peaceful, public reconciliation with the defeated Gallic and Syrian separatist leaders followed his grand triumph. Aurelian freed Zenobia and allowed her to marry a Roman senator so she could live luxuriously in Rome. He arranged for the Senate to appoint Tetricus I governor of Lucania and decreed that Tetricus II would keep his senatorial rank.[46]

The emperor also publicly embraced Syrian culture. After the assistance he believed the sun god had provided him outside of Emesa, Aurelian brought Elagabalus's solar deity back to Rome. This was done much more carefully than when his predecessor had first introduced the sun god two generations earlier. Aurelian reestablished the god in a large temple in the center of the city, enlisted a prominent senator to serve as the restored cult's priest, and returned the god to Roman coins in a form that Romans better understood.

The coins featured an anthropomorphized version of the sun god's likeness, rather than the conical rock of the 220s, and the Latin title "Sol Invictus" (Unconquerable Sun) rather than the Syrian name that had provoked such hostility half a century before. Elagabalus was back in the capital, but in a way that represented a symbolic binding together of the Roman East and West.

Aurelian also addressed some of the long-standing causes of the third century's chronic instability. His reign settled the question of whether the Senate or the army would determine who the emperors would be. Claudius II Gothicus, Quintillus, and Aurelian were all choices of the army—and Aurelian's purge of his senatorial opponents in Rome made clear that the Senate now lacked the capacity to stand against emperors elevated by soldiers.[47]

THIS SHIFT IN who chose the emperor led to a change in the sort of person who ascended to the office. As the son of a tenant farmer who grew up in the Balkan countryside, Aurelian would have faced the same senatorial prejudice that had doomed Maximinus Thrax, another emperor of humble birth from the Balkans, if he had come to power a generation earlier.[48] Aurelian, however, stood at the leading edge of a half-century-long movement entrusting imperial power almost exclusively to Balkan soldiers born to non-senatorial families.

These men did not behave like Decius, who had compensated for his provincial origins by aggressively embracing an ostentatious senatorial conservatism. Beginning with Aurelian, they instead emphasized their distinction from ordinary senators. Aurelian wore "a diadem on his head, and he used gems and gold on every item of clothing to a degree almost unknown in Roman tradition."[49] Trajan, Marcus Aurelius, and other emperors of the past had sought to embody the ideal that the emperor was the first among a group of senatorial equals. Aurelian and the Balkan emperors who followed were instead practical men comfortable with their place in a military aristocracy that sometimes overlapped with but owed little deference to the old Roman senatorial elites.

With the tension between the army and the Senate now decisively resolved in favor of the army, Aurelian took steps to ensure that his newly recentralized Roman administration took better care of Romans living outside of the empire's old Italian core. His policies often tried to strike a delicate balance between spreading more imperial activities to the provinces and maintaining firm central control over what happened there. The mint workers' rebellion and the proliferation of coinage issued from Gallic and Syrian mints during the 260s and early 270s encouraged Aurelian to deemphasize the role of the mint in Rome. He opened or expanded imperial mints in Lyon, Milan, Ticinum (in Italy), Siscia (in modern Croatia), Serdica (in Bulgaria), Cyzicus (in Turkey), Antioch, and Tripoli (in Libya) to ensure the ready supply of coinage.

Aurelian and his successors also replaced many of the civic institutions that had made Rome so resilient in the 260s with centrally funded defensive structures. Palmyra lost its independent army and was turned into a fortified Roman army garrison center.[50] In Athens, the traditional military training given to young Athenian citizens was discontinued, and a new, hastily built wall enclosed the city center.[51] In Gaul, the imperial government undertook a major program of wall building in places as diverse as the northern French city of Senlis, the western city of Bordeaux, and the southern town of Carcassonne.[52] These walls were not just functional, they were also beautiful symbols of the emperor's material dedication to the protection of Romans living near the frontiers.

Not all Roman communities received this level of support. Some, like the province of Dacia, instead experienced a managed retreat. After repeated barbarian incursions that depopulated the lands south and west of the Danube had made the province undefendable, Aurelian withdrew Roman troops to forts along the riverbank and resettled most, but not all, of its Roman citizens in what is now Bulgaria.[53] This was the first time in Roman history that the state had pulled back from territory and left Roman citizens to fend for themselves. It would not be the last.

Even so, the stability Aurelian craved proved elusive. As 275 dawned, he was the most powerful Roman emperor in over half a century. Less than a year later he was dead, the victim of an assassination plot that grew out of a personal grievance nursed by a courtier.[54] Aurelian had done a great deal to update the way the empire functioned, and he had tried to address the needs of its subjects, but the order he created depended a great deal upon his commanding presence.

With Aurelian gone, the Roman Senate and the commanders of the armies spent months trying to agree on a successor. The army, "which tended to create emperors hastily," asked the Senate to nominate one of its members, probably to avoid sparking a power struggle among commanders that might lead to civil war. "The Senate, however, knowing that the emperors it had chosen were unacceptable to the soldiers, referred the matter back to them." The stalemate, which lasted for up to six months, left Aurelian's wife Severina as the state's figurehead until the Senate selected an elderly senator named Marcus Claudius Tacitus.[55] Tacitus died within six months, and by mid-276 Rome had again descended into civil war.[56] Five more emperors would come and go before Diocletian, Rome's next strong sovereign, seized control in 284. It is with him that a new imperial age finally dawned.

PART 4

FROM DIOCLETIAN TO THEODERIC AND JUSTIN I

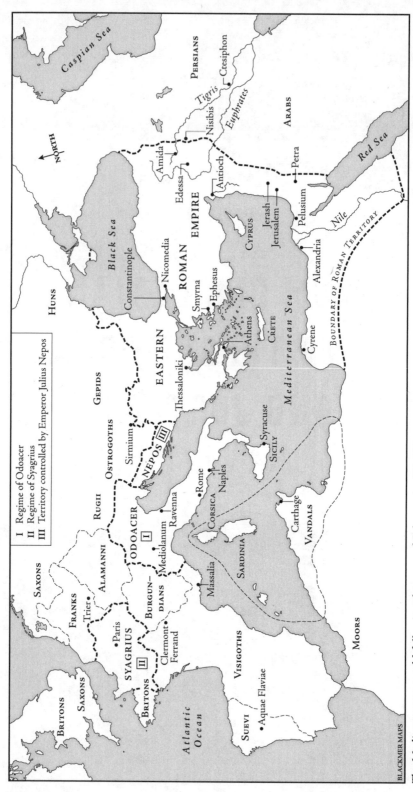

The Mediterranean world following the coup of Odoacer in AD 476

Chapter 22

Diocletian, Constantine, and the Foundations of a New Roman State

284–312

THE ROMAN EMPIRE experienced a strange mixture of foreign military success and domestic instability in the decade between the death of Aurelian and Diocletian's assumption of full control in the summer of 285. There were revolts in Syria, Britain, Germany, southern Egypt, and Asia Minor; barbarian incursions along the Rhine; and a naval raid by the Franks that sacked the Sicilian city of Syracuse, but at the same time Rome saw continued success in its campaigns against Persia, its largest and most dangerous imperial rival. In 282, the emperor Probus set out on a Persian campaign and was assassinated before he reached the border, but Carus, the praetorian prefect who took power after Probus's death, continued the Roman advance until he sacked the Persian capital of Ctesiphon.[1]

By the mid-280s, the Roman military had recovered the ability to capably project power beyond its borders against even the mighty Persian Empire. At the same time, it still had not figured out how to convert this military power into a tool that dissuaded usurpers and prevented barbarian raids across the northern border. Diocletian made it his mission to ensure that Rome retained its military advantage against large, well-organized adversaries like Persia while preventing usurpations and responding quickly to smaller-scale barbarian incursions.

Diocletian had learned from the failed reforms and fallen emperors of the past five decades. He understood that an unclear succession plan or a weak successor represented a mortal danger to a reigning emperor. So, in 286, Diocletian named Maximian, a fellow army officer from the Balkans, as his imperial partner. This arrangement differed from those of the mid-third century in which emperors like Philip I, Trajan Decius, and Valerian had designated their sons as ostensible co-emperors while emphasizing that these sons were subordinate to their fathers. Diocletian had instead returned to the second-century model of adopting a mature, proven heir who fully shared imperial power before an emperor died. Unlike Hadrian, however, Diocletian made this appointment almost immediately after securing power. From that point on, Maximian was fully Diocletian's partner with equal authority and responsibilities. This imperial pairing ensured that any challenge to either Diocletian or Maximian would be met with a robust, forceful, and terrifying response by an adult emperor at the head of a loyal, veteran army.

The imperial pair also enjoyed greater flexibility to deal with regional challenges, because they could each command armies in different parts of the empire simultaneously. Rome had been sporadically moving in this direction since Marcus Aurelius and Lucius Verus had reigned together and campaigned along different frontiers in the 160s, but most of the third-century emperors either ignored this precedent or failed to find a way to make it work in contemporary conditions. Diocletian and Maximian initially arranged their partnership so that each man could lead his army to the regions that most required an imperial presence. Eventually, their areas of responsibility became geographically bounded, with Maximian largely working in the west and Diocletian paying more attention to the eastern provinces.[2]

Diocletian and Maximian expanded this model of shared governance in 293 when they appointed two junior colleagues, Galerius and Constantius, to serve as their deputies. Instead of a pair of emperors, a college of four sovereigns now ruled the empire. Diocletian and Maximian, the two senior members of the imperial college, continued as Augusti. Constantius, Maximian's deputy, and Galerius, who served as Diocletian's colleague, each held the title of Caesar. This system, which would come to be called the tetrarchy (a term meaning "rule by four men"), worked on the principle that each tetrarch individually represented the entire college. Imperial laws were issued in the name of all four men. Coins and statues featured all four tetrarchs together, with identical faces and features, embracing or sacrificing as a group. When their individual portraits appeared on coins, the emperors all looked the same as well.[3]

Diocletian and his colleagues eventually agreed that, after twenty years in power, the senior emperors would retire. Then their Caesars would be promoted to Augusti, and new Caesars would be selected. The guarantee that Galerius and Constantius would each eventually assume power as an Augustus disincentivized them from launching a coup against Diocletian and Maximian. It also communicated that anyone outside the tetrarchy who contemplated rebellion by killing one of them could expect to face a devastating response from the other three. The tetrarchy became both a source of stability in the present and a powerful guarantee of orderly succession in the future.

The tetrarchs also restructured many of the basic operations of the empire itself.[4] Each of the tetrarchs operated out of bases in provincial cities such as Nicomedia, Thessaloniki, and Trier that lay nearer than Rome to the frontiers they defended. The tetrarchs modernized these cities, adorned them with impressive monumental architecture, and expanded their cores into regional administrative centers.

The last decade of the third century and the first part of the fourth saw new administrative layers develop beneath the college of emperors. Diocletian made use of praetorian prefects with expanded powers and responsibilities to execute imperial policies and handle issues that were too complicated for a provincial governor but not serious enough to require imperial attention.[5] Over time, the praetorian prefectures became regularized as the highest administrative divisions of the empire until, by the 340s, there were five prefectures, each with its own financial and judicial staff.

The provinces themselves were redrawn into smaller, more easily governed units so that they could be administered more efficiently.[6] The old Roman province of Asia, for example, was roughly the size of Florida and included more than 2,000 different cities. By the end of Diocletian's reign, it had been divided into seven new provinces, each with a separate military and civilian administration. Diocletian also did away with the administrative inequalities that had for centuries exempted Italians from taxation and required Egyptians to use a separate currency. A lifetime after Caracalla's expansion of universal citizenship in 212, Rome had finally embraced the fact that all its citizens, everywhere, were full stakeholders in the Roman political enterprise.

The new provinces and prefectures of the early fourth century required a large bureaucracy to staff offices designed to be aware of and responsive to the needs of citizens across the empire. The number of permanent new positions would have stunned Romans from previous centuries. They were accustomed to small provincial administrative staffs that governors temporarily supplemented with their own assistants, but by the end of the fourth century there were upward of 40,000 new, permanent bureaucrats staffing the offices of prefects, military commanders, and governors.[7] Whereas the lean government of the early empire had depended largely upon Italians and a narrow group of provincial senators, the professional administration of the fourth century drew upon talented people from everywhere across the empire. It needed to do this because there were not enough qualified Italians.

Roman emperors turned to the empire's schools of rhetoric and law to identify promising young men who could be induced to join the imperial administration. By the middle of the fourth century, teachers like the sophist Libanius were writing hundreds of letters recommending students for government positions.[8] The sons of local aristocrats, who once would have aspired only to leadership in their town councils, could now compete for lucrative positions running the state in what the emperors hoped would be a meritocratic Roman bureaucracy.

As the skills of Roman administrators improved, so, too, did the state's ability to collect taxes and dispense public funds in ways that effectively responded to the needs of its citizens. In 297, the tetrarchs created a new system that regularly reassessed the tax obligations of landholders based upon the current economic condition of their property.[9] Taxes might decrease for someone whose land had fallen out of cultivation and increase when the productivity of the land improved. At around the same time, the tetrarchs decided to combat a bout of hyperinflation by remaking the Roman monetary system. Their new coinage consisted of a pure gold coin that came to be called the *solidus* as well as a new silver coin and three silver washed bronze coins of different sizes. The goal was to create a comprehensive, trimetallic system in which the same coins circulated everywhere in the empire. It would give all Romans the ability to exchange low-value bronze for silver or gold coins at a predictable rate.[10] The number of mints also grew significantly: Fifteen different mints struck upward of 20 million coins a year with the same basic design in locations from London to Alexandria. Fourth-century Roman mints produced so many coins each year that it was not until the early twentieth century that nations again began to produce as many coins as Diocletian did annually.[11] This was the sort of thing that showcased the tremendous competence of the expanding Roman government.

By the time Diocletian and Maximian entered the last part of their second decade in power, conditions in the empire had improved to such a degree that they could begin worrying about preserving the gains they had made. Diocletian and his Caesar, Galerius, started to focus on religious practices, particularly ones that they suspected might turn the gods against the resurgent Roman state. In 302, they ordered the proconsul of Egypt to arrest the leaders of the Manichees, a religious group that had developed around the teaching of a third-century Persian named Mani. These leaders were to be burned alive along with their sacred books.

In 303, Diocletian's measures expanded to target Christians after they were believed to have disrupted a religious ritual in which he was participating. This shocked his Christian subjects, because they believed that Valerian's capture in 260 had effectively demonstrated that the old gods showed no favor to those who persecuted Christians. Persecution had ceased in the territories controlled by Gallienus, Postumus, and Palmyra in the 260s, and had not resumed at any point in the intervening four decades. The decision to effectively tolerate their religious activities had brought Christians out from underground. Churches had begun to appear in cities with large Christian populations. One of the most beautiful of the new churches stood on a hill above Diocletian's palace in the city of Nicomedia.[12] Christians even served openly in the army and at Diocletian's court.[13]

Residents of Nicomedia were then stunned when, on February 23, 303, officials posted an edict outlining a new persecution of Christians. Unlike Valerian and Decius nearly half a century earlier, Diocletian did not want to round up and kill every Christian in the empire. But he did intend to deploy the power of the Roman bureaucracy to destroy the church as an organization by seizing its buildings and decapitating its leadership. Roman officials were told to confiscate church property, burn Christian holy books, strip Christians of any special legal and social privileges they enjoyed, and re-enslave imperial freedmen who were Christians. Diocletian and his co-emperors could not have known that Christianity's steady growth during the forty years when its practices were tolerated meant that the empire was perhaps 10 percent Christian. They did not realize they had targeted a large enough group that Christians in some parts of the Roman world would decide to violently resist the persecution, at least at first.[14]

Their resistance prompted imperial authorities to press Christians even harder. Further edicts followed across the summer and fall of 303 and into early 304. Edicts in 303 mandated the arrest of clergy, and, in 304, the emperors reinstated Decius's requirement that all Romans registered on the public census rolls perform a sacrifice. The Christian authors Lactantius and Eusebius describe mass imprisonment, Christians burned alive, the seizure of Christian structures, and the destruction of Christian scriptures. While these horrors undoubtedly happened, the emperors remained uninterested in targeting ordinary Christians. The *Life of Antony*, a text written about the first Christian monk in the early 360s, recounts how Antony tried to become a martyr by storming into a courtroom and declaring himself a Christian during the tetrarchs' persecution. The bemused judge simply sent him away.[15]

The tetrarchic persecution depended heavily upon the priorities of the imperial officials and local city councilors charged with implementing it. Some documents, such as a receipt given to a lector following the search of his church near the Egyptian city of Oxyrhynchus, show that city councilors followed their orders in the most perfunctory way possible. It is unlikely that the lector was telling the truth when he claimed "that the church had neither gold nor silver nor money nor vestments nor animals nor slaves nor land nor property from gifts nor from testamentary bequests," but the receipt was nonetheless issued.[16] In other cases, Christian church members who were ordered to turn over sacred books gave ignorant or disinterested local officials whatever texts were lying around—including medical books and texts written by heretics.

Although the legal framework for the so-called Great Persecution remained in place until 311, when Galerius issued an edict of toleration, actions against Christians became much more sporadic after the intense bursts in 303 and 304.[17] Much of this had to do with the unraveling of the tetrarchy between 305 and 310.

IN THE FALL of 303, Diocletian journeyed to Rome to persuade Maximian that it was time for them both to figure out how to step aside as Augusti. Diocletian and Maximian originally had planned to name Constantine and Maxentius, the sons of Constantius and Maximian, as Caesars upon their retirement, but Galerius orchestrated things so that he and Constantius became the new Augusti while his friends Severus and Maximinus Daia were elevated to the ranks of Caesar.[18]

Both ancient and modern sources have framed Galerius's actions as a "thinly veiled coup."[19] But nonviolent coups of this sort can certainly work if the political reality they create has time to harden. It is easy to imagine a nonhereditary, term-limited tetrarchy becoming the new Roman normal if Galerius and Constantius reigned for ten years, retired, elevated Severus and Maximinus Daia to the status of Augusti, and allowed them to choose the new Caesars.

This did not happen. Constantius died in 306 while leading his army in Britain, and his troops quickly proclaimed his son Constantine, who had been traveling with them, as Augustus in place of his father. Constantius's army knew Constantine, respected him, and much preferred serving under a commander they trusted to serving under some replacement who would be chosen by the surviving tetrarchs at some point, perhaps months, in the future. It is possible that Constantius himself openly encouraged the army to think of his son as his natural successor. Both the army and Constantine also had the benefit of time. Communications in the Roman Empire moved slowly, and Britain was about as far from the other three tetrarchs as one could be. When word spread across the empire that Constantius had died, there was almost simultaneous news that his army had proclaimed Constantine Augustus in his place.[20]

There was little that the other tetrarchs could do to remove Constantine. Because Constantius's death had left a vacancy in the tetrarchic college that his son had filled with the backing of an army, Constantine had not exactly usurped his position. He and his soldiers had been particularly savvy in how they handled his proclamation. By acclaiming the new tetrarch as an Augustus and not just a Caesar, they had left him room to negotiate his status with the other tetrarchs. In the end, Constantine, Galerius, Severus, and Maximinus Daia reached a compromise. Constantine would be recognized as part of the imperial college by the other three men, but he would join as a Caesar and not an Augustus. Severus, the Caesar chosen to serve under Constantius, would now ascend to the status of Augustus.[21]

This solved the immediate problem of how to handle Constantine, but it sparked a new, much bigger crisis. Maxentius, the son of Diocletian's co-emperor Maximian, recognized that the other tetrarchs' acceptance of Constantine's accession presented him with an opportunity to press his own claim to imperial power.[22] In late October 306, he followed an old blueprint for imperial usurpation by seizing control of the city of Rome with the help of the urban prefect and praetorian guards. If it had been the year 206, that step alone might have been enough to secure imperial power. In the early fourth century, it ensured the wrath of four other emperors, all of them with armies.

Severus, the Caesar who was elevated to Augustus following Constantius's death, attacked Maxentius first from his base in Northern Italy. Italians, however, loathed Severus, because of his role in assessing punitive taxes during a recent census, and his armies deserted him when Maximian returned to Rome from his retirement villa to support his son.[23] Maxentius's forces captured and imprisoned Severus. When Galerius then invaded Italy to support Severus, Maxentius realized that the senior emperor had too few troops to surround Rome and drew him down toward the capital. Galerius recognized he had no good way to counter Maxentius's strategy and withdrew from the peninsula after failing to negotiate a settlement. Almost as soon as he left, Maxentius had Severus killed.

Maxentius benefited from his father's diplomatic savvy during these early years. While Maxentius battled Severus and Galerius, Maximian arranged a marriage that joined Constantine and Maxentius's sister Fausta; he also backed Constantine's elevation to the rank of Augustus after Severus's murder. This was enough to convince Constantine to stay north of the Alps and let affairs in Italy play out.[24]

Maxentius's successful defiance of two different tetrarchs undercut one of the most powerful selling points for Diocletian's institutional reform. The danger of courting multiple attacks from multiple armies loyal to four different sovereigns was supposed to dissuade people from even trying to usurp power. Maxentius, however, had shown that a capable usurper could seize Rome, hide behind its massive walls, and hold on to power as his attacker's soldiers either defected or grew tired of civil war. This was an excellent survival strategy, but it was not one that could lead to a secure position in the imperial college without astute diplomacy.

Sometime in 308, Maximian recognized that his son lacked the patience and skill to walk the long diplomatic path that would lead to his recognition by the other tetrarchs. Maximian attempted a coup against his son, and, when this failed, he sought Constantine's protection in Gaul. With Constantine's assent, Maximian then met Galerius and Diocletian at Carnuntum, a naval base on the Danube near the point where the modern nations of Austria, Slovakia, and Hungary converge. Diocletian had no interest in exercising imperial power again, but he did hope for one final attempt to salvage the tetrarchy. On November 11, 308, the three current and former emperors declared that Diocletian would remain retired; Maximian would again retire to Gaul; Galerius would remain Augustus; Constantine and Maximinus would remain Caesars; and Licinius, another friend of Galerius, would be elevated to the rank of Augustus in place of the murdered Severus. Despite controlling Rome, Maxentius was branded a usurper.[25]

The next three years saw even more upheaval among the tetrarchs. Like Sulla when he had withdrawn from public life 400 years before, Diocletian, in deciding to remain retired, was entrusting others with protecting the integrity of a political system he had created. But they did not value the concept of long-term, collaborative governance as much as he did. Each part of the empire saw different challenges. The governor of Numidia revolted against Maxentius in 308, forcing him to campaign in Africa in 309.[26] In 310, Maximian emerged from retirement and tried to overthrow Constantine. He died in the city of Massalia after Constantine reached its walls.[27] At that point, Galerius's health was failing. When he died in the spring of 311, the tetrarchic college lost its last member who really believed in the system. This freed Constantine, Licinius, Maxentius, and Maximinus Daia, the four men who held a share of imperial power in the empire, to negotiate with and fight against one another.

Licinius and Constantine soon came to an agreement to support one another as they disposed of their rivals. Constantine would back Licinius as he attacked Daia. In return, Licinius drew some of Maxentius's forces to northeastern Italy, by intimating that he might invade, while Constantine led a fast-moving army across the Alps into the Italian northwest. Even with Licinius's help, Constantine's invasion of Italy remained a risky proposition. Maxentius had not only defeated both Severus and Galerius, but had spent the past five years focusing on the defense of Italy, building up his army, and reinforcing the walls of Rome.[28]

According to Eusebius, Constantine believed that "he needed some more powerful aid than his military forces could afford him" if he was to defeat Maxentius, so "he sought divine assistance."[29] He then saw a symbol in the heavens that seemed to be the Christian God's reply to his prayers. His mother and other members of his court were Christians, so, perhaps under their influence, Constantine decided that his invasion would only succeed if his troops fought under the Christian sign that had appeared to him.[30] He ordered that "a likeness of that sign . . . be made" so he could "use it as a safeguard in all engagements with his enemies."[31] If representations on the coins of later fourth-century emperors are a good guide, Constantine's standards now bore the Greek letters X and P (which are the first two letters of "Christ" in Greek) overlayed on top of each other. No one could mistake which God's protection he now claimed.

Although we cannot now say when Constantine's armies first marched under this sign, they advanced with unbelievable speed through Northern Italy and fought extremely effectively. Constantine managed to seize major cities, including Milan and Turin, without having to resort to a siege. He defeated a large field army outside of Verona, and by the end of the summer he had reached Rome. This was more than either Severus or Galerius had managed, despite their greater resources.[32]

Maxentius was prepared, however. He had cut the bridges to the city, done a last set of repairs to the walls, and stocked the capital with supplies to withstand a siege. Then, on October 28, he did something so incomprehensibly stupid that no ancient author could explain it.[33]

Rome was well defended, and Constantine lacked the numbers to surround the city, but Maxentius nevertheless chose to lead his army out of the city to confront Constantine on a field to the north. Fighting with their backs to the Tiber, Maxentius's men were defeated. They retreated to the river, and in the chaos Maxentius drowned. This battle, which is called the Battle of the Milvian Bridge after the Tiber crossing nearest to the fighting, was the moment when Constantine took control of the capital, and when he realized that he had won a most unlikely victory because of his prayers to the Christian God. From this point forward, Constantine was a convinced Christian. The empire was about to learn how much of a difference one man's conversion to Christianity could make.

Chapter 23

Constantine's Invention of
the Christian Roman Empire

312–337

FOLLOWING HIS VICTORY over Maxentius in 312, Constantine took both tangible and symbolic steps emphasizing the beginning of a new era. In Rome, he rehabilitated many of the senators and other officials who had served under Maxentius and appropriated many of the most imposing monuments his rival had built. This included the massive basilica that Maxentius had erected on the east side of the Roman Forum that came to be known as the Basilica of Constantine. It was then and remains today the largest building in the Forum. Constantine also had the face of the enormous statue of Maxentius that his predecessor had intended for the apse of the basilica recarved into his own likeness. This is the famous head that is now found, along with other surviving parts of the so-called *Colossus of Constantine*, in the courtyard of the Capitoline Museum.

The Senate marked his victory by erecting the largest triumphal arch in Roman history on the low ground near the Colosseum that was flanked by the Caelian and Palatine Hills. The arch, which places scenes of Constantine's Italian campaign alongside reused sculptures taken from monuments erected by Trajan, Hadrian, and Marcus Aurelius, was dedicated by "the Senate and people of Rome . . . to the imperator Caesar Constantine Augustus, who, inspired by the divinity and the greatness of his own mind, has, with his army, delivered the Republic from the tyrant."[1] On the inside walls of the central archway are two additional inscriptions. One marks Constantine as the "Liberator of the City." The other speaks of him as the "Founder of Peace."

THE INSCRIPTION'S REFERENCE to "the divinity" that inspired Constantine points to a future very different from the one that most Roman senators had expected. Even in these early days of his Christian faith, Constantine spoke openly of his belief that a divinity had helped him win the war with Maxentius. Christians had no doubt that he was referring to the Christian God, and Constantine immediately took steps to communicate his attachment to Christ to them. In early 313, when he met with his ally Licinius in Milan, they issued a joint edict (the Edict of Milan) restoring property that had been seized in the Great Persecution to the church. They also arranged for Licinius to marry Constantine's Christian half-sister Constantia.[2] That spring, Licinius defeated Maximinus Daia, the last remaining tetrarchic rival in the east, leaving the two new brothers-in-law in control of the entire empire. Notably, Christian sources emphasize that Licinius, too, had a Christian vision—in his case, a dream in which he was instructed to pray to the Christian God before battle.[3]

Eusebius of Caesarea captured the excitement Christians felt in the aftermath of the twin victories of Constantine and Licinius. "When the impious ones were removed, the government was preserved firm and undisputed for Constantine and Licinius," he wrote. They "cleansed the world of hostility to the Divine Being," and they were "conscious of the benefits which He had conferred upon them." Moreover, they "showed their love of virtue and of God, and their piety and gratitude to the Deity," in the way they ruled.[4] But a difference between Constantine and Licinius would quickly become clear in terms of how they expressed their religious views. Both acted in ways that indicated their faith in the Supreme God of Christianity, but in the fourth century being a devotee of that God could take different forms. Constantine was a Christian and understood the power of the Christian God in terms set by Christian leaders. Although Licinius acknowledged the genuine power of the Supreme God, he did so within a more traditional religious framework and took little interest in the Christian church itself. In this he was not far removed from his pagan roots, as pagans could, and often did, agree that Jesus was a god, and that there was a singular, Supreme God—but for them, this god simply reigned over all the others.

While Licinius joined Constantine in issuing the edict restoring confiscated church properties, it was Constantine alone who went further, carefully combining policies that Christians could understand as favorable to their interests with actions that non-Christians could view as consistent with the traditional activities of a pagan sovereign. Constantine intervened militarily to try to resolve an episcopal succession issue in the North African church, for instance, but he also used the same coin design depicting Sol Invictus, the pagan sun god, that Licinius did. Pagans and Christians were allowed to think whatever they wished about the piety of the two emperors.[5]

The alliance between Constantine and Licinius frayed when Constantia bore a son named Licinius in 315. Licinius the elder elevated his son to the rank of Caesar despite Constantine's demand that he refrain from doing so. Constantine then launched an attack on territory that Licinius controlled in the Balkans. On March 1, 317, Licinius agreed to cede most of his European territory to his brother-in-law. Following the peace agreement, Licinius's son (Licinius II), Constantine's eldest son (Crispus), and Constantine's second-born son (Constantine II) were all elevated to the rank of Caesar.[6]

The peace held until 324, when Constantine again mobilized. He advanced through Thrace and defeated Licinius's forces at Adrianople (the modern city of Edirne). After Constantine's son Crispus won a naval victory outside the city of Byzantium, Licinius abandoned that stronghold and fled east. Recognizing the war was lost, Licinius asked his wife, Constantia, to negotiate with her brother. He surrendered once Constantine agreed to spare his life and that of his young son. The emperor's guarantee to his sister and his former ally meant little, however. Within a year, Licinius I and II were both executed on a trumped-up conspiracy charge.[7]

THE THIRTEEN YEARS that elapsed between Constantine's defeat of Licinius and his own death in 337 saw the emperor make a series of decisions that would eventually change the Roman Empire completely. The first was to make the site of Byzantium his new capital. Byzantium stood on the high ground at the end of a peninsula on the southwestern tip of the Bosporus, the narrow waterway linking the Black Sea and the Mediterranean. This location made it a natural center for trade, but, as its long resistance to Septimius Severus more than a century earlier had shown, it also offered its residents unmatched protection from attack. The Bosporus has an extremely strong current that pushes ships right past the peninsula unless their captains know how to navigate its idiosyncrasies. To the north of the peninsula lies a natural harbor, which would come to be called the Golden Horn. It is both large enough and deep enough to serve fleets of merchant ships and warships, but its entry point is narrow enough that it can be blocked off by a heavy chain strung across its mouth. Overall, Byzantium offered Constantine a location for a capital that could not be successfully besieged unless the attacker had control of both the land approach to its west and the sea lanes on its other sides. If properly fortified, Constantine's new capital could resist the attack even of adversaries that managed to cut it off from any relief coming by land or sea.

Work began on the new capital, which Constantine named Constantinople, in November 324.[8] By the time of its dedication in 330, Constantine had built an entirely new city with its own forum, public buildings, and walls that adjoined the old city of Byzantium. To link the old and new parts of the city, his workers tore down Byzantium's main entry point, "built a circular marketplace where the old gate had stood[,] and surrounded it with double roofed porticos." Then, "intending to increase the size of the city, he surrounded it with a wall which was fifteen stadia [a bit less than two miles] beyond the former until it enclosed the entire peninsula," from the Sea of Marmara in the south to the Golden Horn in the north.[9] When the city was again expanded, and surrounded by a new state-of-the-art wall in the fifth century, its defenses became so formidable that they could not be breached by non-Roman attackers for nearly 800 years.[10]

On one level, Constantine's interest in modernizing the infrastructure and expanding the footprint of a strategically important regional center followed the pattern established by many of his predecessors. Diocletian had done this in Nicomedia, Galerius had done it in Thessaloniki, and Constantine himself had built major new buildings in both his old regional capital of Trier and the important Gallic city of Arles. But Constantinople was something different. Constantine very much intended for this to be a second imperial capital, even giving the city its own Senate like that of Rome. It was adorned with artworks taken from all around the empire, including such notable pieces as the Serpent Column set up at Delphi by the Greek cities that defeated the Persians in the fifth century BC. Constantine even ordered every single mint in the empire to flood the state with coins bearing the personifications of Rome, the old capital, and Constantinople, the new one.[11]

Even the Roman Empire struggled to build a city this large in such little time. The instant capital was superficially spectacular but troubled. Many of its hastily erected buildings were so poorly constructed that they had to be demolished soon after opening. Without a large enough population to fill the new space, Constantine had to pay people to move to the city. Writing a generation later, the orator Themistius compared Constantine's Constantinople to "an impatient lover's object of lust." But he agreed that a powerful and wealthy new capital city had sprouted because of Constantine.[12]

Constantine's increasingly public embrace of Christianity and his role in encouraging its growth left an even more profound long-term legacy than the capital he founded. For as long as Licinius was a threat, Constantine had remained relatively restrained in public about how his Christian faith might influence his policies. This made a great deal of sense in a Roman state that had a massive non-Christian majority. After Licinius's defeat, however, Constantine sent a letter to his new subjects in the eastern part of the Roman world outlining a set of priorities that explicitly favored Christians.

In that letter, Constantine removed any ambiguity about the identity of the Supreme God he worshipped. "To all who entertain just and sound sentiments respecting the character of the Supreme Being," he wrote, "it has long been most clearly evident . . . how vast a difference there has always been between those who carefully observe the sacred rules of the Christian religion, and those who treat this religion with hostility or contempt." Christians are "rewarded with abundant blessings," while those who act against Christians "experience results corresponding to their evil choice." Now that Constantine, "a prince who is God's servant," ruled the entire empire, the Roman state would be governed according to policies that favored the church.[13]

Constantine then outlined tangible steps the empire would take so that "the human race, enlightened through me as an instrument, might be called to observe God's holy laws." He described policies regarding the return of exiles from the persecution, the restoration of church properties, and grants of ownership of burial grounds holding the remains of martyrs to the church.[14]

Over the next decade, imperial funds paid for the construction of large churches on the sites where the Apostles Peter and Paul were said to have been buried in Rome. Constantine's mother, Helena, took a celebrated tour of the Holy Land during which she believed she had found the "True Cross" on which Jesus died. While there, she also planned churches on sites identified as Jesus's tomb in Jerusalem and his birthplace in Bethlehem. Constantine was spending imperial money to ensure that his God, the Christian God, would now have monumental sacred sites to rival those of the old gods.

Christian clergy also received significant privileges that matched, or often exceeded, those enjoyed by pagan priests, as well as money and goods they could use to support their congregations.[15] The influx of money and legal dispensations to the Christian church raised an important question that neither Christian leaders nor pagan emperors had previously confronted. Which Christian communities belonged to the church that received these benefits? In the early fourth century, there were many different groups of Christians with a wide range of different beliefs. They practiced different sorts of liturgies, disagreed about issues such as the date of Easter, and refused to accept the legitimacy of each other's clergy. Christianity was not as diverse as paganism, of course, but there was no single, unitary church for the emperor to support. There were many.

This conundrum left Constantine with an important choice. He could do as pagan emperors had done with traditional cults and offer support to a wide range of Christian communities across the empire, both those that he accepted as legitimate and those that he felt were theologically or administratively suspect. All these communities had suffered persecution, after all. It would have been natural for them to all benefit from imperial largesse. But this is not what Constantine decided. He chose instead to anoint one group of Christians across the empire as *the* church and marginalize the others. This was by no means inevitable. The Holy Roman Empire, for example, was able to support more than one church for centuries following the Peace of Augsburg in 1555.[16] The immense goodwill Constantine had earned among Christians as the first emperor to publicly embrace their cult could have allowed him to do the same thing in Rome more than 1,200 years earlier.

But Constantine chose not to support all of them. He had already shown this inclination when he ordered troops in North Africa to resolve a dispute about who was the rightful bishop of Carthage, but issues about episcopal legitimacy mattered even more when Constantine started granting massive buildings and large sums of money to the church. The bishop the emperor regarded as legitimate would control these resources. A rival who lacked imperial recognition would not. Bishoprics across the empire had seen succession crises for centuries, but victory in them now mattered much more than they had before.

When Constantine assumed control of the eastern half of the Roman Empire in 324, he found that the church there had entered into a serious theological conflict that threatened to metastasize across the southeastern Mediterranean, the most heavily Christian part of the Roman Empire.[17] The argument centered on the teaching of an Alexandrian presbyter named Arius who gave biweekly lectures on scriptural interpretation at his parish church.[18] Many of those who attended these lectures had some background in philosophy, and Arius offered himself both as a spiritual guide and an intellectual authority by providing them with an interpretation of the nature of God and Christ that corresponded in its broad outlines with Platonic ideas about the nature of divinity. Platonists in the third and early fourth centuries believed that the Supreme God must be immaterial and disengaged from the physical world, only interacting with physical matter through divine intermediaries.[19]

Christ's incarnation then presented a problem for Christian Platonists, because it described God taking physical form. This would be impossible for the Platonic Supreme God to accomplish, as it would mean that he entered the material world. Arius offered a version of the Trinity that allowed God to remain immaterial while also affirming the divinity of Jesus. In Arius's conception, God had always existed outside of time and space, and Jesus had come into being through a process that God had begun. This gave God priority over Christ, because, while God had no beginning and would have no end, Christ's existence began at a certain point in time.[20] As a result, Arius said, God and Christ must be two distinct entities with two different natures. Christ, he wrote, was "neither equal nor of the same essence with God." The word "of the same essence" that Arius used, *homoousia*, would become extremely important later.

Other Christians objected to Arius's teaching because they believed that God himself had taken on human flesh, suffered, and died so that the sins of mankind might be forgiven and believers might receive eternal salvation. As early as the teaching of the Apostle Paul, it was maintained that this was the act that eliminated the need for individual Christians to follow Jewish law.[21] Arius undermined this foundational Christian idea.

A second problem arose because of what Arius did when he was told to stop teaching about Christ's essence. At some point in 318, Alexander, the bishop of Alexandria, learned what Arius was saying and instructed him that it was inappropriate. Alexander ranked well above Arius in the church hierarchy, but Arius responded to his order by claiming that the church hierarchy did not matter. "I learned these things from participants in wisdom, skillful, and taught by God in every way," Arius continued, and "since I learned from God, I am now no stranger to wisdom and knowledge."[22] No pretentious bishop or artificial church hierarchy could cause Arius to stray from divinely inspired teaching.

Arius's ecclesiastical insubordination was unacceptable to the emperor. Constantine credited God with ensuring his military victories and felt that "internal strife within the Church of God is far more evil and dangerous than any kind of war of conflict."[23] Ending these conflicts was the best way the emperor knew to thank God for his military support. Soon after defeating Licinius, Constantine summoned bishops from across the entire Roman world to what was called an ecumenical church council. The goal was to decide on the propriety of Arius's teachings and his challenge to the authority of the bishop. Invited attendees would all be given permission to use imperially funded transportation in order to meet in the Anatolian city of Nicaea in the late spring of 325.

Church councils were nothing new, but Constantine's Nicene Council was something different. Previous church councils had been regional affairs called to solve geographically limited problems. The 300 or so bishops attending sessions at Nicaea would create a document that bound every church, everywhere, to its findings.[24] This was true even if no one in their home region had ever heard of Arius or thought about the Greek concept of *homoousia* (a word that had no direct Latin translation).

The discussions began in May, and by August the bishops had found a statement of faith they could accept. When the document was presented to Constantine, however, the emperor insisted upon the insertion of a clause indicating that God and Christ were *homoousios* (of the same essence)—a direct contradiction of Arius. Constantine's addition broke the unanimity. Five bishops refused to sign on to the amended document. Others, including the powerful bishop Eusebius of Nicomedia, signed the creed "with hand but not heart," and would later allow their teachings to wander from the agreed upon ideas.[25]

Constantine, however, immediately put the power and prestige of the emperor behind the enforcement of the terms agreed at Nicaea. He sent letters to Egypt informing Christians that, through his efforts, Arius had been condemned, and his books should be burned.[26] By summoning the ecumenical council, inserting himself directly in its deliberations, and using the power of his office to implement its findings, Constantine had now made it the emperor's job to enforce uniformity and orthodoxy within the Christian church. No Roman emperor before him could ever have imagined playing such a role. Few after him would escape it.

Constantine believed that he needed to do even more to catalyze the creation of a Christian Roman state. In an oration now called "To the Assembly of the Saints," he argued that it was his mission to get Romans to embrace "the light of truth" of the Christian God.[27] He maintained that his "brave deeds, victories in war, and triumphs over conquered foes" demonstrated Christianity's power, and he believed that his subjects would also enjoy God's favor if he persuaded them to change their religious behavior.[28] The problem Constantine faced was that no one knew what alchemy would allow an emperor to quickly change the religious orientation of tens of millions of Romans. Christianity had done an excellent job of growing organically from a small group of followers around a Jewish teacher in Judaea during the reign of Tiberius into a community of perhaps 10 million people across the Roman world by the 320s.[29] If Constantine had been patient, a Roman Christian majority probably would have developed on its own.

Constantine was not patient man. As he and his advisers looked for a way to accelerate this process, they decided to use the Roman legal system to express Constantine's strong preference that Romans turn away from sacrifice and stop visiting pagan temples. Eusebius of Caesarea's *Life of Constantine*, a work written soon after Constantine's death, provides a rough sketch of how this Constantinian policy against pagans worked. In 324, Constantine issued a law forbidding provincial governors from offering sacrifices, a law that seems designed to communicate the emperor's religious preferences by eliminating a part of the traditional ceremony through which governors were welcomed to each new city of their provinces. "Soon after this," Eusebius wrote, a law was issued "to restrain idolatrous abominations" by requiring that "no one should erect images, or practice divination and other false and foolish arts, or offer sacrifice in any way." A second law ordered officials to build more churches, because the emperor "expected that, now the madness of polytheism was entirely removed, nearly all mankind would attach themselves to the service of God."[30] Constantine planned to make the empire Christian by de-paganizing it first.

Constantine differed from the Roman emperors who had persecuted Christians in the past by choosing not to use violence or otherwise compel people to embrace Christianity.[31] The laws he issued had no enforcement mechanisms and specified no penalties for those who disobeyed them. Constantine was expressing strong preferences for how he believed his administrators and his subjects ought to behave, but it was up to them how to respond to his suggestions.

The emperor's reliance on persuasion rather than force meant that his new laws had very limited effects. No one was ever prosecuted for sacrificing to or worshipping a pagan god under his reign. Even Eusebius admits that Constantine only ordered the destruction of four temples, three devoted to the goddess Aphrodite and one to Asclepius. One of the temples of Aphrodite, which was located on the supposed site of Christ's resurrection, was replaced by a church. Two others dedicated to Aphrodite were destroyed on moral grounds, because they were centers of ritualized prostitution. Only the fourth, a temple of Asclepius in the city of Aegeae, was closed without obvious reason.[32] The emperor may not have been pagan, but hundreds of thousands of pagan temples remained operational for his entire reign.

Constantine also took care to perform all the traditional religious duties attached to his imperial office. He remained *pontifex maximus* until his death, issued laws reiterating well-established religious practices, and even agreed to the request of the city of Hispellum to construct a temple honoring him and his family.[33] These were the actions of an emperor who believed he had to do the job his fellow citizens expected of him as best he could—and his pagan subjects praised him for it. In 326, not long after Constantine issued his letter disapproving of sacrifice, the pagan Athenian sophist Nicagoras honored the emperor with a graffito written on the wall of the tomb of Ramses VI in the Valley of the Kings. This short text identified its author as "the torch bearer of the most holy mysteries at Eleusis," an unmistakably pagan title, and "gave thanks to the gods and to the most pious emperor Constantine" for making the trip possible.[34] If Nicagoras was aware of Constantine's religious directives, he shows no sign of it here. Similarly, in around 330, the Athenian pagan Praxagoras composed a history of Constantine's reign that made no mention of either his Christianity or his religious policies.[35] Both Athenians thought it perfectly appropriate to honor Constantine in the same way they would any pagan imperial predecessor.

This ambiguity about Constantine's religious significance reflects the final embers of the old pagan Roman model. In this model, when an emperor championed a particular God or cult, people saw it as a reflection of his personal religious preferences. Constantine may have constructed the blueprint for a very different Roman Empire, a Christian one, to emerge in the future, but when he died in 337, he left it up to his successors to determine whether Romans would build upon his model further or discard what he had begun to create.

Chapter 24

Constantius II, Julian, and the Challenges of Making Rome Christian

337–364

A s Constantine neared the end of his life, he designed a succession plan that reflected a singular sort of arrogance. He had reigned for thirteen years as sole Augustus. In 326, he had signed off on the execution of Crispus, his eldest son whose naval victory near Byzantium had won the civil war with Licinius in 324, amid rumors that Crispus may have been having an affair with his stepmother, Fausta. Soon after this, Fausta suspiciously suffocated in a bath house.[1] These executions changed Constantine's succession plan. While Constantine had done more than anyone else to destroy the tetrarchy, he decided that a new tetrarchy would take power after his death. It would be composed of his three sons with Fausta—Constans, Constantine II, and Constantius II—and Flavius Dalmatius (his half-brother).

This arrangement may have made theoretical sense to an old emperor who had risen to political maturity under tetrarchs and who believed that the only thing better than that system was one he headed alone, but his plan had no chance of working. As soon as Constantine I's death was known, agents working on behalf of Constantius

II assassinated Dalmatius as well as most of Constantine's other living male relatives. Two survived—Constantine's nephews Gallus and Julian. Constantius II then took control of Dalmatius's territories in the east. In the west, Constans went to war with Constantine II, a conflict that ended in Constantine II's death and the absorption of his lands by Constans. Within three short years, Constantine's new tetrarchy had degenerated into an empire shared between two of his sons, Constantius II and Constans I.

Even that arrangement lasted only a decade. Constans fell in a coup launched in 350 by a commander of the imperial guard named Magnentius. This prompted a civil war from which Constantius II emerged victorious in 353. From that point on, Constantius II ruled as sole Augustus.

Constantius II then confronted the messy reality that his father's vision of a Christian Roman Empire with twin capitals at Rome and Constantinople had created. It was he, not his father, who ensured that Constantinople grew into a genuine rival of Rome. Magnentius's rebellion had forced Constantius to organize his government around his father's new capital and draw upon the resources provided by its nascent Senate, but it was not until he arrived in Rome in 357 that Romans in the old capital realized the new eastern city was a legitimate rival.

Constantius arrived in the ancient capital that winter on a mission to reconcile with the city and Senate after its support for Magnentius. He performed traditional duties, such as appointing priests to the Roman pagan priestly colleges, and celebrated a triumph during which he confounded Romans by standing immobile like a statue as his chariot passed through the city.[2]

While Constantius's actions pointed to the emperor's desire to reaffirm the continuity of the Roman imperial present and the Roman past, his traveling companion, the Constantinopolitan philosopher and senator Themistius, previewed a dawning new imperial future when he gave an address to his colleagues in the Roman Senate House.[3] Speaking on the emperor's behalf, Themistius explained why Constantius preferred Constantinople to Rome. He conceded that

Constantinople was not yet Rome's equal in honor, but Constantius had made it Rome's peer by building similar urban amenities. And why would he not do this? Since Constantinople had contributed more resources to Constantius's campaigns than the old capital had, it could expect to be rewarded by becoming the administrative equal of Rome.[4]

Constantius then delivered on this promise. He decreed that an urban prefect would oversee the governance of Constantinople, an honor it shared only with Rome itself. Moreover, its Senate would grow in size to match Rome's, and its senators would now share the same titles and legal privileges as Rome's. By 360, the Constantinopolitan Senate and its civic administration were in every way the equal of Rome's. The empire now really did have two capitals, Rome in the west along the Tiber and a New Rome in the east along the Bosporus.[5]

Constantius's approach to Christian doctrine extended his father's view that the empire should recognize one church hierarchy that adhered to a uniform theology across the Roman world. At Nicaea, Constantine had used his personality, prestige, and power to persuade most of the bishops to agree to a creed he had helped to frame. That consensus had begun to fray even before Constantine's death, as Constantine himself seems to have drifted from a strict adherence to Nicene ideas to a position influenced by Eusebius of Nicomedia. Although some Nicene Christians saw Eusebius of Nicomedia as an Arian, it was Eusebius rather than a Nicene champion who had performed Constantine's deathbed baptism.

Not only had Constantine's personal beliefs evolved, but the church had evolved too. Its Nicene faction had become more radical, less forgiving, and increasingly aggressive. In 335, Constantine had been forced to send Athanasius, the combative Nicene bishop of Alexandria, into exile after receiving complaints from Arians and other Egyptian Christians about the bishop's violent followers. When Constantine investigated these charges, Athanasius was reported to have threatened to block the ships providing Egyptian grain to Constantinople.[6] Extreme Nicene faction leaders now looked more disruptive than their rivals.

Near the end of his life, Constantine tried to calm the situation by inviting Arius to return to communion after he agreed, in writing, that the Nicene Creed was orthodox. Arius, who seems to have been as horrified by the direction of the church as the emperor was, traveled to Constantinople, signed a confession of Nicene faith, and then died of a hemorrhage while relieving himself in a public toilet before he could receive the sacrament.[7] Nicene Christians cheered Arius's horrific death as an act of divine justice rather than celebrating his repentant return to the orthodox community as a sign of divine love.

Constantius II dealt capably with the brutal, often violent sectarianism that afflicted the church he inherited from his father. At the time of his accession, Nicenes and anti-Nicenes had "differed in their doctrinal statements," wrote the Arian church historian Philostorgius, but when it came time to worship, they had attended the same churches. They "were accustomed to commune with [each other] in prayers, hymns, and ceremonies." The generation of anti-Nicene leaders that came of age under Constantius, however, "began contending about these points," until a charismatic Syrian teacher named Aetius "persuaded his followers to break the bands of amity and friendship which had formerly bound them" to Nicenes.[8] By the 350s, the Arian conflict had begun to pull the Roman church apart.

Constantius positioned himself between aggressively Nicene figures like Athanasius and militant anti-Nicene leaders like Aetius. He and his allies in the church organized a series of church councils in the later 350s that condemned as nonbiblical both the Nicene term *homoousios* ("of the same essence") that Constantine had pushed in 325 and the Arian alternative *homooisious* ("of similar essence"). They arrived instead at a decision that God and Jesus should be referred to only as *homoios* ("similar"), rejecting the other terms, because, the church historian Socrates Scholasticus wrote, they "were not understood by people and have become a cause of offense."[9]

The bishops who assembled in 360 dramatically understated the impact these arguments were having. Church histories are full of accounts of violence between Nicene supporters and opponents in the major cities of the Roman East, as well as long lists of bishops who were sent into exile for disagreeing with the theology that Constantius II pushed. Athanasius alone suffered exile twice under Constantius, though he delayed his second exile for months by staging displays of popular anger. When imperial troops finally seized the bishop, he was presiding over a marathon midnight service in February 356. They marched in, Athanasius later wrote, carrying "naked swords and javelins and instruments of war," as they stripped virgins, plundered sacred vessels, and killed randomly.[10] This was certainly not the Roman Christian world that Constantine had envisioned or that Constantius was hoping to build.

Constantius's theology proved more appealing to people beyond Rome's borders. In the early 340s, he sponsored a mission by Ulfila, a Christian resident of Gothic lands, who "translated all of the Scriptures into [the Gothic] tongue—with the exception of the book of Kings because that book contains the history of wars[,] while the Gothic people, who are lovers of war, were in need of something to restrain their passion for fighting."[11] Ordained the bishop of Gothia, Ulfila "preached in the Greek, Latin, and Gothic tongues without ceasing," and "left behind in those very three languages several treatises . . . for the use and edification of the willing."[12] Ulfila's teaching about the essence of Christ was in line with Constantius's own ideas. Preferring to teach only "according to the Divine Scriptures," he had no patience for "the sect of the *homoousians*," while "the *homoiousians* too he rejected."[13] Ulfila's translation and missionary work then ensured that the Goths, and eventually most of the other Germanic tribes living adjacent to the Roman frontier, would adopt a version of Christianity based around the theology that Constantius and his allies developed.[14] This would be the emperor's most enduring theological contribution.

Constantius found it even more challenging to encourage Romans to move away from paganism, and Christians, who generally gave Constantine a great deal of leeway to manage de-paganization, lost patience with him. In the mid-340s, Firmicus Maternus, a convert from paganism, urged Constantius and his brother Constans to use "the severest laws so that the deadly error of [pagan] delusion no longer stains the Roman world." "Christ," Maternus wrote, "reserved the extermination of idolatry and the overthrow of the pagan temples for your hands." The emperors only needed to act swiftly, and "the horrid contagion of idolatry will die out and become extinct."[15]

Constantius refrained from acting aggressively against paganism while his brother Constans lived, but after his murder in 350 he adopted the plan Maternus advocated. He issued laws prescribing actual penalties for sacrifices and the use of temples for pagan religious rituals. The first law appeared on February 20, 356, and mandated "capital punishment" for "persons proven to devote their attention to sacrifices or to the worship of images." On December 1 of the same year, another law was added ordering that "all temples should be immediately closed in all cities and access to them forbidden," while warning governors that they "shall be similarly punished if they should neglect to avenge such crimes." As Constantius seems to have feared, governors and almost everyone else seem to have largely ignored these laws. Not only did public festivals involving sacrifice continue throughout the empire, but there is also no record of anyone being charged under either law.[16]

Despite his feelings about sacrifice, Constantius hesitated to destroy pagan temples outright. In fact, in 342, he and Constans mandated that "the buildings of the temples outside of the walls shall remain untouched and uninjured," because they hosted "plays or circus spectacles or contests." Nothing prevented the emperor from transferring pagan temples owned by the emperor to the church, however. The most notable of these was the Caesareum, a large temple of the imperial cult originally built by Cleopatra to honor Julius Caesar. Constantius turned it into Alexandria's cathedral.[17]

Although Constantius ruled as sole Augustus in the late 350s, he recognized that the empire remained too large and complicated for one man to effectively govern alone. He had no sons, and his only living male relatives were Gallus and Julian, the grandsons of Constantius I who had been born to Constantine's half-brother. In 351, Constantius appointed Gallus, the older of the two, as his Caesar in the east, while he himself prepared to lead a campaign against Magnentius in the west. Gallus, however, proved to be so temperamentally ill-suited to ruling that Constantius lured him to a meeting in modern Croatia where he was arrested and killed in 354.[18]

THE MURDER OF Gallus forced Constantius to look to Julian, his last close male relative, as a potential imperial colleague. Julian was an odd young man who did not immediately strike others as emperor material. Constantius and his agents had controlled nearly every aspect of Julian's life for most of the past two decades. Although Julian's murdered father had been a pagan, Julian himself had been raised as a Christian. Early on, he was educated by teachers chosen by the imperial court, but he had "begged his cousin's permission to attend the schools of the sophists and lectures on philosophy." At that point, Gallus had been serving as Caesar, and Constantius had little reason to object if his young cousin wanted to be a scholar.[19]

Julian thus embarked on an intellectual odyssey that took him through the rhetorical schools of Athens and to Pergamum to study Platonic philosophy. He had already been drifting toward an embrace of the old gods, but in Pergamum he became deeply devoted to Maximus of Ephesus, an extremely charismatic philosopher known for his ability to interact so intensely with the gods that he once made a cult statue smile. Under these influences Julian became a convert to paganism—although he dared not let Constantius or anyone close to his cousin know.[20]

Julian's career as a scholar did not last long. Soon after Gallus's execution, "Julian was forcibly removed by Constantius to be his imperial colleague and elevated to the rank of Caesar." He was then "dispatched to Gaul" to supervise its defense. It is hard to imagine someone less prepared to fight along the Rhine frontier than the philosophical young prince. Rather than letting his commanders decide how to conduct the war, however, Julian directed the armies himself, preferring risky and aggressive tactics through which he put his own life in great peril.[21]

In June 356, during one of the first war councils Julian attended, he listened as his generals discussed "the safest route" the army could take to beat back barbarians threatening the Gallic city of Autun. When someone mentioned that a recent commander "had, with considerable difficulty, taken 8,000 auxiliary troops along a path that provided a short cut but was dangerous because it led through dark forests," Ammianus says, Julian "was inflamed with the desire to imitate the example of this bold general." He set out along the trail with "an inadequate escort for a commander." Julian remained calm, despite the risks, even as "the barbarians hurled themselves upon him in successive bands," and "won an easy victory by descending on them" from higher ground. Julian's early triumphs established momentum that cleared barbarians from Gaul and later from Rome's German territories along the Rhine. The campaign culminated in Julian's spectacular defeat of the Alamanni near Strasbourg that settled the frontier for the next decade.[22]

Julian celebrated by giving a panegyric of Constantius in which he ostensibly praised the emperor while implying that Constantius was like Homer's plodding, cautious Agamemnon while Julian stood out as the heroic Achilles.[23] The subtle tension between them that this speech implied soon erupted into the open when an envoy from Constantius ordered Julian to break up his army and send "his Herulian and Batavian auxiliaries," as well as "300 picked men from each of the other divisions of his army," to the east so they could join the army Constantius had gathered to recapture the city of Amida (modern Diyarbakir) from the Persians.[24]

Constantius had military reasons to want to transfer troops from the pacified west to the active war zone in the east, but he designed this order to weaken Julian by destroying the morale that his close-knit forces had developed with one another.[25] There was an additional problem with summoning German auxiliaries to the east. They were non-Roman soldiers who had agreed to serve alongside Romans only under the condition that they would not be transferred below the Alps.[26]

Denarius of 54 BC, issued by Marcus Junius Brutus showing Brutus, the founder of the Republic, and Ahala (private collection/photo by author)

The Appian Way outside Rome (photo by author)

The Roman Forum seen from the Capitoline Hill (photo by author)

The interior of the Colosseum, showing arena floor and seats for senators in distance (photo by author)

The markets built by Trajan as part of the excavation of the slope of the Quirinal Hill during construction of his Forum (photo by author)

The Four Tetrarchs, a porphyry sculpture stolen from Constantinople in 1204, on a corner of Saint Mark's in Venice (Nino Barbieri/Wikipedia)

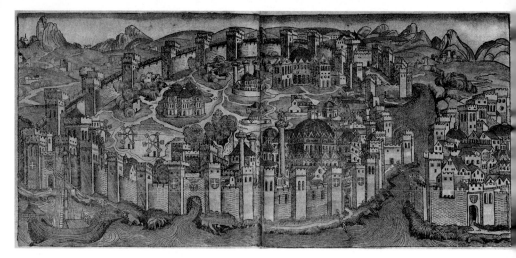

1493 woodcut showing Constantinople and the Golden Horn (*Nuremberg Chronicle*, fol. 129v/130r)

The walls of Constantinople (Johann H. Addicks/Wikipedia)

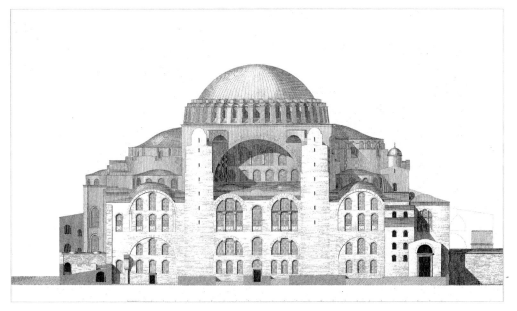

Hagia Sophia exterior (from Wilhelm Salzenberg, *Alt-christliche Baudenmale von Constantinople* [Berlin, 1854])

Hagia Sophia interior (from Wilhelm Salzenberg, *Alt-christliche Baudenmale von Constantinople* [Berlin, 1854])

Southwestern entrance mosaic of the former basilica of Hagia Sophia of Constantinople. The Virgin Mary is standing in the middle, holding the Child Christ on her lap. On her right side stands emperor Justinian I, offering a model of the Hagia Sophia. On her left, emperor Constantine I, presenting a model of the city (Wikimedia)

Solidus of Justinian II featuring the first image of Christ on a Roman coin on the front and an image of Justinian II, identified as Lord Justinian the Servant of Christ, on the reverse (private collection/ image by author)

Image from an illuminated manuscript, the Madrid Skylitzes, showing the use of Greek fire, captioned "the Roman fleet incinerating the fleet of the enemy" (Madrid Skylitzes, fol. 34, via Wikimedia)

Replica of a miniature of Emperor Basil II in triumphal garb, exemplifying the Imperial Crown handed down by Angels (replica of the Psalter of Basil II, the Psalter of Venice, BNM, Ms. gr. 17, fol. 3r, Wikimedia)

Miniature of the Byzantine Emperor Alexius Comnenus being blessed by Christ (Euthymius Zigabenus, *Panoplia Dogmatica*, fol 2v, Wikimedia)

Attack of the Crusaders on Constantinople, miniature in a manuscript of *De la Conquête de Constantinople* by Geoffreoy de Villehardouin, Venetian ms. fol 1r (Wikimedia)

Julian had no choice but to send the 300 Roman troops from each division that Constantius had requested, but he held the German auxiliaries back as he began planning a counterstrike. He set up his winter camp far from the imperial center of Trier so that he could avoid spies sent by Constantius. Basing himself in the more distant, less comfortable city of Paris, Julian summoned the leaders of his auxiliary divisions to a meeting as icebergs floated down the Seine. He hosted them for dinner and then was acclaimed Augustus by their men in a ceremony that was clearly prearranged.[27]

Julian attacked Constantius with the same reckless aggression he had shown against the Alamanni along the Rhine. He wrote letters to major cities across the west assailing Constantius for murdering his family members and sent small, fast-moving detachments of troops into Italy and the Balkans. Julian knew his forces were outnumbered. But like Julius Caesar 400 years earlier, he hoped to quickly secure the west before his cousin mustered his full army.[28]

Unlike Pompey, Constantius was a methodical commander who knew how important patience was when fighting a civil war. Instead of rushing to confront Julian, he spent much of the year preparing. The emperor secured North Africa, the province that provided Italy with much of its grain supply; calmed the eastern frontier; and began moving his larger and better-trained soldiers toward the Balkans. Constantius almost certainly would have annihilated the usurper's army, but the armies never met on the battlefield.[29] Constantius died suddenly of a fever on November 3, 361, at the age of forty-four. As he lay on his deathbed, he supposedly named Julian as his successor. Maybe. But even if he had not, his soldiers would have claimed that he had. Julian was not far away and had an army, and Constantius's men had no alternative candidate to rally around.

Julian was now the sole, undisputed emperor of Rome.

JULIAN KNEW EXACTLY what had caused his rival's untimely death and ensured his own unlikely ascent to power. The old gods, he believed, had "desired to place him in a higher position." Julian wrote that, on the night he was proclaimed Augustus in Gaul, he had "prayed to Zeus" and "entreated [him] to give me a sign." Zeus obliged and told him "not [to] oppose the will of the army." The stunning death of Constantius, then, likely did not surprise Julian at all. It was simply the result of the old gods working to place him on the throne.[30]

In some ways, the convert's zeal that Julian felt for the old gods matched that which Constantine had for Jesus. But, unlike Constantine, Julian wasted little time before "he revealed what was in his heart" to his subjects and "directed in plain, unvarnished terms that the temples should be opened, sacrifices brought to their altars, and the worship of the old gods restored."[31] Julian also removed imperial support from Christian churches, ordered bishops to return any pagan temples that had been converted into churches, and reinstated the Nicene bishops Constantius had exiled.[32] He aimed to reinvigorate paganism while at the same time forcing Christians to fight among themselves over their suddenly diminished resources. This represented a complete reversal of Constantius's religious program.

Julian's pagan revival borrowed structural elements from the Christian church to elevate the emperor's preferred confession. He created a pagan priesthood that resembled Christian bishoprics in which he appointed spiritual governors in a defined region and instructed them "to exhort men not to transgress the laws of the gods." They were to share "money with all men" and distribute to the needy "clothes and food" donated by the government. These regional high priests, in turn, selected priests in individual cities to manage the recovery of temple property, the maintenance of holy sites, and the organization of public festivals.[33]

Julian struggled to realize that, unlike Christianity, paganism was not and never had been a single organized religion. The sheltered emperor thought in the religiously binary terms that Christians had created to distinguish themselves from adherents of traditional religion. He did not understand that such binary thinking was foreign to devotees of traditional religions. Traditional religion was not a system. There were no standard creeds, shared religious calendars, or common practices joining all the pagans across the empire. Some pagans sacrificed regularly. Others did not. Some were passionate devotees of the gods. Others thought very little about the gods. And this diversity of approaches was not only okay. It was what most pagans desired.

Julian had expected an enthusiastic rush of people back to the temples now that Constantius's persecution had ended. He instead got incidents like the one when he turned up for a festival of Apollo at the god's famous shrine in the Antiochene suburb of Daphne. Julian expected to see thousands of eager Antiochenes gathered to celebrate Apollo at his recently reopened temple. He found instead only a single old priest and a goose waiting for him. The emperor could not hide his befuddlement and disappointment.[34]

One of the most disruptive components of Julian's pagan revival was a reform of the empire's education system. As the fourth century progressed, education in the schools of rhetoric and law became increasingly important for ambitious young men looking to begin lucrative careers in imperial service. This training had always centered on the memorization, reproduction, and analysis of classical texts, many of which featured references to the traditional gods. Both Christians and pagans had valued this training, both because of its capacity to mark one as a member of the cultured elite and because it provided a non-confessional path that any Roman could use to begin a public career.[35]

Julian had a different understanding of education. He saw the schools not as centers to credential future bureaucrats but as places of moral instruction offering a path to philosophical enlightenment. As a philosopher and emperor, he felt that he had an obligation to show his fellow Romans how they might embrace a better, more pious way of living. Julian thus decided to transform the education system on which the professional careers of so many elite Romans depended into a tool for pagan religious indoctrination.

Julian's educational reform occurred in two phases. First he issued a law requiring that all "teachers ought to first excel in personal character then in eloquence." He further ordered that a national registry should be created in which "anyone who [wished] to teach" would be evaluated on their moral character and approved by Julian himself.[36] A few months later, Julian issued a second law making clear that he believed teachers had poor character if they taught ideas that they did not believe to be true. This meant that Christian teachers had to choose either to stop teaching or to agree to "persuade" their students that "neither Homer nor Hesiod nor any one of the authors about whom [you] lecture and offer analysis, is guilty of any impiety." In short, Christian teachers had to accept the old gods and evangelize on their behalf or stop teaching. And because of the earlier law he had issued, Julian now had the ability to identify and penalize those who did not measure up.[37]

Julian emphasized that he was not prohibiting Christian students from attending schools. As he wrote to an official who misunderstood the purpose of the law, "Any youth who wishes to attend the schools is not excluded." This would be counterproductive, because, he said, "we ought, I think, to teach but not punish the demented" who were "still too ignorant to know" that the traditional religion was true.[38] The schools should incubate new pagan converts, not exclude those who might be converted.

Julian spent the winter of 362–363 in the Syrian city of Antioch preparing his army for a Persian campaign. He hoped the campaign would prove the superiority of the traditional gods by delivering the sort of dramatic victory that had eluded Constantine and Constantius II. His stay, however, did not go well. The presence of perhaps 100,000 or more men in the city for the whole winter stretched food supplies, causing a spike in prices that Julian was only able to stop when he imported grain from imperial estates. His popularity plummeted.[39]

Many Romans, both pagan and Christian, came to see Julian's religious and administrative policies as too disruptive—even tyrannical. In early 363, Julian published a pamphlet in which he attacked Antiochenes for criticizing him for "turning the affairs of the world upside down."[40] Ammianus, who was from Antioch, greatly admired much of what Julian did, but he felt that the emperor had "dimmed the luster of his many glorious acts by occasional errors."

None of these was so severe as when he had "banned adherents of Christianity from working as teachers of rhetoric or literature." In fact, he said, this was "the one harsh act that should be buried in lasting oblivion." Christian criticism was even more brutal. The Christian bishop Gregory Nazianzen described Julian as "a tyrant who rebelled and has taken a fall worthy of his impiety."[41]

The Roman world never got to see whether the emperor whom Ammianus praised could overcome the hostility that some of his actions caused. When Julian set out on his Persian campaign in the spring of 363, he planned to attack the Persians with the same aggressive, fast-moving tactics that had worked along the Rhine by dividing his forces, sending one group into Mesopotamia along the Tigris River, and sending another, led by Julian himself, along the Euphrates. They were to converge outside of Ctesiphon and attack the Persian capital. The army led by Julian proceeded down the Euphrates, supplied by river boats, and reached the outskirts of Ctesiphon only to learn that the other detachment had been prevented from advancing.

Julian then made the fatal mistake of ordering his army to leave the river, advance into the Persian interior, and burn the supply boats that had accompanied them.[42] Persian forces forced the Romans to retreat by scorching the earth in places the soldiers might otherwise forage for supplies. Finally, Julian was injured in an ambush outside of modern Fallujah as the Romans pulled back. He died on June 26 before he could lead the army back over the frontier. His reign as sole emperor had lasted a little less than twenty months. He had no surviving children and no designated successor.

The commanders of the leaderless army convened and chose Jovian, a member of the imperial bodyguard under both Constantius and Julian, as the new emperor. He was someone whom both "the survivors of Constantius's regime" and Julian's officers could accept. Jovian negotiated a peace treaty that granted Roman land on the far side of the Tigris and the fortified city of Nisibis to Persia in exchange for safe passage home. He then returned to an exhausted Roman Empire, determined to put aside the religious and political dramas of the past decade.[43]

Chapter 25

The Sack of Rome

364–410

THE DECADE FOLLOWING the death of Julian saw the Roman state entrusted to a set of pragmatic and effective rulers who mostly preferred to prioritize its political and security needs above the religious concerns of their immediate predecessors. This pattern began under the emperor Jovian, who was committed to the idea of bridging the divisions caused by the religious militancy of Constantius II and Julian. He "restored some of the best men from all sides to office," according to Themistius, and introduced a policy of religious toleration designed to counteract the tensions that had been created by Constantius's suppression of paganism and Julian's pagan revival. Jovian rescinded Julian's ban on Christian teachers and dismantled the pagan priesthood he had established, but he also "open[ed] up the temples . . . allowing lawful sacrifices." The state then began to financially support both pagan and Christian religious practices.[1]

Romans would likely have appreciated Jovian's moderation if he had lived long enough for them to see its effects. Unfortunately, Jovian never made it back from the Persian frontier. He died on February 17, 364, in Dadastana, a small city in Asia Minor whose overzealous residents accidentally poisoned him when, just before he arrived, they freshly painted a well-insulated building for him to stay in.[2]

The panicked army now had to choose the third Roman emperor in less than seven months—and the fourth in a little more than two years. They struggled with the task, failing to agree on two candidates before they selected Valentinian, the scion of a Pannonian military family whose primary selling point was that he was stationed in nearby Ancyra. Valentinian hastened to Nicaea to link up with the army, but almost as soon as he arrived he was met with calls to appoint a colleague by soldiers terrified of further instability. Valentinian then called for his brother Valens to join him and, three weeks later, proclaimed him co-emperor.[3] They went to Constantinople together and decided that Valens would rule the east while Valentinian took charge of the west. They spent the summer of 364 working together to figure out the details, parting in August. The unified Roman Empire would never again have a single Augustus.[4]

Over the next decade the imperial brothers generally followed Jovian's path of religious toleration, but they had more pressing problems to address. When they came to power they were forced to confront the massive costs of Julian's failed Persian invasion. Not only had the campaign itself been extremely expensive, but the loss of substantial Mesopotamian territory to the Persians in Jovian's peace treaty, and the bonuses that both Julian and Jovian had promised to soldiers, further undercut the government's finances. The emperors therefore undertook a series of unpopular fiscal reforms that increased taxes and restored imperial control over property that Julian had given to cities. They aggressively pursued overdue fines and debts owed to the government by citizens, and they mandated that all tax payments must reach the imperial government in the form of gold ingots, rather than coins, to prevent tax collectors from stealing small amounts of gold by trimming the edges of the coins. These unpopular policies prompted a revolt by Procopius, a cousin of the emperor Julian, in the fall of 365, but the regime survived and emerged in a much stronger fiscal position.[5]

These fiscal and administrative reforms allowed the emperors to focus again on foreign policy in the later years of their reigns. For

Valentinian, this involved the construction of a vast network of fortifications along the Rhine and western Danube frontiers that he reinforced by regular campaigning. Valens, by contrast, blundered into restarting the war with Persia, though the conflict ended with neither side gaining much from the fighting. The successful partnership between the co-emperors lasted for more than a decade, until Valentinian died of a stroke after becoming enraged during a negotiation with envoys sent by the Quadi, a barbarian group from across the Danube that had invaded Roman territory following the construction of forts on their land. His son, the sixteen-year-old Gratian, assumed leadership over the west.[6]

Although Gratian had officially been Valentinian's co-emperor since 367, the death of his father precipitated a set of crises that grew in severity over the next few years. Gratian was in Gaul when Valentinian died, which prompted nervous army commanders along the Danube to summon Valentinian's other son, the four-year-old Valentinian II, and proclaim him Augustus as well. Gratian responded by recognizing his brother's title, but not allotting any territories to him to govern. Looking to install a new set of advisers and administrators he trusted, Gratian then launched a purge of many government officials who had been close to his father as well as the military leadership that had backed Valentinian's elevation.[7]

Valens faced an even more serious problem in the east. In 376, Gothic leaders, terrified by the threat posed by the Huns, petitioned Valens for permission to cross the border and settle in Roman territory. This was different from the Gothic raiders who repeatedly crossed the frontier in the third and fourth centuries to loot Roman lands and return home with booty. The Goths who crossed in 376 came not as warriors but as refugees, bringing both their weapons and their wives and children with them. Their leaders swore to Valens's emissaries that they would live quietly, settle in parts of Thrace that the Romans designated, and serve as auxiliaries in the Roman army if the emperor needed them to do so.[8]

Romans had successfully integrated immigrants for centuries. In fact, their ability to integrate newcomers had formed a central part of the stories that Romans told themselves about the nature of their community. Tarquinius Priscus, Servius Tullius, and the Claudii had all been immigrants. More recently, Marcus Aurelius had supervised a mass immigration of Germans into Italy to help stabilize the population following the large losses caused by the Antonine plague. Romans then knew how to do what the Goths were asking of them, but it required significant planning. When the empire settled migrants, it separated large communities into smaller groups that were then distributed widely across Roman territory.[9] This had the effect of diluting any threat that might be posed by a large, concentrated group of people with preexisting political and military ties while also hastening their integration into the larger Roman world around them.

Valens learned of the Gothic request when he was in Antioch, more than 1,000 miles away from the Danube frontier, so he could manage military operations following the outbreak of renewed hostilities with Persia. He directed his officials in the Balkans to allow one group of Goths, the Tervingi, to cross into Roman territory while they also deployed troops in the region to prevent the crossing of the Greuthungi, a second group that asked for asylum. Fritigern and Alavivus, the first Gothic leaders to arrive, were "given food for their immediate needs and land to cultivate," just as the emperor had promised.[10] The initial reception of the migrants had proceeded as Valens and his officials had planned.

Problems began when far more Tervingi turned up at the border than the Romans had expected. Fearing for their lives, they crossed the Danube en masse using boats and dugout canoes. The most desperate even tried to swim across the river, with many drowning in the swift current.[11] They arrived wherever they landed and did not receive the orderly reception that Fritigern and Alavivus had. Some never met any Roman officials at all. Others arrived after the promised food and land had already been allocated to those who had crossed earlier. Food soon grew short. This was a common problem in the ancient world when large populations entered inland areas unprepared for them. In an era before refrigeration and motorized transport, regions like those into which the Goths crossed could not suddenly increase the food supply.

Roman and Gothic distrust for one another exacerbated the situation. Ammianus talks about Roman officials "collecting all of the dogs they could find" and offering them to starving Goths who were willing to sell their compatriots into slavery in exchange for the animals. The same Roman officials who bartered dogs for slaves also denied Gothic immigrants permission to move to different areas where more food might be available. When the Roman military commander in Thrace invited Gothic leaders to a banquet while at the same time preventing ordinary Goths from entering the walls to buy supplies, the starving Tervingi revolted. Their rebellion forced the Romans to withdraw their troops from the Danube frontier, which allowed the Greuthungi to cross the river, move into Roman territory, and join forces with the Tervingi.[12]

The animosity and fear the situation fueled soon caused Romans to suspect the loyalty of other, earlier Gothic settlers living deeper in Roman territory. Ammianus recounts how two groups, "who had been admitted into our territory much earlier and were assigned to Adrianople [modern Edirne, Turkey]," were ordered to move out of the region immediately. When their request for two days to prepare for the journey was denied, they fought back against an armed and anxious mob of locals who ambushed them and then joined the Tervingi in raiding the Thracian countryside and unwalled towns.[13]

Valens concluded a hasty treaty with Persia so he could shift resources from the eastern frontier to the Balkans and requested reinforcements from Gratian. By the summer of 378, Valens and the Roman army had penned up the Gothic rebels into an area around Adrianople. In August, Valens received a letter from the western emperor requesting that he "wait until Gratian arrived to share the danger and not rashly commit himself to the risks of a decisive action alone."[14]

Valens was unmoved. He was "eager to put himself on the same level as his nephew, whose exploits irked him, by some glorious accomplishment of his own." When he received incorrect intelligence that the Gothic forces had divided, Valens ordered the army to advance toward the Goths on August 9. They marched "eight miles over rough country in the mid-day sun" fully armed and ready for battle. Although the Romans had caught the Gothic cavalry away from the main Gothic camp, Valens allowed the Goths to waste time pretending to negotiate while their cavalry rode back. In the meantime, the Goths had set fires in the countryside so that Valens's men, "who were already exhausted by the summer heat, should also be parched with thirst."[15]

When the battle was joined, the fatigue felt by the Roman army and the mistakes of their emperor led to disaster. The Goths had arrayed a ring of wagons around their camp, and as the Romans moved toward the wagons, the Goths' returning cavalry appeared along the Roman flanks. The Romans, pushed back and surrounded, were pressed in on each other until, as Ammianus vividly describes, "the ground was so drenched in blood that they slipped and fell" as the dead piled up. Perhaps two-thirds of the best troops available in the eastern empire died that day. So, too, did Valens. He had tried to escape the slaughter by taking refuge in a farmhouse, but the Goths burned him alive.[16]

The catastrophe outside Adrianople destroyed the Roman battle army that protected the cities of Thrace. The Goths advanced on Adrianople, and when they failed to capture it they moved east toward Constantinople. The capital withstood them after Valens's widow organized an impromptu defense. As the Goths moved on, however, Roman deserters, runaway slaves, and other barbarians in Roman service defected to them, augmenting their numbers. The enlarged Gothic army then separated, with one group heading toward Gratian's territory in the northern Balkans and the other turning south into Macedonia.[17]

Gratian knew he needed to find a new, capable sovereign to manage the Gothic threat in the Balkans. Although his seven-year-old brother, Valentinian II, held the title of Augustus, he obviously lacked the capacity to lead an army. After deliberating for several months, Gratian agreed to elevate a Spaniard named Theodosius, who assumed power on January 19, 379, in the city of Sirmium. The east-west line established by Valentinian I and Valens gave all the Balkans except for Thrace to the western emperor, but Theodosius received authority over nearly the entire peninsula, so that he could campaign against the Goths in all the regions they had entered. The Gothic war was his.

Theodosius faced a nearly impossible task. The fourth-century Roman state was no longer like that of the earlier Republic. Before Augustus, massive levies of citizen soldiers could quickly replenish losses in the Roman armies, and Rome's strength had depended as much on superior manpower as on fighting skill. After Augustus, Roman armies had won battles because they were more experienced and better trained than the people they fought. But the Battle of Adrianople had destroyed "the bravest and largest detachment of [the eastern] Roman army."[18] This was a massive loss of fighting capacity that no emperor could quickly repair. The Goths, by contrast, now had a larger and more experienced army than the one Theodosius had inherited.

Rome still possessed significant advantages over the Goths. There were perhaps 100,000 people between the two Gothic groups against 60 million Romans.[19] The Goths had no fixed territory in which to settle, no siege engines to capture walled Roman settlements, and no steady food supply beyond what they could steal or gather by foraging. Theodosius spent much of 379 trying to leverage these Roman advantages to contain and defeat the Goths. His propagandists celebrated how he "made the fighting spirit return to the cavalry and infantry" while he transformed "farmers and miners into a terror to the enemy" by recruiting and training these hearty, patriotic peasants.[20] This was, the old philosopher Themistius claimed, "the first turning of the tide," as the "eye of justice [would lead] back to the Romans" and ensure that the "damned villains [would] suffer" for what they had done.[21]

Theodosius's new army failed to deliver on its promise. After a defeat in Macedonia in 380, Gratian summoned Theodosius to a meeting in Sirmium, took back control of much of the Balkans from him, and sent the humiliated emperor scurrying back to Constantinople.[22] It had become clear to everyone that he lacked the capacity to punish the Goths who had killed an emperor, destroyed a Roman army, and plundered a wide swath of countryside in the Balkans.

Effectively forced to spend the next year in Constantinople, Theodosius remade himself into a political and religious reformer. He made the case for political reforms by explaining that "reports of wars and battles of men" were irrelevant because he was setting his mind to making Romans more "harmonious." A well-governed state offered the best "weapons with which men conquer other men."[23] On the religious side, Theodosius redefined himself as a pious, Nicene-adhering Christian emperor who was using his powers to transform Rome into an empire that followed religious practices corresponding to his own. He removed all clergy from Constantinople's churches who did not accept the Council of Nicaea, and then, in May 381, convened an ecumenical council in Constantinople to reaffirm the empire's commitment to the creed of Nicaea.

Theodosius joined this explicit embrace of Nicene Christianity with a renewed push to stamp out paganism, instructing Roman officials to close temples, prohibit sacrifices, and crack down on pagan religious activities. His first antipagan laws appeared in December 381 when he reinstated Constantius II's old prohibition on sacrifices, a law that had been suspended since the accession of Julian, and expanded upon it by forbidding anyone to approach a temple.[24] This began a period of sustained pressure on traditional religion that featured more temple closings as well as campaigns of temple destructions led by monks working in tandem with imperial officials. As attacks leveled rural "shrines of the idols" and pagan temples across Syria, Mesopotamia, and Egypt, gleeful Christian contemporaries praised Theodosius for ensuring that paganism would be "consigned to oblivion."[25]

Theodosius's desperate pivot from the Gothic to the religious battlefield forced the western emperor, Gratian, to take his own strong actions against traditional religion. Starting in 382, he used both legislative and administrative tools to remove the funding that supported the public practice of paganism in Rome. This included the removal of an altar to the goddess Victoria that stood in the Senate House, elimination of imperial funding for the Vestal Virgins, and confiscation of the endowments belonging to temples and religious organizations that had funded pagan rituals for centuries.[26]

By the fall of 382, Theodosius had pivoted again, after the commander of imperial forces in Thrace reached an agreement with the Goths whereby they would end their rebellion in return for land to farm, political autonomy, and an opportunity to serve in the Roman army. These terms, which closely resembled those given to allied states during the Roman Republic, contrasted with the destruction that Theodosius and other Romans had imagined inflicting on Goths who had killed an emperor. But, in the mouth of Themistius, the peace treaty did not represent the emperor's weakness. It instead marked him as a philosopher-king who "ruled in accordance with the will of God."[27]

With a Gothic peace secured, Theodosius began to assert his independence from Gratian. On January 19, 383, the fourth anniversary of his own acclamation, Theodosius made his wife, Aelia Flacilla, an Augusta and his son Arcadius an Augustus. Gratian had not agreed to either move, but circumstances prevented him from challenging it. Then, a few months later, Gratian was seized and killed by forces loyal to Magnus Maximus, the Roman commander in Britain, who hoped that by overthrowing Gratian he might gain the leverage to negotiate some sort of arrangement with Theodosius.[28] When a group of Italian senators, military officials, and bishops instead organized an administration around the figurehead emperor Valentinian II that initially prevented Maximus from crossing the Alps, Theodosius decided to back Valentinian instead.[29] Maximus did eventually take Italy from Valentinian's backers, but Theodosius's army, with its Gothic auxiliaries, defeated Maximus's forces in July 388 and restored Valentinian's power in the west.

The young emperor's regime lasted only four years. In 392, Valentinian II fell from power when the military official Arbogast, whom Theodosius had placed as the effective regent in the west, colluded with pagan senators to kill the unfortunate sovereign and replaced him with a rhetorician named Eugenius.[30] Valentinian died at the age of twenty-two. He had technically been an Augustus for nearly seventeen years but had never actually ruled.

Theodosius intervened again. He marched west and met the forces of Arbogast and Eugenius near the Frigidus River in September 394. He took the field with a larger army that prominently featured units made up of Gothic soldiers serving under the terms the emperor had negotiated in 382. Theodosius decided that he would leverage the numerical advantages he possessed to overwhelm Eugenius's better-positioned defenders, and his Gothic troops were ordered to lead the initial assault. They charged into Eugenius's lines, suffered heavy casualties, and then saw the fighting end inconclusively.[31] Neither side withdrew, however, and Theodosius attacked again the following day, defeating Eugenius and assuming control of the western provinces.[32]

Christian sources written after the battle frame it as a conflict between the paganism of Eugenius's followers and Theodosius's Christianity. The historian Rufinus, for example, wrote that Eugenius catered to pagans, permitted pagan sacrifices before the battle, and was confident he would win because pagan augurs had assured him of this.[33] Theodosius, by contrast, was helped by the Christian God, who responded to his prayers by sending a windstorm that blew "the spears of the enemy . . . back onto them" and ensured Theodosius's victory.[34] But, while Roman Christian propagandists saw the Frigidus as a final vindication of Theodosius's antipagan policies, the Goths saw it as a betrayal. They understood Theodosius's decision to send so many Goths to their deaths as an underhanded way to eliminate the Goths he could not defeat in battle himself.

ALTHOUGH HE NOMINALLY shared power with his sons, Arcadius and Honorius, the victory at Frigidus left Theodosius in effective control of the entire, mostly intact, Roman Empire. He was the last man who could ever claim this. Theodosius, however, did not exercise this unified authority for long. He died a few months later, on January 17, 395, and his demise set off considerable turmoil. The issue was not about who would succeed the emperor. Arcadius, now about eighteen years old, had been an Augustus for over a decade and had stayed in Constantinople to serve as a representative of imperial power while his father went west. Honorius, who had been made Augustus in 393 and was now about eleven, had come to the west with his father. Both sons were, legally speaking, the unquestioned heirs to the empire. But they were also remarkably unprepared and ill-equipped to exercise power.

So while the identities of the new emperors were clear, it was unclear who would run the empire in their names. In the east, there was a regular churn at the top of the imperial administration as courtiers, military officials, and administrators rose and fell until Arcadius's death in 408. Their rapid rises and brutal falls were dizzying. In 395, the military commander Rufinus was killed and replaced by the eunuch Eutropius. Eutropius himself lost power and was executed in 399 when a rebellious Gothic commander, named Tribigild, ordered him to be deposed. Eutropius was replaced first by a courtier named Aurelian, and then another Gothic commander, Gainas, pushed him aside. Gainas fled across the Danube after Arcadius suppressed his attempted coup in 400. As soldiers gave way to eunuchs who gave way to barbarian commanders, the strange shifts in political leadership were nearly as hard for people at the time to follow as they are for us now.

The western situation was even more complicated in 395 than the eastern situation. The stability of the west depended upon Stilicho, a general that Theodosius had brought with him when he marched west to confront Eugenius. Stilicho was of partial barbarian descent and modest social station, but Theodosius had thought so much of his potential that he had arranged for him to marry Serena, his niece and adopted daughter. The general and his wife would become a power couple who capably managed political and military affairs for more than a decade.[35]

Stilicho, however, was not content to serve only as the dominant figure in the west. He claimed authority over both the east and the west and looked for opportunities to exercise the same effective control over the court of Arcadius that he enjoyed in Italy. The figures at the center of political life in Constantinople in the late 390s and early 400s all rejected Stilicho's claims.

Although Arcadius and Honorius remained ostensibly amicable to one another, the contention between Stilicho and the court of Arcadius led to a shadow war between the east and west centered on the western Balkans. This territory, most of which belonged to the prefecture of Illyricum, had historically belonged to the western emperors, but Theodosius had placed it under eastern administration when he advanced on Eugenius. Stilicho, who had moved the western capital from Rome to the Italian city of Ravenna, wanted the territory returned, both because this would mean that the east could not move land forces toward Italy, and because it would enable Stilicho to move on Constantinople if he decided to do so.

There was an added complication. In 395, a Gothic commander named Alaric rebelled. Alaric had led a detachment of Gothic forces at Frigidus, but, following the death of Theodosius, Stilicho had sent him back to the east without a promotion or any sort of official imperial command. Alaric and his men decided to rebel. This must initially have been a small-scale affair that involved only the men already under Alaric's command, but Alaric decided to march on Constantinople. He lacked siege engines, had no chance of capturing the eastern capital, and does not seem to have imagined that he could do so. The attack was instead part of a strategy one might call "negotiation by invasion," through which he hoped to use the threat of attack to get a position of influence for himself and material rewards for his followers. When the formidable defenses of the capital easily repelled him, Alaric then set upon a path of destruction through the more poorly defended cities of Greece.[36]

Alaric's decision to march into Greece was wise. It belonged to the contested prefecture of Illyricum, and the eastern court did not have the military resources positioned to follow him into those lands. Stilicho then led a response from the west that pushed Alaric north into Epirus. Before Stilicho could snuff out the rebellion, however, the eastern court declared Stilicho a public enemy and granted Alaric a military command in Illyricum.[37] They hoped he could keep Stilicho out of the region. Alaric then renounced the agreement in 401 and marched his followers into Italy to besiege Milan.

This was another round of Alaric's negotiation-by-invasion strategy. By 405, Stilicho had pushed Alaric back into Illyricum, but he had also convinced the western court to grant the Goth another Roman military title in the hope that Alaric would secure Illyricum for the west. Stilicho planned to reinforce Alaric with Western Roman troops, and, in preparation for this, Alaric moved his army back down to Epirus to wait for Stilicho's reinforcements.[38]

A series of disasters prevented Stilicho from sending his forces to join Alaric. In 405, barbarian raiders crossed the Alps and penetrated as far as Tuscany. Then, on December 31, 406, large numbers of Vandals, Alans, and Suevi all crossed the Rhine when a cold winter led to large parts of the river freezing solid.

Alaric decided it was again time to renegotiate his agreement. He moved his troops into the Roman province of Noricum (which comprised much of modern Austria), demanded 4,000 pounds of gold, and threatened to invade Italy if the money was not paid. His demand sounds like quite a bit of money, but it was not a huge burden to Roman senators, as many of them personally "received an income of 4,000 pounds of gold per year from their properties."[39] Stilicho understood this and convinced the Senate to pay Alaric, so that he could concentrate on the other military crises afflicting western Europe.[40]

Alaric never got the payoff he expected. Stilicho fell from power in the summer of 408 after he was falsely charged with inciting a mutiny. In reality, Honorius's jealousy of Stilicho's influence induced him to believe courtiers when they whispered that Stilicho aimed to replace the emperor with his own son. Stilicho and his young son were arrested and executed in Ravenna. Honorius and his advisers then compounded the damage their foolishness had caused by ordering the mass execution of Stilicho's barbarian soldiers as well as the wives and children of those men who were stationed outside of Italy.[41]

The death of Stilicho set in motion an utterly avoidable series of catastrophic miscalculations that resulted, two years later, in the sack of Rome. Olympius, the courtier who had Honorius's ear after Stilicho's execution, persuaded the emperor to go back on the deal Stilicho had made with Alaric. Making matters worse, many of the barbarian soldiers who had escaped the massacre Honorius had sanctioned fled to Noricum and joined Alaric's army, while their families were trapped in territory under Honorius's firm control.[42] Although Alaric tried to continue negotiating, it soon became clear that Honorius was not willing to make any new arrangement to pay him, to regularize the military positions of his men, or to allow their surviving family members to leave Italy. Alaric then began another set of negotiations by invasion.

In the winter of 408, Alaric marched his forces into Italy and besieged Rome. Honorius had recently raised the height of the massive walls surrounding the city and reinforced the gates. As in his attack on Constantinople in 395, Alaric lacked the siege engines to break the walls down. Nor did he have the manpower to surround the entire city. Alaric therefore blocked the transport of grain up the Tiber from Ostia instead. This produced such a severe famine that many Romans died; they may have resorted to burying the dead outside of the Colosseum. The Roman Senate first responded by ordering the murder of Stilicho's widow, Serena, a convenient scapegoat, but soon changed course. Negotiating directly with Alaric, the senators then agreed to provide 5,000 pounds of gold, 30,000 pounds of silver, spices and clothes for his followers, and a pledge to advocate for a peace treaty that included releasing the family members of Alaric's followers. Pagan sources claim that the senators raised the money by plundering the treasuries of Rome's pagan temples.[43]

Alaric, confident that the Senate could sway Honorius, lifted the blockade. But the siege had enabled many slaves in the countryside around Rome to escape and join Alaric's army. By the time he withdrew from Latium, his followers were said to number 40,000. Many of these people had joined him following the fall of Stilicho.

Despite this, Honorius still failed to see the urgency of the situation. The Senate sent multiple embassies "to treat of peace," but, as the church historian Sozomen wrote, "the enemies of Alaric at the court of the emperor diligently guarded against the conclusion of any treaty." Honorius was persuaded to begin genuine negotiations only when Pope Innocent I implored him to do so, but these negotiations, too, failed when Honorius's agent, Jovius, the prefect of Italy, proved unable to come to an agreement with Alaric.[44]

Alaric marched on Rome again. In the winter of 409, he seized the harbor at Portus, cutting the supply of grain at a time when there was no local production to draw from. The Senate came to another agreement with Alaric and, with his blessing, acclaimed Priscus Attalus, the urban prefect recently appointed by Honorius, as a rival Roman emperor.[45] Attalus then appointed Alaric as a general, the sort of official position in a Roman regime the Goth had long sought.

Attalus and Alaric also succeeded in securing the defection of significant numbers of Roman troops in Italy. At one point, their actions frightened Honorius enough that he offered to recognize the legitimacy of Attalus's regime and share power with him as co-emperor. Attalus felt secure enough in his eventual victory that he made a counterproposal: Honorius should instead resign and accept exile.[46]

Honorius "kept ships ready to convey him" to Constantinople if escape seemed essential, but he was saved when Attalus and Alaric argued over the emperor's refusal to dispatch Gothic troops to secure the rich grainfields of North Africa. Alaric, suspecting that Attalus and the Senate would prove no more trustworthy than Honorius, dropped his support for Attalus and began working out a new arrangement with Honorius. But Honorius's perfidious idiocy had yet to run its course. As Alaric left a conference with the emperor outside of Ravenna, he was attacked by a Gothic commander in Roman service named Sarus. No more deals were possible with Romans who acted in such bad faith.[47]

"Impelled by rage and terror at this incident," Sozomen wrote, "Alaric returned to Rome."[48] It was now the summer of 410, and on August 24 Alaric "took [Rome] by treachery." Although he still lacked siege engines and sufficient manpower to storm the walls, he and his men were let into the city at the Porta Salaria. "He permitted each of his followers to seize as much of the wealth of the Romans as he was able, and to plunder all the houses," before calling a halt to the sack after three days.[49]

This was the first time since the Gallic sack of 390 BC that an enemy army had captured Rome. But Alaric's sack was very different from that of the Gauls 800 years earlier. Although his men looted houses and captured Roman prisoners (including Galla Placidia, the emperor's sister), the Christian Alaric also guaranteed that churches would provide sanctuary to Roman Christians, and exempted Christian religious centers from plundering. Aside from the Senate House, there was little deliberate burning of the city.[50]

Alaric pulled his punches for a few reasons. First, his army still lacked a homeland to which they could return with the valuables they took. The sack needed to be impactful, but it could not weigh the army down with too much booty, lest Alaric suffer the sort of defeat Brennus's men had as they had tried to carry off all the goods they had taken from Rome. Second—and unlike Brennus—Alaric, the men he commanded, and the families that accompanied them all stood in a sort of netherworld between Romans and barbarians. All of them had lived in the empire for a long time, had served in its armies, and had worshipped in its churches. Many of them, like Alaric himself, even held offices in the Roman army. They wanted a secure place in a Roman Empire that could not quite figure out how to fully embrace or incorporate them.

The Gothic sack of Rome was a completely avoidable catastrophe that reflected the failures of a generation of Roman policy toward the Goths. What makes it even more startling is the fact that, even as Honorius badly and repeatedly bungled the negotiations with Alaric, the eastern empire showed that Rome still had the capacity to peacefully absorb, settle, and integrate newcomers.

In the middle of his narration of Alaric's escapades in the west, Sozomen wrote about a separate barbarian group, led by a man named Uldis, that crossed the Roman frontier and seized a city in the province of Moesia. Roman envoys began public negotiations with Uldis, and when the tribal leaders heard them "discussing the Roman form of government, the philanthropy of the emperor, and how quickly and generously he reward[ed] the best and good men," they broke with their leader and agreed to settle as Romans. Sozomen concluded by saying, "I have seen many [of these people] in Bithynia, near Mount Olympus, living apart from one another, and cultivating the hills and valleys of that region."[51]

By the time Sozomen wrote his account, these Goths had been in the empire for a generation. They were now Romans serving in the army and farming in the hills of northwestern Asia Minor. This was the sort of settlement that Valens imagined he might secure for the Goths in 376. It was what Theodosius had tried to create for them in 382. And it was what Alaric had sought repeatedly since his initial rebellion in 395. The fate of Uldis's followers shows that the fifth-century Roman Empire could still bring people across the frontier and incorporate them into Roman society. This is what makes Honorius's failure to find a place for Alaric so striking. Not only did it lead to the completely avoidable sack of Rome, but it would also hasten the collapse of Roman rule over much of the west. It was as if the western empire had decided to commit suicide.

Chapter 26

The End of the Roman West

410–476

THE SACK OF Rome roused many of the empire's citizens from the illusion that Theodosius I and his sons had inaugurated a new, Christian Roman order in which traditional religion was fading and the Gothic problem was solved. In the late 390s, Christian authors praised the emperors for destroying the "shrines of the idols," replacing famous temples with churches, and leading in a way that caused traditional religion to collapse in on itself. As the Milanese bishop Ambrose once forcefully argued, many had believed it was a moment of Roman Christian progress that promised to make Rome a better and stronger society than it had ever been before.[1]

Theodosius and his sons aspired to create a polity extending from Britain to the Euphrates joined by a common citizenship, a shared history, a universal legal system, and Nicene Christianity as its officially privileged religion. This was a radical idea, but for a few years Theodosius's religious and cultural project looked feasible. The Goths that Theodosius had negotiated with in 382 served loyally in his armies. Many Goths were Arian Christians, but they generally accepted that the best and most impressive churches in the empire were for Nicenes. Even wealthy and powerful pagans usually responded to antipagan laws and temple destructions with flaccid rhetorical denunciations that sounded great but had little tangible effect on policy.[2] Instead of scaling their father's Christian nation-building back after his death, Honorius and Arcadius expanded upon it by issuing laws prohibiting pagan religious processions and requiring governors to confiscate religious images.[3]

Alaric's rebellion revealed how many people living in Roman territory wanted an alternative to the religiously, culturally, and politically unified Roman state of the Theodosians. Barbarians, large numbers of slaves, and many free Romans who were tired of their monotonous life in a stratified, deeply hierarchical society had chosen to join him rather than remain in the system their emperors were creating. Alaric's invasion liberated tens of thousands of slaves in present-day Italy. Though they gained their freedom through these events, their defection to the Goths also meant a loss for Rome, as it removed the contributions of tens of thousands of future Roman citizens from the empire. Slavery was absolutely a dangerous, inhumane, and violent institution, but it also served as a key Romanization tool. Emancipated Roman slaves took on the name and citizenship status of those who sponsored their freedom. Former masters and masters' families became the patrons of these new Roman citizens and took responsibility for them as they established themselves in Roman social and economic life. Alaric's invasion was a long-term catastrophe for a society that for centuries had depended upon the talents of freed men and women to rejuvenate its intellectual, economic, and political life.[4]

Alaric not only freed many Roman slaves, but he also enslaved many free Romans. The most famous of these captives was Galla Placidia, the daughter of Theodosius I and half-sister of the emperor Honorius, who was seized during Rome's sack and compelled to marry Alaric's brother-in-law and successor, Athaulf. Other Roman elites, such as the unfortunate would-be emperor Priscus Attalus, found themselves moving along with the Goths because they no longer had any place in the Roman world. The positions of these Romans were precarious. Gothic leaders eventually returned both Attalus and Galla to Honorius in 415 as part of a peace treaty.[5]

Alaric's campaigns from 395 into the 410s represented the first time since Hannibal that a non-Roman army had stayed in Roman territory long enough to offer the people living there an alternative to Roman rule. In some ways, owing to the incomplete nature of the Theodosian imperial project, Alaric's army had an even more profoundly destabilizing effect than Hannibal's invasion had 600 years before. Hannibal had disrupted a Roman commonwealth made up of legally distinct states bound by political and military ties, whereas Alaric had ripped apart a nascent Christian, Roman nation bound by a common citizenship, a legal system, and centuries of shared history.

In the three decades following Alaric's sack of Rome, this damage spread across the entire Roman West. It was once fashionable to craft maps bearing the title "The Barbarian Invasions," filled with multicolored lines tracing the movements of Goths, Vandals, Alans, and Suevi across the early fifth-century landscape. In a second series of maps, blotches of color spread out from these migration paths by the end of the 430s demarcating the new "barbarian kingdoms" that had consumed Roman Gaul, Spain, and North Africa. By 440, the maps suggest that only Italy and the Mediterranean coasts of Spain and Gaul remained Roman.

The real, more complicated story can only be told by following these armed groups as they moved through the Roman West. It is easiest to begin with the Goths. After their sack of Rome, Alaric's warriors, followers, and their families moved into Southern Italy, which was utterly unprepared for the Gothic attacks. Even so, the Gothic position remained so precarious that they temporarily diverted the Busento River and buried Alaric in its bed when he died near the modern city of Cosenza in late 410. This unmarked and undiscoverable grave was the only way they could prevent angry Romans from desecrating his tomb.[6]

Galla Placidia's husband, Athaulf, led the Gothic band for the next five years as they moved from Italy into Gaul and tried to secure a place within the Roman imperial system. They arrived in Gaul in 412 and joined the native Gallic usurper Jovinus in a fight against Honorius. Dardanus, the prefect of Gaul, induced Athaulf to switch sides in 413 and suppressed Jovinus's revolt with the backing of these Gothic forces. Honorius's inevitable betrayal came once Jovinus was out of the way. The emperor's agents, led by the general Constantius, demanded the return of Galla Placidia and attacked the Goths when they failed to comply. Athaulf responded by proclaiming Priscus Attalus emperor again and working with pliant Gallic nobles to support Attalus's usurpation. When they failed to raise enough money to pay the Gothic troops, Athaulf abandoned Attalus and retreated into northern Spain. He was assassinated outside of Barcelona in 415 and replaced by a new king, Wallia, who negotiated a peace treaty with Constantius. The Romans provided the starving Gothic group with food, and the Goths returned Galla Placidia to Rome. The two sides then agreed to cooperate on a campaign to wipe out the Vandals, Alans, and Suevi.[7]

The Vandals, Alans, and Suevi were the three main barbarian groups that had crossed the Rhine in December 406, and they had all fought for and against the various Roman generals contending with one another in the messy, multifaceted civil war that consumed Gaul between 406 and 413. By 411, the main body of Vandals, Alans, and Suevi had crossed the Pyrenees into Spain. The Suevi and one group of Vandals took the northwestern province of Gallaecia, and the Alans seized the western provinces of Lusitania and Cartaginensis, which encompassed nearly all of Portugal as well as southwestern Spain down to the Mediterranean coast. Another group of Vandals seized Baetica, the province containing Seville and much of modern Andalusia.

In 416, Wallia's Goths and Constantius's Roman forces organized a large-scale attack on barbarian-controlled territories in Spain that inflicted massive casualties on the Vandals, Alans, and Suevi. Fearing that the Goths might take all of Spain for themselves, Constantius called off the attack before Wallia could achieve a total victory. But this time, the Romans followed through on their promise of security for the Goths within Roman territory. Constantius granted the Goths "lands to farm" in Aquitaine that had once belonged either to cities or to imperial estates.[8] The Goths in these lands remained subject to the Gothic king, while the Romans living in the region remained citizens of the empire. Goths were also expected to serve as Roman allies when summoned to fight, just as Italian cities once did during the Republic. Roman authorities could pretend that this arrangement reflected the same sort of Roman domination that the Republic had once enjoyed over its Italian allies, but the reality escaped no one. For the first time since the end of the Republic, Rome had permitted someone who was neither an imperial official nor a Roman to command an army within Roman territory.[9]

The relationship worked in the short term. The Goths did what was expected of them, and Constantius proved a faithful, competent partner. Following the initial Gothic successes in Spain in 417, Constantius wed Galla Placidia, despite the fact that she detested him, and they had a son they named Valentinian in 419. Constantius's military victories and ties to the imperial family convinced Honorius to appoint him as co-emperor in February 421, and he became Constantius III. But not for long: Constantius's death that September again left Rome devoid of effective leadership. Honorius remained as incompetent as ever, and Castinus, the commander who directed the fighting in Spain, was not much better.

The failure of Roman leadership at this delicate moment had catastrophic consequences. In 422, Castinus led Roman and Gothic troops against the Vandals in Spain. The campaign went so well that his army "had reduced [the Vandals] to starvation with an effective siege to the point that they were ready to surrender," but when Castinus "recklessly engaged in open battle," his Gothic auxiliaries and some of his Roman troops defected to the Vandals. He was defeated, forced to retreat to Tarraco (modern Tarragona), and reduced to observing the Goths, Vandals, and Suevi contest with one another for influence over the peninsula.[10]

The political vacuum left in Rome by the death of Constantius III encouraged Romans to focus on internal conflicts rather than the elimination of these nascent barbarian statelets in Spain. Galla Placidia, who "was surrounded by a host of barbarians because of her marriages to Athaulf and Constantius," became their first target. The recently humbled Castinus and other members of Honorius's court convinced the emperor to exile Galla and her son Valentinian to Constantinople in late 422. Unfortunately, Honorius died in August 423 without leaving an obvious heir. A courtier named Johannes initially seized power with the backing of Castinus, but the eastern court in Constantinople sent Valentinian and Galla Placidia back to the west with an army. Johannes was decapitated, and the six-year-old Valentinian III was acknowledged as the western Augustus on October 23, 425. He was then betrothed to the daughter of the eastern emperor, Theodosius II.[11]

There was a problem, however. Johannes had sent a Roman military commander named Aetius, who had once been a hostage at the court of the Hunnic king, to the Huns, so that he might secure a detachment of soldiers that Johannes could use in the civil war against Valentinian III. Aetius convinced the Hunnic king to send the troops, but he arrived in Italy after Johannes's death. Aetius's Huns gave him enough leverage to persuade Galla Placidia to give him command over the Roman forces in Gaul and pay the Huns to return home. This created a new dynamic, where Galla Placidia would dominate Valentinian III's court while Aetius, backed implicitly or explicitly by the Hunnic court, emerged as the leading military figure of the age. Their precarious partnership provided the shrinking Western Roman Empire with the executive and military skill that it needed to survive the calamities to come.

The later 420s largely belonged to Galla, who was able to play the ambitions and suspicions of the generals Felix (based in Italy) and Boniface (in North Africa) against those of Aetius (in Gaul). This arrangement collapsed when Felix tried and failed to displace Boniface from Africa in 427, a move that prompted Aetius to arrest and execute Felix and his wife in 430. Boniface then returned to Italy and defeated Aetius, but died shortly afterward. Aetius left Roman territory, gathered a group of Hunnic soldiers, and returned to seize command of the Roman army.[12]

The years of infighting that preceded Aetius's consolidation of power proved costly for the Western Roman state. His campaigns in

Gaul held back Gothic and Frankish advances on Roman-controlled territory, but internal turmoil in Italy prevented him from responding to an appeal for help from Spanish leaders against the Vandals. This meant that Aetius could not prevent the political rot from spreading to North Africa. In 429, the Vandals, a group that had only ever lived inland, crossed into Africa and devoted most of their military strength to capturing the lightly defended Roman North African provinces (which now make up much of modern Tunisia and coastal Algeria). By 439, they had left Spain and taken control of Carthage, the productive farmland around it, and the most important port in the southwestern Mediterranean. Western Roman control over North Africa ended in 442 when Rome signed a peace treaty recognizing the full independence of the Vandal kingdom.[13]

It is largely due to Aetius that the Western Roman state survived the loss of North Africa. Nearly every annual entry in the chronicle written by the Spaniard Hydatius describes a new victory by the general in the later 430s. In 436, Aetius vanquished the Burgundians who sought to expand in Gaul. In 437, he defeated another Burgundian force, inflicting 20,000 casualties. In 438, he defeated the Goths and killed 8,000.[14] Then, in the 440s, Aetius preserved the state by harnessing the talents of Roman aristocrats, including Flavius Merobaudes. A senator of Frankish ancestry, Merobaudes owned land in northern Gaul and southern Spain and commanded Roman armies in both regions. He also wrote poems describing life at Valentinian's court, delivered an oration praising the achievements of Aetius, and served as a senator in Rome. He even gifted an estate to a monastery outside the Gallic city of Troyes. His service led Valentinian III to approve the erection of a bronze statue of him in the Forum of Trajan, above a base praising him as "a man of ancient nobility" who possessed "equal measures of strength and learning," and who was "as capable of doing things worthy of praise as he was of offering praises for the things done by others."[15]

Merobaudes, like much of the aristocracy around him, was intensely loyal to Aetius, whom he praised as a man who wore a breastplate "as a way of life." He said that Aetius had accomplished so much that "not even our own Cato . . . would not admire his deeds." Aetius not only won battles, but he also built Roman-led coalitions of barbarian allies to defend what remained of the western empire's European territory. The result, Merobaudes wrote in 443, was that Aetius had "returned with the Danube at peace," and the "Rhine [had] produced treaties that make the wintry world Rome's servant."[16]

Events in the later 440s required a new set of diplomatic approaches. The Huns with whom Aetius cooperated in the 420s and 430s became much more aggressive when the brothers Bleda and Attila took control of the Hunnic Empire around 440. The Huns had always deployed cavalry of unmatched skill, but under Attila they developed the capacity to storm well-fortified Roman cities—an advantage that groups like the Goths and Vandals lacked.[17] In 441, Attila's Huns captured Viminacium in modern Serbia, and the following year they stormed Naissus (modern Niš). Both were well-protected cities located in lands controlled by the eastern court of Theodosius II. By early 443, Theodosius had concluded that he could not defeat the Huns in the field and instead agreed to pay an annual tribute. Attila increased the tribute in 447, after the empire reneged on the treaty and suffered two severe defeats during a Hunnic reprisal raid into the Balkans. Priscus of Panium, the ambassador sent to negotiate a new tribute arrangement, wrote that the Roman commanders' "overwhelming fear" of Attila had "compelled [the ambassadors] to accept every condition, however harsh, in exchange for peace."[18]

Attila then turned his attention to the west. His invasion of Western Roman lands began in the spring of 451 with attacks on the modern German cities of Trier and Metz, both of which fell by the end of April. In early summer, Attila's forces spread out across central Gaul, sacking the cities that resisted them and trying to lure barbarians serving under Roman command to switch sides.[19]

Aetius led the Western Roman response with a level of diplomatic and technical skill few Roman commanders had ever displayed. Shorn of North Africa, much of Spain, and large parts of Gaul, the western empire could marshal only a fraction of the monetary and military resources of the east. But Aetius understood that the barbarian kingdoms sprouting on formerly Roman land were led by men at least as terrified of Attila as they were of the Roman court in Italy. Aetius then built an army led by Romans but supplemented by large numbers of well-trained, experienced Goths and Burgundians that defeated Attila in what is now northeastern France.[20]

In 452, Attila responded by attacking the well-fortified Italian cities in the Po Valley. The result was a grinding campaign made up of sieges and urban assaults for which Attila's army was not adequately supplied. Attila was forced to withdraw when famine and disease began to ravage his troops. As he retreated toward the Danube, much of the Hunnic army "was slaughtered by troops . . . under the command of the duke Aetius."[21] Aetius, the Western Roman army, and the coalition of allies he assembled had done what the richer, more populous, and stronger east could not. They had defeated Attila and destroyed much of the Hunnic Empire's combat power. Attila died in the early winter of 453 before he could get revenge.[22] Within twenty years of his death, the Hunnic Empire had collapsed.[23]

ONE MIGHT IMAGINE that Aetius's victories over Attila, which capped three decades of distinguished service to the Western Roman state, would buy him the privilege of finishing his political and military career in whatever fashion he chose. But Valentinian III's idiocy, and the venality of his advisers, denied the general this ending.

Aetius fell from power suddenly and brutally in 454, just one year after Attila's passing ended the Hunnic threat to the empire and less than a year before the thirty-five-year-old Valentinian III would mark his thirtieth year as emperor. The recent, disastrous reign of Honorius had shown Romans how dangerous it could be to entrust actual decision-making to a foolish man who spent his entire life surrounded by sycophants. Galla Placidia had managed the behavior of her son by cocooning him in a world dominated by rituals and complicated protocols so long and boring that just the acclamations senators chanted at every imperial ceremony took forty minutes to complete.[24] She had hoped that the sheer numbing dullness of court life could sufficiently occupy her son so that he might refrain from interfering in the plans of the grownups upon whom the Roman state depended.

Galla Placidia's death in 450 had removed the most significant barrier preventing Valentinian from exercising the considerable power he legally possessed, but, by then, the cowardly emperor's fear of Attila was enough to prevent him from acting rashly. Aetius was given the freedom to meet the Hunnic threat however he wanted, but some of his decisions had irritated the isolated, ignorant emperor. Valentinian could not understand why Aetius refused to act on his fantastical idea to personally lead Western Roman forces to Constantinople and reunify both empires under his sole authority.[25] He also objected to the marriage alliances Aetius had arranged for Valentinian's only two living children. One secured Rome's southern flank by pledging Valentinian's daughter Eudocia to Hunneric, the son of the Vandal king Geiseric. The second would join Aetius's son Gaudentius to Valentinian's daughter Placidia, a marriage that, if consummated, would link Aetius's family to the imperial dynasty and position Gaudentius as imperial heir.[26]

Aetius badly miscalculated when he took away the emperor's ability to choose his successor while, at the same time, disappointing Roman elites who hoped they or their heirs might marry Placidia.[27] As soon as the death of Attila made Aetius seem expendable, an ambitious senator named Petronius Maximus conspired with Valentinian to eliminate the general. On September 21, 454, "Aetius was in the palace preparing for a meeting" when the murder occurred. "Valentinian leapt at him" just as Aetius began "explaining the budget and calculating tax revenues." Valentinian then "drew his sword from his scabbard . . . and rained blows on [Aetius's] head and killed him." After this, Priscus writes, Valentinian "could not avoid ruin because he had destroyed the bulwark protecting his empire."[28]

Valentinian relished the freedom to make bad decisions that he now enjoyed. Although Petronius Maximus had helped to plan Aetius's murder, Valentinian sidelined the powerful senator because he believed that "he ought not to again transfer his power to others," now that he was "freed from the oppression of Aetius." Maximus responded by conspiring with two close associates of Aetius to over-throw the emperor. On March 16, 455, Valentinian was killed in the Campus Martius while on his way to practice archery. The chronicler Hydatius reported that his attendants and bodyguards stood frozen in the field while "a swarm of bees settled on the blood that had run onto the ground . . . and sucked it all up." This event foreshadowed the Western Roman state's paralysis as two decades of bloodshed descended upon it.[29]

Petronius Maximus set the tone early. He seized power in Rome immediately following Valentinian's assassination, both by bribing the Roman population with gifts and by forcing Eudoxia, Valentinian III's widow (and the daughter of the late eastern emperor Theodo-sius II), to marry him.[30] She hated her new husband, but the hatred became even more visceral when Maximus broke off the engagement of her daughter Eudocia to Hunneric, the heir to the Vandal king-dom, and betrothed her instead to his own son. Hunneric's father, the Vandal king Geiseric, had originally arranged the match with Aetius, and it had been intended to compensate Geiseric for breaking a treaty with the Goths in order to make an alliance with Rome. By breaking the engagement, Maximus had robbed the Vandal king of his payment.[31]

Geiseric responded by sailing a massive fleet, manned largely by sailors who had once considered themselves Roman, to a spot out-side Rome. Some contemporary sources even suggest that Eudoxia had summoned Geiseric to rescue her and her daughters from Max-imus. When the Vandal fleet disgorged its army near the end of May 455, Maximus "panicked, mounted his horse, and fled," until, Priscus wrote, "someone threw a rock that hit him in the head and killed him." He fell just as Geiseric was about to enter Rome.[32]

Geiseric's sack of Rome was far more destructive than that of Alaric forty-five years earlier. Unlike Alaric, Geiseric controlled ships in which he could haul off plunder, and he had a kingdom to which that plunder might be taken. He had "found the city bereft of all defenses" so his men could loot the city at their leisure. "For fourteen days, through an untroubled and open search, Rome was emptied of all of its wealth and many thousands of captives." The staggering riches stolen from the Palatine and Capitoline Hills alone included "a huge amount of gold and other imperial treasures" from the emperor's palace, as well as the gilded bronze roof of the Temple of Jupiter Capitolinus. Eudoxia and her daughters, Eudocia and Placidia, "were abducted to Carthage," and Eudocia married Hunneric soon after the fleet returned to Africa.[33]

The death of Petronius Maximus prompted a Gallic nobleman named Avitus, an ambassador at the court of the Gothic king Theoderic, to seize the vacant Roman throne with Gothic backing. Once Avitus arrived, his Gothic support became as much of a political liability in Rome as it was a military asset outside of it. Italians resented the emperor, who protected himself with a Gothic bodyguard and staffed his administration with Gallic peers. He struggled to restore the food supply and urban infrastructure that the Vandals had disrupted. Priscus wrote that Italians "blamed Avitus for the famine at that time," and "forced him to send away . . . the people he had brought from Gaul" as well as "the Goths . . . he had brought as his own guard." Stripped of his Gothic protection, Avitus fled Rome in the summer or early fall of 456.[34]

It took around six months for the western senators and military commanders to agree on a new emperor. This was the first of four western interregna between 456 and 473, including one vacancy that lasted from August 465 until April 467, a longer period than the entire reigns of more than twenty previous emperors.[35] As the Senate and its army commanders jostled for power in Italy, the western empire continued to shrink. By the mid-470s, it had lost all of the major Western Mediterranean islands to the Vandals save Sicily. Roman holdings in Gaul were reduced to eastern Provence. Goths, Burgundians, Franks, and an independent Romano-Gallic ruler named Syagrius held the rest of the Gallic provinces.[36] The Goths moved into Spain, seized Tarragona, and eliminated the Roman presence in the Spanish peninsula in 472. At that point, Rome controlled less territory in the Western Mediterranean than it had at any point since Scipio Africanus had taken the field in the Second Punic War.

It was perhaps inevitable that someone would decide that the much-reduced west no longer needed its own Roman emperor. In August 476, the barbarian general Odoacer seized Italy and overthrew the child emperor Romulus Augustulus.[37] Odoacer had the Roman Senate send an embassy to Constantinople carrying the western imperial regalia and bearing the message that "one shared emperor was sufficient for both territories."[38] Instead of selecting a new western emperor, Odoacer would serve as the imperial agent governing Italy in the name of the eastern emperor Zeno.

At this moment, an Eastern Roman chronicler wrote decades later, "the Western Empire of the Roman people, which the first emperor Octavian Augustus had begun to rule in the 709th year from the foundation of the city, perished with this Augustulus."[39] He was correct that no other Roman emperor would rule a Western Roman state based in Italy. But the end of the line of Western Roman emperors based in the peninsula did not mean the end of the Roman's state's Italian story. A new, and much more complicated, Roman Italian experience was about to begin.

Chapter 27

Western Romans Outside
the Roman State

476–526

THE LINEAR NARRATIVE of the barbarian invasions, conquests, and consolidation of Western Roman lands does not correspond to the actual experiences of Roman and non-Roman people living through the fifth century. The stories told to us by the generation experiencing these changes in Gaul, Spain, and Africa more closely resemble those told by Italians during the Second Punic War. For many centuries, the Roman Empire had provided an overarching political structure that managed local competitions for influence between cities and prominent individuals. Rome set the rules, intervened when rivalries became too intense, and offered a more lucrative set of empire-wide rewards and honors that the most ambitious could pursue. And, just as Hannibal allowed Italian cities to break out of the old Italo-Roman commonwealth, so too did the non-Roman armies marching across the fifth-century western empire strip away the imperial structures that encouraged local Gallic, Spanish, and African notables to behave.

The areas that fell outside of central Roman control in the first part of the fifth century became steadily less Roman as the imperial system broke down and sporadic atrocities shredded the fabric of their communities. In 414, for example, the Gothic group marauding through Gaul "ravaged the villages all around," wrote Gregory of Tours. "They set fire to farm buildings and ruined vineyards and grain fields by driving livestock into them." They also captured the slaves and peasants working on these farms, a theft of labor that prevented landowners from repairing the infrastructure destroyed in a raid.[1]

This violence was not random. The barbarian attacks in these regions often were carefully calibrated attempts to exploit local divisions and induce some members of a city's or region's elite to cooperate more closely with the armed groups nearby. The raids on farms, the taking of captives, and the destruction of cash crops often represented a deliberate effort by local elites to permanently reduce the status of a local rival. In some cases, an attack was provoked by nothing more than a rumor about someone's wife. In 410, according to the chronicler Fredegar, the city of Trier "was captured and burned [through the efforts] of the faction of one of the senators in the city" whose wife was said to be having an affair.[2] Another chronicler, Hydatius, described how his city of Aquae Flaviae in northern Spain was "betrayed by informers" who allowed "a band of Sueves" to enter and take him prisoner before they "overwhelmed the same [district] causing massive destruction."[3] This civil strife was no different from the petty civic jealousies that Hannibal had exploited in the 210s BC—except that, this time, Roman control seldom returned.

The Roman social order was splintering, largely due to the activities of armed barbarian groups. But places in the west where no barbarians were present had their own set of problems. The fifth century saw the return of a mysterious movement called the Bacaudae that had first emerged in Gaul during the tumult of the late third century. In their third-century manifestation, the Bacaudae were described as "inexperienced farmers [who] sought military garb," "ravaged the countryside far and wide," and "assailed many cities."[4] The early fifth-century Bacaudae first appeared in the Alps following the Rhine crossing of the Vandals, Alans, and Suevi, when they blocked a mountain pass and compelled a Roman general to pay for passage.[5] The scope of Bacaudae activity soon expanded dramatically. According to a fifth-century Gallic chronicler, northern Gaul "was separated from Roman society" for more than two years around 435 by a "rebellion precipitated by Tibatto" in which "nearly all of the slaves of Gaul conspired in a Bacauda."[6] In Spain, Hydatius wrote of the suppression of Bacaudae activities four different times in the thirteen years between 441 and 454.[7]

The bishop Salvian of Marseille explained that, as the barbarians advanced, corruption became common among the local elites charged with collecting taxes. The Roman state depended upon these local leaders to keep the revenues flowing, but they took advantage of their position to "plunder" the less fortunate and "increase their private fortunes." As a result, Salvian claimed, "the greater part of the Spaniards and no small proportion of the Gauls" were left "despoiled, afflicted, and murdered by wicked and bloodthirsty magistrates." He concluded that "the overwhelming injuries poor men suffer compel them to wish to become Bacaudae" because the Roman state lacked the capacity to provide the legal protections its citizens needed and expected. It was only "after they had lost the rights of Roman citizens," Salvian wrote, that oppressed people gave up "the honor of the Roman name" by taking up arms against their local—Roman or non-Roman—oppressors.[8]

With the central administration only sporadically able to provide military support to prop up Roman authority in Gaul and Spain, communities used whatever local social capital they controlled to police elite behaviors. In 453, a church council held in the city of Angers held that anyone "involved in the betrayal or capture of cities ought both to be excluded from communion and from feasts" within the city.[9] In other words, a local bishop or aristocrat who gave the city over to anyone, Roman or non-Roman, would be religiously and socially ostracized by the community. Because the central government now lacked the capacity to punish such treachery, locals figured out how to deter it themselves.

Small, local decisions like those made in Angers show why Rome's military, political, and administrative retreats encouraged a slow process of de-Romanization throughout the west. This was, in a sense, an inversion of the path that many of the ancestors of these fifth-century Gallic, British, German, Spanish, and North African people had followed to become Roman in the Julio-Claudian and Flavian periods. Just as the Roman state in the first century AD had spread Roman names, amphitheaters, and law across the west by honoring and rewarding local elites, so, too, did the barbarian leaders based in Gaul, Spain, and North Africa bestow monetary rewards and prestige on Roman notables willing to work with them.

The results affected all aspects of life. Amphitheaters, the most prominent markers of Romanization in the first and second century AD, faded into irrelevance. Outside of Italy, the few that survived into the fifth century were remade into fortifications as the funding necessary to hold games dried up and the infrastructure for them crumbled. In the British town of Cirencester, the disused amphitheater was repurposed as a defensive structure. Its entrances were closed or narrowed, protective ditches were dug around the southern wall, and a timber building was constructed within it.[10] In the French town of Senlis, the minor axis of the amphitheater was walled off so that the disused building also became a fortification.

Other public structures lost the funding or expertise required for their continued operation. In the early sixth century, the Gothic king Alaric issued the *Breviarium*, an updated version of the mid-fifth-century Roman *Theodosian Code*, that contained the text of the original Roman law and interpretations of how each law applied to an early sixth-century Gothic context. The fifteenth book reproduces a Roman law issued by the emperors Arcadius and Honorius mandating that cities use income from "farms belonging to the municipality" to "pay for the upkeep of public works and the heating of baths." The Gothic interpretation reads, "Whenever it shall be necessary to repair buildings ruined by age, the royal treasury shall pay a third part from its resources toward such repair."[11]

While both laws concern the maintenance of city infrastructure, the differences between the Roman law and the Gothic version are simultaneously subtle and glaring. In the Gothic kingdom, cities no longer have a sustainable, predictable source of revenue from

municipally owned farms to pay for the regular, preventive maintenance of their buildings or the heating of public baths. Instead of preventing things from falling into disrepair using their own resources,
as they had under Roman rule, cities in the Gothic kingdom had to
wait for structures to fall into ruin before they could apply for rebuilding aid from the king, and even then, the funding would amount to
only one-third of the cost of repairs. Presumably they simply had to
hope they could somehow gather the rest of the money needed. However, most of the time they could not find this additional funding.

Funding was only part of the problem with maintaining a Roman
way of life outside of the empire. Western cities cut off from the core
of the Roman state also faced serious problems attracting the necessary engineering talent to build or maintain complicated infrastructure. In the second century AD, for example, Pliny had to ask
the emperor Trajan to send surveyors, engineers, architects, and
other specialists from the army or the central administration to the
major cities of Asia Minor when structures like aqueducts and baths
required extensive maintenance.[12] The highly trained technicians
who handled complicated repairs to large structures worked for the
emperor and were no longer available in the smaller barbarian kingdoms scattered across the post-Roman west.

While these new barbarian kingdoms lost access to the talents
of the best Roman designers and technologists, many local Romans,
especially those with military and administrative training, chose to
work with the new barbarian leaders in formerly Roman lands. The
naval power that enabled the North African Vandal kingdom to sack
Rome in 455 grew out of the regime's ability to induce sailors who
had once considered themselves Roman to serve on ships that fought
against Rome. The post-Roman states in Gaul took over the Roman
administrative structures in their territories and appointed Romans
to manage them. In 461, for example, the Gothic king Theoderic II
arranged for the Roman aristocrat Arborius to replace Nepotianus as
the commander of joint Roman and Gothic forces fighting in Spain.
Nepotianus had been chosen in 458 by the Roman emperor Majorian
when the territory was under Roman control. Theoderic appointed

his successor following Majorian's murder in 461, stepping seamlessly into the leadership vacuum left by the political upheaval in the empire.[13]

By the 470s, Gothic kings had renamed these offices in which Gallo-Romans and Hispano-Romans served but had not dramatically changed their duties. Dukes of Aquitaine and Spain commanded Gothic armies in those regions, while Namatius of Saintes commanded the Atlantic fleet as he defended the coast from "the serpentine ships of Saxon pirates."[14] Gallo-Romans and Hispano-Romans also served the Gothic regime as provincial governors, envoys, and royal counselors. Some of them, like the jurist Leo of Narbonne, worked closely with the Gothic kings Euric and Alaric, the new non-Roman leaders of southern Gaul. Leo was Euric's spokesman, propagandist, and legal adviser. When Alaric's *Breviarium* was drafted in 506, a group of jurists with Latin names worked under the supervision of a senior official with a Gothic name.[15]

Roman aristocrats who wished to avoid serving directly under barbarian leaders sometimes decided to serve their home cities by joining the clergy. Sidonius Apollinaris, the son-in-law of the emperor Avitus and scion of a Gallic senatorial family, first rose to prominence in 456, when two imperial panegyrics that he delivered at the age of twenty-six earned him a statue in the Forum of Trajan.[16] In 468, the emperor Anthemius appointed Sidonius urban prefect of the city of Rome, the highest office that a senator could hope to hold, after he delivered another impressive speech praising the emperor.[17] By the early 470s, however, Euric's Goths had stormed into eastern Gaul, captured the Auvergne, and changed Sidonius's status from that of a Roman senator, patrician, and former urban prefect to someone who no longer lived in a Roman state.

Sidonius had already adjusted. Sometime after 468, he agreed to assume the title of bishop of Clermont-Ferrand.[18] It was in this capacity that he helped to organize the defense of his home region against the Goths, actions for which he was imprisoned for a year when the Auvergne fell in 475.[19] When he returned to his city, Sidonius used the talents that once had enchanted Roman emperors to serve the

Christians of Clermont.[20] Sometimes this involved praising God, but he also wrote pieces dripping with classical allusions that flattered the intellectuals of the Gothic court.[21] This naked appeal to men like Leo of Narbonne worked well enough that Sidonius again gained the favor of his sovereign, though, in this case, it was the Gothic king Euric rather than a Roman emperor. By the time he died sometime in the 480s, Sidonius had positioned his son Apollinaris to serve the Gothic regime as courtier and military commander.[22] In 515, Apollinaris followed his father's example and was ordained bishop of Clermont.[23]

Unlike the messy, decades-long erosion of Roman control over western Europe, the Vandal conquest of North Africa unfolded systematically over a few years, but it presented North African Christians with a profound quandary. Although many Roman sailors and civilians worked with the Vandal regime, just as their compatriots cooperated with the Goths in Gaul and Spain, the Vandals were Arian Christians who attacked the Roman clergy and elites who resisted them. When Carthage fell in 439, many North African clergy fled to Italy so they could stay within Roman imperial territory. Others, such as the Carthaginian bishop Quodvultdeus, were tortured and sent to Italy "naked and despoiled on broken ships," according to the militantly anti-Vandal bishop Victor of Vita.[24] Another wave of refugees turned up in Constantinople in the 480s, after the Vandal king Hunneric ordered their tongues to be cut out as a consequence of their open defiance of his rule. These exiles began conducting public events in which they called for the eastern emperor to send forces to North Africa so the province could return to Roman imperial control.[25]

The continued existence of the powerful, although much diminished, Western Roman state exempted fifth-century Italians from the awkward choices their colleagues in Gaul, Spain, and North Africa confronted. Much of this was due to Odoacer, the barbarian general who seized control of Italy in 476, and his recognition of the military and economic power that remained in Italy, the most urbanized and prosperous region in the entire west. Odoacer tried to maximize these resources by governing in a way that maintained established procedures, preserved cordial relations with the Roman Senate, and protected the rights and property of his subjects.[26]

Perhaps most importantly, Odoacer reinforced Italy as the center of Roman life in the Western Mediterranean by welcoming Romans fleeing insecurity in other regions. Not only did he receive individual migrants, such as bishops persecuted by the Vandals in North Africa, but he also arranged the transfer to Italy of most of the Roman population of the transalpine province of Noricum when he judged that the military could no longer protect them.[27] While other parts of the west shed their Roman character, the barbarian Odoacer fortified it in Italy.

Although the eastern emperor Zeno never accepted Odoacer's proposal to abolish the western empire and replace it with a regime in which Odoacer served as Zeno's agent, Odoacer pretended he had. He diligently acknowledged Zeno's superiority, displayed Zeno's portraits in Rome, and issued coinage bearing the image of Zeno.[28] Odoacer's public submission to Eastern Roman authority extended so far that he sent a formal embassy congratulating Zeno on a victory that Odoacer had won in Zeno's name against a barbarian group called the Rugians. Left unsaid, but understood by all, was that the Rugian war had happened because Zeno's agents had encouraged them to invade and depose Odoacer.[29]

The Rugian attack failed to dislodge Odoacer, but Zeno found another ruler he could send against the Italian regime. This was Theoderic, the king of a Gothic group in the east that historians call Ostrogoths (Eastern Goths) to distinguish them from the Visigoths (Western Goths) who had established themselves in Spain and Gaul. Theoderic had been a hostage in Constantinople during his youth, led an abortive attack against the well-defended eastern capital in 487, and was redirected to Italy by Zeno. If his invasion of Italy succeeded, Theoderic would solve Zeno's Odoacer problem. If it failed, Odoacer would solve Zeno's Gothic problem.[30]

Odoacer reacted to Theoderic's invasion of Italy in 489 by emphasizing the Roman character of his regime and appointing his son Thela as Caesar, a position that officially made Thela a junior emperor under Zeno.[31] Odoacer's non-Roman lineage meant that he might invite resistance if he were to claim imperial power himself, but his son was born Roman and could serve as a symbol of his father's defense of Roman autonomy against the attacks of Theoderic's Goths. This move touched off a brutal war that inflicted serious damage across the Italian Peninsula before it ended on March 5, 493, when Odoacer and Theoderic agreed to rule Italy jointly.[32] The peace lasted for ten days. On March 15, Theoderic personally slaughtered Odoacer at a dinner party held in the Italian capital of Ravenna to celebrate the agreement.[33]

Theoderic built upon Odoacer's success in stabilizing what had once been the Western Roman Empire by emphasizing its Roman character and institutions. He governed alongside a Roman Senate that he empowered to rebuild and reform the capital. Material conditions in Italy improved as Roman resources and specialists turned their efforts back to the Italian core. Large-scale repairs were made to Italian churches and public buildings, a striking contrast to the managed decay that Visigothic kings had enforced in Spain. While the rest of the cities in the west closed their amphitheaters or made them into forts, Theoderic renovated his. He sponsored elaborate games in the Colosseum and paid for chariot races in circuses across the peninsula.[34]

Theoderic also improved the military position of the Roman West. After the territorial losses of the last western emperors and Odoacer's retrenchment, Theoderic again expanded Roman control. At its peak, his domains extended to the old Danube frontier in the northeast and deep into Provence and the southern Rhône Valley in Gaul. For a time, he even assumed effective control over the Visigothic kingdom in Spain by serving as regent for his grandson, the young Visigothic king Amalaric.[35] Where he could not secure power himself, Theoderic used marriage alliances with the Franks and Vandals to establish the supremacy of his regime over that of the other Roman successor kingdoms in the west.

Theoderic always remained a Gothic king, but, as the sixth-century Eastern Roman historian Procopius put it, "he governed two nations, Goths and Romans, in one."[36] This led "both Goths and Romans to love him greatly." It also permitted Theoderic to staff his military with Goths and draw upon the experienced Italo-Roman senatorial and aristocratic elite to run his government.[37]

Theoderic's Roman subjects responded eagerly. They took to comparing him to the top tier of Roman leaders from centuries past. His conquests made him a new Trajan to some while, to others, his commitment to the traditions of Rome made him a new Cato.[38] In 507, Ennodius of Pavia compared Theoderic to Alexander the Great because under his rule "the Roman empire [had] returned to its former boundary" and "the wealth of the Republic [grew] along with private prosperity."[39] The senator Cassiodorus, who worked for a time writing letters on the king's behalf, once teased the Burgundian king Gundobad that he should be happy that Theoderic had sent him a water clock like the one he "once saw in the city of Rome," because, without it, he would fall back into "the habit of beasts" who could "feel the hours by their bellies' hunger."[40] Theoderic's regime, Cassiodorus was implying, retained all that was good about the Roman past, while the other kingdoms he dealt with would slip back to animalistic barbarism without his help.

Theoderic also deftly managed the religious differences between the Arian Christian Goths he led as king and the Nicene Christian Romans he governed. "Although he was himself of the Arian sect," a contemporary wrote, "he nevertheless made no assault against the Catholic religion."[41] As he remade the city of Ravenna into a gleaming new capital, he built religious structures that served each community separately. This offered an important, and deliberate, contrast with the religious persecutions of Nicene Romans in places such as Gaul and, especially, North Africa. Theoderic understood the advantage of maintaining the sort of pluralistic, inclusive political culture that had defined Roman life for more than 1,200 years. In the words of Procopius, "Although in name Theoderic was a usurper, yet in fact he was as truly an emperor as any who have distinguished themselves in this office from the beginning."[42]

Theoderic, however, was fated to rule for too long. He had enjoyed good relations with Zeno, and he had generated so much trust in

Constantinople that Zeno's successor, Anastasius, sent the western imperial regalia back to Italy in 497, an action seen in the west as an acknowledgment that Theoderic effectively (though not officially) ruled as a Roman emperor.[43] When Anastasius died in 518, however, a much less favorable climate descended upon Constantinople. Justin I, the new eastern emperor, was a Latin speaker from the Balkans. He and Justinian, his nephew and eventual successor, mounted a few sporadic naval raids on western territory as Theoderic's forces bumped up against the Eastern Roman frontier.[44]

These tensions with the east prompted an unfortunate response from Theoderic. In 523, he ordered the arrest of the philosopher Boethius and his father-in-law, Symmachus. Boethius and Symmachus "were men of noble and ancient lineage, and both had been leading men in the Roman Senate and had been consuls," wrote Procopius. They "practiced philosophy and pursued justice in a manner surpassed by no other men," and had "relieved the poverty of both citizens and strangers by generous gifts of money." Their political prominence and philanthropy led to a rumor that "they were plotting a revolution," and "Theoderic, believing the slanders, put the two men to death . . . and confiscated their property."[45]

This was a serious mistake. Boethius and Symmachus belonged to the Anicii clan, one of the most powerful families in Italy, but one that also had an eastern branch with connections high up in the Constantinopolitan court.[46] Their unjust execution encouraged their Constantinopolitan relatives to work with other Italian exiles who loathed what the Gothic regime had become during Theoderic's senescence.[47] In these last paranoid years of his life, Theoderic had created a set of Roman senatorial martyrs plucked from a family that was uniquely well positioned to transform their outrage at his "act of tyranny" into military action by the Eastern Roman state.[48] The scene was now set for the Eastern Roman Empire to bring the Roman state back to the west, if and when its sovereigns wished to do so.

Chapter 28

The Roman Christian Empire
of the East in the Fifth Century

395–491

THE EASTERN ROMAN Empire thrived while Roman rule across most of the west collapsed amid barbarian invasions, civil wars, and aristocratic shortsightedness in the fifth century. Much of the success in the east was due to the region's historical and geographical advantages. If one were to consider the richest regions in the entire Roman world, all, bar Italy and North Africa, were in the east. And, except for Carthage and Rome itself, the wealthiest and most populous cities were also in the empire's eastern territories. The eastern region included the large and opulent cities of Asia Minor, such as Ephesus and Nicomedia; beautiful, fortified cities such as Edessa and Amida; the Syrian metropolis of Antioch; the increasingly important Christian religious sites in and around Jerusalem; and Egypt, home to some 500,000 residents in the great city of Alexandria and the most populous and agriculturally productive of all the Roman provinces.

The crown jewel of the eastern empire was Constantinople. Fifth-century Constantinople was a marvelous showcase for what a Christian Roman capital could be. Constantine's shoddy insta-capital of the 330s matured into an impressive imperial center under

Theodosius I and Arcadius. As its importance grew, so too did the Roman effort to enhance its already formidable natural defenses by expanding its footprint.

But Constantinople also benefited from one incredible stroke of luck that freed it from the reliance on German generalissimos that so distorted fifth-century Western Roman life and convinced its leaders to build a fortification system that made it impregnable for centuries. In 400, the emperor Arcadius tasked a Gothic general named Gainas with tamping down an insurrection by another Gothic leader, but Gainas chose to join forces with the rebel instead of suppressing him. When these troops tried to seize the capital under cover of darkness, Arcadius, who was in Constantinople at the time, declared a public emergency. Gainas was repelled by the combined efforts of the troops guarding the city walls, shopkeepers protecting their wares, and the general public.[1] Lacking a naval force, most of Gainas's followers were then cut down when they tried to cross to Asia in rafts.[2]

In 402, the grateful city began work on a column with a carved frieze celebrating Arcadius's victory over Gainas that resembled the ones built for Trajan and Marcus Aurelius in Rome 300 years earlier. But Arcadius had another, much more important response as well to Gainas's attack.[3] He undertook the construction of a wall incorporating the most state-of-the-art methods in the world to protect the city from future attacks. His successor, Theodosius II, continued the work, and by the time of Theodosius II's death in 450, the wall system stretched for nearly four miles and included a wide moat, a lower outer wall, and a high inner wall. These fortifications represented a revolution in defensive technology that made the land approaches of the eastern capital effectively impregnable.

The security Constantinople provided fostered remarkable political stability in the eastern empire. Only ten men ruled in Constantinople between Theodosius I's death in 395 and Justinian I's death in 565. None of these emperors campaigned abroad during their reigns, and most of them spent the majority of their time in and around the capital. This centralized the eastern administration around the imperial palace and forced the emperor to work closely with the

Constantinopolitan bishop who presided over the worship services he attended.

The power of Eastern Roman bishops differed significantly from that of their western counterparts in the fourth and fifth centuries. The great eastern cities of Alexandria, Antioch, and Ephesus all had Christian communities dating back to the time of the apostles, and they all became Christian-majority communities earlier than the large cities of the west. Alexandria, for example, may have had a Christian majority by 360. The rapid growth of Constantinople in the fourth century meant that it, too, was a Christian-majority city early on, by 400, if not sooner.

Much of the growth of Christianity in the east during the later fourth century occurred organically as individual Romans encouraged their friends, neighbors, and family members to embrace the faith. One can trace this slow but steady progression through the growing tendency for parents to name their children after biblical figures or Christian saints, as well as through the replacement of traditional invocations of pagan divinities with phrases such as "To the One God" on tombstones.[4]

But paganism persisted. So, beginning with Theodosius I's antipagan actions in the 380s, imperial policy tried to further the organic growth of the church. When the punch of Theodosius's legislative and physical attacks on centers of pagan worship failed to end traditional Mediterranean religion, he—and later, his sons—targeted pagan practices beyond sacrifices in temples. In the 390s, new laws restricted binding trees with ribbons, erecting altars of turf, and offering honors to gods within a household.[5] The next decade saw prohibitions extend to festivals and banquets in which the traditional gods were recognized, because Christians might be induced to participate in the fun.[6] Then, in an indication of how difficult the process of suppressing paganism was becoming, the emperors entrusted bishops with monitoring local compliance. Any governors who blocked the enforcement of this law would be fined twenty pounds of gold. Bishops and their agents were now freed to police religious activities in their communities.

Theodosius and Arcadius looked away as bishops began mounting violent attacks on pagan temples. The most notorious such incident occurred in 392, when Theophilus, the bishop of Alexandria, orchestrated the destruction of the city's Serapeum, a massive Alexandrian temple, following a riot. When the temple came down, Theodosius helped pay for the construction of a large shrine containing the supposed remains of the prophet Elisha and John the Baptist. He also funded the establishment of a monastery to be filled with monks who would discourage any furtive prayers by devotees of Serapis within the god's old sacred precinct.[7] Similar actions undertaken by bishops and monks in Apamea, Gaza, Menouthis, and Canopus destroyed monumental pagan temples and placed churches on their sites.

Millions of pagans remained in the fifth-century Roman East, and hundreds of thousands of shrines, temples, and religious images were scattered across its lands. But their numbers were shrinking rapidly as older pagans died and shrines fell into disrepair.[8] Even in cities such as Athens, which probably retained a pagan majority into the mid-fifth century, pagan practices moved underground. Most Athenian pagans prayed privately, in their own homes, with people they trusted, while making rare, furtive trips into shuttered temples to pray before images of the old gods when they most needed divine help. Meanwhile, the power of Athenian bishops had grown so great that, by 450, they could preside over services in a church constructed within the Library of Hadrian and intimidate pagan philosophers and rhetoricians.[9]

The role that bishops played in managing the decline of paganism in the fifth-century east coincided with the growing preference of younger Romans for attending church, but the deep and distinctive histories of eastern bishoprics could provoke conflicts between them that imperial authorities struggled to control. The churches of Alexandria, Antioch, and Constantinople had each developed ways of exercising local authority and projecting power beyond their territory. The church of Alexandria was particularly potent because Athanasius, the fourth-century bishop, built a network of urban supporters by distributing imperial grants to the needy and extending offers of employment to laborers. As the fourth century progressed, he developed strong relationships with leaders of the growing Egyptian monastic movement like St. Antony, a hermit who lived a solitary life devoted to God in the high desert, and Pachomius, the creator of the first communities in which monks lived together. The bishop supported these monks, and in return the monks would flood the city to support him in times of crisis.

While the bishop of Alexandria was the most powerful Christian figure in the Roman East for most of the fourth century, emperors also acknowledged and respected the influence of the bishops who represented Antioch, Alexandria's ancient urban rival. Early in 387, an antitax riot broke out during which a crowd of citizens burned down part of the imperial palace in Antioch and destroyed bronze statues of the imperial family.[10] In accordance with imperial law, all the members of the city council were arrested and held in the council chamber until an imperial commission could decide whether to hold them responsible.[11]

Their bishop, Flavian, mobilized to save the city. He traveled to Constantinople to convince the emperor to pardon the Antiochenes, and he had local monks inundate the city when the imperial commissioners arrived.[12] Flavian's deputy John Chyrsostom then delivered a sermon to an anxious audience saying that the monks "would not depart until the judges spared the entire city."[13] When Theodosius decided to pardon the rioters and city councilors, he let it be known that Flavian and the monks had persuaded him to do so. Large crowds filled Antioch's main church each day for the better part of three weeks to hear Chrysostom praise the emperor's mercy and piety.

The centralization of the eastern imperial court in Constantinople gave its bishop a different sort of power. Unlike the churches of Alexandria and Antioch, the Constantinopolitan church possessed no long-standing control over the churches of a large province. Nor did it have an army of monks it could mobilize. Its power came instead from its proximity to the imperial court and the bishop's access to the emperor. But the moment that redefined the Constantinopolitan church came when Theodosius I summoned the second ecumenical council to the city in 381. The Council of Constantinople's first, most important goal was to reaffirm the emperor's commitment to the Council of Nicaea, but the bishops assembled there also made two other important rulings limiting the episcopal power of Alexandria and Antioch while expanding that of Constantinople. First, they specified that bishops of Alexandria had no jurisdiction beyond Egypt and that no bishops from any episcopal see should involve themselves in affairs beyond their home regions. More importantly, they affirmed that "the Bishop of Constantinople . . . shall have the prerogative of honor after the Bishop of Rome; because Constantinople is New Rome."[14] From this point forward, the bishop of Constantinople and the church he headed would hold a primacy in the east that rivaled only that claimed by the pope in Rome.

The Constantinopolitan bishops struggled to assert the power they had been given, however. When the capital's bishop died in 397, the Alexandrian bishop Theophilus tried to install a pliant ally in his place. If this had happened, it could have effectively negated Constantinople's primacy over Alexandria in the hierarchy of eastern Christian churches. Eutropius, the eunuch who was at that moment the dominant figure in the imperial court, wanted a dynamic, powerful, and relatively young new bishop with the talent, confidence, and charisma to forcefully defend Constantinople's position. And, as the man with the ear of the emperor, Eutropius got his man. He sent a team to Antioch to recruit John Chrysostom.[15]

Eutropius seemed to have made an excellent choice. Socrates Scholasticus explains that Chrysostom had been "an inner circle student of the sophist Libanius" who had trained to become a lawyer before abandoning his secular career and its material comfort to live as a monk in the hills outside Antioch.[16] He had accepted a position in the clergy only because, one of his admirers later wrote, "his stomach had been deadened" by his ascetic practices and "the functions of his kidneys were impaired by the cold."[17] The ravages that monastic life had inflicted on his body gave Chrysostom's words an instant credibility to Christian audiences, but it was the power of his rhetoric that made him such an effective preacher. Chrysostom was bombastic, charismatic, and a master stylist whose rhythmic cadences and crisp metaphors enchanted and inspired audiences. Secretaries attended his sermons and faithfully transcribed every word he said so that their beauty, forcefulness, and inspiration would survive forever. And they have. More words spoken by John Chrysostom survive today than those of any other Greek author who lived before him.

Although Chrysostom had the pedigree and rhetorical skills to excel as bishop of Constantinople, he lacked the temperament to succeed in the job. His time in the desert had convinced him of his righteousness, and the rigors of his full days of prayer had deadened his patience just as thoroughly as the rough diet had deadened his stomach. He spoke freely about whatever he believed to be true with a naivete that would have been endearing if it hadn't been so "offensive to a great many" people of influence. Chrysostom, though, "lived free of any fear of the future" because he trusted in "the rectitude of his way of life" and blasted away at the wealthy and mighty of the empire with words his mind seldom filtered.[18] He was a time bomb.

Chrysostom began making enemies almost immediately after he was ordained bishop of Constantinople on February 26, 398. That summer, he publicly criticized Eutropius, the man to whom he owed his job, over a law that limited the ability of criminals to claim protection from arrest by entering a church. When Eutropius fell from power the following year and took refuge in Constantinople's majestic Church of the Holy Wisdom (better known by its Greek name Hagia Sophia), Chrysostom humiliated him by preaching a sermon about the vanity of worldly honors while the fallen courtier quivered and clutched the church's altar a few feet from the pulpit.[19]

In 401, Chrysostom stumbled into an even more serious conflict with Theophilus of Alexandria.[20] Theophilus had condemned the ideas of a group of Egyptian monks called the Tall Brothers, who had then fled to Constantinople and requested Chrysostom's help. Taking his status as the highest-ranking bishop in the east seriously, Chrysostom summoned Theophilus to defend himself before a church synod in the capital. Theophilus delayed turning up for two years, and when he finally arrived he successfully shifted the focus of the synod from his own conduct in Egypt to Chrysostom's in Constantinople. When Chrysostom refused to attend, he was deposed.[21]

Popular outrage forced the emperor to restore Chrysostom to his see in the fall of 403. He reluctantly resumed his duties only to soon fall into another controversy. It began when a celebration held beneath a column supporting a silver statue of the empress Eudoxia disrupted services at Hagia Sophia. When Chrysostom learned what had caused the commotion, he delivered a speech in the church comparing the empress to Herodias, the biblical villain who had her daughter Salome dance before King Herod Antipas and ask that he order the murder of John the Baptist as her reward. "Again Herodias raves," John said to his congregation. "Again she dances; and again she desires to receive John's head on a plate."[22] This charge proved too explosive for the emperor Arcadius to ignore. John was again deposed and exiled. John's followers rioted and set Hagia Sophia on fire, a display revealing the power that a talented bishop of Constantinople could wield if he chose to go rogue.[23]

Chrysostom died in exile in 407, but his followers remained a potent force in Constantinople. Ultimately they secured his posthumous rehabilitation and he became one of the most revered saints in the Eastern Orthodox Church. His fate also cemented Constantinopolitan suspicions about the motivations of Alexandrian bishops.[24]

All the main characters in the empire had changed when the next round in the battle between the churches of Constantinople and Alexandria was joined in the 420s. When Arcadius died in 408, he was replaced by his seven-year-old son Theodosius II. Although Theodosius II would rule for forty-two years—the longest tenure of any Roman emperor up to that time—he proved to be a largely indifferent emperor who preferred riding horses to governing. He left many decisions to his much more capable and intelligent sister, Pulcheria. In Alexandria, Theophilus's nephew Cyril seized control of the church after a burst of street fighting that followed his uncle's death in 412. And in Constantinople, the admired bishop Atticus, who ran the church from 406 until 425, displayed a moderation that contrasted with Cyril's combustibility and prevented serious conflicts from arising.[25]

Nestorius, the next Constantinopolitan bishop of consequence, shared none of Atticus's moderation. Like John Chrysostom a generation earlier, Nestorius was a Syrian cleric "distinguished for his excellent voice and fluid speech," with both a monastic background and a reputation for delivering impressive, moving sermons.[26] He arrived in Constantinople in early 428 and almost immediately clashed with Cyril over what title one should use to refer to Mary, the mother of Jesus. One camp, which held that Mary had given birth to God, who took human form, said that she should be called *Theotokos* (a Greek word meaning the "One who Gave Birth to God"). The other camp rejected this notion because they believed it to be impossible for God to be physically born. When Nestorius inserted himself into the argument and condemned anyone who used the title *Theotokos*, Cyril and the bishop of Rome warned him to recant or face removal from office. Nestorius appealed to Theodosius II, who summoned a church council in the city of Ephesus to discuss the issue.[27]

The Council of Ephesus in 431, the third ecumenical council of the church, unfolded unlike any before it. Egyptian sources write that Cyril journeyed to Ephesus alongside an army of Egyptian ascetic supporters. One of these monks was Shenoute, the eighty-three-year-old head of a monastic community in Upper Egypt, who hit Nestorius on the head with the Bible when he first saw the Constantinopolitan bishop.[28]

Nestorius had no good way to respond to Cyril's impressive show of force. He was counting on significant support from allies in Syria, but they were delayed, and Cyril and his supporters won a vote to depose Nestorius before the Syrians arrived. When the Antiochenes finally reached Ephesus, their outraged bishop tried to organize a motion to censure Cyril for deposing Nestorius before the whole council had assembled. Cyril responded by having the council vote to depose him as well.[29] Finally, fearing that this dissension might permanently rupture the unity of the eastern church, Nestorius shouted, "Let Mary be called *Theotokos*, if you want, and let all disputing cease." It did no good. No one acknowledged that he had recanted, and he remained deposed. He was banished to an oasis in the Egyptian desert, where he lived for the last two decades of his life.[30]

Nestorius's removal did permit Cyril to reconcile with the bishop of Antioch, but this only delayed the splintering of the church for a couple of decades.[31] While the Council of Ephesus in 431 had determined the proper way to refer to Mary, it had opened up new questions about how the human and divine natures of Jesus combined together in the baby she bore. After 431, one could not say Jesus had two, separate natures, one human and the other divine. But how could his distinctive human and divine natures fit together in a physical body?

A Constantinopolitan monastic leader named Eutyches proposed an answer in the mid-440s. He argued, in essence, that Christ had one nature that, like an alloy, was a blend, comprising both his fully human nature and his fully divine nature. Just as one could not take a piece of bronze and pull out the tin and copper from it, one could not take Christ and disentangle the human from the divine.

Eutyches's ideas became widely known only after the deaths of many of the men who had rebuilt ecclesiastical peace after the Council of Ephesus. Bishop Domnus had taken over the see of Antioch in 441. Cyril had died in 444 and had been succeeded in Alexandria by the ruthless Dioscorus. Even Constantinople had a new bishop, Flavian, who took office in 447. The only major player at Ephesus who remained as bishop in his original see was Juvenal, the ambitious leader of the church of Jerusalem.

Trouble began when a local synod presided over by Flavian in Constantinople in November 448 condemned Eutyches for claiming that Jesus possessed "two natures" before they came together when he took a human body, but "one nature afterwards."[32] Although Bishop Domnus in Antioch and Pope Leo in Rome both supported Flavian's finding, Eutyches's condemnation incited a furious response from Dioscorus, the bishop of Alexandria, who convinced Theodosius II to call another council at Ephesus to address the matter.

When that council assembled in 449, Dioscorus used a combination of imperial guards and Egyptian monks to force attendees to exonerate Eutyches and depose Flavian.[33] Fearing for his life, Flavian sought sanctuary at a church altar, but Dioscorus's supporters dragged him away and beat him so badly that Flavian died a few days later. Pope Leo's legate to the council fled back to the west when Dioscorus refused to allow the reading of the Tome of Leo, a letter sent by the pope. And Domnus of Antioch was deposed after he stopped turning up to the synod. Only the opportunistic Juvenal of Jerusalem stayed loyal to Dioscorus. Outraged that his Tome had not been read, and disgusted by Dioscorus's use of force, Leo dismissed the gathering at Ephesus as a "Robber Council."[34] But when Theodosius II agreed to abide by the council's result, it represented a horrible, seemingly final, moment of total Alexandrian victory over the churches of Constantinople and Antioch.

The victory did not last long. Theodosius II died in a riding accident in 450 and was succeeded by Marcian, a former military official, who married Theodosius's sister Pulcheria and then joined with Pope Leo to overturn the Robber Council of Ephesus. In 451, Marcian convened a new council in Chalcedon, just across the Bosporus from Constantinople. This council, now known as the Council of Chalcedon, was charged with returning order to the church by dismantling the decisions made at Ephesus two years earlier. The assembled bishops rehabilitated Flavian of Constantinople and tried Dioscorus for misconduct. Dioscorus refused to appear for his trial, but the council summoned a host of witnesses to complain about the bishop's tyrannical behavior and then deposed him. They sent him into exile for his failure to answer the charges. The next session of the council accepted Leo's Tome as the basis for its confession of faith. This was good politics, but poor theology. The Tome was written in Latin, a language that lacked the vocabulary to capture the nuances of a discussion about the nature of Christ conducted in Greek. Its adoption only added more ambiguity to an already fraught theological controversy.[35]

Some supporters of Dioscorus steadfastly refused to endorse the Tome, but the emperor secured one very important defector.[36] Juvenal of Jerusalem, the stalwart supporter of the Alexandrian position at the two Ephesian councils, abandoned Dioscorus and served on the committee that drew up the creed that all who accepted the council's findings would say aloud.[37] In return, the council's seventh session elevated the see of Jerusalem so that, like Rome, Constantinople, Antioch, and Alexandria, it had jurisdiction over the churches of multiple provinces. By the sixth century, the five churches privileged at Chalcedon became the pentarchy, a group made up of the five great patriarchates of the Roman world.

Marcian, his wife Pulcheria, the papacy, and the clergy in Constantinople all saw Chalcedon as an important victory. It punished Dioscorus's violence and restored proper theological and political balance to the church. Many Eastern Romans disagreed. Asia Minor, Syria, and Phoenicia all saw isolated opposition to Chalcedon emerge among clergy and monks, but the Chalcedonian results proved particularly hard for Egyptians and Palestinians to accept. Crowds of anti-Chalcedonian monks, enraged at Juvenal's betrayal of Dioscorus, met the bishop upon his return to Palestine, forced him to flee, and appointed a new, anti-Chalcedonian bishop of Jerusalem to serve in his place. Marcian ultimately sent imperial troops to restore Juvenal in 453, a mission they accomplished only after massacring a crowd of anti-Chalcedonian monks in Nablus.[38]

The situation in Egypt was even more tense. Proterius, Marcian's choice as the new pro-Chalcedonian bishop of Alexandria, arrived in Alexandria with a group of imperial commissioners and soldiers sent by the emperor. When he summoned Egyptian clergy to a meeting in which they were to pledge their support of Chalcedon, a man named Macarius stood up, chastised Proterius for accepting the legitimacy of the Tome of Leo, and challenged the orthodoxy of Chalcedonian Creed.[39] One of the imperial couriers then kicked Macarius in the genitals.[40] Macarius fell dead on the spot, the first Alexandrian martyr for the anti-Chalcedonian cause, and the people of Alexandria took up the body, wrapped it in fine clothes, and placed it in the shrine dedicated to John the Baptist and Elisha that had been built on the old Serapeum site.[41]

The situation in Alexandria finally stabilized in 482, when the emperor Zeno and Alexandria's anti-Chalcedonian bishop Peter Mongus signed the *Henotikon*, a document drafted by Peter and Acacius, his Constantinopolitan counterpart.[42] The *Henotikon* was, in essence, an agreement by the leaders of the two churches to stop fighting one another about the Tome of Leo, the Council of Chalcedon, and the nature of Christ. It did not try to resolve the theological issues of the past five decades. The *Henotikon* instead created a cooperative framework through which the leaders of the two churches could stop arguing about theology, accept each other's legitimacy, and return to communion with one another. Peter and Acacius also believed that their agreement could serve as a template to bring the rest of the churches of the east back together with one another. Not only did they now accept each other, but they also agreed to "receive and hold communion with all the other bishops who would accept the *Henotikon*," regardless of their views on Chalcedon and the Tome.[43] And the *Henotikon* succeeded in calming the fighting and restoring all the major eastern churches to communion with one another.[44]

One major church did not endorse the *Henotikon*, however. In Rome, the *Henotikon* was seen as a betrayal, because it failed to explicitly uphold Chalcedon and the orthodoxy of the Tome of Leo, Acacius and the Constantinopolitan church had traded the interests of the Roman church for peace with Alexandria. But Zeno ruled in Constantinople as the head of a Roman Christian Empire, and Rome sat far away, under the control of Odoacer. Alexandria and the unity of the east mattered more to the emperor in Constantinople than the far-off, former capital of the fallen west. The papacy could complain. Constantinople, however, was not terribly interested in listening. Yet.

Chapter 29

Anastasius, Justin I, and the Old Men at the End of the World

491–527

I N EARLY APRIL 491, a public spectacle unfolded in Constantinople that showed how fully the Eastern Roman Empire embraced
its Christian character. When the emperor Zeno died on the night of
April 9, his widow, the Augusta Ariadne, stood as the sole figure in
the Roman state who still legitimately held an imperial title. This was
not a new situation for Romans. In 450, when the Augusta Pulcheria had been in a similar situation, she had chosen Marcian to serve
as both the next emperor and as her husband. But Ariadne had an
even more impressive claim than Pulcheria as the keeper of imperial
legitimacy. She had grown up in the imperial palace as the daughter
of the emperor Leo I, and she was not only Zeno's wife, but also the
mother of the short-lived Leo II. No one alive understood the job of
ruling the empire better than she did. And, perhaps just as importantly, Zeno had legally established that a portion of the private funds
that flowed to emperors was controlled directly by "our wife, the most
serene Augusta."[1]

Constantinopolitans knew that Ariadne was a powerful and
wealthy woman entitled to select her own husband.[2] They were also

aware that whoever she married would likely be the next emperor. But, constitutionally, the office of emperor remained a public one. Rome was an empire, but as emperors like Tiberius and Pescinnius Niger had realized, no emperor or member of the imperial family owned the imperial title. It was entrusted to them by the public, and if public confidence dissipated, their legitimacy could dissipate as well.

This is what makes the scene in Constantinople on that day so impressive. Writing nearly 500 years later, the emperor Constantine VII Porphyrogenitus describes how Ariadne came before an assembly of all the Roman people in the city during which "the magistrates, senators, and the bishop assembled in the portico before the Grand Hall of the palace, [and] the people gathered in the Hippodrome in their assigned places, as did the soldiers." The palace in Constantinople had a passageway to the imperial box of the Hippodrome, and as soon as the crowds saw Ariadne clad in the garb of a high imperial official and accompanied by the bishop of Constantinople, they began chanting. "Ariadne Augusta, may you be Victorious!" rang out first. Next came the call, "Many long years for the Augusta." And then, "An orthodox emperor for the empire!" And finally, after the empress had acknowledged them, "An emperor who is Roman for the entire world."[3]

The courtiers read out Ariadne's response: "Even before your requests, we have ordered the most glorious magistrates and the Senate, with the unanimous approval of our valorous armies, to choose a man who is Christian, Roman, and possessed of all the virtues of an emperor." The crowd then shouted its approval: "Oh Empress, may you lead a pious life! May all good things come to you! You are Roman, nothing foreign! May the race of Romans be raised up!"[4]

In 491, Constantinopolitans understood what their orthodox Christian Roman Empire was. It extended east along a line running roughly from the western Balkans down to the Libyan desert. It was a state in which the bishops of all the major cities were in communion with one another, according to the terms of Zeno's *Henotikon*. The west was lost, and the papacy was not in communion with the bishop of Constantinople, but those were foreign affairs beyond the immediate control of their emperor. The east was strong and prosperous—and they wanted to keep it that way.

Once Ariadne received this demonstration of popular support, she and her retinue returned to the palace and summoned Anastasius, a roughly sixty-year-old imperial official who seemed to be a good match. Although he inclined toward anti-Chalcedonian ideas, he swore to Ariadne that he would uphold the doctrines decided at the Council of Chalcedon. He was miserly but did not crave money so much as he hesitated to spend it. And, most importantly, he was Roman through and through. In a little more than a day, everyone returned to the Hippodrome to see Anastasius present himself to the Roman people. When they married a month later, Ariadne, "who had made him emperor[,] . . . administered the empire" alongside Anastasius just as she had done with Zeno.[5] They formed a ruling team until her death in 515.

Ariadne and Anastasius complemented each other. She was a veteran of court politics who could help steer him away from problems. She was a Chalcedonian Christian, and Anastasius a moderate anti-Chalcedonian, but the tenuous religious peace that Zeno's *Henotikon* created allowed each of them to effectively ignore the other's view of the council. But, most of all, the arrangement worked because both Ariadne and Anastasius were imperial caretakers. Ariadne's job, as the widow Augusta who had survived her husband but had no living children, was to find an emperor who could bring immediate stability to the realm. And Anastasius, who was also childless, seemed like a perfect short-term placeholder emperor until a new dynasty might establish itself.

Then the unexpected happened. Anastasius ruled for twenty-seven years, a welcome period of stability for a large segment of Eastern Roman Christians who believed that the world would end in or around the year 500.[6] They had calculated that the world was 6,500 years old at the time of Jesus's birth. Since the world was created in seven days, they believed it likely that it would last only 7,000 years total. They were expecting Christ's return and the end of times to come imminently.

This idea was particularly pronounced in the anti-Chalcedonian communities of Egypt and Gaza, for whom the ecclesiastical divisions caused by what happened at Chalcedon were proof that the end of time approached. In one case, a Palestinian monk named John Rufus even reported a prophecy that the Council of Chalcedon was "the precursor of the Antichrist." It had "called the anger of God upon all the earth," so that "the Roman Empire now reaches its end." If, as these anti-Chalcedonian militants believed, the world was about to end, why should they or anyone else really care how energetically the Roman emperor was attending to things? The early years of Anastasius's reign, then, were not moments when Romans demanded revolutions in how their state worked.[7]

None of this meant that Anastasius was indolent. He fought—and won—two civil wars, and he superintended a Roman victory over the Persians in 506 that forced them to return the city of Amida, which they had unexpectedly captured in 502. He also brought about dramatic improvements in the Roman monetary system by reforming the bronze coinage, which had become so small that the coins no longer had room for the name of the emperor who issued them. They were worth so little that, for most purchases, a buyer had to drop a bag of bronze coins on the counter so that a merchant could weigh them and assess their value. It was very difficult to accumulate enough bronze coins to trade for a gold solidus—and sometimes even difficult to determine what number of bronze coins equaled a solidus.

In 498, Anastasius issued a new set of bronze denominations, each clearly marked to show their value, and stabilized the exchange rate between gold and bronze.[8] For the first time since the tetrarchy, Romans could save their small change and exchange it for high-value coins at a predictable and stable rate. Not coincidentally, the imperial coffers swelled under Anastasius's stewardship, so much so that he accumulated a treasury surplus worth over 320,000 pounds of gold during his reign.[9]

Twenty-seven years is a long time to govern, and the world changed as Anastasius aged. The furor over the possible end of times began to die down by the 510s, and as it did, a younger, much more militant generation of anti-Chalcedonians came of age in the monasteries of Palestine. Their most prominent voice belonged to Severus, a monk who had once studied in Alexandria while Peter Mongus governed the church and Zeno's *Henotikon* determined its theology. Severus first came to imperial attention in 508, when he led a group of monks to Constantinople to complain that Elias, the bishop of Jerusalem, had unjustly expelled them from their monasteries.[10]

Anastasius, too, became more willing to challenge the pro-Chalcedonian figures in the capital. In 511, he removed Macedonius, the popular Chalcedonian bishop of Constantinople, after Macedonius refused to permit language favored by Severus to be used in the liturgy. Fearing that this move might prompt acts of resistance, Anastasius distributed money to the army and stationed soldiers outside the Constantinopolitan walls to prevent angry Chalcedonian monks from entering the city.[11]

The anti-Chalcedonian revolution crested after Anastasius replaced Flavian, the patriarch of Antioch who supported the *Henotikon*, with Severus. He took this step, according to the sixth-century historian Evagrius Scholasticus, following a riot in which anti-Chalcedonian monks from the Syrian countryside "burst into the city . . . to force Flavian to anathematize Chalcedon." When Flavian's supporters responded with "a great slaughter of the monks," Anastasius had the necessary pretext to depose the bishop. He forced him into exile and appointed Severus to oversee the city's churches in 512. With Severus's ascension, all of the major sees in the eastern empire (save those in Palestine and Egypt) were occupied by anti-Chalcedonian bishops who no longer wanted to uphold the *Henotikon*.[12]

This proved to be a deeply unstable situation. There remained considerable anger against Severus among the people of Antioch and the pro-Flavian monks living near the city. Even worse, in November 512, Anastasius provoked a serious disturbance in the capital when he added an anti-Chalcedonian phrase to the liturgy. When crowds began chanting for a change in the imperial regime, Anastasius, who was then in his late eighties, "was compelled to come to the Hippodrome in a pitiful state, without his crown." Evagrius Scholasticus says that he offered to abdicate, but "on seeing this spectacle, the populace turned back . . . and begged Anastasius to put on his crown again." He did, and he punished those he deemed responsible for the rioting, but the emperor also allowed the offending phrase to be taken back out of the liturgy. Ariadne, for her part, found his behavior degrading—and told him so.[13]

The religious policies of the empire changed rapidly following the death of Anastasius on July 9, 518. Anastasius had no sons, and Ariadne's death in 515 meant that he had no surviving empress. While three of his nephews had enjoyed a prominent role in his administration, none was designated his successor.[14] Anastasius's death then set off a fast-moving scramble to seize power. The reports about what transpired over the next day diverge greatly. The most plausible account describes negotiations in the Hall of 19 Couches, the large audience hall in the palace used for ceremonial occasions, that lasted an entire day. Justin, the head of the imperial bodyguard, apparently stationed his men outside to prevent anyone from leaving until a new emperor was chosen. After a long period of deliberation, Justin emerged as the consensus choice.[15]

Another, much more salacious, account appears in later sources (including Evagrius Scholasticus). They claim that Amantius, the eunuch in charge of the imperial bedchambers, gave money to Justin to purchase the loyalty of his men so that Amantius's preferred candidate could take power, but that Justin instead used the money to buy support for his own bid. Whether or not this story is true, Justin clearly believed Amantius to be a threat. Justin took the oath of office on July 10. Within ten days, Amantius and his favored candidate were, in Evagrius's careful phrasing, "eliminated from the ranks of men."[16]

Justin cut a very different sort of figure from Anastasius. He was a distinguished soldier, devoted Chalcedonian, and native Latin-speaker born of peasant parents in Badar, a town outside the modern North Macedonian capital of Skopje. Justin had come to the capital in the 470s to join the military, and while he knew Greek, his meager education and background in the empire's northwest made him ill-disposed toward the Greek-centric theological arguments made by figures like Severus of Antioch.[17] The reaction to his accession in Constantinople certainly made Justin feel more confident that others too shared these sentiments. Within a week of being sworn in as emperor, Chalcedonian mobs in the capital had begun calling for the deposition of Severus.[18]

Not long after that, Justin summoned a prominent Chalcedonian and former military commander named Vitalian to the capital. Vitalian had once rebelled against Anastasius because of the former emperor's religious policies. Justin elevated Vitalian to the position of *magister militum* (a top military command), where he became an extremely useful ally in the early years of Justin's reign.[19] Not only did his military skill insulate Justin from rebellions, either by Chalcedonians loyal to Vitalian or by anti-Chalcedonians who feared him, but his reputation as a fierce opponent of Severus gave Justin cover to act against those who supported Severus in the capital. Soon word began spreading through the capital that Vitalian had demanded that Severus be expelled from his bishopric and either put to death or subjected to having his tongue cut out. Fueled by popular anger and Vitalian's demand, a synod convened on July 20 that deposed Severus, who then fled to a monastery in Alexandria that had long been the epicenter of Egyptian resistance to the Council of Chalcedon.[20]

By 520, Vitalian had outlived his usefulness. That July, he and some of his closest advisers were summoned to the imperial palace to meet with Justin. Accompanying them was Justinian, the emperor's nephew and adopted son, who had recently been promoted to the position of *magister militum* alongside Vitalian. As Vitalian and his party approached the palace, they were stabbed and killed. Thus began a forty-five-year period when Justinian would dominate the direction of life in the Roman world.[21]

It had been clear from the beginning of Justin's reign that Justinian would play an important part in how his uncle ran the state. Justinian's name had even been floated as a possible successor to

Anastasius, though he and his uncle both agreed that it was premature to suggest such a high position for him.[22] Justinian was chosen as one of the consuls in 521. Three years later he secured patrician status, the highest standing a male could enjoy, and had arranged for his wife, the actress Theodora, to receive the title of patricia, its female equivalent.[23] Justinian was made Caesar the following year, and in April of 527 Justin and Justinian began issuing laws jointly and appearing together on coins bearing the legend "Our Lords Justin and Justinian, Perpetual Emperors."[24] Justinian was now Justin's co-emperor.

Justinian's rise did cause one significant long-term problem for the Roman state. Aside from the war they fought in 502–506 and a brief conflict in the 440s, Roman and Persian relations had generally been peaceful since the 370s. At times they had even been friendly. In 525, Justin received a unique proposal from the Persian king Kavad I to formally adopt his son Chosroes. Kavad himself had been forced from power by rivals, and he feared that Chosroes, his third-oldest son but his first choice for a successor, might face similar challenges from his brothers. Kavad hoped that Justin's adoption of Chosroes would both "preserve stability in government," by protecting his son from Persian rivals, and "put an end to causes of war" with Rome.[25]

Justin and Justinian both initially seemed favorably inclined toward the proposal and brought it to the Constantinopolitan Senate as well as to Justin's circle of close advisers. They were warned, however, that the request seemed like it could be a ruse, because under Roman law, a legal adoption by Justin would give Chosroes a possible claim to the Roman imperial throne.[26] Justinian himself was advised that he should oppose the proposal so it would not interfere with his own path to the emperorship.[27] Justin and Justinian therefore decided that concerns over a contested succession in Constantinople trumped the possible benefits of securing good relations with Persia.

This short-term thinking had serious long-term consequences. In Procopius's account, when a delegation sent by Justin to negotiate the possible adoption stated "that the adoption of Chosroes must take place just as is proper for a barbarian," the young prince became "deeply injured at what had transpired, and vowed revenge on the Romans for their insult to him."[28] In part because of the wounded pride this incident produced, low level hostilities between Rome and Persia commenced in 526 and erupted into a large scale war in 530. The fighting would last until 532, at which point Rome had to effectively purchase a peace treaty on Persian terms. A proposal that could have secured many decades of Roman-Persian peace instead seeded an unnecessary, quite expensive conflict.[29] Unfortunately, this was the first of many instances where Justinian acted without appreciating the long-term costs of his decisions. This made his reign one of the most revolutionary in Roman history—for good and for ill.

PART 5

FROM JUSTINIAN TO CHARLEMAGNE AND IRENE

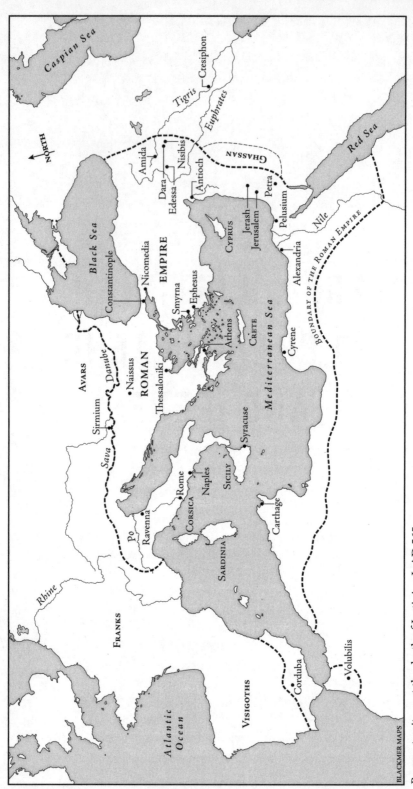

Roman territory at the death of Justinian I, AD 565

Chapter 30

Justinian

527–565

W AR WITH PERSIA still lay in the future when Justinian took
power following the death of his uncle in August 527. Instead
of focusing on the frontier, the new emperor looked first to repair
domestic politics. Justinian realized that Rome's strength lay in its
ability to constantly reinvent its state and political community so that
both could take best advantage of the resources the Roman people
possessed. Lethargic old emperors and the popular belief that the
world might soon end had stalled this process over the past thirty-
five years, but Justinian was determined to jolt the drifting state back
onto the dynamic path that had made it great. God, he believed,
demanded it of him.

Justinian began work almost immediately. One of his first tasks
involved the most audacious reform ever made to Rome's nearly
1,000-year-old legal system. Written Roman law had begun with the
Twelve Tables, the law code issued by the decemvirs between 451 and
449 BC, and had then grown in complexity as Roman society did.
Each year, the praetors of the Republic had issued an edict laying out
the elements of legal interpretation that required clarification. With
the advent of imperial power, emperors began issuing legal edicts as
well as rescripts, which were legally binding answers to tricky legal
questions forwarded to them by their subjects. By the second century

AD, prominent legal scholars called jurists were adding their own interpretations of the law that guided later practices. All these legal materials were useful, but unless a new law explicitly contradicted an old one, each new edict, rescript, or definitive juridical text simply expanded and deepened Roman law. As in British common law or the legal system in much of the United States, nothing new replaced or invalidated anything that preceded it unless it did so explicitly. Until Justinian.

Over the course of five years, Justinian's advisers produced three important texts that revolutionized the Roman legal system. The first of these, the *Justinianic Code*, edited and systematized all the existing rescripts and edicts that had been issued by emperors since the second century AD and rendered all laws that did not appear in the text invalid. This was the first time in Roman history that such a step had been taken. Next, the legal advisers synthesized the vast corpus of Roman juridical writings into one, definitive work called the *Digest*. As he did in the *Code*, Justinian then invalidated every jurist's opinion that the *Digest* did not include. The *Institutes*, the codification project's third phase, created a standardized textbook that would be used in all the law schools across the empire. This work, too, carried the force of law and rendered obsolete the entire intellectual infrastructure that had preceded it. Instead of starting with the Twelve Tables, Roman law now restarted with Justinian.[1]

Justinian's arrogance had pushed him beyond the practical problem of clarifying an old, complicated legal system. He relished the fact that his reforms disrupted Roman traditions. Roman lawyers had long talked about the *quinquaginta decisiones*, fifty intractable legal questions that involved complicated and often conflicting legal interpretations.[2] These had effectively become exercises in legal reasoning that tested the ability of Roman lawyers and law students to frame legally binding arguments and counterarguments. Between 529 and 534, however, Justinian issued laws that resolved them all.[3] On one level, this was completely pointless. These cases were exercises in legal theory rather than active controversies. But by solving the insolvable,

Justinian anointed himself as Rome's premier lawgiver. It mattered little to him that he had also destroyed a long-standing component of Roman legal culture.

Justinian believed that it was his divine duty to remake Roman law because God's support for the state was contingent upon him doing so. "The supreme protection of the Roman state rests upon two props, arms and laws," he wrote, and this is why Rome had "dominated all nations in the past as, with the aid of a propitious God, it will do in the future."[4]

Because God had helped the emperor reform the Roman legal system, Justinian believed he was obligated to regulate how Romans worshipped God. His predecessors had regulated religious practices, but aside from Julian's discredited education law, they had focused on what their subjects did, not what they believed. Romans who believed in the old gods or who held Christian beliefs not sanctioned by a church council did wrong only if, for example, they made a sacrifice in a temple or held communion with a bishop who was outside of the imperially recognized church hierarchy. Christian orthodoxy was action. What one believed was largely beside the point.

For Justinian, however, orthodoxy depended upon both what one did and what one believed. Beginning with a law issued in the first months of his reign, his legislation contained doctrinal statements mandating what orthodox Christians must believe.[5] Justinian continued to do this in subsequent laws, with the statements of correct belief growing in length and complexity.[6] Justinian wrote that it was the purpose of "imperial edicts and laws to correct false belief" so that Romans would "promote, acknowledge and honor the only true and saving faith of the Christians."[7]

Justinian targeted the rights of pagans and Jews even more aggressively. In 529, agents acting in Justinian's name closed the Athenian Platonic school, ending nearly a millennium of unbroken philosophical instruction in Athens.[8] He then prevented pagan-led institutions from receiving financial gifts and blocked pagans from holding office or teaching.[9] If pagans thought to escape these penalties by converting to Christianity disingenuously, Justinian promised to strip imperial offices and social ranks from anyone who "embraced the true and orthodox faith only in pretense."[10]

These laws changed what it meant to be Roman. For the first time since Caracalla's extension of universal citizenship, the empire now had categories of people who understood themselves to be Romans but who lacked the full legal protections and privileges of other Romans. Pagans, Jews, and "heretical" Christians now had fewer rights than their fellow citizens.

Some shocked Romans took action to try to change their second-class status. Justinian brutally suppressed a Samaritan revolt in Palestine in 529 that erupted "when they learned of the emperor's anger against them."[11] Two years later, a group of seven famous pagan philosophers fled across the Persian frontier because "they were prohibited by law from exercising their citizen rights because they did not follow the established religion."[12] One of the exiles, the philosopher Simplicius, justified his departure from Justinian's empire by writing that a philosopher "in corrupt states . . . ought to ask to be an exile from these incurable affairs" and immigrate "to another, better state."[13] The sympathetic historian Agathias wrote that the philosophers returned to Roman territory only when Justinian signed a peace treaty with Persia in 532 that guaranteed that they could "return to their homes and live out their lives in peace without being compelled to alter their ancestral religious beliefs."[14]

MANY ROMANS SHARED Simplicius's anger toward an emperor who felt like he was not bound by the rules that had long governed Roman life. Earlier in 532, a serious disturbance broke out in Constantinople after Justinian failed to exercise the clemency that Romans expected of their sovereign. The cause was mundane. Chariot racing was the most popular sport in the capital, and the Hippodrome, the massive U-shaped space that hosted the races and abutted the imperial palace, doubled as the main venue for regular Romans to collectively make public appeals to the emperor. The city had two chariot-racing teams, the Blues and the Greens, each of them with hundreds of thousands of fans and professional cheerleaders who led the fans in chants. They also had bands of hooligans who battled each other in the streets like modern-day football ultras.

In late 531, the city prefect convicted seven Blue and Green supporters of murder, but on the day they were scheduled to be executed the scaffolding holding their nooses broke. Two men, one a Blue supporter and the other a Green, survived the hanging. Their injured bodies were quickly gathered up by monks and carried away to a monastery, but the prefect then sent troops to arrest the two men if they left the monastery. The standoff was still ongoing on January 13, 532, when Justinian presided over twenty-two chariot races in the Hippodrome. When the competition began, supporters of both teams chanted appeals for the emperor to grant clemency to the two men, a normal request that custom dictated the emperor would grant, but which Justinian ignored. That evening, supporters of both factions rioted, burning the office of the prefect and part of the imperial palace. It then spread to Hagia Sophia, incinerating the church in the center of the city that had been built on the site of the cathedral destroyed in the rioting following the exile of John Chrysostom.[15]

Justinian deployed every tool available to Roman emperors to try to stop the violence, aside from admitting fault. He arranged for another set of races the following day, but the mob responded by burning part of the Hippodrome. He sent senators to calm passions; he dismissed the prefect and other imperial officials who had angered the circus factions; and he deployed soldiers to suppress the unrest. None of it worked. More fires were set each day as disorder and destruction fell on ever wider parts of the city center. During those tense nights, the rioting factions took to using the word *Nika*, Greek for "victory," as a code word to differentiate the opponents of the emperor from the agents Justinian sent to infiltrate their ranks. Thus the violence would come to be called the Nika Riot.

By January 18, Justinian realized that the popular anger centered not on the fate of the two prisoners but on his refusal to behave as Romans believed their emperor should. He decided to follow the example of Anastasius by going into the Hippodrome and asking his people to forgive his arrogance.[16] Justinian excused the misconduct of the crowd and assured them that "there is nothing on your head. . . . For my sins have made me deny you what you asked of me in the Hippodrome."[17] The offer of a pardon attracted some favorable chants instigated by agents loyal to Justinian, but the positive chants were soon drowned out by a negative one: "You are forsworn, ass!"[18] Justinian then retreated into the palace as the crowd proclaimed Hypatius, an anti-Chalcedonian nephew of Anastasius, as the new Roman emperor.[19]

Justinian's wife, Theodora, saved his throne. When the emperor and his advisers began to discuss whether he should flee the capital, Theodora interjected that "it is unendurable for one who has been an emperor to be a fugitive." She told her husband that he could flee if he wanted to, but she would not be going with him. She knew what it felt like to be looked down upon—born of low status, she had worked as an actress earlier in life and was dogged by rumors about her past and her sexually libertine behavior—and she never wanted to go back. "Let it never happen," Procopius records the empress saying, "that I ever live a single day in which those around me do not call me empress."[20]

"When the empress had spoken in this way," Procopius continues, "all were filled with boldness," and they arrived at a plan where soldiers loyal to Justinian would storm the Hippodrome through the main gate opposite where Hypatius sat enthroned.[21] As the terrified crowd scattered, Justinian's general Belisarius broke into the imperial box. Hypatius was seized and executed, and his body was thrown into the sea.[22] Estimates of the number of casualties caused by the Hippodrome assault and related violence range from 30,000 to 80,000 people, out of a total Constantinopolitan population of perhaps 400,000.[23] But "no longer did any faction member appear anywhere" because "all of Constantinople was quiet and no-one dared to go outside."[24]

The Nika Riot nearly ended Justinian's regime, but it did nothing to deter his ambitions. He decided to rebuild all of the public spaces that had been destroyed in the riot so that they were even more impressive than before. The new Hagia Sophia was to be the jewel of this urban renewal program. According to Procopius, "the emperor, thinking nothing of cost . . . began to gather all the artisans from the whole world" to create a magnificent domed structure unlike anything the earth ever had seen.[25] When the church was dedicated in 537, the astonished audience walked into a massive open space capped by a broad dome that measured about 100 feet across and 180 feet tall. (It would ultimately reach 200 feet in height after its reconstruction following an earthquake in 558.) No columns or supports intruded into the church's 165-foot-long open central space; the dome instead "seems to float in the air on no firm basis," supported only by piers set back to the sides.[26] It would remain the largest masonry dome in the world for a millennium.

The massive church was elaborately decorated with a range of materials from around the empire. Its walls were covered with images of vines, birds, and baskets of fruit made from rare stones cut from quarries scattered across the Mediterranean basin. Other surfaces were coated in silver, and large silver discs bearing images of Christ, angels, the disciples, the Virgin Mary, and the symbols of the emperor and empress hung on the church's huge columns.[27] A few years later, Justinian's subjects would sing a hymn in Hagia Sophia celebrating the church as a symbol of Romans' repentance following the Nika Riot. The city had been saved, the congregants sang, only because "the emperor and empress . . . lifted their eyes in hope toward the Creator," repented alongside other Romans, and ordered the reconstruction of Hagia Sophia to reaffirm God's protection of the empire's citizens and its rulers. The hymn concludes with a prayer for the salvation of the imperial couple and the entire polity—a prayer one must imagine many of Justinian's traumatized subjects in the capital would have said half-heartedly.[28]

THEODORA'S PROMINENT ROLE in the construction of Hagia Sophia mirrored the high profile she enjoyed in religious policy discussions. Justinian championed the Council of Chalcedon, but Theodora maintained strong relationships with anti-Chalcedonian leaders.

In the months following the Nika Riot, she helped the repentant emperor organize a gathering to discuss his disagreements with anti-Chalcedonian clergy. Although Severus of Antioch declined the invitation, he sent a letter indicating his political support for Justinian. The exiled bishop assured his sovereign that loyalty to the Roman state and its emperor trumped any concerns he might have about Justinian's theology.[29] Both sides were apparently eager to find a mutually acceptable way forward, and many anti-Chalcedonian leaders remained in the capital after the initial discussions concluded. With Justinian's approval, Theodora housed them in the Palace of Hormisdas, the residence where she and Justinian had lived during the reign of Justin I. That group would eventually grow into a community of as many as 500 anti-Chalcedonian clergy and monks living in the capital under Theodora's protection.

Justinian and Theodora continued to visit and discuss theology with the anti-Chalcedonians assembled in the Hormisdas until, in March 533, Justinian issued an edict condemning both Nestorius and Eutyches and ceasing to mention Chalcedon.[30] This was enough to induce Severus of Antioch to come out of hiding, travel to Constantinople, and spend the winter of 534/535 in the Hormisdas negotiating with the emperor. In the following year the bishops of both Constantinople and Alexandria were replaced by anti-Chalcedonians personally selected by Theodora.

These developments brought the two sides close to an agreement to solve the Chalcedonian conflict, but they never quite reached it—and then the moment slipped away. Some of this was personal. Z'ura, an anti-Chalcedonian monk who had once sought a deeper connection with God by living atop a pillar outside of Amida, had been forced to descend to the ground by local Chalcedonians. He fled to Constantinople, took up residence in the Hormisdas Palace, and then got into a heated argument with Justinian when the emperor came to visit him.[31] This made Justinian so angry that Theodora eventually moved Z'ura from Constantinople to a site in Thrace. While Z'ura antagonized the emperor, Theodosius, the new Alexandrian patriarch, and Anthimus, his Constantinopolitan counterpart, also struggled to secure their positions in their respective cities. Divisions within the Alexandrian anti-Chalcedonian community so vexed Theodosius that he was forced to request military support from Justinian so he could be installed in his see. The emperor could be forgiven for doubting whether his anti-Chalcedonian partners had the power to deliver the theological peace he sought.

Justinian found a new episcopal partner the following year when Agapetus, the bishop of Rome, arrived in Constantinople and demanded Anthimus's deposition. Justinian agreed. Anthimus was quickly replaced by a new Chalcedonian patriarch named Menas. Anthimus moved into the Hormisdas Palace, where he could remain protected by the empress. Later in 536, a council convened by Justinian condemned Severus, Anthimus, and Z'ura, and then Justinian ordered Theodosius of Alexandria deposed.[32]

Until that moment, both Chalcedonians and anti-Chalcedonians had refrained from creating parallel church hierarchies in which a single city would have both a Chalcedonian and an anti-Chalcedonian bishop. The camps disagreed theologically, but they retained some hope of eventually coming back together. In the 540s, however, two anti-Chalcedonian clergy became so concerned that Justinian might snuff out all the remaining ordained anti-Chalcedonians in the empire that they began ordaining anti-Chalcedonian priests and bishops for cities that already had Chalcedonian clergy, so that they could head their own, separate anti-Chalcedonian congregations in Egypt, Syria, and parts of Mesopotamia. Once they separated, these churches never again came together. Justinian's actions created the fissure that, to this day, still separates the Greek Orthodox church from its Syrian Orthodox and Coptic Orthodox cousins.

JUSTINIAN'S EMBRACE OF Pope Agapetus doomed his effort to reunify the churches of the east, but it provided him with an important ally in an even more ambitious endeavor. While his elderly predecessors had done little to reverse the fifth-century loss of Rome's western territories, Justinian believed that Constantinople should use its military and economic superiority to restore the west to the empire. He was not alone in thinking this. North African refugees fleeing the Vandals had made public appeals for Constantinopolitan relief in both the 480s and, more recently, during the early years of the emperor's regime. In the 520s, the Italian king Theoderic's executions of the prominent senators Boethius and Symmachus incited members of the Anicii family, which had representation in both the Roman and Constantinopolitan Senates, to agitate for eastern intervention in Italy.[33] There had even been fighting between Italian and Constantinopolitan armies in the 520s, when eastern forces conducted naval raids against western ports and the western regime responded by capturing the eastern city of Gratiana, on the south bank of the Danube.[34] It also helped that Justinian, as a native Latin speaker from the Balkans, saw similarities between his own culture and that of the lost western territories.

The natural appeal of a western campaign to a figure like Justinian coincided with a shift in eastern thinking about what, exactly, had happened in Italy during the last quarter of the fifth century. When Odoacer had seized power in 476, Constantinopolitans had understood it as yet another instance in which a western warlord was declaring himself the *generalissimo* in charge of the Italian Peninsula. But eastern thinking changed as Theoderic's regime began projecting power outside Italy. By the 510s, eastern writers, led by Justinian's friend Marcellinus Comes, had recast the history of the 470s so that Odoacer's coup was the moment when "the Western Empire of the Roman people . . . perished." And, so that no one mistook why this mattered, Marcellinus deliberately misidentified Odoacer as "the king of the Goths" so he could pin blame for the end of the western empire on the people who now controlled Italy.[35] The reconquest of Gothic Italy was now squarely in the sights of the Roman court in Constantinople.

Although eastern propagandists like Marcellinus were laying the intellectual groundwork for a reconquest of Italy, Justinian's western reconquest began in North Africa. When the Vandal king Hilderic, who was also the grandson of the emperor Valentinian III, was overthrown in 530, Justinian had sufficient pretext to launch a hybrid military and political campaign against the Vandals.

The war began three years later when Roman agents sparked local revolts against Vandal rule in Sardinia and the Libyan province of Tripolitania, followed quickly by the dispatch of Roman troops to support the rebels. A Roman army then landed about 150 miles from Carthage. As they marched toward the Vandal capital, Belisarius, the general leading the expedition, instructed his troops not to loot or pillage the land because "the Libyans, who are Romans by descent, do not trust and are hostile toward the Vandals." On September 13, 533, Belisarius defeated a Vandal army 10 miles outside of Carthage. He entered the city two days later and proclaimed it liberated. North Africa was Roman again.[36]

The last embers of Vandal resistance flickered out when their new king, Gelimer, was captured in March 534. Justinian then staged a triumphal procession displaying the treasures that Geiseric and his men had seized when they had sacked Rome in 455, including the imperial insignia of the Western Roman Empire, and, apparently, according to Procopius, the temple menorah, the Ark of the Covenant, and the other "treasures of the Jews that Titus . . . had brought to Rome after the capture of Jerusalem" in AD 70.[37] Gelimer and his family were led into the Hippodrome to bow before Justinian, who granted him an imperial estate in Asia Minor. The former king would live there with his family until his death in 553. This well-choreographed act of imperial mercy for a Vandal contrasted dramatically with the carnage Justinian had inflicted on Romans in that same space a few years before.[38]

Justinian hoped that the choreography on that day would induce Italy's Gothic leadership to submit peacefully to Roman rule rather than risk an armed conflict. But, if armed intervention was needed, Justinian could use two possible pretexts. First, the Vandals had possessed a toehold of Sicilian territory that the Italian regime prevented Constantinople from occupying.[39] Second, the assassination of Amalasuntha, the Gothic queen and Roman ally, permitted Justinian to claim that the purpose of a Roman invasion was to avenge the death of a friend of the empire.

The emperor did not wait long to attack. In late 535, 7,500 troops commanded by Belisarius landed in Sicily, while another Eastern Roman army attacked western holdings in Dalmatia. Dalmatia fell to the east the following summer. Sicily fell even faster. By late 536, Belisarius had taken the island, crossed to Southern Italy, and advanced to Rome. That December, the city opened its gates and the Gothic garrison retreated. As Procopius put it, "Rome became subject to the Romans again after a time of sixty years."[40]

Unfortunately for Justinian, Rome's capture did not end the war. The Goths were more entrenched in Northern Italy and held Ravenna, the well-defended Italian capital, which was surrounded by swamps. Ravenna's defenses were not as impenetrable as those of Constantinople, but the city was not much easier to capture than the eastern capital. Its resistance gave the Goths time to regroup under a new king named Vitigis, and they held out until eastern forces took Ravenna in 540. At that point, Justinian tried to end hostilities through the same choreographed acts of surrender and reconciliation that had concluded the Vandal campaign. Vitigis was given an honorific Roman title and a comfortable pension. Some of his courtiers, like the Latin author Cassiodorus, even moved to Constantinople to integrate themselves into Justinian's empire.

But the Italian war had lasted too long to be resolved so cleanly. While it fought the Goths, Justinian's empire was hit with an almost unfathomable series of catastrophes. Antioch, the third-largest city in the east, and the place where Roman armies often gathered when preparing to fight in the east, was hit by four major earthquakes between 525 and 532. They destroyed much of the city and its defensive walls. Then, in 536, a strange cloud of dust, possibly caused by the impact of a comet or an unknown volcanic eruption, dimmed the sun over the Northern Hemisphere for an entire year. Cassiodorus described it producing "a winter without storms, spring without mildness, and summer without heat." The sudden shift in the climate resulted in food shortages that made it effectively impossible for the empire to manage the complicated logistics of a war of conquest.[41]

Justinian's challenges increased as the 540s began. The Roman advance toward Ravenna and the likelihood that Italy might again fall under Constantinople's control prompted Chosroes, the Persian king, to break the so-called Eternal Peace he had signed in 532 and launch a surprise attack across the Euphrates. Because Justinian's best troops were in Italy, Chosroes's army advanced quickly into Syria, poured through the ruined walls of Antioch, and led much of the great city's population back across the Persian frontier as slaves. Justinian was forced to recall Belisarius from Italy to fight in the east, but the general's departure reignited the Italian war. With Belisarius gone, Gothic forces swept down as far as Southern Italy. The city of Rome suffered particularly badly in this phase of the conflict. The Goths captured it in 546, lost it the next year, retook it two years later, and finally lost the city for good in 552. The fighting in Italy did not conclude until the last Gothic holdouts were reduced in 562, the same year that Justinian signed a treaty with Persia that ended hostilities in exchange for a large annual subsidy.

The Persian invasion was only part of the reason the war in Italy dragged on for so long. A bigger problem appeared in 541/542 when the first known outbreak of bubonic plague swept through the Mediterranean. Procopius remarks that, at its height, the plague killed between 5,000 and 10,000 people a day in Constantinople, forcing authorities to bury the bodies in mass graves. Chosroes even suspended campaigning against Rome out of fear that the plague might devastate his armies.[42]

A law issued by Justinian in 542 offers a chilling indication of the plague's toll. It describes a Roman financial system thrust into turmoil because "the danger of death has penetrated every place." So many lenders and debtors had died in the past year that no one was quite sure who owed what to whom. The legal heirs of many of the deceased either did not know about the loans or claimed not to have any records of the contracts laying out their terms.[43] At the same time, so many bankers had died that borrowers and heirs who did acknowledge loans had no idea whom they should pay. Any Roman emperor would have struggled to deal with a credit market suddenly filled with uncollectable loans, but this was a major problem for Justinian, because more than any sovereign before him, he had used bonds to fund his long wars and expensive construction projects.[44] If the empire's credit market seized up, everything from the Italian war to progress on the buildings he was constructing might suddenly stop.

It is to the emperor's immense credit that he managed imperial institutions so expertly that they weathered these combined disasters. Not only was he able to continue the war in Italy, but he opportunistically seized part of southern Spain from the Visigothic kingdom. By the time of his death in 565, Justinian had restored the North African coast, southern Spain, and all of Italy to Roman rule. He had arrived at a peace treaty with Persia, rebuilt Constantinople, and constructed a series of defensive works across the Adriatic, the Balkans, and the Middle East designed to protect his restored empire.

All of this had come at a tremendous cost. Justinian's interest in the west had made it more difficult for him to arrive at a solution that might have reintegrated his Chalcedonian and anti-Chalcedonian subjects into one Christian community. The divisions in the east that his alliance with the pope exacerbated never healed. Italy, too, suffered in the aftermath of his reconquest. Multiple sieges and sacks had depopulated the city of Rome and destroyed much of its infrastructure.[45] Milan was "razed to the ground" by Goths, who killed all its men and enslaved all its women.[46] The Italy that Justinian finally took control of in 562 was utterly unlike the urbanized, sophisticated place it had been in 536. Italy was Roman again, but it had not been so completely devastated since at least Hannibal's invasion.

Everyone from sixth-century Romans to modern observers have struggled to understand Justinian. In his *Secret History*, a work full of slander and gossip, Procopius speaks about Justinian's head vanishing and his body flickering whenever the restless emperor stood up from his throne. "Indeed," Procopius famously concluded, "how was this man likely to be anything but an evil spirit, who never knew what it was like to have enough drink or food or sleep, but . . . roamed the palace at unseemly hours of the night?"[47] Justinian himself confirms part of this picture when he speaks about laws he issued "after thinking them out with great care, during sleepless nights, guided by our devotion to God."[48] Whereas Procopius framed the emperor as a demon wandering through the night, the emperor saw himself as a sovereign who reigned with the pious devotion of a Christian ascetic. Neither could imagine a reign like Justinian's unfolding without some supernatural aid.

They were right to marvel. Justinian held power for thirty-eight years, longer than all other previous emperors save Theodosius II and Augustus, and no emperor except Augustus had devoted more energy to changing the systems through which the Roman state operated. Justinian's actions during his reign reflected his persistent optimism that the Roman state and its people would return to the glory they had historically enjoyed if he, acting through God's design, gave them the chance to do it. The 1,300 years of Roman history preceding Justinian made him optimistic that Rome could reabsorb its western citizens, rebuild the cities his wars had destroyed, and recover from the combined effects of natural disasters, Persian sacks, and plague. We now know that Justinian's optimism was misplaced, and that because he aimed so high, his failures were even more spectacular. And once Roman optimism dissipated, it would take a long time for it to return.

Chapter 31

After Justinian

565–602

MANY OF THE consequences of Justinian's manic activities already were clear during his lifetime. On the positive side, he rapidly built a new class of Roman elites, joining the glitterati of Constantinople and the east to the aristocrats of Rome, Ravenna, and Carthage. Many of these figures, like the senator Cassiodorus in Italy and the African poet Corippus, had loyally served non-Roman rulers until Justinian forcibly reabsorbed them into the Roman state. Others, such as the historian Jordanes, exemplify how Justinian created spaces for people to be simultaneously proud of their Gothic descent, loyal to the Roman state, and passionate about a Christian faith in line with the Council of Chalcedon. Jordanes, for example, concluded his history of the Goths with the moment when his "praiseworthy people ceded to an even more praiseworthy emperor[,] . . . the victorious and triumphant emperor Justinian."[1]

Justinian deserves credit for facilitating this elite reintegration, but his efforts to revitalize Italy also short-circuited the natural resilience of Italian communities by centralizing Roman administration in Ravenna.[2] As a result, prestigious offices held by Roman senators, including the urban prefecture of Rome, faded in importance, until they disappeared entirely by the end of the sixth century.[3] The demise of the urban prefecture in Rome was emblematic of a wider trend in which Italians turned increasingly to the Eastern Roman military governors for protection and guidance while the organs for local resilience in Italy atrophied.[4] This deeply compromised the Italian recovery from Justinian's war.

Internal and military affairs were no easier to manage in the core territories of the Roman East. Theodora's death in 548 profoundly affected Justinian on both a personal and a political level. Not only had she been a courageous and devoted spouse, but her death had robbed him of a connection to the empire's leading anti-Chalcedonians at a moment when his policies had fostered the emergence of a parallel anti-Chalcedonian ecclesiastical hierarchy. Militarily, Justinian bought peace with the Persians and barbarians along the northern edges of Roman territory while fortifying cities and monasteries far from the front line.[5] In 562, he negotiated a fifty-year peace with Persia. According to the treaty, Persia renounced its claims to the kingdom of Lazica, the location of much of the recent fighting between Romans and Persians, in return for an annual payment of 30,000 solidi. Justinian even paid the first seven years' tribute up-front as a lump sum, more of an indignity than a financial hardship to an empire that minted more than a hundred times that number of gold coins a year. Nevertheless, the agreement did reek of the sort of desperate surrender that an elderly emperor concerned with his immediate legacy might make.[6]

Justinian also bequeathed his successor new challenges to Roman control of its frontiers. The 550s saw the first significant incursions by Slavs in the Balkans. Although the defenses Justinian had constructed around major cities generally held, the Slavs advanced so deeply into the countryside that they briefly caused panic in Constantinople.[7] Then, in 558, the Romans were introduced to the Avars, a powerful, well-organized group based around the Sea of Azov that was moving west in response to pressure from the Turks. The Avar threat remained remote under Justinian, but it would become much more serious by the 570s.

Justinian, although no longer the young man that courtiers once breathlessly compared to a demon incapable of rest, retained both a formidable intellect and an even more acute survival instinct well into his eighties. He weathered a number of attempted coups during the last decade and a half of his rule, but none stung as much as the one organized by a group of bankers in November 562. Justinian had granted new legal privileges to the financiers, and he relied upon them to pay for his wars and construction projects. But the access he had given them to positions of power ultimately led one of them, the banker Marcellus, to pay a palace attendant fifty pounds of gold to let an assassin gain access to the emperor. When the plot was discovered, Marcellus and his accomplices committed suicide rather than endure whatever punishment Justinian might devise.[8]

FORTUNATELY FOR ROMANS, there was no contested succession when Justinian died on the night of November 14, 565. Before his death was publicized, the court's chief eunuch and a small group of senators went to Justinian's nephew Justin, who was then serving as the head of the palace guards, and had him crowned emperor Justin II.[9] Then, as rumors of a new emperor spread through Constantinople on the morning of November 15, citizens filled the Hippodrome so they might greet him.[10] Few Constantinopolitans would have been old enough to have mature memories of any emperor but Justinian.

Justin was married to Sophia, Theodora's niece, and understood the importance of having a wife with connections to anti-Chalcedonian leaders. Like her aunt, Sophia had grown up anti-Chalcedonian before converting to Chalcedonianism in 562, so that Justinian might appoint her husband as his successor. Some anti-Chalcedonians still thought highly of her at the time of the accession, however.[11] Perhaps for this reason, Sophia featured prominently alongside Justin in the public activities connected to his accession and appeared alongside him on coins issued by the new emperor.[12]

Justin soon disrupted the carefully balanced domestic and foreign policies Justinian had crafted during his last years. Some of this had to do with the fact that Justin's power rested on a narrow constituency of courtiers, palace guards, and a faction of senators.[13] The loyalties of the armies, their commanders, and the bankers—all the people essential to the success of Justinian's domestic initiatives and frontier policies—were still uncertain.

Justin quickly moved to limit any challengers from these quarters. His main military rival, another member of Justinian's family confusingly also named Justin, was an exceptional commander whose military talents far surpassed his political acumen.[14] This Justin had a much more impressive record than the man who became emperor. He was one of the last figures other than an emperor to serve as consul, and he had fought impressively against barbarians for many years. However, when one of his deputies was implicated in an extortion scheme, the new emperor used it as a pretext to order the general's execution. Removing the general responsible for "preventing the Avars from crossing the Danube" did not make the empire any safer, but it probably did make Justin II feel more secure.[15]

Justin and Sophia took other drastic actions that they believed helped them personally even though they had negative consequences for the state. In 566, they paid off the debts to the bankers from whom Justinian had borrowed, "reclaimed his bonds," and then staged a ceremony in the Hippodrome to show the public that the power of these financiers had been broken.[16] Justin claimed that these debts had burdened the treasury "until it was totally exhausted," but the ready availability of capital to pay off so many loans at once suggests that there was no shortage of funds.[17] While Justin and Sophia pretended that they were championing regular Constantinopolitans over the financial elite favored by Justinian, they had in fact drained the state's cash reserves to prematurely retire bonds the state could have paid over time. This measure took away the interest payments that the bankers had counted on receiving and depleted the capital held in their banks. It thus made it much more difficult for the emperor to raise capital in the future, because the financiers became much less likely to trust him. The imaginary fiscal crisis that Justin and Sophia had pretended to solve quickly transformed into a real one with effects so severe that Justin resorted to selling imperial offices and priesthoods.[18]

JUSTIN'S APPROACH TO foreign policy was similarly misguided. Just seven days after he took power, he received an embassy from the Avars asking him to "send our king the gifts that he is due."[19] Justin denied the request, telling the envoys, "We do not allow arrogance," and warning that their nation would be "extinguished by a sudden thunderbolt" if it dared to attack Rome.[20]

The Avars then allied with the Lombards against the Gepids, a barbarian group friendly to the Romans, but whom they attacked "as if they were fighting against Justin."[21] When the Avar forces overwhelmed the Gepids, their power terrified the Lombards, too. The Lombards then invaded Italy and overcame the unprepared Roman garrisons, many of them stretched thinly across cities whose defenses had not yet been fully repaired following Justinian's long Italian war. By the late 580s, Italy was primarily under Lombard control, though these lands were divided between the main Lombard kingdom, based in the Po Valley, and semi-independent Lombard duchies in Central Italy and Campania. The Romans retained control of the strip of land linking Rome to Ravenna and Naples as well as the Southern Italian regions of Apulia and Campania. Justin's petty slight of the Avar ambassadors then set off a chain reaction that shattered Italian unity and Roman control over the peninsula. The former condition would not return until the 1870s. The latter never did.[22]

The Avar conquest of the Gepids created problems in Rome's Balkan provinces as well. The Gepids had seized control of the old Roman administrative center of Sirmium (modern Sremska Mitrovica in Serbia) when Justinian invaded Italy, but Justin had reoccupied the city when the Gepid kingdom collapsed.[23] The Avars, however, claimed that they should control all that had once belonged to the Gepids. When they attacked Sirmium not long after the Lombard invasion of Italy, Justin lacked the capacity to reinforce the city. Bonus, the Roman general defending Sirmium, felt compelled to negotiate, but he feared agreeing to something without the permission of his "emperor, who is terrible and very stern." Justin was forced to pay a much larger indemnity than what the Avar envoys had requested in 565.[24]

Part of the reason Justin felt compelled to pay was that, while fighting raged in Italy and the Balkans, the emperor made the absurd decision to breach the fifty-year peace treaty with Persia after a group of Turks requested that he "join them in their war against the Persians." Justinian's peace treaty required an annual tribute payment by Rome to Persia, but Justin had not made the installment due in 571, and had rudely rebuffed the Persian envoy sent to check on the emperor's intentions. Evagrius Scholasticus wrote that Justin "had made no preparations for war," but he nevertheless ordered Marcian, the general in command of Rome's eastern forces, to advance into Persian territory in the fall of 572 without "either an army fit for battle nor any other equipment for war."[25]

Marcian had some initial successes against the equally unprepared Persians, but his advance stalled when Justin rashly ordered him to besiege the well-fortified city of Nisibis, and then inexplicably relieved him of his command in the middle of the night without telling the army or its officers who would now be leading them. They were forced to abandon the siege. With the Roman offensive blunted and the empire's eastern defenses in shambles, the Persian king Chosroes was able to lead a separate force into Roman territory. He invested Dara, a strategic fortress city that the emperor Anastasius had constructed to serve as a Roman counter to the Persian Nisibis. The city fell in November 573.[26]

The catastrophic loss of Dara broke Justin. "When Justin had heard about these events," Evagrius wrote, "he had no healthy or sane thoughts . . . but he fell into mental disorder and madness."[27] Although he still had occasional moments of lucidity, Justin was no longer capable of managing the empire's affairs. Sophia then stepped in to run the state in her husband's stead, selecting Justin's associate Tiberius to serve as her co-regent.

SOPHIA AND TIBERIUS assumed control, said Evagrius, when "Roman rule, together with the state itself, was in danger of collapsing" because of Justin's catastrophic mismanagement.[28] The Roman state had developed increasingly sophisticated, mutually reinforcing political, financial, and military systems over a period of many centuries. These systems capably identified the resources it possessed, collected them from around the empire's vast territory, consolidated them in administrative centers, and redirected them in a fashion that leaders identified as best serving Rome's interests. They worked well when the state administered the same territories without interruption for a long enough time period that the revenue and resources became predictable. In these stable periods, administrators could predict with good accuracy what the empire produced as well as what each region needed. Rome's genius was in creating a culture of expertise so that the people managing the distribution of resources and executing the policies of the state were well trained and understood their areas of responsibility.

One way to grasp the sophistication of the Roman imperial system Justin inherited is to compare its capacities to those of the Roman Republic of the mid-first century BC. In the Republic, Roman senators governed provinces using a very small staff, usually drawn in part from their own households. Doctors, courtroom advocates, and even philosophers were not trained in any systematic manner. Some had attended unregulated private institutions, while others, such as jurists and sometimes doctors, had learned their crafts through apprenticeships. In Justin's world, doctors, lawyers, teachers, and aspiring bureaucrats attended universities, such as the massive complex of classrooms that filled some three city blocks in the center of Alexandria. The empire's largest universities employed upward of fifty professors, whose expertise the imperial government certified and whose salaries it paid. Government officials monitored student progress, so that, as Justinian once promised the most capable among them, "when you have completed your course of study . . . you may be able to govern the portions of our empire which are entrusted to you."[29]

In the Republic, the talents of these teachers and students drawn from around the Mediterranean would have been effectively wasted by a Roman state unable to identify capable administrators and unwilling to employ provincials in this capacity. The empire, by contrast, built elaborate systems to nurture its gifted young citizens and maximize their contributions across their lifetimes.

The smaller, more competent sixth-century Roman military also differed dramatically from the massive citizen armies of the late Republic, which could, and often did, deploy many tens of thousands of troops to win wars on multiple fronts simultaneously. These earlier Roman armies had been citizen levies drawn from a large but largely untrained population of young men. They were massive, but inexperienced and inefficient. Justin's armies were far smaller, but they were made up of trained, mature, often veteran soldiers whose superior capabilities and experience made them much more formidable than the volunteers fielded by Marius or the draftees serving under Pompey.

In the most basic terms, the sixth-century Roman Empire approached problems differently than the Republic. It relied on a smaller but much more capable group of experts to run its administration, economy, diplomacy, and military forces. The quality of their training meant that fewer people were needed to do these things. This freed the millions of Roman citizens, who might once have been drafted into military service against the Persians in Syria, the Avars in Sirmium, or the Lombards in Italy, from the disruptions of their lives and economic activity that military service would have entailed. But these experts were also extremely valuable and difficult to replace. They needed to be empowered to use their skills, and deployed judiciously so their talents could have the most effect. And this is where Justin failed the Roman state most seriously.

In a few short years, Justin undermined the interdependent systems that had long supported Roman economic, diplomatic, and military activity. Justin first marginalized the bankers who ran the capital markets that had enabled the state to fund its armies and make tribute payments. Then, concerned about the lack of money that had resulted from his actions, he violated the terms of multiple treaties that required him to pay specified sums to outside states. Then he had to deploy limited military resources, including valuable and difficult-to-replace veteran soldiers, in numbers too small for them to decisively win any of the three wars he had caused. This led to a set of conflicts in which Rome could neither prevail militarily nor resolve diplomatically while they steadily leaked precious manpower and money from an empire struggling to cope with the demands its capricious emperor had placed upon it.

SOPHIA AND TIBERIUS had few good options for resolving the overlapping crises Justin had created. In early 574, a Persian envoy arrived in Constantinople offering a truce because their king "thought that the Romans would give whatever the Persians wished." Sophia then settled on a plan to buy time.[30] The empress broke with protocol and met personally with Chosroes's envoy, telling him Justin was ill, and then sent her own envoy to the Persian king with a message that "bewailed her husband's misfortunes and the state's lack of a leader." She implored Chosroes not to "trample upon a widowed woman." This (and a payment of 45,000 solidi) won the empire a one-year truce.[31] Then, on December 7, 574, Sophia took advantage of one of Justin's fleeting moments of lucidity to have her husband appoint Tiberius as his Caesar and heir-designate.[32]

Tiberius and Sophia were then able to negotiate a short treaty that restored peace to the Syrian and Mesopotamian frontier for three years in exchange for an annual payment of 30,000 solidi while allowing for fighting to continue in the Caucasus and in the Arabian deserts. Then, in 576, in an attempt to force them into making a permanent peace, Chosroes invaded Asia Minor with an army that included war elephants. The Romans defeated this incursion, but they lacked the manpower to follow up on their victory. The war degenerated into a prolonged slog in which both sides traded victories and defeats while hoping to induce their opponent to negotiate from a position of weakness. The Roman victory of 576 was followed by a defeat in Armenia in 577. The Romans volleyed back in 578 by turning away a Persian invasion of Asia Minor and then striking into the highlands of Persian-controlled Armenia. In 580, the Roman general Maurice raided across the Tigris. The next year, however, the Persians turned away an invasion force with which Maurice hoped to attack Ctesiphon. Most absurdly, it seems that both sides perpetuated the fighting simply so that they might get a better deal in whatever peace agreement was ultimately signed.[33]

For Rome, the long Persian conflict prevented the deployment of the empire's best troops to the Balkan and Italian theaters. The situation became so serious that, in 578, the Roman Senate sent 3,000 pounds of gold (the equivalent of 309,267 solidi) to Tiberius, "to beg the Caesar to mount an expedition to defend Italy, which was exhausted by Lombard raids." Citing the demands of the Persian war, Tiberius returned the money to Rome and suggested that the Senate use it either to "persuade some of the leaders of the Lombard people . . . to switch allegiance to the Romans," or, if that failed, to "make an alliance with the leaders of the Franks by giving them the money."[34] The papacy even joined in by asking that the leader of the Burgundians attack the Lombards. All of this was outside the normal system of taxes, diplomacy, and military deployment, and none of it could reverse the Lombard gains.

The situation in the Balkans deteriorated even more significantly than the one in Italy. The overstretched imperial armies could not prevent Slavic raids deep into Greece. Tiberius then appealed to the Avars to remove the Slavs from Roman territory, but when the Avars saw how weak the Roman state had become, their leader, called the Chagan, decided instead to extort protection money from the emperor. In 579, the Chagan collected the 80,000 solidi in annual tribute that Rome owed them and then, Menander reports, "without seeking an excuse or a pretext or even troubling to invent a false charge against the Romans . . . suddenly broke the treaty he had made with Tiberius." The Chagan attacked Sirmium, isolated the city, and began a blockade that resulted in the city's fall three years later.[35] While the Romans struggled to relieve Sirmium, Avar armies moved on to other cities in the northern Balkans as Slavic migrants streamed across the Danube and settled in parts of modern Bulgaria and Greece. The Balkans were quickly becoming lost.

NEITHER THE EAST nor Italy nor the Balkans improved when Maurice, Tiberius's top general, succeeded his patron in 582. Maurice was an exceptional military tactician, but he struggled to manage the empire's many concurrent crises in the 580s. His Italian strategy, to the degree he had one, involved encouraging the Franks to attack the Lombards from the north. It was not until 586 that the Romans even secured a durable Italian truce. In the Balkans, the combination of Avar pressure and Slavic migration led to a near complete breakdown of Roman state control outside of territory that could be resupplied by sea. When Rome raised its tribute to the Avars to 100,000 solidi a year in 582 in exchange for a two-year pause on their attacks, Slavic groups pressed even harder. In 585, Slavic attacks reached all the way to Athens and the Long Walls that Anastasius had built in Thrace to serve as the outer defense of the Constantinopolitan region. The next year Slavic forces sacked Corinth and besieged Thessaloniki while the Avars broke their treaty with Rome and resumed their expansion in the northern Balkans. Maurice could do little more than pay them off and then march an army around Thrace in the autumn of 590 to make a show of force after the Avars withdrew.

Then, suddenly, everything changed. In early 590, a rebellious commander overthrew the young Persian king Chosroes II, and Chosroes fled to Roman territory. Maurice agreed to help him return to power and sent Roman forces to join with troops loyal to Chosroes in an invasion of Persia. Resistance quickly collapsed, Chosroes was restored, and he agreed to a treaty with Maurice that returned the fortified city of Dara to Rome and gave Rome control of much of the territory in the Caucasus that the two empires had fought over in the past.

This eastern settlement permitted Maurice to use Rome's best troops to retake the Balkans.[36] Campaigns over the next three years saw Roman forces push west along the Danube while reestablishing links to Roman territory farther south and launching attacks on the river's banks to discourage Slavic crossings. By the end of 595, Roman soldiers were able to directly challenge the Avars in what is now Serbia.[37] The chastened Avars then shifted their focus to attacking Frankish territory in Germany, which suddenly looked much more inviting than Roman lands.[38] By 602, Avar military defeats and the constant pressure that Roman forces were exerting on the Chagan caused a rebellion by Avar subjects.[39]

IN THE DECADE following Chosroes's restoration, Maurice demonstrated remarkable skill as a military strategist and tactician. It is no wonder that he is widely credited as the author of the most comprehensive guide to strategy and campaigning to survive from the Roman world.[40] But even these military successes could not reverse the damage that had been done to the Roman state over the past generation. Justin had caused a deep and profound rot in the banking system, and from all indications the system continued to deteriorate well into the reign of Maurice. This was especially true in Italy, where, in 600, Pope Gregory the Great had to personally intervene to keep the very last banker's stall open in the Roman Forum.[41]

These financial problems, combined with plunging tax revenues, forced Maurice to defend the empire without paying his soldiers a full salary in cash. In 587, he sent a message to the eastern commander ordering him to cut the pay of his troops by 25 percent, perhaps in exchange for a shift in the terms of their service. Only the exceptional interpersonal skills of the commander prevented a full mutiny.[42] Then, in 594, Maurice "ordered the general Peter to give the Romans one-third of their pay in gold, one-third in weapons, and the remaining third in clothing," rather than the full salary in cash they expected.[43] Another revolt was avoided only when Peter announced that any orphans of a service member would receive their father's rank. Ostensibly, Maurice claimed to be concerned about soldiers spending their allowance on things he thought frivolous. But his model of in-kind compensation did promise to make the state more resilient if it ever faced a shortage of cash.[44] By the later 590s, Maurice began to simultaneously repopulate the Balkan countryside and provide for its defense by forcing large numbers of Armenian cavalrymen and their families to migrate to the area. Once they arrived, they were given farmland they would be expected to defend, a solution that promised to keep the soldiers fighting in the Balkans even if a new war with Persia erupted or if the state lacked the funds to pay them.[45]

A clear pattern emerges across these efforts. Because Maurice could no longer compensate the military with the resources from taxes and bonds, he was shifting the empire away from the sophisticated, flexible, professional armies of Justinian that civilians had paid for and back toward the systems of payment-in-kind and settlements of citizen soldiers once used by the Republic. This military revolution did not inspire great confidence among the soldiers.

It also made Maurice's decision in late 602 to order his soldiers to spend the winter in Slavic territory beyond the Danube particularly reckless. The emperor once wrote that "it was preferable to mount attacks against [the Slavs] in the winter when they [could not] hide among the bare trees."[46] This was a sound strategy, but he failed to take into account that his changes to the professional status of his armies made them less willing to do what he ordered without question. He should have known better, especially when the group he sent north in 602 complained that their horses were exhausted and the plunder they had seized in the recent campaigns might be lost.[47]

Discontent was evident as letters pinged back and forth from the front to the capital during the march toward the Danube. What had begun as a request by the soldiers for the emperor to improve the conditions of service grew into a serious problem proportionate to the emperor's intransigence and parsimony.[48] The army sent one final request, asking him to reconsider his orders as they approached the river crossing. When he did not relent, they rebelled.

The situation then quickly deteriorated. Many army units abandoned their positions along the Danube and marched to Constantinople under the leadership of a soldier named Phocas. Lacking regular troops to defend the capital, Maurice tried to organize supporters of the Blue and Green chariot-racing teams to guard the city walls. Soon, however, calls within the city, and the presence of Phocas's mutineers outside the capital, convinced Maurice that he could preserve himself only by fleeing. While people in the capital acclaimed Phocas as the new emperor, Maurice and his family sailed across to Asia. The fugitive emperor even ordered his son Theodosius to go to Persia to request help from Chosroes, but before he could act on this, forces loyal to Phocas captured Maurice and most of his family. Maurice was decapitated on November 27, 602, after being forced first to witness the murder of his children. Their bodies, and his, were cast into the sea.[49]

In the early spring of 603, when the snows covering the Anatolian mountain passes had melted sufficiently that a messenger from Constantinople could safely travel into Persian territory, Phocas sent an envoy to Chosroes, "since it was customary for the Romans and Persians to do this whenever they ascended to royal power." Enraged when he heard about Maurice's murder, the Persian mobilized his army on the "pretense of upholding the pious memory of the emperor." And this, the historian Theophylact Simocatta wrote, "became the undoing of the prosperity of both the Romans and Persians."[50]

So began the war that would end the ancient world.

Chapter 32

The New World of Heraclius

602–631

PHOCAS, WHOM THE chronicler Theophanes described as a "rebellious, insolent, and cowardly" soldier of middling rank, had none of the skills or social connections required to lead the Roman Empire in a world war. He did not even know how to be emperor. Five days after he took power, members of the Blue circus faction and their Green rivals got into a turf war. Phocas sent Alexander, a member of his military staff, to defuse the situation. Instead of resolving it, Alexander "came to blows with Kosmas, the leader of the Blues," who then began chanting, "Go away and learn the protocol! Maurice is still alive." These words were simultaneously insulting and threatening to a new, inexperienced regime.[1]

They were also true. Although Phocas disposed of Maurice soon after this incident and forced everyone in the city to view his head (and the heads of his dead family members) in a public square "until they began to smell," this did not change the fact that neither the new emperor nor any of those around him knew how to manage the capital.[2] The situation in the provinces was scarcely better. The Egyptian chronicler John of Nikiu complained about "the great quantity of blood shed by Phocas," as well as the "great terror that prevailed among all of the officers" of the state, its cities, and the church.

Phocas's agents, he added, "strangled some of them, burned others, drowned others, and gave still others to wild beasts."[3]

The terrors caused by Phocas's purges depleted the empire of the qualified administrators who could have repaired its damaged administrative and logistical systems. In the early 600s, Rome did not suffer from a lack of resources but from an inability to move those resources to the places they were needed. This was especially true in the Balkans, where instability along the Danube disrupted the military supply chain that Justinian had put in place. Rome could still get resources to its Balkan armies, but they arrived in such a haphazard fashion that the soldiers stationed there often carried a mismatched supply of goods that were both extremely valuable and insufficient to meet their basic needs.

At an extraordinary Easter celebration in 600, for example, Rome's Avar enemies gifted the Romans 400 wagons of grain so that they might not starve on the holiday. The Roman commander then "sent in return various Indian goods to the barbarians, namely, pepper, Indian cloves, costus spice, cinnamon, and other rare goods."[4] The Roman troops had no food, but they had plenty of expensive spices and seasonings to use on it if some ever arrived from Constantinople. Phocas, of course, had no solution to this problem, and his decimation of the empire's leading administrators made it unlikely that he would find one.

Phocas's manifest incompetence and the looming threat of a Persian invasion prompted Narses, the formidable and intimidating commander of Roman forces based in Edessa, to rebel in 603.[5] Phocas's response was a huge blunder. Assuming that "the Avar nation was at rest" and unable to attack, he withdrew his armies from Europe and "sent one against the Persians and the other to besiege Edessa."[6] But the Avar nation was not at all at rest, and it had repeatedly shown a willingness to break or renegotiate treaties with Rome whenever a Persian threat loomed. In addition, the Slavs in the Balkans remained a constant threat because they lacked a coherent, unifying political structure, which meant it was difficult for the Romans to negotiate with them. Phocas had left the Balkans open to Avar raids and migrations by armed Slavs that could not be effectively countered.

Phocas also failed to effectively utilize his experienced soldiers once they arrived in the east. While Narses eventually surrendered, Persia began a series of slow advances that pushed its line of control deeper into Roman territory each year. In 604, Dara fell after a siege lasting more than a year. The Armenian historian Sebeos reports that the Persians destroyed the city "and put all of its inhabitants to the sword," rather than take the risk that Rome might recapture it.[7] With this keystone of Roman frontier defenses now eliminated, the Persian army pushed into Roman Armenia and Mesopotamia. In 609, it captured Edessa, the last major fortified city in Roman Mesopotamia before one reached the Euphrates.[8] Its capture meant that Persian forces could cross into Syria without fear that Roman troops might counterattack from Mesopotamia and cut their supply lines.[9]

Phocas faced serious internal problems, too. The purges of 602 and 603 foreshadowed a larger pattern according to which the incompetent and paranoid emperor responded to perceived threats with ghastly violence. He had the leader of the Green faction in Constantinople burned alive in the main street of the capital following a riot.[10] After Phocas detected a possible conspiracy, he ordered the beheadings of nine senior officials, and then commanded that Maurice's widow Constantina and her female children be pulled out of the convent where they were living and had them beheaded as well.[11] In 609, according to Theophanes, the emperor responded to mockery of him in the Hippodrome by ordering the city prefect to "maim many persons and hang their limbs from the Sphendone," the outer part of the curved section of the Hippodrome stands.[12]

These tyrannical displays prompted Heraclius, one of Maurice's former generals who controlled civil and military affairs in Africa, to rebel. The rebellion was deliberately planned and moved slowly, but, in a notable twist, the elderly commander put his thirty-five-year-old son, also named Heraclius, forward as its leader.[13] After capturing

Alexandria and cutting off the supply of Egyptian grain to Constantinople, the younger Heraclius led a fleet to the capital.[14]

Heraclius arrived on Saturday, October 3, 610, and anchored his ships just offshore so that the entire population could see his armada. Phocas, who had planned for an assault by land, was shocked and withdrew to the imperial palace within the city walls. Panic descended upon Phocas's loyalists. Bonosus, one of the emperor's most loathsome associates, fled the city and was captured and killed.[15] Finally, after three days of growing anxiety, Phocas and his detested lieutenant, the chamberlain Leontius, were dragged from the palace. Phocas was stripped, placed on a small boat, shown to Heraclius and all of the sailors onboard his ships, and then beheaded. "His head was placed on a pole," according to John of Nikiu, and "the rest of his body was dragged along on its belly" to the Hippodrome, where it and the corpse of Leontius were burned.[16] Heraclius was crowned emperor by Sergius, the patriarch of Constantinople, that same morning.

A NEW ERA in Roman history began with his crowning, but Heraclius inherited an empire in deep crisis. Theophanes succinctly encapsulated Rome's military condition, writing, "Heraclius found the affairs of the Roman state undone, for the Avars had devastated Europe while the Persians had destroyed all of Asia and annihilated the Roman army in battle."[17] In the Balkans, John of Nikiu noted, "the barbarians . . . devastated Christian cities and carried off their inhabitants," so that "no city escaped save Thessaloniki only; for its walls were strong." Elsewhere, "the province was devastated and depopulated."[18]

Phocas's fall roughly coincided with the Persian crossing of the Euphrates and the collapse of the last of Rome's eastern defenses. In 611, Persian armies entered the Anatolian plateau, pressed into Cappadocia, and seized its capital of Caesarea.[19] Their advance prompted Heraclius to send "messengers with splendid treasures and letters to king Chosroes to request peace." Chosroes supposedly responded,

"The [Roman] kingdom is mine," and said that the embassy had done nothing more than "offer us our own treasure as a gift." He then seized the riches Heraclius sent, killed the ambassadors, and refused to reply further to the message.[20] Although Heraclius recaptured Caesarea in 612, he was defeated in early 613 outside of Antioch.[21] This defeat and another at the Cilician Gates, the pass separating the southeast coast of Anatolia from Syria, severed the last land routes linking Constantinople to the Levant. Chosroes now had the freedom to advance into the rich, poorly defended cities of coastal Syria, Palestine, and eventually Egypt.[22]

The next big blow for the empire came in 614, when Chosroes seized Palestine and the city of Jerusalem. "For three days," Sebeos wrote, "they put to the sword and slew all of the populace of the city" as well as the refugees who had sought safety behind its walls.[23] The death toll must have been immense, because Jerusalem was both a place of refuge and a fortress. It anchored a defensive network of garrisons and fortified monasteries spanning the Galilee and both sides of the Jordan Valley. Its fall caused that entire defensive system to collapse, and when it did, Rome lost the Christian empire's spiritual heartland as well as the holy sites and relics there.

No relic was more precious than the True Cross on which Jesus was believed to have been crucified, an object supposedly rediscovered by Constantine's mother Helena in the 320s. It was still venerated in the Church of the Holy Sepulcher that had been constructed at her direction.[24] Although Chosroes evidently did not damage the church, he took the cross and entrusted it to his Nestorian Christian wife Shirin.

The Roman loss of the Holy Land and the True Cross reverberated across the empire unlike any event since perhaps Alaric's sack of Rome more than 200 years earlier. It seemed inconceivable that a Roman state, governed by an emperor who claimed to be divinely selected, could have so totally lost the favor of God unless its rulers or its citizens had done something dreadfully wrong.

The Palestinian monk Antiochus Strategos listed the possible things that might have caused God to "send on us the evil Persian race as a rod of chastisement and medicine of rebuke." God may have been upset because of the Nika Riot under Justinian, the violence and murders committed by underlings of Phocas, or even the bad behavior of the Blue and Green circus factions.[25] But the "rod of chastisement" continued to strike in 615 when Rome sent another embassy to Chosroes that included the praetorian prefect, the prefect of the city of Constantinople, and a high clerical official. Instead of coming back with a peace treaty, they were arrested and died in Persian captivity.[26]

The peeling away of so much territory deeply disrupted the reeling Roman administrative systems. The loss of most of the east meant that, by the middle of the 610s, Heraclius ran out of gold to coin. He responded by introducing a new silver coin, and "imperial payments were made in it at half their old rates."[27] Soldiers were now paid in bronze rather than gold and silver, but Heraclius even lacked enough bronze to pay them at pre-crisis rates. He was forced to melt down a large bronze ox in the Theodosian forum and shrink the size of the follis just to make payroll.[28] The follis had weighed more than twenty-one grams in the 540s. It was reduced to eight grams by 615 and a puny five grams in the mid-620s. The state also took to clipping the edges of older issues, melting that surplus bronze down, and reissuing the old, misshapen coins with a lower weight.[29]

None of this made the empire any stronger. The Persian advances into Asia Minor were followed by attacks on Roman Egypt. In 619, Alexandria was captured and Rome lost control over the Nile Valley. The fall of Egypt—and the loss of its grain—devastated imperial economic life as much as the capture of Jerusalem had shattered its spiritual equilibrium. Heraclius was forced to suspend the city's grain dole, which caused famine and exacerbated an outbreak of bubonic plague among the weakened Constantinopolitans.[30] In 621, the dire conditions compelled Heraclius to melt down church treasures to get the bullion necessary to run the state.[31]

Chosroes then turned his attention to the conquest of Asia Minor, a campaign he hoped would culminate in the capture of Constantinople and the collapse of the entire Roman state in the Eastern Mediterranean. Heraclius led an army into northern Asia Minor that summer, but then he was compelled to return to Constantinople and negotiate with the Avars, who had laid siege to Thessaloniki and raided as far as the walls of Constantinople. Having seized 270,000 Roman captives, they agreed to a ceasefire only after Heraclius paid them 200,000 solidi and delivered his illegitimate son as a hostage.[32]

Affairs were becoming desperate as the campaigning season began in 624. With the Avar situation seemingly under some control, Heraclius launched another offensive against the Persians that had a different rhetorical justification than any that Romans had used previously. He left Constantinople on the day of the Annunciation, celebrated Easter in Nicomedia, and then met his army at Caesarea in Cappadocia, where he spoke to them about the war in new terms. This was not a war between states or a conflict between two kings, the emperor claimed, but a holy war. His men, Theophanes quotes him as saying, were to "fight to avenge the insult done to God."[33]

In words that are as chilling as they are inspirational, Heraclius said to the soldiers, "Let us stand bravely against the enemy who have inflicted many terrible things on Christians. Let us respect the sovereign state of the Romans and oppose the enemy who are armed with impiety. Let us be inspired with faith that defeats murder." The emperor then concluded, "Our danger is not without reward; instead, it leads to eternal life. Let us stand bravely, and the Lord our God will assist us and destroy the enemy."[34]

The Persian war had become a conflict in which all Romans, from the emperor to the common soldier, now fought not for their state but for their God. The rewards they received for fighting were not the worldly honors and monetary bonuses an emperor could give, but eternal life, a gift that only God could bestow upon them. The fate of the empire, the success of its emperor, and the durability of the Christian religion were now seen as effectively the same.

As Heraclius's army advanced into Persia, it became clear that this religious war would be fought differently from previous Roman invasions and would have different strategic goals. Chosroes himself was at the head of a Persian army of some 40,000 men, and he intended to lead them into Roman territory. His military governors controlled Cilicia and Mesopotamia, the corridors through which one would usually lead an army from Constantinople to Persian territory. And yet Heraclius did not march his army to Cilicia or Mesopotamia, as conventional strategy dictated. He marched north, into the Caucasus, with the intention neither of blunting Chosroes's advance nor of liberating Roman territory. He marched instead into Persia.

No one, least of all Chosroes, expected Heraclius to attack from that direction, and the route the emperor took was not well defended. As he advanced, Heraclius also undertook a campaign of religious vengeance. His army ravaged towns and villages as they progressed through Persian Armenia, and then, when Heraclius learned that Chosroes was in Ganzak, he set upon that city.[35] Chosroes fled, his troops scattered, and Heraclius captured the stragglers. Then he led the army to Thebarmais, which housed a famous Zoroastrian fire temple of particular importance to the Persian king. Heraclius extinguished the sacred fire, polluted the sacred lake near the temple with corpses, and, Theophanes wrote, "burned down the entire temple of fire as well as the entire city."[36]

When the weather turned cold, Heraclius asked his soldiers to purify themselves, so that they might all seek God's help about where to spend the winter. Some in the army wanted to keep pressing on deeper into Persia, while others wanted to winter in Caucasus. None advocated returning to Roman territory. Heraclius then pulled out a Bible "and found a passage that directed him" to spend the season in the Caucasus. He retreated there and released the 50,000 Persian prisoners he held, a prudent action insofar as it limited the supplies he needed. This decision earned him the gratitude of men who, "with tears in their eyes, prayed that he should become the savior of Persia and slay Chosroes, the destroyer of the world."[37]

Heraclius could not match these successes the following year. The Persians had too many troops, and they knew his location. They were thus able to effectively prevent him from making any major advances. Heraclius's biggest success was in keeping his army together, outmaneuvering the forces Chosroes sent against him, and then defeating a large Persian field army when it thought his forces were fleeing.[38]

The war's momentum turned in 626, when the Persians mounted a massive attack on Constantinople. The Persian king sent two armies from the east that were to converge in Asia Minor; meanwhile, the Avars, who had broken their treaty with Rome at his urging, would attack Constantinople from the northwest with both an army and a fleet of canoes.[39] A combined naval and land onslaught like this was the only way Constantinople could fall, but Heraclius and his predecessors had augmented the city's natural defenses to prepare for just this sort of assault. There were large cisterns that stored water in case the aqueduct was cut, granaries stuffed with emergency food in case land or sea approaches to the city were blocked, and fleets of small boats that could, if necessary, swarm and disable any attempt by the Avars to attack the city's seawalls or ferry Persians to Europe.

When Heraclius learned of the threat to Constantinople, he dispatched some troops to reinforce the city. But he did not himself return to it.[40] Instead, he led the bulk of his army in a rapid march along the Euphrates, through the Cilician Gates along the Mediterranean coast, and up into the Anatolian plateau, where he met and defeated one of the two Persian armies that was to attack Constantinople. He then stayed in the east, perhaps hoping that his presence there might induce the remaining Persian forces to quickly withdraw from the Bosporus when their initial assault failed.[41] Heraclius entrusted Constantinople's defense to the soldiers he sent; to the regent Bonus, whom he had left to administer military affairs in the city; and to the patriarch Sergius, who assumed responsibility for marshaling the city's divine protectors. All would play key roles in saving the empire.

By the late spring of 626, a Persian army under the control of Shahrvaraz, one of Chosroes's most powerful generals, arrived on the Asian side of the Bosporus. He and his men captured Chalcedon and began building a camp within view of Constantinople. At the end of June, a cavalry contingent that Heraclius had dispatched retreated to Constantinople rather than face a 30,000-man Avar vanguard in Thrace.[42] About ten days later, these Avars reached the outskirts of the city, "made themselves visible to the Persians," and began communicating "with each other using fire signals."[43] On Tuesday, July 29, 626, the Avar Chagan reached the walls of Constantinople. Patriarch Sergius responded by organizing a procession of priests praying to the Virgin Mary.

The Avar assault began two days later with attacks on two spots along the city's land walls, but the Romans held firm. They continued to do so after a hard day of fighting on Friday, August 1, and another on Saturday, the 2nd. As night fell that Saturday, the Chagan summoned Roman ambassadors to an audience where he sat with three Persians. The unimpressed Romans left the embassy, intercepted the Persians as they were trying to sail across the Bosporus, and beheaded them. One of the heads was sent to the Chagan. Another was placed on the beach at Chalcedon in response to Chosroes's own execution of Roman envoys a decade earlier.[44]

The key moment in the siege came on Sunday. The Avars lacked a proper navy, but the Slavs serving under them were expert at navigating with canoes that could be launched quickly. That morning, a flotilla of Slavic canoes set out to cross the Bosporus and ferry Persian troops to join the Avar attack. Roman sailors, however, intercepted most of the canoes, drowning as many as 4,000 Persian soldiers.[45] After another failed naval assault on Thursday, August 7, the Slavic soldiers in the Chagan's army decided to head home, and "the Chagan was also forced to retreat and follow them."[46] The city was saved.

Heraclius, Bonus, and the soldiers who defended the capital received much-deserved credit for saving the empire, but to the people of Constantinople, the city also owed its salvation to another, much more powerful force. They had been told for years that they were fighting a holy war on behalf of the Christian God. It was then not at all surprising that witnesses reported that it was God who, through "the welcome intercession of his unblemished Mother," Mary, had "saved the city from the utterly godless enemies who encircled it." One report described the Virgin Mary herself fighting attackers atop the city walls.[47] Another claimed she was "present everywhere" when the Avars tried to assault the city by land, and that on August 7, she had "safeguarded the city and all its inhabitants" by sinking Slavic boats before they could assault the seawalls.[48] This victory, the clergyman Theodore Syncellus argued, showed to all the nations of the world the true power of the Christian God to protect his chosen people.[49] It seemed to validate Heraclius's claim that the Romans were fighting both for and with God.

The victory at Constantinople also helped Heraclius to secure a powerful new ally as he returned to offensive operations in 627. A Turkish army at least 40,000 strong attacked the Persians in the Caucasus, and Heraclius joined them as they were besieging Tiflis (modern Tiblisi, in Georgia). The combined force then marched down into Mesopotamia, where Chosroes had positioned troops to block Heraclius from turning west to reconquer Roman land the Persians were occupying. But Heraclius did not turn west. He moved deeper into Persian territory, and he continued to do so even as winter weather descended on the region.

On December 12, a date much later than Roman soldiers usually were in the field, Heraclius ambushed a Persian contingent outside the city of Nineveh and pressed on toward the Persian capital of Ctesiphon. After pausing briefly to celebrate Christmas, he captured at least three royal palaces after Chosroes fled them for the safety of the capital. According to Theophanes, he seized, among other treasures, "300 grain-fed ostriches, 500 grain-fed gazelles, and 100 grain-fed wild asses," as well as "silken garments, rugs, and woven carpets" that he burned because they were too heavy to carry with him.[50] Heraclius also liberated enslaved Roman "captives from Edessa, Alexandria, and other cities" who were held on these sites. Then, after he left each palace, "he demolished these priceless, wonderful, and astonishing structures so that Chosroes might learn how great was the pain the Romans had suffered when their cities were laid waste and burned by him." Heraclius and his soldiers then "thanked God for having wrought such wonders."[51]

Heraclius made one last attempt to negotiate an end to the conflict, but the Persian king rebuffed him and instead ordered his nobles to call up more men. "The hatred of the Persian people against him grew" because of this, but an even more serious threat emerged after Chosroes contracted dysentery following his hasty flight from his winter palaces to Ctesiphon. Fearing that the illness would kill him, Chosroes angered his firstborn son, Siroes, when he announced that one of his younger sons should succeed him instead of his eldest child. Siroes then initiated a plot to overthrow his father. He sent a message to Heraclius in which he promised to end the war and withdraw from Roman territory if Heraclius backed off in order to let the coup attempt play out.[52] Heraclius withdrew toward the Zagros Mountains and waited.

Chosroes was captured and deposed on the night of February 23/24, 628, but heavy snows prevented word of his downfall from reaching Heraclius for another month. In Siroes's letter informing the emperor of his father's death, he made peace with Heraclius, "handed back to him all of the imprisoned Christians and the captives held in every part of Persia," and returned "the precious and life-giving Cross that had been taken from Jerusalem."[53] The emperor then sent a dispatch to Constantinople informing his fellow citizens that the war had ended. The emperor's letter, which is preserved in the *Chronicon Paschale*, began with an exhortation: "Let all the earth raise a cry to God . . . For fallen is Chosroes, opponent of God."[54] Chosroes's son Siroes, the emperor continued, "killed the ingrate, arrogant, blaspheming opponent of God by a most cruel death," so that all might "might know that Jesus, who was born of Mary . . . is God almighty."[55]

Heraclius withdrew to Armenia, and his envoy negotiated a treaty reestablishing the Persian-Roman frontier along the lines agreed in 387. Rome regained the territory in Asia Minor, Mesopotamia, Syria, Palestine, and Egypt that had been taken by Chosroes during the 610s, and Persia resumed control over the lands Maurice had taken as compensation for restoring Chosroes to the throne in 591.[56] The implementation of the treaty proved difficult, however. Shahrvaraz, the Persian general in command in Egypt, refused to leave Roman territory, and Heraclius lacked the capacity to force him to do so.[57] When Siroes died a few months later, Heraclius agreed to back Shahrvaraz's bid to seize the throne if his army would retreat across the newly agreed upon border.

Shahrvaraz lost the throne less than two months after winning power in April 630, but the new sovereign, Boran, updated the agreement with Heraclius, so that Rome gained more Persian territory in exchange for security guarantees. Although the border between the two empires now returned to where it had been before Phocas's coup, the immense destruction caused by this last great war between Rome and Persia left both empires far weaker than they had been for centuries.[58] And with Islamic armies consolidating power in Arabia, this was the worst possible time for both major Near Eastern powers to have exhausted themselves.

Chapter 33

The Coming of Islam

631–690

O N MARCH 21, 630, Heraclius led a procession of soldiers and members of the imperial family to Jerusalem, carrying with him the locked, unopened box containing the True Cross that he had taken back from the Persians.[1] After parading through the city, Heraclius returned the sacred object to its rightful place and "distributed alms and money for incense to all the churches and inhabitants of the city."[2] Instead of waiting to celebrate his own prowess in the capital, he had undertaken a new sort of Roman imperial triumph—one in the empire's holiest city and designed to mark the end of a Christian holy war.

But a more traditional triumph also awaited at the end of the army's long march to Constantinople. The ninth-century Constantinopolitan patriarch Nicephorus describes how Heraclius entered the capital to cheering crowds. They flocked to greet him, to view the "four elephants which he paraded at the Hippodrome," and to gather up the coins he distributed to those in the stands. Heraclius then began restoring the church treasures he had taken to fund the later stages of the war with funds seized "from the royal treasury" of Persia.[3]

It was easy to imagine the dawn of a new Golden Age from the unconquered capital of a restored Christian Roman Empire, but the effects of a generation of warfare were harder to ignore in the provinces to which Roman rule now returned. Although Heraclius had both lost and regained Mesopotamia, Syria, Palestine, and Egypt, Rome had been absent from these lands for a long time. A baby born on the day that Jerusalem had fallen to the Persians would have been nearly seventeen years old when Heraclius led the True Cross back to the city. This meant that an entire generation of people in the Levant had grown up not as Roman citizens but as Persian subjects living under Persian institutions. They did not automatically see a Roman restoration as something natural, or even as something good. The Persians simply vanished, and until the Romans returned, the people of these lands lived in an administrative vacuum with no state exercising any real control over them at all.

A group of Jews in northern Mesopotamia decided to take advantage of this vacuum by seizing Edessa. Sebeos reports, "When they saw that the Persian army had departed from them and had left the city in peace, they shut the gate, fortified themselves within it, and did not allow the army of the Roman Empire to enter." Heraclius laid siege, and the Jewish leaders negotiated an agreement to open the city gate in exchange for permission to remain safely in their homes. Nevertheless, the Jews did not trust the emperor and went south to the Arabian Peninsula to seek protection from a group of Arabs inspired by the religious teachings of "a certain man from among the sons of Ishmael whose name was Mahmet."[4] We know him as Muhammad.

The Jewish seizure of Edessa illustrates how state power evaporated in the Eastern Roman world of the early 630s. Edessa was a well-fortified city equipped to sustain itself through long and difficult sieges mounted by armies, and it had been many years since no soldiers were in the area. But the Persians were gone, the Romans lacked the manpower to quickly regarrison cities like it, and no civilian administrators would turn up without military support. The Roman Empire had worked for centuries to govern its citizens with capable administrators, ensure their rights with the best legal system in the ancient world, and protect their lives and property with a professional army. None of this was true any longer. None of the people living in Syria, Palestine, Mesopotamia, or Egypt had seen a Roman governor or used the Roman legal system for a decade or more. And no one, anywhere, had much faith in the Roman professional army.

Heraclius provoked an additional crisis as he tried to restore the systems of government that had once made the Roman state work. He was a Chalcedonian Christian emperor hoping to reintegrate a set of provinces that, aside from Palestine, were both overwhelmingly anti-Chalcedonian and accustomed to dealing with a Persian ruler who did not care about their views on the nature of Christ. Heraclius did attempt to reconcile the various Christian groups in his state through symbolic steps, such as taking Communion from the leader of the Nestorian church that had split from Constantinople following the Council of Ephesus two hundred years earlier, and meeting with the anti-Chalcedonian patriarch of Antioch.[5] But Heraclius, who was told that he was quite literally "adorned by God with victories" like King David, had little patience for the protestations of "heretical" church leaders.[6] He quickly tired of the seemingly endless theological divisions among his citizens.

After an abortive first attempt to push a theological compromise on his newly restored empire, Heraclius and Sergius, the heroic patriarch who had led the defense of Constantinople against the Avars, began advocating an alternative doctrine called *monotheletism*.[7] Monotheletism held that Christ possessed a single, unified will that transcended his human and divine natures. Because it focused on Christ's will rather than his nature, they hoped it might attract universal support. It did not. Anti-Chaldeconian populations in Egypt and Syria resisted this new formulation and, losing patience, Heraclius turned the power of the empire against them. Sources in both Syria and Egypt describe forces loyal to Heraclius seizing church property, exiling bishops, and forcing monks to agree to the doctrine.[8] Once rumors of a persecution of anti-Chalcedonians began to spread, Heraclius's theological compromise was doomed.

The emperor could perhaps have chipped away at this resistance, but, just as Roman authority was returning to the Near East, Arab armies inspired by the prophet Muhammad began testing Roman frontiers. The prophet himself is said to have sent a message of peace to Heraclius informing him of the revelations of Islam, but if the message was sent, Heraclius failed to appreciate its significance. Instead of a negotiation, Muslim-Christian relations in Rome's historical territory began with violence, when a group of Christians killed an early Muslim convert at a fortified location east of the Dead Sea in 628. Arab forces invaded the newly restored Roman province of Arabia the following year, but they were defeated by the local Roman commander and Arab auxiliaries allied with him near Karak in modern Jordan.[9]

Arab pressure on Roman territory increased after Muhammad died in 632. In 634, a large group of raiders erupted across the Roman frontier near Areopolis (the modern Jordanian city of Rabba), a strategic site on the road linking Syria to Arabia. They seized the city while other Arab forces advanced as far as Gaza and Caesarea. They did not capture either city, but the Arabs did score several victories, first defeating a Roman detachment sent to confront them in Palestine and then a field army commanded by Heraclius's brother in Syria. Roman troops scattered to garrison the walled cities of the region, but they could not protect all of them. Over the next two years, Arab armies seized Bostra, the provincial capital of Scythopolis, and the strategically important Syrian cities of Damascus and Emesa.[10]

Emesa's capture forced Heraclius to organize a large Roman field army that could confront the invaders.[11] The Muslim Arab general Khalid ibn al-Walid pulled his scattered forces out of the Syrian cities and concentrated their manpower near the Yarmouk River to prevent the Romans from moving south into Palestine and Roman Arabia.[12] When the two armies finally engaged, the battle played out over the course of a few days in the summer of 636 until, on August 20, the Arab cavalry charged as a strong wind blew dust in the faces of the Romans. The disoriented Roman heavy cavalry left the infantry unprotected along their flanks, and their lines collapsed. Many Roman soldiers were trampled by Arab horses. Others fell into ravines as they tried to escape. All told, perhaps as many as 40,000 Roman troops lost their lives in the ensuing slaughter.[13]

Heraclius learned of the devastating Roman defeat at Yarmouk while he was still in Antioch. He responded rationally by ordering Roman forces in Syria and Mesopotamia to fall back to more defensible territory in southeastern Anatolia while he reinforced Roman Egypt with forces drawn from the Balkans. A Syriac chronicle says that, as Heraclius departed Syria, "he was supposed to have said: 'Farewell Syria!' as if he despaired of ever seeing her again." But the emperor also understood that the rest of the empire could still be saved if he pulled back what remained of the Roman army. The retreating soldiers were ordered "to ravage indiscriminately, as if Syria was already enemy territory," so as to establish a no-man's-land between Roman defenses and the cities the emperor had effectively abandoned to the Arabs.[14]

Romans in Syria did not quite know how to react after the Arabs rushed back in. Residents of Damascus held out for as long as they could, but, "seeing that there was no one who could save them," they finally surrendered.[15] In Emesa, residents "expected reinforcements to come and rescue them, but none came. Then they lost their will to fight and sued for peace." Meanwhile, in Palestine, "the Palestinians and the inhabitants of coastal settlements all congregated within the walls of Jerusalem," but Jerusalem too eventually capitulated, probably in later 637.[16] Gaza and Ascalon also fell that year. By the end of 638, Arab armies had seized or negotiated the surrender of Antioch, Aleppo, and the inland Syrian cities. The Roman navy continued to resupply some coastal cities, but in 640, Caesarea, the last provincial capital in Syria and Palestine still under Roman control, finally fell.

In the meantime, Heraclius repositioned Roman forces. He stationed troops along the edge of the Anti-Taurus mountain range that protected southern and eastern Anatolia, in the eastern Anatolian and Armenian highlands that protected northern Asia Minor and Roman Armenia, and around the Egyptian city of Pelusium so they could prevent Arab troops from entering Roman Egypt.

The Anatolian lines held, but Arab armies captured Pelusium in late 639. By early 640, Arab forces had advanced as far as Egyptian Babylon on the site of modern Cairo, the location of a fortress that represented the key node in Roman defenses separating the Nile Delta from the fertile lands and cities of Upper Egypt. When Babylon fell in December, the Nile Valley fell with it. Then, in late 641, the empress Martina negotiated the handoff of Alexandria and the rest of Egypt to the Arabs in exchange for the peaceful withdrawal of Roman forces.[17] Aside from a brief reoccupation of Alexandria by Roman marines in 645, Egypt was permanently lost to the empire.

HERACLIUS DIED ON February 11, 641, after more than three decades in power. He was succeeded by his son Heraclius Constantine, but the new emperor died a few months later. Heraclius's second wife, Martina, and her son Heraclonas briefly took over, but they were deposed, mutilated, and sent into exile. By the end of the year, the new Roman emperor was Heraclius's grandson, the eleven-year-old Constans II.

Constans II ruled from 641 to 668, and his son Constantine IV ruled from 668 to 685. The nearly relentless Arab assaults on Roman territory and the paucity of surviving Roman literary and documentary evidence, however, make it difficult to reconstruct these four decades. In some cases, even the years in which major events occurred are disputed. These years do, however, reveal the general ways in which the Roman state refashioned itself administratively, economically, and spiritually into a smaller, more homogeneous polity. By doing so, it became better equipped to survive in a world where, for the first time in nearly 1,000 years, it was competing against a larger, richer, and more powerful adversary.

The headline stories across those four decades center on the loss of imperial territory to the Arabs in the southern Mediterranean and the regular raids that Arab armies launched into Asia Minor. After the Romans surrendered Egypt, Arab armies advanced along the coast and quickly absorbed Cyrenaica. Tripolitania fell in 643, and Arab forces came within 250 miles of Carthage before retreating in 648. In Asia Minor, Arab raiders penetrated deep into Cappadocia and Phrygia in 647. Three years later, Arab navies forced the Romans to abandon Cyprus. In the meantime, Arab soldiers also pushed to the east, and by 651 their caliph also controlled the entirety of what had been the Persian Empire. One could now begin to question whether Rome would soon disappear just as Sassanian Persia did.

An Arab civil war gave the Romans a reprieve between 656 and 661, but raids began again after it concluded. These built up to a series of attempts to capture Constantinople in the late 660s and 670s. In the most serious of these, which most historians believe began in 674, the Romans beat back a land assault and then destroyed much of the Arab fleet with a new weapon called Greek fire. Although the precise formula for Greek fire is no longer known, it was apparently a napalm-like incendiary substance that Romans pumped onto ships with hoses and ignited. They used it to burn the vessels as well as the horses, men, and anything else on board. It even burned on water.[18] Although Greek fire was both terrifying and effective against naval attacks, it still took years of fighting before the Romans could expel the Arabs from the last of their forward bases in Anatolia. In 678, the Romans and Arabs agreed to a peace treaty that required the Arabs to pay the trivial sum of 3,000 solidi a year (which is about what one would pay for a single thirty-five-acre farm in Egypt at the turn of the seventh century).[19] The peace broke down in the early 680s, but a new agreement was signed in 688 or 689 after some Roman successes saw them push back into Cilicia.

The empire also struggled to maintain authority over territory on other fronts. The Avar defeat outside of Constantinople in 626 had created a vacuum in the southern Balkans that the empire's preoccupation with the east prevented it from exploiting. Instead of Roman rule returning to these lands, the new Slavic settlers and what remained of the indigenous Roman population in the interior of the peninsula spent most of the seventh century frozen in a state-less anarchy, where Slavic chieftains, rather than Roman governors, regulated local affairs. It was only in the fortified coastal settlements that Constantinople could resupply by sea that one found a Roman imperial presence, though even this could seem tenuous. The well-fortified city of Thessaloniki, for example, came under assault repeatedly in the later seventh century. The most serious attack, an unsuccessful siege by a collection of Slavic tribes in 677, prompted the composition of a literary work in which locals credited the city's salvation to St. Demetrius, a warrior saint with the power to guide merchant ships filled with grain to the city. The saint was even said to ride out to engage in battle with the invaders himself. He was there always, whereas the Roman state could only intervene when the situation in the east was calm.

The Bulgars, a new, much more potent player, entered the Balkan scene around 680. They had been subjects of the Avars, but had shaken off Avar control with Roman help. They asked the emperor Constantine IV for permission to settle in territory beyond the Danube that was ostensibly Roman but was in practice ungoverned land. Constantine denied this request, and the Bulgars went there anyway. Constantine then led Roman troops to try to dislodge them. When Constantine left before the campaign concluded, however, the panicked soldiers were defeated. They were compelled to recognize Bulgar control over the land they were occupying and to pay an annual tribute to them.

The situation in Roman Italy was similar, though Roman losses were less dramatic there. The empire was only able to engage sporadically in offensive operations in Italy, but the most notable of these, a failed attempt by Constans II to reconquer Lombard areas in 663, proved so costly that the emperor "dismantled all the city's bronze decorations" when he visited Rome and "removed the bronze tiles from the roof of the church of *Sancta Maria ad Martyres* [the Pantheon]."[20] Constans was assassinated in the Sicilian city of Syracuse in 668 amid rumors that he might try to move the capital from Constantinople. The west would never again see this sort of sustained attention from a Roman ruler.

Constans's stay in the central Mediterranean represents the most dramatic attempt to recalibrate how the Roman state utilized the resources it still possessed, but it was not the only such effort. Rome still required large, well-trained armies to defend its southeastern and northeastern frontiers from Arab attacks, but the loss of Syria, Palestine, and Egypt had devastated Roman revenues. It has been estimated that these lost territories in the Eastern Mediterranean may have contributed as much as three-quarters of the total taxes collected in the empire in the year 600. Additional territory was lost between 650 and 700, so that by the turn of the eighth century the Roman Empire was likely generating only 15 percent of the annual revenue it had been collecting a century earlier.[21]

This collapse in revenues forced the state to change the way it compensated its soldiers. It could no longer afford to pay them a regular salary, so instead it provided troops with irregular cash payments, tax privileges, and in-kind compensation that included some form of property ownership.[22] In lieu of large field armies traveling great distances to fight wherever they were needed, the later seventh-century empire had armies based in specified regions that were tasked with the long-term defense of their assigned areas. Anatolian soldiers were placed in one of two armies, the Armeniakon in the north and the Anatolikon in the south. A third army, the Thrakesion, was stationed in western Asia Minor. The Opsikion army, which included the imperial bodyguard, took responsibility for the area around Constantinople and northwestern Asia Minor. Another branch of military personnel manned the Roman fleets. When the armies engaged in offensive actions or the government otherwise needed to direct large quantities of supplies to a region, a group of officials called *kommerkiarioi*, who were ostensibly connected to the customs offices, handled the collection and distribution of materials.[23]

This system of support created a new type of Roman army. Even into the reign of Heraclius, Roman soldiers were heterogeneous groups of people drawn from all over the empire who assumed they might be ordered to campaign far from home. The later seventh-century Roman soldier, however, stayed in the same region for years. Many of these men married local women, had children who grew up in the same place their fathers had lived, and left their property in these towns to their children. Many of the children born of these relationships later enlisted. In the course of a couple of generations, these developments transformed the regionally diverse, extremely mobile Roman armies of the high empire and late antiquity into much more homogeneous forces that were closely tied to the places in which they were based.[24]

Because soldiers and their commanders now lived, worshipped, and grew up in the areas where they served, they also shared the religious and cultural ideas of the people around them. This posed a new challenge to the emperors in Constantinople, who were used to working on theological questions with bishops, not soldiers. Soldiers, however, were living with and suffering alongside the people in the borderlands that the emperors could no longer protect. They had little patience for the sorts of claims of ultimate imperial religious authority that had seemed compelling in the age of Justinian. This was especially true for Roman Christians who believed the misfortunes that arose in the empire could be due to the impiety of their fellow citizens or their emperor.

It was the army's new, regionally specific theological concerns that ultimately doomed the Roman experiment with monotheletism, the theological formula Heraclius had introduced to bring Syria and Egypt back into communion with Constantinople in the heady days after his Persian victory. Monotheletism had always struggled to gain a footing among Latin speakers in the west, but the Arab conquests and the collapse of Roman imperial power in the Middle East further undercut its appeal. One prominent monothelete opponent named Maximus the Confessor even claimed that the "barbarous desert people overrunning" the empire emerged "because of the great number of our sins" as impious Romans embraced a heretical idea.[25]

These criticisms of monotheletism were so powerful that they helped catalyze the revolt of the North African army in the 640s and another in Italy in the 650s.[26] Both revolts failed, but the western armies' hostility to monotheletism was balanced by an equally enthusiastic embrace of it among Eastern Roman soldiers. When Constantine IV called an ecumenical council in 680–681 to condemn the doctrine, he ended up arresting, imprisoning, and mutilating some of the leaders of the Anatolikon army in order to suppress a coup by angry monotheletes.[27] This did not calm the political churn caused by the disconnection between the religious policies of the emperor and the beliefs of his armies. The people of the empire agreed that they had angered God, but they did not agree about how they had angered Him and were unsure how to return to His good graces. And while Romans struggled with this question, Arab leaders began preparing for their greatest attack yet on the empire.

Chapter 34

Iconoclasm

690–775

IN 692, CONSTANTINE IV's son, the Roman emperor Justinian II, made the foolish decision to scrap a peace treaty that he had agreed to with the Arab caliph Abd al-Malik three years earlier. That agreement was a brilliantly balanced document that forced both sides to abandon their most optimistic war ambitions. Rome accepted that it would not recover Syria or other lost lands in the Eastern Mediterranean, and the Arabs accepted that they would not seize Constantinople.

The treaty also required both sides to surrender some of the strategic assets that had helped them in the conflict that just ended. The Arab Empire was now much larger and wealthier than the Roman Empire, so the caliph agreed to pay the significant subsidy of 1,000 gold coins a day, a sum that may have represented almost 20 percent of the Roman Empire's annual budget in the late 680s.[1] The Romans agreed to allow at least 12,000 Mardaites, a group of Christian rebels that the Arabs had failed to suppress, to move from Arab to Roman territory.[2] The two empires also agreed to share the tax revenue collected from the island of Cyprus equally. In exchange for abandoning unrealistic war goals, the Romans became richer and the Arabs consolidated control of the Lebanese and Syrian highlands. The revenue sharing in Cyprus gave both empires incentives to keep the peace going forward.

Individual Romans trusted the agreement enough that they began to return to the no-man's-land along the Anatolian frontier and the devastated coastal Roman cities that had been depopulated by the Roman-Arab fighting. The calm on the eastern frontier enabled Justinian to redeploy some of his troops to the west, because they were no longer needed to guard against the Arabs. When he led this army through Thrace and Macedonia to open a land corridor between Constantinople and Thessaloniki, it was the first time Roman forces had been able to do this in decades. Roman forces also seized tens of thousands of Slavic prisoners that Justinian forcibly moved to the part of Western Anatolia where the Opsikion army was based.[3] He then "raised an army of 30,000" from among them "whom he equipped and named 'the Chosen People,'" and placed them under the command of one of their noblemen.[4]

The 30,000 "Chosen People" gave Justinian a field army that could campaign beyond its home region, and this made Justinian overconfident. He soon began to test the limits of what Abd al-Malik would permit him to do without attacking. In 690 or 691, Justinian undermined the agreement to share tax revenue from Cyprus by moving a segment of the Cypriot population to the city of Cyzicus, which had been devastated when it had served as the base of operations for an earlier Arab attack on Constantinople.[5] He also refused to accept as tribute any new coins minted by Abd al-Malik. Until the 690s, Arab coins had human figures on their fronts, in imitation of the Roman and Sassanian Persian coins that had circulated in the western and eastern parts of their empire before the Muslim conquests. Justinian II, however, had placed a large portrait of Christ, rather than an image of the emperor, on the front of Roman solidi. This was a coin design the Muslim caliph could not reasonably imitate. Thus he had started to replace the Christ images with "the name of their prophet, Muhammad," written in Arabic, on one side, "and, on the other side, . . . the name of Abd al-Malik."[6]

When Justinian refused to accept the new coins, Theophanes reports that the caliph's envoys "begged that peace should not be broken" and explained that the coins remained the same weight and purity but simply had a different appearance, because "the Arabs could not endure the Roman imprint on their own currency." Justinian "mistook this plea as a sign of fear" and mobilized his army to head east.[7] The emperor was counting in particular on his new force of Chosen People to overwhelm what he believed to be a numerically inferior Arab force.

The armies met near Sebastopolis, and although Justinian's army was well positioned, the fight turned into a rout. Some Roman troops fled, and Justinian's band of Chosen People defected to the Arabs. Justinian had gambled that he might do better than what the peace treaty had given him—and lost, badly. Now he was stuck fighting a war against a larger, richer adversary while struggling to make up the revenue and manpower his recklessness had cost the empire. The patriarch Nicephorus's history echoes a fear that many Romans shared that something more severe than fiscal and military deficiencies awaited Rome. They believed Justinian had broken both secular and sacred law when he had violated Rome's peace with the Arabs. They therefore understood the defections of Roman forces at Sebastopolis to be a sign that God disapproved of the emperor's conduct.

This sense of divine anger contributed to Justinian II's fall from power, followed by mutilation, and then by exile to Crimea in 695. Following his departure, the empire saw six different short-lived emperors rise to power and fall over a period of just 22 years, a degree of imperial turnover completely unfamiliar to Romans who had known only 13 Roman emperors in the preceding 204 years. The two decades between the accession of Leontius in 695 and the fall of Theodosius III in 717 also differed from the preceding two centuries because the regional Roman armies, which were manned by people who increasingly shared the same religious outlook, took the lead in facilitating regime changes. Leontius, for example, lost power in 698 because of a coup by naval officers based in southern Anatolia.[8] Local commanders of Anatolian armies also overthrew the emperor Philippicus in 713, his replacement Anastasius II in 715, and Anastasius's replacement Theodosius III in 717.

The two most notable, and dangerous, innovations in this Roman game of musical thrones involved Justinian II's restoration in 705, when he returned from exile to depose and kill Tiberius III, the emperor who had been elevated in the naval officers' coup of 698. Justinian took the capital with the support of an army of Bulgars sent by their king Tervel, the first time a Roman emperor had taken over the state using a non-Roman force since the fifth century AD. And Justinian II's return was much more brutal than the fifth-century, barbarian-backed coups by figures such as Avitus.[9] Justinian not only broke with the recent tradition of mutilating and exiling former emperors by killing his two immediate predecessors. He also purged regional military commanders and mutilated the patriarch of Constantinople. He rewarded Tervel with expensive presents, "invested him with an imperial mantle, and proclaimed him Caesar."[10]

When the emperor Philippicus overthrew Justinian II in 711, he did so in a fashion that combined the regionally specific religious rebellions of the seventh century with the new willingness to involve non-Romans in Roman civil wars. He advanced on Constantinople with help from the Khazars, a powerful group based in what is now southern Ukraine, and the backing of Roman devotees of monotheletism who lived in Crimea.[11] Once he took power, he restored monotheletism by delegitimizing the councils called by Constantine IV and Justinian II in which it had been condemned.[12] When he fell from power in 713, the empire pivoted again, restoring the authority of those councils and renouncing the theology favored by Philippicus's backers. The deacon Agathon, who lived through this political and religious chaos, lamented "the frightful troubles which have come to pass . . . as a result of our sins" and the "massive destruction" that was now threatening the survival of the state.

Fears of Rome's collapse surfaced because of how its internal instability coincided with a rapid deterioration in its military capabilities. The Roman state that had fought the Arabs to a standstill in the 680s could not easily rebuild the manpower and skilled personnel it had lost at Sebastopolis. Although there were some scattered successes, the long-term trajectory of Rome's war with the Arabs was not positive.[13] The empire lost Carthage to the Arabs in 698, a defeat that quickly led to the collapse of Roman Africa.[14] Then, in 713, Roman envoys visiting the caliphate's capital of Damascus saw evidence that the caliph was amassing land and sea forces that appeared to be building up for an attack on Constantinople. The next year, news reached the capital that an Arab "fleet had sailed up from Alexandria to Phoinix [probably in Lebanon] with a view to cutting cypress wood" that they might use to build more ships.[15]

It is to his immense credit that, despite the precarity of his own position, the emperor Anastasius II decided to prepare the capital to resist what he believed would be a major Arab attack intended to capture Constantinople and eliminate the Roman state. According to Nicephorus, he ordered that "each inhabitant of the City [of Constantinople] could remain only if he had provisions for a period of three years," while anyone else should flee to wherever they felt safest. He then "carefully restored the wall of the City, refurbished the military engines, stored a great quantity of provisions in the City, and fortified it" so it would be prepared to withstand an attack.[16] When the Arab army and fleet eventually arrived, only the defenses of the capital would allow the empire to survive.

DESPITE HIS CAREFUL planning, neither Anastasius II nor his successor Theodosius III held the throne when the Arab assault began. It was instead a third emperor, Leo III, who led Constantinople's defense. Born in Commagene, Roman territory that sat alongside the empire's frontier with the Arabs, Leo was conversant, and maybe fluent, in Arabic and had spent time as a young man in the border region where Christian Roman and Muslim Arab influences overlapped.[17] As an adult, he had served as the commander of the troops of the Anatolikon army, the group drawn largely from areas around his hometown. He was so familiar with developments in the caliphate of Abd al-Malik and his successors that later authors called him "Saracen-minded Leo" and criticized him for "his Arab mentality."[18]

Leo took power on March 25, 717, when Arab forces were already beginning their advance. That summer, their armies captured Pergamum and Sardis on the Aegean coast of Asia Minor and then advanced on the capital, supported by an armada of 1,800 ships.[19] On August 15, the Arabs arrived outside Constantinople and began a siege that would last for thirteen months.

Although the Arab attackers far outnumbered the Roman defenders, they were hindered by the challenges of overcoming the formidable natural defenses of Constantinople while enduring weather unlike anything most of them had experienced. The Arab lines prevented any supplies from entering the city by land, but Constantinople was surrounded on three sides by the treacherous currents of the Bosporus and protected by Roman ships equipped with Greek fire. After an early battle saw the emperor "burn twenty Arab ships after breaking their lines," Nicephorus reports, Arab fleets completely avoided the straits in fear of "the artificial fire of the Romans."[20]

Roman naval prowess sustained the city during the summer and fall, forcing the Arabs to endure a "very severe winter in which so much snow fell that the ground was invisible for 100 days." Large numbers of men, horses, camels, and other supply animals starved. When spring came, the Roman navy sprang back into action, capturing the food and weapons carried by a flotilla that the caliph had sent from Egypt to resupply his army and then destroying the ships.[21]

This victory opened the sea up for Roman fishing boats to bring food to the capital and severed the supply lines of the Arabs. The chronicler Theophanes vividly describes Arab soldiers reduced to eating their dead camels and bread made from "their own dung, which they leavened." Malnutrition and poor hygiene led to a plague in the Arab camp, and while it was raging the Bulgars decided to attack the weakened invaders. In the end, they "massacred 22,000 Arabs," forcing the rest of the beleaguered Arab army to retreat. They left the city on August 15, the date that Romans celebrated the Dormition of the

Virgin Mary (commemorating how she was taken into heaven while asleep). Roman sources dutifully credited "God and His all-holy virgin Mother" for "fulfilling those who truly call on him" despite their sins.[22] No Arab army would ever again threaten Constantinople.

LEO'S VICTORY AT Constantinople left him strong enough to break the fever of rebellion that had so disoriented Romans for most of the past generation. One challenge, which arose when the military commander of Sicily and Southern Italy elevated one of his soldiers named Basil as emperor during the period when Constantinople was besieged, collapsed in 718 as soon as messengers loyal to Leo arrived in Syracuse and informed the soldiers that the capital remained Roman. The Syracusans "immediately acclaimed Leo as emperor and surrendered both Basil and the magistrates who had been appointed by him." They promptly beheaded the revolutionaries, "[preserving] their heads in vinegar so they could be sent to the emperor."[23]

The following year, Leo suppressed a revolt in which the former emperor Anastasius II "attempted to regain the empire" with help from the Bulgars. Leo's agents intercepted letters Anastasius sent to the Bulgars, "confiscated his possessions," and sent Roman supporters of the revolt into exile. The Bulgars were told "that they should embrace peace and surrender [Leo's] enemies." They did. The Bulgars asked for the emperor's forgiveness and "sent [Anastasius] along with the archbishop of Thessaloniki and many other captives to the emperor." Leo ordered them beheaded and "performed an equestrian race in which he paraded their heads affixed to poles through the Hippodrome."[24] Everyone, both Roman and non-Roman, now understood that usurpations would be punished most brutally.

While Leo could suppress revolts and cordon off Roman internal politics from the military intervention of non-Roman neighbors, many Romans still felt stalked by disasters they did not know how to escape. Some of these fears grew out of the conflict with the Arabs, which was still unresolved. Even after their victory at the walls of Constantinople, the Romans remained on the defensive into the 720s. The Arab strategy had shifted from knocking out the empire with one great blow to progressively chipping away at Roman control of Asia Minor. In 727, Arab armies advanced as far as Nicaea, a city less than 100 miles from Constantinople.[25] As they went, they forced Romans to shelter behind city walls, leaving their fields to be plundered and their homes destroyed.

Terrifying natural disasters also shook Roman territory. In the summer of 726, the caldera below the volcanic island of Thera (modern Santorini) began to emit "a vapor as from a fiery furnace" until "pumice stones as big as hills" shot into the air. These fell all around the Aegean, "so that the entire surface of the sea was filled with floating pumice."[26] Nicephorus describes how, near Thera, the volcano raised a new island in the sea and caused the water to become "so hot that one could not even touch it."[27]

Listing these misfortunes is one thing. Experiencing them is something very different. Subsistence fishermen, farmers, and merchants in the Aegean struggled to support their families as pumice rained down from the sky, clogging the waterways and damaging the boats of the people desperate enough to venture out to sea. Many starved while waiting for things to return to normal. The Romans who were stuck in besieged cities had a different sort of terrifying experience. Being trapped in Constantinople may have been slightly less horrifying than in other places. The city was immense, but by the eighth century its population was much smaller than it had been under Justinian I, when perhaps 500,000 Romans had lived there.[28] Although it would still have been extremely uncomfortable for people confined to the city at this time, the large cisterns, the huge expanse of land between the city center and the land walls, and the resupply missions by sea moderated some of the worst effects of a siege.

Sieges were much harder to endure in the smaller cities of Asia Minor that the Arabs attacked in the 720s. Their fortified urban cores were much smaller than Constantinople, and when they came under siege their tightly packed areas housed both urban families and residents of the countryside. In the city of Nicaea, for example, the fortified area was so small that it took less than twenty minutes to walk along the city's main street from the western gate of the seawalls to the eastern gate that travelers used from the land side. A trip along the city's main north-south axis took about the same amount of time. If the city was besieged, tens of thousands of people had to fit into this constrained space where they could not walk more than a mile in any direction—for days or months at a time. The food supply dwindled, and the risk of disease spiked. People struggled with the unknowable question of how long the siege would last. In their darkest moments, Roman families wondered when the city would fall. And, if it did, whether they would be killed, raped, enslaved, or permanently separated from one another.

Eighth-century Romans believed that the Aegean boiled, the sky rained stones, and the Arabs advanced because Romans, collectively, had sinned and failed to repent. They continued to pray to the Christian God, his saints, and the angels, in some cases using icons with the images of divine figures to focus their prayers. As the disasters continued, many Romans began to doubt that this sort of prayer alone sufficed. They prayed, but the catastrophes around them seemed to say that the way they prayed no longer worked. God remained angry.

Some of the stories that appear in later Roman sources describing the 710s and 720s show the lengths Romans went to in their efforts to alleviate their desperation and terror. Nicephorus describes a terrifying scene in Pergamum in 717. As a large Arab army encircled the walls, "the inhabitants of the city took a pregnant girl who was about to give birth to her first child, cut her open and, removing the infant inside of her, boiled it in a pot of water, into which the men who were about to fight dipped their sleeves." Unfortunately, this vile ritual only made God angrier. The Pergamene defenders "were overtaken by divine wrath so that their hands were incapable of taking up weapons and, because they could do nothing, the enemy took the city without a fight." Strange, brutal human sacrifices clearly did not help.[29]

In 727, however, a Roman soldier defending the city of Nicaea during an Arab siege tried something different that appeared to work. An Arab army of perhaps as many as 100,000 soldiers surrounded the city. On the day before their final assault, Theophanes writes, a soldier named Constantine "saw an icon of the Mother of God" posted above the city gate. "He picked up a stone and threw it at the icon and, after [the icon] fell, he broke it and trampled it." When the Arabs attacked the following day, the city held out until the Arabs withdrew.[30]

Unlike the human sacrifice that had precipitated the fall of Pergamum to the Arabs in 717, the trampling of the icon of the Virgin Mary in Nicaea seemed to have saved the city, despite the size of the Arab force and the breaches in its walls. And the emperor noticed. When Leo heard of the disasters afflicting the empire, Nicephorus reports, he "considered them to be signs of divine wrath and pondered what might have caused them."[31] Theophanes tells us that the events in Nicaea prompted Leo to assume that the Roman use of religious images lay at the heart of the empire's problems, and that Leo "blamed all the emperors, bishops, and Christian people who lived before him for committing idolatry in worshiping the holy and venerable icons."[32] He then summoned Germanus, the patriarch of Constantinople, and told him to agree to "the removal of the holy icons."[33] Germanus refused to do this without an ecumenical council endorsing the change, so Leo replaced him with a more pliant patriarch. "From that time forward," the pro-icon patriarch Nicephorus wrote, "many pious men who would not accept the imperial doctrine suffered many punishments and tortures."[34] This religious revolution is known today as *Iconoclasm*, a term that literally means the "destruction of images."

The vociferous later Roman reaction against Iconoclasm and the loss of most of the sources that supported the suppression of images has largely obscured the exact path of the empire under Leo.[35] It is hard to say for certain what Leo believed; what specific actions he undertook to shape the empire so that its religious practices might conform to those beliefs; and in what chronological order those actions occurred. We can, however, say that Leo sought to deemphasize icons and instead to elevate the symbolic power of the cross, an image that Iconoclasts would say had the power to "turn the enemy to flight and slaughter the barbarians," as an inscription put it.[36] We can also say that, whatever else he did, Leo led a military revival. It culminated in 740, when the armies led by Leo and his son, the future emperor Constantine V, defeated the Arabs in battle outside of Akroinon in Asia Minor, killing thousands of soldiers and two Arab commanders. This victory, the most substantial battlefield defeat the Romans had inflicted on the Arabs to date, seemed to vindicate Leo's theological path.

OUR PRO-ICON SOURCES' opacity about exactly what happened and when becomes even more problematic when they describe the reign of Leo's son, Constantine V, who acted much more aggressively against icon veneration than his father ever did. Constantine shared his father's suspicion of religious images, and when he took power following Leo's death in 741, pro-icon authors recount a coup launched by Constantine's brother-in-law Artabazos, the military commander of the Opsikion army, that aimed to "give him the empire because he was orthodox."[37] Artabazos spread a rumor that Constantine had died while leading forces to the east. He then entered the capital without opposition "and speedily restored the holy images of the saints."[38]

In one way, Artabazos's rebellion harkened back to the theologically infused insurrections of the later seventh and early eighth centuries. It does seem that the Constantinopolitan populace and the Opsikion soldiers in the area around the capital were more favorably disposed to icons than people living in other parts of the empire. This, however, meant that Constantine could counter Artabazos by returning to the southeast and securing the backing of the Anatolikon soldiers, men who lived in the shadow of Arab disdain for religious images. He also quickly gained the support of the Thraskesian soldiers in western Anatolia.[39] If the revolt itself was an anti-Iconoclastic movement of the northwest and the capital, those supporting the emperor's reaction were more geographically (and potentially religiously) diverse.

Constantine could not immediately dislodge Artabazos from the capital, but he defeated armies loyal to him outside of Sardis and Nicaea, and then he cut off supplies to Constantinople until a "severe famine racked the inhabitants." Constantine, for his part, received all defectors who asked to leave the city "with favor and treated them very well." Artabazos eventually fled to Nicaea, where he was captured along with his sons. They were blinded, publicly flogged, and sent into exile. Many other prominent officers were killed, and the patriarch Anastasius, who had backed the coup, was forced to endure public jeering as he was paraded around the Hippodrome on an ass and flogged. It was hard to argue that God favored Artabazos's devotion to icons.[40]

Other events in Constantine's reign similarly showed the emperor's great talent for turning events that might seem to signal divine disapproval into opportunities to reinforce the impression of Iconoclasm's effectiveness. Between 746 and 751, a severe plague outbreak raged through the empire. "The pestilence was particularly intense" in Constantinople, the empire's densest and largest city, where, Nicephorus says, people lost their minds and "imagined that they were accompanied by certain hideous strangers," or were surrounded by "people striking each other with swords." "These misfortunes," everyone agreed, "were inflicted by God's wrath," and those who survived had done so "surely because of God's will."[41]

Not everyone agreed what to do next. Nicephorus and other later anti-Iconoclast thinkers felt that God had sent the plague to punish the Iconoclasts. Constantine, however, felt that divine wrath had fallen on Rome not because of the actions that he and his father had taken against icons, but because those actions had not gone far enough. When the plague subsided, Constantine set to work on a public campaign to persuade his subjects that the continued presence of icons in Roman religious life had caused the empire's most recent catastrophes.[42] He wrote texts against icon veneration, arranged public meetings to discuss them, and then, in 754, summoned an ecumenical council that sanctioned his approach to religious images.[43] This council agreed with the emperor that one could not "paint a picture" of Christ "as if it were that of a mere man" without dividing his divine nature from its material representation.[44] From that point forward, "anyone who presumes to manufacture an icon, or to worship it, or to set it up in a church or a private house," would be "deemed guilty under imperial law as a foe of God's commands."[45]

Later sources suggest that Constantine ruthlessly enforced these prohibitions by covering up or replacing figural mosaics in churches, pulling down other iconographic representations of Christ, compelling soldiers to swear they would not make use of icons, and punishing monks and clergy who opposed him.[46] The most striking moment came in October 767, when the emperor ordered the arrest and public humiliation of a former patriarch of Constantinople in front of Hagia Sophia. His face, head, and eyebrows were shaved before he was seated backward on an ass, led into the Hippodrome to be jeered at and spat upon, and then executed. His head then hung for three days at the Milion, the ceremonial center of the city, as an example to the impious.[47]

These events certainly did occur, but the scope of Constantine's violence is also greatly overstated by later anti-Iconoclast sources. Theophanes, for example, claims that Constantine was "polluted with so much Christian blood" that "he reached a pinnacle no less than Diocletian," the supposed author of the Great Persecution, with whose reign Theophanes began his massive chronicle.[48] But there is no sign of the sort of resistance to Constantine's religious policies that would have necessitated such widespread violence.[49]

In fact, conditions in the Roman state had improved rapidly after Constantine's council of 754 that ratified his stance against icons. Romans could see this evidence all around them, but it was especially clear in Constantinople. Constantine was brutally efficient in repopulating the capital following the plague by forcing Christians to move there from elsewhere in the empire.[50] His rebuilding program repaired the damage to the city walls and other structures, such as the church of Hagia Eirene. It also reconnected and expanded the aqueduct of Valens, a key feature of the city's water infrastructure that had channeled fresh water over 160 miles into the capital's cisterns until it was cut by the Avars during the siege of 626. Even Theophanes, one of his most vociferous critics, admitted that "Constantine made the city prosper."[51]

Constantine V did more than simply repair damage to the empire's cities. He also restored the capacity of the Roman military to mount offensive operations, enabling it to recapture Roman lands in the Balkans and Asia Minor. He launched nine expeditions into Bulgar territory between 759 and 775, and he took advantage of the civil war that saw the Abbasid dynasty overthrow the Umayyads to end the joint administration of Cyprus and recapture the cities of Theodosioupolis and Melitene in what is now eastern Turkey.

Constantine's approach to these captured lands more closely resembled that of Justinian II than that of first- and second-century emperors such as Claudius and Trajan. When Roman conquerors of the later Republic or early empire took territory, they had worked to absorb it by co-opting the local elite and inducing them to cooperate with their new Roman rulers. Constantine, by contrast, wanted the people of these cities to live under his rule and he wanted to control their lands, but he did not want the people to stay in those lands he now controlled. He forcibly removed his new subjects from the east, leaving the frontier a depopulated wasteland that made it difficult for Arab armies to provision themselves if they tried to raid Roman territory.[52] He then resettled them as colonists in lands that, technically speaking, belonged to the Bulgars. When Bulgars asked for compensation, Constantine refused to pay. He defeated the Bulgars when they tried to reclaim the territory, forcing them to abandon their claims.

Constantine's achievements across the thirty-four years of his reign were real, significant, and transformative, both for the empire at large and, in particular, for its capital of Constantinople. The empire was indeed stronger at his death in 775 than it had been for nearly 150 years before him, and even hostile, anti-Iconoclastic sources acknowledge the ways in which his efforts improved it. He was so popular among Constantinopolitans and the clergy that the 754 council "acclaimed him as the 'New Constantine' . . . who had abolished idolatry."[53]

At the same time, the empire could only be restored so much in these three decades. Beyond its monumental center, Constantinople remained a shrunken, depopulated shadow of the city it had been 200 years earlier. That city once had a bustling university district with more than forty publicly supported professors supervising hundreds of associate instructors and thousands of students drawn from around the empire. We do not know exactly when it closed, but the university, its professors, and its students were all long gone by the reign of Constantine V.[54]

So, too, was the robust banking and financial system that had powered the empire until the seventh century. Although the decline of this system is harder to trace than the collapse of university education, its effects were much more profound. As the empire recovered, its money supply failed to keep pace with the growth in its economy. This lag had not been a problem when most of the empire's money was held in bank accounts. But without a strong banking sector to hold deposits and produce financial instruments, Constantine needed to produce coins in order to expand the money supply. He could not do it fast enough. The result was a deflationary spiral. Theophanes describes how Constantine's actions "caused goods to abound," but the limited availability of coins forced farmers, merchants, and craftspeople "to sell off cheaply the supplies that derive from God."[55] This is deflation of the sort one would expect in a Roman world that was rapidly becoming more stable and prosperous, but that lacked the infrastructure to manage that prosperity. Constantine had achieved a great deal. But the empire needed more than a single ruler, regardless of his skills, to rebuild the institutions that made it strong. Rome's recovery from its most difficult century was only beginning.

Chapter 35

The Secession of the City of Rome from the Roman State

c. 720–814

PEOPLE IN CONSTANTINOPLE happily proclaimed Constantine V the "new Constantine," but the farther one moved from the capital and the empire's Anatolian heartland, the more likely one was to find people who had a much more negative view of the emperor. In no place was this more strongly felt than in the city of Rome itself.

Although the eastern part of the empire had seen a steady improvement in its security since Constantine had begun speaking against icons in the 750s, the city of Rome saw no similar benefits. For nearly 500 years, Rome had been the world's largest metropolis, a densely populated city of 1 million that took nearly two hours to traverse by foot. It had been at the center of an empire that extended for hundreds of miles in every direction. By the eighth century, it had shrunk into a small frontier city of a few tens of thousands of people. Farmland, water mills, and other features of the Italian countryside were springing up in spots that had once featured paved streets and monumental buildings. And during the reign of Constantine V, Rome effectively divorced itself from the Roman state it had birthed.

The problems that led to this separation had begun well before Constantine took power in 741. The city of Rome had become the center of a duchy after the Lombard invasions splintered Roman Italy apart, but by the early eighth century its dukes had little power or freedom of action. They answered to the exarch of Ravenna, controlled few troops of their own, and seldom stayed in their position for more than two or three years at a time.[1] As Lombard pressure on Ravenna combined with the Arab advances on Constantinople in the later 710s, the papacy stepped in to fill the power vacuum left by the reeling Roman state.[2]

Relations between the bishop of Rome and the emperor in Constantinople only deteriorated further as the empire's control over Central Italy became more precarious in the 730s. The emperor Leo III responded to the growing Lombard threats to Ravenna and Rome by reorganizing Italy so that it might defend itself using its own resources. He mandated the creation of a registry listing the names of all Italian male children living under imperial control and redirected revenues from papal lands in Italy and Sicily to the imperial treasury.[3]

Leo's actions deeply antagonized the new pope, Gregory III, a prelate who was already upset about the emperor's attitude toward icon veneration. Gregory took office in February 731 and organized a local council that condemned Iconoclasm that November. Leo may have responded by transferring control over the churches of Sicily and Calabria from the pope to the patriarch of Constantinople. Roman emperors in Constantinople and their subjects presiding over the church in Rome had been disputing various matters for hundreds of years, but conditions at this point were different from anything that had come before. While Leo's administrative and fiscal reforms stabilized Southern Italy, they came too late to save Roman Ravenna and the exarchate based there. The city first fell to the Lombards in 739, and, while the empire quickly took it back, it had become clear to Pope Gregory III that the Roman state no longer had the military capacity to protect its Central Italian territory from the Lombards. Ravenna again fell out of imperial control, this time permanently, in 751, when the last Roman exarch defected and went into exile under Lombard protection in Naples.[4]

Gregory had already begun searching for an exit from the empire in the 730s. After negotiations with the southern duchies of Benevento and Spoleto did nothing more than telegraph to the Lombard king, Liutprand, that he need not fear Roman imperial intervention if he attacked Rome, Gregory appealed to the Franks, Liutprand's much more formidable northern neighbors. The pope sent multiple requests for help to Charles Martel, the Frankish official who ran affairs in the kingdom on behalf of the Frankish king, in which he warned that God might punish him if he "turns deaf ears to my plea."[5] He got nowhere. Charles was respectful but noncommittal, and Gregory died in 741 with Rome's security situation still unresolved.

The new pope, Zacharias, continued to negotiate with the Lombards and Franks as well as the emperor in the east to try to find some diplomatic formula that might protect his city. Soon after taking office, Zacharias contacted Liutprand and agreed to suspend all military cooperation with Benevento and Spoleto in exchange for Liutprand turning over four towns to him that he had seized from the empire. Zacharias also wrote to Constantinople to inform Constantine V about his election. He made no move to assert papal independence during the civil war between Constantine V and Artabazos.

Zacharias was not naïve, and he knew that neither Liutprand's goodwill nor blind loyalty to Constantinople would keep Rome safe. So he kept developing the papacy's diplomatic connection with the Franks. In 749, a delegation sent by Pippin, the son of Charles Martel, arrived in Rome. Pippin, like his father before him, effectively ran the Frankish kingdom, but he answered to the nominal king, Childeric. He hoped to secure papal religious support for a coup that would depose Childeric and place himself on the Frankish throne. Sensing that this was an opportune time to finally secure a durable alliance with the Franks, Zacharias "commanded by virtue of his apostolic authority that Pippin should be made king."[6]

Zacharias died before Pippin could offer him any substantive reward, but his successor, Pope Stephen II, took office amid a crisis that threatened to completely reshape the politics of Central Italy. After the Lombard king Aistulf captured Ravenna and the duchy of Spoleto, he set his sights on the city of Rome. Stephen then negotiated a truce with the Lombard king that was supposed to spare the city for forty years.[7] It didn't. Aistulf broke the truce in less than a year. After Constantinople denied Stephen's request for imperial reinforcements, Stephen demanded permission from Aistulf to cross the Lombard-Frankish frontier so that he might meet with Frankish leadership. A biography of Stephen claims that this made Aistulf "gnash his teeth like a lion," but, fearful of provoking Pippin, the Lombard king ultimately granted his request.[8]

If he hoped to return to a Rome free of Lombard domination, Stephen knew he would need to do so behind a Frankish invasion force. The pope spent the winter lobbying the Frankish nobles who would need to commit troops if Pippin decided to invade Italy. When they finally agreed to a military alliance with the pope the following summer, Pippin wrote to Aistulf demanding that he "return the property of the holy church of God of the Roman Republic," including the Roman imperial territory around Ravenna that he had just seized. This formulation made it clear that the pope had declared himself to be the head of his own, new Roman state under Frankish protection. Stephen then repaid the king by presiding over a ceremony that confirmed Pippin as Frankish king. Both Pippin's pledge of support and Stephen's anointing of the king took place in Frankish territory, before an assembly of Frankish nobles, so that no one in the kingdom had any reason to question the validity of either man's claim on the other.[9]

The new Roman Republic, headed by Stephen as pope and protected by the Franks, now had a public claim on Ravenna, which was controlled by the Lombards, and Rome, which was officially still ruled by the emperor in the east. Pippin now needed to use Frankish soldiers to secure both territories for his new ally.

He first turned his attention to the Lombards. When Aistulf refused an offer to sell the lands Rome claimed to the pope, Pippin defeated him in battle and forced the Lombard king to agree to a treaty that bound "Romans, Franks, and Lombards" and compelled Aistulf to "return the city of Ravenna" to the Roman Republic led by Stephen, a brand new principality that had never possessed the city.[10] Pippin then withdrew back across the Alps as Stephen went back to Rome.

As soon as the Frankish forces departed, Aistulf mobilized "all the people of his kingdom" to attack Rome and snuff out the papal Roman Republic before the Alpine passes thawed sufficiently for Frankish forces to march south.[11] But Rome's defenders held out until Pippin returned to Italy. When he did, his soldiers again routed the Lombards and forced Aistulf to pay reparations, surrender the territory Stephen claimed, and deliver one-third of the Lombard treasury to the Franks.[12]

Constantine V lacked the manpower and the resources to take Rome back from its papal leader and Frankish protectors. But he understood how to leverage the soft power that accompanied his status as the head of the genuine, 1,500-year-old Roman state. For most of the preceding 800 years, Roman emperors had hesitated to arrange for members of the imperial family to marry non-Romans. The exceptions usually came during moments of crisis, as in 626, when Heraclius had betrothed his daughter to a Turkish leader as the Avar and Persian attack on Constantinople loomed. But Constantine knew firsthand the benefits of strategic marriages. He had married a Khazar princess to secure an alliance with her father's kingdom, hoping to protect the empire from having its Arab and Bulgar adversaries link up against it.

By the later 750s, Constantine had begun courting the Franks in the hope that a marriage alliance with his son Leo might induce them to abandon their papal ally. The dance began with the exchange of envoys bearing beautiful gifts. In 757, one such delegation traveled from the empire to the Frankish court bearing an organ, a novelty for people north of the Alps, who had not possessed one since the empire's fifth-century retreat.[13] Finally, in 767, Constantinopolitan envoys proposed a marriage between Leo and Pippin's daughter Gisela, in the hope that the sliver of Central Italy Pippin had recently given to the pope would be Gisela's dowry.[14]

The papacy counterattacked. Stephen and his successor, Paul, started writing to Pippin to affirm that popes alone could confer legitimate Roman status. The empire in Constantinople, they wrote, was not Roman, but "Greek," and an "orthodox king" like Pippin ought to avoid the "impious wickedness of the heretical Greeks" who "destroy[ed] the holy orthodox faith" by attacking icons.[15]

In 767, Pippin summoned what Frankish sources called "a great council . . . with Romans and Greeks" to decide whether the Franks would agree with Constantine's efforts to limit the veneration of icons. This theological decision would also serve as a proxy for how Pippin positioned himself in the political conflict between Rome and Constantinople.[16] Although Pippin may already have decided that the genuine Romans were those sent by the pope, some Frankish clergy were as suspicious of icon veneration as their eastern counterparts were. In one notorious incident, a bishop in Marseille had smashed icons that he felt his parishioners were worshipping.[17] Pippin needed the council to publicly affirm his theological fidelity to the pope almost as much as the papacy needed it to solidify their political ties. The council concluded by officially endorsing the papal position that icon usage was permissible and consistent with traditional Christian practices.

This decision slowed Constantine V's courting of Pippin and increased papal efforts to solidify the popes' political independence. The popes began to promote a document now known as the *Donation of Constantine*, which claimed that the emperor Constantine I had granted the pope "supremacy" over all the other bishops in the church; relinquished to him "the city of Rome and all the provinces, districts, and cities of Italy and of the western regions" to rule as he wished; and entrusted him with the western imperial crown and regalia.[18]

These claims were, of course, utterly ludicrous. Any Roman lawyer in the east or west who saw the text of the *Donation of Constantine* would know immediately that it was a forgery that could not contain the text of any genuine early fourth-century law. The popes knew this as well, but a poor documentary justification of their claim to political authority was better than none at all.

Despite the claims made by the *Donation of Constantine*, the deaths of Pope Paul in 767 and Pippin in 768 threw the alliance of their two states into chaos. In Rome, factions allied with the Lombards and Franks battled one another to determine the political orientation of their new republic, while in Francia, Pippin's kingdom was divided between his two sons, the seventeen-year-old Carloman and the twenty-six-year-old Charles, better known now as Charlemagne. It is not clear whether they ever got along, but Charlemagne and Carloman quickly stopped cooperating with one another after their father's death.[19]

The new Frankish sovereigns understood that their positions were too precarious to offer much real protection to the papal state. Not only did the Lombard kingdom sit between Frankish lands and the new Roman Republic under their protection, but many Franks remembered political life before Pippin had become king, and had yet to fully accept the rule of the new Carolingian dynasty he had started. Carloman could not risk sending troops out of his domains, and Charlemagne could not even travel to the Italian border without first traversing his brother's territory.[20]

Charlemagne—or, more accurately, his mother, Bertrada—turned to marital diplomacy to alleviate some of these problems. She arranged for Charlemagne to marry the daughter of the Lombard king, Desiderius, who hoped to enlist the young Charlemagne as an ally. Fearing that this marriage prefigured a Frankish betrayal, Pope Stephen III attacked it as "an unrighteous coupling with a foreign race" that would "pollute" the Frankish people by mixing them with the "most foully stinking Lombards . . . from which the stock of lepers is known to have sprung."[21]

The pope need not have worried, however. By 771, Charlemagne had sent away his new bride and seized control of Carloman's lands, after his brother died of a suspiciously serious bloody nose.[22] When Carloman's wife and young sons fled to Desiderius, Charlemagne had a pretext to attack Lombardy. Desiderius proved utterly unprepared for both the power of Charlemagne's army and the speed with which it could advance. He entered Lombardy in late 773, placed Pavia under siege, and then traveled to Rome for Easter while the Lombard capital held out. There he met the new pope, Hadrian, and negotiated a treaty that would divide the Lombard lands between them. Charlemagne would take the lands that had historically belonged to the Lombard kingdom in Pavia, while St. Peter, through his agent the pope, would assume control of the old Roman territories around Ravenna, Venice, Istria, and Tuscany. Aside from Ravenna and the lands in Tuscany that connected it to Rome, much of this territory remained the possession of the Roman Empire in Constantinople.[23]

Once Pavia surrendered, however, Charlemagne both refused to relinquish the agreed upon territory to the papacy and indicated that he had no intention of fighting the Roman Empire over its Italian lands. Frustrated by Charlemagne's refusal to abide by the treaty they had signed, Hadrian invoked the *Donation of Constantine* in a letter to Charlemagne, asking him to come back to Italy and return the "power over the West granted by the most pious Constantine" to the papacy.[24] Charlemagne ignored him for a time, but, in 781, Charlemagne agreed to give Hadrian a swath of land that stretched across Italy, from Ravenna in the east to Rome and parts of Campania in the west.[25] This grant became the core of the medieval papal states. From Charlemagne's perspective, it was an effective way to simultaneously shut the pope up and create a buffer between Frankish Lombardy and the Roman imperial territory in the south.

CHARLEMAGNE SPENT MOST of the middle years of the 780s and the early 790s dealing with issues north of the Alps, including expensive and time-consuming military campaigns in Saxony and Brittany.[26] Aside from a military intervention in 787, the king's attention to Italian affairs waned until a violent attack on Pope Leo III in 799 forced the prelate to flee Rome and seek refuge with Charlemagne.[27] Charlemagne met Leo in Paderborn that September and sent him back to the city with an armed Frankish escort.[28]

Charlemagne himself decided to travel to Rome at some point the following year to show his support for Leo. The king arrived at the steps of St. Peter's Basilica on November 24, 800, along with a baggage train carrying a solid silver table, a 55-pound bejeweled gold crown, and over 200 pounds of other gold and silver objects that he intended to give to the church.[29] As if this did not make the king's support for the pope clear enough, Charlemagne presided over two meetings, one in early December and another on the 23rd, designed to exonerate Leo of all the charges his opponents had leveled against him in order to justify his violent deposition.

Leo reciprocated on Christmas Day when he arranged a ceremony during which he placed "a precious crown" upon Charlemagne's head and then arranged for a crowd of people in the city to "cry out with one voice: 'To Charles, pious Augustus crowned by God, great and pacific emperor, life and victory.'"[30] This acclamation, which derived from what was chanted to Roman emperors in Constantinople, meant that Charlemagne was "now called Emperor and Augustus."[31] The *Donation of Constantine* had supposedly given the popes ownership of the western imperial crown and imperial regalia, items that the pope could use himself or grant to whomever he wished.[32] And Leo was so full of gratitude for Charlemagne's support that he decided to bestow Constantine's crown and the western empire upon the Frankish king, or so he claimed.

It is easy more than 1,200 years later to misunderstand the significance of what happened that Christmas in the city of Rome. No one, not the pope, not Charlemagne, not even his court propagandists, imagined that Leo's declaration had magically transformed Charlemagne's various realms into a Roman Empire.[33] This was only another title for Charlemagne to enjoy alongside that of King of the Franks and King of the Lombards. Each of these titles reflected his personal authority over diverse peoples and lands. None of them corresponded to any sort of unified Roman state. Charlemagne, and Charlemagne alone, served as the unifying factor. Charlemagne was, in a very real sense, claiming to be a Roman emperor without a Roman Empire.

In 800, the actual Roman Empire was not the property of an individual but the product of nearly 1,600 years of collective labor undertaken by a citizen body of Romans who had built the state, developed its institutions, created its legal system, and superintended its evolution. Continuity mattered to those Romans. Their political project was the same one that Appius Claudius Caecus, Cicero, Marcus Aurelius, and Justinian had all taken turns leading. But they had taken turns. None of those figures had owned the Roman state. They, like their fellow citizens, were stakeholders in a very old, very successful collective enterprise.

Charlemagne had received a Roman imperial title given to him by a pope whose predecessors had used a forged document to appropriate it. To be sure, this title, and the Roman legacy it allowed him to claim, meant a great deal to the Frankish king. As his energy and health declined, Charlemagne spent more and more time in Aachen, the German spa town that he renamed Future Rome, and that he refashioned into a sort of Roman theme park complete with an octagonal church decorated with columns scavenged from the old Roman buildings in Italy.[34] But this was a German king playacting the part of a Roman emperor. Aside from the stretch of Central Italy administered by the pope, Charlemagne did not rule over many people who thought themselves Roman, and the lands he controlled barely cohered together in any sort of unified state.

This is why, after Charlemagne's death in 814, the entire enterprise began to fall apart. His son Louis faced regular civil conflicts from the time he took power, and, after Louis's death, the Frankish Empire was divided among Charlemagne's grandchildren like a private estate. It would never come back together. Even the imperial title was treated more like a private honor than a public office. There would continue to be sovereigns holding the title of Roman emperor (and, later, Holy Roman emperor) until the nineteenth century, but the title was applied chaotically for the first few centuries after Charlemagne's coronation. Not only were there times when multiple claimants used the title of Roman emperor, but there were also periods of a decade or more when no one used the title at all.[35]

The kingdoms of these German sovereigns, who sometimes bore the title of Roman emperor, and the regimes of the popes who governed the city of Rome offer interesting and compelling perspectives on the legacy of Rome in Western Europe. But none of those stories are the stories of the Roman state with which this book is concerned. That state, the real Roman Empire, remained powerfully headquartered in Constantinople. We will now return to its story.

Chapter 36

Rome's First Empress and the First End of Iconoclasm

775–802

T HE CORONATION OF Charlemagne as Roman emperor coincided with a series of political and religious crises that disrupted
the Roman recovery Constantine V had led from Constantinople.
When Constantine died on September 14, 775, the empire passed
to his sickly son and successor Leo IV. Constantine buttressed Leo's
position by marrying him to Irene, an orphaned Athenian girl
from the Sarantapechos family. The Sarantapechos clan had been
a local power in Central Greece at a time when Constantine V had
begun slowly expanding Roman power back into the Greek interior
that Rome had long ago abandoned to Slavic settlers. Constantine
believed that joining his son to a Greek family could both help the
empire return to Central Greece and provide the future emperor with
a non-Constantinopolitan power base. A strong influence in Central
Greece might also help him fend off any challenges to his rule.[1]

The nineteen-year-old Irene arrived in the capital on November
1, 769, at the head of a flotilla of silk-adorned warships. The trip must
have been quite spectacular for a girl raised in eighth-century Athens,
a shriveled city of ancient ruins and fewer than 10,000 inhabitants.[2]
The capital had shrunk, too, but was much larger, more modern, and
more impressive than any city Irene had visited before. The ceremony

greeting her only reinforced this majesty. When she disembarked, Irene "was met by the prominent men of the city and their wives, who led the way before her" into a city filled with more people than the girl had ever seen in one place in her life. Her betrothal was celebrated two days later. The whirlwind journey from Athenian orphan to empress ended on December 17, when she participated in another day of ceremonies in which she "was crowned empress" and then celebrated her marriage to Leo.[3]

The betrothal, coronation, and marriage ceremonies were extremely important, highly choreographed public events. Constantinopolitans expressed their loyalty to the regime and its newest member in a fashion that visually reinforced the hierarchies and organization of communal life in the capital. Irene was on display. She had not yet needed to do anything to merit the long and enthusiastic chants praising her.[4] But, unlike many young imperial brides who saw only a blur of new faces bowing to the floor before them in the palace and singing up to them from the Hippodrome, Irene recognized that each of these subjects was also a potential ally in a city where she knew no one. Within a few years, she had constructed a network of powerful supporters in the capital.

One sentence chanted to Leo and Irene on that December day pointed to the most important thing that could happen to permanently secure Irene's presence at court: "May God bless you, with your wife, and may God grant you children born in the purple."[5] And Irene and Leo fulfilled the crowd's hope for an heir "born in the purple" very quickly, as she became pregnant a few months later. On January 14, 771, Leo and Irene welcomed their first child, a boy they named Constantine, in a room in the palace with walls of purple stone, or *porphyry*, accented by purple fabric.[6] He was what Romans called a *porphyrogenitus*, a baby born into the royal purple, both literally and figuratively.

Constantine VI's birth not only firmly cemented Irene's connection to the imperial family but also made Leo IV well positioned to assume power when his father died. The former emperor had married twice after the death of Leo's mother, Tzitzak, and left behind five more sons with his third wife Eudokia.[7] Although Eudokia's presence

at court and her ability to support the ambitions of her sons complicated matters, the birth of Leo's heir made any direct challenge to
Leo's succession difficult. If any of his half-brothers wanted to take
his place as emperor, they would have to overthrow him and kill his
infant son.

Leo IV was able to take power without evident incident, but
a challenge did emerge the next year.[8] This happened when Leo,
ostensibly bowing to demands orchestrated by leaders of the armies,
appointed his five-year-old son as his successor, effectively removing
Leo's half-brothers from the line of succession. Understanding that it
might prompt a reaction, he forced his half-brothers to participate in
Constantine VI's coronation at Hagia Sophia, swearing allegiance to
the child as Irene watched the ceremony from the gallery above.[9]

Leo's half-brothers were now effectively boxed in. Not only would
any coup attempt transgress their publicly sworn oath to support Leo
IV and Constantine VI, but any possible co-conspirators knew that
the emperors had the support of both the military command and the
Constantinopolitan people. Nevertheless, Nicephorus, one of Leo's
half-brothers who had been given the title of Caesar by their father,
decided that his position would only get worse if he did not try to seize
power then. He was denounced, tried, and sent into exile in Crimea.[10]
It may or may not be a coincidence that his mother, Eudokia, also
never again appears in our sources.[11]

Over the next four years Leo IV emerged as a steady, largely effective leader, while Irene settled in as the only living Augusta. Leo's
generals kept the papal Roman Republic off balance by launching
naval raids on some of its Campanian territory. They also executed
a successful invasion of Arab Syria. But a diplomatic initiative led to
the emperor's most notable achievement.[12] In 777, Leo welcomed the
exiled Bulgar king Telerig in Constantinople, "made him a patrician [and] joined him in marriage to a cousin of his wife Irene." He
then sponsored the exiled king for baptism.[13] This alliance shows an
evolving Roman policy of deterring attacks by new regimes by housing members of displaced royal houses. Telerig's marriage to a member of Irene's family also points to her growing importance in her

husband's empire, as well as her ability to collect powerful allies of her own.

Irene's influence increased even more following Leo's death on September 8, 780. Although he was not yet ten years old, her son Constantine VI was now Roman emperor, though a regency would legally rule the empire until he reached majority. We don't know for sure whether this regency involved a council, but the first coins issued under the new emperor made it clear that Irene effectively controlled whatever arrangement was made.[14] The last batch of coins issued by Leo IV featured dynastic propaganda emphasizing the continuity of his regime with those of his father Constantine V and grandfather Leo III, as well as the promise of a bright future under Constantine VI. They showed Leo IV and Constantine VI standing together on the front, while Leo III and Constantine V stood together on the reverse. After Leo IV's death, he was moved to the back of the coin alongside his two distinguished predecessors. Irene now joined her son on the coin's front, the first imperial woman to appear on the front of a Roman coin since Heraclius's second wife, the empress Martina, nearly 150 years before.[15]

Fearing her growing power, a group that included the current or former heads of fleets, regional armies, and the palace guard plotted to bring back the former Caesar Nicephorus and make him emperor. The plot was quickly detected, and Irene "had them scourged, tonsured, and dispatched to various places." Nicephorus and his brothers were effectively disqualified from further imperial office when she forced them to enter the priesthood. On Christmas morning of 780, the empress and Constantine VI watched triumphantly in the church as the emperor's humiliated uncles administered Communion—a display that left no doubt about their new clerical statuses and ineligibility for imperial office.[16]

Irene's early time as regent reveals some of the powerful relationships she had been building with prominent Constantinopolitans over the past decade. She replaced many of the people implicated in the recent plot with people close to her, including a court eunuch whom she sent to oversee the military response to an Arab invasion in June 781. In 782, Irene sent two other court eunuchs out as military commanders. She tasked one with putting down a revolt in Sicily. Another, Staurakios, who Theophanes claims "was at that time the head of everything and administered all matters," took over as commander on the Arab front that year. Although Staurakios countered the Arab advances effectively, he made a series of careless mistakes that compelled Irene to agree to a much more onerous treaty than otherwise would have been necessary.[17]

Peace on the eastern frontier opened up the possibility of redeployment elsewhere, and Irene sent Staurakios to Greece the following year. Over the course of two years of campaigns, his armies restored the land route to Thessaloniki and then pushed south until his troops "penetrated the Peloponnese," a peninsula whose interior areas had been separated from imperial control for centuries. By the spring of 784, conditions had improved so much that Irene and her son were able to tour Thrace and travel to Beroia (modern Stara Zagora in Bulgaria), "which she ordered to be rebuilt and renamed Eirenoupolis."[18]

Irene also relied heavily on palace eunuchs for diplomatic missions to the west. The most memorable of these came in 781 when she sent one of them named Mamalos to lead a delegation to Charlemagne to negotiate the betrothal of the king's daughter Rotrud to the emperor Constantine VI.[19] Both the bride and groom remained too young to marry, but they were vital symbols of a union that, if consummated, would offer additional protection to Constantine VI and Irene if there were any internal challenges to their position.

By the early 780s, one can begin to see how Irene and her allies worked strategically to secure her position as the de facto ruler in Constantinople. In its broadest outlines, the pattern is a familiar one. It replicated how Roman regimes in the past had established themselves by shunting aside established military and administrative figures tied to their predecessors while elevating capable but socially marginal figures who could serve as their replacements. Emperors like Septimius Severus and Phocas had done this when establishing a new dynasty, but Irene's project was more akin to what Claudius I had done in the first century AD, and what Justin II had done in the sixth. Like those emperors, Irene was not founding a new dynasty but instead laying the groundwork to change an existing one in fundamental ways. And to do this, she had to disempower entrenched family members and advisers and replace them with ambitious men who owed their power and positions to her.

What did Irene hope to achieve by remaking the empire? Most obviously, she wanted to stay alive and stay in power. Although eighth-century emperors and empresses usually mutilated, exiled, and blinded the sort of insurrectionists that Julio-Claudian or Flavian emperors would have executed, revolution remained an extremely high-stakes game in the Roman state. The best way for a leader to stay alive was to deter people from trying to have them killed. As a young woman from the provinces who ran the empire on behalf of a child, Irene needed to place enough people loyal to herself in enough positions of authority that any challengers would fear to act.

As the 780s progressed, however, it became clearer that Irene was remaking the imperial administration for reasons that went beyond self-preservation. She did not want to just survive. She wanted to dismantle Iconoclasm.

Her first moves in this direction came in 784, when Paul, the patriarch of Constantinople, fell ill, abruptly resigned his position, and retired to a monastery. When Irene asked him why he had resigned, Paul supposedly began weeping and spoke of his great regret that he had "sat on the throne of the priesthood while God's Church was suffering oppression" because of Constantinople's Iconoclasm. She then orchestrated a visit to the monastery by members of the Senate and a group of nobles who had all interacted closely with the patriarch during previous church services and other public events. They were thus presumably savvy enough to understand what they were to do when Paul told them that "they would not find salvation unless an ecumenical council took place and the error that is in your midst is corrected."[20] Rather conveniently, Paul died soon after this meeting, becoming a figure around whose blessed memory the anti-Iconoclasts could organize a movement.

Irene decided to tap Tarasius, another of the palatine officials with whom she had developed a relationship, as the new patriarch. Despite his status as a layman, Tarasius evidently understood the role he was to play and refused to accept ordination and elevation to the patriarchate unless something was done to reverse the Iconoclastic policies that had "divided and torn asunder" the church in the capital from the Christians in both the east and the west who continued to venerate icons. The solution, Tarasius concluded, was a council attended by leading bishops from around the Roman Empire that would reverse the Iconoclastic synod held by Constantine V in 754.[21]

Tarasius spoke, but his message reflected Irene's strategic brilliance. Whereas Constantine V's Iconoclastic synod had essentially been a gathering of church leaders drawn from within the empire, Irene assembled a genuinely ecumenical gathering in which the patriarchs of Antioch, Alexandria, Jerusalem, Constantinople, and Rome (the ancient group called the *pentarchy*) would all condemn Iconoclasm. If Constantine could push Iconoclasm on the shrunken empire by assembling a council that reflected its internal church leadership at that moment, Irene could trump him by inviting the bishops who represented the greatness of the entire Roman world as it once was.[22]

Irene's gathering failed to accurately represent the true nature of the Christian world, however. One problem concerned the guest list. The members of the pentarchy came from what had been the five most important centers in the fifth- and sixth-century Christian world, a world in which the largest populations of Christians had resided in Rome and the huge cities of the Roman East. But by the end of the eighth century, war, conquest, and conversions to Islam had diminished the power of the bishops of Alexandria, Antioch, and Jerusalem. The bishops serving congregations in Charlemagne's Frankish territories now likely had larger flocks and more clout than these traditionally important bishops.[23] But no one from Francia was invited.

Irene also misread popular opinion within the capital itself. As the council attendees were taking their seats in the church of the Holy Apostles on August 1, 786, Iconoclast officers in the *tagmata*, the regiments of soldiers based in Constantinople, ordered their men to storm the building. They "bared their swords . . . threatening to kill the archbishop" as well as the other priests and abbots in the building, while a small group of Iconoclast bishops began shouting "Victory!" Tarasius was forced to dissolve the council.[24]

Irene and Tarasius responded quickly and deftly. A little more than a month after the failed conference in Constantinople, the empress arranged for Staurakios to meet with one of the armies stationed in Thrace that he had recently commanded. They agreed to help the empress expel the disruptive soldiers from the capital, and, Theophanes reports, Irene was able to equip them by "pretending to be undertaking an expedition to the east against the Arabs as if they had invaded." The provincial soldiers were then able to enter the capital peacefully. They disarmed the rebellious Constantinopolitan tagmata, and Irene "placed them and their families in boats and exiled them from the City." She then "formed a new tagma with officers who were loyal to her," and in May 787 she sent messages inviting the bishops to gather again, this time in the city of Nicaea.[25]

The Second Council of Nicaea, the seventh (and, to this day, last) ecumenical council recognized by both the modern Catholic and Greek Orthodox Churches, convened on September 24, 787. Over the course of about three weeks of meetings, the nearly 500 assembled bishops and monks engaged in a choreographed condemnation of Iconoclasm that saw none of the raucous energy, violence, or debate typical of earlier councils. "The synod," Theophanes later observed, "introduced no new doctrines but maintained unshaken the doctrines of the holy and blessed Fathers while it rejected the new [Iconoclasm] heresy."[26] The choice of Nicaea, the location where the first ecumenical council had met under Constantine I over 450 years earlier, and the emphasis on traditionalism in the council's findings were both deliberate. Iconoclasts had attacked icon veneration as an innovation unknown to the earliest Christians and claimed it had no support in biblical text or in the writings of early Christian authors. The council counteracted this argument by producing and authenticating earlier texts affirming icon veneration and condemning the Iconoclasts' arguments as innovations. It was a deliberately backward-looking theological discussion.

It also had little immediate tangible effect. Irene did erect a symbolically important image of Christ on the gatehouse of the imperial palace, but redecorating churches was expensive and it could not be done immediately. Even Constantine V, who had enjoyed a full treasury, had prioritized curtailing the production of new icons and images of people in churches over finding and destroying existing figural representations.[27] Irene, who was in a much weaker financial and political position than Constantine V, could do little to quickly change the appearance of churches. But the council did allow for the return of private icon production, and Romans who favored icon veneration built monasteries on family land that included richly decorated scenes of the saints and martyrs.[28] The decorative schemes of these locations for private worship could be more quickly revised than those found in the massive cathedrals of the capital. These must have been the places where Romans felt the effects of the Second Nicaean Council, if they felt them at all.

The restoration of icons represented a wager that the empress had made with full awareness of its risks. She knew that her position of influence would be compromised if Romans perceived her as recklessly abandoning a religious practice that had served their empire well. If the empire thrived under Irene's religious policy, the empress from Athens, and the son in whose name she (theoretically) acted, would earn the titles "New Constantine and New Helena" that the messengers coming from Nicaea had given them.[29] But Irene desperately needed Romans to believe that God was happy with the outcome of the council.

The following years gave Romans precious little evidence that God approved of the synod the empress had orchestrated. In the east, Arab raiders breached the Roman frontier, defeated a Roman army sent to meet them, and killed some of its commanders. In a naval attack on Cyprus the Arabs captured and killed another Roman general. In Thrace, a Bulgar force captured and killed the general Philetos.[30] Irene's effort to build an alliance with the Franks also collapsed under papal pressure that weakened Frankish resolve to go forward with her son's marriage to Rotrud.[31] When the engagement fell apart, Irene responded by sending Roman troops to make the duchy of Benevento a Roman protectorate before possibly challenging Charlemagne's hold on Northern Italy. Unfortunately, Irene's army was soundly defeated, and her chosen general was captured and executed by the Franks.[32]

These defeats shook Roman confidence in the empress's leadership and the capacities of Staurakios and the other advisers on whom she depended. Constantine VI was now a twenty-year-old adult and saw that everyone was still effectively ignoring him while consulting with Staurakios about everything. In February 790, Constantine ordered Staurakios's arrest and banishment. But his men moved too slowly, and Irene learned of the order before it could be carried out. With Staurakios's assistance, she had her son's men flogged, tonsured, and sent far away from Constantinople. Constantine himself was seized, flogged, and confined for a few days. After the emperor was spanked and sent to his room, Irene compelled the army in Constantinople to swear an oath to her: "As long as you are alive, we shall not permit your son to rule." As Theophanes wrote, "Everyone swore these words and no one dared to object."[33]

Fear is a powerful but brittle foundation for a sovereign's legitimacy. The farther one moved from the capital, the less Romans feared Irene. When a messenger arrived to administer the required oath to the soldiers of the Armeniac army, they refused, saying that they would "not ever place the name of Irene before that of Constantine." It was an explicit challenge to the extralegal supremacy over her son that Irene had seized. She sent a second embassy that was to either persuade or arrest them, but the soldiers instead deposed their own commander and "acclaimed Constantine as sole emperor." When other provincial armies heard that the Armenian soldiers no longer acknowledged Irene's authority, they, too, overthrew the commanders she had selected and "proclaimed Constantine sole emperor." The spontaneous revolt quickly became more organized when several different military groups assembled in Bithynia that October and "unanimously asked for the emperor Constantine." Realizing that she could not effectively resist "the impetus of the army, Irene let him go."[34]

As HE PREPARED to meet the troops, Constantine sent a messenger ahead, tasking him with getting the soldiers to swear yet another oath, this time affirming that "they would not accept his mother Irene as *basileus*," the masculine Greek noun that means emperor. They swore the oath, and when Constantine returned to the capital that December, he imprisoned Irene in a Constantinopolitan palace and purged the eunuchs and commanders loyal to her. This shift in leadership did little to improve the political or military fortunes of the state, however. Constantine's generals proved no more able than those appointed by his mother, and battlefield failures against the Bulgars and the Arabs eroded Constantine's confidence in his ability to manage the empire on his own. On January 15, 792, "after receiving entreaties from his mother and many people in authority," Theophanes tells us, "the emperor once again pronounced her empress."[35]

Everyone in Constantinople acquiesced, but the Armeniac army rebelled against the restoration of an empress they had sworn they would never accept. Constantine was forced to march against the very body that had enabled him to regain power. The Armeniac army was devastated. Their officers were killed, as was a sympathetic bishop. The unit itself was disbanded, and "the emperor put 1,000 men in chains," brought them to Constantinople, and "had their faces tattooed in ink with the words 'Armeniac plotter.'" Then he shipped them off to Sicily.[36]

Constantine would have been better off had he listened to their protests. Unlike his mother, the emperor failed to realize that each political pivot he made could earn him support in new quarters, but it usually bled support from others. The Armeniac troops could be fickle, but their actions had secured his power over his mother. He returned their loyalty by decimating the unit, humiliating its members, and turning to the very forces in Constantinople upon whom his mother's influence rested. This error might not have been a fatal one if Constantine had proved himself a capable commander or an effective politician, but he possessed neither of these traits. Nor did he understand how shallow his support was among the nobles, courtiers, soldiers, and clergy in the capital.

In 795, Constantine made a decision that caused much of this support to bleed away, too. Tired of his wife, Constantine dissolved the marriage and compelled her to become a nun so he could marry one of his mother's attendants named Theodote. Following an outcry in the capital, the emperor made a symbolic pilgrimage of atonement to the church of the Evangelist in Ephesus, but he nevertheless married Theodote that August. The patriarch Tarasius signaled his discomfort with this arrangement by refusing to perform the ceremony, but the strongest resistance came from anti-Iconoclast religious figures close to Irene. The most notable of these was Theodote's uncle, a monk named Plato who headed the Sakkoudion monastery and had participated in Irene's Council of Nicaea. Although Constantine tried to reconcile with Plato, their relations continued to deteriorate until the emperor ordered Plato's arrest, along with the arrests of ten other monks, in February 797.[37]

The monks' conflict with Constantine demonstrated his incompetence to Irene. She saw that his growing list of enemies imperiled both his life and her position and began working with leaders of the tagmata to "help her depose her son and become sole ruler herself." On July 17, 797, members of the tagmata tried to apprehend Constantine as he left a race at the Hippodrome. He managed to elude them and boarded a warship. He ordered the crew to take him across the Sea of Marmara to the Anatolic army, but Irene had co-opted the sailors, too, and they returned him to the capital. On August 19, the emperor was blinded, on his mother's orders, in "the Porphyra," the purple chamber in the palace where he had been born. The blinding was performed in the most "cruel and grievous manner with a view to making him die." It is not clear how much longer he lived after this.[38]

Irene reigned alone as sole sovereign for the next five years, mostly with the same middling success as her son. She tried, and failed, to negotiate some sort of permanent peace with the Abbasid caliph Harun al-Rashid upon taking over the empire. Arab raids instead intensified, with attacks reaching as far west as Ephesus.[39] In the west, Charlemagne's coronation as Roman emperor by Pope Leo in 800 prompted another challenge to Roman rule in Italy and the Adriatic region. Carolingian propaganda declared that the "title of emperor had become extinct among the Greeks and a woman [had] claimed the imperial authority," while Charlemagne prepared for a land and sea attack on Roman positions in Italy, Dalmatia, and Sicily. Fortunately for the Romans, nothing came of his plans aside from a few naval skirmishes around Venice. Instead, the Carolingian and Roman courts again began exchanging ambassadors, leading to rumors in Constantinople that the empress was considering a marriage to Charlemagne that would unite the Christian world.[40]

Even if the ambassadors did raise this possibility, there is little chance that these rumors reflect a serious attempt to formalize a marriage between the empress and the Frankish king. They were, however, extremely useful tools for Irene to deploy within Constantinople at a time when people had begun to contemplate her overthrow. Among the plotters were the brutally disfigured four sons of Constantine V's second marriage, who twice more tried to seize power. After the first attempt, they were exiled to Athens, so that Irene's relatives could watch over them. Then, after a Slavic chieftain from the area around Volos tried to free the four sons from Athens, Irene ordered her nephew and brother to arrest and blind her brothers-in-law.[41]

By this point, she was showing some of the strains from more than three decades at the center of Roman political life. She contracted a serious illness in May 799 that set off a series of intrigues among her inner circle. She survived them, but she fell from power three years later following a palace coup incited by Nicephorus, the head of the imperial fiscal department. Irene was exiled and died on the island of Lesbos on August 9, 803.[42]

Irene spent more than half her life playing—and, mostly winning—a series of high-stakes political games in Constantinople. Many Roman women had shared effective power over the Roman state with their husbands or sons over the preceding 1,500 years. They included figures as diverse as Tanaquil, the wife of the sixth-century BC king Tarquinius Priscus, who had helped her husband establish himself and then arranged for the succession of Servius Tullius, and Sophia, who had ruled Rome when the emperor Justin II had fallen into madness more than 1,000 years later. Others, such as Tiberius Gracchus's mother Cornelia, Augustus's wife Livia, Nero's mother Agrippina, and Theodosius II's sister Pulcheria, had used their tremendous skills, political acumen, and personal talents to remake the Roman world around them in ways that suited their interests. But none had ruled in their own right.

Irene showed that, while their gender made it more difficult for an extremely talented woman to supplant an incompetent man, it did not preclude them from doing so. Irene also established an administrative language that worked for a female Roman sovereign. The coins she issued during her solo reign showed her—crowned and holding a cruciform scepter—with a legend describing her as a *Basilissa*, an empress. They left no doubt that Irene was both a woman and the supreme sovereign in the state. In legal and other state matters, however, she continued to use the masculine term *Basileus*, or emperor. The laws she issued and the judgments she passed emphasized not the particularity of her gender but the long, unbroken tradition affirming the timeless quality of the imperial office. It was a state office, entrusted to generations of sovereigns by the Roman people, and she tied herself to a tradition of imperial service stretching back to Augustus. She had decoded how a woman could rule Rome directly and in a fashion that simultaneously displayed her femininity and maintained continuity with an office established by and for men. Irene was the first, but not the last, to do so. Other Roman imperial women would follow in her path—and learn from her mistakes.

PART 6

FROM NICEPHORUS I TO ROMANOS IV

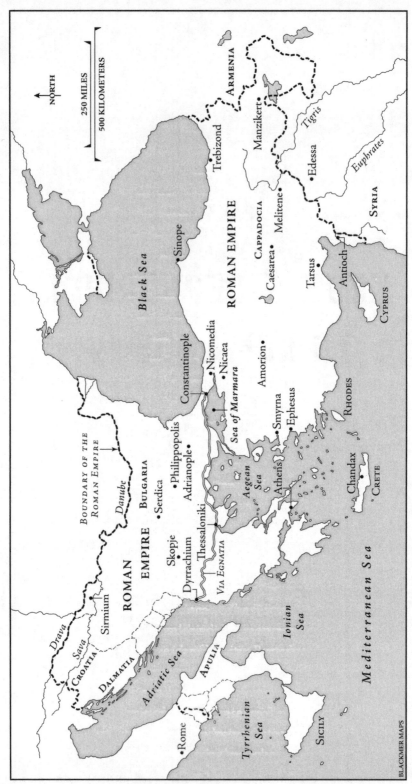

The Eastern Roman Empire and its dependencies, c. AD 1025

BLACKMER MAPS

Chapter 37

The Medieval Roman State Takes Shape

802–814

IRENE'S SUCCESSOR, THE emperor Nicephorus I, belonged to a new group of Roman elites that had grown up as Constantine V began to stabilize the state following the volatility of the later sixth, seventh, and eighth centuries. Their backgrounds and fortunes differed significantly from the Constantinopolitan glitterati of the sixth century, who had possessed estates scattered across different regions, enjoyed access to the credit networks through which money flowed, and could depend upon publicly funded schools to train their children for state administrative service. This world disappeared alongside Roman political control of the eastern and southern Mediterranean as territorial shrinkage, economic collapse, and the coups and countercoups of the late seventh and early eighth centuries eventually exhausted the systems that supported the intergenerational wealth, power, and privileges of the old Roman imperial elite.

The new elite to which Nicephorus belonged included Armenians, Persians, and Syrians who crossed into Roman territory as Arab armies threatened their lands in the seventh century, as well as Bulgars and Slavs who came later. By the mid-eighth century, nearly 20 percent of the people known to hold the old senatorial titles of *patrikios* (patrician) and *hypatos* (consul) came from families with origins outside what were now the empire's borders.[1] These were not humble people rising through the ranks. They were instead figures like the members of the Boilades family, a clan of Bulgar émigrés that became prominent in the ninth century and joined the Roman state under conditions that preserved the prerogatives to which they had become accustomed in their homeland.[2] A not entirely inapt parallel could be drawn with the Claudii, the old Italian clan that entered both Roman life and the Roman elite during the unsettled period following the initial establishment of the Roman Republic in the late sixth century BC. In both cases, a destabilized Roman state benefited by granting high Roman status to prominent émigrés looking to join it.

Nicephorus himself came from one of these families. He was Syrian and had descended from members of the royal line of Rome's old Arab allies, the Ghassanid family, who had taken refuge in Cappadocia during the seventh century.[3] But his influence and wealth derived much more from his position in the growing, increasingly capable imperial service than from his old noble lineage. The Roman state of this period had a far smaller and less expansive bureaucracy than it had in the Constantinian or even Justinianic periods. While those imperial administrations had employed many tens of thousands of civil servants, the empire of Irene had a staff of perhaps 1,000, mostly concentrated in the capital. But these were good positions that offered steady pay in cash, access to either the emperor or his immediate subordinates, and noticeability in a city that contained fewer than 100,000 people.[4]

The families that established themselves in imperial service in the eighth and early ninth centuries did their best to pass that elite status across generations. Public education had not yet returned to the capital, but their children served in administrative apprenticeships that provided essential training, and often they entered imperial service in the same department as their relatives.[5] Once they began to accumulate wealth, elite Constantinopolitans began buying estates in areas such as the Bithynian coast of the Sea of Marmara, Paphlagonia, or the Black Sea coast of Pontus—areas that the regular Arab attacks of the seventh and early eighth centuries had once largely cut off from the economy of the capital. Church and imperial officials also returned to resume ownership of properties in the countryside that they had abandoned a century before.[6] This process disrupted the functioning of regions that had once existed as an archipelago of micro-economies in which Roman soldiers lived and secured their supplies.

It is not at all surprising then that Nicephorus I threw himself into a comprehensive administrative reform of the Roman state after he overthrew Irene in 802. He had been an imperial fiscal official, and the coup that brought him to power was backed by a host of other palace and military officials with substantial financial and administrative knowledge. He and his team understood very well how the state operated and how those operations could be improved, but the reforms took a bit of time to develop. One key part involved balancing a steady expansion of imperial territory in the Balkans and Greece with effective campaigning against the Arabs, whose raids continued to exact a toll on the Roman forces and people. Nicephorus was able to fight the Arabs to a standstill in Asia Minor, but damaging naval raids on Cyprus in 806 forced him to make a treaty in which he agreed to pay the caliph 30,000 solidi a year.[7] When the caliph died in 809, the ensuing civil wars eliminated any immediate Arab threats. This lent added momentum to Nicephorus's efforts in the Balkans, which included successful campaigns against the Bulgars and the suppression of a revolt by Slavs in Greece that threatened the new Roman administrative center established in Patras.

Nicephorus soon began to rationalize Roman administrative structures in Asia Minor and to redeploy military resources from that theater to secure and better defend the empire's recovered territory in Europe. He developed a new system of military and provincial administration based around existing military districts called "themes" (*themata* in Greek). Nicephorus had inherited the late Roman system, in which military officials commanded troops divided by regions while civilian governors remained in charge of provinces based around the old Roman administrative boundaries. This structure had become quite outdated. Old Roman provinces and ninth-century military regions did not always have the same boundaries, and their administrators lacked an effective way to determine exactly how much money, labor, and supplies existed in the places under their jurisdiction.

The theme system blended the old provincial civilian and military command hierarchies into one organized structure. Nicephorus gave generals ultimate authority in the themes and clearly designated the old civilian administrators as their subordinates. Those civilians now served as judges in the region, while fiscal officials operating in each theme assumed responsibility for the collection of taxes and the distribution of military supplies. In order to minimize local corruption, the fiscal officials in the themes also reported directly to the central administration in Constantinople. While the reform initially appears to have affected only five themes in Asia Minor, the theme structure was quickly extended to Roman territories in the Balkans and Adriatic.

Nicephorus then ordered a comprehensive census of the property held by all citizens of the empire. The objective was to ascertain who legally owned what land and to accurately assess each person's ability to pay taxes. Any tax remissions granted in the past were canceled, and impoverished people who paid low taxes were to pay more if their fortunes recovered. According to Theophanes, Nicephorus even taxed buried treasure, so that "everyone who in the previous twenty years had discovered any kind of jar or vessel" containing money would now owe back taxes on what they had found.[8]

All of these measures were designed to address the economic changes that had been unleashed by the empire's burgeoning recovery. Tax remissions had been used for centuries by Roman emperors to keep local money in communities that were hit by military or natural disasters. Nicephorus's reversal of these remissions, then, was a sign of his optimism that the economies of many stricken communities had now stabilized. The tax on buried treasure, however, is the most telling sign of the expansion of calm, settled spaces within Roman territory in the early 800s. Just like the proverbial American who keeps money under a mattress, Romans had routinely kept clay pots filled with coins under the floors of their homes to hide the cash they had saved. The "jars or vessels" containing treasure that Nicephorus taxed were not like the pirate's treasure that children try to dig up on the beach. They were household savings buried beneath homes that had been abandoned decades or even centuries before. The fact that the emperor was choosing to tax such discoveries strongly suggests that they were now becoming quite common as Romans returned to depopulated areas of the empire.

Some of Nicephorus's other reforms also suggest a recovery of Roman commercial activity, and perhaps even an effort by the emperor to spark the rebirth of an imperial financial sector. Shipowners were ordered to buy vacant land in Asia Minor so that some of their wealth could be redirected back into agricultural production. In addition, people who purchased slaves from merchants who had not gone through the imperial customhouse in Adydos were ordered to pay the unpaid custom dues, and leading merchants in Constantinople were given loans of twelve pounds of gold apiece from the imperial treasury at an interest rate of 16.67 percent. This last measure, which resembled the scheme Nerva and Trajan had used to spur sustainable investment in Italian communities 700 years earlier, compelled these wealthy Constantinopolitans to find ways to generate even more income that exceeded the interest rate they were paying. And, of course, Nicephorus intended to also tax the profits they made.

Nicephorus took additional steps to support the continued expansion of Roman control over the Balkans. Some of these moves yielded short-term political gains. Prior to embarking on his reform program, Nicephorus had patched up relations with Irene's family by arranging for Theophano, a relative of the late empress, to win a beauty pageant that determined the bride for his son and heir Staurakios. This mollified her powerful Athenian clan at a time when the emperor's interests in Greece required their support.[9]

Other moves provided a framework that he hoped would enable Rome to expand the theme system to the reconquered territories of the Balkans. Theophanes describes how Nicephorus "removed Christians from all the themes," and made them sell their land in their home regions, move to the Balkans, and settle the new territory

Rome had taken from the Slavs there.[10] The new communities in which these transplants settled also took on responsibility for providing equipment and financial support for the armies that defended them.[11] This offered a ninth-century update to the system of establishing colonies of military-trained men and their families that had been used over 1,000 years earlier to permanently garrison territory seized by Roman field armies and secure Liguria and the Po Valley.

By 810, Nicephorus had crafted a well-integrated system designed to sustainably fund a Roman military made up of citizen soldiers based in and supported by the communities they defended while simultaneously encouraging economic growth and increasing tax revenues. This system would eventually evolve into one that allowed the Roman Empire to reemerge as the most powerful polity in the Mediterranean over the next few centuries. But even the best designed, most resilient systems are sometimes challenged by events their architects never anticipated.

In the summer of 811, Nicephorus and Staurakios, his son and heir, led an army into Bulgar lands. Theophanes reports that their soldiers were "gathered not only from Thrace but also from the Asian themes[,] as well as many poor men armed at their own expense with slings and sticks."[12] They enjoyed an initial wave of success. By mid-July, Nicephorus's forces had burned the Bulgar capital, seized its treasury, and forced Krum, the Bulgar khan, to propose a peace treaty. But Nicephorus refused Krum's offer. Then, on the night of July 26, Krum's forces attacked the Roman camp while most of the soldiers were asleep. They killed Nicephorus, the governors of the Anatolikon and Thracian themes, the head of the imperial guard, and a huge number of officers and ordinary soldiers. Staurakios escaped the battle but suffered a serious wound to his spine that left him paralyzed below the chest. "Seeing himself to be in an incurable condition, Staurakios sought to secure the empire for his wife," who "hoped to obtain the empire for herself in the manner of Irene," but this plan was thwarted by a group of courtiers.[13] They instead arranged for Michael Rhangabe, the husband of Staurakios's sister, to be proclaimed emperor by both the Senate and the soldiers in Constantinople as dawn broke on October 2, 811. Staurakios resigned the throne, took up residence in a monastery, and died three months later.[14]

Michael Rhangabe had inherited an impossible situation, and he handled it poorly. As Krum's forces advanced into Thrace and Macedonia, Michael tried to mobilize the soldiers stationed in these new themes to defend their lands. They instead "rebelled out of fear of war" and abandoned most of the towns and forts that Nicephorus had established, ceding the territory to the Bulgars. The result was that Nicephorus's "ostensible achievements" in capturing and settling the Balkans "quickly collapsed."[15]

These sudden, shocking losses prompted Romans to wonder once again whether they had somehow angered God. When Irene had restored the veneration of icons, some wondered if perhaps she had also snapped the state back into a cycle of military crises spawned by religious conflicts. The first sign of this unease came when a group in the capital tried to restore Iconoclasm. According to Theophanes, they plotted to "abduct" the old, brutalized, blinded sons of Constantine V, who still lived as prisoners on an island in the Sea of Marmara, in the middle of the night, and "bring [them] before the army," in the hope that the army might respond by overthrowing Michael.[16]

Michael managed to put down this poorly planned revolt. But the next year saw an even more spectacular Iconoclast provocation when a crowd of former soldiers in Constantinople rigged the mausoleum of Constantine V so that it appeared to open spontaneously. Theophanes says that they called on the dead Iconoclast emperor to "arise and help the state that is perishing" because of Krum's advances. They then claimed to have seen Constantine himself, saying he "had arisen on his horse and set off to fight the Bulgars."[17] The prefect of the city tortured them until they confessed that they had orchestrated the whole thing, but this punishment failed to calm the feeling in the capital that the state was again drifting toward catastrophe.

On June 22, 813, the catastrophe the anti-icon forces predicted materialized. Krum defeated another Roman army outside of Adrianople, put that city under siege, and then marched on Constantinople. By the time Krum arrived outside the walls, the Roman state had a new emperor. The generals and their soldiers decided to replace the overwhelmed Michael with Leo V, the commander of the Anatolikon theme. Michael was sent to a monastery, and Leo assumed control over the defense of the city. When Krum arrived outside the capital, he was "struck" by the immensity of its walls, "gave up hope of the siege," and "made some tentative proposals for peace." Instead of negotiating, Leo decided that this was a good moment to try to assassinate the Bulgar leader, but the assailants "merely wounded Krum." Krum then burned an imperial palace outside the walls, sacked Adrianople, and returned home. The wound, however, proved so debilitating that the Bulgar leader died the following April.[18]

Krum's death came too late to stop Leo from responding to military defeats as his eighth-century predecessors had. Although the new emperor had pledged to respect the canons of the Second Nicaean Council before the patriarch crowned him, the popular calls for a return to Iconoclasm proved hard to ignore.[19] At some point in late 814, Leo empaneled a commission to look again at the use of icons in Roman churches. He appointed the scholar John the Grammarian, who headed a monastery connected to the church of Sergius and Bacchus in the capital, to lead the discussions. That December, Leo then went to the patriarch Nicephorus and told him that soldiers were blaming icons for the recent military defeats. He requested that the patriarch begin removing icons from the churches as a compromise, but if he refused to do so, he needed "to explain . . . why you venerate them when the Scripture nowhere requires this."[20]

The patriarch responded by resigning and going into exile. A new patriarch, Theodotus Kassiteras, inaugurated on April 1, 815, convened a church council that repudiated Irene's council. The new council reinstated the findings of the Iconoclastic church council called by Constantine V in 754. It also ordered the removal of any bishops who would not agree to abide by these doctrines. Icons, the bishops held, could remain in place, but they could no longer be prayed to.

With Iconoclasm restored, Leo offered his own proof that God was again content by avenging the defeats of 811 and 813. These successes came about when he ambushed and annihilated a Bulgar force commanded by Krum's successor, Omurtag. The two sovereigns then negotiated a thirty-year peace treaty that demarcated the boundary between their territories, permitted the Bulgars to construct an eighty-mile-long earthen trench separating their lands, and enabled the Romans to resume the resettlement of Thrace.[21] Iconoclasm was back. It seemed to work. But Rome was about to enter a period where the strengths of its new administrative, economic, and military systems rendered this kind of interpretative science irrelevant. It would soon no longer be necessary to use recent events as signs of whether God was happy with Rome's religious practices. The empire would emerge much stronger than it was before.

Chapter 38

The Roman System Abides

815–842

L EO V INHERITED an empire in crisis, but one that also stood on the cusp of a remarkable recovery of its power and influence. Although we can now see the signs of this shift in the 810s, no one could have imagined such a brilliant Roman future at that time. As the decade began, Rome faced an Arab caliphate that stretched from India to Tunisia, a Frankish state headed by Charlemagne that extended from Spain to the Balkans, and a Bulgar kingdom that had just killed the Roman emperor and annihilated most of his best troops. By 820, all of Rome's formidable competitors were much reduced. The tensions between the Romans and Franks, which lessened significantly following a peace treaty signed between Nicephorus and Charlemagne, decreased even further following the great Frankish king's death in January 814. Krum's death in March of the same year ultimately led to a peace treaty that calmed the Balkans. And, although war with the Abbasid dynasty would resume after the Arab Empire resolved the civil conflict that followed the death of the caliph Harun al-Rashid, the long-term trend inclined toward the Romans.

The calming effects of growing stability take a long time to permeate the psyche of a population shocked by unexpected disasters, but the empire had already changed enough that its second embrace of Iconoclasm unfolded much differently than its first. When Constantine V organized and implemented his anti-icon policies in the mid-eighth century, he did so in a reeling state in which few people outside the clergy had the capacity to mobilize independently against his religious policies. Many of the great monastic establishments of the fourth and fifth centuries that had once engaged in doctrinal combat now lay in territory ruled by Muslims, while those that remained in lands under imperial control lacked the drive and resources to meaningfully resist the emperor's policy.

This was no longer true in the ninth century. The opponents of Iconoclasm were now well resourced, well connected, and greatly motivated by a zealotry that made them prize principled confrontation and court martyrdom. None embraced this approach more heartily than Theodore the Studite. Theodore belonged to the same class of well-trained imperial administrators that Nicephorus's reforms had empowered, but he had decided to walk away from elite Constantinopolitan life and become a monk at a monastery his uncle had founded on family land in Bithynia. He was a cousin of Theodote, the second wife of the emperor Constantine VI, and his criticism of that marriage had led the emperor to send him into exile in Thessaloniki. Irene had recalled Theodore and tasked him with repopulating the largely empty Stoudios monastery in Constantinople with anti-Iconoclast monks.[1] By the time Leo V took power, Theodore governed 1,000 monks, and most of them hated the idea of Iconoclasm. None of them had any land, titles, or property they feared losing. And there were no barriers to the sort of mischief they could make.[2]

Leo struggled to control the Stoudites as he tried to rebuild an empire-wide consensus against icon veneration in 814 and 815. He sent Theodore back to Bithynia after the monk led a demonstration in favor of icon veneration, but this just allowed the abbot to describe himself as a persecuted defender of Christ in powerfully written letters he sent to supporters around the empire. Theodore kept writing after Leo ordered him to be flogged and sent into exile at a site with a harsh climate and inadequate food. Eventually, the fed-up emperor forced Theodore to walk to the city of Smyrna along the Aegean coast, a rigorous and dangerous journey that the emperor must have again hoped might lead to Theodore's death. It did not. But Theodore spent the next twenty months imprisoned in the old Smyrene city council chamber under the supervision of an Iconoclastic bishop. Theodore's skill in advertising his eager and open resistance to imperial persecution meant that Leo's punishments only amplified the monk's message. The emperor was unwittingly creating an anti-Iconoclast celebrity.[3]

Despite the conflict with Theodore and his supporters, Leo proved to be an exceptionally effective emperor. Even later pro-icon historians admitted that he "was a highly competent administrator of public affairs" who rebuilt the armies devastated by the losses in 811 and 813 and "reestablished from their foundations cities all over Thrace and Macedonia" that had been lost following Nicephorus's death.[4] Leo had even been planning for his succession by proclaiming his son Symbates as his co-emperor in 814 and then renaming him Constantine.[5] No less an authority than Patriarch Nicephorus, whom Leo had removed from office for not agreeing with Iconoclasm, once said that "even if he was a scourge" to the church, Leo "nevertheless took great care of the affairs of the commonwealth."[6]

In 820, Leo's regime succumbed to the sort of personal rivalries that sometimes doomed even the most effective Roman leaders. The problem started with Michael, an old friend of Leo's from the eastern stronghold city of Amorion, whom Leo had appointed as commander of the palace guards.[7] Following a series of outbursts in which Michael went so far as to threaten to depose the emperor, Leo had him arrested and charged with treason. He was spared execution after Leo's wife intervened, but this mercy convinced Michael and the members of the guard to do away with the emperor before he had time to reconsider. The conspirators attacked Leo as he entered church on Christmas Day. Leo, a strong fighter, "took hold of the cross" in the church, "as he had no other defensive weapon." He managed to "deflect the blows to his body" until a giant of a man sliced off the hand that held the shattered cross and then severed the emperor's head.[8] The plotters arrested Leo's family and castrated his son Constantine so he would be ineligible to rule.[9] They then placed Michael on the throne.

The new emperor, Michael II, began trying to consolidate control over the stunned Roman populace by reaching out to some of the figures Leo had antagonized. In mid-821, however, the armies of the Anatolikon and Kibyrraiotai themes rallied around a commander named Thomas who had also been close to Leo. Thomas seized the tax revenues from those regions, and the troops rose in revolt against Michael. Not all the commanders supported Thomas, and his rebellion sparked a civil war that lasted nearly three years. Roman troops killed each other in numbers not seen since perhaps the revolt of Heraclius more than 200 years earlier. Thomas "took over the entire Roman armada, except for the so-called imperial fleet," and used it to ferry 10,000 troops across the straits, putting Constantinople under a combined land and sea siege for two years. The combat between these Roman fleets saw the first sustained use of Greek fire by Romans against other Romans. The two contenders even invited outside powers to intervene in a Roman civil war for the first time in over a century. Thomas appealed to the Arabs for support, while Michael received reinforcement from the Bulgar khan Omurtag. When the Bulgars devastated Thomas's forces in a battle along the Sea of Marmara, Michael was able to secure what was left of Thomas's fleet. He then marched through eastern Thrace, captured Thomas, and snuffed out the revolt by dismembering its leader.[10]

Michael's victory resulted in a stronger emperor but a momentarily weaker Roman state. The battles had depleted the Roman armies, damaged the walls of Constantinople, and shattered the fleet. None of this could be repaired quickly. While Rome struggled to rebuild, outside forces took advantage of its deficiencies. At some point in the 820s, a small group of Arab adventurers who had been expelled from Spain landed on Crete, which had been left unprotected by the loss of so many ships in the civil war. They seized the island and began to use it as a base from which to attack shipping and raid the islands of the Aegean. Although Michael sent seventy ships against them, he could not dislodge the invaders.[11]

The civil war also left Sicily dangerously underprotected. In 826, a military commander named Euphemius rebelled after the emperor ordered his detention following an illicit love affair.[12] Euphemius's soldiers prevented the arrest, Euphemius declared himself emperor, and then he invited Arab forces from North Africa to land in Sicily to back his claim.[13] Euphemius was beheaded while trying to capture Syracuse, but the Roman state would never eliminate the Arab military presence in Sicily that he introduced. Although the state held on to parts of the island for much of the next century, the weakness of the Roman navy there, as in Crete, meant that the imperial center could not prevent the Arabs from using Sicily as a base for continued attacks on the Italian Peninsula.[14] Arab raiding even reached Ostia and the city of Rome in 846. The empire was, of course, no longer responsible for the protection of its historical capital, but its vulnerability shows how deeply the naval losses sustained in Thomas's rebellion destabilized the northern Mediterranean.

MICHAEL DIED IN 829, leaving the empire to his son and successor Theophilus. This was the emperor under whom Romans first really began to feel the compounding benefits of the administrative reforms launched at the beginning of the century. After two centuries of relative frugality, it is striking to see the wealth of the state he controlled. The anonymous continuator of Theophanes's chronicle devotes six full manuscript pages to descriptions of the palaces Theophilus built for family members and the renovations he made to the imperial palace in Constantinople. He carefully notes the different types of marble used in each room, the types of gold tiles used on the ceilings, and the designs created when different types of marble and precious stones were combined. One palace had a beautiful staircase made entirely of Carian marble; another featured Egyptian porphyry columns that "transmitted an undistorted echo" around a cave-like niche; and a third was designed to mimic the architecture and interior design of the Abbasid palace in Baghdad.[15]

The most remarkable thing of all, however, is that Theophilus spent lots of money, because his attention to the rule of law and the recovery of commerce gave him lots of money to spend. Each week he rode out from the palace along the main street of Constantinople to make himself available to hear any petitions, "so that people might always be able to make their complaints and not be hindered by wicked men fearing punishment." And some stories, like one about the time when Theophilus intervened to prevent a general from stealing the horse of a common soldier, became so well known that their circulation reinforced the perception of an emperor who helped the weak and those who had been mistreated by the powerful.[16]

Each week Theophilus would "go through the marketplace," review what was for sale, and learn about their prices. He did this not only so that he could be approached, but also, and more importantly, because it gave him a sense of the availability of "all that might nourish people," so that he could use his funds to intervene quickly if food scarcity loomed.[17] These were the actions of a prudent administrator. He wanted everyone in the capital to see that he cared for his fellow citizens and had the resources to intervene if circumstances necessitated it. And, in a Constantinople whose population again approached 100,000 people, Theophilus could project the majesty of an emperor while remaining accessible enough that any who wanted to see him could do so.

Theophilus was equally perceptive about the condition of the wider empire he governed. He rebuilt the defenses of the Roman state to reverse the damage that had been done by the civil war between Michael II and Thomas. This included a reconstruction of the walls of the capital, so it would be protected if Arab raiders from Crete reached it; a reorganization of the armies that built upon the reforms of the themes begun by Nicephorus a generation earlier; and a recruitment drive that resulted in a massive growth in the size of Roman forces.[18] By the end of his reign, the empire could field as many as 120,000 troops, a 50 percent increase over what Constantine V could marshal half a century earlier.[19]

Theophilus augmented this growth with a willingness to incorporate non-Romans who would fight for the Roman state. In 834, a group of 7,000 fighters from the Khurramite community of Azerbaijan entered Roman territory and joined the Roman army as auxiliaries. The Khurramites, who practiced a religion blending elements of Persian Zoroastrianism and Islam, had first rebelled against the Abbasid caliphate in 816/817. In 833, when they had suffered a significant defeat, a leader of the rebel forces named Nasr realized that they would have a better chance of defeating the caliph as part of the Roman state. Nasr led his army across the border, converted to Christianity, and took the name Theophobos. He then received the rank of patrician and married Theophilus's sister. His followers were "enrolled in the Roman state" and granted "ranks and military land holdings" like other Roman soldiers in the theme system.[20] Four years later, another, even larger, wave of Khurramites, numbering some 16,000, arrived in Roman territory following the final defeat of their rebellion.[21]

The Khurramite resettlement was just the largest in a series of migrations to Rome in the ninth century by groups looking for a safe place to live. Unlike other states, Rome had a reputation for protecting the refugees who came to it, even if that meant fighting against the rulers from whom they had fled. A generation earlier, Nicephorus I had allowed Bulgarian refugees to settle in Roman territory as part of his expansion into Thrace and Macedonia. After Nicephorus was captured and killed, the Bulgar leader, Krum, had demanded that "Bulgar as well as Roman refugees should be returned to their countries" as part of any peace agreement. When the emperor Michael I mentioned this condition to the Senate, the senators reacted with genuine horror. No one, they argued, could ever consider delivering a person who "fled for refuge . . . to the Roman state" back to whatever "dreadfulness and savagery" they had chosen to leave behind. Rome, the senators argued, was a place to which the oppressed should "flee continuously," not only because of "our civility and mildness," but also because accepting these refugees benefited Rome by leaving enemy land "depopulated to our advantage."[22]

Small groups of Bulgar exiles, however, differed significantly from the more than 20,000 armed Khurramites that Theophilus welcomed into the empire. And yet the Khurramites were just the latest manifestation of a pattern that had seen leaders migrate with trained soldiers, who then offered service to Rome in exchange for Roman honors and positions of influence. In fact, one of the most interesting points of continuity is that Appius Claudius in 504 BC and Theophobos in AD 834 both negotiated patrician status as one of the conditions for bringing their soldiers into Rome. At the same time, Rome often struggled to manage the initial phases of this process without drama, as the defection of Justinian II's Chosen People to the Arabs at the Battle of Sebastopolis showed. There was always a risk that asking groups of new Romans to fight and die for a state they had recently joined might push them away from a political system whose rules they were still learning.

Theophilus did his best to manage these challenges, but he also hesitated to send large numbers of Roman troops to fight in the Caucasus when a bigger group of Khurramites, under the leader Babak, faced annihilation. Theophilus responded to Babak's plea for Roman assistance by mobilizing his army, calling up the men who had crossed the frontier with Theophobos, and launching an invasion that penetrated deep into Syria and destroyed Sozopetra, which Roman sources describe as the home city of the Abbasid caliph.[23] Theophilus hoped that the Roman attack would divert any Arab troops from the campaign to suppress the Khurramites, but the gambit did not work. Instead, Babak's rebellion was crushed, Babak was killed, and the incensed caliph mobilized a massive army to launch a revenge attack against Theophilus's hometown of Amorion, a strongly fortified city that formed a key node in Rome's eastern defenses.

The Arabs assembled at Tarsus, linked up with 10,000 Turkish troops based in Melitene, and marched into Roman territory. Theophilus met them with a large army of his own, made up of Khurramites as well as troops taken from themes in both Europe and Asia, but he was defeated in the field and could do nothing to help Amorion when the Arab forces placed it under siege.[24] Its walls held out against the caliph's siege weapons, but the city was ultimately betrayed by one of its defenders. Most people were killed, while "anyone who remained alive, namely officials and important men in the themes, were sent to Baghdad," in case someone might ransom them.[25] The site of Amorion then sat abandoned for a generation.

The loss of Amorion shocked all Romans, but it particularly shook Theophobos in his conviction that leading his countrymen to Rome was the right decision. Rumors began spreading that he had been negotiating an agreement to defect to the Abbasids. While these rumors were probably not true, Theophobos faced a dilemma. Ultimately he decided to withdraw his men and their wives and children to the Roman city of Amastris, arousing considerable suspicion about his loyalty to the emperor. After Theophilus sent a fleet to blockade Amastris, Theophobos surrendered and was executed. Remembering the painful lessons that Romans had learned from Alaric's Goths in the fourth century AD, the Khurramites were never again allowed to assemble as a single force under one of their own commanders. Theophilus instead ordered them separated into smaller groups of 2,000 that he "dispatched to each theme, to be enlisted in the service of the appointed governors, and he appointed brigade commanders to be in charge of them."[26] They were given lands tied to military service and were forced to marry Roman wives. Thereafter, they "almost entirely vanished" as a distinct group of people, quickly blending into the Roman world around them.[27] The only trace of the Khurramites noted by later historians was the title of "Persian" that continued to be held by their brigade commanders for at least a century after their incorporation into the theme armies.[28]

This bumpy but ultimately successful integration of tens of thousands of new Romans underlines a fundamental ambiguity of Theophilus's reign. This was an age that set the stage for considerable long-term Roman successes, but it was also one punctuated by moments of acute disappointment that sapped the short-term confidence that both newly arrived and long-established Romans had in the empire.

Nowhere did this dynamic play out more powerfully than in the bitter, ongoing conflict about Iconoclasm. Theophilus, the sixth (and last) Iconoclast Roman emperor, surpassed the others in the level of pro-icon resistance he faced as well as in his harsh punishment of dissidents. Many of the stories told about imperial persecutions of people who venerated icons are creative retellings, but those connected to Theophilus often feel grounded in reality. One such story involved an icon painter and monk named Lazarus who practiced his craft even though it was forbidden. Lazarus was discovered, told to stop, and then tortured and imprisoned when he refused. When Theophilus heard that Lazarus had resumed painting, "he commanded that his palms should be burned with irons." Lazarus was eventually released from prison and, in a detail that lends plausibility to the tale, he was given the honor of replacing the image of the Virgin above the Chalke gate when Iconoclasm again ended.[29]

Lazarus belonged to a new breed of monks who took up the pro-icon fight after Theodore the Studite died in the 820s. Although Lazarus seems to have been a native-born Roman, other leaders came from abroad to foment a different, more dramatic sort of resistance during Theophilus's reign. From the east came a group of monks who fled the St. Sabas monastery in the Palestinian desert outside of Jerusalem and sought refuge in Constantinople. Some acquired such a following that they were brought to the imperial palace for an audience with the emperor. When they behaved in a disrespectful way toward the sovereign they regarded as a heretic, Theophilus ordered the tattooing of "frivolous iambic verses" that he had composed on the foreheads of two anti-Iconoclastic monks.[30]

Methodius, the most important anti-Iconoclast leader to come from the west, took a much less conventional but more effective approach to undercutting Theophilus. Instead of arguing directly against Iconoclasm, he began to write prophetic works that predicted disaster for Rome if it continued to ban icons. The first of these, written in April or May of 820, correctly predicted the imminent death of Leo V and apparently circulated within the empire before the event occurred.[31] In 829, Methodius wrote another pamphlet that

mentioned the Arab invasion of his home island of Sicily and predicted the violent death of Michael II. A third pamphlet, predicting
Theophilus's death, appeared in the 830s.[32]

Methodius's most audacious stunt involved an imperial chamberlain named John who planted an obscure, seemingly ancient document in the imperial library that Methodius had written in a sort
of code. Theophilus found the work and asked both the patriarch of
Constantinople and the empire's leading scientist what it said. When
neither could read it, John suggested that the emperor ask Methodius for help. Methodius was duly summoned and wrote Theophilus
an interpretation of the document. Theophilus thanked the monk,
ordered his release from prison, and gave him special quarters in the
imperial palace. From that point forward, Theophilus "always kept
[Methodius] somewhere nearby so that he might resolve obscure
things unknown to most men." Theophilus remained a committed
Iconoclast, but he also came to deeply value Methodius's insights,
despite their disagreements about icons.[33]

The unlikely (and probably rather one-sided) friendship between
the Iconoclast emperor and the iconophile prophetic holy man
pointed to the coming intellectual and political bankruptcy of the
Iconoclast movement. When Leo V had begun to again attack the
veneration of icons a few decades earlier, part of his rationale had
been the sudden, striking decline of Roman fortunes after the Second Council of Nicaea in 787 condemned the Iconoclasm that had
been championed by successful emperors such as Constantine V. But
Methodius's prophetic texts contradicted that rationale. He showed
how recent military and personal failures had not provided robust
evidence of divine endorsement of Roman religious policies. Leo
V had been assassinated. Michael II had presided over a civil war,
the siege of Constantinople, the loss of Crete, and the introduction
of Arab forces into Sicily. Theophilus's Iconoclasm had led to the
destruction of Amorion. By the time Theophilus died in 842, Methodius's prophecies had shown Romans that Iconoclasm was no longer
necessary.

Rome's second embrace of Iconoclasm had begun as a panicked, passionate reaction to what seemed like a failed pro-icon policy that endangered the state. By the 840s, no one any longer doubted the empire's strength or integrity, and, even if they did, they had to admit that ninth-century Iconoclasm did not seem to work particularly well as a tool for ensuring Roman victory. At that point, Iconoclasm could be replaced by an imperial regime that focused on managing a functional Roman system rather than on trying to guess what divine path might avert the next existential system. This was the task on which the next regime immediately set to work.

Chapter 39

The New Macedonian Dynasty

842–912

WHEN THEOPHILUS DIED in 842, Michael III, the two-year-old son he had fathered with his wife Theodora, nominally succeeded him as emperor. In practice, however, Theodora ran the empire at the head of a group of carefully chosen advisers. And, like Irene, Theodora decided to use her control over the Roman state to turn it away from Iconoclasm. She summoned pro-icon religious figures to Constantinople so that they could engage in public debates about icons. She then called a synod that reiterated the orthodoxy of Irene's Second Council of Nicaea, removed her husband's patriarch of Constantinople, and ordained Methodius, the mystic whose prophecies had done so much to undermine Iconoclasm, as his replacement. Many bishops who had cooperated with the Iconoclast emperors and the priests who served under them were allowed to repent and retain their positions. And, this time, the spotty military record of the second wave of Iconoclast emperors meant that there was no upwelling of anger in the armies as images of Christ, the Virgin, and Christian saints returned to churches.[1]

It was entirely coincidental but extremely fortuitous that the restoration of icon veneration coincided with a revival of Roman military fortunes during Theodora's regency. The raid that led to Amorion's capture was the last major invasion of Roman territory mounted by the Abbasids before infighting splintered their empire's political integrity. By the 850s, it was Roman armies, not Arab raiders, who were on the offensive. Roman attacks now penetrated deep into Arab-held lands in Cilicia, Mesopotamia, and northern Syria. Theokistos, Theodora's most trusted general, mounted an invasion of Crete, and although he failed to retake the island, his campaign began a period when Roman naval forces undertook offensive operations across the Eastern Mediterranean. Most notably, the Roman navy twice attacked and raided the Egyptian port of Damietta in the 850s to block shipments of weapons to Crete.[2]

Theodora's regency ended like so many others in Roman history when the young emperor in whose name she was managing the state decided to assert himself. Sometimes, as when Constantine VI had temporarily sidelined Irene in the 780s, a disagreement about the military had prompted an emperor to break with a protector. At other moments, as when Nero turned on Agrippina because she forbade him from seeing his mistress, the cause was much more personal and heartfelt. Unfortunately for Theodora, Michael was more like Nero than Constantine VI. Michael fell in love with a girl named Eudocia Ingerina, but Theodora wanted him to marry another woman whose family she believed to be a better political match. Theodora's brother Bardas sensed Michael's anger and persuaded him to sideline his mother and execute her ally Theokistos. Michael agreed to do this, and Theokistos was killed in November 855. Theodora was then removed from power, and she and her five daughters were all sent to a convent.[3]

Bardas replaced Theodora as the real power in the state. He directed military policy while participating personally in Roman attacks against Samosata and Crete. He organized spaces for secular learning in the capital that could train imperial administrators and established a philosophical school within the imperial palace.[4] Bardas capped all of this by having Michael proclaim him Caesar in 862.

The empire scored even greater successes under Bardas's direction when it shepherded the conversion to Christianity of the non-Romans who had settled in what had once been Roman Illyricum. Roman tradition held, quite wrongly, that the Serbs, Croats, and other Slavic people in that land had once been converted to Christianity under the emperor Heraclius. What had instead happened was that, as Rome had lost control of all but the coastal areas of Illyricum, the ecclesiastical structure inland had effectively ceased to exist. The functional churches along the modern Croatian coast remained under the control of the pope for the rest of the seventh century, but the abandoned inland areas were an afterthought. Then, in the eighth century, the emperor Leo III had removed Illyricum from papal authority and placed it under the control of the patriarch of Constantinople. This move had prompted a furious papal reaction, but the popes could do nothing as long as coastal Illyricum remained under imperial control and the inland areas were pagan. In the ninth century, however, the increasingly settled situation in the Balkan interior steered the leaders of the emerging non-Roman states in the inland parts of the peninsula to consider converting to Christianity.

Bulgaria, the name historians use for the Bulgar kingdom after its Bulgar and Slavic subjects adopted Christianity, was the first of the Balkan kingdoms to convert. Commerce and personal exchanges between Bulgars and Romans grew steadily following the peace treaty they signed in 816. As these individual relationships deepened, so too did the penetration of Christianity.[5] By the early 860s, Boris, the leader of Bulgars, indicated to both Rome and Constantinople that he was interested in converting to Christianity, effectively asking the papacy and the patriarchate to compete for his allegiance. Constantinople had a head start, because Cyril and Methodius, two missionary brothers working with its support, had created the Cyrillic alphabet that enabled Slavic speakers to read Christian texts and celebrate Mass in their native language. This was a major advantage for the Eastern Roman church. When Boris converted in 864, he did so in a fashion that placed him in communion with Constantinople. He even took the Christian name Michael to honor the emperor.[6]

The papacy was livid. Pope Nicholas sent Boris a long letter laying out why Catholic practices were preferable to those of the east and explaining how Bulgars needed to change their behaviors and practices to conform to Christian standards. The papacy's tactics backfired, however, and Boris responded by requesting that a council of bishops rule that the church in his kingdom was not subject to Rome. Despite vehement papal protests, the bishops of Constantinople, Alexandria, and Antioch all granted this request from the Bulgarian leader. The Constantinopolitan patriarch then named an archbishop for Bulgaria, and the council ordered that all the Catholic missionaries and priests connected to the western church leave Bulgarian lands.[7] This was a major cultural and religious victory for Constantinople.

Less well documented, but no less consequential, are Roman interactions with the Rus under Michael. In June 860, a fleet of Rus ships emerged from the Black Sea and attacked Constantinople. Skilled navigators of the mighty rivers of Russia and Ukraine, the Rus sailed down into the Black Sea and then moved toward the capital, "plundering every region and all the monasteries" they found while "killing all the people they captured."[8] Because the imperial fleet (and the Greek fire it carried) was in the Aegean, the Rus threatened the city for more than a month until some combination of Michael's arrival and a freakishly strong summer storm led to their withdrawal. Not long after this, the Rus sent an embassy "begging that they might become participants in divine baptism." By 867, the Constantinopolitan patriarch Photius could claim that the Rus had embraced "the purifying and genuine religion of Christians."[9] If this did indeed happen, the conversion did not stick. But the contacts between Rome and the Rus that began with a terrifying raid under Michael evolved into something much more measured by the end of the decade.

Michael had done well under Bardas, but by the middle of the 860s his attention was drifting toward a new favorite person at court. This was Basil, a Macedonian peasant descended from Armenian migrants who had been forcibly settled in Thrace by the emperor Nicephorus I sixty years earlier.[10] An enormous man, Basil possessed uncommon physical strength. When he arrived in Constantinople to seek his fortune, he attracted the attention of an abbot who recommended his services as a bodyguard to a nobleman. That man often hosted Bardas at his home. During one of these visits, Bardas watched as Basil defeated all the imperial attendants in a wrestling competition.[11] Bardas recommended Basil to Michael, and the emperor enrolled Basil in his cavalry escort before quickly raising him to patrician status and head of the imperial guard. Michael then arranged for Basil to marry Eudocia Ingerina so he might cover his own affair with her.

None of this would have been possible without the changes in Roman life unleashed in the early ninth century. Without Nicephorus's forced resettlement of Thrace, Basil would have been born hundreds of miles away in a remote eastern theme with little chance of making his way to the capital. The reemergence of Constantinopolitan monastic life gave Basil a place to establish himself when he arrived in the capital. The monasteries' connection to families of imperial courtiers and functionaries gave him a point of entry into the world of the Roman nobility. Finally, when Basil's skills attracted imperial attention, he swiftly climbed the ladder of imperial offices. One hundred years earlier he would have spent his life a farmer in a small village. Now he was the master of the imperial guard, the husband of a noblewoman, and a trusted confidant of an emperor.

Michael did not realize how ambitious and extremely dangerous his new friend Basil was. As the two men became closer, Basil began turning the impressionable emperor against Bardas in much the same way that Bardas had turned him against Theodora. Basil personally killed Bardas in 866 and then persuaded Michael to elevate him to serve as co-emperor. This arrangement did not last even a year. In April 867, Basil orchestrated the murder of Michael, a reprehensible betrayal that inaugurated Rome's Macedonian dynasty, a line of emperors and empresses descended from him that would last for nearly 200 years.

BASIL I, ONE of the most disreputable characters to rule the Roman state, benefited from the best work of image rehabilitation since the emperor Nerva had been transformed from a murderous incompetent into the divinized founder of Rome's most revered dynasty. At the same time, Basil's predecessor, the feckless emperor Michael III, had his character and achievements attacked so unfairly that it makes the mistreatment of Domitian by Tacitus, Pliny, and Suetonius seem mild.

This historical distortion began when the patriarch Photius contrasted the dynamism that the new emperor supposedly embodied with the lethargy of Michael, and compared the coup that brought Basil to power to the Jewish king David overthrowing Saul in the Bible. Later figures wove even more elaborate tales to explain away the murder. Genesius, who wrote a series of imperial biographies in the tenth century, framed Basil's murder of the emperor as a giant misunderstanding caused by courtiers, who supposedly "conspired to destroy [their] harmony and love" by convincing each man that the other meant to kill him. Even so, Basil refused to kill Michael himself, wrote Genesius, because "the thought of murder made him swoon." Thus it fell to his associates "to kill Michael themselves, fearing that otherwise they would be killed along with Basil."[12]

None of these stories could really hide Basil's identity as a violent and insecure man who showed no loyalty or love even for his benefactors. At the same time, his personal disreputability did not prevent him from notching some real achievements during his eighteen years in power. Basil lost the Sicilian city of Syracuse to the Arabs, marking the first time it had been out of some form of Roman control since the war against Hannibal.[13] But he compensated for its loss with an aggressive set of campaigns that removed Arab forces from the Italian mainland and provided the Greek-speaking Roman refugees fleeing Syracuse with a safe haven.[14] In Greece, his officials defeated and destroyed a raiding fleet of thirty ships sent from Tarsus and a set of naval attacks launched from Crete. In Asia Minor, his son-in-law ended a war with the Paulicians, a sect of rebellious Christians, by capturing and decapitating their leader, Chrysocheir.[15] Then, in an action that was totally on-brand, Basil received the severed head and shot three arrows into it. He proclaimed his archery practice "an offering . . . to God . . . on behalf of the multitudes Chrysocheir had killed."[16]

One of the most consequential projects Basil undertook was one that involved updating Roman law so that it better suited the conditions of the later ninth century. While the comprehensive law code Justinian had introduced 350 years earlier still held sway over the empire, Rome's territorial contraction since then meant that, in many places, legal texts had become impossible to find. When they were available, most people lacked knowledge of the legal Latin in which they were written.[17]

Basil decided to undertake a comprehensive "cleansing" of Roman law by removing outdated laws, updating the Justinianic code with the laws issued since its publication, and translating the new document into Greek.[18] The resulting text, the *Prochiron*, first appeared in the 870s. Its prologue explains that, since the time of the Old Testament patriarchs, God had entrusted rulers with the task of providing people with law and justice in a fashion that appropriately organized their lives. The Iconoclast emperors of the eighth century had tried to do this, but their impiety overthrew "legislation piously written by many emperors" and their work needed to be discarded.[19] Basil promised that the *Prochiron* would replace their tainted publications with a new one that translated older concepts from Latin into Greek and introduced new legislation that better reflected current conditions in the empire.[20] Then, in the 880s, he published the *Eisagoge*, the second work of his legal codification project, that pivoted from the Old Testament to a philosophical explanation of the need to update the legal code in a fashion that "cleansed everything remaining in the breadth of the ancient laws" of impious or irrelevant ideas.[21]

But Basil's successes continued to be overshadowed by his loathsome behavior. In the 880s, his most notable victim was his own son, the future emperor Leo VI. Since Basil had married Michael III's mistress, Eudocia Ingerina, it was widely rumored that Leo, his first son with Eudocia, was in fact Michael's child. Basil therefore made it clear early in his reign that he wanted his son Constantine, the child of his first wife, to be his heir. Constantine, however, died in 879.[22] Basil was then forced to elevate Leo and his third son, Alexander (whose parentage was not in doubt, because he was conceived after Michael's death), to the status of co-heirs.[23] In 883, Basil "imprisoned Leo in the Pearl Hall of the palace and intended to have him blinded." The patriarch Photius convinced him not to take his son's sight, but Leo spent the next three years locked away, "writing countless pleas to the emperor" without great effect. Leo was finally restored to his position on July 21, 886, after Basil suppressed a coup supported by sixty-six senators concerned about Alexander's manifest unfitness to take the throne. The cold, calculating emperor released Leo only because his return to the line of succession might help to preserve his own power.[24]

Even Basil's most earnest propagandists could do little to cleanse the stain of his initial order to unjustly imprison and blind his son. In one of the more remarkable understatements in all of Roman history, Genesius wrote simply that "malicious men managed to curb natural affection and Basil's fatherly love for Leo cooled a little."[25] If locking away and nearly taking the eyes of one's son is just a small cooling of the affection, one shudders to think what Basil's genuine anger looked like.

A biography of Basil attributed to Leo's son, the emperor Constantine VII Porphyrogenitus, offers an even more absurd story. While Leo was imprisoned, a pet parrot kept in the palace disrupted a dinner party Basil was having with some senators by "uttering the words 'Alas, Alas, Lord Leo' over and over again."[26] The guests eventually fell silent, and when Basil asked the senators what troubled them, they said they could not eat as long as the bird kept reminding them of what Leo was experiencing in the same building, while they dined in luxury.[27] It was at that point that Basil "promised to look into the matter" that had led to Leo's arrest, and shortly afterward he had Leo released from custody.[28] If one chooses to accept this story of the divinely gifted parrot changing the emperor's mind, we must then wrestle with the question of why, exactly, Basil had failed to investigate the charges against his son for the preceding three years.

Fortunately, Basil died before he could again change his mind about Leo. It happened on August 29, 886, following a bizarre hunting accident where he was gored by a stag, dragged for miles, and then freed by an attendant who cut the emperor's belt. Basil survived the goring but died of an infection not long afterward. The emperor did live long enough, however, "to order that the man who had cut off his belt should have his head cut off for having drawn his sword before the emperor."[29] No ending seems more appropriate for Basil than unjustly killing the man who had tried to save his life.

Leo VI RULED for nearly twenty-six years and displayed a mild character so unlike that of his father that he came to be known as Leo the Wise. But Leo, like Basil, firmly believed that the emerging Roman institutions of the ninth century needed updated documents that explained how those systems functioned. One of the first such publications he sponsored represented a third phase in the legal codification project begun by his father. This is the *Sixty Books*, a text also known by its Greek title the *Basilika* that appeared on Christmas in 888. Its preface claims again to "eliminate the difficulty of studying the laws" by assembling all the laws that remained valid in six volumes and then, like Justinian, voiding all the ones that did not make the cut. Like Justinian before him, Leo then kept the legal texts current by issuing a set of 120 new laws that changed, amended, or even replaced elements of the Justinianic legal edifice that Leo had inherited.[30]

Leo's interest in documenting, updating, and organizing the old administrative texts from late antiquity extended well beyond the legal codification project. Sometime just before the turn of the tenth century, he began work on the *Book of the Prefect*, a document containing a set of rules governing the commercial, banking, and guild activities that took place in and around Constantinople which were overseen by the prefect of the city.[31] At roughly this same time, he also elected to update the Roman military manual that the emperor Maurice had assembled 300 years earlier to reflect its approach to new tactics and military threats that Maurice could never have anticipated.[32]

In the *Taktika* (as the resulting military manual was called), Leo devoted significant attention to naval warfare and the use of Greek fire, a technology that did not exist during Maurice's lifetime, as well as larger strategic initiatives involving coordinated land and sea attacks. If, for example, Arabs attacked by sea from Cilicia, a region with which the empire shared a land boundary, Leo advised that the response should involve defensive action by sea and an attack by land. Alternatively, if an Arab army coming from Cilicia breached the land frontier, the Roman navy should mount an attack on areas near the major Cilician cities of Tarsus or Adana. If Romans faced coordinated attacks from Cilicia, Syria, and Egypt, they should gather ships in Cyprus and try to destroy the Arab fleets before they left port.[33]

The later years of Leo's reign show that the *Taktika*'s plans were not just theoretical discussions of what Romans should do but a set of strategies they actually used. Between September 909 and September 910, the Roman admiral Himerius gathered a fleet in Cyprus that he used to mount raids on Syria following an Arab attack that came from Cilicia.[34] In 911, Himerius directed a large-scale attack on Crete that involved 177 ships and over 12,000 soldiers, apparently trying to apply the *Taktika*'s combined land and sea assault strategy to the Arab-held island. The campaign failed, but the approach it took shows that Leo wanted his generals, like his lawyers, to use the texts he commissioned to improve Roman performance in this new age.

Leo died in 912, leaving the throne to his brother and nominal co-emperor, Alexander. Alexander proved to be a disaster. He dismissed the admiral Himerius and the patriarch of Constantinople, provoked a war with Bulgaria by refusing to pay the annual tribute mandated by law, and then died after less than thirteen months in power. Alexander, who apparently struggled with both alcoholism and impotence, left no heir. Hence Leo's eight-year-old son, Constantine VII, took over as the next emperor.[35]

Constantine's position was simultaneously constitutionally secure and practically weak. He was born in the purple chamber in the palace on September 2, 905, and was immediately proclaimed a porphyrogenitus. This name was attached to Constantine for his whole life and has remained the most common title used for him to this day. No Roman emperor needed the title more. Because, while Constantine

VII Porphyrogenitus was the son of a Roman emperor, born in the imperial palace to Zoe Karbonopsina, a woman who would be an Augusta, his father and mother were not married at the time of his birth. And when the wedding did occur, it was among the most controversial weddings in Roman imperial history.

Zoe Karbonopsina (literally "Zoe with Charcoal Eyes") was Leo's fourth wife, and fourth marriages were not permitted under Roman canon law. Even third marriages were problematic. Leo was not entirely to blame for this situation, however. As sometimes happened with Roman emperors, Leo had little choice about who his first wife would be. He had begun a relationship with Zoe Zaoutzaina, the daughter of a nobleman who would have been a perfectly suitable bride, but his mother had staged a beauty pageant in her son's absence and chosen Theophano Martinakia as his bride. Basil I agreed she was a perfect choice. Leo did not. They were married in 882, and Leo promptly began an affair with Zoe Zaoutzaina. When Theophano reported this to the emperor, Basil had his son and heir beaten and forced Zoe to marry another man. After his father died, Leo could afford to be so brazen in his liaisons with Zoe that they spent the nights together while his wife slept in a separate part of the palace. The empress had little choice but to permit this, but she did have the ability to refuse to grant her husband a divorce. They remained married until her death almost fifteen years later.[36]

Roman church law allowed widowers to marry a second time, but not if the second marriage was used to legitimate an adulterous relationship that had begun before the first marriage ended. Leo could remarry, but not to Zoe. He tried to force the issue, but he was reduced to compelling a priest working in the palace to conduct the ceremony because the patriarch refused to do so. Zoe bore Leo a daughter, but she succumbed to an illness only two years after the wedding. Leo quickly married a third wife named Eudokia. The church grudgingly permitted widowers to marry a third time, but this marriage did not last long either. Eudokia died roughly a year later during the birth of a stillborn boy, whom the emperor named Basil.[37] Leo was now thrice a widower—and, more importantly, he had no male heir.

Zoe Karbonopsina came into Leo's life in 903, first as a lover, and then, in September 905, as the mother of Constantine, his only living son. Although it seems that Leo and Zoe had lived together before Constantine's birth, they were not married, and Leo knew that church approval of the union would be extremely difficult to secure.[38] He then negotiated an agreement through which the patriarch Nicholas I agreed to baptize Constantine on the condition that Leo would sever all ties with Zoe. Leo promised to do this, but, Nicholas would write, "three days after the baptism[,] . . . the mother was introduced into the palace with an escort of guards, just like the wife of an emperor."[39] Leo then risked splintering the church, enraging the patriarch, and inciting public anger by trying to get church approval for a union with Zoe.

All of these things happened. Leo got his fourth marriage, but it required him to depose Nicholas I, agree to an eight-year penance, and issue legislation prohibiting any future fourth marriages.[40] Even so, the church split over the issue. When Leo's brother Alexander took over as emperor, he exploited the division to bring Nicholas back as patriarch and expel Zoe from the palace. It was even rumored that he intended to kill his nephew but was talked out of it by Leo's friends, who reminded him that "Constantine was just a child" who was innocent of anything his father had done.[41]

This was the world the eight-year-old Constantine inherited upon his uncle's death. He was the legitimate emperor, but his mother had been exiled and the regent who would run the empire in his name was Nicholas, the patriarch his father had deposed in order to marry his mother. Constantine, though, was a porphyrogenitus. The systems that his father and grandfather had so diligently cataloged meant that, in the tenth century, his status as a porphyrogenitus ensured that he would stay alive and remain a part of the imperial college. But it was not enough to ensure that he would ever actually rule. Instead, Constantine's accession began a long period during which emperors born in the purple struggled to assert any sort of direct control over the empire they supposedly led.

Chapter 40

The Age of Impotent Emperors

913–976

THE ELEVATION OF Constantine VII began a reign of nearly fifty years. During this period, he offered Romans the glorious facade of an emperor who belonged to the Macedonian dynasty while effective power lay instead with someone else who had a much less impressive family background. The jockeying for power began just three days after his uncle Alexander died. Although Alexander had selected a regency council led by the patriarch Nicholas, a man named Constantine Doukas tried to seize power with a detachment of soldiers he was supposed to lead against Bulgaria. Doukas was killed following an impromptu defense of the emperor by the residents of Constantinople and the imperial guards. But the terrified regents began a series of brutal reprisals that ended only when some of the judges in Constantinople asked the patriarch and the other regents, "How do you presume to do such things when the emperor is still a child and you cannot get his order for it?"[1] The regents had no answer.

Their question highlighted an essential feature of tenth-century Roman political life. Killings, exiles, and political turmoil—which would have normally disgusted Romans if emperors ordered them—seldom dented the people's love for the Macedonian dynasty, whose emperors sat in the palace while other men and women ran the state, ostensibly on their behalf. As long as a member of the dynasty lived somewhere, Romans could tolerate a surprising amount of violent political jockeying between the generals, commanders, and even foreigners competing to actually run the state in his name. Suddenly the long-term survival of an inept or disinterested sovereign became an asset to those seeking power.

Surprisingly, one of the first people to realize that Rome now depended more heavily upon the presence of a ceremonial emperor than it did on his actual decision-making was not a Roman at all. In August 913, Simeon of Bulgaria arrived outside the walls of Constantinople with an army and began negotiations with the regency council while the eight-year-old Constantine VII had dinner with Simeon's sons. Simeon asked the patriarch to make him a member of the Roman imperial college, a proposition that Nicholas denied (as Simeon no doubt expected he would). Nicholas instead prayed over Simeon and "then put his monastic cowl on Simeon's head instead of a crown," a gesture that evidently marked the Bulgarian as a "brother" of the Roman emperor.[2] This was enough for Simeon, who realized that this nebulous title enabled him to meddle in future Roman affairs whenever he wished by claiming that he was only intervening to protect his new imperial sibling.

At this point Constantine VII's mother, Zoe Karbonopsina, staged a political comeback. Alexander had exiled her when he took power, but she now saw that the weakness of the regency council threatened the position of her son. Soon after Simeon departed, she arranged for word to leak out that "because the emperor Constantine was a child, he wanted his mother," and she needed to return to the palace. Zoe then purged the regency council of the members appointed by Alexander and installed her own allies as part of a reconstituted group.[3]

Zoe dominated Roman political life for the next five and a half years. Although her son was the official ruler, Zoe made sure that Romans knew who was directing affairs. The bronze coins issued during that time showed her and Constantine together, grasping a cross and identified as Augustus and Augusta. Zoe is the larger figure, standing on the right in a position that conveys her authority.[4] This styling resembled the way Irene had presented herself during the reign of Constantine VI, making it clear that Zoe was angling to come as close to Irene's position as any woman had in more than a century.

Zoe handled imperial affairs well while they were hers to manage, but she made a crucial mistake when she entrusted a complicated attack against Bulgaria to a general named Romanos Lekapenos. Her diplomats had secured an alliance with the Pechenegs, a Turkic group from Central Asia that had traveled to the northern side of the Danube. Romanos was supposed to sail a fleet up the Danube and transport the Pechenegs across the river so they could attack Bulgaria alongside the Romans. When the Pechenegs arrived at the river, however, they lost faith in the Roman generals, after seeing Romanos quarreling with another commander, and went home.[5] The Bulgarians defeated the outmanned Roman soldiers, and Romanos did nothing to help rescue survivors. When he returned to Constantinople, "there was even a vote passed by his enemies to have him deprived of his eyesight," but he was saved by Zoe's intervention.[6]

ROMANOS REPAID ZOE by launching a revolt that led to her downfall.

The story our sources preserve is nearly as ornate as it is hard to follow, but Romanos supposedly reached out to the young emperor via an associate at court and suggested that he should take him "into his personal service" to protect himself against coups. The thirteen-year-old Constantine then gave Romanos the power to act to protect him, and Romanos immediately arrested the eunuch in charge of the imperial bedchamber, one of Zoe's key supporters. Taken completely by surprise, Zoe summoned the patriarch Nicholas to the palace so that the regency council could organize a response. She also tried to rally the Constantinopolitan populace to support her. But instead of helping Zoe, Nicholas induced Constantine VII to strip his mother of all power so that he could advise Constantine instead. The following morning, it became clear that Constantine wanted no such thing.

"Crying and shedding tears," he embraced his mother and pleaded, "Let my mother be with me!"[7]

What the emperor actually wanted mattered little in the days that followed. His male regents had no popular or military support, and his mother's position collapsed when Leo Phocas, the commander of the army units in Constantinople, defected to Romanos. On March 24, 919, Romanos sent two emissaries to the palace to explain that what he had done "was not an act of rebellion," because he had acted in defense of the emperor. The following day he removed the patriarch and other regents from power. Having "prostrated himself before the emperor," he swore loyalty to him in a public ceremony.[8]

Like Basil I two generations earlier, Romanos descended from an insignificant family that had moved as settlers to reconquered Roman land during his father's lifetime.[9] Constantine would later describe Romanos as "a common, illiterate fellow" who "was not of noble or imperial stock." But Romanos understood that any path to a sustainable imperial dynasty would have to go through the family of the weak, reigning sovereign.[10] He began to act toward Constantine VII much like a fig seedling does to a mature tree, slowly strangling its host as it sinks its own roots into the ground.

In April 919, Romanos arranged for the engagement of the fourteen-year-old emperor and his own ten-year-old daughter, Helena, and they wed a month later. Romanos then sent Zoe to a convent on a spurious charge that she had tried to poison him soon after the ceremony, and convinced his isolated son-in-law to name him Caesar. In December 920, Romanos Lekapenos was named co-emperor. The following May, Romanos's son Christopher Lekapenos joined the imperial college, and not long after that Romanos used a coup attempt "as a pretext to demote the emperor Constantine, make him second in rank, and promote himself to the foremost position" in the state.[11] Then, on Christmas of either 923 or 924, Romanos "crowned his sons Stephan Lekapenos and Constantine Lekapenos in the Great Church."[12] By the end of the decade, Constantine VII had been reduced to appearing in ceremonial processions alongside his brothers-in-law.[13] The Macedonian dynasty continued, but its sole living member was seldom seen in public and no longer even appeared on coins.

Constantine VII also became an afterthought in foreign affairs as Romanos began to direct Roman foreign and military policy. In the east, he and his generals conquered Melitene (modern Malatya), a major Muslim center of power in a valley that lay just outside of the last range of mountains separating Asia Minor and the plains of Syria and Mesopotamia.[14] In the Balkans, he negotiated a peace treaty with the Bulgarians that would join his granddaughter Mary to the Bulgarian leader Peter. During the wedding feast, Peter, perhaps at Romanos's encouragement, insisted that Mary's father, Christopher, "should be acclaimed" before the Macedonian dynast Constantine. He wanted everyone in Constantinople to understand that the Bulgarians and their sovereign would support Christopher over Constantine VII in any succession struggle should Romanos die or fall from power.[15] "By now," the eleventh-century historian John Skylitzes wrote, "Constantine had only the appearance and name of emperor, for he was deprived of all the privileges." This happened even though Constantine was the most senior emperor and the rightful heir of the Macedonian dynasty.

Fortunately for Constantine VII, Christopher died in 931 before the Bulgarians had cause to intervene in the imperial succession.[16] Then, in December 944, Romanos himself fell from power in a complicated set of coups orchestrated by Constantine and his wife, Romanos's own daughter, Helena. This episode began when Constantine arrived at a plan to "set the sons against the father" and reached out to Stephan Lekapenos. Working through intermediaries in the court, Constantine manipulated Stephan into exiling his father. When Stephan then tried to assume power himself, Constantine's wife Helena and her half-brother, the eunuch Basil, organized a secondary coup backed by the general Bardas Phocas (now commonly called Bardas Phocas the Elder to distinguish him from his grandson). Stephan and Constantine Lekapenos were taken by surprise, "arrested while they were at the table dining" with Constantine, sent into exile, and forcibly made clerics.[17]

IT IS HIGHLY unlikely that Constantine VII possessed the political acumen to execute two such complicated coups in the span of a little more than a month on his own. Not only was he "addicted to wine," according to Skylitzes, but, once he seized power, he "was indifferent to the promotion of officials." He left it to Helena and Basil to choose the men who would run the state. It was also Helena and Basil, not Constantine, who arranged for his son, who bore the name Romanos, to be crowned as co-emperor and successor-designate.[18] While Constantine was now officially the sole ruler of the empire, the children of Romanos Lekapenos were still effectively running much of its domestic affairs.

Bardas Phocas the Elder and his family assumed control of military affairs. Bardas became the chief commander of the Roman army, while his sons Nicephorus and Leo led the armies in the Anatolikon theme and Cappadocia, respectively. Bardas, said Skylitzes, "showed himself to be a fine commander when he served under others, but he brought little or no benefit to the Roman state once authority over the entire force depended on his judgment."[19] In 955, Constantine finally lost patience and replaced him as chief commander with his son Nicephorus Phocas. Nicephorus and his nephew John Tzimiskes then restored Roman military fortunes in a fashion that primed the state for rapid expansion in the 960s.

The surviving Lekapenoi secured their authority in two different arenas. Helena managed affairs for her husband and guarded the position of their son, Romanos II. Her eunuch half-brother, Basil, of course, had no interest in the next generation, since he physically could produce no children, but he proved remarkably adept at becoming indispensable to the empire's rulers. He served as the guardian of the imperial bedchamber and used this position to amass political influence and tremendous wealth. Contemporary Roman authors speak about Basil living in an impressive house in Constantinople that had once belonged to the fifth-century commander Aspar. More recently, it had housed an exiled Armenian king.[20] Basil also owned "fertile and prosperous places along the eastern frontier" and employed a private guard of more than 3,000 that he could mobilize if his interests were threatened.[21]

While members of these great families ran domestic and military affairs in his name, Constantine VII devoted much of his time to intellectual pursuits. An anonymous historian writing in the early 960s praised the emperor for his educational reforms, which brought to the capital teachers who "adorned and enriched the Roman state with their wisdom." The emperor himself loved to meet their students and gave them stipends so they could focus on their studies without concern for their finances. His goal was to "align the state on a more intellectual course" by improving the quality of the teachers in the capital and ensuring that the students they trained had the skills necessary to operate its institutions.[22]

Like his father before him, Constantine had something of an obsession with documenting the proper, effective operation of the court and other institutions in the capital. His indifference to governing left him a lot of time to organize the production of a massive collection of texts that remain central to our understanding of how the Roman Empire functioned in the sixth through tenth centuries.[23] Contemporaries describe Constantine as an insatiably curious researcher who requested that his governors write historical and geographical reports of the places they were stationed. In addition, he questioned visitors from abroad at great length when they visited the palace.[24] He, or people working under his direction, then wrote treatises assembling information about the empire's themes, the origins of the peoples whose lands neighbored the empire, the history of agricultural practices, and the career of Basil I. He also initiated a project that excerpted, assembled, and organized extracts from the historical works covering Greek and Roman antiquity that could be found in the empire's libraries.

Two works in particular stand out in this vast literary corpus. One of these, *On the Ceremonies*, gathered and systematized descriptions of imperial ceremonial events, processions, and festivals with the same meticulous precision that Basil I and Leo VI had applied to their works on Roman law and military tactics. Constantine even explained the need for the project in similar terms to those used by Leo in the *Basilika* and the *Taktika* by claiming that knowledge of Roman ceremonies "[had] been neglected and [had] become . . . moribund." Older accounts of imperial ceremonies, he added, needed to be updated to reflect current practices, so that the ceremonial aspects of Roman life could be revivified and rediscovered. This was essential work, the emperor argued, because ceremonies were what showed Roman imperial rule "to be more beautiful, more noble, and awe-inspiring both to our own people and to non-Romans."[25]

A second work, *De Administrando Imperio* (On the empire's administration), spoke more directly to his concern for the future of his dynasty. Constantine exhorted his newly elevated son Romanos II to take its lessons to heart because it collected "those things which I think you should not be ignorant about so that you will be wise when you take control of the government." He intended the work to be a comprehensive guidebook for Romanos, one that he could easily consult so he could determine if he was receiving good, well-informed advice from those around him. In domestic affairs, it recorded how state institutions had evolved over time. It also detailed the resources, capabilities, national origins, customs, geographical characteristics, and historical interactions with Rome of every non-Roman nation.[26] Not only was Romanos supposed to learn how to rule, he was also supposed to appreciate why his empire was superior to all other states in the world.

FEW COULD DENY that Constantine, in his own unique fashion, had done all he could to prepare Romanos II to rule the empire when he succeeded his father in 959. Romanos inherited his father's nominal authority over the Roman state as well as the cadre of advisers who actually administered Rome's affairs. He did institute some changes by dismissing the powerful eunuch Basil, allowing his mother Helena to fill the vacuum this left, and "appointing officials who were fervently loyal to him." He also followed the pattern of his father and grandfather by elevating an heir as soon as he could, crowning his young son Basil on Easter in 960. In 961, he had a second son, Constantine, who would eventually also be enrolled as co-emperor.[27]

Romanos II knew enough not to interfere with Nicephorus Phocas's command over the Roman military. In 961, Roman forces under Nicephorus recaptured Crete, more than 130 years after it had fallen under Arab rule.[28] This was both somewhat unexpected and a source of great excitement in Constantinople. Troops drawn from Asia, who had been transported to Crete alongside Roman ships equipped with Greek fire, had stormed the Cretan beaches in full armor. The defeated Cretan defenders had withdrawn to their fortified capital of Chandax, where they withstood a siege for much of the winter of 960/961. Nicephorus then stunned them by collapsing a large section of the city wall and storming the city.

Nicephorus next embarked on a set of actions designed to reintegrate Crete into the empire. This involved the violent suppression of the Muslim defenders in Chandax and other cities as well as a set of campaigns in the countryside against Cretans, most of whom were likely Christian.[29] Nicephorus constructed a fortified settlement called Temenos for the soldiers garrisoning the island. They were given land with which to support themselves and allowed to maintain it in exchange for continued military service under the same terms that bound garrison soldiers to lands in other themes across the empire. Nicephorus also transferred "bands of Armenians, Romans, and others" to the island so they could settle there and re-Romanize it.[30] Not long afterward, a monk named Nikon embarked on a church building and evangelization campaign designed to correct Cretan religious practices and reimplant the church hierarchy and community structures that had atrophied during the century Crete sat outside of the empire under Muslim rule.[31]

The capture of Crete was the beginning of a series of mostly successful Roman campaigns designed to return lands under Muslim rule to Roman control. Romanos, however, did not live to see them. He died on March 15, 963, less than four months after Roman armies under the command of Nicephorus and John Tzimiskes captured the Syrian city of Aleppo. Because Romanos's mother, Helena, had died two years earlier, his passing left the official control of the state to the child emperors Basil II and Constantine VIII. And it left effective control up for grabs.

The game then began again. Tzimiskes arranged for Roman armies in Cappadocia to proclaim Nicephorus emperor so he could serve alongside the impotent Macedonian sovereigns. After court figures tried to resist, Basil the eunuch unleashed his private army to secure the capital for the new claimant to the throne. When Nicephorus finally arrived in Constantinople later in the summer, he reconstituted a very familiar-looking structure around Basil II and Constantine VIII. He had already promised that he would not overthrow his young colleagues, but he also made clear that he would run affairs in the state while they provided the Macedonian window dressing that gave his regime legitimacy.[32] As had been the case under both Constantine VII and Romanos II, Nicephorus entrusted the empire's major military commands to members of the Phocas family. His brother Leo assumed control of the fleet, while Tzimiskes took control of the armies along the eastern front. Nicephorus returned Basil the eunuch to a position of influence in the palace and installed him as the president of the Constantinople Senate. He then secured a family connection to the Macedonian dynasty by marrying Theophano, the beautiful and brilliant widow of Romanos II.

Nicephorus then went to war. In a series of offensives between 963 and 969, he reconquered Tarsus, recaptured Antioch, and pressed deeply into coastal Syria. The victory over Tarsus in 965 proved particularly violent. The Romans destroyed all the vegetation around the city, defeated an army sent from the city outside its walls, and then starved the citizens into submission. When the city surrendered, Nicephorus carried out an ethnic cleansing in which he forced its Muslim inhabitants to flee to Muslim lands in Syria, "taking only themselves and necessary clothing."[33] The city's main mosque was converted into a stable, and its territory was settled by Roman soldiers placed in a set of new military themes.[34] Nicephorus also arranged for the migration of a large group of Syrian Orthodox Christians, who left Muslim territory in order to settle in underpopulated areas around Melitene.

These campaigns were expensive. The needs of large armies campaigning abroad ate into the Roman state's ability to provide for its own citizens in Constantinople. As food prices rose, rumors spread through the capital that Nicephorus and his brother Leo "were making private profits off of the sufferings of the masses."[35] The money Nicephorus raised was actually going to pay the army, but inflation and a higher tax burden combined with overly aggressive riot suppression to make the populace hate Nicephorus despite his conquests.[36] He was assassinated during the night of December 10, 969, by conspirators led by the empress Theophano and John Tzimiskes, the man who went on to take Nicephorus's spot as co-emperor. Some mourned Nicephorus, while others criticized Tzimiskes, but the child emperors Basil II and Constantine VIII were held blameless. In fact, they were hardly mentioned at all in the sources that recounted the processions and acclamations that accompanied the coronation of John Tzimiskes.[37]

When Constantinople awoke on December 11, 969, it did so to the calls of "corps of picked men passing through the streets of the city, proclaiming Tzimiskes as the emperor of the Romans." They were followed at some distance by Basil the eunuch, "the bastard son of the emperor Romanos [Lekapenos]." By noon, Tzimiskes and Basil the eunuch had replaced Nicephorus's administrators in the capital and sent messengers out with word about who would replace his provincial governors. The replacement of one non-Macedonian emperor with another went so smoothly, Leo the Deacon wrote, that, aside from the deaths of "the emperor Nicephorus and one bodyguard . . . no one else received so much as a slap on the face." Tzimiskes also dispatched Theophano to a monastery after making her the scapegoat for her husband's murder.[38]

Tzimiskes proved to be an exceptionally good leader. He reigned for a little more than six years, but that was enough time for him to amass a trove of significant military and political achievements. In the military arena, he seized a large chunk of territory in the Balkans after he defeated Russian forces that looked poised to overwhelm Bulgaria. He also built upon Nicephorus's successes in the east. Antioch became a forward base for Roman armies, which penetrated so deeply into Syria and Mesopotamia that they sacked cities such as Nisibis, Damascus, and Beirut that had not been touched by Roman arms for centuries. Aleppo, now a Roman protectorate and buffer state, pledged to prevent hostile forces from crossing into Roman territory. When the Fatimid caliphate in Egypt tried to take advantage of the chaos in Syria, Tzimiskes's forces thwarted their attempt to storm Antioch and then defeated them in the field.[39]

Tzimiskes proved equally adept at managing the internal challenges that such rapid expansion caused. The new territories in the east and the Balkans were organized into small themes over which a more senior general exercised collective authority, a system that added complexity to the theme structure but enhanced the empire's ability to identify and mobilize resources in these new lands. Tzimiskes also addressed some of the internal problems that had led to Nicephorus's downfall, using the immense plunder he had secured from Syria and from the defeated Russians to eliminate his predecessor's unpopular taxes.

It was all quite a lot to pack into a relatively short reign. On the night of January 10–11, 976, Tzimiskes died in Constantinople at the age of fifty-one. His death left the eighteen-year-old Basil II as the only adult emperor who could legally exercise power. The age of the impotent emperors was now nearing its end, but only because Basil II was willing to fight harder for the throne than any other Macedonian emperor in almost a century. And the fight would become very, very messy before one of Rome's most accomplished emperors finally seized full control of the state.

Chapter 41

Basil II, the System, and the Peak of the Macedonian Dynasty

976–1025

T HE UNEXPECTED DEATH of John Tzimiskes in January 976 prompted a power struggle that profoundly shook the foundations of the Roman state. Very little of Rome's success under the Macedonian emperors of the mid-tenth century had derived from their middling military and political capacities. It had instead been fueled by a sophisticated administrative system that welded the ceremonial power of the Macedonian sovereign to the decision-making prerogatives of co-emperors, experienced advisers at court, and military commanders. These figures communicated policy and military goals to a professional, well-trained class of administrators and soldiers who effectively executed their leaders' commands in their emperor's name.

It had taken a long time to build this system. Its foundations had been laid by the administrative reforms of Nicephorus I in the first years of the ninth century, and had been further developed by the palace schools that emerged to train future bureaucrats under Michael III. The legal, administrative, diplomatic, and military treatises sponsored by Basil I, Leo VI, and Constantine VII had explained to these professionals how they should do their jobs. The military leadership had benefited from another shift: The decline of the Abbasid dynasty ended the regular raiding of Asia Minor that had necessitated keeping the semiprofessional soldiers of the themes close to the lands that supported them. Thanks to the growing revenue generated by its well-administered territory, the Roman state could again field well-equipped professional armies capable of conquering territories across the Mediterranean, the Balkans, Armenia, and the Middle East.

As in other moments of rapid Roman expansion, the fruits of these conquests were unequally distributed. Prominent families like the Lekapenoi and the Phokades used their decades at the center of tenth-century Roman political life to amass large landholdings in their home regions. So, too, did relative newcomers, including John Tzimiskes, from the Armenaikon theme, and Bardas Skleros, whose family estates were in Mesopotamia.[1] Their families came to possess a potent combination of wealth and influence within their home regions. In some cases, they had a multigenerational hold over important military commands. These were the sort of men that the emperor Basil II needed to displace if he was going to take real control over the empire.

It was by no means inevitable that Basil would try to do this. In fact, it is not clear that Basil initially did anything on his own at all. After Tzimiskes's death, Basil's great-uncle, Basil the eunuch, returned to the palace to run imperial affairs just as he had during the reigns of Constantine VII, Nicephorus Phocas, and Tzimiskes. Basil the eunuch immediately began looking for people who might try to seize the position of co-emperor that Tzimiskes had left vacant. He particularly feared Bardas Skleros, supreme commander of the army, who had helped Tzimiskes seize power in 969. Basil the eunuch trusted neither Skleros's judgment nor his loyalty and demoted him to regional commander of the forces in Mesopotamia. Skleros responded by orchestrating his proclamation as emperor by the Mesopotamian troops. He followed this up by seizing the tax revenues in the region and arresting wealthy people so he could take their property.[2] After depositing these stolen funds in a fort located near modern Harput in eastern Turkey, he negotiated alliances with the

Arab rulers who controlled the territories adjacent to his. From that point forward, wrote John Skylitzes, "Skleros had his mind set on one thing: his desire to be emperor."[3]

While at many other times in Roman history such a statement certainly would have meant a desire to overthrow or kill the reigning emperors, it is not entirely clear that this is what Skleros meant in 976. Skleros, like Romanos Lekapenos and John Tzimiskes, may well have simply sought to again reduce the Macedonian dynasts Basil II and Constantine VIII to a ceremonial role while he actually ran the state.[4] Whatever ambiguity existed in the first weeks of the revolt dissipated, however, after all their supporters first skirmished in a mountain pass not far outside of Caesarea in Cappadocia. After losing the commander of his cavalry in a bloody fight, Skleros ordered attacks into Asia Minor. Meanwhile, other forces exerted pressure on Antioch to the south and on the city of Attaleia, the base of the imperial fleet in the region.[5] Skleros was an Armenian, so forces loyal to Constantinople responded by killing "every Armenian they captured without quarter because these had been the first to join the uprising."[6] This brutality did not change the course of the war. Skleros's forces captured Nicaea and Abydos the next year, causing Constantinopolitans to fear that their food supply might be disrupted.[7]

Things had become desperate enough by the spring of 978 that Basil the eunuch appealed for help from the Phocas family, which had been sidelined since Tzimiskes's coup had killed Nicephorus Phocas.[8] Nicephorus's nephew, Bardas Phocas the Younger, arranged for a few thousand troops from Georgia to reinforce the imperial army, and by the early spring of 979 Skleros's army had been defeated in eastern Anatolia.[9] Skleros then fled to Baghdad, where he was taken into custody so that he could be used as a bargaining chip in the future.[10]

Skleros's presence in Baghdad, however, made the emperor Basil II so nervous that he agreed to trade the tribute paid to Rome by the kingdom of Aleppo for Skleros during a period when Basil the eunuch had fallen ill. This led to rumors that the outraged eunuch might try to overthrow the emperor.[11] Basil II heard these rumors, placed Basil the eunuch under house arrest, and promoted Bardas Phocas to serve as commander of Roman forces in Antioch. He tasked Bardas with renegotiating the treaty with Baghdad so the Aleppine tribute would again be paid to Constantinople.[12] As a result, Skleros remained in Baghdad, still a threat to the emperor.

Without any general strong enough to assert a claim as a co-emperor, and with his brother Constantine VIII perfectly comfortable standing back from exercising power, Basil II now controlled the direction of Roman imperial policy. This was the first time in nearly twenty-five years that a member of the Macedonian dynasty would direct state policy—and Basil II's first actions did little to inspire confidence. In 986, he launched a campaign against the Bulgarians led by a new group of commanders, who, though less accomplished, were presumably more loyal to him than the men he had recently dismissed. Once the Romans reached the area around Serdica (modern Sofia), they "settled down and kept watch over the city for 20 days" rather than organizing an effective attack. Not only did they fail to take the city, but, as Leo the Deacon suggests, they were so inept that the Bulgarians were able to burn their siege engines, ambush their foraging parties, and then defeat the main army in a battle where they also seized "the imperial command tent . . . and all the army's baggage."[13]

This failure had the predictable result of encouraging all the notables with access to armies to press their own claims to power. Skleros asked the ruler in Baghdad to free him and give him money to recruit Bedouins, Kurds, and Armenians to accompany him into Roman territory.[14] Bardas Phocas too soon entered the fray. He lent his troops first to Skleros, then betrayed his new ally and launched his own bid for power backed by a Georgian monarch.[15]

Basil II was much savvier than his adversaries expected him to be. The eleventh-century historian Yahya of Antioch records that Basil "asked for help from the ruler of the Russians," and, in exchange for military aid, committed to betroth his sister to their king, Vladimir, if Vladimir would agree to be baptized "along with all of the people in his country."[16] With Basil at its head, this mixed Russian and Roman force defeated and killed Bardas Phocas on April 13, 989. Bardas Phocas's "head was brought to Constantinople and paraded around," and then Basil sent it, rotting, on a tour of the provinces, so that all could see what happened to someone who challenged the emperor.[17]

This convoluted civil war pointed to the complex world that had grown up alongside the reemergence of Roman military power as an international force. That Roman renaissance had been guided by powerful families like the Skleroi and the Phokades who enjoyed great wealth, regional power bases, and long terms in military commands and administrative positions. These families had benefited disproportionately from Rome's victories and amassed large properties in or near areas that Roman armies had just reconquered. Basil II remained more powerful than these families, but only just, and the emperor knew this balance of power might shift if he left great Roman magnates in command positions while allowing their wealth to continue to grow.

Basil II tried to limit both the danger these elites posed to his position and the growth of their fortunes. In 996, he issued a law that gave the emperor the power to investigate any transaction through which an imperial officer or title holder assumed ownership of property belonging to someone with less wealth.[18] This served as both a statement of legal principle and a warning to other powerful figures: The emperor would use the power of the state to break up their landholdings if he was given cause to do so.[19]

Two families, the Phokades and the Maleinoi, particularly concerned the emperor because of their involvement in the recent revolt of Bardas Phocas.[20] The Phokades, of course, remained suspect because Bardas was one of them. The Maleinoi are both more interesting and more indicative of the nuanced strategy Basil had decided to pursue in order to neuter the powerful families he distrusted. The head of the family, Eustathios Maleinos, had hosted the gathering at which Bardas Phocas was proclaimed emperor. When Basil was traveling through Eustathios's home region of Cappadocia following the suppression of the revolt, Skylitzes describes how Eustathios "received him and his entire army as his guests, giving him and his men whatever they needed without counting the cost." Imperial visits were notoriously expensive, and this sort of superficially deferential display of generosity doubled as an implicit statement about the family's wealth. Basil pretended to be grateful and invited Eustathios to Constantinople so that the emperor could reciprocate. Then, once Eustathios was in the capital, the emperor prevented him from ever leaving it again, making "generous provision for his needs but [holding] onto him as though he were raising a wild beast in a cage until he reached the end of his life." When Eustathios died, "all his property was appropriated by the state."[21]

Basil did not want or need to kill the barons who had collectively almost toppled his regime. He understood that these men were dangerous only when they could combine their wealth and their power as local patrons with imperial offices. They could be controlled through administrative barriers that prevented these assets from coalescing.[22] This is why Eustathios Maleinos was imprisoned in a gilded, Constantinopolitan cage but allowed to keep his property in Cappadocia for the rest of his life. His money did not matter if it could not be used to buy local villages to augment his power. It also did not matter if he held no authority over armies or tax collection. A man who was merely wealthy did not threaten Basil. The same was true of men who just held commands, or men who were locally influential. But Basil would no longer tolerate the accretion of distinct, overlapping forms of power like that wielded by his rivals in the 980s. As a result, "Basil found himself playing the game of power politics most successfully," once he realized how to put "the great families . . . on an equal footing with the rest."[23]

Basil also kept the great families from rising again by playing a much more direct role in running the empire and managing its military campaigns than his recent predecessors had done. He "spent the greater part of his reign on campaign" and "hardened himself against the most extreme cold and heat of summer" so that he could fight year-round, breaking with the practice of most emperors, who usually joined military campaigns only when the weather was conducive to travel.[24]

Basil's armies began to outperform those led by other commanders as they became accustomed to the demands of their emperor. When the armies of the Egyptian Fatimid caliphate won a series of battles against Roman forces based in Antioch, Basil himself led a segment of the Roman field army across Anatolia in the spring of 995 and induced the Fatimids to retreat.[25] Three years later, he responded to a Roman defeat outside Antioch with such extensive, brutal attacks on Fatimid territory in Syria and Lebanon that the Egyptians agreed to a peace treaty that held for nearly two decades.[26]

Basil's actions in the Caucasus followed a similar path. As along the eastern frontier, Basil preferred to regulate Roman relations with his neighbors in Georgia and Armenia through diplomacy rather than warfare. But there were moments during the emperor's long reign when he was forced to lead armies into these regions. The emperor's relationship with Prince David of Tao shows that he could deftly balance diplomacy and the threat of military intervention to first secure a sovereign's loyalty and eventually his kingdom. David had provided a detachment of troops that helped Basil defeat Skleros in 979 and, in return for this service, Basil rewarded the Georgian with control over some Roman border towns. But David then chose the wrong side in Bardas Phocas's revolt.[27] After an imperial army loyal to Basil defeated David's troops, he was allowed to retain his throne and territory, but forced to name Basil as his heir. When news of David's death in 1000 reached Basil, the emperor immediately sent soldiers from Antioch, quickly "took possession of all of the Georgian's lands," and "appointed Roman governors" before any resistance could coalesce.[28]

Basil's relationship with Bulgaria provides the clearest example of how the emperor's growing skill as a commander began to alter both the outcomes of Roman conflicts and the power of Roman diplomacy.[29] After the ill-prepared emperor had led Roman forces to disaster in 986, the dynamics of Roman-Bulgarian relations had started to change. Although Rome had been the dominant power in the region before this defeat, Bulgaria now began to challenge Roman control over the southern Balkans. Bulgarian raids extended east into the territory that John Tzimiskes had seized from the Russians and south to the outskirts of Thessaloniki. On one occasion, they even reached as far as the Isthmus of Corinth.[30]

Basil led armies against the Bulgarians in the Balkans for much of the early 990s without much success, though one of his commanders did win a battle in 995 that led to the wounding of the Bulgarian leader Samuel and the capture of 12,000 soldiers.[31] Beginning in 1000, however, Basil began a military offensive that would eventually lead to the Roman recovery of all the Bulgarian kingdom's lands. The war commenced with an advance on Serdica that separated Samuel's eastern territory from his territory in the west. The eastern region quickly came under Roman control as far as the Danube, but the fighting was much more prolonged in the western half of Bulgaria. The next four years saw the Romans press north and west before the intensity of the combat slowed significantly in 1005.[32]

In 1014, Basil led the Roman field army back into Bulgaria and confronted the Bulgarian army near a pass called Kleidion (the Key) that Samuel had fortified with a wall. Basil then sent a detachment of commandos through the mountains so that they could emerge behind the Bulgarians as Basil attacked the wall head-on. When the commandos appeared during the assault, wrote Skylitzes, the "panic-stricken Bulgarians turned to flee, the emperor broke through the abandoned wall, and Samuel barely managed to escape." Basil then "blinded the Bulgarian captives—around 15,000 it is said—and he ordered every 100 to be led back to Samuel by a one-eyed man." Samuel fainted when he saw the horror done to his army, then "had a heart attack and died two days later."[33]

The Bulgarian defeat at Kleidion and its gruesome aftermath started four years of brutal warfare through which Basil eventually conquered the entire Bulgarian kingdom. Although it began with a terrible mutilation of Bulgarian captives that would eventually earn Basil the sobriquet "the Bulgar Slayer," the final Roman absorption of Bulgaria in 1018 came about through diplomacy rather than violence.[34] Basil's brutality had been very real, but the emperor understood that brutality worked best as a tool to sufficiently terrify an adversary who otherwise might not be willing to negotiate. Eventually, wrote Yahya, "the Bulgarian chieftains came to meet Basil" and gave him "possession of their fortresses" without a fight. In return,

Basil "awarded each an appropriate [Roman] title" and a position in the territory's new Roman administration.[35] Basil then rapidly consolidated control of the countryside without having to destroy any of its fortifications. He installed a Roman administration staffed by people loyal to him who knew the region because they had once belonged to the Bulgarian nobility.[36]

Basil understood that the integration of new lands and the people living in them began with the integration of the elites who held sway over these domains. This process is clearest in the case of Bulgaria. After the initial shock caused by their defeat at Kleidion, Basil shifted the allegiances of Bulgarian notables by framing a stark choice for them. They could willingly join Rome in return for Roman titles, offices, and stipends, or they could resist and risk destruction.[37] Both the rewards and the threats needed to seem quite real for Basil's approach to work. The stories from Kleidion (however exaggerated they may have been) proved sufficiently alarming that Basil secured the defection of the coastal city of Dyrrachium, thirty-five mountain forts, and some well-defended towns in exchange for a few grants of Roman patrician status to their Bulgarian governors and their sons.[38]

The defectors increased in number and prominence as the war progressed. In early 1018, the Bulgarian official in charge of Skopje turned the city over to Basil in exchange for Roman titles.[39] Basil received the surrender of the Bulgarian royal family in Ochrid as well as that of several commanders, who, Skylitzes reports, each "came with a detachment of troops," again in exchange for Roman imperial honors.[40] When the pacification of Bulgaria was complete, wrote Yahya, the emperor "returned to Constantinople, where he married Roman sons to Bulgarian daughters and Bulgarian sons to Roman daughters." Basil hoped that these unions would bring "an end to the ancient animosity that had existed between them."[41]

Basil used a similar approach in his new Armenian territories. There, too, elites were given Roman titles, brought into midlevel administrative positions, and encouraged to marry Romans.[42] Their status as members of the Roman polity also freed Armenians to move, settle throughout Anatolia, and intermarry with the Romans living there. Although many Armenians did not accept the Council of Chalcedon, none of the Armenian migrants belonged to autonomous communities or asserted any sort of collective political independence. When Armenians moved deeper into Anatolia, they worked to integrate themselves into existing communities rather than setting themselves apart.[43]

It is much more difficult to describe how Basil's empire treated the Muslims who remained in areas like Crete, Syria, Cilicia, and Melitene that it had reconquered. The emperors in the 960s had expelled Muslims from some of these territories, though this was effectively impossible to do on islands such as Crete. Our evidence is not abundant, but there are scattered reports of cities that contained both churches and mosques. This included Constantinople itself, though it is not clear whether the people praying in its mosques were locals or visitors to the city. There are no known cases of Muslims serving within the imperial administration proper, though it is certainly possible that some Muslim converts may have done so.[44]

As Basil neared the end of his life in 1025, one could see the outlines of a very familiar Roman story. After six remarkable decades of expansion, the Roman state now contained its most religiously, ethnically, and linguistically diverse population since the seventh century. This was still a Roman state, but it now had substantial Bulgarian, Armenian, and even Muslim subjects that the emperor had bound to it by trading Roman honors for their loyalty.[45]

Basil had employed a very old strategy not unlike what Julius Caesar had done in Gaul a millennium earlier. But attracting elites was only the beginning of a much longer process that created Roman populations out of diverse groups of conquered peoples. The next steps required sustained cultural, social, and marital interactions between Romans and non-Romans, so that gradually the lines separating non-Roman and Roman individuals slowly faded away. It took generations, not minutes, to unfold, but Romans had historically excelled at facilitating this sort of transformation. As long as they had the time to do so.

Chapter 42

From the Apogee to the Nadir

1025–1071

THE MEDIEVAL ROMAN state reached its peak by the end of the reign of Basil II. Basil had expanded its borders in all parts of the Mediterranean save Italy. His administrative reforms had neutered the great families that once constrained the emperor's power, and his astute diplomatic skills had brought in new elites from Bulgaria, Armenia, and Syria whose descendants could populate future Roman administrations. Romans old and new had begun building communities, congregations, and even families together in both the newly conquered territories and in historically Roman areas. Established Roman families moved into the new places, new Roman families moved into old ones, and all these people lived under the capable and robust administrative state that the emperors of the ninth and tenth centuries had built. The foundations appeared to have been laid for Rome to sustain itself going forward as the primary power in the Eastern Mediterranean and Balkans.

And yet the empire squandered what Basil II had achieved in less time than it had taken for him to build it. Much of the decline resulted from choices Basil himself had made. The emperor had never married and had no children. He had also done little to prepare his brother and co-emperor, Constantine VIII, for the responsibility of running the state. To be fair, Constantine had shown little interest in the job. He spent most of his time living luxuriously in Constantinople, playing checkers and dice while his brother traveled with the army. Constantine had married and was the father of three daughters, Eudokia, Zoe, and Theodora. Eudokia entered a convent, interested neither in power for herself nor in exercising influence through a marriage to whatever grandee her father or uncle wanted to reward. Basil tried to arrange a diplomatic marriage for Zoe, but after an engagement linking her to the son of the German emperor Otto III fell apart, Basil and his brother made no further efforts to marry her abroad. Zoe and Theodora made no plans of their own to marry, in the hope that a path to power in Constantinople or abroad might open, but this meant that both were still single when their father died. Because their uncle and father had both lived so long, they were past the age when they could have children. Rome's longest-lasting dynasty would die with them.

Zoe and Theodora became the central figures in Roman political life as the zombie Macedonian dynasty limped to its conclusion. Four different emperors ruled between Constantine VIII's death in 1028 and the death of Theodora in 1056, a total that does not include the two months during which Zoe and Theodora reigned together and the year and a half when Theodora ruled alone. Zoe, however, was the dominant figure for much of this time. Strikingly beautiful well into her sixties, Zoe was also "most imposing in her manner and commanded respect" from all those who approached. She also understood how her membership in the imperial family enabled her to leverage these personal qualities to secure and maintain political power.[1]

Zoe, however, had little say over the first act in her imperial story. As Constantine VIII lay dying, he initially determined that the throne should pass to Constantine Dalassenus, a formidable military commander whose skills disquieted those in Constantinople who had become accustomed to the dying emperor's indifference.[2] They argued instead for Romanos Argyros, an older man of around seventy whom courtiers believed would be much easier to manipulate. Constantine VIII acquiesced and agreed to a marriage that would link Romanos to one of his daughters and position him as imperial heir. He then forced Romanos's wife of more than fifty years to leave her husband and enter a convent, an act that so angered Theodora that she refused to marry Romanos.[3] Zoe had no such reservations. She married Romanos three days before her father's death, and then followed her new husband as he ascended to power.[4]

Although Zoe was nearly fifty and Romanos was twenty years older than her, the new emperor compelled her to undertake a host of fertility treatments so that they might found a dynasty together. The philosopher and historian Michael Psellus reports that these included "fastening little pebbles on her body, hanging charms about herself, and decking herself with all sorts of nonsense."[5] When, predictably, none of it worked, Romanos began ignoring his wife. He limited her access to imperial funds and cut her off sexually. By 1033, both Romanos and Zoe had taken lovers. Soon after Zoe became attached to a strapping young Paphlagonian named Michael, the brother of a court eunuch named John Orphanotrophos (the Orphanage Keeper), Romanos mysteriously fell ill. On April 11, 1034, Romanos was found dead in his bathtub.

As rumors flew that Zoe had poisoned her husband, she and Michael tried to convince the patriarch to marry them and crown Michael emperor that same evening.[6] When the patriarch "stood there speechless," wondering whether he could refuse to perform a marriage between two adulterers and potential murderers, John and Zoe offered a bribe of fifty pounds of gold to the patriarch and clergy, a sum large enough to convince them to perform the ceremony.[7] So began the reign of Michael IV.

It quickly became clear that Zoe had miscalculated when she assumed "she would have a slave and servant rather than a husband" on the imperial throne. She was not wrong that Michael was too simple and weak to push back against her as she moved trusted courtiers into the palace and "took a closer interest in state affairs." But she had misjudged how savvy his brother John, the court eunuch, could be. John, Skylitzes wrote, "was an energetic man of action" who knew that Romanos had died after trying to sideline Zoe, and he feared what the empress might do to his brother. He "expelled the empress's eunuchs from the palace," appointed women from his family to watch over her chambers, and restricted her movements.[8]

John attempted to return to the days when Constantinople had a Macedonian dynast sitting in the palace while someone else managed the state. His plan rested entirely on Michael's robust health, but Michael's condition declined precipitously after he took power. He soon became "too sluggish and lethargic to undertake affairs of state," leaving everything to John.[9] This proved to be a disaster. Word began to spread through the capital that John was selling offices and mistreating his subjects. And then a series of earthquakes, storms, and even a plague of locusts afflicted the empire.[10] Perhaps because of the unease these events caused and the emperor's frailty, John decided to entrench his family in the imperial hierarchy even more thoroughly by installing his nephew, also named Michael, as Caesar and imperial heir-designate. In the meantime, "the emperor Michael spent most of his time in Thessaloniki," visiting the tomb of St. Demetrios "in the hope of finding relief from his illness."[11]

On the rare occasions when Michael IV did intervene in imperial affairs, he "was so inexperienced and incompetent in exercising his authority that he brought disorder everywhere." In 1040, a Bulgarian named Peter Deleanos appeared in Belgrade and claimed to be a long-lost grandson of the Bulgarian king Samuel. He quickly attracted disgruntled Bulgarians to his cause and they marched south until they placed Thessaloniki under siege. Michael fled the city, returned with reinforcements, captured Deleanos, and reasserted Roman authority over Bulgaria. The exertion of campaigning exacerbated his illness to such a degree, however, that he decided to resign from office and live out his days as a monk. He died on December 10, 1041, and was buried in a monastery that he had founded.[12]

ZOE, THE SIXTY-THREE-YEAR-OLD daughter of the last Macedonian dynast, seized effective power. She had in Irene, Theophano, and Zoe Karbonopsina models of how an empress might run the Roman state, but none of them exactly fit her situation. They had all married into an imperial dynasty and tried to exert influence by managing the careers of their young, weak, or idiotic sons, but Zoe linked the Roman present to the nearly 200-year-old Macedonian dynasty. Her authority then did not depend on a son or a husband. Their authority derived from her.

Zoe began by forcing John to join a monastery, recalling her father's eunuchs to help her administer the government, and summoning the young Caesar Michael so he could be installed as emperor. He would become Michael V. Before this happened, however, she brought precious relics before Michael and "bound him with powerful oaths . . . to do whatever she commanded." But John was not yet beaten. Zoe had a hobby of experimenting with chemicals in her private chambers, ostensibly for cosmetic purposes, and John seized on this by writing to the young emperor and warning him to beware of her, "lest he suffer the same fate as his uncle, the emperor Michael [IV,] and Romanos, his predecessor, who had been killed by sorcery."[13]

This unsubtle reference to Zoe's mysterious chemistry experiments convinced Michael "to hatch a plot against her." The emperor arranged a splendid spectacle in which he processed through the city on Easter, soaked in the cheers of Constantinopolitan residents, and, he hoped, created a sense that his popularity was so great that none would challenge it. That night he arrested Zoe, exiled her to an island in the Sea of Marmara, and ordered her jailers to forcibly tonsure her. They were then supposed to "bring the cut hair back to Michael" to prove that it had been done.[14]

When Michael dispatched the city prefect to announce Zoe's expulsion, however, the Constantinopolitan population responded with outrage at the emperor's low birth and the fact that he had broken the sacred oaths he had sworn. Chanting, "We don't want a cross-trampling caulker for an emperor," they armed themselves with rocks and pieces of broken statues and rioted.[15]

Zoe's courtiers and the prominent senators who supported her realized they needed a member of the imperial dynasty present in

Constantinople immediately, lest they squander the momentum this popular revolt was creating. Zoe was secreted on an island, but her sister Theodora was in the Constantinopolitan convent that she had joined when Zoe had married Romanos. Rather than run the risk that Zoe might be delayed or killed before Michael could be toppled, the senators brought Theodora to Hagia Sophia, "where they dressed her in imperial purple and proclaimed her empress, along with Zoe."[16]

Michael then tried to salvage his reign by bringing Zoe back and restoring her, but the damage had been done. After a couple of days of intense street fighting that killed 3,000 people, Michael V fled to the monastery where Zoe had exiled his uncle John. Zoe then gave a speech to the Constantinopolitan populace in which she thanked them for supporting her and asked them what they thought should happen to Michael. Although the crowd cried out "Impale him! Crucify him! Blind him!," Zoe "shrank from punishing him." Theodora did not. She ordered the blinding of both Michael and John in April 1042, ending their hopes of founding Rome's next imperial dynasty.[17]

The two empresses then decided to live together in the palace, with Theodora conceding that Zoe remained the more senior figure and agreeing to sit slightly behind her sister when they conducted meetings. This arrangement worked in the moment, but the state felt stagnant. The empresses were both in their sixties, the last members of the Macedonian line, and they had no husbands or heirs. This alarmed Constantinopolitan senators, who began pressuring the women to empower a sovereign who, Psellus records, "would make provision for the future and prepare long before" any domestic or external problems erupted.[18]

Zoe again stepped forward. After consultation with her allies in the Senate, she agreed to marry Constantine Monomachos.[19] The Monomachoi were an old aristocratic family that had first become prominent when one of its members had governed Sicily under the empress Irene more than 200 years before. Constantine was a nephew by marriage of Zoe's first husband, Romanos III, but John had exiled him after his uncle's death. Zoe recalled Constantine after Michael V's fall, placed him in charge of the theme of Hellas, and then quickly summoned him to Constantinople so they could marry on June 11, 1042. On June 12, he was crowned emperor Constantine IX Monomachos.

Neither spouse had any illusions about what their marriage meant. Zoe was a beautiful woman in her mid-sixties who had a robust romantic life. Monomachos had his own mistress, Maria Skleraina, the great-granddaughter of Bardas Skleros, whose rebellions had troubled Basil II.[20] People within Constantinople feared that Monomachos might try to dispose of the empresses in the same way that Michael V had. In 1044, popular anger erupted after Constantine arranged for Maria to be addressed as *despoina* in public, a title reserved for empresses.[21] As the emperor was processing through the city, crowds began chanting, "We don't want Skleraina for empress! We don't want our mothers Zoe and Theodora, born in purple, put to death on her account."[22] The situation calmed only when Zoe and Theodora appeared on a balcony to assure the crowd that they were fine. Had they not "calmed the crowd, many would have perished, possibly including the emperor himself."[23]

Despite the riot, Constantine IX Monomachos was a skilled emperor who knew how to handle the sorts of tasks that Roman emperors of the early eleventh century confronted. He faced down rebellious nobles and captured an Armenian kingdom that was supposed to pass into Roman control when its sovereign died. He defeated a Russian naval attack on Constantinople using Greek fire, and he invested in the educational life of the capital. None of this looked particularly odd to those familiar with the dynamics of the Macedonian dynasty. In fact, when Zoe died in 1050, the city remained so quiet that contemporary historians barely mention her passing.[24] At the moment, Monomachos seemed to be doing exactly what Romans expected a good emperor to do.

IN RETROSPECT, CONSTANTINE IX Monomachos was the Alexander Severus of his day, a perfect ruler for yesterday's world. Everything was changing dramatically around him, but neither Monomachos nor any of the other elites in the capital fully grasped this. All Romans in 1050 realized that the Macedonian dynasty was nearing its end, but few recognized the revolutionary developments that were shaking the world outside of their state.

One of Rome's greatest qualities over the preceding 1,800 years had been its ability to withstand, adapt to, and then profit from major shifts in the geopolitical environments surrounding it. This was true when Servius Tullius and the leaders of the early Republic had created new political structures enabling Rome to survive the hoplite revolution that destroyed so many principalities in the sixth century BC. Rome had survived the emergence of the Goths and Persians in the third century AD by building a more robust and responsive imperial administration under the tetrarchs. Rome had even absorbed the massive blows inflicted upon it by the Arab expansions of the seventh and early eighth centuries by redesigning its military and civilian institutions. It then returned in force to recapture significant portions of the territory it had lost to the Arabs in Anatolia, Syria, and northern Mesopotamia. In all of these cases, Rome survived an initial shock, arrived at a way to reorganize its society so it could better sustain itself, and then went on the offensive once the world had rebalanced.

The middle of the eleventh century forced Rome to confront yet another age of revolutionary upheaval that would buffet the empire simultaneously from the west and the east. But this time, the steps Rome took to survive would end up weakening the state. As Psellus put it, these upheavals sickened an empire with "a thoroughly strong constitution which [was] not altered by the first sign of illness . . . until, by slow degrees the malady grew [into a fatal ailment]."[25]

The challenge in the west came from the Normans, descendants of Vikings who had settled in Northern France. The Normans developed a military profile centered on heavily armed cavalry and a remarkable ability to capture fortified cities. These skills made Norman mercenaries highly valued, but they also made these same mercenaries uniquely dangerous. Norman soldiers were notoriously prone to rebellions, and when they rebelled, their talent for capturing cities and seizing territory led to a series of conquests across Europe and the Mediterranean.[26]

The Norman attacks on Roman territory began in Italy, when a group of mercenaries recruited to help retake Sicily rebelled after they were discharged from Roman service. They defeated Roman forces in 1041 and began a campaign to capture the Roman-held cities of Southern Italy during Constantine IX Monomachos's reign. While the exact course of the fighting is not well documented, the Norman armies moved so quickly that, after more than 500 years of rule from Constantinople, Roman Italy collapsed in a single generation.

The eastern threat came from the Seljuk Turks, another serious adversary that the empire was, in theory, much better equipped to confront. Seljuk attacks on Roman territory also began in the 1040s, with border raids into some of the extreme eastern areas of Armenia over which Rome had recently taken control. By the end of the decade, the initial raiders had been reinforced by additional troops from Transoxiana. When they defeated a Roman regional army and captured its commander, Monomachos negotiated a treaty with the Turkish sultan. "But the raiding did not stop," the eleventh-century historian Michael Attaleiates reported, because the sultan asserted that "he did not know the identity of these plunderers." Even if he did, he was not powerful enough to stop them.[27]

Two extremely consequential actions taken in 1054, the last year of Monomachos's reign, compounded the empire's long-term problems with both western Christians and Turks. The first involved a delegation sent to Constantinople by Pope Leo IX to coordinate a response against the Normans. It arrived in April, stayed until July, and made a total mess of ecclesiastical relations between Rome and Constantinople. Incited by a letter they falsely believed to have been written by the Constantinopolitan patriarch, the papal legates inserted themselves into an argument that Greek bishops were having with their Armenian counterparts about the propriety of the Armenian (and Catholic) practice of using unleavened bread during Communion. Two days before they left for Italy in mid-July, the Catholic visitors excommunicated the Constantinopolitan patriarch for his stance on unleavened bread and other errors.

The excommunication had no legal validity, because Pope Leo, in whose name they issued it, was already dead, but this fit of pettiness began the Great Schism that has divided the Catholic and Orthodox churches to this day. The initial breach, however, was so inconsequential at the time that contemporary Constantinopolitan sources barely mention it. Although it is now often assumed that the Constantinopolitan church responded to its leader's excommunication by doing the same to the pope, Monomachos and the patriarch instead called a synod that ended up asserting that the whole affair had been due to miscommunications and bad translators.

The emperor and his bishops could not combat the ill-will the legates' actions had created, however. Despite their efforts to smother the controversy, Greek-speaking Romans began to circulate texts laying out the theological, liturgical, and procedural errors they saw in Catholic teaching and practice. They had long overlooked their disagreements with Catholics over clerical celibacy, the insertion of the phrase *filioque* (Latin for "and from the son") into the Latin Nicene Creed, and, of course, the use of unleavened bread in Communion. After 1054, they increasingly chose not to do so. It did not matter much at that point, but it would have catastrophic consequences in the future.[28]

The second problem arose from an extremely shortsighted decision Monomachos made to increase tax revenue by disbanding the structure that bound his Iberian army (which was based in an area roughly overlapping parts of the modern state of Georgia) to the land they defended. Instead of providing troops in exchange for the lands they farmed, people in the region now paid taxes to the state that supposedly would be used to compensate soldiers in cash. This increased revenue but removed the service obligations from around 50,000 landowners who otherwise would have provided Rome with soldiers.[29]

The reform had little immediate effect; these forces performed extremely well in beating back a Seljuk attack on Roman Armenia in

1054.[30] In the long term, however, the replacement of a frontier army composed of soldiers tied to the land with taxes paid by the land's residents had a seriously corrosive effect. Not only did those serving in Iberia now have less connection to the territory they were defending, but future emperors would inevitably be tempted to redirect the tax revenue raised in those regions and spend it for purposes other than their defense. Within a generation, what Attaleiates had described as "a formidable army [that] used to be stationed in Iberia and drew its support and supplies from the neighboring public lands" shrank away. As it did, Roman allies in the region stopped trusting Rome to protect them and made agreements with the Turks instead.[31]

As Constantine IX Monomachos lay on his deathbed in the Mangana monastery in 1055, no one yet knew that Roman Italy would collapse, that Turkish commanders would turn Rome's allies against it, or that the Greek and Latin churches would permanently divorce. The main concern in the capital was who would succeed him as emperor. The eunuchs in the palace decided to summon Nikephoros, the governor of Bulgaria, so that he might be presented to the Senate, the people, and the armies as the next emperor. Before he could arrive, however, the old Macedonian empress Theodora turned up at the imperial palace, supported by a member of one of the oldest noble families in Constantinople. She was restored to the position of ruling Roman sovereign before Monomachos died on January 8, but her seizure of power did absolutely no one any good. According to Skylitzes, she "immediately pursued with vengeance those who had plotted to make [Nikephoros] ruler" and soon began descending into her final illness as effective control of the empire fell increasingly on the eunuchs around her.[32] She died in August 1056, and the Macedonian dynasty died with her. It had lasted almost twice as long as any other Roman imperial dynasty.

THE NEXT FIFTEEN years showed how unmoored Roman political life could become without a dynastic ruler presiding at its center and limiting the ambitions of powerful local barons. Power passed first to

Michael VI, an elderly bureaucrat from a modest family best known for managing military budgets. He was chosen by palace eunuchs confident, Skylitzes wrote, that "he would only have the appearance and name of emperor while they conducted affairs as they wished."[33] Instead, his selection prompted members of more powerful families to try to take power themselves. A cousin of Monomachos was the first to attempt it. His ill-planned rebellion went nowhere, but Michael fell not much later when an aristocratic revolt replaced him with Isaac Comnenus, the husband of a member of the former Bulgarian royal family, in 1057.[34] Isaac was an effective leader, but he did not last long either. In 1059, he fell ill following a campaign in the Balkans and retired to the Stoudios monastery, where he died six months later.[35]

The new emperor, Constantine X Doukas, a leading member of another powerful aristocratic family, prevailed in the palace jockeying over who would replace Isaac. Although he tried to secure his succession by designating his young sons as heirs and appointing his brother as Caesar, neither step prevented disgruntled figures in Constantinople from trying to overthrow him the following year.[36] Their plot, which ranks among the most absurd in Rome's long history of moronic coup attempts, unfolded on April 23, 1060. It involved creating a disturbance in the city, inducing the emperor to get on a specific ship, and then casting him into the sea to drown. It had little chance of success. Constantine X simply boarded another boat when he found no imperial barges waiting, and refused to change ships when the conspirators' boat pulled up next to his. They tried to sink his ship by ramming it, but he made it back to the palace and had his brother arrest those involved.[37]

Constantine X Doukas's escape from the doomed ship was the highlight of a reign dogged by his failures as a manager of military finances and defense strategy. He discharged some of Rome's most experienced soldiers because they were too expensive to retain, sent lightly equipped troops into battle, and lost the fortress city of Ani to the Turks in 1064, after he privatized the provision of grain to its garrison and gave the contract to a corrupt official.[38] The city fell, Attaleiates concluded, "along with all of its villages and their lands[,] on account of the greed of the emperor."[39] In 1067, the year of Constantine X's death, Turkish attacks led to the capture of the Roman governor of Edessa, the sacking of the Cappadocian city of Caesarea, and raids that penetrated Cilicia and the countryside around Antioch.

THE RAPID DETERIORATION in Rome's eastern position convinced Doukas's widow, Eudokia, along with the patriarch and members of the Constantinopolitan Senate, that allowing his heir, the eighteen-year-old emperor Michael VII, to take power "would harm the common good and contribute to the destruction of the Roman state."[40] The state, after all, was not his by right but a public institution that belonged to citizens who needed a capable ruler. The delegation of notables persuaded the young emperor that this new ruler should be Romanos Diogenes.

Romanos IV Diogenes married Eudokia and took the imperial oath in Constantinople on January 1, 1068. He then spent the next two years trying to stabilize the empire's borders. The rapid expansion of the previous century and the professionalization of much of the Roman army had severed the connection of soldiers to the frontier lands they had once guarded. It had also demilitarized the themes in the interior of Asia Minor and Greece.[41] This created a situation not unlike that faced by Romans in the last quarter of the fourth century AD. The army fought very effectively when it took the field, but the state struggled to quickly recruit and train soldiers to fill armies depleted by military defeats. In Antioch, for example, the magister Nicephorus Botaniates tried to build an army made up of local recruits, "but they were unable to do anything noteworthy because they had no experience in war, could not ride a horse properly, and were practically without weapons."[42] There was little chance that these raw local recruits could gain the skills and confidence they would need to hold the Roman East if Romanos failed to secure its borders with his field army.

In 1070, Romanos IV and Eudokia turned their attention to buttressing their defenses against political machinations in the capital. While the Turkish emergency had induced Michael VII to cede authority to Romanos, it remained a strong possibility that Michael and his relatives in the Doukas family might try to take this authority back should Romanos show any weakness. The long-term solution to this, of course, would be for Romanos to have an adult heir who commanded enough authority to defend the regime from a challenge. But the emperor and empress had only two infant sons who would not be able to play this role for at least another twenty years. In the meantime, the emperor reached out to the Comneni clan, the family of the former emperor Isaac, and arranged for the marriage of a son from Romanos's first marriage to Isaac's niece. He then dispatched Isaac's nephew Manuel to the east to direct that year's campaign.[43] These moves prompted a significant enough shift that the Caesar John Doukas, the brother of Constantine X, decided to leave Constantinople.

In 1071, Romanos IV himself led a large and powerful army made up of Roman professional soldiers, local levies, and western mercenaries into the east. That August, as they approached the city of Manzikert (modern Malazgirt in eastern Turkey), which had recently fallen to the Turks, Romanos decided to attack the city with part of the army while also sending a detachment of elite Roman infantry and Frankish and Russian mercenaries to try to retake the town of Chliat. A Turkish force was in the field nearby, but if they attacked, Romanos trusted that he could instruct the detachment sent to Chliat to break off the siege and return while his own personal bodyguard protected him.[44] Manzikert fell to Romanos on August 23, but Turkish troops began harassing the Romans soon after they entered the city. A confusing multiday engagement ensued in which Romans and Turks skirmished while Romanos waited in vain for the troops sent to Chliat to appear.

The turning point came on August 26, when Romanos himself led soldiers out into the field. His Turkish opponents fell back, and after a pursuit lasting much of the afternoon, the emperor decided to order a retreat. He commanded that "the imperial banner be turned around" to signal that the men should turn around but, as Attaleiates explains, when those farther back in the army saw the banner flip, they were misled about its meaning. Andronicus Doukas, Michael VII's cousin, who "had previously plotted against [Romanos], spread the word among the soldiers" that the emperor had died. Doukas then pulled his men from the field. As his units retreated, a large portion of the Roman army melted away with them.[45] Romanos tried to rally the troops, but "no one was listening to him." While the "entire imperial army" fled, Romanos fought on, nearly alone. He "vigorously defended himself against his attackers," but "he had been wounded on the hand and his horse had been shot by many arrows, so he was fighting on foot."[46] At dusk, when the emperor finally surrendered, the sultan decided to take him prisoner rather than kill him.[47] The Seljuk sultan Alp Arslan held Romanos for eight days, negotiated a favorable peace treaty with him, and then sent him back to Roman territory to implement its terms.[48]

No Roman military disaster had ever before occurred because a commander pulled his troops from the field so that a non-Roman army could destroy his leader. But, before Andronicus Doukas, no Roman military commander had ever so selfishly and cynically placed the short-term profit of his own family above the long-term good of his state. And it was this cynicism, rather than the defeat at Manzikert, that placed the Roman state on the eventual path to its destruction.

PART 7

FROM ALEXIUS COMNENUS TO NICETAS CHONIATES

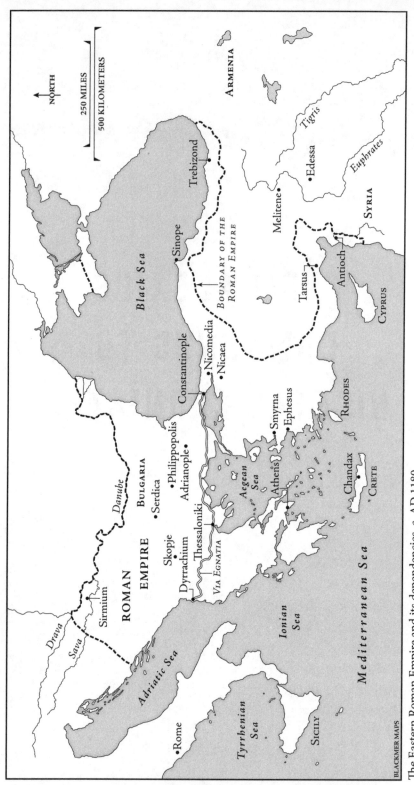

The Eastern Roman Empire and its dependencies, c. AD 1180

Chapter 43

Alexius I Comnenus and the Roman State's Last Great Revival

1071–1118

T HE BATTLE OF Manzikert stands out among the military
catastrophes suffered by the Roman state. Legendary defeats
like those at Cannae in 216 BC and Adrianople in AD 378 shattered
Roman armies by destroying their leadership and killing tens of
thousands of soldiers. Manzikert was different. The casualty numbers were relatively low. While some of the hired mercenaries had
switched sides, the battle was lost primarily because of the treachery of Andronicus Doukas, who had left the emperor Romanos to
fight nearly alone. Most of the Romans escaped the field. Manzikert
is now a turning point in Roman history not because of the number
of Romans who died there, but because it gave people like John and
Andronicus Doukas, Michael VII Doukas, and Romanos IV Diogenes cause to kill lots of Romans later.

The Doukas family and their supporters assumed that Romanos
had died in the fight they had fled. The Caesar John Doukas returned
to Constantinople, sent Eudokia into exile, and placed Michael VII on
the throne. The Doukas family believed they had returned to power
without any violence in the capital at all. But then they learned that
Romanos had not died. He was gone for a week, returned, and began
behaving like he was still emperor. Rome suddenly faced a question it

had never encountered: What happened constitutionally when a captured emperor returned?

Rome had no good answer. Only one emperor, Valerian in 260, had ever before been captured alive—and he had never returned to Roman territory. Additionally, unlike the French king Francis I, who returned to his throne in 1526 after a year in Spanish captivity, no Roman emperor had an inherent right to resume the office he held. The state belonged to its citizens, and as the recent examples of Isaac Comnenus and Michael VII showed, leading citizens could ask an emperor to stand aside in favor of another, more capable person. After Manzikert, the Doukas family could be forgiven for thinking that Romans had every right to move on from Romanos IV.

But Romanos IV had no intention of giving up his claim. He belonged to a powerful Cappadocian family, and when he resolved to fight for his throne, he could count on considerable support in the east. The eastern armies that he needed for a civil war, however, were the same forces that were needed to defend Roman territory in Asia Minor. When Romanos drew them to the west, the east was poorly protected. Turkish bands moved in quickly, displacing populations and sending Roman refugees fleeing west. Perhaps the only fortunate thing was that the civil war ended quickly. Romanos's forces lost a series of engagements before he surrendered in June 1072.

Michael VII had few answers for the social and economic problems the collapse of Roman control in Asia Minor presented his regime. He and his relatives mended relations with the Comneni by placing a member of their family in command of an expedition to Asia Minor. He also placated some nobles who had lost estates in Asia Minor by giving them land in the Balkans. But plunging tax revenues forced him to cut spending and dramatically reduce the purity of the gold coinage. Michael's weakness also encouraged the Frankish mercenaries in Roman service to test the empire's strength. In 1073, a Frankish mercenary cavalry commander named Roussel de Bailleul rebelled, and 3,000 of the empire's Frankish mercenaries soon joined him. Michael was forced to summon another group of Turkish mercenaries to put down the revolt.[1]

The Franks and Turks were not the only ones to see opportunities in Michael's weakness. Beginning in 1077, the state fell again into a sprawling, complicated set of civil wars that further decimated its remaining armies made up primarily of Romans. Michael's regime fell when the elderly general Nicephorus III Botaniates seized the throne with the help of Seljuk Turkish troops, but Nicephorus lost power four years later, when Alexius Comnenus, his most trusted general, seized control of the state for himself.[2] It was only with Alexius's arrival that some semblance of political stability returned to Constantinople.

In her history of Alexius's reign, called the *Alexiad*, his daughter Anna Comnena wrote about what she described as a series of "mortal plagues" in Rome at this time as "pretenders" both inside and outside of the empire fought for the throne. But "God preserved [Alexius] Comnenus, like some precious object," she adds, because God "wished for him to revive Roman power."[3] Much of Anna's account of her father's life overstates his brilliance, but she was not exaggerating the dreadful conditions he inherited. Alexius had taken over a Roman state that was broke, failing, and at war with itself. None of the great ninth- and tenth-century administrative manuals written to instruct emperors in how to run the Roman administrative system offered any guidance for how Alexius might extricate the state from these serious, overlapping crises.

And yet Alexius—and the empire—survived. He ruled for thirty-seven years and managed to stop the deterioration of Roman power, not by following the dictates of Leo VI's or Constantine VII's great management tomes but through a long series of improvised measures. One of the biggest challenges Alexius faced in 1081, and one he would continue to face until his death in 1118, was how to manage the expectations of the large, diverse group of aristocrats who helped him reach and keep the throne. Anna again neatly summed up her father's problem. These people required something in exchange for their support, and, while Alexius "was exceptionally generous and very ready to give, he did not have a great abundance of money."[4]

What Alexius did have was a monopoly on the Roman imperial honors and titles that his supporters valued, and he granted these liberally in moments when his predecessors might instead have given monetary rewards to their supporters. Gregory Pakourianos, the Armenian general who had supported his coup, was promoted to Alexius's old rank.[5] Alexius brought the Melissenos clan into the fold by offering the title of Caesar and authority over Thessaloniki to Nicephoros Melissenos. He also invented a series of titles derived from *sebastos* (the Greek translation of Augustus) to give to his brothers Isaac (whom he made *sebastokrator*) and Adrian (*protosebastos*).[6] This title inflation happened in large part because the emperor could no longer afford to pay the stipends that had previously been attached to the offices these elites already claimed. The honors then needed to be more impressive because the material rewards attached to them were disappearing.

Honors alone would not suffice for long, however, because most of Alexius's important backers belonged to families whose ancestral property lay in parts of Asia Minor that the empire no longer controlled. These elites remained influential, but, like the empire they served and the emperor they supported, they were also broke. Alexius created a solution through a series of improvised measures that stabilized their fortunes by giving them revenue from imperial estates. When Melissenos was given control of Thessaloniki, for example, he also received a portion of the tax revenues derived from land in that area. Melissenos and others like him took this money directly, before it was passed along to the emperor. When these revenues were combined with the tax exemptions the emperor granted to his associates, they effectively stabilized or even increased the incomes of the beneficiaries.[7]

This new system of administrative compensation sidelined elites in the Balkans who depended on the salaries connected to the titles they had received when they had agreed to join the Roman administrative system in the earlier decades of the eleventh century. Most of these figures did not belong to the Comnenian inner circle, and the emperor felt little need to compensate them, at least initially. After

Alexius ran out of imperially owned estates to back the tax concessions he was granting to his followers, he began confiscating land
from churches, monasteries, and individual senators.[8] Alexius had
not intended these actions to be transformative, but they inadvertently created a system that enriched his favorites with "cartloads of
public money" that otherwise would have funded the government.[9]
The long-term consequences of this system would prove quite dire,
although it is hard to imagine how Alexius could have survived
without it.

Alexius also scrambled to find creative short-term solutions
to problems with the Pechenegs, Normans, and Turks, groups that
endangered the survival of the state. Constantine IX Monomachos
had allowed a group of Pechenegs to settle in the Balkans. Although
they had rebelled in the 1070s, the Pechenegs posed little independent risk to the Roman state until they joined forces with a group of
Romans living around Philippopolis (modern Plovdiv) who belonged
to the long-persecuted Paulician heretical sect that had once vexed
Basil I. With Paulician help, the Pechenegs began raiding Thrace.[10]
Alexius tried to break apart this Roman dissident–Pecheneg alliance by "writing conciliatory letters full of promises," but the weak
emperor's pledges held little appeal for either the Pechenegs or the
Paulicians.[11]

His response to the Pecheneg attacks prefigured his approach
to the Normans and Turks. He first tried to eliminate the Pecheneg
problem using Roman forces, but Roman victories in 1086 simply
induced the Pechenegs to retreat, leaving their Paulician allies to face
Alexius's retribution on their own. The Pechenegs returned in 1087,
reinforced by additional Pecheneg migrants from across the Danube and some forces loyal to the deposed king of Hungary. Alexius
again tried to negotiate, but the conflict ended only when he reached
an agreement with the Cumans, a group that lived on the northern
coast of the Black Sea, to join the war on Rome's side.[12] On April 29,
1091, a combined Roman and Cuman force commanded by Alexius won an overwhelming victory in which, Anna wrote, "a whole
nation . . . together with their wives and children was completely

wiped out" either by death or through enslavement. As news of the victory reached Constantinople, people began singing "a little burlesque song." It went, "Just by one day did the Scythians [an old, classicizing name used for northern barbarians] miss seeing the month of May."[13]

This military success masked a much more serious problem with the Roman Empire. As its security situation declined, the state that had successfully integrated new and diverse populations for almost two millennia was no longer doing this very well. People from other regions no longer wanted to become Roman. And people who were already Roman started wanting to leave.

Alexius's Norman problem arose from coordination between disgruntled Romans and outsiders looking to take advantage of imperial weakness. And, like the Pechenegs, the Normans would be defeated only when Alexius negotiated to receive outside help. The threat began when the last Roman governor of Dyrrachium appointed by Nicephorus III asked Robert Guiscard, a Norman duke based in Southern Italy, to protect him from Alexius's new regime.[14] As the governor fled his post, Robert Guiscard sailed across the Adriatic and seized Roman islands and ports. His first targets were places like Corfu, but by mid-June he had besieged Dyrrachium, a key Roman administrative center on the Adriatic mainland. If it fell, a Norman force of perhaps as many as 10,000 soldiers and 1,300 knights would have a base on which to disembark and begin attacking inland Roman cities.[15]

Alexius scrambled to respond. He cobbled together a field army by combining the Roman soldiers remaining in the Balkans with western mercenaries (including Englishmen displaced by the Norman Conquest of England in 1066), Turks, and Roman forces that he had withdrawn from garrisons in Asia Minor. Although his decision to abandon these garrisons effectively ceded Asia Minor to Turkish invaders, it did not help the emperor against the Normans. Alexius's motley army had no experience fighting together. It was defeated following a cavalry charge by Robert's knights, and Dyrrachium fell in

February 1082. Norman attacks on sites in Epirus and Thessaly soon followed.

Alexius then pivoted. If he could not defeat the Normans in the Balkans, he could try to short-circuit their attack by putting pressure on the supply lines connecting them to their bases in Italy and Sicily. He decided to work on two fronts. On the Italian mainland, he encouraged revolts in the Southern Italian territory the Normans had recently conquered. Robert had to return to Italy, but his departure did not stop the Norman expansion in Epirus, and eventually Thessaly. It was not until 1083, when Alexius appeared with an army fortified by 7,000 Turkish troops, that he was able to begin pushing the Normans back. By the winter of 1084–1085, the combination of Roman victories in battle and an epidemic that killed perhaps 40 percent of Robert's knights put an end to the invasion.[16]

The land battles were only a part of Alexius's anti-Norman strategy. He also depended heavily on a naval alliance with the Republic of Venice, a polity that shared Rome's discomfort with Norman expansion in the Adriatic.[17] While Alexius's army campaigned on land, Venetian ships fought alongside the Roman navy to hinder Robert's ability to resupply his forces. Venetian marines captured Dyrrachium (which they returned to the emperor), while the Romans took back some Adriatic islands they had lost. Like many of Alexius's ventures, his alliance with Venice had clear short-term benefits that helped ensure the empire's survival.

The Venetians, however, leveraged their naval support in the 1080s into significant long-term concessions. On a personal level, the Venetian doge received a package like that which Alexius had granted to other favored notables. He was given the rank of *protosebastos* (the same rank that Alexius had earlier given his own brother) and recognized as the duke of Dalmatia and Croatia. The Venetian patriarch was also given a Roman imperial title and an annual allowance of twenty pounds of gold.[18]

Venetian merchants received Alexius's most significant concession. Since he lacked the cash to pay the Venetians, Alexius replicated the model he had used to compensate Roman administrators when he could not pay their salaries. He confiscated coastal property owned by Roman monasteries along Constantinople's Golden Horn, granted warehouses there to the Venetians, and gifted Venetian merchants three docks in Galata (the land across the Golden Horn from Constantinople) from which they could conduct trade without paying any taxes or custom duties. The Venetians operating in the city "were completely free of Roman authority," and their tax status could not easily be changed.[19] Alexius's concessions ultimately laid the foundations for Venetian traders to inflict deep damage upon the once vibrant Roman merchant economy. He had also given Venice a pretext to start a war if Rome ever tried to alter the agreement's terms.

The Turkish conflict in the east was much bigger and much more difficult to resolve than the Norman and Pecheneg attacks in the west. Some of this had to do with Alexius's decision to pull Roman troops from Asia Minor so he could confront the Normans. When Roman forces moved to the Balkans, Alexius chose to rely heavily on non-Romans to garrison the cities and fortresses in western Asia Minor. His plan worked initially, but in 1085 his most trusted Turkish commander died on campaign in Syria, and the commander's son, to whom Alexius had entrusted the defense of the well-fortified city of Nicaea, rebelled. He seized Nicaea for himself and then began a campaign to reduce other Roman cities in the region. By the early 1090s, he had conquered most of northwestern Asia Minor—including the city of Nicomedia, less than 100 miles from the capital. Antioch, Edessa, and other cities in the southeast fell too. On the Aegean coast, the empire saw Smyrna pass out of Roman control for the first time in 1,200 years. After an alliance with the sultan of Baghdad failed to stem the attacks, Roman clerics in the capital began openly speaking about Alexius's failures and the imminent divine punishment that awaited the empire.[20]

Alexius then made his most consequential long-term error. In 1095, he sent envoys to Pope Urban II requesting that he organize a force of western knights and infantry to come east and fight for the empire. Although the Great Schism of 1054 still divided the church of Rome from that of Constantinople, Alexius and Urban had been working to bring the churches back together. As part of this process, they had even jointly issued a call for the Croatian king to send knights to fight on behalf of the beleaguered Roman Empire in 1090.[21]

Alexius's broader and more desperate call for help in 1095 was shrewdly framed to resonate among eleventh-century Europeans who cared little about Rome's Anatolian frontier but had become increasingly fixated on the holy city of Jerusalem. Urban followed the emperor's lead by preaching about the threats to Jerusalem while distributing large numbers of religious relics sent by Alexius to the west. This included a suspiciously large quantity of fragments of the True Cross.[22]

Both sides had something to gain. Alexius hoped to get military support from the west that included knights, the well-armored heavy cavalry that effectively supplemented the emperor's own powerful infantry. Urban sought a way to rally western Christians around a cause that only he could champion. If they heeded his call, the pope could demonstrate a unique sort of international authority unmatched by other western European political leaders. This cooperative appeal by the pope and the Roman emperor for a western Christian army to fight in the east began what we now call the Crusades.

Urban's call succeeded beyond anyone's expectation. The pope himself was involved in recruiting knights and even administering oaths that bound them to the expedition. But so many other Europeans headed east that their numbers far outstripped the supplies available for them. Many even organized excursions on their own. So it was that, when the first wave of Crusaders arrived at the Roman frontier, Anna described them as "a host of civilians . . . carrying palms and bearing crosses on their shoulders" rather than armor and weapons.[23]

This group, the so-called People's Crusade led by Peter the Hermit, was ill-supplied, poorly disciplined, and not terribly useful as a fighting force unless they were attacking civilians. And they attacked a lot of civilians. The People's Crusade massacred Jews as they crossed Germany and plundered Roman towns and villages after they entered imperial territory. Alexius had the good sense to send Peter's crew quickly into Asia Minor, where, in October 1096, they encountered a much larger and more capable Turkish force. The Turks defeated the soldiers who followed Peter, captured most of the civilians, and either killed them or forced their conversion.[24] Many in the west soon came to believe that Alexius "rejoiced greatly" when he learned of this defeat.[25] He did not, but the fate of Peter's followers planted the seed of a narrative of "Greek" treachery that would eventually consume the crusading movement.

Urban helped choose the more capable and disciplined troops who formed the second wave of Crusaders, but these figures brought Alexius a different set of problems. Some encountered bandits, whose attacks they blamed on the emperor. Others inadvertently provoked conflict with Roman imperial naval or land forces.[26] And when the petty nobility and royal second sons of Europe began arriving in Constantinople, their overbearing arrogance grated on their hosts even as Alexius tried to receive them with the honors they expected. The emperor had a civil conversation with Robert Guiscard's son Bohemond, against whom he had fought in the 1080s, and even kept his composure when a Frankish knight provoked him by sitting on the Roman imperial throne.[27] The emperor's diplomacy worked well enough that nearly all the Crusaders swore to return any captured territory to the emperor.

In early 1097, a combined force of Romans and Crusaders set out for Nicaea. The city surrendered to Alexius as Crusader siege engines battered its walls. Alexius then used the Crusaders' progression through central Asia Minor as a shield behind which he could recapture most of the western coastal cities that had recently fallen to the Turks. The empire recovered Smyrna, Ephesus, and most of the other cities it had lost along the Aegean coast, but the cooperation between Crusaders and the emperor broke down that summer. As the Crusaders reached southeastern Anatolia, they began taking territory for themselves and refusing to return it to the emperor. Then, in the autumn, they put Antioch under siege. The attack proved difficult, and the imperial assistance they requested did not materialize. When the Crusaders finally captured the city the following summer, they refused to return it to Alexius.

The consequences of Alexius's decision to request western military aid in this way now became clear. After the Crusaders captured Jerusalem in July 1099, they established a string of kingdoms stretching from the Egyptian border to Edessa in southeastern Anatolia. Because some of these Crusader states abutted the empire and comprised territory the Crusaders had sworn to return to Alexius, there was inevitable border tension, which only increased animosity between the two sides. The Norman Bohemond, who had taken control of Antioch after its capture, even arranged an attack on Roman territories from Italy in 1107. Alexius beat the attack back, but the peace treaty revealed how the Crusades had now linked conflicts along Rome's eastern and western frontiers. Although Alexius's victory was won outside Dyrrachium, on the Adriatic coast, the peace compelled Bohemond to agree to make the Syrian principality of Antioch a Roman vassal. The threat of renewed Norman attack from the west, however, meant that Alexius never displaced the Norman descendants of Bohemond from Antioch.[28]

In the final decade of his reign Alexius worked to strengthen Rome's position in the Adriatic by deepening and diversifying its network of allies. Venice's rival Pisa signed a treaty with the emperor in 1111 that gave the Pisans a dock, preferred tax status, and preferential seating in Hagia Sophia.[29] The papacy was, as always, an unpredictable ally, with its political orientation shifting as each new pontiff replaced the other, but Alexius continued to try to work with Urban's successor, Paschal II, on some framework that might lead to a church reconciliation. Instead of having to make desperate appeals, as he had a generation earlier, Alexius was now negotiating from a position of security, if not exactly one of strength.

The situation in Asia Minor improved following the Roman reconquests of coastal areas enabled by the Crusaders. Turkish attacks resumed in 1109, after the Turks adapted to the shocking conquests of the First Crusade, but Roman defenses had recovered enough that Alexius's governors were able to beat them back using their own Roman forces. Then, in 1116, two years before his death, Alexius mounted a final campaign into the interior of Asia Minor that aimed to stop these raids by capturing Iconium (modern Konya), the Seljuk capital. He did not reach Iconium, but Alexius's success induced the sultan to sign a peace treaty.[30]

Anna was clear-eyed about what her father had accomplished by the time of his death in 1118. She wrote, rightly, that "not one of the former emperors . . . had ever been met with such complicated issues," but she believed that Rome had survived them all because of Alexius's leadership.[31] Alexius may have saved the empire, but the complicated, short-term measures he had taken to do so would work in the long term only if men of equal talent adjusted and sustained them. As Anna concluded, "After him things were different and everything was turned into confusion," and "his efforts were rendered vain after his death by the stupidity of his successors."[32] Their stupidity meant that, as Alexius neared death, the first Romans who would outlive their state had just been born.

Chapter 44

The Stupidity of the Successors

1118–1185

THE DOMESTIC ALLIANCES that Alexius Comnenus built to underpin his regime were no less complicated than the foreign ones he negotiated. The Comneni were a large, prominent, and powerful family whose members were uncommonly fecund. Alexius and his wife, Irene Doukas, had three boys and four girls whom they married strategically to scions of other leading Roman families. This locked up the loyalties of many other elites while Alexius lived, but it also stored up problems for his successor.

Irene made this situation even more fraught than it ordinarily would have been. Alexius made it clear that he wanted his eldest boy, John, to be emperor after his death, but Irene hoped that Anna Comnena's husband Nicephorus Bryennios might take power instead.[1] John outmaneuvered her, however. When a fatally ill Alexius entered the Mangana monastery to die, John snuck into the room, "embraced his father as if in mourning, and secretly removed the signet ring" that conveyed imperial legitimacy from his finger, evidently with Alexius's permission. The ring enabled John and his advisers to force their way into the imperial palace on August 15, 1118, as crowds of supporters in the streets acclaimed John as the new emperor John II Comnenus. Irene and Anna were reduced to pleading with him to step down and even asked the dying Alexius to call him back. Neither appeal worked, and Alexius died the next day.[2]

John's position was so precarious, reports Nicetas Choniates, that he "hugged the palace like an octopus clinging to the rocks" rather than join Alexius's funeral procession. Within a few days, however, he consolidated a team of supporters headed by his own brother Isaac. Isaac's support neutralized a possible rival for the throne, but the new emperor depended most heavily on John Axuch, a Turk who had been captured by the Crusaders in 1097. John Axuch was the same age as John Comnenus and had been "his playmate and dearest friend" when they were both children.[3]

The inevitable challenge from Bryennios and Anna came a year later, after both John II Comnenos and John Axuch had already shown themselves capable military leaders. The details of the plot remain obscure, because Choniates, our main source, spends nearly as much time discussing Anna's vagina and Bryennios's penis as he does the coup attempt.[4] Whatever they actually tried to do, the emperor decided not to punish them. He instead made it known that, while he thought about confiscating his sister's property, John Axuch had talked him out of doing so because Anna "remain[ed] the sister of a virtuous emperor."[5] This seemed like an admirable act of clemency, but John had forgotten the lesson that Cicero had taught more than a thousand years earlier when he cautioned that Roman political life would degenerate if the narrow concerns of a family overtook higher, nobler concerns about the common good of the state.[6]

John's stage management was masterful. He made it clear that he had the support to sniff out and suppress coups. And he had demonstrated his clemency by effectively pardoning Anna in a way that emphasized that this reprieve happened only because she was family. No other plotters could expect the same treatment—unless they, too, were his relatives. The message had the desired effect, at least among nonfamily members. The only other plots of any significance during the twenty-five years that John II Comnenus ruled centered on his brother Isaac. Like Anna, Isaac was spared execution. Unlike Anna, he wandered to neighboring principalities trying to build support for an invasion that might topple his brother. None came. And yet John refused to break with the principle that family members were to be pardoned, not punished, even when they committed acts of sedition. It was now the Comnenian way, and the empire would eventually suffer grievously for it.[7]

John II's powerful military reputation explains why Isaac struggled to attract support from non-Roman military commanders.[8] John spent most of his reign campaigning, mostly successfully, in the Balkans, Asia Minor, and even into northern Syria. In the Balkans, he defeated the last big Pecheneg attack on Roman territory, beat back a Hungarian invasion, and captured large numbers of Serbian marauders that he forcibly settled in Asia Minor. He fought vigorously against the Turks and reestablished Roman power along the Mediterranean and Black Sea coasts of Anatolia. He even managed to conquer Cilicia again for the empire, march to Antioch, and nearly secure its surrender from the Crusaders.

And yet even these largely successful campaigns across the 1120s, 1130s, and early 1140s could not reverse the changes that had occurred in Asia Minor and northern Syria since the massive territorial losses of the 1070s. In all of these areas, there were two or even three generations of Romans who had never lived under a Roman state. In one incident near the end of John's life, the emperor was forced to confront some of them. In 1142, he set out into the countryside around Attaleia in Phrygia and approached Lake Pousgouse, a large body of water containing islands "inhabited by colonies of Christians" who maintained strong personal and commercial ties with the Turks living on the mainland. When John sought their submission, they joined with the Turks and "looked upon the Romans as their enemies." He did eventually capture the islands, though at significant loss of Roman life, but the empire could not hold the area. The lesson, Choniates affirmed, was that "custom, reinforced by time, is stronger than race or religion."[9]

Choniates understood something that John did not. Rome no longer looked like a government that was reuniting Romans with fellow citizens from whom they had been temporarily separated. It looked more like a warring power that could plunder cities and take land but could not hold on to its conquests.

This new reality meant that John's impressive victories did little to fundamentally change Rome's position in Asia Minor. By the time of his death in 1143, the land our maps show to be ostensibly under Roman control again looks quite impressive. But the people living in the land that he believed he was reconquering did not necessarily see themselves as natural members of the state he led. This was similar to the situation in the Western Mediterranean under Justinian I when significant populations of ethnic Romans had no interest in being forcibly brought back under the control of a state they did not know.

John's military policy faltered in one key conflict. In 1119, John refused to extend the agreement Alexius I had made with the Venetians. Evidently their free use of the port facilities and "their immoderate enrichment" from their tax-free status had led them to behave arrogantly. In 1122, Venice then unleashed its fleet against Roman islands in the Aegean, capturing Chios, Rhodes, and Lesbos, while attacking and plundering any Roman ships or ports they could reach. Venetian raids ended only when John "admitted them again on the previous terms" to their Constantinopolitan quarter and reinstated their tax status in 1126.[10]

The conflict with the Venetians was the first indication of a new dynamic that would govern relations between the east and the west in coming years. Alexius's two biggest initiatives in the west, the alliance with the Venetians and the call for the crusade, had begun with the Roman Empire occupying a superior position, but one determined as much by its mystique as by its power. The empire had a wealth of cultural, scientific, and religious artifacts that far surpassed anything in the west outside of, perhaps, what remained in the city of Rome itself. It was remote, exotic, and different in a way that provoked complicated feelings of envy and insecurity in the western visitors with whom Alexius negotiated.

John's failure to end Alexius's concessions to the Venetians showed that, while the empire remained rich, it was no longer intimidating. Nor was it remote. The Roman state now sat in between the kingdoms, cities, and principalities of western Europe and their cousin kingdoms implanted in the Eastern Mediterranean by the Crusaders. Venice had now shown that Roman emperors could be bullied in a way that sucked their empire's wealth and vitality northwestward. The Crusaders had shown that Romans lacked the power to bar their territory to western armies that wanted to pass through. And the rest of the west was watching.

WHEN JOHN II Comnenus died during a Cilician boar hunt gone wrong on April 8, 1143, he left a superficially strong empire that had no solutions for the longer-term problems it faced. One of those problems arose from his own family. John had four sons and had arranged for Alexius, his eldest, to become his successor-designate early in his reign. Unfortunately, both Alexius and John's second-born son, Andronicus, died in 1142. As John lay dying in Cilicia, he instructed his advisers that they were to prefer Manuel, his youngest son, over Isaac, his third-born, because "Manuel would be the better administrator of the empire."[11]

John was right about this, mostly. Manuel Comnenus revealed himself to be one of the most charismatic and creative emperors Rome would ever have. He used these talents to leverage the still-considerable wealth and prestige of the empire in ways that compensated for the steady erosion of the systems that had once made it so rich and powerful. Although the state had lost the Anatolian highlands and the tough local warriors who lived in them, the economic engines of Asia Minor were the lowland cities and agricultural areas along the Aegean coast that Alexius and John II Comnenus had restored to Roman control. Manuel could also draw on the productive lands in Greece and the Roman Balkans. Nearly a half century of relative calm there had fueled the growth of large-scale olive oil, wine, ceramics, and silk production in Greece as well as the prosperity of port cities such as Athens and Corinth.[12]

These cities and farms generated lots of potential tax revenue, but Manuel allowed corruption to creep into tax collection. Like his father and grandfather, he granted concession-holders the right to take a portion of the payments for themselves before the remainder went on to the treasury. But Manuel's empire had more such figures, and, as Choniates observed, "the inhabitants of the provinces, who in the past had to pay the imperial tax-collector," would now pay their taxes to some "half-Turkish, half-Greek barbarian" military officer rather than to the state. The result was that "everyone wanted to enlist in the army," going so far as to pay bribes to recruiters so that they, too, could become officers granted the revenues from "parcels of dewy land and wheat-bearing fields."[13] Regular Romans, however, began to flee the areas that provided the revenues Manuel had granted to these new military leaders because their farms and trades did not pay enough for them to provide for themselves and pay the taxes assessed to them. Manuel's cronyism was hollowing out the countryside by crippling the systems designed to protect its residents.[14]

Manuel's powerful armies fought extremely well, however. In the 1140s, they beat back attacks from the Crusader kingdom of Antioch, the Seljuk Turks, the Cumans, and the Normans. In the 1150s, they defeated attacks from Serbs, Hungarians, and Armenians and launched offensives in Italy and against the Crusader kingdom of Antioch. Between 1159 and 1161, they inflicted such sustained pressure on the Seljuks that they reduced the sultan to a Roman subordinate. In the late 1160s and early 1170s, victories in the Balkans forced the leaders of both Serbia and Hungary to become Roman vassals.

Aside from retaking Sirmium and coastal lands in Dalmatia from the Hungarians, these military victories resulted in little territorial gain. Perhaps because of the trouble his father had encountered in getting even Romans whose land he conquered to accept the rule of the Roman state, Manuel was much more interested in performing his superiority through public spectacles than in doing the hard work of absorbing the lands of those he defeated. When he came to Antioch following his victories in Cilicia, for example, he did not assume control of it. He instead entered the city with "[their king] Reginald and the nobles of Antioch running on foot around the imperial horse" like petty lords.[15] When he participated in a jousting tournament following the procession, Manuel personally dashed two Frankish knights to the ground in a display that "filled the Antiochenes with admiration for his manly courage."[16] Then he left and handed the city back to the Crusaders.

Manuel treated other sovereigns similarly. In 1161, his victories over the Turks led the sultan to affirm that he "would without hesitation do everything commanded by the emperor."[17] The sultan even journeyed to Constantinople the following year and participated in a ceremony where Manuel displayed the empire's riches while sitting on the throne, lording over the sultan who sat on a low stool below him.[18] But this was just a pantomime. No large swathes of territory changed hands, and the sultan's allegiance proved short-lived and fickle. Another war followed less than two decades later.

In each of these cases, Manuel used displays of Roman military power to bind the leaders of foreign powers to him as allies rather than absorbing their people as subjects. But, just as the Samnite decision to humiliate the Romans following their victory at Caudine Forks in 321 BC had inspired Rome to attack again, Manuel's displays of ritual submission made the embarrassed sovereigns more, not less, likely to challenge Rome in the future.

Fortunately, warfare was only one of the foreign policy tools Manuel used. When he could not fight, or the adversary was too far away to defeat, he used marriage to build alliances.[19] No fewer than ten Comneni were married to foreign spouses, including Manuel himself. His first wife, Bertha of Sulzbach, belonged to the family of the Holy Roman emperor Conrad. His second wife, Maria of Antioch, was a princess from the Crusader kingdom. He then arranged for his son Alexius II Comnenus to marry Anna, the daughter of King Louis VII of France. And his daughter Maria Comnena was betrothed first to Bela, the future king of Hungary; then to William of Sicily; and finally to Renieri of Montferrat.[20]

The clear affinity that Manuel had for westerners reflected changes in a Roman Empire that hosted increasingly large numbers of western travelers, merchants, and soldiers traversing Roman territory as they went from the Catholic west to the Crusader states in the east.[21] Small groups of pilgrims, monks, and priests caused little concern, but Romans remained understandably nervous when groups of armed westerners entered their lands.

No such moment caused greater anxiety during Manuel's reign than the Second Crusade. The Second Crusade, led by King Louis VII of France and the emperor Conrad III of Germany, was intended as a response to the fall of the Crusader kingdom of Edessa in 1144. As their armies advanced toward the Roman frontier in 1147, Manuel, having heard rumors that they planned to assault Constantinople and install a Catholic patriarch, called Roman forces back to the capital and paid for the repair and reinforcement of its walls.[22] He avoided any direct conflict with the German and French armies by arranging markets for them to provision themselves, getting them to swear that they would not attack Romans, and then shadowing them with a Roman army as they moved through the Balkans. Finally, when the French and Germans arrived outside Constantinople, they found Roman troops stationed on the walls wearing "coats of mail" and "armed with brazen lances," while other Roman soldiers followed behind the westerners to prevent them from trying to plunder farms, shops, or businesses.[23] It worked well enough. The German troops agreed to be ferried across to Asia after Manuel commandeered "every rowboat, ferryboat, fishing boat, and horse transport" to quickly get them away from the capital.[24] When the French arrived, Manuel similarly hurried them across the straits.

The crusade became a fiasco soon after the soldiers reached Asia. Short of provisions, the German and French armies took to plundering Roman territory before getting mauled by Turkish armies. Conrad fell ill in Ephesus and retreated to Constantinople to recover. After fighting on to Attaleia, Louis decided to take a ship to Antioch and left the army to march on its own overland. He made it to Antioch and then Jerusalem, but few of his soldiers survived to join him. The French collectively (and unfairly) blamed Manuel for failing to provide the support they needed to reach the Holy Land. Conrad accepted Manuel's grant of ships and equipment to travel on to Palestine, but Conrad's story of Roman cooperation was quickly subsumed in the west by Louis's self-serving tale of Roman perfidy. And, among Romans, the memory of the crusading armies threatening Constantinople and ransacking towns in Asia was impossible to forget.

Romans felt a different sort of unease about the Italian communities that grew rapidly during Manuel's reign. Small Italian merchant enclaves in Dyrrachium or Rhodes were tolerable, but Constantinople hosted large colonies of thousands or even tens of thousands of Genoese, Pisans, and Venetians sustained by the favorable trade treaties Manuel and his predecessors had made. The empire struggled to figure out how these Italian merchant communities fit into the larger life of the capital. On one hand, Romans reacted strongly against Italians who tried to integrate too quickly by taking "for themselves Roman wives and dwelling like other Romans in their houses outside of the residential areas granted to them by the emperor."[25] On the other hand, they deeply disliked Italians who failed to integrate at all. The worst example of the latter happened in 1170, when Venetians attacked the Genoese who were living in Constantinople, pulled down their houses, and then refused to pay for repairs when Manuel ordered them to do so. Manuel then sent letters across the empire instructing every Roman governor to arrest all the Venetians in his territory at precisely the same time on March 12, 1171. This mass arrest prompted another round of Venetian attacks on Roman islands, but this time Manuel's fleet largely repelled them.

As the events of 1171 show, Romans had been extremely lucky to be led by someone with Manuel's unique combination of skill, personal charisma, and savvy. His military successes, diplomatic marriages, and staged displays of Roman superiority could—only just barely—control the foreign challenges, internal corruption, and popular anger that threatened the empire. But Rome's luck ended with Manuel's death on September 24, 1180. At that point, Choniates wrote, "the affairs of the Romans were borne on an errant and helpless course."[26]

MANUEL'S COUSIN ANDRONICUS Comnenus deserves most of the blame for the sudden, catastrophic decline of the Roman state that occurred over the next five years. Andronicus was the son of Isaac Comnenus, the roguish brother of the emperor John II, and he had inherited his father's sense of entitlement, his gift for turning perceived slights into long-term grudges, and his talent for fomenting insurrections against whatever family member held power. Although Andronicus had a mediocre record as a commander that Manuel "bitterly abused" in private, the emperor honored him publicly and kept appointing him as a regional military governor into the early 1150s.[27] Andronicus eventually became angry when Manuel elevated his nephew to the rank of *protosebastos*, which Andronicus felt should have been his instead. "From that point on," said the historian John Kinnamos, Andronicus "continually worked at and plotted treachery."[28]

His first attempt came when he governed Cilicia and convinced the Crusader king of Palestine as well as the Turkish sultan to back an insurrection. It was detected, but Manuel did nothing to punish Andronicus. When Andronicus was given a command in the Balkans, he wrote a letter to the king of Hungary promising to give up all Roman claims to the territory he governed if the king "would take part in his attempt to carry out his intended usurpation." Manuel again found out about the plot but "abstained from doing him harm." Andronicus next tried to have Manuel assassinated during a boar hunt. The emperor escaped, but again did not punish his cousin. Their relationship only reached a breaking point when Andronicus nearly killed another family member in the emperor's presence in 1155. According to Manuel's bizarre code of family conduct, rebellion was a lesser infraction than physically attacking a relative. Finally, an enraged Manuel punished Andronicus for the assault on his other cousin by placing him under house arrest in the palace.[29]

Andronicus escaped from prison in 1159, was recaptured in a hut along the Sakarya River in western Asia Minor, and was then reinstalled in the prison.[30] Not surprisingly, Andronicus escaped a second time by making wax copies of the keys to his cell, giving them to his wife and son, and having them make iron copies that he could use to open the cell door. He fled to Russia, but in 1165 Manuel welcomed him back and gave him a command in a war against the Hungarians.[31] In 1166, Manuel further honored his troublesome cousin by sending him back to govern Cilicia. He granted him the taxes collected in Cyprus in addition to those from Cilicia so that, as Kinnamos put it, he "might be able to engage in lavish expenditure" while away from the capital. Andronicus had an affair with the empress's sister Philippa, but he "abandon[ed] her without any reason." Then he fled to the Crusader kingdom of Jerusalem with the tax money Manuel had granted him.[32]

Andronicus's saga continued in the Crusader kingdom of Jerusalem. There he met Theodora, the daughter of another Comnenian cousin and the widow of Baldwin III, Jerusalem's recently deceased king. Andronicus seduced her and then ran off with her, fleeing first to a neighboring Arab state and then into Turkish territory. Now a pariah in Jerusalem, Andronicus began "making frequent raids against Roman territory and took many men captive, rendering the spoils to the Turks."[33] Eventually, Manuel granted Andronicus amnesty. When the rascal arrived in Constantinople in July 1180, wrote Choniates, "the emperor . . . was moved to tears" and gave Andronicus an estate along the Black Sea coast.[34] He was, after all, family.

So it was that, after Manuel's death that September, Andronicus decided to mount a coup against the weak and unstable regime of Manuel's eleven-year-old son, Alexius II Comnenus. Manuel had named Alexius II as his successor and selected the empress and Crusader princess Maria of Antioch, Alexius II's mother and Manuel's second wife, to serve as his regent. Maria soon took Alexius II's cousin as a lover, a terrible decision that coincided with an attempt to overthrow Alexius launched by his half-sister Maria Comnena and her husband Ranieri of Montferrat, a member of a French aristocratic family. Their plot failed, and as one would now expect, its Comnenian leaders were pardoned.

Andronicus realized that he now had "an opportune and plausible excuse for seizing the throne."[35] He said he had sworn an oath to protect the honor and persons of Manuel and Alexius II. Ranieri's coup and Maria of Antioch's affair made Andronicus duty-bound to replace the regency with his own regime.

For much of the next year, Andronicus mobilized armed supporters while regularly sending letters to the capital filled with what Choniates called "silver-tongued wheedling" in which "he professed his zeal to do what was right and expounded on the need to liberate the emperor" Alexius II from the regency. As Andronicus and his soldiers advanced in Asia Minor, he began securing significant defections to his cause. After the commander of the army defending Nicomedia lost a battle against Andronicus, he packed his wife and six sons into a boat and sailed to join Andronicus's force.[36] When these forces reached Constantinople, the admiral who had been placed in command of the imperial fleet sailed all his ships over to Andronicus. His defection led to the collapse of the regime, and when he took the city, Andronicus ordered that Maria's lover should have his eyes gouged out.[37]

Andronicus inflicted even greater brutality on the Italian communities that had rallied to fight on behalf of the old regime in Constantinople. He incited mobs of people in the city to attack any Italians they could find, and then sent his own commandos to assist in the pogrom. Genoese, Pisans, and other Italians, wrote Choniates, "attempted to save themselves as best they could by leaving behind their homes[,] . . . scattering throughout the city, seeking asylum in the homes of the nobility, or boarding ships manned by their countrymen." Those who could not flee or hide were slaughtered while every home known to belong to an Italian was looted. The Genoese and Pisans who made it onto their ships sailed out of the Golden Horn and then took vengeance by "inflicting as much injury as possible on Romans" whose islands they passed as they journeyed to Italy. In an ominous sign of future trouble, Andronicus did nothing to stop them.[38]

The reprisal raids undertaken by the Italian refugees forced from their homes reflected a larger erosion of Roman power across the Balkans, Asia, and the Mediterranean that Andronicus could not stop. The Hungarian king Bela, who had once been a ward at Manuel Comnenus's court, seized upon the chaos in Constantinople to retake Sirmium and the Dalmatian territories that Manuel had captured in the 1170s. In 1183, Hungarians captured Belgrade and advanced as far as Serdica before being checked. The Crusader state of Antioch slipped from Roman domination and seized control of Cilicia. The Turkish sultan, Kilij Arslan, recaptured Sozopolis, which the Romans had held since early in the reign of John II, and cut the Roman land access to Attaleia.[39] The successes of the past sixty years had unraveled in a matter of months.

Then, almost impossibly, things got worse. Andronicus began a reign of terror against people he suspected of opposing him. He expelled many of them from office, sent others into exile, imprisoned still more, and even gouged out the eyes of some. The mere discussion of "the calamities that had befallen the Republic," Choniates tells us, led to noblemen being "seized on the spot, blinded, and thrown into a dark prison."[40] Andronicus also decided to break with family tradition and actually punish members of the Comnenian family. Manuel's daughter Maria Comnena and her husband Ranieri were poisoned. Manuel's second wife, Maria of Antioch, the mother of Alexius II Comnenus, was strangled. Andronicus even murdered Alexius II Comnenus and arranged to marry his wife, the daughter of the king of France, whom Choniates described as a "red-cheeked and tender spouse who had not yet completed her eleventh year of life."[41]

This all proved unbearable to many prominent Romans. In 1183, the brothers Isaac and Theodore Angelus led rebellions in Nicaea and Prusa. Andronicus secured the surrender of Nicaea the following spring in a particularly disgusting way. Choniates describes how Andronicus arrested Isaac's mother in Constantinople, brought her to Nicaea, and then placed "her on top of the battering ram as though it were a carriage and moved the engines of war up to the walls."[42] Isaac surrendered the city after Andronicus agreed to spare her life and give him safe passage back to Constantinople. Theodore was not so lucky when Prusa fell. Andronicus blinded him and dispatched him over the Turkish border, alone, on an ass that would lead him aimlessly around until they both "became food for wild animals." He was saved only because Turkish scouts found him, took him to their tent, and tended his wounds.[43]

Some Comnenian family members were more successful in evading Andronicus's wrath. In 1184, when Isaac Doukas Comnenus arrived in Cyprus with a group of supporters, he showed the Cypriots imperial letters that supposedly named him governor of the island.[44] The only problem was that he had forged them. Once he secured the island, he named himself emperor and began running Cyprus as its own state. Andronicus lacked the men and ships he needed to retake the island, so instead he arrested, condemned, and ordered the stoning of two of the rebel's most prominent relatives. Then, in early 1185, another Alexius Comnenus fled Roman territory after Andronicus claimed that he, too, had engaged in a plot. He made it to Sicily and sought help from the Norman king, William II.

It is only fitting that Andronicus, a Comnenian who plotted with multiple foreign powers, would see his own regime collapse after he forced a different Comnenian prince to seek help from the Normans. William II responded to Alexius's call with an invading army. It entered the Balkans in the summer of 1185 and arrived outside of Thessaloniki on August 6. It was joined by a fleet on August 15. And then, on August 24, these forces captured the city after its governor, David Comnenus, handed it over because he feared Andronicus.[45] At least 7,000 people died in the city and many more were enslaved.[46]

The Norman capture of Thessaloniki laid bare the utter bankruptcy of both Andronicus's regime and the Comnenian model of imperial governance. The entitled Comnenian princelings had been too small a group to pose a threat under Alexius I. They became a manageable challenge under John II, and were still only a nuisance under the strong and capable regime of Manuel. But in less than five years, they had nearly torn the empire apart. One Comnenus had split Cyprus off from the empire. Another had joined with the Normans to pursue a spurious claim on imperial power. A third had betrayed the empire's second-largest city to the Normans because, evidently, he was petrified with fear. And Andronicus, the worst of the group, had not only created the conditions that had prompted all these betrayals but displayed such remarkable brutality that Romans everywhere turned against him.

In one sense, Rome was lucky. Andronicus was so terrible that he fell from power before the Normans reached the capital. On September 11, 1185, Andronicus went back on his pledge to safeguard the life and property of Isaac Angelus, the leader of the rebellion in Nicaea, whose safety the emperor had guaranteed two years earlier. When Andronicus sent men to "grab Isaac by his hair or seize him by the beard so they could bring him down from his room in disgrace," Isaac instead got on his horse, raised his sword, and charged at the official whom Andronicus had sent. He crushed his skull with the sword and then rode as fast as he could to Hagia Sophia, shouting out to all who could hear that he had killed one of the emperor's agents with his sword.[47]

Sometimes all it takes is one person's public defiance to break a tyrant's spell. And so it was that night. As Isaac entered Hagia Sophia seeking sanctuary, the few people who saw his display blocked the doors to keep Andronicus from seizing him. The next morning, Choniates wrote, "there was no inhabitant of the city who was not in attendance and who did not pray to God that Isaac might reign as emperor and Andronicus be dethroned."[48] By the middle of the day, the angry crowd had broken into the prisons and liberated the members of illustrious families who had been locked up for an "insignificant fault or incidental remark."[49] The burgeoning crowd then armed itself, acclaimed Isaac as emperor, and stormed the palace. Andronicus fled, but he was soon captured and arrested.

The Comnenian dynasty had fallen. But the Roman state would never again control the anarchic forces its last members unleashed.

Chapter 45

Two Decades of Roman Collapse

1185–1203

THE POPULAR UPRISING that toppled Andronicus Comnenus unleashed a frenzy of looting and violence unlike anything Constantinopolitans had ever experienced. No one, least of all Isaac Angelus, could contain the passions of a Roman mob that had just overthrown an emperor. The crowd flowed into the palace "without any difficulty because there was no one to obstruct them or to prevent them from doing what they wanted," wrote Nicetas Choniates. They first plundered the mint, stealing all the coins already minted as well as thousands of pounds of raw gold and silver. They then looted the palace armory of all the weapons it contained before "despoiling the churches inside the palace," stealing the holy relics and stripping precious metal off the icons. Never before had a change in power led average Romans to loot the treasury, the palace, and the sanctuaries that belonged to the commonwealth as if they were the personal property of a fallen emperor.[1]

The mob's sadism surpassed its greed. When Andronicus was brought to the capital, an orgy of vicious humiliation ensued. The former emperor was imprisoned "with two heavy chains weighing down his proud neck, the iron collars used to fetter caged lions, and his feet were painfully shackled." As he was led to the new emperor, Isaac, "he was slapped in the face, kicked in the butt, his beard was torn out, his teeth pulled out, his head shaved." Random people began hitting him as he passed, with the wives of men he had killed taking turns punching him in the face. Eventually, someone cut off his right hand and he was thrown back into the prison with the wounds left untreated.[2]

Andronicus's ordeal had only begun. When he did not die of an infection, he had one of his eyes gouged out, and then he was paraded around the Forum on a mangy camel, dressed in rags like a beggar. Some people began to feel sympathy for the fallen emperor, but the mob was not done. They clubbed him over the head, threw stones at him, spread cow dung under his nostrils, poured ox vomit and human excrement over his eyes, and doused his once-handsome face with boiling water. When he reached the city's theater, Andronicus was taken down from the camel and hung upside down by his feet from two columns. The crowd stripped him naked, while some Latins who had escaped Andronicus's ethnic cleansing "raised their swords with both hands above his buttocks and, standing around him, brought them down to see whose cut was deeper." He died "with his right arm extended in agony and brought to his mouth so that it seemed to many that he was sucking out the still-warm blood dripping from his recent amputation." His body was left exposed for several days until it was "pitched into one of the vaults of the Hippodrome like an animal carcass."[3]

These horrific details are worth repeating because even Vitellius, Pupienus, Leontius, and other fallen emperors whose bodies had been publicly mistreated did not endure such prolonged, sadistic, and humiliating public torture. And, as Choniates noted, people disfiguring, beating, and sodomizing the emperor "gave no thought to the fact that, but a few short days earlier . . . they had confirmed their loyalty and devotion to him" by oath. Andronicus's fate suggests that something profound had broken in the Roman state.

ROMANS THEN TURNED to Isaac II Angelus, the man whose brave defiance of Andronicus had sparked the riot that led to his downfall, to rebuild their faith in the systems that had governed their lives. Isaac gathered together Andronicus's victims in order to restore to them whatever property remained in the imperial treasury and pay them compensation. Although this prompted some "to look upon Isaac's reign as the transition from winter to spring," his symbolic actions could not cover up the profound challenges he faced.[4]

The most significant of these challenges came from the Norman army, which had recently captured Thessaloniki and was still moving toward the capital. In those initial heady days, volunteers turned out enthusiastically to help the new emperor turn back the Sicilian invasion. On November 7, 1185, the general Alexius Branas routed the Normans near the Strymon River in northern Greece. He captured their leaders, 4,000 soldiers, and the Comnenian figurehead who had invited them into Roman territory in the hope that they might place him on the imperial throne.[5]

This initial success against the Normans was, unfortunately, the high point of Isaac Angelus's reign. Despite his last name, the new emperor was connected to the Comnenus family through his paternal grandmother, and he was strongly influenced by the family's practice of placing its members in positions of power regardless of their qualifications. Isaac, though, took this nepotistic tendency to a ridiculous extreme when, in 1186, he sent a fleet to Cyprus to dislodge Isaac Doukas Comnenus, the man who had used fake documents to seize control of the island under Andronicus. The emperor chose as his generals the elderly Alexius Contostephanus and a Comnenian family member who had "had his eyes cut out by Andronicus and thus was considered unfit for battle." The invasion led by the blind admiral went as well as one would expect. A Norman commander who had come to help the Cypriot regime found the seventy ships the emperor had sent sitting on the beach after the sailors and marines they had carried had joined in the fighting on land. The ship captains "readily surrendered" their vessels, which represented most of the Roman navy, and they were sailed off to Sicily. So it was that the Roman navy, which had gotten its start almost 1,500 years earlier by capturing and copying a Carthaginian warship wrecked off Sicily, was reduced to insignificance when a Sicilian stole most of its ships.[6]

At roughly the same time, the Roman state began to lose control of Bulgaria. In late 1185 or early 1186, Isaac decided to pay for his wedding to the daughter of the king of Hungary by instituting a special tax on the flocks tended by the Vlachs, a Romance-language-speaking people possibly descended from the old Roman inhabitants of the Balkans.[7] The Vlachs living in this rugged area had remained loyally Roman despite the upheavals of the eleventh and twelfth centuries, but the new taxes on their flocks were unacceptable.

In early 1186, two Vlach brothers named Peter and Asan met with Isaac to negotiate some sort of accommodation. They knew the ways of the Comnenian dynasty, however, so instead of asking for tax relief on behalf of all the Vlachs, they proposed to join the Roman army as officers in exchange for control of "a certain estate in the vicinity of Mount Haemus that would provide them with a little revenue." The request represented an attempt at blackmail, but Peter and Asan were far from the first nobles to ask for a slice of imperial tax income from Roman towns. It had been the primary method of binding important local leaders to the Roman administrative system ever since Alexius I Comnenus had pioneered the system a century earlier. And if their last name had been Comnenus, the brothers would not even have had to ask. But, for unknown reasons, Isaac denied their request and had Asan slapped in the face "for his impudence." Insulted by this indignity, the brothers went home and plotted an insurrection.[8]

Their small rebellion gained strength because of Roman mistakes and imperial arrogance. On April 21, 1186, Isaac II Angelus won a significant victory over the Vlachs when they became terrified of an eclipse, but he squandered it by quickly withdrawing his army and failing to pursue Peter and Asan after they fled across the Danube. When Asan returned that summer with troops reinforced by auxiliaries provided by the neighboring Cumans, Isaac II Angelus first dithered and then decided against leading the Roman army himself. This proved a catastrophic mistake. The first general he sent rebelled and tried to seize the Roman throne for himself rather than confronting Asan's army. The second general lost many men when he tried to attack Asan's mountain fortresses. Isaac then sent Alexius

Branas, the victor over the Normans in 1185. Branas, too, rebelled, securing the support of the Roman troops based in Adrianople and marching on Constantinople before Isaac stopped him by using Latin forces commanded by Conrad of Montferrat.[9] The emperor then held a celebratory feast where, Choniates reports, he "ordered Branas's head brought forward" so it could be "tossed back and forth like a ball."[10]

Isaac pretended to be magnanimous and agreed to pardon those among Branas's supporters who would swear oaths to him. But soon after they did, he sent a mob of Constantinopolitans to loot and burn the houses of people living in suburbs perceived to have supported Branas. Conrad's French soldiers marched out of the city the following morning and took their own turn plundering what remained in the razed buildings and monasteries. The French looting provoked a counterattack by Constantinopolitans, who thought they could seize back the property the French had taken just as easily as they had stolen from the Italians under Andronicus. This time, however, the urban mob attacked soldiers rather than civilians. Conrad's men set up barricades, defended them professionally, and "mauled" the Romans.[11]

This chaos helped doom Isaac's fight against the Vlachs and the Bulgarians, who were now joining their revolt. In September 1187, Isaac himself had to return to the front at the head of a smaller, less experienced Roman army and without his French allies.[12] Although he now confronted an enemy that had seized even more territory in the plains and threatened major cities, Isaac remained a disinterested commander. He fought for a couple of months, left his army in barracks in the field, and went back to Constantinople for the winter. He returned to the front briefly the following spring, but soon headed to the capital because, Choniates claims, he preferred "the delights of the Propontis and the pleasurable resorts along her shores" to life in a military camp.[13] With his departure, eastern Bulgaria was now effectively lost to the empire. Within a few years, the nascent Vlacho-Bulgarian state would stretch from the Black Sea to Belgrade, the fruits of a revolt that Isaac could have avoided if he had granted

Peter and Asan the tax concessions they had requested in 1186. Isaac's mismanagement of the situation stands out as one of the most consequential blunders in all of Roman history.

Isaac's problems were now so overwhelming, wrote Choniates, that "not a single year elapsed without bringing some public horror."[14] In 1188, the "horror" came from Isaac's mismanagement of the Third Crusade. This was an armed expedition planned by the German emperor Frederick Barbarossa, the French king Philip II, and the English king Henry II following the fall of Jerusalem to the Kurdish general Saladin in October 1187. The three kings set off separately, with the French and English contingents traveling by sea, though the English were delayed by Henry's death and the coronation of his successor Richard I. When the Germans arrived, Isaac at first gave Frederick permission to pass peacefully through Roman territory. But the paranoid emperor soon began to suspect that Frederick might be aiming at his throne and tried to block the mountain passes to prevent Frederick's advance. He also harassed the German foraging parties, effectively forcing them to fight their way through Roman territory. Frederick responded by plundering and temporarily occupying Philippopolis, Beroe, and Adrianople as he advanced on Constantinople. In March 1190, Isaac finally felt compelled to meet Frederick's demands and ferry his army across to Asia.[15] The German threat ended after Frederick drowned in a river in Asia. But the Crusaders further damaged Roman interests when Richard I of England seized Cyprus from Isaac Doukas Comnenus and granted it to the former king of Jerusalem in 1192.[16]

By the mid-1190s, the empire had tired of the annual parade of horrors Isaac was inflicting on his fellow Romans while "he delighted in dirty jokes, lewd songs, and silly dwarves" in comfortable Constantinopolitan palaces.[17] Choniates details at least nine different plots against Isaac between 1187 and 1195 led by generals, Comnenian family members, and even an imposter who looked and talked like the murdered emperor Alexius II Comnenus. One of these plots finally succeeded. In the spring of 1195, Isaac decided to lead a Roman army against the Vlachs following yet another Roman defeat about

100 miles west of Constantinople. As the army was assembling at Kypsella on April 8, Isaac went out hunting. By the time he returned, a group of aristocratic supporters, the emperor's courtiers, members of the Senate, and the entire army had acclaimed his brother Alexius as the new emperor. Isaac's eyes were gouged out at a convent founded by the father of Andronicus Comnenus, and he was starved for many days in the hope that he might die. When he did not, he was imprisoned and kept on a diet of "wine and measured bread" that would slowly starve him until it drove him mad.[18]

The emperor Alexius III Angelus—also known as Alexius Comnenus, the regnal name he chose to distinguish himself from his brother—took control of the empire "peacefully and without factional strife," said Choniates. His first act was to call off the campaign against the Vlachs that Isaac had planned, disbanding the army and distributing the money intended to pay for the war as rewards to "the entire population for going over to him so readily and avoiding political strife."[19]

The strife came soon enough. The Seljuk Turkish regime was fragmenting, and Roman pretenders—including Isaac Doukas Comnenus, the former ruler of Cyprus, and a second person masquerading as the long-dead emperor Alexius II—found Turkish emirs willing to gamble on the chance that one of them might seize the Roman throne. When Alexius III tried to lead a Roman army north to confront the Vlachs in 1196, the troops mutinied and demanded that the emperor "lead us back to our own land." This was a particularly striking statement, because the foreign territory they wanted to retreat from had been Roman less than a decade ago.[20]

Pressures also came from the west. In 1196, Choniates reports, Frederick Barbarossa's son Henry VI, who had inherited his father's empire and seized Norman Sicily, sent a message to Constantinople in which he "laid claim, as the present ruler of Sicily, to all the Roman provinces between Epidamnos and the famous city of Thessaloniki," because they had been seized in the 1180s when the Normans had tried to overthrow Andronicus Comnenus.[21] Henry threatened to invade unless the Romans paid him a huge ransom. This was simple blackmail, but, as Frederick Barbarossa's march through Roman territory a few years earlier had shown, the weakened Roman state could not resist the Germans if the Germans chose to attack.

Alexius III knew he had to pay, but he stupidly chose to receive the German envoys on Christmas Day while wearing "his imperial robe set with precious stones." He had ordered Roman senators present at the meeting to wear their purple garments with gold embroidery that marked their senatorial status. He hoped to intimidate the Germans by "extolling the wealth of the Roman Empire," but instead the Germans saw the expensive clothing as a sign that their price had been too low. Their demand to leave the empire in peace rose to 5,000 pounds of gold.[22]

Alexius did not have the money. To meet the demands, said Choniates, he "taxed the provinces, imposing a so-called German tax" on them. Meanwhile, he forced everyone in Constantinople to pay a tax that amounted to a percentage of their net worth. This prompted rioting directed at Alexius, in part because people believed he had wasted public funds by giving handouts to his supporters, and that he had undercut revenue collection by distributing governorships in the provinces "to his worthless kinsmen." He was reduced to confiscating all the gold and silver votive offerings left outside churches to thank saints for miraculous healings. When even this did not produce the needed funds, he ordered the imperial tombs in Constantinople to be opened, so they could be stripped of everything of value. Finally, Choniates recounts, "the only things left of those ancient Roman emperors . . . were their coats of stone." The treasures of 800 years of imperial burials were "consigned to the smelting furnace" and readied to be sent to Germany. And it was all for nothing. Henry died on September 28, 1197, before the money could be sent. Rome, yet again, had escaped disaster.[23]

The years afterward were, Choniates wrote, "no different from what went before . . . listless and spiritless." The armed forces were undermanned and exhausted, while gout limited Alexius III's activity. Neither the emperor nor his armies had the vitality necessary to stop Roman control from bleeding away in the northern Balkans as

Hungarian, Serbian, and Vlacho-Bulgarian conquerors carved up the land.[24] By 1202 the empire had also lost the Black Sea port of Varna and was defending against raids into Thessaly. Things were no more stable internally. At least four more revolts flared up between 1197 and 1202, while Romans in the capital began proposing possible successors to Alexius III.[25] Less than a generation had passed since Manuel Comnenus had left his son a wealthy and powerful empire extending from Sirmium to Syria. That same empire was now nearly bankrupt and had contracted back to Greece, the Aegean, and western Asia Minor.

This was the condition of the Roman state when Pope Innocent III contacted Alexius III to negotiate conditions for a Fourth Crusade. Between 1198 and 1202, the pope and emperor exchanged eight diplomatic missions and twelve official letters in which they tried to fashion a working arrangement that would prevent more German extortion of Constantinople, formalize Roman imperial help for the crusade, and bring the eastern church back into communion with Rome.[26] When nothing was agreed, the Crusaders decided instead to travel by sea, conquer Egypt, and then use it as a base to retake Jerusalem. In April 1201, they contracted with Venice for the construction of a massive fleet that would "carry 4,500 horses and 9,000 squires." Other ships would "accommodate 4,500 knights and 20,000 foot soldiers," as well as "all the sustenance they require for nine months." The Crusaders would pay 94,000 marks and agreed to evenly split the anticipated spoils with the Venetians.[27]

When the Crusaders arrived in Venice, however, there were far fewer of them than anyone had anticipated, and they lacked the funds to pay the Venetians what they owed.[28] The nobility leading the crusade first turned over the silverware and other items made of precious metals that they had hoped to carry along to the Holy Land, but when that failed to resolve their debts, they reluctantly agreed to fight on Venice's behalf. Despite an explicit papal prohibition, the Crusaders first captured the Christian, Croatian city of Zadar for the Venetians. When the plunder from Zadar also proved insufficient, the Doge of Venice suggested that they move on to attack Roman territory.[29]

The rolling dysfunction of the Roman state gave the Crusaders a pretext for war. Their leader, Boniface of Montferrat, was the cousin of Philip of Swabia, a claimant to the German imperial throne who had married Isaac II Angelus's daughter Irene. They had been hosting her brother Alexius Angelus while he traveled around western Europe looking for someone who might back him in a coup attempt. Boniface told the other Crusaders that he had met Alexius at a Christmas party and, because he was the son of the former emperor Isaac II, they could bring him to Constantinople, claim that "this young man [was] the rightful heir" to the Roman throne, and install him as emperor, wrote the French chronicler Robert de Clari. Then they could "take provisions and other things" from the Romans to help pay off the Venetians.[30]

The monarchs, princes, and kings of the west saw no problem with this option, because, by the logic of western Europe, a son was the natural inheritor of a title his father had possessed. But Romans understood the office of the emperor differently. The emperor Alexius III had even explained this to the pope, reminding him that the Roman throne was "not conferred through [hereditary] succession but through the election of the nobles" who represented the Roman state. Because Alexius Angelus was a private citizen, he "could not lay claim to any right to the imperial throne." The Roman Empire, as Alexius hoped to make clear, remained a state in which rulers were entrusted with their authority by Romans, not one in which they were owed that authority by accident of birth.[31]

The pope remained officially noncommittal, but he communicated in April 1203 that he disapproved of the Crusaders' plan "to depart for Greece with the son of the former emperor of Constantinople." His letter, however, arrived well after the Crusaders had sent for Alexius Angelus.[32] When Alexius joined the Crusader army, he "agreed to demands which were impossible to fulfill," wrote Choniates. These included a pledge to contribute "seas of money" the empire did not have as well as heavily armed Roman troops and warships that did not exist, along with a promise to pursue a union of the churches under terms set by the pope that his countrymen would never accept.[33] It was a recipe for disaster.

Alexius III had known about the Crusaders' movements for months, but he had done nothing to prepare for their arrival. It was, Choniates wrote, "as though his advisers were talking to a corpse" when they asked him to stockpile weapons, repair fortifications, or build ships. It was only when he learned that Alexius IV Angelus was really being put forward as an imperial rival that "he began to repair the rotting and worm-eaten small ships, barely twenty in number," that were the remnants of the once-proud Roman navy. He also had no time to summon the armies back to the capital or repair the walls. The best he could do was to order the destruction of houses that abutted the outside of the walls so that no one assaulting the city could use them to scale its fortifications. It was much too little, much too late.[34]

The ignorant young Alexius and his Crusader puppet masters first made landfall at the former Roman city of Dyrrachium. When the residents learned that Alexius Angelus had arrived, they greeted him as the emperor Alexius IV Angelus.[35] After they left Dyrrachium, Alexius and the Crusaders put in on Corfu for the first three weeks of May. They passed around the Peloponnese in June, stopping on the Aegean islands of Euboea and Andros, before arriving outside Constantinople on the night of June 23, 1203.[36]

The Crusaders were awestruck. Geoffrey of Villehardouin wrote that "when they saw the heights of its walls and their powerful towers, they could not even imagine that it was possible for so powerful a city to exist in the entire world." They were equally astonished by "its superb palaces, tall churches, the likes of which it was not possible to believe existed if one had not seen them with their own eyes, and the length and extent of the city."[37]

The Crusaders and their Venetian allies were perhaps just as surprised when they brought Alexius Angelus before the walls of Constantinople and told the Romans, "Behold your natural ruler!"

Nothing could be less tone deaf than telling Romans that they had a natural ruler. Indeed, as Villehardouin confesses, no one, "not a single person," made any show of support for the would-be emperor.[38]

The disappointed Latin forces then decided to land at Chalcedon, across the Bosporus from Constantinople, so they could plan how they might assault the city. They were expecting a robust Roman defense that would probably include stretching the great metal chain across the Golden Horn, the strategy that had foiled so many naval attacks in the past. When the Crusaders landed and attacked the fortress to which the north end of the chain was attached, the Romans just ran away.[39] The Crusaders then broke the chain, and the powerful Venetian-led fleet entered the harbor, where it overwhelmed the Roman navy on July 5.[40]

The Crusaders took the next three days to plan their assault on the land. After a week of inconclusive skirmishing along the walls, they decided on July 17 to either storm the city or try to come to terms with the emperor. After a combined land and naval assault led to the Crusaders occupying some of the towers, they beat back a Roman attempt to push them outside the walls by setting a massive fire. Although it burned 125 acres, the fire was only a tactical victory. Enough Romans survived that the city could possibly still have withstood the attack. The emperor Alexius III, however, decided that night that all was lost. He gathered whatever treasure he could carry and fled the city. As Choniates wrote, it was "as though he had worked as hard as possible to make a miserable corpse of the City and bring her to utter ruin."[41]

The Crusaders were the first non-Roman army to breach the nearly 800-year-old Constantinopolitan city walls, but they had not yet captured it. They awoke the next morning to two pieces of news. First, Alexius III had fled. And second, Roman courtiers had taken Isaac II Angelus, the father of the pretender whom the Crusaders hoped to place on the throne, from his prison cell in the palace, and reinstalled the blinded, mentally broken man as emperor.[42] Maybe, Roman elites hoped, this desperate move could save the empire.

Chapter 46

The Death of the Roman State

1204

T HE DECISION TO pull Isaac Angelus from prison and restore him to imperial power took the Crusaders entirely by surprise. If Isaac was again emperor, their pretext for attacking and looting Constantinople had evaporated. But, Choniates wrote, they "made no changes in their expectations" and forced Isaac "to agree to fulfill all the promises Alexius had made them."[1] Alexius entered the city and was crowned emperor Alexius IV Angelus alongside his father while the Latin lords sat with the Roman senators. Isaac II and Alexius IV then had to find a way to pay the Latins what Alexius had promised them. They "took possession of what little was in the imperial treasury" after the flight of Alexius III, stole all the money the former emperor's wife and family possessed, and melted down the precious objects remaining in the churches. It still was not nearly enough.[2]

The Crusaders' imposition of an emperor that no Romans wanted prompted another explosion of anti-western sentiment in the city. Choniates describes how Constantinopolitan mobs "senselessly razed and reduced to ashes the dwellings of western people . . . making no distinction between friends and foes." This was counterproductive, he added, because the Genoese and Pisans living in Constantinople were "totally disgusted by the wickedness and recklessness" of the Crusaders and their Venetian masters and could have been Roman allies if they had been enlisted in the fight. Instead, the Pisans evacuated the city and sailed across the Golden Horn, where they joined with the Venetians.[3]

On August 19, 1203, a group of French, Venetian, and Pisan soldiers launched a revenge attack against a mosque used by merchants and the capital's community of Roman Muslims that was located north of the church of Hagia Eirene in the modern Sultanahmet district. Constantinopolitan Muslims and other Romans living around the mosque grabbed whatever weapons they had and beat the attackers back, but the Crusaders lit a large fire that they hoped would level the neighborhood around the site and cause its defenders to scatter. The flames quickly spread through the monumental core of the city, torching the Forum of Constantine, the Hippodrome, and two southern harbors on the Sea of Marmara, before ultimately burning all the way across the city until it reached the Golden Horn. Choniates reports that most of the city's wealthiest residents "were stripped . . . of their possessions" by the blaze, which burned through Constantinople's most densely populated and richest areas.[4]

The emperors Isaac II Angelus and Alexius IV Angelus could do nothing to help their people recover. Instead, they again plundered whatever precious metals and jewels they could find in churches and tombs so that they could continue to pay the westerners.[5] On the day of the fire, Alexius IV even offered the Crusader Boniface additional money that he did not have to march to Adrianople and confront the deposed Alexius III, who was trying to rally resistance forces there.

By the end of August, the desperation of the capital's leaders and the anger of its citizens had begun to consume the treasures that linked the Roman present to its glorious past. Still desperate to pay the Crusaders, Isaac II and Alexius IV removed and melted down all the gold and silver ornaments in Hagia Sophia that created the magnificent optical effects in Justinian's church.[6] Outside the church, crowds angry about the heavy taxes they had to pay to the Latins rioted in the burned-out Forum of Constantine, smashing a thirty-foot-tall bronze statue of Athena that stood there on a pedestal.[7] This statue, which had been sculpted by Pheidias around 456 BC, had been taken from the Athenian Acropolis and erected in Constantinople under the emperor Leo I so it could be protected as an artistic treasure.

By early winter, sporadic acts of resistance to Alexius IV and his Crusader protectors began to pop up as popular anger rose. On January 1, 1204, fifteen burning ships were sent during the night toward the Crusader fleet anchored outside the city. The Venetian pilots managed to avoid the attack and then added a charge to the bill Alexius owed them "for the service they had rendered him."[8] Then, six days later, Alexius Doukas attempted to "win the throne and the citizens' favor" by charging his horse into Crusader troops. His horse slipped when he charged, but his defiance prompted some young Romans to fire a volley of arrows to give him time to escape.[9]

Doukas's charge inspired a wider rebellion that culminated in a remarkable assembly held in Hagia Sophia a little more than two weeks later. At this meeting, the Senate, the bishops, and the clergy came together to select a new emperor who might seize power from the Angeli duo and their Crusader protectors. No one wished to be chosen, but finally, after two days of deliberation, the assembly settled on a man named Nicholas Kannavos "against his will."[10]

The Roman state had only a few months left to live, and even as it neared its end, the Romans followed a process according to which the citizens and their representatives decided on their ruler. But for the first time in centuries, the state was too weak to ensure the safety of that ruler. Choniates writes that Kannavos, like everyone else in that meeting, knew that "whoever was proposed for election would be led out the very next day like a sheep led to slaughter."[11]

Alexius IV behaved just as expected. His father had fallen ill, so the emperor summoned Boniface and agreed that Crusaders should be brought inside the city walls to save his regime.[12] That evening, however, Alexius Doukas bribed the imperial guards to allow him into the emperor's chambers. He convinced Alexius IV that armed men waited outside to kill him, and his life would be saved only if he followed him out of the palace.[13] The simple-minded young man went with Doukas, chanting psalms to himself, and was seized when he emerged from the palace "as Doukas decked himself with the imperial insignia."

The joint reign of Isaac II and Alexius IV Angelus had ended. Within a couple of weeks, both father and son would be dead. The former probably died of natural causes.[14] The latter most decidedly did not.[15]

On the morning of January 28, Constantinople awoke to the news that it now had two exceedingly weak emperors. One of them, Kannavos, did not want the job, and the other one, Doukas, was remarkably ill-suited to do it. Kannavos, whom Choniates describes as "gentle by nature, keenly intelligent, and versed in generalship," holed himself up in Hagia Sophia and refused to do anything to consolidate his authority.[16] His support quickly ebbed away, and within a week Doukas arranged to be formally proclaimed emperor. He had his rival arrested.

Conflict between Alexius V Doukas and the Crusaders camped outside the city was now inevitable. When they learned of the deaths of their puppets, the Crusaders, the Doge of Venice, and the clergy accompanying them held a conference to decide how they might proceed. According to Villehardouin, the clergy observed that "the Greeks as a people had seceded from the Church of Rome," then declared the new emperor guilty of murder and condemned the entire population of Constantinople as accomplices in his crime. As a result, the conference asserted, a Crusader attack on Constantinople and the seizure of all the empire's lands would be both "just and lawful."[17]

Unlike his two predecessors, Alexius V Doukas immediately began working energetically to protect Romans from the Crusaders. He ordered the reinforcement of the walls that the Crusaders had broken through the previous year, though the wooden beams the impoverished emperor could afford were a poor substitute for the strong stone and brick that had once protected the city.[18] Alexius V also decided to compensate for the weakness of the city's defenses by going on the offensive against the Crusaders. At some point in February, he rode out against Baldwin, the count of Flanders, with Roman forces evidently recruited from within the city, but his raw Roman recruits fled when they saw the French knights.[19]

On April 8, the Venetians' largest ships took up positions along the seawalls next to the ground that had been cleared by the fires the preceding summer. An initial probing advance on April 9 was pushed back by Roman archers. After resting for the weekend, the Venetians attacked again on April 12. They seized a single tower, the one nearest the Petria Gate, about two-thirds of the way up the Golden Horn from the harbor's mouth, after the Romans barely put up a fight. The Crusaders then breached the wall of beams that Alexius V had hastily constructed and set another large fire to clear the buildings along the seawalls.

This fire, the third large blaze to cut across the city in a year, left so many people homeless that they "wandered aimlessly about" in a sort of collective shock, unable to do anything to fight back against the Crusaders.[20] So Alexius V did what Alexius III had done. He returned to the palace, boarded a fishing boat, and sailed away from the city on the night of April 12–13.

When they learned of the emperor's flight, the Roman notables held a very hastily arranged assembly in Hagia Sophia, which was still nearly four miles away from where the Crusaders had breached the walls. Here, they selected Constantine Laskaris as the new head of the Roman state. But Constantine would not accept the imperial insignia or don the imperial robe. He had no interest in being the last Roman emperor of a falling city. Instead he intended to spark resistance to the Crusader attack—inside the city, if possible, or outside of it, if necessary.

Constantine agreed to go with the patriarch to the Milion, the symbolic stone from which all distances in the empire were once measured. There he tried to inspire the people gathered to fight the Crusaders, but, as Choniates wrote, "not a single person from the populace responded to his appeals." The city had not fallen so much as it had given up.[21]

When the Crusaders entered Constantinople on April 13, they were greeted by a defeated population. People were holding "crosses and venerable icons of Christ," Choniates reports, in the hope that their shared Christian faith might calm the Christian holy warriors. It did not. The Crusaders took over the houses that still stood after the fires and used them as bases. From these bases they set out on expeditions to seize everything they could find.[22] They looted churches, dismantled public monuments, and sent a flood of ancient treasures back to western Europe.[23]

THE DEATH OF the Roman state came neither from the looting of the Roman capital nor the surrender of its citizens. The state died when the Crusaders assembled to decide what would happen next. They could, in theory, have behaved as Theoderic did when he had decided that Roman institutions, laws, and ways of living would all continue after he seized control of Italy from Odoacer in 493. To all who lived in it, Theoderic's Italy remained a Roman state—at least until Justinian's propagandists began trying to convince them otherwise. If the Crusaders had agreed to appoint an emperor who would govern in a Roman way, following Roman laws, one might be able to argue that the Roman state continued after their conquest.

The Crusaders instead behaved like the Normans had when they had seized Roman Italy. They held a meeting to choose twelve electors, all from the west, who met in a palace that the Doge of Venice had requisitioned. No Romans were consulted or involved in the decision of who their new ruler would be. The electors chose Baldwin, a count from Flanders, as the new Latin emperor of Constantinople and celebrated his coronation on May 16. Along with his fellow Crusaders and their Venetian backers, Baldwin partitioned the empire and assigned its lands to Venice and the other Crusaders.[24] In his arrogance, Baldwin even refused to meet with Roman officials from the military and civil bureaucracy or any provincial governors, the very sorts of steps that would have established continuity between his regime and the Roman past.[25] He did not think this necessary and did not care to get their advice about how to rule or run the state. The Romans were his subjects, not his fellow citizens, and he felt that he had nothing to learn from them.

Much of the territory that is now part of modern Greece fell under the control of Crusader lords. Roman cities such as Thessaloniki and Athens became Crusader fiefdoms, their Roman citizens reduced to the status of subjects of the western lords who claimed them. The Crusaders also made quick work of Alexius III Comnenus and Alexius V Doukas, the last two living Roman emperors. Doukas had joined up with Alexius III in Thrace after he fled Constantinople, but Alexius III had him blinded.[26] Both men were subsequently captured by the Crusaders. Doukas was taken to Constantinople and thrown down from the top of the Column of Theodosius.[27] Alexius III was captured and imprisoned until 1209 by the Crusader lord who had seized Thessaloniki.[28] He lived until 1211, but he never again exercised any real political authority.

The significance of Baldwin's refusal to reach out to Roman elites soon became clear to the Crusader lords as they fanned out to take control of the fiefdoms they had arrogated to themselves. Romans who had no real role in the leadership of the new Latin empire began to resist its authority. The far eastern Roman principality of Trebizond, which two members of the Comnenus family had separated from the Roman state sometime after the Comnenian dynasty fell in 1185, completely eluded Crusader control. Although it was never very large in terms of either territory or population, the Roman regime based in that city was protected by mountains that enabled it to remain independent until 1461.

A more vital center of Roman resistance to the Crusaders emerged in Epirus, a mountainous area of northwestern Greece and southern Albania, where the military and diplomatic skills of Michael Comnenus Doukas, a cousin of Alexius III, prevented a Crusader conquest of the region. A savvy and inspiring leader, Michael induced a Bulgarian-Vlach attack on the Crusaders in Thrace, took Dyrrachium from the Venetians, and recaptured some of Thessaly from its Crusader lord. By 1224, Epirus had seized Thessaloniki from the Crusaders, which led its leader, Theodore, to proclaim himself emperor. His actions suggest that the Epriate Roman resistance movement had matured into a Roman state, but it clearly did not begin as the continuation of the one the Crusaders captured.

The most successful Roman resistance developed in Asia Minor under the leadership of the Lascarid family. Theirs was a movement inspired in part by an idea that Constantine Lascaris expressed when trying to rouse the Romans to defend their city. Even if their state fell on that day, Constantine claimed, the Romans should have faith, "because God both kills and restores life."[29] He believed that Romans could rise again as part of a different state than the one that had ended when the Crusaders pushed east into the city. And as the Latins advanced in Constantinople, Constantine Lascaris fled to Nicaea.

It was in Nicaea that the new Roman state that Constantine had prophesized was born. Constantine there joined his brother Theodore and organized an armed Roman resistance to the Latin Empire in Asia. The Lascarid movement initially struggled to hold the Crusaders back, suffering a major loss when Constantine Lascaris died following a defeat outside the city of Adramyttion in 1205.[30] The Epirote and Bulgarian attacks in Europe, however, forced the Crusaders to pull back from Asia and permitted Theodore Lascaris to consolidate power around Nicaea. By the early 1230s, the Nicene Empire had expanded to include territory in Europe. A little more than a decade later, Nicene armies and diplomacy had made Epirus a Nicene vassal and Thessaloniki a Nicene possession. They had also removed the Bulgarians from Thrace. Then, in 1261, the Nicene Romans took back Constantinople from the Crusaders. They would hold the city until 1453.

These victories over the Crusaders were Roman triumphs, led by Roman generals, who fought on behalf of two different Roman states. But, as Constantine Lascaris knew, the Roman people were now surviving without the 2,000-year-old state into which they had been born. Other Romans knew that too. The leaders of Trebizond had already separated from the main Roman state before it fell; Michael Doukas in Epirus hesitated to claim the Roman imperial title until his regime had a signature victory that merited it; and, when the Lascarids eventually claimed the title of emperor in 1205, they did so without using the conventions for selection that had been used in the past. Theodore Lascaris was instead "proclaimed emperor of the Romans by all the eastern cities," a subgroup of independent Romans that reflected the shattering of a unitary Roman polity.[31]

The Comneni of Trebizond, the Doukas family in Epirus, and the Lascarids in Nicaea were Roman leaders of new Roman states, the descendants of the state that died in 1204. But when the Crusaders killed the old state, they severed the direct institutional line joining Romulus, Julius Caesar, Justinian, and Alexius V Doukas.

THE LOSS OF the institutional connection that joined the Roman present to eighty generations of Romans in the past mattered to the kings, senators, and emperors who have been the most prominent figures in this book. But the end of the Roman state also shattered the lives of more modest people who depended upon the rules, patterns, and paths to prosperity that Rome had offered before the Crusaders destroyed them.

The historian Nicetas Choniates, for example, writes movingly about the life he had built prior to April 13, 1204, and the terrible things that happened to him afterward. Born around 1155, Nicetas and his older brother Michael grew up in the Anatolian frontier town of Chonai (modern Khonaz).[32] Both showed potential in their early schoolwork and were sent to secondary schooling in Constantinople in the hope that their talents and the connections they made in the capital might place them among the imperial elite. Both men succeeded. Michael ultimately became the bishop of Athens, while Nicetas joined the imperial administrative service. Nicetas's talents in rhetoric led to a position as a tax official in Pontus and two terms as imperial undersecretary in Constantinople. His career further accelerated when Isaac II Angelus chose him to give the oration marking the emperor's marriage to the daughter of the king of Hungary. This honor led to further promotions, until, in 1195, he was named "the most grand logothete who governs all things."[33] He apparently held this position until he was removed from it by Alexius V Doukas in 1204.[34]

The Roman system enabled every step of Nicetas Choniates's three-decade rise from a child living in a remote provincial town to the figure at the very center of the Roman administrative state. It was what made him "a living tablet of the law code" when he served as a judge.[35] It was what marked him as the capital's most eligible bachelor, and led to his marriage to the sister of his best friend, the aristocrat John Belissariotes.[36] And it was what allowed him to purchase a beautiful three-story mansion adorned with gold mosaics in Constantinople's magnificent Sphorakion district just northeast of the Forum of Constantine and Hagia Sophia.[37]

The collapse of the Roman state immediately rendered all his wealth and honors worthless, along with the accoutrements of power that Choniates and many other Romans like him had accumulated over the decades. He wrote movingly of becoming homeless as the second of the Crusaders' two massive fires swept through the city. He found refuge with a Venetian wine merchant named Dominicus, but even this personal relationship proved unable to bear the strain of the Crusader attack. Dominicus housed Choniates and his pregnant wife for a time, but eventually he sent them away, fearing that he could no longer keep the Crusaders from arresting Choniates and raping his wife. Once they were back out on the streets to fend for themselves, Choniates's family servants fled, leaving Choniates and his wife "to carry on our shoulders the children who could not yet walk and to hold in our arms a male infant at breast."[38]

Choniates and his family left the city on April 17 along with other refugees as the last snows of winter descended on Constantinople. When they walked through the city gates, the party passed Crusader soldiers "loaded down with spoils" who were strip-searching the refugees to see if they had hidden anything of value under their clothes. Other Crusaders leered lecherously at young girls. Choniates "instruct[ed] the young girls to rub their faces with mud to conceal the blush of their cheeks," so that they might avoid being raped. Despite these precautions, a soldier snatched the daughter of a Roman judge who had joined Choniates's group. Her elderly father, tripping as he tried to save his daughter, "fell into a mudhole, laying on his side wailing and wallowing in the mire." The humiliation of these noble refugees grew worse as they reached the countryside, where people taunted them, saying their poverty and nakedness proved the "equality of Roman citizen rights," because now all Romans, even the elite, were equally poor.[39] "Such was the fate," Choniates wrote, "that befell us and those of our rank" after the Roman state collapsed.[40]

Choniates led his family to Nicaea, hoping to rebuild his fortune by offering his skills to the Nicene resistance led by Theodore Lascaris. But with the Roman system collapsed, there was no need for someone trained to manage it. Choniates and his family ended up living in squalid homes with other Constantinopolitan refugees in Nicaea. "We chose to reside," he wrote, "as though we were captives . . . huddled about the churches[,] where we were looked down upon as aliens [rather than Roman citizens]."[41]

THIS IS WHAT it feels like to live through the death of your state. Every credential you earned loses its meaning. Every honor or mark of social status you received is rendered worthless. Every loving personal relationship you ever formed risks being transformed into a transaction. And, worst of all, the very protections of life and property that every state guarantees its citizens no longer exist. It happens so suddenly that Choniates—who had followed the rules of the Roman system for his entire life, working hard to become an eloquent, rich, and powerful man—lost everything in less than a week. On April 12, 1204, Choniates was a fixture of the Roman establishment. On April 17, he was a penniless refugee carrying his children as he walked in the mud through a Constantinopolitan city gate to an unknown future. Choniates himself had not changed. But the context in which he lived had changed so much that his skills, talents, and connections no longer mattered. It is in these first moments of its absence that we see clearly the true power the Roman state had for most of its citizens.

Conclusion

The Resilience, Not the Fall, of Rome

Most Roman histories end the same way. Something falls. Books about the Roman Republic end with its transformation into the Roman Empire. Roman imperial history ends with the fall of the Western Roman Empire, either to Odoacer in 476 or to Justinian in the sixth century. The Eastern Roman Empire's story often ends with the Ottoman capture of Constantinople in 1453, the moment when that city finally falls out of Roman control forever. Every story needs an ending, and the fall of Rome offers the natural, dramatic conclusion to a narrative that can neatly highlight the lessons contemporary readers should learn from the Roman past.

This has always been true. In the first century BC, Sallust places his readers in a late Republic overwhelmed by a pandemic of political corruption that infected everyone who touched Roman public life. In the third century AD, Cassius Dio ends his history by tracing Rome's slow degeneration into cacophonous anarchy as strange-looking emperors, non-Italian military units, and ill-disciplined soldiers ruin the state by letting their appetites overwhelm their rationality. In sixth-century Constantinople, the pagan Zosimus rails against the abandonment of the old gods that caused the sack of Rome while the Christian Marcellinus Comes imagines the fall of the west at the hands of the barbarian Odoacer. Even Choniates uses the story of Constantinople's capture in 1204 to emphasize the dire consequences of the sinfulness of his fellow citizens.

This book, too, ends with a fall of Rome that offers some lessons to us. While I do not agree with Choniates that sinfulness caused the Crusader evisceration of the Roman state in 1204, I do believe that the seizure of Constantinople resulted from a long series of choices made decades or even centuries before Choniates's time that changed the way Roman leaders and systems behaved. Basil II's decision to marry his sister to the Russian ruler Vladimir in exchange for military help probably saved his throne, but it broke a taboo against marrying imperial family members to people from what Constantine VII Porphyrogenitus called "these infidel and dishonorable tribes of the north."[1] This event in the 980s began a pattern of intermarriage that linked Roman families with northerners such as Philip of Swabia and established the precedent that non-Romans could send troops to support the imperial claims of their in-laws just as Vladimir had once done for Basil II.

Alexius I Comnenus made even more consequential changes to the rules governing Roman life in the dangerous period after he took power in 1081. He allowed commanders and officials whom he could not pay to compensate themselves directly from imperial revenues. He prevented family members from rebelling by placing them in administrative positions based on their bloodlines rather than their competence. He also ceded Roman sovereignty to outsiders by granting Venetians real estate in the capital and permitting armed Crusaders to transit Roman territory. All of Alexius's decisions made sense at the time. They prevented the collapse of the Roman army, consolidated his authority after a time of anarchic civil war, and even helped the empire retain or regain territory. The state might not have survived into the 1100s if Alexius had not made such radical shifts in Roman policy. But the Crusader capture of the city in the 1200s would have been impossible to imagine if Alexius had not made these concessions a century earlier.

Decisions made by Basil II in the 980s and Alexius I Comnenus in the 1080s and 1090s proved so consequential in 1204 because they undermined customs and institutions that would have otherwise prevented their successors in the later 1100s from making terrible choices that damaged the empire. Alexius I Comnenus did not compel Manuel I Comnenus to keep appointing Andronicus Comnenus to governorships, showering him with funds, and granting him the estate from which he launched the coup that shook the Roman state. But Alexius created the conditions that made Manuel think that these actions were somehow normal.

It is particularly hard to fault emperors of the tenth and eleventh centuries for young Alexius IV Angelus boasting about his right to the Roman throne at a Christmas party in 1201. But their willingness to pay western armies to fight in Roman civil wars encouraged Boniface of Montferrat and his Venetian allies to take Alexius IV Angelus seriously when he offered them rich rewards for their help. Alexius IV's predecessors had made his outlandish promises seem credible. In one sense, the Roman state fell because the systems, institutions, and customs that walled its internal political life off from outsiders had been allowed to decay until they could no longer defend Romans from Crusaders, Venetians, Normans, and others.

BUT THE DEATH of Rome is not the story on which we should focus. All states die. No others lasted for 2,000 years. Understanding why the Roman state died is a much less important exercise than explaining what made it last for so long. If, as Niccolò Machiavelli once wrote, Roman history should be "compared with modern events" so that people can learn to better understand their own worlds, then we should use Roman history to learn how a society that changed so much lasted so long.[2]

From the very beginning of their history, Romans knew that their state's power grew out of the twin virtues of openness and adaptability. They believed that Rome had begun as a transformative place in which exiles, brigands, and captives formed a community by focusing on the positive things they could contribute tomorrow rather than the crimes and misfortunes that defined them yesterday. They continued to find places for newcomers for millennia. This was as true of the Roman Republic that welcomed the Claudii in 504

BC as it was of the Roman Empire that accepted Armenian populations arriving in its territory 1,600 years later.

Romans were equally good at recognizing valuable new ideas and creating ways for the state to adapt and improve them. So it was that Romans observed the phalanx in the sixth century BC, adopted the practice themselves, and eventually modified it to create the more powerful Roman maniple. They then did the same thing, over and over again. In the fifth century BC they built a legal system patterned on Greek models that proved so flexible that it evolved into something that held together a Mediterranean-spanning empire. In the third century BC, Roman shipwrights copied Carthaginian designs, figured out how to produce ships based on them, and gained a naval superiority over the Mediterranean that it did not lose for nearly 1,000 years. One hundred years later Roman bankers built a financial system that drew upon Greek roots but was far more sophisticated and long lasting than anything that had come before.

Roman religious history also shows its people's remarkable ability to repeatedly create, expand, and adapt existing institutions to serve new needs. Roman citizens believed that Rome's success and safety depended upon their collective devotion to the God or gods that looked over their state. This basic principle endured for two millennia even as the identity of these gods, and the manner in which one showed devotion to them, dramatically changed. Some of the changes also grew out of the same principle of incorporating anything new that might help make Rome stronger. So Juno joined Rome after the capture of Veii, Cybele was welcomed during the Second Punic War, and Isis arrived at some point during the later Republic.

When Christianity developed in the empire of Augustus and Tiberius, it spread beyond Judaea both because of the roads and maritime networks the Julio-Claudian dynasty maintained and because of Romans' historical openness to new, potentially better ways to do things. Christianity promised a novel, personal way to interact with God and a more powerful divine protector for the state. Constantine's conversion and his decision to use imperial resources to protect and promote the church joined the administrative capacity of the Roman state with the enthusiasm of its rapidly growing Christian populations. This started a multi-century process through which the church grew into an institution that unified Romans religiously as well as the state unified them politically.

No Roman in the eighth century BC would have understood much of anything about Roman life in the thirteenth century AD (or, in many cases, even a single word that was said by a Roman at that time). And yet Romans in the thirteenth century would agree with their distant political ancestors that they shared a common history as citizens of the same Roman state. This is because the openness to newcomers and new ideas that served as the accelerator for Roman expansion and prosperity existed alongside a deep respect for tradition that governed how fast Roman life changed. It was neither rare nor accidental to see panegyrics like that in which Merobaudes of Gaul in the fifth century AD bridged 600 years of Roman history to compare the general Aetius to "our Cato," when he praised his ability to preserve "our customs and integrity" in a changing world.[3] Romans understood the great power that came from preserving the attributes that made them so distinctive across the millennia.

This fundamental continuity highlights one of the most important reasons why Rome endured for so long. States must have mechanisms that bring new figures into their citizen body, new ideas into their polity, and new people into their leadership, but they must also continue to empower voices that advocate for ties to the past. Both Gaius Gracchus and Cato the Elder must have a place in a healthy polity. No society can thrive if it is in a perpetual state of revolution, nor can it survive if it does not embrace new people and ideas. There must be a balanced interplay between the old and the new, the progressive and the conservative, for citizens to remain engaged and trusting of their state.

ROME ALSO OFFERS a second, related lesson. Because healthy societies evolve deliberately in a fashion consistent with the consensus opinions of their citizens, no one should ever want to live in a place where the systems and institutions governing their lives fail. When that happens, the survival of their state becomes a matter of chance. Rome lasted for 2,000 years because its culture managed change very well, but it was also helped by good luck in those few moments when existential disasters threatened. When Rome faced possible extinction during the Second Punic War, Romans were fortunate to have Fabius Cunctactor and Scipio Africanus, two very different military visionaries, from two different generations, managing two very different phases in the war. Both men were essential to Rome's victory— but Rome could never have counted on either figure appearing at precisely the moment when his particular talent was most needed. Rome was lucky again when Augustus emerged in the first century BC, Diocletian in the third century AD, and Alexius I Comnenus in the eleventh century. All these people possessed exactly what Rome needed to survive the crises they inherited and rebuild the institutions it needed in order to thrive afterward. But none of them were inevitable. Any one of these crises could have ended Rome's story had someone less skilled led the state in their place.

Rome's secret was not that it knew how to produce great, visionary leaders. Their appearance is always a historical accident. It was instead that Roman society created systems that minimized the moments when Romans were forced to hope that such a person might materialize to save them. The greatest Roman leaders were not the people who destroyed the institutions that made Rome strong. They were the men and women who changed those institutions and made them work better. States cannot determine whether they will be lucky, but strong states with strong institutions and cultures of consensus building can minimize the need for exceptional leaders. And the reason that the need for such leaders is infrequent in these states is that the systems regulating citizens' lives are both strong enough to endure and flexible enough to adapt and evolve to new conditions.

No society should seek out, eagerly await, or even welcome the figures whom Thomas Carlyle once called "the Great Men" of history.[4] These transformative characters should be—and will be— exceedingly rare in states with strong institutions and cooperative political traditions. States that evolve steadily and organically are repelled by the sudden, unpredictable jolts such characters provide. As they should be. Charismatic disruptors are incredibly dangerous figures who break out from a rules-based order and try to bend the world around them to their wills.

Rome was not a society of Carlylean Great Men. It was a society whose greatest strength came from its robust political, social, religious, and economic institutions. These institutions in fact limited the number of people able to seize unconstrained control and enhanced Roman citizens' willingness to push back forcefully when such people emerged.

Rome's most important lesson to us is that no one, in any society, should ever want their own Sulla or Augustus or Justinian to blow up the systems of the past. A society that rolls the dice with the unchecked power of a single person may get a sophisticated, stable, and new order. But it probably won't. Marcus Aurelius is much less likely to appear than an arrogant king like Tarquinius Superbus; a paranoid, broken emperor like Commodus; or a vicious nihilist like Andronicus Comnenus. No society that hopes to last even a fraction of Rome's 2,000 years should ever willingly trade robust, inclusive, and slowly evolving systems for the dramatic disruptions promised by a single individual.

ACKNOWLEDGMENTS

This project was born out of the weird combination of isolation and ambition that the COVID-19 lockdowns produced. I had just finished writing *The Eternal Decline and Fall of Rome*, a book that covered the 2,200-year history of an idea about Rome, during the first months of the lockdowns, when historians had little choice but to retreat to the past because the present was so dismal. In that strange moment, I thought that it couldn't be much more difficult to write a full Roman history from the state's beginning to its end.

But it was.

When students ask me what it's like to write a book, I tell them that it feels a bit like creating a horcrux in Harry Potter's universe. Every book contains a small piece of you that you willingly gave up because the project meant so much to you. This book took out a pretty big piece. I started it when my son, Nate, was a freshman in high school and my daughter, Zoe, was still in middle school. Now, as I finish it, Nate is about to start his junior year of college and Zoe is figuring out which one she will attend. Our niece, Ava Rose Grosely, graduated from high school and is now halfway through college. These members of our family, and above all my wife, Manasi, have given nearly as much to this book as I have. Manasi in particular has suffered through me being miserable, moody, or preoccupied by random Romans from whatever century I'm writing about that month. There were also precious parts of their lives that I missed because of the travel this project required. It's with great sadness that I think about the baseball games I did not attend, the speech and debate tournaments I did not judge, the college move-in days I didn't help with, the Home Start events I could not volunteer at, and the TV broadcasts I had to watch from 8,000 miles away. Manasi, Nate, Zoe, and Ava, you are the most wonderful family anyone could have. I am so glad that, when the final words were written in this book, you were all in Rome with me as I wrote them. Nothing has ever meant more to me.

There are many other people who deserve thanks for all they have done to make this project happen. The list starts with Brian Distelberg, who took on this project for Basic Books, gave me an almost impossibly large word limit and long deadline, and then stuck with me for the past four years when I blew past the generous limits he set. My dear friend Eric Schmidt, with whom I have worked for twenty years, first at the University of California Press and now at Basic, received this manuscript when it was 337,000 words and 1,100 pages long. He spent most of the last part of 2024 helping me make it so much more concise. I can't say enough how grateful I am for his patience, his frankness, and his willingness to read so closely. Katherine Streckfus picked up where Eric left off and did an excellent job of smoothing out all of the roughness left after so many cuts. Kate Blackmer, perhaps the world's most diligent and attentive mapmaker, produced the maps that begin each section of the book. My agent, Andrew Stuart, has been a wonderful resource for me as I thought through what I wanted this book to do and how I might ensure it does it. And Tim Debold of Atramenti Editing did a thorough, final fact check.

I also benefited from conversations with many colleagues and friends over the past four years. This includes my University of California colleagues Nate Aschenbrenner, Mira Balberg, Denise Demetriou, Karl Gerth, Mark Hanna, Dana Velasco Murillo, Micah Muscolino, and Patrick Patterson (all in San Diego) and Emily Albu, Diliana Angelova, Beth Digeser, Susanna Elm, Erich Guren, Carlos Noreña, and Michele Salzman (across the rest of the UC system). The same is true of so many other friends around the United States and the world. The ideas about the role of Roman women in this book are deeply informed by the Elite Women reading group of Julia Hilner, Meaghan McEvoy, Natalie Novella, Michele Salzman, Joost Snaterse, and Cristiana Sogno that I have been so lucky to participate in for the past few years. Lisa Bailey, Han Baltussen, Dan Osland, Shunsuke Kosaka, Mark Masterson, and the rest of the Trans-Pacific Partnership in Late Antiquity offered generous feedback on early ideas— even when they were not exactly late antique. The same is true of Giovanni Cecconi, Barbara Del Giovane, Adalberto Magnelli, Carlo Slavich, and all the colleagues in Florence with whom I have worked so closely for the past eight years.

I appreciate the many other people who have shared publications, hosted lectures, read chapters, or just spent an afternoon talking with me about Rome. This includes longtime friends and mentors Cam Grey, Susan Harvey, Anthony Kaldellis, Michael Kulikowski, Scott McGill, and Joe Pucci as well as brilliant students such as Matt Crum, Maria Lubello, Jamie Marvin, and Amanda Tarkington. Few people alive know more about late antiquity than the incredible trio of Lieve Van Hoof, Peter Van Nuffelen, and Marco Formisano in Ghent, and I had the great fortune to visit with them when I was working through some of the very chapters in which they are experts. The same is true of Jan Willem Drijvers, who not only convinced me to visit Salvation Mountain but also taught me a lot about Helena and Jovian on the way. Philippe Blaudeau in Angers was an extremely generous host and conversation partner who got me to think of Chalcedon in new ways while we toured the Loire Valley. Audiences at Rice University, the American Academy in Rome, and the State University of New York at Binghamton, as well as in Coimbra, São Paulo, Jerusalem, Venice, Crete, Oxford, Macquarie, Würzburg, Fordham, and Bakersfield, have also given me valuable feedback and ideas. The same is true of a great many public audiences around the United States and Europe.

My favorite public audience has always been the San Diego Greek community, where Alexia Anas and the Hellenic Cultural Society have done so much to support my work over the past twelve years.

I owe particular thanks to Carol Vassiliadis and her family. Carol has been a wonderful friend to me and my family since we arrived in San Diego. She has always encouraged me to be as ambitious as I can in my scholarship and has supported that work better than I could have ever imagined possible. It is for these reasons that the book is dedicated to her.

NOTES

The translations of ancient sources in this book generally follow the most widely available English translations, adapted for clarity. This includes the Loeb Classical Library volumes for most classical texts; the Ante-Nicene, Nicene, and Post-Nicene Fathers series for patristics; the Translated Texts for Historians series for late antiquity; and Dumbarton Oaks series for many medieval Greek texts.

Introduction

1. A. Kaldellis, *Romanland: Ethnicity and Empire in Byzantium* (Cambridge, MA, 2019).

2. Kaldellis, *Romanland*, ix (self-identification and state name), 31 (language), 3–37 (broader context).

3. Dionysius of Halicarnassus 3.47.

4. Livy, *Ab urbe condita* 39.6–7 (title omitted hereafter).

5. H. Flower, *Roman Republics* (Princeton, NJ, 2010).

6. Cicero, *De re publica* (*Rep.* hereafter), 1.39.

Chapter 1. Foundations

1. R. Peroni, "From Bronze Age to Iron Age: Economic, Historical, and Social Considerations," in *Italy Before the Romans*, ed. D. and F. Ridgway (London, 1979), 24–25; T. Cornell, *The Beginnings of Rome* (London, 2012), 32n7.

2. On Mycenaean pottery, see Cornell, *Beginnings*, 40.

3. Cornell, *Beginnings*, 48.

4. Cornell, *Beginnings*, 51, 57.

5. Cicero, *Rep.* 2.3–4.

6. Pliny, *Natural History* (*NH* hereafter), 3.67–70.

7. J. Poucet, "Le Septimontium et la Succusa chez Festus et Varron," *Bulletin de l'Institut Historique Belge de Rome* 32 (1960): 25–73.

8. Cornell, *Beginnings*, 73–75.

9. Dionysius of Halicarnassus 1.9.4.

10. Dionysius of Halicarnassus 1.31; cf. Livy 1.7; *Origo gentis Romanae* (*OGR* hereafter), 5.

11. Dionysius of Halicarnassus 1.34, 1.44 (soldiers settling), 1.39 (pasturing cattle); cf. Virgil, *Aeneid* 8.184–279; Livy 1.7; *OGR* 6–8.

12. Dionysius of Halicarnassus 1.45–65 tells of Aeneas. The most famous discussion is that of Virgil's *Aeneid*. On Aeneas, see Livy 1.1–2; *OGR* 9–16. On the foundation of Alba Longa, see Livy 1.3.

13. Dionysius of Halicarnassus 1.73; *OGR* 19–23.

14. On the rape of Rhea Silvia, see Dionysius of Halicarnassus 1.77; Livy 1.4; *OGR* 19.1–7 (for multiple variations of the story).

15. Dionysius of Halicarnassus 1.79 (she-wolf story), 1.84.4 (Lupa as a prostitute; cf. *OGR* 21.2); Livy 1.4 (both wolf and prostitute); *OGR* 21.2 (explanation of confusion).

16. Dionysius of Halicarnassus 1.79.12–83; Livy 1.5.

17. Dionysius of Halicarnassus 1.85–89; Livy 1.6. *OGR* 23 presents multiple variations on the narrative, including one in which Remus outlives Romulus.

18. Dionysius of Halicarnassus 1.89.2.

19. Dionysius of Halicarnassus 1.89.1.

20. Livy 1.8.

21. Livy 1.9; see also Cicero, *Rep.* 2.7.13.

22. Livy 1.9–13.

23. Livy 1.7, 1.16, 9.29; Dionysius of Halicarnassus 1.79.8–11. On the statue, see Livy 10.23; Cicero, *In Catilinam* 3.19; Cicero, *De Divinatione* 1.20, 2.47.

24. Cicero, *Rep.* 2.1.2.

25. Cicero, *Rep.* 2.7.13–2.8.14 (council chosen), 2.9.15 (Senate and expansion).

26. Cicero, *Rep.* 2.12.23 (interregnum), 2.12.24 (virtues), 2.13.25 (foreigner); cf. Livy 1.17.

27. Cicero, *Rep.* 2.14.26–27.

28. Cicero, *Rep.* 2.21.37; Livy 2.1.2.

Chapter 2. The Roman Revolution of Servius Tullius

1. Cornell, *Beginnings*, 81.

2. Cornell, *Beginnings*, 100.

3. *Ineditum Vaticanum*, ed. H. von Armin, *Hermes* 27 (1892), 118–130 = Jacoby, FrGH 839, fr. 1, following the translation of Cornell, *Beginnings*, 170, adapted for clarity.

4. Aristotle, *Politics* 1310a–1311a; *Athenian Constitution* 16.

5. Aristotle, *Politics* 1311a; *Athenian Constitution* 13.5; Herodotus 3.60, 5.67–68, 5.92; Diogenes Laertius 1.99.

6. On dating questions, see Dionysius of Halicarnassus 4.6–7. For mid-sixth century, Cornell, *Beginnings*, 121–126.

7. Cicero, *Rep.* 2.19.34; Livy 1.34; Dionysius of Halicarnassus 3.46–48.

8. Livy 1.34–35; Cicero, *Rep.* 2.20.35.

9. Cicero, *Rep.* 2.20.35–36; Livy 1.35–36; Dionysius of Halicarnassus 3.67; Granius Licinianus, Bk. 26 B. 1–8.

10. Livy 1.35.

11. Livy 1.39; Dionysius of Halicarnassus 4.2; Cicero, *Rep.* 2.21.37; cf. H. Dessau, *Inscriptiones Latinae Selectae*, 3 vol. (Berlin, 1892–1916) (*ILS* hereafter), 212.1.8–27.

12. Livy 1.39; cf. Dionysius of Halicarnassus 4.2.

13. Cicero, *Rep.* 2.21.37; cf. Livy 1.39.

14. Dionysius of Halicarnassus 4.3.

15. Cornell, *Beginnings*, 132.

16. *ILS* 212.I.16–24.

17. Dionysius of Halicarnassus 2.36.2.

18. Cornell, *Beginnings*, 135–141.

19. *ILS* 212.I.24.

20. Livy 1.41. See also Cicero, *Rep.* 2.21.38; Dionysius of Halicarnassus 4.4–5.

21. Cicero, *Rep.* 2.21.38; Dionysius of Halicarnassus 4.9.6–9, 4.10.1–3; Livy 1.41, 1.46.

22. Dionysius of Halicarnassus 4.14–15; Livy 1.43. See Cornell, *Beginnings*, 173–179.

23. Aulus Gellius 6.13; Livy 1.43; Cicero, *Rep.* 2.22.39–40; Dionysius of Halicarnassus 4.16–20.

24. In the Republic, the legions had 3,000 men each. Cornell (*Beginnings*, 182) proposes that this reflects an early division of the regal 6,000-man legion into units of equal sizes commanded by two consuls.

25. Cicero, *Rep.* 2.22.40.

26. Strabo, *Geographica* 5.3.7.

27. Cornell, *Beginnings*, 202.

28. Dionysius of Halicarnassus 4.27.7, 4.40.7; Ovid, *Fasti* 6.570; Pliny, *NH* 8.194, 197.

Chapter 3. Counterrevolution and the Dawn of the Republic

1. Dionysius of Halicarnassus 4.29–30; Livy 1.46–47. For clarity, I will use the name Tarquin for Lucius Tarquinius.

2. Livy 1.47.

3. On the stabbing, see Dionysius of Halicarnassus 4.39; on being thrown by Tarquin, Livy 1.48.

4. Livy 1.46.

5. A point twice highlighted by Dionysius of Halicarnassus (4.7–7, 4.30.2).

6. Livy 1.49; Dionysius of Halicarnassus 4.41–43; Cicero, *Rep.* 2.25.46.

7. Livy 1.51–55; Dionysius of Halicarnassus, 4.41–51, 4.59; Cicero, *Rep.* 2.24.44.

8. Cicero, *Rep.* 2.24.46.

9. Livy 1.56.

10. Livy 1.58; Dionysius of Halicarnassus 4.64–67.

11. Livy 1.59; cf. Dionysius of Halicarnassus 4.70.

12. A. Feldherr, *Spectacle and Society in Livy's History* (Berkeley, 1998), 194–203.

13. Cicero, *De Officiis* 1.17.53–58 (principle of state superseding family); Cicero, *Rep.* 2.26.47–48 (Tarquin in particular). See also Feldherr, *Spectacle and Society*, Chapter 4.1 (section with notes 18–26).

14. Dionysius of Halicarnassus 4.72–76 (debate), 4.76.2 (consulship defined).

15. Dionysius of Halicarnassus 4.84.2.

16. Dionysius of Halicarnassus 5.8.5.

17. Livy 2.2; Dionysius of Halicarnassus 5.9–12.

18. Livy 2.6.

19. Livy 2.9–13.

20. Livy 2.18–20.

21. Livy 2.21.

22. Livy 2.23; cf. Dionysius of Halicarnassus 5.63.

23. Livy 2.31.

24. Livy 2.33; cf. Dionysius of Halicarnassus 6.72–90.

25. Polybius 3.22; Cornell, *Beginnings*, 210–214.

26. Livy 2.16.

Chapter 4. The Heroes of the Early Republic

1. Festus 519–520 L, quoted in A. V. Koptev, "The Making of Plebeian Secessions in Roman Historiography," *Vestnik of Saint Petersburg University: History* 63 (2018):

842. On the *ver sacrum*, see L. Aigner Foresti, "La tradizione antica sul ver sacrum," in *Coercizione e mobilità nel mondo antico*, ed. M. Sordi (Milan, 1995), 141–147.

2. Herodotus 7.170; Cornell, *Beginnings*, 305.

3. Livy 2.22.

4. Dionysius of Halicarnassus 6.95; Cicero, *Pro Balbo* 53–54.

5. Livy 2.40–41; Dionysius of Halicarnassus 8.69.1. On the Hernician League, see Livy 9.42.

6. Livy 4.11.5–7.

7. On Latin citizenship reciprocity, see Cornell, *Beginnings*, 297.

8. Livy 3.9–21; Dionysius of Halicarnassus 10.14–16.

9. Livy 3.26–29.

10. Dionysius of Halicarnassus 10.25.3.

11. Cornell, *Beginnings*, 268.

12. Cornell, *Beginnings*, 281–283.

13. Dionysius of Halicarnassus 10.32.2.

14. Livy 4.13–14.

15. Dionysius of Halicarnassus 12.1.5–6.

16. Dionysius of Halicarnassus 12.1.9.

17. Dionysius of Halicarnassus 12.1.13–14.

18. Dionysius of Halicarnassus 12.4.2. Dionysius is here relying on the work of L. Cincius Alimentus (specifically FGrH 8104 F4), written around 200 BC, and the second-century history of Calpurnius Piso Frugi that depended on Cincius's work (fr. 4P). See G. Forsythe, *The Historian L. Calpurnius Piso Frugi and the Roman Annalistic Tradition* (Lanham, MD, 1994), 69, 301–310.

19. Cicero, *Catiline* 1.1.3; cf. Cicero, *Pro Milone* 3 and *De senectute* 56.

20. Livy 3.31.8.

21. Cicero, *Rep.* 2.36.61.

22. Livy 3.33.

23. Cornell, *Beginnings*, 273.

24. Livy says that no plebeians took part (3.32), but one of the first group of decemvirs, Titus Genucius, has a plebeian name.

25. Livy 3.33.

26. Cicero, *Rep.* 2.36.61.

27. Livy 3.34–35.

28. Livy 3.36.

29. Cicero, *Rep.* 2.37.63. The law prohibiting intermarriage appeared on Table 11.

30. Livy 3.37.

31. Livy 3.44–57; Dionysius of Halicarnassus 11.28–44. Cicero, *Rep.* 2.37.63 cuts off after the plebs secede.

32. Livy 3.54.

33. For the quote, see Livy 3.55; for discussion, Cornell, *Beginnings*, 276–277.

34. Livy 4.26–30.

Chapter 5. Rome Becomes Rome

1. Cornell, *Beginnings*, 310–312.

2. Livy 4.58.

3. Livy 4.58.

4. Livy 8.8.3–9; Cornell, *Beginnings*, 186–189.

5. Livy 4.59–60; Diodorus Siculus 14.16.5.

6. Livy 5.2–7 (campaigning), 5.4.11 (Troy).

7. Livy 5.27.8.

8. C. Kraus, "Fabula and History in Livy's Narrative of the Capture of Veii," in *Historical Consciousness and the Use of the Past in the Ancient World*, ed. J. Baines, H. van der Blom, Y. S. Chen, and T. Rood (Sheffield, 2019), 345–358.

9. Livy 5.20.

10. C. Kraus, "'No Second Troy': *Topoi* and Refoundation in Livy, Book V," *Transactions of the American Philological Association* 124 (1994): 283.

11. Livy 5.19; Plutarch, *Camillus* 5.3.

12. Livy 5.21–22.

13. Livy 5.21–22; Plutarch, *Camillus* 6.1–4.

14. Livy 5.25; cf. Plutarch, *Camillus* 7.5.

15. Livy 5.24.

16. Livy 5.30.8; Diodorus Siculus 14.102.4.

17. Plutarch, *Camillus* 14.2; Livy 5.32. See also Kraus, "Fabula," 355.

18. Livy 5.32.

19. Polybius 1.6.1; Dionysius of Halicarnassus 14.117.8.

20. Livy 5.35–36; cf. Dionysius of Halicarnassus 13.10.11; Polybius 2.17. Plutarch (*Camillus* 15–16) rather absurdly attributes the Gallic migration in part to their taste for wine.

21. Cornell, *Beginnings*, 316.

22. Livy 5.36; Plutarch, *Camillus* 17.3–5.

23. Livy 5.36; Diodorus Siculus 14.113.4–6.

24. Plutarch, *Camillus* 18–19; Livy 5.37–38.

25. E.g., Diodorus Siculus 14.115.2; Livy 5.38–40.

26. Livy 5.41; Plutarch, *Camillus* 22.

27. Livy 5.47; Diodorus Siculus 14.116.6; Dionysius of Halicarnassus 13.7; Plutarch, *Camilllus* 27; John Lydus, *De magistratibus reipublicae Romanae* 1.50; N. Horsfall, "From History to Legend: M. Manlius and the Geese," *Classical Journal* 76, no. 4 (1981): 298–311.

28. Livy 5.42–55; cf. Diodorus Siculus 14.116.8; Plutarch, *Camillus* 23–29.

29. For discussion, see Horsfall, "History to Legend," 299–304.

30. V. Rosenberger, "The Gallic Disaster," *Classical World* 96, no. 4 (2003): 365–373, at 370.

31. H. Bellen, *Metus Gallicus-Metus Punicus: Zum Furchtmotive in der römischen Republik* (Mainz, 1985), though note W. V. Harris, *War and Imperialism in Republican Rome, 327–70 BC* (Oxford, 1979), 176. For discussion, see Rosenberger, "Gallic Disaster," 366.

32. Cornell, *Beginnings*, 318; Horsfall, "History to Legend," 305–306.

33. On the capture of the Capitoline, see Ennius, *Annales* 227–228; Tacitus, *Annals* (*Ann.* hereafter), 11.23; Horsfall, "History to Legend," 304.

34. Livy 5.55.

35. Justin, *Historia Philippicarum* 20.5.1–6; Diodorus Siculus 14.117.7; cf. Strabo, *Geographica* 5.2.3.

36. On the extension of citizenship, see Livy 6.4.4. On new tribes, Livy 6.5.8. For discussion, Cornell, *Beginnings*, 319–320.

37. Livy 5.50.3 (Caere); Justin 43.5.4–10 (Massalia).

38. Livy 6.26.8.

39. Cornell, *Beginnings*, 351.

40. Cornell, *Beginnings*, 348–352.

41. Cornell, *Beginnings*, 336, provides a chart showing the years when Rome had consuls and the years when it had consular tribunes.

42. Livy 6.37.5.

43. Livy 6.34–42; Plutarch, *Camillus* 39–42; Cassius Dio 7.28; Zonaras 7.24. For ease of consultation, all references to Dio follow the book and chapter divisions in Cary's Loeb edition. Although Zonaras often epitomizes Dio, his text will be cited separately when it is the primary source on which I depend. In places where Zonaras overlaps with Dio, I have preserved the reference to Zonaras, with cross-references to the fragments of Dio where essential.

44. Livy 6.35.1–5.

45. Livy 6.35.10, 6.38.3.

46. On 500 *iugera*, see Varro, *Rerum rusticarum* 1.2.9; Livy 6.35.4.

47. Livy 6.40.11–6.42.2; G. Pellam, "A Peculiar Episode from the 'Struggle of the Orders'? Livy and the Licinio-Sextian Rogations," *Classical Quarterly* 64 (2014): 288–290.

48. Livy 7.42, 8.12.

Chapter 6. Roman Domination of Italy

1. Livy 9.1–10; N. Horsfall, "The Caudine Forks: Topography and Illusion," *Papers of the British School at Rome* 50 (1982): 45–52.

2. On the increase to four legions, see Cornell, *Beginnings*, 354; on formations, Polybius 6.19–25.

3. Livy 9.45.

4. On Abruzzi, see Livy 9.45.18, 10.3; Diodorus Siculus 20.101.5. On Narnia, Livy 10.9.8. On the new tribes, Livy 10.9.10.

5. Cornell, *Beginnings*, 360.

6. Livy 10.28–12.28.

7. Livy 10.29.19.

8. Livy 10.30.9.

9. Polybius 6.53–54; H. Flower, *Ancestor Masks and Aristocratic Power in Roman Culture* (Oxford, 1996), 36–38.

10. On mentality, see Polybius 6.53–54; on Barbatus, *Corpus Inscriptionum Latinarum* (hereafter *CIL*), 1.2.7; Flower, *Ancestor Masks*, 176–177.

11. On "father of Latin prose," see Cornell, *Beginnings*, 373. On his writings, Cicero, *Brutus* 61 (oration on Pyrrhus); Pomponius, *Digest* 1.2.2.7 and 36 (juridical writing); Pseudo-Sallust, *Epistulae ad Caesarem* 1.1.2 (bon mot). On his career, B. MacBain, "Appius Claudius Caecus and the Via Appia," *Classical Quarterly* 30 (1980): 356–372.

12. Festus, *De verborum significatu* 290 L lines 12–16, trans. Cornell, in *Beginnings*, 248; T. Cornell, "The Lex Ovinia and the Emancipation of the Senate," in *The Roman Middle Republic: Politics, Religion, and Historiography, c. 400–133 BC*, ed. C. Bruun (Rome, 2000), 69–89.

13. Festus, *De verborum significatu* 290 L.

14. Livy 9.46.11; Diodorus Siculus 20.36.5.

15. Diodorus Siculus 20.36.1; Livy 9.29.6; Frontinus, *De aquis urbis Romae* 1.4–5.

16. Diodorus Siculus 20.36.2.

17. MacBain, "Appius," 363–372.

18. Diodorus Siculus 20.36.4.

Notes to Chapter 7

19. Diodorus Siculus 20.36.6; cf. Livy 9.46.12–14, L. Calpurnius Piso Frugi, *Historiae*, Book 3, Fr. 29, in T. Cornell, ed., *The Fragments of the Roman Historians*, 3 vols. (Oxford, 2013), vol. 2 = fr. 27P; Cornell, *Beginnings*, 375.

20. Livy 9.33.4–9.34.3.

21. Plutarch, *Pyrrhus* 14.2–7.

22. Plutarch, *Pyrrhus* 16.6–17.5; Dionysius 19.12; Livy 13.

23. Plutarch, *Pyrrhus* 17.4–5.

24. Plutarch, *Pyrrhus* 18.1–5.

25. Plutarch, *Pyrrhus* 18.6.

26. *CIL* 6.40943, 11.1827; Cicero, *De Senectute* 6; Cicero, *Brutus* 61.

27. Plutarch, *Pyrrhus* 19.4.

28. T. Parkin, *Old Age in the Roman World: A Social and Cultural History* (Baltimore, 2003), 104.

29. M. Fronda, *Between Rome and Carthage: Southern Italy During the Second Punic War* (Cambridge, 2010), 13–34.

30. Plutarch, *Pyrrhus* 21.14–15.

Chapter 7. Rome and Carthage

1. Diodorus Siculus 22.7.5, 22.10.6; Livy 13.10; Polybius 3.25.

2. Polybius 1.8.

3. Polybius 1.10.1–2.

4. Polybius 1.11.1–2; B. D. Hoyos, *Unplanned Wars: The Origins of the First and Second Punic Wars* (Berlin, 1998), 51–66.

5. Diodorus Siculus, 23.1.2; Polybius 1.11; cf. Suetonius, *Tiberius* 2, Seneca, *De brevitate vitae* 13.4; Velleius Paterculus 1.12; Valerius Maximus 2.4.7.

6. Diodorus Siculus 23.1.2; Polybius 1.11.

7. Polybius 1.11–12; Diodorus Siculus 23.3.1–4.

8. For the quotes, see Polybius 1.16; on indemnity, Diodorus Siculus 23.4.1.

9. Polybius 1.17.

10. Polybius 1.20.

11. Polybius 1.21.

12. Polybius 1.22.

13. Polybius 1.23.

14. Polybius 1.26.

15. Diodorus Siculus 23.12.

16. Diodorus Siculus 23.15.5.

17. Polybius 1.32–33; A. Goldsworthy, *The Fall of Carthage: The Punic Wars, 265–146 BC* (London, 2006), 89–90.

18. Polybius 1.57.

19. Diodorus Siculus 23.14.4; Polybius 1.39, 1.49–52.

20. Polybius 1.59.

21. Polybius 1.62–63.

22. On Libya, see Polybius 1.65–88. On Utica, see Diodorus Siculus 25.3.2; Polybius 1.70.9, 1.83.11.

23. Polybius 3.10; cf. Polybius 1.88.8–12.

24. Solinus 5.1. On other experiments, see Livy, *Periochae* (hereafter *Per.*), 19. For more context, see T. C. Brennan, *The Praetorship in the Roman Republic* (Oxford, 2000), 1:91–95.

25. J. Serrati, "Garrisons and Grain: Sicily Between the Punic Wars," in *Sicily from Aeneas to Augustus*, ed. C. Smith and J. Serrati (Edinburgh, 2000), 122–126.

26. Polybius 2.19–20; R. Feig Vishnia, "A Case of 'Bad Press'? Gaius Flaminius in Ancient Historiography," *Zeitschrift für Papyrologie und Epigraphik* 181 (2012): 27.

27. Feig Vishnia, "A Case of 'Bad Press'?," 29–33.

28. Livy 21.63.2–8; Polybius 2.24–25, 2.28–31.

29. Cicero, *de Senectute* 11. On Fabius as augur, see Livy 30.26.7; Pliny, *NH* 7.165; Valerius Maximus 8.13.3; Feig Vishnia, "A Case of 'Bad Press'?," 41.

30. Zonaras 8.20; Polybius 2.32; Plutarch, *Marcellus*, 4.1–3; Livy 21.63.2.

Chapter 8. Fabius, Scipio, and Hannibal

1. Polybius 3.10.

2. Polybius 2.1.5, 3.11.

3. Polybius 2.1.7–8.

4. Cassius Dio 12.48.

5. On the Ebro treaty, see Polybius 2.13.1–7; Appian, *Spain* 2.7.

6. On the Saguntum agreement, see Polybius 3.30.1–2; Appian, *Spain* 2.7; N. Rosenstein, *Rome and the Mediterranean* (Edinburgh, 2012), 120.

7. Livy 21.3–5; Zonaras 8.21; Polybius 3.13.

8. Appian, *Spain* 10; Livy 21.6; Polybius 3.15.

9. Livy 21.6; cf. Polybius 3.15; Appian, *Spain* 11–13.

10. Livy 21.16.

11. Appian, *Spain* 13; cf. Livy 21.18; Cassius Dio 13.10; Zonaras 8.22 (following Cassius Dio).

12. Livy 21.19; cf. Cassius Dio 13.56.

13. Livy 21.20.

14. Livy 21.20; Appian, *Spain* 14.

15. Livy 21.17.

16. Rosenstein, *Rome and the Mediterranean*, 129; Livy 21.23.

17. Cassius Dio 13.54; Livy 21.25.

18. Livy 21.25–26.

19. Livy 21.29.

20. Livy 21.31–32.

21. Livy 21.39.

22. Polybius 3.33.18, 3.56.4, with numbers based on an inscription that Hannibal himself erected in Italy.

23. Polybius 3.70.

24. Polybius 3.65.1–3.66.2; Livy 21.39–46.

25. Polybius 3.67.

26. For "pretexts," see Polybius 3.68; Appian, *Hannibalic War* (*Hann.* hereafter), 6.

27. Polybius 3.69.

28. Appian, *Hann.* 6.

29. Livy 21.54.

30. On the number of survivors, see Rosenstein, *Rome and the Mediterranean*, 133.

31. Livy 21.62–63; Plutarch, *Fabius Maximus* 2.2–3; Cassius Dio 14.7.

32. Livy 21.63.

33. Plutarch, *Fabius* 2.4.

34. Rosenstein, *Rome and the Mediterranean*, 135.

35. Polybius 3.80.
36. Zonaras 8.25.
37. On the battle, see Polybius 3.82–86; Zonaras 8.25; Appian, *Hann.* 10; Livy 22.4–7. On casualties, Rosenstein, *Rome and the Mediterranean*, 136.
38. Cassius Dio 14.8; Zonaras 8.25; Polybius 3.87; Livy 22.7; Appian, *Hann.* 12; Plutarch, *Fabius* 4.1.
39. Cassius Dio 14.9.
40. Plutarch, *Fabius* 7.3–5.
41. Plutarch, *Fabius* 8.3.
42. Plutarch, *Fabius* 14.2.
43. Plutarch, *Fabius* 14.2; Livy 22.36.
44. Plutarch, *Fabius* 14.5.
45. Plutarch, *Fabius* 16.1; Livy 22.49–54; Polybius 3.116–117; Cassius Dio 15.22–27; Zonaras 9.1–2; Appian, *Hann.* 18–25.
46. Livy 22.49.
47. Estimates of casualties varied: 70,000 dead (Polybius 3.117); 60,000 (Quintilian, *Institutio Oratoria* 8.6.26); 50,000 (Plutarch, *Fabius* 16.8; Appian, *Hann.* 4.25); 48,200 (Livy 22.49). For modern estimates, see P. A. Brunt, *Italian Manpower, 225 BC–AD 14* (Oxford, 1971), 419n4; Rosenstein, *Rome and the Mediterranean*, 143–144.
48. Appian, *Hann.* 4.26.
49. Appian, *Hann.* 4.27.
50. Plutarch, *Fabius* 17.4–18.3.
51. Livy 22.57.
52. Livy 22.53–54.
53. Livy 22.51.1.
54. Livy 23.6.1–2; Fronda, *Between Rome and Carthage*, 103–125.
55. Polybius 7.9.1–17; Livy 23.33.1–12.
56. On regional and local dynamics, see Fronda, *Between Rome and Carthage*.
57. N. Rosenstein, *Rome at War* (Chapel Hill, NC, 2004), 90.
58. Livy 24.34.
59. On the capture of Syracuse, see Livy 25.23–31; Appian, *Sicily and the Other Islands (Fragments)*, 4. On currency reform, M. Crawford, *Roman Republican Coinage* (Cambridge, 1983), 3–46.
60. Livy 26.35–36, 28.45–46.
61. Rosenstein, *Rome and the Mediterranean*, 163–165.
62. Livy 28.12.
63. Livy 28.38.
64. Livy 28.38.
65. Livy 28.38, 28.41.
66. Livy 28.45.
67. Livy 28.46.
68. Livy 30.32–35; Polybius 15.9–14.
69. Livy 30.40.
70. Livy 30.43.
71. Livy 30.44.
72. Livy 30.45.
73. Livy 31.49.4–5.
74. Livy 37.3.7.

75. Livy 31.46.
76. Livy 31.47.
77. Valerius Maximus 5.3.2b; cf. Livy 38.53.8.

Chapter 9. Economic Inequality, Political Opportunism, and Gaius Gracchus

1. Appian, *Macedonian Wars* 4; Livy 31.2–6. On the Battle of Cynoscephalae, see Appian, *Macedonian Wars* 8; Polybius 18.1.1–18.12.5; Zonaras 9.16.
2. Polybius 18.46.
3. Polybius 18.47; Livy 33.30; Zonaras 9.16.
4. Varro, *Rerum rusticarum* 1.2.9; Livy 6.35.4.
5. The numbers for 234/233 appear in Livy, *Per.* 20. Those for 209/208 are found in Livy 27.36.7. See S. Hin, *The Demography of Roman Italy* (Cambridge, 2013).
6. P. Kay, *Rome's Economic Revolution* (Oxford, 2014), 43–58.
7. On credit, see W. Harris, "A Revisionist View of Roman Money," *Journal of Roman Studies* 96 (2006): 1–24; Kay, *Rome's Economic Revolution*.
8. Livy 39.6–7; Calpurnius Piso, *Historiae fr.* 34.
9. This discussion is based on the larger arguments of Rosenstein, *Rome at War*.
10. Cicero, *Rep.* 1.39.
11. Cicero, *Laws* 3.35–36; Cicero, *Brutus* 97; Livy, *Oxyrhynchus Epitome* 54.193; A. Yakobson, "Secret Ballot and Its Effects in the Late Roman Republic," *Hermes* 123 (1995): 426–442.
12. Appian, *Spain* 13.83; Plutarch, *Tiberius Gracchus* (*Ti. Gracchus* hereafter), 7.
13. Plutarch, *Ti. Gracchus* 8.
14. Plutarch, *Ti. Gracchus* 8; Appian, *Bella Civilia* (*Civil Wars*, hereafter *BC*), 1.1.7. See also Rosenstein, *Rome at War*, 141–169.
15. K. Bringmann, *A History of the Roman Republic* (Cambridge, 2007), 151.
16. Plutarch, *Ti. Gracchus* 8.
17. Plutarch, *Ti. Gracchus* 10.
18. Plutarch, *Ti. Gracchus* 10.4–6.
19. Plutarch, *Ti. Gracchus* 11–12; cf. Appian, *BC* 1.12.5; D. Stockton, *The Gracchi* (Oxford, 1979), 65–67.
20. Plutarch, *Ti. Gracchus* 14–15.
21. Plutarch, *Ti. Gracchus* 16; Appian, *BC* 1.2.15.
22. On the last murder of a Roman officeholder in 414 BC, see Livy 4.49–50.
23. Cicero, *Rep.* 1.36.
24. Appian, *BC* 1.2.17.
25. Velleius Paterculus 2.7.3.
26. Plutarch, *Ti. Gracchus* 20.3.
27. Plutarch, *Ti. Gracchus* 20.2–4; Sallust, *Jugurtha* 31.7.
28. Sallust, *Jugurtha* 31.7.
29. Plutarch, *Ti. Gracchus* 21.1; Appian, *BC* 1.27.121–124.
30. On Italian economic integration, see S. Roselaar, *Italy's Economic Revolution* (Oxford, 2019).
31. Cicero, *De officiis* 3.47. On dating to 126, see Cicero, *Brutus* 109. For further discussion, Roselaar, *Italy's Economic Revolution*, 217.
32. Cicero, *De officiis* 3.47; Valerius Maximus 9.5.1.
33. Appian, *BC* 1.34; H. Mouritsen, *Italian Unification* (London, 1998), 109–113.
34. Valerius Maximus 9.5.1; Appian, *BC* 1.34.

35. On the Fregellae revolt, see Mouritsen, *Italian Unification*, 119; C. Steel, *The End of the Roman Republic* (Edinburgh, 2013), 20n48.

36. Cicero, *Brutus* 109.

37. Cicero, *Brutus* 125–126; Plutarch, *Gaius Gracchus* (*G. Gracchus* hereafter), 3.2.

38. Plutarch, *G. Gracchus* 2.4, 3.1.

39. Plutarch, *G. Gracchus* 3.1.

40. Plutarch, *G. Gracchus* 3.3–4.

41. Plutarch, *G. Gracchus* 6.3.

42. On the grain dole, see Appian, *BC* 1.3.21; Cicero, *Sestius* 103; Livy, *Per.* 60.

43. Roselaar, *Italy's Economic Revolution*, 217–219.

44. Plutarch, *G. Gracchus* 8.

45. On Carthage, see Plutarch, *G. Gracchus* 8; Appian, *BC* 1.23; Eutropius, *Breviarium* (hereafter *Brev.*) 4.21; Orosius 5.12.1; Velleius Paterculus 1.15.

46. Appian, *BC* 1.23.

47. Plutarch, *G. Gracchus* 9.1.

48. Plutarch, *G. Gracchus* 10.1.

49. Cicero, *Brutus* 99; Plutarch, *G. Gracchus* 8.3; Appian, *BC* 1.23.

50. Cicero, *Brutus* 99–100; cf. Plutarch, *G. Gracchus* 8.2.

51. Appian, *BC* 1.23; Plutarch, *G. Gracchus* 9.3.

52. Plutarch, *G. Gracchus* 12.1–2.

53. Plutarch, *G. Gracchus* 13.1–2.

54. Plutarch, *G. Gracchus* 13.3.

55. The term is first used quite late—by Julius Caesar in *Commentaries on the Civil War* 1.5—but the institution took shape in the second century. On the SCU, see B. Straumann, *Crisis and Constitutionalism* (Oxford, 2016), 57–60, 89–92.

56. Plutarch, *G. Gracchus* 15.1.

57. Plutarch, *G. Gracchus* 17.3.

58. Plutarch, *G. Gracchus* 18.1.

59. Plutarch, *G. Gracchus* 17.6.

Chapter 10. Marius and Sulla

1. Sallust, *Jugurtha* 41.9.

2. Sallust, *Jugurtha* 8.1, 13.7.

3. Sallust, *Jugurtha* 26 (Cirta), 29.1–3 (bribery).

4. Sallust, *Jugurtha* 31.2 (cabal), 40.5 (bitterness).

5. Sallust, *Jugurtha* 64.2; cf. Plutarch, *Marius* 8.

6. Cicero (*Rep.* 2.40) indicates that the lowest property class eligible for military service possessed at least 1,500 bronze asses, a modest amount equaling less than 150 denarii.

7. Or so says Sallust (*Jugurtha* 84.4). For the step of enrolling the landless, see Plutarch, *Marius* 9; Sallust, *Jugurtha* 86; Valerius Maximus 2.3.1; Gellius 16.10.10.

8. Sallust, *Jugurtha* 84.1–4 (spoils). On landless recruits, see Plutarch, *Marius* 9; Sallust, *Jugurtha* 86; Valerius Maximus 2.3.1; Gellius 16.10.10.

9. For casualties, see Livy, *Per.* 67 (80,000); Granius Licinianus Bk. 33 (70,000). On the battle, Sallust, *Jugurtha* 114; Plutarch, *Camillus* 19.7; Plutarch, *Lucullus* 27.7; Cassius Dio 27.91.1–3.

10. Plutarch, *Marius* 14.

11. Plutarch, *Sulla* 4.

12. Plutarch, *Sulla* 4.3.

13. Plutarch, *Marius* 28.1.

14. Livy, *Per.* 69; Velleius Paterculus 2.12.6; Plutarch, *Marius* 29; Appian, *BC* 1.29.

15. Appian, *BC* 1.30.

16. Appian, *BC* 1.32–33.

17. Appian, *BC* 1.33.

18. Plutarch, *Sulla* 5.1.

19. Sallust, *Jugurtha* 95.3.

20. Plutarch, *Sulla* 2.

21. J. P. V. D. Balsdon, "Sulla Felix," *Journal of Roman Studies* 41 (1951): 1–10; A. Keaveney, *Sulla: The Last Republican*, 2nd ed. (New York, 2005), 33–34.

22. Sulla, *Memoirs*, fragment 10 (Cornell, *Fragments of the Roman Historians*) = Plutarch, *Sulla* 5.1.

23. Plutarch, *Sulla* 5; Keaveney, *Sulla*, 27–35.

24. Plutarch, *Sulla* 6.1.

25. Plutarch, *Sulla* 5 (extortion case), 6 (Bocchus statue).

26. The most recent such law was the Lex Licinia Mucia (Cicero, *De officiis* 3.47). For discussion, see Steel, *End of the Republic*, 35–36.

27. Appian, *BC* 1.35–36. For discussion, see H. Mouritsen, *Italian Unification*, 90, 142–151.

28. Velleius Paterculus 2.14.

29. Velleius Paterculus 2.14; Appian, *BC* 1.36.

30. On Asculum, see Appian, *BC* 1.38; Velleius Paterculus 2.15. For background, Mouritsen, *Italian Unification*, 130–142.

31. Asconius 22C; Steel, *End of the Republic*, 82.

32. Appian, *BC* 1.49.

33. Appian, *BC* 1.49; Cicero, *Pro Balbo* 21.

34. Cicero, *Pro Archia* 4.7.

35. Asconius 3C.

36. Plutarch, *Sulla* 6.

37. Appian, *Mithridatic Wars* 22; Valerius Maximus 9.2.3; Plutarch, *Sulla* 24.4; Cassius Dio, fr. 109.8. This fragment of Dio belongs somewhere in books 30–35 of his history, but its place in the individual books is not always easily distinguished. For ease of reference, subsequent references to material from these books will correspond to the marginal numbers in Cary's Loeb edition.

38. Cicero, *De Imperio Cn. Pompei* 19; Kay, *Rome's Economic Revolution*, 243–252.

39. Plutarch, *Marius* 34.

40. Plutarch, *Sulla* 8.

41. On the anti-Senate, see Plutarch, *Marius* 35; Plutarch, *Sulla* 8.2.

42. Appian, *BC* 1.55.

43. Appian, *BC* 1.56.

44. Appian, *BC* 1.57.

45. Appian, *BC* 1.57.

46. On the Esquiline Gate, see Appian, *BC* 1.58.

47. For the "passion" quote, see Plutarch, *Sulla* 9.7. On the capture, Appian, *BC* 1.58; Velleius Paterculus 2.19.

48. Appian, *BC* 1.59.

49. Appian, *BC* 1.60.

50. Appian, *BC* 1.60; Plutarch, *Sulla* 10.3.

51. Appian, *BC* 1.62.

52. Cassius Dio 102.7.

53. Appian, *BC* 1.66–69.

54. Appian, *BC* 1.72–74; Cicero, *De oratore* 3.8–10.

55. E. Badian, "Waiting for Sulla," *Journal of Roman Studies* 52 (1962): 52.

56. Plutarch, *Sulla* 24.

57. Plutarch, *Sulla* 12.

58. Appian, *Mithridatic Wars* 1.51–3; Badian, "Waiting for Sulla," 57.

59. Appian, *BC* 1.77.

60. Appian, *BC* 1.82.

61. Velleius Paterculus 2.27.1–3; Appian, *BC* 1.93; Plutarch, *Sulla* 29.

62. Plutarch, *Sulla* 31.1.

63. Plutarch, *Sulla* 31.1.

64. Plutarch, *Sulla* 30.2.

65. Cicero, *Rep.* 1.39.

66. Appian, *BC* 1.79.

67. Plutarch, *Sulla* 33.1.

68. Sallust, *Catiline* 28; Appian, *BC* 1.96.

69. Appian, *BC* 1.101.

70. Plutarch, *Sulla* 36.2.3.

Chapter 11. Sulla's Children

1. Sallust, *Histories* 1.49.1.

2. Sallust, *Histories* 1.49.2.

3. Appian, *BC* 1.66–68; Plutarch, *Pompey* 1. For discussion of his career, see A. Keaveney, "Pompeius Strabo's Second Consulship," *Classical Quarterly* 28 (1978), 240–241.

4. Plutarch, *Pompey* 4–5; A. Keaveney, "Young Pompey: 106–79 BC," *L'Antiquité classique* 51 (1982), 111–139, at 113–117.

5. Appian, *BC* 1.66–68; Plutarch, *Pompey* 1; R. Seager, *Pompey the Great: A Political Biography*, 2nd ed. (Oxford, 2002), 20–23.

6. Appian, *BC* 1.80; Plutarch, *Pompey* 8.

7. Valerius Maximus 6.2.8.

8. Plutarch, *Pompey* 13. See also Seager, *Pompey*, 28–29.

9. Plutarch, *Pompey* 14.

10. Plutarch, *Pompey* 17.

11. Cicero, *Pro Balbo* 19, 32ff., 38.

12. Sallust, *Histories* 2.17–18.

13. On Crassus's wealth, see Plutarch, *Crassus* 2; Cicero, *De officiis* 1.25; Cassius Dio 37.56.4; Velleius Paterculus 2.44.2. On his jealousy, Plutarch, *Crassus* 6.

14. Cicero, *In Verrem* 1.45.

15. Cassius Dio 38.5; Plutarch, *Lucullus* 34.

16. Plutarch, *Crassus* 12; Appian, *BC* 1.121 (soothsayers).

17. Appian, *BC* 1.121.

18. Cassius Dio 38.12.7.

19. Cassius Dio 38.12.7. On his courtroom skills, see J. Osgood, *Lawless Republic* (New York, 2025).

20. Plutarch, *Cato* 4.1; F. Drogula, *Cato the Younger: Life and Death at the End of the Roman Republic* (Oxford, 2019), 9–22.

21. On his priesthood, see Velleius Paterculus 2.22; Florus 2.9. On Sulla, Plutarch, *Caesar* 1; Suetonius, *Caesar* 1.

22. On evidence of these views of Sulla, see Cassius Dio 36.34.4; Appian, *BC* 1.104.

23. Plutarch, *Caesar* 5.2. Suetonius, *Caesar* 6.1, preserves a small section of the speech on Julia.

24. On his spending on the campaign, see Plutarch, *Caesar* 5–6. On notions about his unsustainable popularity, Plutarch, *Caesar* 4.5.

25. On the campaign of 63, see Sallust, *Catiline* 35.3–4; Cicero, *Pro Lucio Murena*; Steel, *End of the Republic*, 154.

26. Plutarch, *Cicero* 15, Crassus 13.3; Cassius Dio 37.31.1–3.

27. Sallust, *Catiline* 47–48; Cicero, *Catiline* 3.15.

28. Sallust, *Catiline* 48–49.

29. Sallust, *Catiline* 51.23, 51.32–34.

30. Sallust, *Catiline* 52.22–23, 52.36.

31. Sallust, *Catiline* 54.2–6.

32. Sallust, *Catiline* 51.7.

33. On the death of Mithridates, see Cassius Dio 37.10–14; Appian, *Mithridatic Wars* 16.111.

34. Cicero, *Epistulae ad familiares* 5.7.1; Plutarch, *Pompey* 43.1.

35. Cassius Dio 37.20.4, 37.20.6; cf. Plutarch, *Pompey* 43.2.

36. Plutarch, *Pompey* 44.

37. Cassius Dio 37.50.6.

38. Cicero, *Epistulae ad Atticum* 1.17.8–9.

39. Plutarch, *Crassus* 7.6.

40. Plutarch, *Caesar* 11–12; Cassius Dio 37.52.

41. Plutarch, *Cato* 31.3; Plutarch, *Caesar* 13.2; Cassius Dio 37.54.2; Suetonius, *Caesar* 19.1–2.

42. Plutarch, *Crassus* 14.2.

43. Cassius Dio 37.57.1; Livy, *Per.* 103; Plutarch, *Crassus* 14.1–3; Plutarch, *Caesar* 13.1–2; Plutarch, *Pompey* 47; Plutarch, *Cato* 31.2–5; Suetonius, *Caesar* 19; Velleius Paterculus 2.44.1; E. Gruen, *The Last Generation of the Roman Republic* (Berkeley, 1974), 88–90.

44. Cassius Dio 38.3.

45. Plutarch, *Pompey* 47; Plutarch, *Caesar* 14.

46. T. P. Wiseman, "The Publication of De Bello Gallico," in *Julius Caesar as Artful Reporter*, ed. A. Powell and K. Welch (Swansea, 1998), 1–9.

47. Cicero, *Rep.* 5.2, 1.36.

48. Cicero, *Laws* 3.18.42.

49. Cassius Dio 40.48.

50. Asconius 30C–42C; Cassius Dio 40.46.

51. Cicero, *Pro Milone* 70; Asconius 35–36.

52. Cicero, *Rep.* 3.13.23.

53. R. Morstein-Marx, "Caesar's Alleged Fear of Prosecution and His 'Ratio absentis,'" *Historia* 56 (2007): 159–178; cf. Steel, *End of the Republic*, 193–194.

54. On Curio, see Cicero, *Epistulae ad familiares* 8.6.5.

55. Appian, *BC* 2.30.

56. Appian, *BC* 2.31; cf. Caesar, *Civil War* 1.4.

57. Caesar, *Civil War* 2.

58. Caesar, *Civil War* 1.7.

59. Caesar, *Civil War* 1.14–27; Appian, *BC* 2.36–39; Cassius Dio 41.5–13.

60. Appian, *BC* 2.49; Caesar, *Civil War* 3.3. In *End of the Republic*, 197, Steel lists the imperium holders. Cassius Dio 41.43.2 speaks of 200 senators.

61. Appian, *BC* 2.63; Caesar, *Civil War* 3.73–74.

62. Caesar, *Civil War* 3.88–89; Appian, *BC* 2.70.

63. On Pompey's fate, see Plutarch, *Pompey* 77–80; Appian, *BC* 2.83–86; Caesar, *Civil War* 3.103–104; Velleius Paterculus 2.53.

64. Appian, *BC* 2.91; Plutarch, *Caesar* 50 (Greek translation); Cassius Dio 42.48.1 (paraphrase). Latin: Suetonius, *Caesar* 37.

65. Appian, *BC* 2.94.

66. Cassius Dio 43.45.

67. Cassius Dio 47.1.

68. These coins are RRC 480/2a–c (DICT QUART); 480/3, 480/4, 480/5a–b, 480/17 (variations of IMP); and 480/6–15, 480/18 (variations of DICT IN PERPETUO).

69. E.g. Appian, *BC* 2.112.

70. RRC 433/1 and 2.

71. Plutarch, *Brutus* 8–10.

72. On Cassius's role, see Plutarch, *Brutus* 8–10.

Chapter 12. Rome's First Emperor

1. Appian, *BC* 2.114.

2. Sallust, *Catiline* 51.12–14.

3. Appian, *BC* 2.122; Cassius Dio 45.21.

4. Cicero, *Epistulae ad Atticum* 14.10.1 (call the Senate), 15.11 (kill Antony).

5. Plutarch, *Caesar* 67.7; Appian, *BC* 2.137–142; Cicero, *Epistulae ad Atticum* 15.1a.

6. Nicolaus of Damascus, *Vita Augusti* (hereafter *VA*) 27.

7. Cassius Dio 44.34.6.

8. Cassius Dio 44.22.3; Appian, *BC* 2.126–129; J. Osgood, *Caesar's Legacy* (Cambridge, 2006), 13–14.

9. Appian, *BC* 2.128.

10. Cassius Dio 44.35.1–4; Appian, *BC* 2.143; Plutarch, *Caesar* 68.

11. Appian, *BC* 2.143.

12. Appian, *BC* 2.144–147; Cassius Dio 44.35; Plutarch, *Caesar* 68; Suetonius, *Caesar* 84.

13. Cassius Dio 44.35.4; Appian, *BC* 2.147.

14. Appian, *BC* 2.147.

15. Appian, *BC* 3.4–5.

16. Cicero, *Rep.* 3.13.23.

17. Appian, *BC* 3.10–11; Nicolaus of Damascus, *VA* 18, Suetonius, *Augustus* 3.

18. Appian, *BC* 3.11.

19. Nicolaus of Damascus, *VA* fr. 130.108; Appian, *BC* 3.28.

20. Cassius Dio 45.5.3–4; Florus 2.15.2–3.

21. Appian, *BC* 3.22.

22. Appian, *BC* 3.21.

23. Plutarch, *Brutus* 24; Cicero, *Philippics* 10.8.16.

24. For "brute beast," see Cicero, *Philippics* 2.12.30; on prostitution, 2.18.44–45.

25. Appian, *BC* 3.45.

26. Cicero, *Philippics* 14.8.22–13.35.

27. Appian, *BC* 3.80–81.

28. Cicero, *Epistulae ad familiares* 10.23=Ep. 890.

29. Appian, *BC* 3.88–92.

30. Appian, *BC* 3.94 (adoption), 3.95 (indictment of murderers); Velleius Paterculus 2.69.5 (Caesar's murder a crime).

31. On the triumvirs' entry, see Appian, *BC* 4.7; Cassius Dio 47.2. On Cicero's capture, Appian, *BC* 4.19–20; Cassius Dio 47.8, 11; Plutarch, *Cicero* 47–48; Plutarch, *Antony* 20. On the initial killings, Appian, *BC* 4.5; Livy, *Per.* 120; Plutarch, *Antony* 20; Cassius Dio 47.3–14.

32. Appian, *BC* 4.8–10.

33. Josephus, *Jewish Antiquities* 14.272; Josephus, *Jewish War* 1.220; Cassius Dio 47.28–37; Appian, *BC* 4.64–81.

34. Augustus, *Res Gestae* (hereafter *RG*), 2; Cassius Dio 47.37–49; Appian, *BC* 4.107–138; Suetonius, *Augustus* 13; Plutarch, *Brutus* 43–53; Velleius Paterculus 2.71.1.

35. Osgood, *Caesar's Legacy*, 152–166.

36. Appian, *BC* 5.122ff; Cassius Dio 49.12.4; Velleius Paterculus 2.80.4.

37. Osgood, *Caesar's Legacy*, 329–330.

38. Pliny, *NH* 36.121.

39. Cassius Dio 49.40; Plutarch, *Antony* 50.4.

40. Cassius Dio 50.2.7–50.3.5.

41. Augustus, *RG* 25.2.

42. Osgood, *Caesar's Legacy*, 357–364.

43. D. Rathbone, "Egypt, Augustus, and Roman Taxation," *Cahiers du Centre Gustave Glotz* 4 (1993): 81–112, at 99–110.

44. Cassius Dio 51.21.4.

45. Cassius Dio 53.11; Strabo, *Geographica* 17.3.25.

46. Augustus, *RG* 34.

47. Cassius Dio 53.16.8, 53.18.2; Suetonius, *Augustus* 7.2; Velleius Paterculus 2.91.1.

48. Cassius Dio 53.31.1, 54.3.4–8.

49. Cassius Dio 54.1.1–2.

50. Cassius Dio 54.6.1–4, 54.10.1–5.

51. Horace, *Odes* 4.15.5–20.

52. Augustus, *RG* 1.1–3.

53. Augustus, *RG* 6.

54. Augustus, *RG* 6.

Chapter 13. The Terrors of Tiberius

1. Cassius Dio 53.30.2.

2. Cassius Dio 53.31.4.

3. Cassius Dio 54.31.1.

4. Cassius Dio 54.31.2.

5. Suetonius, *Tiberius* (*Tib.* hereafter), 7.2.

6. Suetonius, *Tib.* 7.3, 11.4.

7. Suetonius, *Tib.* 10.2.

8. Suetonius, *Augustus* 65; Cassius Dio 55.10.

9. Cassius Dio 55.10.

10. Tacitus, *Ann.* 1.3.

11. Appian, *BC* 4.34. See also B. Hopwood, "Hortensia Speaks: An Authentic Voice of Resistance?," in *Appian's Roman History: Empire and Civil War*, ed. K. Welch (Swansea, 2015), 305–322.

12. Tacitus, *Ann.* 3.1; Cassius Dio 55.32.2.

13. On responsibility for Agrippa Postumus's death, see Suetonius, *Tib.* 22 (Augustus, Livia, or Tiberius); Cassius Dio 57.3.5 (Tiberius); Tacitus, *Ann.* 1.6.1 (Livia).

14. Tacitus, *Ann.* 1.7.1.

15. Cassius Dio 57.2.3.

16. Suetonius, *Tib.* 24; cf. Cassius Dio 57.2.4; Ovid, *Ex Ponto* 4.13.27.

17. Tacitus, *Ann.* 1.7.1.

18. Cassius Dio 57.8–9, 18; Tacitus, *Ann.* 4.38; Suetonius, *Tib.* 26.

19. Tacitus, *Ann.* 15.

20. Tacitus, *Ann.* 1.7; Cassius Dio 57.7.2.

21. Cassius Dio 57.7.3; cf. Suetonius, *Tib.* 31.

22. Suetonius, *Tib.* 28.

23. Tacitus, *Ann.* 1.2.1, 3.65.

24. On expansion in Germany, see Velleius Paterculus 2.97; Cassius Dio 54.25, 54.32–33; R. Seager, *Tiberius* (London, 2004), 18–23.

25. On the battle, see Velleius Paterculus, 2.118–119; Cassius Dio 56.21. On Augustus's reaction, Suetonius, *Augustus* 23. On Tiberius's response, Suetonius, *Tib.* 17–19.

26. Tacitus, *Ann.* 1.31.4; cf. Cassius Dio 57.5.4.

27. Tacitus, *Ann.* 1.32; Cassius Dio 57.5; Suetonius, *Tib.* 25.

28. On the Pannonian mutiny, see Tacitus, *Ann.* 1.16–30; Cassius Dio 57.4.

29. Tacitus, *Ann.* 1.16.

30. Tacitus, *Ann.* 1.47.

31. Tacitus, *Ann.* 1.29–30.

32. On suppression of the rebellion, see Tactius, *Ann.* 1.48–49; Cassius Dio 57.5. On the invasion of Germany, Cassius Dio 57.6.

33. Tacitus, *Ann.* 4.6.

34. Tacitus, *Ann.* 1.75; Suetonius, *Tib.* 33.

35. Tacitus, *Ann.* 2.29.2.

36. Suetonius, *Tib.* 46–47.

37. Tacitus, *Ann.* 2.87.

38. On Asia Minor, see Cassius Dio 57.17.8; Tacitus, *Ann.* 2.47. On the Aventine, Tacitus, *Ann.* 6.45.

39. Tacitus, *Ann.* 6.16–17; Cassius Dio 58.21; Suetonius, *Tib.* 48. For more discussion, see Kay, *Rome's Economic Revolution*, 262–264.

40. Tacitus, *Ann.* 4.13; cf. Cassius Dio 57.22.3.

41. Tacitus, *Ann.* 6.46.

42. Cassius Dio 57.19; cf. Tacitus, *Ann.* 6.51.

43. Tacitus, *Ann.* 4.67; Suetonius, *Tib.* 41–42. For more discussion, see Seager, *Tiberius*, 174.

44. Tacitus, *Ann.* 1.72.

45. Tacitus, *Ann.* 1.72–74.

46. On Cordus's case, see Tactius, *Ann.* 4.34; Cassius Dio 57.24.2–4; Suetonius, *Tib.* 61.3; Seneca, *Dial.* 6.1.3, 6.22.4–7, 6.26.1–3. On the joke, Seneca, *Dial.* 6.22.4. On the charge and defense in the Senate, Tacitus, *Ann.* 4.34.

47. Cassius Dio 58.4.1.

48. Cassius Dio 58.4.2 (administration), 58.2.7 (birthday), 8 (envoys).

49. Cassius Dio 58.5.1.

50. Cassius Dio 58.6.3–5.

51. Cassius Dio 58.7–8.

52. Cassius Dio 58.10.1.

53. Cassius Dio 58.10.3–8.

54. Cassius Dio 58.11.4.

55. Cassius Dio 58.11.5–7; Tacitus, *Ann.* 5.9.

56. Tacitus, *Ann.* 6.10.

57. Tacitus, *Ann.* 6.24–25; Suetonius, *Tib.* 53–54; Cassius Dio 58.22.

58. Cassius Dio 58.16.3.

59. Cassius Dio 58.12.

60. Tacitus, *Ann.* 6.50.5; Cassius Dio 58.28. Suetonius, *Tib.* 73.2 claims Caligula poisoned him.

61. Tacitus, *Ann.* 6.51.

Chapter 14. Caligula and Claudius Stumble Toward a New Rome

1. Philo, *Legatio* 2.8–11; Suetonius, *Gaius* 13–14.

2. Suetonius, *Gaius* 17–18.

3. Cassius Dio 59.9.1–6; Suetonius, *Gaius* 16.1.

4. Cassius Dio 59.6.7. On the dating of the consulship to July, see Suetonius, *Gaius* 17.1.

5. On Antonia and Agrippina, see Cassius Dio 59.3.4–6; Suetonius, *Gaius* 15.1–3. On the shrine of Augustus, Cassius Dio 59.7.1.

6. Cassius Dio 59.3.7.

7. Suetonius, *Gaius* 15.3; Cassius Dio 59.8.1.

8. Philo, *Legatio* 3.15–19.

9. Philo, *Legatio* 23.155.

10. Philo, *Legatio* 23.157 (Augustus), 24.161 (Tiberius).

11. Caesar, *Gallic Wars* 1.10–11, 3.11 (support for Caesar), 7.75 (revolt).

12. Strabo, *Geographica* 4.2.2 (capital), 4.6.11 (roads).

13. *CIL* 13.1036.

14. Philo, *Legatio* 3.19.

15. Suetonius, *Gaius* 51; Philo, *Legatio* 4.22.

16. Cassius Dio 59.8.1–3; Suetonius, *Gaius* 23; Philo, *Contra Flaccum* 3.11; Philo, *Legatio* 4.22–5.31.

17. Philo, *Legatio* 6.32–8.61; Cassius Dio 59.10.6.

18. Cassius Dio 59.8.4–7; Philo, *Legatio* 9.62–71; Suetonius, *Gaius* 23.

19. Cassius Dio 59.3.

20. Suetonius, *Gaius* 37; Cassius Dio 59.2.6.

21. Cassius Dio 59.17–18.

22. On his sexual depravity, see Suetonius, *Gaius* 36. On incest, Suetonius, *Gaius* 24; Cassius Dio 59.11.1. On Incitatus, Cassius Dio 59.14.7; Suetonius, *Gaius* 55.

23. Cassius Dio 59.16.8, 59.10.7.

24. Cassius Dio 59.10.5 (bloody games), 5.14 (selling gladiators), 5.15 (roads); Suetonius, *Gaius* 38, 40.

25. Cassius Dio 59.28.11; Suetonius, *Gaius* 41.

26. On taxes, see Cassius Dio 59.21. On seashells, Suetonius, *Gaius* 46.

27. Cassius Dio 59.28.1–5; Suetonius, *Gaius* 22; Philo, *Legatio* 13.93–16.114.

28. Philo, *Legatio* 16.115.

29. On rioting, see Philo, *Legatio* 17.119–20.138.

30. Philo, *Legatio* 29.188–194 (temple in Jerusalem), 31.207–34.260 (Petronius).

31. Philo, *Legatio* 45.367.

32. Cassius Dio 59.29.2.

33. Cassius Dio 59.29.7.

34. Suetonius, *Claudius* 10.3; Cassius Dio 60.1.1–3; Josephus, *Jewish Antiquities* (*JA* hereafter), 19.1–4.

35. Suetonius, *Claudius* 10.4.

36. Cassius Dio 60.1.4.

37. Suetonius, *Claudius* 4.2.

38. Suetonius, *Claudius* 8.

39. *Roman Imperial Coinage* (*RIC* hereafter), 1. Suetonius, *Claudius* 113.

40. Cassius Dio 60.3.5, confirmed by Suetonius, *Claudius* 11.1.

41. Cassius Dio 60.3.6–7.

42. Cassius Dio 60.4.5 (destroying documents), 60.6.3 (returning funds).

43. Josephus, *JA* 19.5.3. Cassius Dio 60.6.7 sees these actions differently.

44. Cassius Dio 60.21.2 (elephants), 60.20.3 (Vespasian).

45. Cassius Dio 62.2.1.

46. The inscription is *ILM* 116, *IAM* 2448. For further discussion, see D. Fishwick, "The Annexation of Mauretania," *Historia* 20 (1971): 467–487.

47. Cassius Dio 60.17.7.

48. Tacitus, *Ann.* 11.23.3–4.

49. Tacitus, *Ann.* 11.25.2.

50. Seneca, *De Beneficiis* 6.19.2.

51. Tacitus, *Ann.* 11.26–27.

52. Tacitus, *Ann.* 11.37–38; Cassius Dio 61.31.

53. Tacitus, *Ann.* 12.66; Cassius Dio 61.34.1–3 (mushroom specifically mentioned); Suetonius, *Claudius* 43–44.

Chapter 15. Nero

1. Cassius Dio 61.1.2, 61.7; Tacitus, *Ann.* 13.15–6.

2. J. Malitz, *Nero* (Malden, MA, 2005), 11.

3. First speech of Nero, in Malitz, *Nero*, 16; Cassius Dio 61.3.1.

4. Malitz, *Nero*, 18.

5. Cassius Dio 61.7.1; Tacitus, *Ann.* 13.13; *CIL* 10.6599.

6. Tacitus, *Ann.* 13.14.

7. Cassius Dio 61.7.1; Suetonius, *Nero* 28.

8. Tacitus, *Ann.* 14.1; Cassius Dio 61.12.

9. Tacitus, *Ann.* 14.3.

10. Cassius Dio 61.12.2; Tacitus, *Ann.* 14.3.

11. On the calm seas, see Tacitus, *Ann.* 14.5.

12. Cassius Dio 61.14.

13. Cassius Dio 61.14.

14. Pseudo Aurelius Victor, *Epitome de Caesaribus* (*Epit. de Caes.* hereafter), 5.1–4.

15. Cassius Dio 61.11.1.

16. Tacitus, *Ann.* 14.52.1.

17. Cassius Dio 61.15.1–4.

18. Suetonius, *Nero* 39.

19. Cassius Dio 61.16, 61.22.

20. Cassius Dio 62.2.

21. Tacitus, *Ann.* 15.38–42 (quote at 15.40); Cassius Dio 62.16–18; Suetonius, *Nero* 38.

22. Cassius Dio 62.16–18.

23. Tacitus, *Ann.* 15.39; Suetonius, *Nero* 38.

24. Tacitus, *Ann.* 15.42.

25. Suetonius, *Nero* 31.

26. Tacitus, *Ann.* 15.44.

27. Tacitus, *Ann.* 15.44.

28. Suetonius, *Nero* 16.

29. Tacitus, *Ann.* 15.48–74.

30. Tacitus, *Ann.* 15.60.64, 15.63; cf. Cassius Dio 62.24–25.

31. Tacitus, *Ann.* 16.21.

32. Tacitus, *Ann.* 16.22.

33. Tacitus, *Ann.* 16.34–35; Plato, *Phaedo* 115b–118a.

34. Cassius Dio 63.9.

35. Strabo, *Geographica* 17.1.11.

36. Romans had destroyed Corinth in 146 BC but Julius Caesar had refounded it as a Roman colony in 44 BC.

37. For the decree, see *ILS* 8794. My translation follows Malitz, *Nero*, 92.

38. E.g., Roman Provincial Coinage 1.1238–1244. See E. Manders and D. Slootjes, "Linking Inscriptions to Provincial Coins," *Latomus* 74 (2015): 1000.

39. Cassius Dio 63.12; Suetonius, *Nero* 23.

40. Cassius Dio 63.19.

41. Suetonius, *Nero* 25.

42. Cassius Dio 63.20; Suetonius, *Nero* 25.

43. Cassius Dio 63.20.

44. Suetonius, *Nero* 40.

45. Josephus, *Jewish War* 4.8.1; Pliny, *NH* 4.106, 4.109; Tacitus, *Histories* (*Hist.* hereafter), 1.51.6, 4.17.5.

46. Cassius Dio 63.23; Plutarch, *Galba* 4–5.

47. On the coins, see *RIC* 27 (Libertas) and 72 (Salus). On propaganda, Suetonius, *Nero* 41.

48. Cassius Dio 63.24.4; Plutarch, *Galba* 6.4; Suetonius, *Galba* 11.

49. Cassius Dio 63.24; Plutarch, *Galba* 6.3.

50. Plutarch, *Galba* 6.1; Plutarch, *Otho* 18.3; Cassius Dio 63.25.1.

51. Plutarch, *Galba* 6.4.

52. Suetonius, *Nero* 42.1.

53. Suetonius, *Nero* 44.1.

54. Suetonius, *Nero* 44.2–45.2.

55. Plutarch, *Galba* 2.2.

56. Suetonius, *Nero* 50.

57. Tacitus, *Hist.* 1.4.

58. Cassius Dio 64.3.4; Suetonius, *Galba* 15.1–2; cf. Plutarch, *Galba* 16.1–4.

59. Cassius Dio 64.3.3; Tacitus, *Hist.* 1.6; Suetonius, *Galba* 16.1.

60. Tacitus, *Hist.* 1.6; Cassius Dio 64.3.2; Suetonius, *Galba* 12.2.

61. Tacitus, *Hist.* 1.7.

62. Suetonius, *Galba* 16.1.

63. Tacitus, *Hist.* 1.12.

64. Tacitus, *Hist.* 1.15.

65. Tacitus, *Hist.* 1.18.

66. Tacitus, *Hist.* 1.21–49; Suetonius, *Galba* 19–20.

67. Tacitus, *Hist.* 1.51.

68. Cassius Dio 64.10.

69. Cassius Dio 64.13.1–2.

70. Suetonius, *Otho* 10.1. For other versions of his last words, see Cassius Dio 64.13.1–2; Tacitus, *Hist.* 2.47; Plutarch, *Otho* 15.3–6; Martial, *Epigrams* 6.32.

71. Tacitus, *Hist.* 3.68; Suetonius, *Vitellius* 15.1–3.

72. Cassius Dio 65.19–21; Tacitus, *Hist.* 3.71–74; Suetonius, *Vitellius* 15–7.

Chapter 16. The Flavian Empire of the New Roman Elite

1. Suetonius, *Vespasian* 1.2–4.

2. P. A. Brunt, "The Revolt of Vindex and the Fall of Nero," *Latomus* 18 (1959): 531–533.

3. Tacitus, *Hist.* 4.1, 4.11.

4. Cassius Dio 66.2.5.

5. Cassius Dio 66.9.1–2.

6. *CIL* 6.930; M. H. Crawford, ed., *Roman Statutes*, vol. 1 (London, 1996), 549–553.

7. Suetonius, *Vespasian* 9.2.

8. Tacitus, *Hist.* 4.43–44.

9. Cassius Dio 63.14.3; Tacitus, *Hist.* 1.8; Pliny, *Epistulae* 9.19.5 (individual letters in letter collections are hereafter abbreviated as *Ep.* for Pliny and all other authors); B. Levick, "Cluvius Rufus," in *The Fragments of the Roman Historians*, ed. T. J. Cornell, vol. 1 (Oxford, 2013), 549–560.

10. Tacitus, *Hist.* 4.9.

11. Cassius Dio 66.10.2.

12. *CIL* 6.1257–1258 (*ILS* 218).

13. Suetonius, *Vespasian* 8.5.

14. Cassius Dio 65.15.1; cf. Suetonius, *Vespasian* 9.1.

15. C. F. Norena, "Medium and Message in Vespasian's Templum Pacis," *Memoirs of the American Academy in Rome* 48 (2003): 25–43; R. Taraporewalla, "The Templum Pacis: Construction of Memory Under Vespasian," *Acta Classica* 53 (2010): 145–163.

16. Josephus, *Jewish War* 7.159–162.

17. On Galba, see Cassius Dio 64.5.3; Suetonius, *Galba* 14.2. On Otho, Cassius Dio 64.9; Suetonius, *Otho* 7.1. On Vitellius, Cassius Dio 65.16–17, 65.20; Suetonius, *Vitellius* 15.2.

18. Tacitus, *Ann.* 13.47; *CIL* 6.5863.

19. Suetonius, *Vespasian* 9.1.

20. Suetonius, *Vespasian* 15.1.

21. Cassius Dio 66.12.2.

22. Suetonius, *Vespasian* 15.1.

23. Dio Chrysostom, *Discourse* 21.10.

24. Tacitus, *Hist.* 2.8–9; Cassius Dio 64.9.

25. Cassius Dio 66.19.3; Zonaras 11.18; John of Antioch fr. 104.

26. On the third pretender, see Suetonius, *Nero* 57.2; Tacitus, *Hist.* 1.2.1.

27. Suetonius, *Titus* 8.1.

28. Suetonius, *Titus* 8.3–4.

29. Cassius Dio 66.25.1.

30. Cassius Dio 66.25; Suetonius, *Titus* 7.3.

31. Cassius Dio 66.25.5.

32. Cassius Dio 66.26.1; Suetonius, *Titus* 10.1.

33. Cassius Dio 68.3.2.

34. Cassius Dio 67.3.5–4.2; Tacitus, *Agricola* 39; Suetonius, *Domitian* 6.1.

35. B. Jones, *The Emperor Domitian* (London, 1992), 150–153.

36. E.g., Tacitus, *Agricola* 39; Suetonius, *Domitian* 6.

37. Suetonius, *Domitian* 4.1–2; Cassius Dio 67.8.1–4.

38. On the gifts, see Suetonius, *Domitian* 4.5. On banquets, Cassius Dio 67.8.5, 67.9.1. On confiscations and taxes, Cassius Dio 67.5.4–5; Suetonius, *Domitian* 12.1–2.

39. Suetonius, *Domitian* 3.1, 20.1.

40. Cassius Dio 67.2.4.

41. Suetonius, *Titus* 7.1.

42. Suetonius, *Titus* 6.2.

43. Suetonius, *Domitian* 10.3–4; Cassius Dio 67.13.

44. Suetonius, *Domitian* 10.2.

45. Suetonius, *Domitian* 6.2; Cassius Dio 67.11.1–2.

46. Cassius Dio 67.11.2.

47. K. H. Waters, "The Character of Domitian," *Phoenix* 18 (1964): 76n62; Jones, *Domitian*, 192.

48. Cassius Dio 67.4.3.

49. Juvenal, *Satire* 3.13–16, 3.60–61, 3.62–65; cf. Athenaeus, *Deipnosophistae* 120b–c. 3.75ff. For context, see E. Courtenay, *A Commentary on the Satires of Juvenal* (Berkeley, 2013), 126–165.

50. Jones, *Domitian*, 61.

51. J. Grainger, *Nerva and the Succession Crisis of AD 96–99* (London, 2004), 77–88.

Chapter 17. Nerva, Trajan, Hadrian, and the Adoptive Dynasty

1. Suetonius, *Domitian* 14–17; Cassius Dio 67.15–17.

2. *RIC* 2.Nerva 7.

3. Suetonius, *Domitian* 23.

4. Cassius Dio 68.1.

5. Cassius Dio 68.1.

6. Grainger, *Nerva*, 41–44.

7. R. Syme, "The Imperial Finances Under Domitian, Nerva, and Trajan," *Journal of Roman Studies* 20 (1930): 55–70.

8. Cassius Dio 68.2.3.

9. Cassius Dio 68.1.3.

10. Syme, "Imperial Finances," 61.

11. Cassius Dio 68.3.2.

12. Cassius Dio 68.3.3.

13. C. P. Jones, "Sura and Senecio," *Journal of Roman Studies* 60 (1970): 98–104, at 99; J. Bennett, *Trajan: Optimus Princeps* (Bloomington, IN, 1997), 46.

14. Cassius Dio 68.3.3.

15. Cassius Dio 68.4.1–2.

16. Grainger, *Nerva*, 73–88.

17. Grainger, *Nerva*, 101.

18. Eutropius, *Brev.* 8.2.

19. Martial 10.7; Pliny, *Panegyricus* (*Pan.* hereafter), 10–11.

20. Pliny, *Pan.* 11; Eutropius, *Brev.* 8.1.

21. Cassius Dio 58.5.4.

22. Pliny, *Pan.* 21–23.

23. Cassius Dio 58.5.5; Pliny, *Pan.* 23.6.

24. Ammianus Marcellinus (Ammianus hereafter), 16.10.15.

25. *RIC* 2.Trajan 471 (Portus), 246–248 and 255–257 (Forum façade), and 307 (Trajan's Column).

26. Pliny, *Pan.* 40.5.

27. *CIL* 9.1455 and 11.1147; Pliny, *Pan.* 82.4; Bennett, *Trajan*, 81–82; P. Garnsey, "Trajan's Alimenta: Some Problems," *Historia* 17 (1968): 367–381.

28. P. Lambrechts, "Trajan et le récruitement du Sénat," *L'antiquité classique* 5 (1936): 105–114.

29. Pliny, *Ep.* 6.19.4–6.

30. Cassius Dio 67.7.4.

31. Grainger, *Nerva*, 24.

32. Pliny, *Pan.* 12.2–4 suggests that the war probably ended by 99. The war itself is extremely poorly documented. For reconstruction of events, see Grainger, *Nerva*, 112–116.

33. G. W. Bowersock, *Roman Arabia* (Cambridge, MA, 1983), 79.

34. Cassius Dio 68.14; Ammianus 14.8.13.

35. Bennett, *Trajan*, 163–165.

36. Bennett, *Trajan*, 167.

37. Bowersock, *Roman Arabia*, 85n28.

38. Ammianus 14.8.13.

39. K. Czajkowski, *Localized Law: The Babatha and Salome Komaise Archives* (Oxford, 2017).

40. Pliny, *Ep.* 10.79–80, 112, 114, 115; Cassius Dio 37.20.2.

41. *RIC* 2.Trajan 324–325.

42. Cassius Dio 69.1.3–4.

43. *Scriptores Historiae Augustae* (hereafter SHA), Hadrian 5.3.

44. Cassius Dio 68.33; cf. Fronto, *Principia Historiae* 8–9; Eutropius, *Brev.* 8.6; Festus, *Breviarium* 14.3; SHA.Hadrian 5.1–8, 9.1.

45. SHA.Hadrian 5.1.

46. Eutropius, *Brev.* 8.6.

47. L. Revell, *Roman Imperialism and Local Identities* (Cambridge, 2009), 57–61.

48. Philostratus, *Vitae Sophistarum* (*Lives of the Sophists*, VS hereafter) 481.

49. Philostratus, *VS* 489. Regarding "two gendered and a hermaphrodite," this is my attempt to translate Greek words that do not easily conform to modern sensibilities or terminology.

50. Quotes: Philostratus, *VS* 489, 491–492. On Favorinus, M. Gleason, *Making Men* (Princeton, NJ, 1995).

51. Philostratus, *VS* 489.

52. Philostratus, *VS* 530.

53. Philostratus, *VS* 533.

54. Cassius Dio 69.12.1.

55. Cassius Dio 69.14.1–3.

56. Cassius Dio 69.

Chapter 18. Pius and Marcus

1. Cassius Dio 69.17.1; SHA.Hadrian 23.10–16.

2. *RIC* 2.Aelius 428–444.

3. Cassius Dio 69.17.2–3, SHA.Hadrian 25.9.

4. SHA.Hadrian 23.10.15; Cassius Dio 69.20.1.

5. SHA.Hadrian 24.7.

6. Cassius Dio 69.21.1–2; SHA.Hadrian 24.1–3.

7. Cassius Dio 69.22.1–3.

8. SHA.Hadrian 24.9.

9. Cassius Dio 70.1.

10. Cassius Dio 70.2; SHA.Hadrian 27.4.

11. J. H. Oliver, "The Ruling Power," *Transactions of the American Philosophical Society* 43, no. 4 (1953): 887.

12. Aristides, *Orationes* 26.6–13. (This work and other collected orations by other authors will be abbreviated *Or.* hereafter.)

13. Aristides, *Or.* 26.30, 26.36, 26.63, 26.102.

14. Aristides, *Or.* 26.59, 26.66, 26.84.

15. Ps. Aurelius Victor, *Epit. de Caes.* 15.6.

16. SHA.Pius 5–6.

17. *RIC* 3.Pius 284; SHA.Pius 8.5.

18. Aristides, *Or.* 26.107.

19. Marcus, *Meditations*, Book 1.16.

20. Marcus, *Meditations*, Book 1.16.

21. Philostratus, *VS* 528, 577, 589.

22. Philostratus, *VS* 570–571.

23. Philostratus, *VS* 567.

24. Aristides, *Or.* 18.

25. Aristides, *Or.* 19; Philostratus, *VS* 582.

26. Philostratus, *VS* 549.

27. Cassius Dio 73.5.3–6.5.

28. Philostratus, *VS* 559–562.

29. On the outbreak, see SHA.Verus 8.1–2. On symptoms, Galen, *Methodus medendi* 5.12; Galen, *De atra bile* 4.

30. C. Elliott, *Pox Romana: The Plague That Shook the Roman World* (Princeton, NJ, 2024).

31. Aristides, *Or.* 48.38.

32. Lucian, *Alexander the False Prophet*, 36.

33. Pseudo-Galen, *De Theriaca, ad Pisonem* 16 (vol. 14.280–281 in Kuhn edition); K. Harper, *The Fate of Rome* (Princeton, NJ, 2017), 99–100.

34. SHA.Marcus 21.6–9.

35. See, generally, Harper, *Fate of Rome*, 99–100. On the Germans, see Cassius Dio 72.11.

36. Cassius Dio 72.34–35.

37. Cassius Dio 72.34.

38. Cassius Dio 72.22; SHA.Marcus 24–26; SHA.Avidius Cassius 9.5–10.

39. SHA.Avidius Cassius 8.

40. Herodian 1.5.5.

41. On the joint emperorship, see SHA.Marcus 37.5; *RIC* 3.Marcus 1554–1587. On the joint campaign, *CIL* 2.4114, 6.8541, 10.408. On the joint triumph, SHA.Commodus 2.5.

42. *RIC* 3.Marcus 1260.

43. Cassius Dio 72.36.

Chapter 19. Commodus, Septimius Severus, and the Age of Rust

1. See O. Hekster, *Commodus: An Emperor at the Crossroads* (Leiden, 2002), 1, 39.

2. Galen, *De Praenotione* 12 (vol. 14.661–663 in Kuhn edition); Hekster, *Commodus*, 33.

3. SHA.Marcus 37.5; *RIC* 3.Marcus 1554–1587.

4. Herodian 1.4.3–6; Hekster, *Commodus*, 39.

5. Cassius Dio 73.1.

6. Cassius Dio 73.4.3.

7. Hekster, *Commodus*, 31–32.

8. Herodian 1.8.3–4.

9. Herodian 1.8.6; SHA.Commodus 4.3; Cassius Dio 73.4.5; Hekster, *Commodus*, 51–54.

10. Herodian 1.8.3.

11. Herodian 1.8.7.

12. Herodian 1.17.2.

13. Cassius Dio 73.1.1.

14. Cassius Dio 73.9.1.

15. Herodian 1.8.8.

16. Cassius Dio 73.5.3; SHA.Commodus 4.9–11.

17. Herodian 1.10.1–3; SHA.Commodus 16.2; *CIL* 11.6053; Hekster, *Commodus*, 65–67.

18. Cassius Dio 73.9.4.

19. Cassius Dio 73.12.3.

20. Cassius Dio 73.14.3.

21. Cassius Dio 73.13.6; Herodian 1.12.4.

22. Herodian 1.11.5.

23. Herodian 1.15.6.

24. Hekster, *Commodus*, 145.

25. Cassius Dio 73.21.

26. E.g., *RIC* 3.Commodus 221, 253, 254, 427.

27. Cassius Dio 72.24, 73.15.2; Herodian 1.14.2–6; Galen, *De Indolentia* 8, 18, 23; Galen, *De compositione medicamentorum per genera* 1.1, Galen, *De antidotis* 1.13; Cassius Dio 72.24.

28. Herodian 1.15.8.

29. Herodian 1.17.12.

30. SHA.Pertinax 5.7.

31. Herodian 2.1.1.

32. SHA.Pertinax 4.

33. Cassius Dio 74.1.

34. SHA.Pertinax 4.4.

35. Cassius Dio 74.1.

36. SHA.Pertinax 5.2–3.

37. Cassius Dio 73.9.2a, 74.4.1.

38. Cassius Dio 74.1.1, 74.3.4.

39. Cassius Dio 74.5.4.

40. Cassius Dio 74.8.4.

41. Cassius Dio 74.9–10.2; Herodian 2.5.7.

42. Cassius Dio 74.11.2–6.

43. Cassius Dio 74.12–13.

44. Cassius Dio 74.13.3.

45. SHA.Julianus 4.2.

46. Herodian 2.7.7–8.

47. Herodian 2.8.4.

48. *L'Année épigraphique* (hereafter *AE*), 1928.86 (altar); Herodian 2.9–10.1.

49. Herodian 2.9.9.

50. Cassius Dio 74.15.2.

51. Cassius Dio 74.15; Herodian 2.11–12.

52. Cassius Dio 75.1–2.

53. Cassius Dio 75.2.5–6.

54. Cassius Dio 75.4; Herodian 2.10.1, SHA.Pertinax 15.2. For discussion, see C. Ando, *Imperial Rome: AD 193–284* (Edinburgh, 2012), 26–27.

55. Cassius Dio 73.23.1–5.

56. SHA.Severus 7; Herodian 2.14.4.

57. Cassius Dio 74.6.3.

58. Cassius Dio 75.8.3.

59. Cassius Dio 75.10–14; Herodian 3.1, 3.6.9.

60. Cassius Dio 76.7.4; SHA.Severus 10.3–6. For numismatic evidence of the 196 date, see *RIC* 3.Caracalla 1–5.

61. Divinization of Commodus: Cassius Dio 76.7; *RIC* 3.Severus 72A; Commodus as Severus's brother: *CIL* 6.1031, line 2.

62. This break seems to coincide with his eleventh acclamation as imperator, in late 198 or early 199 (beginning with *RIC* 3.Severus 122).

63. Herodian 3.5.2–3.

64. Cassius Dio 76.4.4.

65. *CIL* 6.1031 (Theater of Pompey); *CIL* 6.896 (Pantheon).

66. On the rebuilding, see SHA.Severus 23; *CIL* 6.896, 935, 938, 1031, 1034. On the marble plan, see the Stanford Digital Forma Urbis Romae Project, https://formaurbis .stanford.edu/docs/FURmap.html, accessed February 6, 2025. On the coin, *RIC* 3.Severus 288. On the games, Herodian 3.8.10.

67. Cassius Dio 76.9; Herodian 3.8.5, 3.9.9–11.

68. *CIL* 14.4380.

69. Cassius Dio 76.15.1.

70. Herodian 3.10.7.

71. Herodian 3.10.8.

72. Herodian 3.11–12.12.

73. Herodian 3.14.9–15.1.

74. Cassius Dio 77.15.2.

75. Cassius Dio 78.2.3.

Chapter 20. Caracalla's Empire of Romans

1. Herodian 4.4.4.

2. Herodian 4.4.5.

3. Herodian 4.4.7; Cassius Dio 78.3.2.

4. SHA.Caracalla 2.9–11; Herodian 4.5.2.

5. Cassius Dio 78.12.6.

6. Herodian 4.5.7.

7. Herodian 4.3.2–4.

8. Ando, *Imperial Rome*, 51; Cassius Dio 78.2.6.

9. Cassius Dio 78.3.4; Herodian 4.6.1; SHA.Caracalla 3.3–4.9.

10. Herodian 4.6.3; cf. SHA.Caracalla 3.8, 4.8.

11. Cassius Dio 78.4–5; SHA.Caracalla 4.1–10.

12. *Papyrus Gissensis* 40.

13. Ando, *Imperial Rome*, 57; Gilliam, "Dura Rosters and the 'Constitutio Antoniniana,'" *Historia* 14 (1965): 74–92.

14. The best holistic reading of this document is A. Bryen, "Reading the Citizenship Papyrus (P. Giss. 40)," in *Citizenship and Empire in Europe, 200–1900*, ed. C. Ando (Stuttgart, 2016), 29–44.

15. These translations follow those of Bryen, "Reading the Citizenship Papyrus," 33.

16. O. Irshai, "How Do the Nations Relate to Israel? Rabbis, the Conversion of the Goyim, and the *Constitutio Antoniniana*," in *In the Crucible of Empire: The Impact of Roman Citizenship Upon Greeks, Jews and Christians*, ed. K. Berthelot and J. Price (Leuven, 2019), 165–180, at 175–177.

17. Sifre Deuteronomy 344, 401; y. Baba Qamma 4:3 (4b) and b. Baba Qamma 38a. For discussion, see Irshai, "How Do the Nations Relate to Israel?," 172.

18. Irshai, "How Do the Nations Relate to Israel?," 178–179.

19. Cassius Dio 78.9.4–5.

20. C. Davenport, "Cassius Dio and Caracalla," *Classical Quarterly* 62 (2012): 797–800, 809.

21. Cassius Dio 78.15.3–7; Herodian 4.7.1, 4.8.3, 4.12.4.

22. Cassius Dio 78.13.6, 78.24.1; Herodian 4.7.7.

23. D. Potter, *The Roman Empire at Bay, AD 180–395*, 2nd ed. (London, 2014), 144.

24. Cassius Dio 78.22.1–78.23.3; Herodian 4.8.7–4.9.7.

25. Herodian 4.13.5; cf. Cassius Dio 79.4; SHA.Caracalla 7.1–2.

26. Cassius Dio 79.11.

27. Cassius Dio 79.30.2.

28. Cassius Dio 79.41.

29. Herodian 5.5.6.

30. Herodian 5.5.7–8; *RIC* 4b.Elagabalus 195.

31. Herodian 5.6.1–5 (quotes); Cassius Dio 80.9.1–4.

32. On his dancing, see Cassius Dio 80.13.3. On priestly dress, Cassius Dio 80.11.2. For similar comments, Herodian 5.5.3, 5.5.5–9; SHA.Elagabalus 26.1.

33. Cassius Dio 80.14.4 (makeup); see also Cassius Dio 80.13.1–4.

34. On his marriage to Hierocles and adultery fetish, see Cassius Dio 80.15.1–4. On Zoticus, Cassius Dio 80.16.1–6. On the vagina, Cassius Dio 80.16.6.

35. This is especially true when Cassius Dio tells many of the same types of anecdotes about Nero's relationship with Sporus (Cassius Dio 62.28.3).

36. Cassius Dio 80.11.1.

37. Cassius Dio 80.17.1–2; Herodian 5.6.1–4.

38. SHA.Alexander 3.1.

39. Herodian 5.6.4.

40. SHA.Alexander 34, 41.

41. Cassius Dio 80b.20; Herodian 5.8.4–10; SHA.Elagabalus 17.1–7; SHA.Alexander 15.2.

42. Herodian 6.1.2; Cassius Dio 80b.1–2.2; SHA.Alexander 15.6, 31.3. On Ulpian, see Potter, *Empire at Bay*, 158–163.

43. Cassius Dio 80b.2.2–3.

44. Cassius Dio 80b.4.1; Herodian 6.4.5. Although, see Potter, *Empire at Bay*, 222–225.

45. Potter, *Empire at Bay*, 166.

46. Herodian 6.5.1, 7.

47. Herodian 6.4.7.

48. Herodian 6.5.7–10. For analysis of the results, see Potter, *Empire at Bay*, 167.

49. Herodian 6.5.9.

50. Herodian 6.7.9.

51. Herodian 6.8.3–4.

52. Herodian 6.9.4–5.

53. SHA Lives of the Two Maximini 1.5, 2.6, 6.8; Herodian 7.1.1–2.

54. SHA Lives of the Two Maximini 4.1.

55. Potter, *Empire at Bay*, 168–169.

56. Herodian 7.9.1–11.

57. Herodian 7.10.1–8.

58. Herodian 8.5.8–9.

59. Herodian 8.8.8.

Chapter 21. The Third-Century Crisis

1. Potter, *Empire at Bay*, 237.

2. *RIC* 4c.Philip 69; Zosimus 1.19; SHA.3 Gordians 31.3, Eutropius, *Brev.* 9.2.3.

3. *RIC* 4c.Philip.25, 40b, 70.

4. SHA.3 Gordians 33.1.

5. D. L. Bomgardner, *The Story of the Roman Amphitheater* (London, 2001), 215; Augustus, *RG* 22.

6. SHA.3 Gordians 33.1.

7. D. Kehoe, *Law and the Rural Economy in the Roman Empire* (Ann Arbor, MI, 2007), 59–62. On habitat loss and its effect on Mediterranean mammals, see G. Barham, "Echoes of Extinction: Analyzing the Impact of Classical Civilizations on the Sardinian Pika, Greek Lion, and North African Elephant" (Undergraduate Honors Thesis, University of California, San Diego, 2025).

8. Zosimus 1.19.2; Potter, *Empire at Bay*, 238.

9. *Codex Justinianus* (hereafter *CJ*), 2.26.3; Potter, *Empire at Bay*, 239.

10. Zosimus 1.20–21.

11. *Sibylline Oracles* 13.82.

12. J. B. Rives, "The Decree of Decius and the Religion of Empire," *Journal of Roman Studies* 89 (1999): 137n13.

13. Pliny, *Ep.* 10.97.

14. Eusebius, *Historia ecclesiastica* 6.41.11–13. This and the multiple other ecclesiastical histories by different Roman authors will be abbreviated *HE* subsequently.

15. Dexippus fr. 26.7–10; C. Davenport and C. Mallan, "Dexippus' 'Letter of Decius,'" *Museum Helveticum* 70 (2013): 57–73.

16. Zosimus 1.23; Zonaras 12.20.

17. Harper, *Fate of Rome*, 136–139; Zosimus 1.36; SHA.Gallieni 5.5; Eusebius, *HE* 7.21.

18. *Res Gestae Divi Saporis* 9–17.

19. *Sibylline Oracles* 13.119–129, trans. Potter; Potter, *Empire at Bay*, 243–245.

20. SHA.Valerian 5–7; SHA.3 Gordians 9.7.

21. Potter, *Empire at Bay*, 248.

22. *RIC* 5a.Valerian.71–74, 121, 190, 251–253, 285.

23. Eusebius, *HE* 7.10–12; *Acta Proconsularia Sancti Cypriani* 1.1–6.

24. Cyprian, *Liber de lapsis* 5–6.

25. Lactantius, *De mortibus persecutorum* (*DMP* hereafter), 5.

26. Potter, *Empire at Bay*, 256, following SHA.2 Gallieni 1.3.

27. SHA.30 Tyrants 9.1, 10.1.

28. Zosimus 1.38.2; SHA.30 Tyrants 3.9; Aurelius Victor, *De Caesaribus* (hereafter *De Caes.*), 33.8; Eutropius, *Brev.* 9.9; J. Drinkwater, *The Gallic Empire* (Stuttgart, 1987), 24–28.

29. *AE* 1993 1231.

30. N. Andrade, *Zenobia* (Oxford, 2019), 127–132; D. Potter, *Prophecy and History in the Crisis of the Roman Empire* (Oxford, 1990), 381–394.

31. Zonaras 12.24.

32. Zosimus 1.39.2; SHA.Gallienus 10.3–6, 12.1; *Sibylline Oracles* 13.155–171; Potter, *Prophecy*, 341–346.

33. John of Antioch, fr. 152.2 (Odaenathus); Zosimus 1.41; Zonaras 26.1 (Postumus).

34. Potter, *Empire at Bay*, 267–268.

35. *RIC* 5a. Aurelian 381; Potter, *Empire at Bay*, 263.

36. Zosimus 1.42; SHA.Aurelian 18.1; SHA.Claudius 6–9, 11.3–4, 11.6–9, 12.1.

37. On the reign of Quintillus, see Zosimus 1.47; Potter, *Empire at Bay*, 268.

38. Zosimus 1.48–49.1; Potter, *Empire at Bay*, 269.

39. On the mint worker revolt, see Eutropius, *Brev.* 9.14. On the "tsunami," Ammianus 30.8.8. On the killing of senators, SHA.Aurelian 21.5–7; Aurelius Victor, *De Caes.* 35.6; Ps. Aurelius Victor, *Epit. de Caes.* 35.4; Zosimus 1.49.2.

40. SHA.Aurelian 32.1–3; SHA.Firmus 3.1.

41. SHA.Aurelian 25.2–5.

42. Zosimus 1.54.2–55.3.

43. SHA.Aurelian 33.3; SHA.30 Tyrants 24.1–2; Eutropius, *Brev.* 9.13; Drinkwater, *Gallic Empire*, 42–43, 90–91.

44. Ps. Aurelius Victor, *Epit. de Caes.* 35.2.

45. SHA.Aurelian 34.2–3.

46. On Zenobia, see SHA.30 Tyrants 30.27. On Tetricus I and II, Aurelius Victor, *De Caes.* 35.5; Ps. Aurelius Victor, *Epit. de Caes.* 35.7; Eutropius, *Brev.* 9.13.

47. SHA.Aurelian 50.5; SHA.Tacitus 1.1–2.6.

48. Ps. Aurelius Victor, *Epit. de Caes.* 35.1.

49. Ps. Aurelius Victor, *Epit. de Caes.* 35.5.

50. Andrade, *Zenobia*, 217.

51. G. Fowden, "City and Mountain in Late Roman Attica," *Journal of Hellenic Studies* 108 (1988): 53.

52. On Senlis, see M. Durand, *La muraille antique de Senlis* (Beauvais, 2005).

53. Eutropius, *Brev.* 9.15.

54. Zosimus 1.62.

55. On the interregnum, see Aurelius Victor, *De Caes.* 35.10–13; Ps. Aurelius Victor, *Epit. de Caes.* 35.10; SHA.Tacitus 1.1–2.6. For quotes, SHA.Tacitus 2.5–6. On Severina, *RIC* 5a, pp. 253–254.

56. Eutropius, *Brev.* 9.16; SHA.Tacitus 13.5.

Chapter 22. Diocletian, Constantine, and the Foundations of a New Roman State

1. Zosimus 1.66–71; SHA.Aurelian 13.5; Carus 8.1; Zonaras 12.29–30; Eutropius, *Brev.* 9.14; Festus, *Breviarium* 24.
2. Aurelius Victor, *De Caes.* 39.12.
3. On the rationale for the tetrarchic model, see Aurelius Victor, *De Caes.* 39.19–22.
4. S. Corcoran, *The Empire of the Tetrarchs*, 2nd ed. (Oxford, 2000).
5. C. Kelly, "Bureaucracy and Government," in *The Cambridge Companion to the Age of Constantine*, ed. N. Lenski (Cambridge, 2006), 185–187.
6. Lactantius, *DMP* 7.4.
7. P. Heather, "New Men for New Constantines?," in *New Constantines*, ed. P. Magdalino (Aldershot, 1994), 18–21.
8. *Theodosian Code* (hereafter *CTh*) 14.9.1.
9. L. Depuydt, "AD 297 as the Beginning of the First Indiction Cycle," *Bulletin of the American Society of Papyrologists* 24 (1987): 137–139.
10. K. Harl, *Coinage in the Roman Economy* (Baltimore, 1997), 148–151. On further modification, see Potter, *Empire at Bay*, 385–386.
11. Harl, *Coinage*, 3.
12. Lactantius, *DMP* 12.3.
13. *Papyri Fiorentini* 171; *Oxyrhynchus Papyri* (hereafter *P. Oxy*), 1357. The most prominent Christian at court was Lactantius, who served as a tutor to the sons of Constantius and Maximian. For others see Eusebius, *HE* 8.1.4, 8.6.2–4; Lactantius, *DMP* 15.2.
14. Eusebius, *HE* 8.2.3–4, 8.6.8; Lactantius, *DMP* 13.1; Potter, *Empire at Bay*, 337; Corcoran, *Empire of the Tetrarchs*, 179–181.
15. Lactantius, *DMP* 15.1–7; Eusebius, *HE* 8.6–13; Athanasius, *Life of Antony* 46.
16. *P. Oxy.* 2673.
17. Lactantius, *DMP* 33–34.
18. Lactantius, *DMP* 18–20; Eutropius, *Brev.* 9.27.1; Potter, *Empire at Bay*, 340–341.
19. Potter, *Empire at Bay*, 662n36.
20. Lactantius, *DMP* 24.5–8; *Anonymous Valesianus*, pt. 1 = *Origo Constantini* 2.4; *XII Panegyrici Latini* (henceforth *Pan. Lat.*), 7 (6).5.3.
21. Lactantius, *DMP* 25.3–5.
22. Zosimus 2.9.2.
23. Lactantius, *DMP* 23.6.
24. Potter, *Empire at Bay*, 346–350.
25. Eusebius, *Vita Constantini* (*VC* hereafter), 1.26.
26. Zosimus 2.12.1–3.
27. Lactantius, *DMP* 29.8.
28. *Pan. Lat.* 12.3.3; Potter, *Empire at Bay*, 357.
29. Eusebius, *VC* 1.27.
30. Eusebius, *VC* 1.29; cf. Lactantius, *DMP* 44.5–6; *Pan. Lat.* 6 (7).21.3–7.
31. Eusebius, *VC* 1.29.
32. Potter, *Empire at Bay*, 357.
33. For an attempt to explain this failure, see Lactantius, *DMP* 44.

Chapter 23. Constantine's Invention of the Christian Roman Empire

1. *ILS* 694.
2. Lactantius, *DMP* 45.1, 48.1; Eusebius, *HE* 10.5.4. On Constantia's Christianity, see Jerome, *Ep.* 133; Rufinus, *HE* 1.11; Philostorgius, *HE* 1.9.

3. Lactantius, *DMP* 46.6. For discussion, see Potter, *Empire at Bay*, 366.

4. Eusebius, *HE* 9.11.9.

5. Eusebius, *HE* 10.5.1; Lactantius, *DMP* 48; D. Potter, *Constantine the Emperor* (Oxford, 2012), 172–182, 193–203.

6. *RIC* 7.Rome 51–58, 63–77, 97–103, 129–244.

7. Zosimus 2.20–28.

8. On this date, see Potter, *Empire at Bay*, 381.

9. Zosimus 2.30.4.

10. A. Kaldellis, *The New Roman Empire* (Oxford, 2024), 166.

11. S. Bassett, "The Antiquities in the Hippodrome at Constantinople," *Dumbarton Oaks Papers* 45 (1991): 87–96; P. Stephenson, *The Serpent Column* (Oxford, 2016).

12. Zosimus 2.31–32; Themistius, *Or.* 3.47c–48a; P. Heather and D. Moncur, *Politics, Philosophy, and Empire in the Fourth Century* (Liverpool, 2001), 134n278.

13. The "Letter to the Eastern Provincials" is reproduced by Eusebius at *VC* 2.24–42 and partially preserved in *P. London* 878. See T. D. Barnes, *Constantine: Dynasty, Religion, and Power in the Later Roman Empire* (Malden, MA, 2011), 108.

14. Eusebius, *VC* 2.28–42.

15. Eusebius, *VC* 2.46.

16. A. Gotthard, *Der Augsburger Religionsfrieden* (Münster, 2004).

17. R. Williams, *Arius* (Cambridge, 1987), 48–81.

18. Epiphanius, *Panarion*, 3.153.16; Socrates Scholasticus, *HE* 5.22.

19. R. Gregg, "Review of Williams, Arius," *Journal of Theological Studies* 40 (1989): 252.

20. Arius, *Thalia* (in Athanasius, *De synodis Arimini*, 15.3.6).

21. E.g., Galatians 4.3–7.

22. Arius, *Thalia*, in Athanasius, *Orationes tres*, 26.20.44–21.3.

23. Eusebius, *VC* 3.12.

24. Eusebius, *VC* 3.9, counts 250 bishops, but the conventional number is 318 (Athanasius, *Ad Afros* 2).

25. Socrates Scholasticus, *HE* 1.8; Rufinus, *HE* 10.5.

26. Socrates Scholasticus, *HE* 1.9.

27. On the oration, see J. Schott, *Christianity, Empire and the Making of Religion in Late Antiquity* (Philadelphia, 2008), 113–117.

28. Constantine, "Oration to the Assembly of the Saints," 22.

29. On the number of Christians, see R. Bagnall, "Religious Conversion and Onomastic Change in Early Byzantine Egypt," *Bulletin of the American Society of Papyrologists* 19 (1982): 105–124; R. Stark, *The Rise of Christianity* (Princeton, NJ, 1996), 11–13.

30. Eusebius, *VC* 2.4–5.

31. Eusebius, *VC* 2.60.

32. Eusebius, *VC* 3.54; Potter, *Constantine*, 276.

33. Zosimus 4.36; *CTh* 16.10.1; *CIL* 11.5265; Potter, *Constantine*, 281.

34. J. Baillet, *Inscriptions grecques et latines des Tombeaux des Rois Syringes à Thebes* (Cairo, 1920–1926), no. 1265; G. Fowden, "Nicagoras of Athens and the Lateran Obelisk," *Journal of Hellenic Studies* 107 (1987), 51–57.

35. Photius, *Bibliotheca*, Codex 62; Barnes, *Constantine*, 195–197.

Chapter 24. Constantius II, Julian, and the Challenges of Making Rome Christian

1. On their deaths and suspected adultery, see Zosimus 2.29; Philostorgius, *HE* 2.4; Zonaras 13.2.38–41. For discussion, D. Woods, "On the Death of the Empress Fausta," *Greece and Rome* 45 (1998): 70–86.

2. Ammianus 16.10; Symmachus, *Relationes* 3.7.

3. Heather and Moncur, *Politics, Philosophy, and Empire*, 117; Ammianus 16.10.

4. Themistius *Or.* 3.42d, 3.45b.

5. G. Dagron, *Naissance d'une capitale* (Paris, 1974), 213–239; Heather and Moncur, *Politics, Philosophy, and Empire*, 122–123.

6. Athanasius, *Festal Letter* 4.5, 8; Athanasius, *Defense Against the Arians* 60.4, 86–87; Festal Letters, Index 3; Sozomen, *HE* 2.25.

7. Socrates Scholasticus, *HE* 1.38; E. Muehlberger, "The Legend of Arius's Death," *Past and Present* 227 (2015): 3–29.

8. Philostorgius, *HE* 3.14.

9. Socrates Scholasticus, *HE* 2.30–41.

10. Athanasius, *Arian History* 81.

11. Philostorgius, *HE* 2.5.

12. *Letter of Auxentius* 39 [61], in P. J. Heather and J. Matthews, *The Goths in the Fourth Century* (Liverpool, 1991), 142.

13. *Letter of Auxentius* 28 [47], in Heather and Matthews, *Goths in the Fourth Century*, 138.

14. Heather and Matthews, *Goths in the Fourth Century*, 126–132.

15. Maternus, *De errore*, 16.4, 20.7.

16. *CTh* 16.10.4, 16.10.6. On sacrifices continuing see Ammianus 19.12. On implementation, S. Bradbury, "Constantine and Anti-Pagan Legislation in the Fourth Century," *Classical Philology* 89 (1994): 137.

17. *CTh* 16.10.3; Rufinus, *HE* 11.22; Sozomen, *HE* 7.15.

18. Ammianus 14.7, 14.11; J. Matthews, *The Roman Empire of Ammianus*, 2nd ed. (Ann Arbor, MI, 2007), 406–408.

19. Julian, *Misopogon* 252a–254c; Eunapius, *Lives of the Sophists and Philosophers* (hereafter *VS*), 473–474.

20. Eunapius, *VS* 475.

21. Eunapius, *VS* 476.

22. Ammianus 16.12; Zosimus 3.3.

23. Julian, *Or.* 2; see S. Elm, *Sons of Hellenism* (Oakland, 2012), 63.

24. Ammianus 20.4; cf. Libanius, *Or.* 12.58–61; Julian, *Letter to the Athenians* 279.

25. For discussion, see Elm, *Sons of Hellenism*, 63.

26. Zosimus 3.8.3; Ammianus 20.4; Matthews, *Roman Empire of Ammianus*, 93–103.

27. Ammianus 20.4.14; Libanius, *Or.* 12.61, 13.33; Julian, *Letter to the Athenians* 279–282; Potter, *Roman Empire at Bay*, 502–506.

28. Julian, *Letter to the Athenians* 270–272, 276; Ammianus 21.8.

29. Ammianus 21.7.3.

30. Ammianus 20.5; Julian, *To the Cynic Heraclius*, 231B–234C; Julian, *Letter to the Athenians* 272, 284.

31. Ammianus 22.5; Eunapius, *VS* 473.

32. Julian, *Ep.* 60; Misopogon 346B; Rufinus, *HE* 11.22.

33. Julian, *Letter to a Priest* 288D, 290D, 291C; Julian, *Ep.* 62–63. For discussion, see Elm, *Sons of Hellenism*, 321–324.

34. Julian, *Misopogon* 362a–b.

35. E. Watts, *City and School in Late Antique Athens and Alexandria* (Berkeley, 2006).

36. *CTh* 13.3.5.

37. Julian, *Ep.* 42.

38. Julian, *Ep.* 42.

39. Julian, *Misopogon* 368D–370A; Elm, *Sons of Hellenism*, 271–273.

40. Julian, *Misopogon* 360D.

41. Ammianus 22.10.7; Gregory Nazianzen *Or.* 4.1.

42. Ammianus 24.7.

43. Ammianus 25.5–7; Themistius, *Or.* 5.65b–67a; Heather and Moncur, *Politics, Philosophy, and Empire*, 150–152.

Chapter 25. The Sack of Rome

1. Themistius, *Or.* 5.67c–70c; *CTh* 13.3.6.

2. Eutropius, *Brev.* 10.18; Ammianus 25.10.13; Sozomen, *HE* 6.6.

3. Ammianus 26.4.

4. In 378–379, Gratian effectively ran the empire as a sole Augustus, but his brother Valentinian II also had the title. The same is true in 394–395, when Theodosius I effectively ruled alone but shared the title of Augustus with his sons Arcadius and Honorius.

5. On the bonuses, see Ammianus 24.3, 30.8; Libanius, *Or.* 18.168–170; Zosimus 3.13. On taxes, Eunapius, *History* fr. 31; Libanius, *Ep.* 1184–1186, 1436, 1439. On properties, *CTh* 5.13.3, 10.1.8; *AE* 1906 30. On debts, Ammianus 26.6.7. On ingots, *CTh* 12.6.12. On Procopius, Ammianus 26.6–9; Themistius, *Or.* 7.91a–c; Philostorgius *HE* 9.5; Zosimus 4.8.

6. Ausonius, *Mosella* 454–460; Ammianus 30.6–10; Zosimus 4.19; Ps. Aurelius Victor, *Epit. de Caes.* 46.10.

7. Ammianus 28.1.57, 30.10; E. Watts, *Final Pagan Generation* (Oakland, 2015), 169–173.

8. Ammianus 31.3–4; Eunapius, *History* fr. 42; Socrates Scholasticus, *HE* 4.34; Sozomen, *HE* 6.37; M. Kulikowski, *Rome's Gothic Wars* (Cambridge, 2007), 123–138.

9. P. Heather, *Goths and Romans, 332–489* (Oxford, 1991), 128–135.

10. Ammianus 31.4; Heather and Moncur, *Politics, Philosophy, and Empire*, 200; Kulikowski, *Rome's Gothic Wars*, 131–132.

11. Ammianus 31.4.

12. Ammianus 31.4–5.

13. Ammianus 31.6–8.

14. Ammianus 31.12.

15. Ammianus 31.12.

16. Ammianus 31.12–4; Theodoret, *HE* 4.32; Kulikowski, *Rome's Gothic Wars*, 139–143.

17. Socrates Scholasticus, *HE* 5.1; Ammianus 31.16. For discussion, see Heather and Moncur, *Politics, Philosophy, and Empire*, 205–207.

18. Philostorgius, *HE* 9.17.

19. On Gothic numbers, see P. Heather, *The Fall of the Roman Empire* (Oxford, 2005), 145, 507.

20. Themistius, *Or.* 14.181b.

21. Themistius, *Or.* 14.181b–c.

22. Heather and Moncur, *Politics, Philosophy, and Empire*, 207; Themistius, *Or.* 15.

23. Themistius, *Or.* 15.197b.

24. *CTh* 16.10.8.

25. Theodoret, *HE* 5.20–21. On the temple attacks, see Libanius, *Or.* 30; G. Fowden, "Bishops and Temples in the Eastern Roman Empire, AD 320–435," *Journal of Theological Studies* 29 (1979): 53–78.

26. Symmachus, *Relationes* 3; Ambrose, *Ep.* 17 and 18.

27. On the treaty, see Heather and Moncur, *Politics, Philosophy, and Empire*, 259–264; Kulikowski, *Rome's Gothic Wars*, 152–153. For the quote, Themistius, *Or.* 16.207b.

28. Gregory of Tours, *Historia Francorum* 1.43; *Chronica Minora* 1.646.7.

29. N. McLynn, *Ambrose of Milan* (Berkeley, 1994), 154.

30. On the status of Eugenius, see Socrates Scholasticus, *HE* 5.25 (grammarian); Zosimus 4.54.1 (rhetorician). For discussion, B. Croke, "Arbogast and the Death of Valentinian II," *Historia* 25 (1976): 235–244.

31. Zosmius 4.58.2–3; Socrates Scholasticus, *HE* 5.25.

32. For battle narratives, see F. Paschoud, ed., *Zosime: Histoire Nouvelle*, vol. 2.2 (Paris, 1979), 474–500; A. Cameron, *The Last Pagans of Rome* (Oxford, 2011), 93–131.

33. Rufinus, *HE* 11.33; Cameron, *Last Pagans*, 100–110.

34. John Chrysostom, *Patrologia Graeca* 63.491; Cameron, *Last Pagans*, 107–108.

35. C. Sogno, *Serena and Stilicho*, forthcoming.

36. Socrates Scholasticus, *HE* 7.10; Zosimus 5.5.4; Kulikowski, *Rome's Gothic Wars*, 165.

37. Claudian, *In Eutropium* 2.211–218. For discussion, see Kulikowski, *Rome's Gothic Wars*, 167.

38. Sozomen, *HE* 9.4.

39. Olympiodorus of Thebes, fr. 44.

40. M. Salzman, *The Falls of Rome* (Cambridge, 2021), 99.

41. Zosimus 5.35.

42. Zosimus 5.35–36.

43. Sozomen, *HE* 9.7; Olympiodorus of Thebes, fr. 7.3; Zosimus 5.38–41. For discussion, see Salzman, *Falls of Rome*, 102.

44. Sozomen, *HE* 9.7–8; Zosimus 5.41–45; Salzman, *Falls of Rome*, 102; Kulikowski, *Rome's Gothic Wars*, 173–174.

45. Philostorgius, *HE* 12.3–4.

46. Sozomen, *HE* 9.8.

47. Sozomen, *HE* 9.9; Philostorgius, *HE* 12.3. For discussion, see Kulikowski, *Rome's Gothic Wars*, 176–177.

48. Sozomen, *HE* 9.9.

49. Sozomen, *HE* 9.9.

50. Heather, *Fall of the Roman Empire*, 227.

51. Sozomen, *HE* 9.5.

Chapter 26. The End of the Roman West

1. Socrates Scholasticus, *HE* 5.20; Rufinus, *HE* 11.27–28; John Chrysostom, *in Babylam* 13; Ambrose, *Ep.* 18.23.

2. Symmachus, *Relationes* 3. For the "flaccid rhetorical denunciations," see Libanius. *Or.* 30.

3. *CTh* 16.10.19.3.

4. K. Harper, *Slavery in the Late Roman World* (Cambridge, 2011), 241–246, 463–493; J. A. Harrill, *The Manumission of Slaves in Early Christianity* (Tübingen, 1995).

5. On Galla Placidia, see Jordanes, *Getica* 160. On Attalus, Zosimus 6.12.3; Sozomen, *HE* 9.8.11. On the return of Attalus and Galla, Olympiodorus of Thebes, fr. 13; Philostorgius, *HE* 12.4–5; Orosius, *History Against the Pagans*, 7.42.9; H. Sivan, *Galla Placidia: The Last Roman Empress* (Oxford, 2011).

6. Olympiodorus of Thebes, fr. 10; *Gallic Chronicle of 452*, 69; Jordanes, *Getica* 157–158.

7. *Gallic Chronicle of 452*, 69; Olympiodorus of Thebes, fr. 19, 20, 22, 26; Sidonius Apollinaris, *Ep.* 5.9.1; Jordanes, *Getica* 164; P. Brown, *Through the Eye of a Needle* (Princeton, NJ, 2012), 391–392.

8. Philostorgius, *HE* 12.4–5; Olympiodorus of Thebes, fr. 26.2.

9. Heather, *Fall of the Roman Empire*, 242–243; Kulikowski, *Rome's Gothic Wars*, 183.

10. Hydatius, *Chronicle* (*Chron.* hereafter), 40.28. For discussion, see A. Merrills and R. Miles, *The Vandals* (Malden, MA, 2014), 46.

11. Olympiodorus of Thebes, fr. 38, 43.2. For discussion, see Heather, *Fall of the Roman Empire*, 258–261.

12. Hydatius, *Chron.* 41.6–8.

13. Hydatius, *Chron.* 41.6–8, 41.15; Quodvultdeus, *In Barbarian Times* 2.5; Merrills and Miles, *The Vandals*, 52–55; Heather, *Fall of the Roman Empire*, 267–289.

14. Hydatius, *Chron.* 41.12–14.

15. On the statue's base, see *CIL* 6.1724. On Merobaudes's commands, *CIL* 6.1724.9 (Gaul); Hydatius, *Chron.* 41.19 (Spain). For his oration, Merobaudes, *Panegyric* 1 fr. IIA.

16. Merobaudes, *Panegyric* 1 fr. Ia 9–14, fr. IIb, 20–24; Merobaudes, *Panegyric* 2.2–8.

17. See Heather, *Fall of the Roman Empire*, 301–304.

18. Priscus, fr. 9.3. For discussion, see Heather, *Fall of the Roman Empire*, 306–312.

19. Jordanes, *Getica* 195.

20. Jordanes, *Getica* 38.197–41.218.

21. Hydatius, *Chron.* 42.29.

22. Priscus, fr. 24.1; Theophanes 5946.

23. Heather, *Fall of the Roman Empire*, 351–384.

24. Heather, *Fall of the Roman Empire*, 370.

25. Priscus, fr. 30, lines 18–21.

26. Merrills and Miles, *The Vandals*, 112–116.

27. Placidia may have already been engaged to the future western emperor Majorian before Aetius arranged her betrothal to Gaudentius. Sidonius Apollinaris, *Carmina* (*Carm.* hereafter), 5.203–206.

28. Priscus, fr. 30.

29. On the murder and aftermath, see Priscus, fr. 30, lines 58–72. On the army being frozen around him, Hydatius, *Chron.* 42.31.

30. Priscus, fr. 30, 72–82.

31. On the engagement and its context, see J. Conant, *Staying Roman: Conquest and Identity in Africa and the Mediterranean, 439–700* (Cambridge, 2012), 23–29.

32. Priscus, fr. 30, 91–100. See also Hydatius, *Chron.* 42.31. For discussion, see Salzman, *Falls of Rome*, 153.

33. Prosper, *Chronicle* s.a. 455, from Salzman, *Falls of Rome*, 148; Procopius, *Wars* 3.5.3–4.

34. Priscus, fr. 32; cf. Sidonius Apollinaris, *Carm.* 7.399–434; Salzman, *Falls of Rome*, 159–162.

35. There were four western interregna between 456 and 473: October 456 until April 457; August to November 461; August 465 until April 467; and November 472 to March 473.

36. On Syagrius, see Gregory of Tours, *History of the Franks* 2.27.

37. Procopius, *Wars* 5.1.4–8; Ennodius, *Life of Epiphanius* (hereafter *VE*), 95–100; *Anonymous Valesianus* (*Anon. Val.* hereafter), 8.37–38; Eugippius, *Vita Sancti Severini* 4; Marcellinus Comes, *Chronicle* s.a. 476; Jordanes, *Getica* 242; Jordanes, *Romana* 344. For discussion, see B. Croke, "A.D. 476: The Manufacture of a Turning Point," *Chiron* 13 (1983): 81–119.

38. Malchus, fr. 14; *Anon. Val.* 12.64.

39. Marcellinus Comes, *Chronicle* 476.2.

Chapter 27. Western Romans Outside the Roman State

1. Gregory of Tours, *Glory of the Martyrs*, 12, quoted in Brown, *Eye of a Needle*, 395.

2. Fredegar, *Chronicle* 3.7; Brown, *Eye of a Needle*, 397.

3. Hydatius, *Chron.* 44.4 (Majorian).

4. *Pan. Lat.* 10.4.3; Eutropius, *Brev.* 9.20; Aurelius Victor, *De Caes.* 39.12; Potter, *Empire at Bay*, 281.

5. Zosimus 6.3.

6. *Chronicle of 452*, a.c. 435, following the edition of R. Burgess, "The Gallic Chronicle of 452," in *Society and Culture in Late Antique Gaul*, ed. R. W. Mathisen and D. Shanzer (Abingdon, 2017), 52–84, at 78. For discussion, see Brown, *Eye of a Needle*, 403–404.

7. Hydatius, *Chron.* 41.17, 41.19.

8. Salvian, *De gubernatione Dei* 5.6.

9. On the Council of Angers in 453, see C. Munier, ed., *Concilia Galliae, a. 314–506* (Turnhout, 1963), 138. For more discussion, see R. W. Mathisen, *Roman Aristocrats in Barbarian Gaul* (Austin, 1993), 79.

10. "Historic England Research Records," Heritage Gateway, www.heritagegateway.org.uk/Gateway/Results_Single.aspx?uid=1089343&resourceID=19191, accessed on May 22, 2023.

11. *CTH* 15.1.32 = *Breviarium* 15.1.2, trans. C. Pharr. For discussion, see J. Matthews, *Laying Down the Law* (New Haven, CT, 2000).

12. Pliny, *Ep.* 10.17, 10.37.3, 10.39.6.

13. Sidonius Apollinaris, *Carm.* 5.553–557; Hydatius, *Chron.* 45.1. For discussion, see Mathisen, *Roman Aristocrats*, 126.

14. Mathisen, *Roman Aristocrats*, 126–127; Sidonius Apollinaris, *Ep.* 8.16.13–18.

15. Sidonius Apollinaris, *Ep.* 8.3.3, 8.16.13–8; Mathisen, *Roman Aristocrats*, 126–129; J. Harries, "Not the Theodosian Code: Euric's Law and Late Fifth-Century Gaul," in Mathisen, *Society and Culture in Late Antique Gaul*, 48–50.

16. On his family background, see Sidonius Apollinaris, *Ep.* 1.3.1. On his panegyrics, Sidonius Apollinaris, *Carm.* 6 and 7. On the statue, Sidonius Apollinaris, *Carm.* 8.7–8; Sidonius Apollinaris, *Ep.* 9.16.

17. Sidonius Apollinaris, *Ep.* 1.9.6.

18. Sidonius Apollinaris, *Ep.* 3.1.2; Gregory of Tours, *Historia Francorum* 2.21.

19. Sidonius Apollinaris, *Ep.* 9.3.3.

20. Sidonius Apollinaris, *Ep.* 9.12.1.

21. Sidonius Apollinaris, *Carm.* 9.302–317.

22. Avitus of Vienne, *Ep.* 24, 36.

23. Gregory of Tours, *Historia Francorum* 3.2.

24. Victor of Vita, *History of the Vandal Persecution* 1.5; J. Conant, "Europe and the North African Cult of the Saints, Circa 350–900," *Speculum* 85 (2010): 1–3.

25. Aeneas of Gaza, *Theophrastus* 66.15–67.10.

26. A. Chastagnol, *Le Sénat romain sous le règne d'Odoacre* (Bonn, 1966), 52–56.

27. Eugippius, *Vita Sancti Severini* 44.

28. On Zeno's portrait, see *Anon. Val.* 9.44. On coins, *RIC* 10.3601–3667.

29. John of Antioch, fr. 214; *Anon. Val.* 10.48.

30. *Anon. Val.* 11.49; Procopius, *Wars* 6.6.10–11.

31. John of Antioch, fr. 214a.

32. *Anon. Val.* 12.55, 57, 60; John of Antioch, fr. 214a; Agnellus of Ravenna 39; Procopius, *Wars* 6.6.24.

33. Procopius, *Wars* 5.1.24; *Anon. Val.* 12.60.

34. Ennodius, *VE* 101–105; *CIL* 6.31957.

35. On the Gallic campaign, see J. Arnold, *Theoderic and the Roman Imperial Restoration* (Cambridge, 2014), 262–294. On the protectorate over Spain, Procopius, *Wars* 5.12.54–57.

36. Procopius, *Wars* 6.6.26.

37. Procopius, *Wars* 6.6.29.

38. On Trajan, see *Anon. Val.* 60. On Cato, Ennodius, *Panegyric of Theoderic* (hereafter *PanThe*), 60–69.

39. Ennodius, *PanThe* 58–69, 79.

40. Cassiodorus, *Variae* 1.46.

41. *Anon. Val.* 12.60.

42. Procopius, *Wars* 6.6.29.

43. *Anon. Val.* 12.64. For discussion, see Arnold, *Theoderic*, 70–71.

44. A. Sarantis, "War and Diplomacy in Pannonia and the Northwest Balkans During the Reign of Justinian," *Dumbarton Oaks Papers* 63 (2009): 21–22.

45. Procopius, *Wars* 6.6.32–34.

46. S. Bjornlie, *Politics and Tradition Between Rome, Ravenna, and Constantinople* (Cambridge, 2013), 138–141.

47. Priscian, *In laudem*, 239–245; Lydus, *De magistratibus* 3.28.4.

48. *Anon. Val.* 86–87.

Chapter 28. The Roman Christian Empire of the East in the Fifth Century

1. Socrates Scholasticus, *HE* 6.6; Sozomen, *HE* 8.4.

2. Sozomen, *HE* 8.4.

3. On the column, see J. F. Matthews, "Viewing the Column of Arcadius in Constantinople," in *Shifting Cultural Frontiers in Late Antiquity*, ed. D. Brakke, D. Deliyannis, and E. Watts (Aldershot, 2012), 212–223. On the date, see Theophanes 5895.

4. F. Trombley, *Hellenic Religion and Christianization*, vol. 2 (Leiden, 2001), 247–316.

5. *CTh* 16.10.12.2.

6. *CTh* 16.10.19.3.

7. Rufinus, *HE* 11.27–28; *Storia della Chiesa di Alessandria*, vol. 2, 14.10–16.2; Sozomen, *HE* 7.15; E. Watts, *Riot in Alexandria* (Berkeley, 2010), 196–198.

8. Maximus of Turin, *Sermon* 91.2.

9. Marinus, *Life of Proclus* 11 (private worship), 15 (intimidation), 29 (temple).

10. Libanius, *Or.* 22.4–7; John Chrysostom, *Homilies on the Statues* 3.7, 5.3, 8.4; Sozomen, *HE* 7.23; Zosimus 4.41; Theodoret, *HE* 5.20.

11. Libanius, *Or.* 22.29–31; Chrysostom, *Homilies on the Statues* 17.2.

12. Chrysostom, *Homilies on the Statues* 21.1, 21.6, 21.8–18.

13. Chrysostom, *Homilies on the Statues* 17.3.

14. Following the translation of P. Schaff, *A Select Library of Nicene and Post-Nicene Fathers of the Christian Church*, 2nd ser., vol. 14, *The Seven Ecumenical Councils* (New York, 1916), 178.

15. Palladius, *Dialogue on John Chrysostom* 5.

16. Socrates Scholasticus, *HE* 6.3.

17. Palladius, *Dialogue on John Chrysostom* 5; Socrates Scholasticus, *HE* 6.4.

18. Socrates Scholasticus, *HE* 6.3.

19. Socrates Scholasticus, *HE* 6.5; Sozomen, *HE* 8.7; John Chrysostom, *Contra Eutropium* 1 = PG 52.392.

20. S. Wessel, *Cyril of Alexandria and the Nestorian Controversy* (Oxford, 2004), 23–31.

21. Palladius, *Dialogue on John Chrysostom* 7–11; Socrates Scholasticus, *HE* 6.7, 6.9–18; Sozomen, *HE* 8.11–23.

22. Socrates Scholasticus, *HE* 6.18. For the speech itself, see John Chrysostom, *Patrologia Graeca* 54.485.

23. Palladius, *Dialogue on John Chrysostom* 10; Socrates Scholasticus, *HE* 6.18.

24. Socrates Scholasticus, *HE* 6.7–15; Sozomen, *HE* 8.9–19. For discussion, see Wessel, *Cyril of Alexandria*, 23–30.

25. Socrates Scholasticus, *HE* 7.15.

26. Socrates Scholasticus, *HE* 7.29.

27. Socrates Scholasticus, *HE* 7.32.

28. *Storia della Chiesa di Alessandria*, vol. 2, 46.20–27; Besa, *Life of Shenoute* 129.

29. Socrates Scholasticus, *HE* 7.34.

30. Socrates Scholasticus, *HE* 7.34.

31. Cyril, *Ep.* 39.

32. *Gesta Constantini* 527; *Acta Conciliorum Oecumenicorum* 2.1.1, 143.

33. *Acta Conciliorum Oecumenicorum* 2.1.1.858–862. For discussion, see M. Gaddis, *There Is No Crime for Those Who Have Christ* (Berkeley, 2005), 299–309.

34. Leo, *Ep.* 95; Cyril of Scythopolis, *Euthymius* 27 and *Sabas* 56.

35. Gaddis, *There Is No Crime*, 310–322.

36. E. Honigmann, "Juvenal of Jerusalem," *Dumbarton Oaks Papers* 5 (1950): 241–242.

37. *Acta Conciliorum Oecumenicorum* 2.1.2.125.

38. Zacharias Scholasticus, *HE* 3.1–5; Evagrius Scholasticus, *HE* 2.5; John Rufus, *Plerophories* 10, 21–22, 56; *Panegyric on Macarius of Tkow* 7–8.

39. *Panegyric on Macarius of Tkow* 15.5–8.

40. *Panegyric on Macarius of Tkow* 15.8; cf. *Synaxarion of the Coptic Church*, Baba 27.

41. *Panegyric on Macarius of Tkow* 16.1.
42. Zacharias Scholasticus, *HE* 5.7–8; Evagrius Scholasticus, *HE* 3.14; cf. Liberatus, *Breviarium causae Nestorianorum et Eutychianorum* 17.
43. Zacharias Scholasticus, *HE* 5.7; cf. Evagrius Scholasticus, *HE* 3.12.
44. Zacharias Scholasticus, *HE* 5.7.

Chapter 29. Anastasius, Justin I, and the Old Men at the End of the World

1. *CJ* 10.32.64; B. Croke, "Ariadne Augusta: Shaping the Identity of the Early Byzantine Empress," in *Roman Emperors in Context* (London, 2021), 153–168.
2. Croke, "Ariadne," 162–163.
3. Constantine VII Porphyrogenitus, *De Ceremoniis aulae Byzantinae* (*De Cer.* hereafter) 1.92.
4. Constantine VII Porphyrogenitus, *De Cer.* 1.92.
5. Constantine VII Porphyrogenitus, *De Cer.* 1.92.112–137; Ps. Zacharias, *Chronicle* (hereafter Ps. Zacharias) 7.13.
6. M. Meier, *Das andere Zeitalter Justinians* (Göttingen, 2003), 16–21.
7. John Rufus, *Plerophories* 17, 20, 88–89.
8. D. Sear, *Byzantine Coins and Their Values* (London, 1974), 12–25.
9. Lydus, *De magistratibus* 3.51; Procopius, *Anecdota* (*Anec.* hereafter) 19.5.
10. Evagrius Scholasticus, *HE* 3.33.
11. Ps. Zacharias 7.7–8; Theophanes 6002; Zacharias Scholasticus, *Vita Severi* 103–108.
12. Evagrius Scholasticus, *HE* 3.32–33; Ps. Zacharias 7.10.
13. Evagrius Scholasticus, *HE* 3.44; Malalas 16.18; Theophanes 6005; Theodore Lector, *HE* 508.
14. Evagrius Scholasticus, *HE* 4.1; Ps. Zacharias 7.14.
15. Constantine VII Porphyrogenitus, *De Cer.* 1.93. For discussion, see B. Croke, "Justinian Under Justin: Reconfiguring a Reign," in Croke, *Roman Emperors in Context*, 172–173.
16. Evagrius Scholasticus, *HE* 4.2.
17. Ps. Zacharias 7.14, 8.1; Malalas 17.1; Procopius, *Anec.* 6.11–16.
18. Constantine VII Porphyrogenitus, *Excerpta de insidiis* 43, following a lost portion of Malalas 17.2. For discussion, see A. A. Vasiliev, *Justin the First* (Cambridge, MA, 1950), 136–160.
19. Malalas 17.5; Ps. Zacharias 8.2; Evagrius Scholasticus, *HE* 4.3; Theophanes 6011.
20. Evagrius Scholasticus, *HE* 4.4; Theophanes 6011; Ps. Zacharias 8.2.
21. Ps. Zacharias 8.2; Victor Tonnenensis, *Chronicon* 103; Theophanes 6012; Evagrius Scholasticus, *HE* 4.3; Malalas 17.8; Procopius, *Anec.* 6.28. For discussion, see Croke, "Justinian Under Justin."
22. Croke, "Justinian Under Justin," 173.
23. Croke, "Justinian Under Justin," 192–194.
24. Victor Tonnenensis, *Chronicon* 109; Sear, *Byzantine Coins*, 114–133.
25. Procopius, *Wars* 1.11.6–7; Theophanes 6013.
26. Procopius, *Wars* 1.11.18. For discussion, see G. Greatrex, *Rome and Persia at War* (Leeds, 1998), 135n43.
27. Procopius, *Wars* 1.11.16. For discussion, see Croke, "Justinian Under Justin," 195.

28. Procopius, *Wars* 1.11.30.

29. On the cost of Persian peace, see Procopius, *Wars* 1.22.19; Malalas 18.56.

Chapter 30. Justinian

1. *Institutes* 3.2.

2. T. Honore, *Tribonian* (London, 1978), 22.

3. *CJ, De emendatione* 1.

4. *CJ, De Iustiniano Codice Confirmando*, Pro. 2.

5. *CJ* 1.1.5.1 and 2.

6. *CJ* 1.1.6.1–6, 1.1.7.6–11.

7. *CJ* 1.5.18.1.

8. Malalas 18.47.

9. *CJ* 1.11.9.1.

10. *CJ* 1.5.18.5 (pretense), 1.5.18.10 (investigation).

11. Malalas 18.35.

12. Agathias 2.30.3–4.

13. Simplicius, *In Enchiridion* 32.65.35.

14. Agathias 2.31.2–4.

15. *Chronicon Paschale* (*CP* hereafter) 622; Malalas 18.71; Procopius, *De aedificiis* (*Aed.* hereafter) 1.20–22.

16. *CP* 507, 622–628; Malalas 475.11–16.

17. *CP* 623–624.

18. *CP* 624.

19. Malalas 18.71.

20. Procopius, *Wars* 1.24.32–37.

21. Procopius, *Wars* 1.24.51.

22. *CP* 627–628.

23. For casualty estimates, see Malchus, fr. 46; *CP* 627; Lydus, *De magistratibus* 3.70; Ps. Zacharias 9.14.

24. *CP* 627–628.

25. Procopius, *Aed.* 1.23.

26. Procopius, *Aed.* 1.27–28.

27. Paul the Silentiary, *Description of Hagia Sophia* 605–615, 682–719.

28. Romanus the Melode, *Hymn* 54.25.

29. Ps. Zacharias 9.15–16.

30. *CP* 630–633; *CJ* 1.1.6. For discussion, see F. Millar, "Rome, Constantinople, and the Near Eastern Church Under Justinian: Two Synods of C.E. 536," *Journal of Roman Studies* 98 (2008): 69.

31. John of Ephesus, *Lives* 2, in *Patrologia Orientalis*, 17:18–35. For discussion, see S. Harvey, *Asceticism and Society in Crisis* (Berkeley, 1990), 84–86.

32. D. Potter, *Theodora: Actress, Empress, Saint* (Oxford, 2015), 176.

33. Merrills and Miles, *The Vandals*, 196–223; Procopius, *Wars* 4.5.8; Aeneas of Gaza, *Theophrastus* 66.15–67.1; Ps. Zacharias 9.17.

34. Procopius, *Wars* 5.3.14–18.

35. Marcellinus Comes 476.2.

36. Procopius, *Wars* 3.16.3, 3.20.17.

37. Procopius, *Wars* 4.9.

38. Procopius, *Wars* 4.9.12–14.

39. Procopius, *Wars* 4.5.11–25.

40. Procopius, *Wars* 5.14.14.

41. Cassiodorus, *Variae* 12.25; Michael the Syrian 9.26.296; John Lydus, *On Portents* 9c.

42. Procopius, *Wars* 2.23–24; Ps. Zacharias, 10.9; Evagrius Scholasticus, *HE* 4.29.

43. Justinian, Edict 7, preface.

44. Corippus, *In laudem Iustini* 11.

45. Procopius, *Wars* 7.17.12–14.

46. Procopius, *Wars* 6.21.39–40.

47. Procopius, *Anec.* 12.

48. Justinian, *Novellae* 15.

Chapter 31. After Justinian

1. Jordanes, *Getica* 315.

2. Salzman, *Falls of Rome*, 299ff.

3. Salzman, *Falls of Rome*, 310.

4. For discussion, see Brown, *Gentlemen and Officers* (Rome, 1984).

5. Procopius, *Aed.* 4.1.4, 11.20.

6. Menander Protector, fr. 6.

7. Agathias 5.11–20.

8. Malalas 18.141; Theophanes 6055.

9. Corippus, *Iustini* (*Iust.* hereafter), 1.66–185.

10. Corippus, *Iust.* 1.294–367.

11. John of Ephesus, *HE* 2.10.

12. Corippus, *Iust.* 1.187–293, 2.1–83. On coins, see Sear, *Byzantine Coins*, 357–361.

13. Corippus, *Iust.* 1.15–27, 3.220–332.

14. S. Lin, "Justin Under Justinian," *Dumbarton Oaks Papers* 75 (2021): 121–142, at 129–131.

15. Continuator of Marcellinus Comes 540.1; Agathias 4.21.5–22.7; Evagrius Scholasticus, *HE* 5.1.

16. Corippus, *Iust.* 2.361–430.

17. Justin II, *Novellae* 146, preface.

18. Evagrius Scholasticus, *HE* 5.1–3.

19. Corippus, *Iust.* 3.305–307.

20. Corippus, *Iust.* 3.339–340, 369.

21. Menander, fr. 12.1.

22. Chris Wickham, *Early Medieval Italy* (London, 1981), 28–32.

23. Procopius, *Wars* 7.33.8 (Gepids); Menander 12.2 (Romans).

24. Menander 12.4–7, 15.5.

25. Evagrius Scholasticus, *HE* 5.7–8.

26. Evagrius Scholasticus, *HE* 5.9–10; Theophylact Simocatta 3.10.6–7.

27. Evagrius Scholasticus, *HE* 5.11; John of Ephesus, *HE* 3.4; Menander 18.

28. Evagrius Scholasticus, *HE* 5.11.

29. Justinian, *Institutes*, preface 7.

30. Menander 18.1.

31. Evagrius Scholasticus, *HE* 5.12; Menander 18.2.

32. Evagrius Scholasticus, *HE* 5.13.

33. Menander 23.9, 26.1. For discussion, see M. Whitby, *The Emperor Maurice and His Historian* (Oxford, 1988), 268–274.

34. Menander 22.

35. Menander 21, 25.
36. Whitby, *Maurice*, 158–165.
37. Theophylact Simocatta 7.10–11.8.
38. Theophylact Simocatta 6.3.6–7.
39. Theophylact Simocatta 8.5–6.
40. George T. Dennis, *Maurice's Strategikon: Handbook of Byzantine Military Strategy* (Philadelphia, 1984).
41. Gregory the Great, *Ep.* 11.16.
42. Evagrius Scholasticus, *HE* 6.4; Theophanes 6080.
43. Theophanes 6088.
44. Whitby, *Maurice*, 167. Note Maurice, *Strategikon* 1.6.11, on proper maintenance of gear.
45. Sebeos 20. For discussion, see Whitby, *Maurice*, 167–168.
46. Maurice, *Strategikon* 11.4.
47. Theophylact Simocatta 6.10.1–3, 8.6.2.
48. John of Nikiu 102.10–11; Theophylact Simocatta 3.2.8; Theophanes 6094. 286–287.
49. Theophylact Simocatta 8.8–11; *CP* 694.1–5.
50. Theophylact Simocatta 8.15.7.

Chapter 32. The New World of Heraclius

1. Theophanes 6094.286–290.
2. Theophanes 6095.291.
3. John of Nikiu 104.1–3, 105.1–6.
4. Theophanes 6092.
5. Theophanes 6095; Sebeos 31.106–107; Michael the Syrian 2.379.
6. Theophanes 6096.
7. Sebeos 31.107; C. Mango and R. Scott, *The Chronicle of Theophanes Confessor* (Oxford, 1997), 422n4, following Michael the Syrian 2.378 and Theophanes 6118.323.
8. *CP* 609.
9. Theophanes 6102; Sebeos 33.111.
10. *CP* 603; Theophylact Simocatta 8.15.1.
11. *CP* 605; Theophanes 6099 (conflating the two suspected plots).
12. Theophanes 6101.
13. Nicephorus, *Breviarium* (*Brev.* hereafter), 1.20–30, 2.1–15.
14. Sebeos 31.106; *CP* 610; John of Antioch, fr. 218e–f; John of Nikiu 109.25–110.9.
15. *CP* 610.
16. *CP* 610; John of Nikiu 110.6; Nicephorus, *Brev.* 1.35–51.
17. Theophanes 6103.
18. John of Nikiu 109.18.
19. Sebeos 33.112. All translations, chapters, and section numbers for Sebeos follow those in R. W. Thomson, *The Armenian History Attributed to Sebeos* (Liverpool, 1999). See also Theophanes 6103.
20. Sebeos 34.113. See also Theophanes 6105, which is less detailed than Sebeos, but correctly has the embassy follow the fall of Caesarea rather than occurring at the time of Heraclius's accession.
21. Sebeos 34.114–115.
22. J. Howard-Johnston, "Heraclius' Persian Campaigns and the Revival of the East Roman Empire, 622–630," *War in History* 6 (1999): 1–44, at 1–3.

23. Sebeos 34.115.

24. J. W. Drijvers, "Evelyn Waugh, Helena, and the True Cross," *Classics Ireland* 7 (2000): 25–50, at 30.

25. Antiochus Strategos, translated in F. C. Conybeare, "Antiochus Strategos's Account of the Sack of Jerusalem in A.D. 614," *English Historical Review* 25 (1910): 502–517.

26. *CP* 615; Nicephorus, *Historia Syntomos=Breviariaum* (*Brev.* hereafter), 6–7, 15.25–29.

27. *CP* 615.

28. M. Whitby and M. Whitby, *Chronicon Paschale* (Liverpool, 1989), 158n441.

29. G. Bijovsky, *Gold Coin and Small Change: Monetary Circulation in Fifth-Seventh Century Byzantine Palestine* (Trieste, 2012), 374–375; C. Morrisson, "Byzantine Money: Its Production and Circulation," in *The Economic History of Byzantium from the Seventh through the Fifteenth Century*, ed. A. Laiou (Washington, DC, 2002), 909–966, at 929.

30. *CP* 618; Nicephorus, *Brev.* 12.7–9.

31. J. Haldon, *Byzantium in the Seventh Century* (Cambridge, 1990), 224.

32. *CP* 623; Nicephorus, *Brev.* 10, 13.

33. Theophanes 6114.

34. Theophanes 6114.

35. Theophanes 6114.308.

36. On the desecrations, see Howard-Johnston, "Heraclius's Persian Campaigns," 16–17. For the quote, Theophanes 6114.

37. Theophanes 6114.

38. Theophanes 6115.

39. Nicephorus, *Brev.* 13.

40. *CP* 626.718.

41. Howard-Johnston, "Heraclius's Persian Campaigns," 19–20.

42. *CP* 626.717.

43. *CP* 626.718.

44. *CP* 626.722–723.

45. *CP* 626.723–724; Sebeos 38.123.

46. *CP* 626.725.

47. *CP* 626.716, 725.

48. Theodore Syncellus, *Homily on the Siege of Constantinople* (*Hom.* hereafter), 19, 24.

49. Theodore Syncellus, *Hom.* 40.

50. Theophanes 6118.322–323.

51. Theophanes 6118.321–323.

52. Theophanes 6118.325–327.

53. Theophanes 6118.327.

54. *CP* 628.727–728.

55. *CP* 628.729.

56. Sebeos 39.128; Howard-Johnston, "Heraclius's Persian Campaigns," 28.

57. Nicephorus, *Brev.* 15–17; Sebeos 40.

58. Sebeos 41.131.

Chapter 33. The Coming of Islam

1. For the date of March 21, see Antiochus Strategos 516.

2. Sebeos 41.131.

3. Nicephorus, *Brev.* 19.1–9.

4. Sebeos 42.134–135.

5. *Chronicle of Seert* 93.

6. Theodore Syncellus, *Hom.* chap. 52.

7. P. Booth, *Crisis of Empire* (Oakland, 2014), 188–200.

8. John of Nikiu, *Chron.* 115.9, 116.10–12; *History of the Patriarchs of Alexandria*, "Benjamin," 490–492; Michael the Syrian 11.3.

9. Al-Tabari, *Hist.* 1.1562–1568; Theophanes 6123.335; W. Kaegi, *Byzantium and Early Islamic Conquests* (Cambridge, 1992), 69–74.

10. Nicephorus, *Brev.* 20; Theophanes 6125; Kaegi, *Byzantium and Early Islamic Conquests*, 93, 110.

11. *Chronicle of 1234*, 48, in *The Seventh Century in the West-Syrian Chronicles*, trans. A. Palmer (Liverpool, 1993). All references to the *Chronicle* follow the translation and numbering of Palmer's text.

12. *Chronicle of 1234*, 66; Nicephorus, *Brev.* 20; Kaegi, *Byzantium and the Early Islamic Conquests*, 119.

13. Theophanes 6126.338; *Chronicle of 1234*, 54; Kaegi, *Byzantium and the Early Islamic Conquests*, 112–136.

14. *Chronicle of 1234*, 68.

15. *Chronicle of 1234*, 63.

16. *Chronicle of 1234*, 64.

17. Haldon, *Empire That Would Not Die*, 32.

18. Theophanes 6165; Nicephorus, *Brev.* 34. On dating, see Haldon, *Empire That Would Not Die*, 42–43.

19. Based on figures in K. Harper, "People, Plagues, and Prices in Roman Egypt," *Journal of Economic History* 76 (2016): 820.

20. *Liber Pontificalis* 1.344, quoted in Haldon, *Empire That Would Not Die*, 41.

21. Haldon, *Empire That Would Not Die*, 26–29.

22. Haldon, *Empire That Would Not Die*, 149.

23. Haldon, *Empire That Would Not Die*, 259–264.

24. Haldon, *Empire That Would Not Die*, 150–151.

25. Maximus Confessor, *Ep.* 14. See also P. Booth, *Crisis of Empire*, 278–279.

26. Haldon, *Empire That Would Not Die*, 37.

27. *Chronicle of 1234*, 122–123; Theophanes 6173.360; Michael the Syrian 2.468; Haldon, *Empire That Would Not Die*, 45.

Chapter 34. Iconoclasm

1. M. Hendy, *Studies in the Byzantine Monetary Economy* (Cambridge, 2008), 168–171.

2. Theophanes 6178.363; Nicephorus, *Brev.* 38; *Chronicle of 1234*, 128.

3. Theophanes 6180.364.

4. Nicephorus, *Brev.* 38; cf. Theophanes 6184.366.

5. Theophanes 6183.365.

6. *Chronicle of 1234*, 135; M. Humphreys, "The 'War of Images' Revisited: Justinian II's Coinage Reform and the Caliphate," *Numismatic Chronicle* 173 (2013): 229–244.

7. Theophanes 6183.365.

8. Theophanes 6190.370–371; Nicephorus, *Brev.* 41.

9. Theophanes 6196.373–375; Nicephorus, *Brev.* 42.1–44.

10. On the gifts, see Theophanes 6198; on Caesar, Nicephorus, *Brev.* 42.60–65.

11. Nicephorus, *Brev.* 45.35–75.

12. L. Brubaker and J. Haldon, *Byzantium in the Iconoclast Era* (Cambridge, 2011), 20.

13. Theophanes 6192.371; Michael the Syrian 2.473–474.

14. W. Kaegi, *Muslim Expansion and Byzantine Collapse in North Africa* (Cambridge, 2010).

15. Theophanes 6207.385. The location of Phoinix is unknown, but it is probably a reference to Phoenicia (which is famous for its cypress wood).

16. Nicephorus, *Brev.* 49.9–17.

17. Theophanes 6209.391, 395. For Leo as an Arabic speaker, see W. Ball, *Rome in the East* (London, 2000), 489.

18. Theophanes 6218.405 ("Saracen-minded"), 6224.410 ("Arab mentality").

19. On the capture of Pergamum, see Nicephorus, *Brev.* 53.

20. Nicephorus, *Brev.* 54.15–31.

21. Nicephorus, *Brev.* 54.35.39; Theophanes 6209.397.

22. Theophanes 6210.397–399; V. Grumel, "Homélie de Saint Germain sur la deliverance de Constantinople," *Revue des études byzantines* 16 (1958): 188–205.

23. Theophanes 6210.398.

24. Nicephorus, *Brev.* 57; Theophanes 6211.400.

25. Theophanes 6218; J. Herrin, *The Formation of Christendom* (Princeton, NJ, 1987), 321–322; Brubaker and Haldon, *Byzantium in the Iconoclast Era*, 75–76.

26. Theophanes 6218.404–405.

27. Nicephorus, *Brev.* 59.

28. Nicephorus, *Brev.* 68, speaks of "the city having become deserted" by the middle of the eighth century.

29. Nicephorus, *Brev.* 53.

30. Theophanes 6218.406.

31. Nicephorus, *Brev.* 60.

32. Theophanes 6218.406.

33. Nicephorus, *Brev.* 60.

34. Nicephorus, *Brev.* 62.

35. Brubaker and Haldon, *Byzantium in the Iconoclast Era*, 79–155.

36. Quoted in Brubaker and Haldon, *Byzantium in the Iconoclast Era*, 140.

37. Theophanes 6232.413.

38. Nicephorus, *Brev.* 64.35–38.

39. Theophanes 6233.414–415.

40. Nicephorus, *Brev.* 67; Brubaker and Haldon, *Byzantium in the Iconoclast Era*, 156–161.

41. Nicephorus, *Brev.* 67; Brubaker and Haldon, *Byzantium in the Iconoclast Era*, 182n129.

42. Brubaker and Haldon, *Byzantium in the Iconoclast Era*, 182–184.

43. On the Council of 754, see Theophanes 6245.427–428; Brubaker and Haldon, *Byzantium in the Iconoclast Era*, 189–197.

44. G. D. Mansi, ed., *Sacrorum Conciliorum Nova et Amplissima Collection* (Mansi hereafter), xiii.257E.

45. Mansi xiii.328B–C.

46. Theophanes 6257.437–438, 6253.432, 6259.441–443; Brubaker and Haldon, *Byzantium in the Iconoclast Era*, 201–212.

47. For details of these tortures, see Theophanes 6259.441–443.
48. Theophanes 6267.448.
49. Brubaker and Haldon, *Byzantium in the Iconoclast Era*, 5–6.
50. Theophanes 6237.422, 6247.429.
51. Theophanes 6259.443.
52. E.g., Theophanes 6237.422. For this objective, see Brubaker and Haldon, *Byzantium in the Iconoclast Era*, 166.
53. P. Magdalino, "The Distance of the Past in Early Medieval Byzantium," in Centro italiano di studi sull'alto medioevo, *Ideologie e practice del reimpiego nell'alto medioevo* (Split, 1999), 141.
54. The 710s are the most likely endpoint. See Nicephorus, *Brev.* 52.3–4; Theophanes 6204.382, 6218.405.
55. Theophanes 6259.443.

Chapter 35. The Secession of the City of Rome from the Roman State

1. Herrin, *Formation of Christendom*, 347.
2. T. F. X. Noble, *The Republic of St. Peter* (Philadelphia, 1984), 25–26.
3. Theophanes 6224.410.
4. *Codex Diplomaticus Langobardiae*, ed. C. R. Brühl, 3.1, no. 23 (Rome, 1973), 111–115.
5. *Codex Carolinus* (*CC* hereafter), 1 (pp. 476–477 in the *Monumenta Germaniae Historica* [*MGH*] edition) and 2 (pp. 477–479).
6. *Royal Frankish Annals* 749.
7. *Liber Pontificalis* (*LP* hereafter), 1.442.
8. *LP* 1.446.
9. *LP* 1.449; *Royal Frankish Annals* 754; Noble, *Republic of St. Peter*, 87–88.
10. *LP* 1.450–451; cf. Einhard, *Vita Karoli* (*VK* hereafter), 6; *CC* 6.489.
11. *LP* 1.451; Noble, *Republic of St. Peter*, 91.
12. *LP* 1.454.
13. On the organ, see *Royal Frankish Annals* 757; *Fredegarii Continuatio*, chap. 40.
14. Kaldellis, *New Roman Empire*, 462.
15. *CC* 32.539.
16. *Royal Frankish Annals* 767; cf. *Annals of Einhard* 767; *CC* 37.549.
17. Gregory I, Register 9.209. For discussion, see Kaldellis, *New Roman Empire*, 448.
18. J. Nelson, *King and Emperor: A New Life of Charlemagne* (New York, 2020), 353–356. For a translation of the text of the Donation of Constantine, see E. Henderson, *Select Historical Documents of the Middle Ages* (London, 1910), 319–329.
19. Nelson, *King and Emperor*, 93–100.
20. Nelson, *King and Emperor*, 100–102.
21. Quoted in Nelson, *King and Emperor*, 104–105.
22. Einhard, *VK* 18. For the larger context, see Nelson, *King and Emperor*, 105–110.
23. *LP* 1.498.
24. *CC* 60.587.9–18. See also Nelson, *King and Emperor*, 355.
25. *Ludovicianum* 1–7. See also R. Davis, *Lives of the Eighth-Century Popes* (Liverpool, 2007), 112–113.
26. Nelson, *King and Emperor*, 181–209 (Saxony), 227 (Brittany).
27. *LP* 2.4.
28. *LP* 2.6.

29. *LP* 24.

30. *LP* 2.7, trans. Davis, adapted.

31. *Royal Frankish Annals,* AM 801.

32. This provision of the *Donation of Constantine* is laid out in Henderson, *Select Historical Documents,* 325, 327.

33. *Annales Laureshamenses* xxxiiii.801.

34. On the Ravenna materials, see D. Deliyannis, *Ravenna in Late Antiquity* (Cambridge, 2010). On Aachen as New Rome, see Moduin of Autun, *Ecloga* 192.24–31; Herrin, *Formation of Christendom,* 448n5.

35. The overlaps included Guy and Lambert (April 892–December 894), and Lambert and Arnulf (February 896–October 898). Vacancies included 877–881, 888–892, 899–901, 905–915, and 924–936.

Chapter 36. Rome's First Empress and the First End of Iconoclasm

1. J. Herrin, *Women in Purple: Rulers of Medieval Byzantium* (Princeton, NJ, 2001), 53–58.

2. A. Kaldellis, *The Christian Parthenon* (Cambridge, 2009), 68–74.

3. Theophanes 6261.444; Herrin, *Women in Purple,* 59–64.

4. Constantine VII Porphyrogenitus, *De Cer.* 1.40 (R206).

5. Constantine VII Porphyrogenitus, *De Cer.* 1.39 (R198) (text of chant), 1.41 (R211) (its use in the combined nuptial and Augusta crowning ceremony).

6. On the birth, see Theophanes 6262.445. For a description of the room, Anna Comnena, *Alexiad* 6.8.

7. Nicephorus, *Brev.* 88; Theophanes 6260.443–444.

8. On Constantine V's death, see Theophanes 6267.448.

9. Theophanes 6268.449–450.

10. Theophanes 6268.449–451.

11. Herrin, *Women in Purple,* 67–68.

12. *CC* 64.591–592; Theophanes 6270.451–452.

13. Theophanes 6269.451.

14. On the regency council, see Herrin, *Women in Purple,* 75. On the possibility of no council, Kaldellis, *New Roman Empire,* 464.

15. Sear, *Byzantine Coins,* 1583–1584, 1586–1587, 1590, 1591, 1596.

16. Theophanes 6273.454; Herrin, *Women in Purple,* 77.

17. Theophanes 6273–6274.

18. Theophanes 6276.457. For discussion, see Kaldellis, *New Roman Empire,* 465; Herrin, *Women in Purple,* 81–82.

19. Theophanes 6274.455; cf. Einhard, *VK* 19; Noble, *Republic of St. Peter,* 165; Brubaker and Haldon, *Byzantium in the Iconoclast Era,* 256–259; Herrin, *Women in Purple,* 78–80.

20. Theophanes 6274.457, generally echoed by *Vita Tarasius* 397–398; Nicephorus, *Apologia minora,* PG 100.837C. For discussion, see Herrin, *Women in Purple,* 83–84; Brubaker and Haldon, *Byzantium in the Iconoclast Era,* 249–250, 263 (with doubts about his sincerity).

21. Theophanes 6277.459–460.

22. Brubaker and Haldon, *Byzantium in the Iconoclast Era,* 262–286.

23. On the invitations, see Theophanes 6279.461 (not mentioning Jerusalem).

24. Theophanes 6278.461–462; Mansi, xii.990C–991B.

25. Theophanes 6279.462.

26. Theophanes 6280.463.

27. Kaldellis, *New Roman Empire*, 456.

28. Brubaker and Haldon, *Byzantium in the Iconoclast Era*, 314–316.

29. Brubaker and Haldon, *Byzantium in the Iconoclast Era*, 352–354.

30. Theophanes 6281.463–464, 6282.465.

31. On papal efforts to sabotage union, see CC 74.605.10–18. For discussion, Brubaker and Haldon, *Byzantium in the Iconoclast Era*, 254.

32. Theophanes 6281.464.

33. Theophanes 6282.465.

34. Theophanes 6283.466.

35. Theophanes 6285.469; Herrin, *Women in Purple*, 94–95.

36. Theophanes 6285.469; Herrin, *Women in Purple*, 94–95.

37. Theophanes 6287.469–6288.471; Theodore the Studite, *Ep.* 443; *Vita B* of Theodore the Studite, 253A–D; Herrin, *Women in Purple*, 96–97.

38. Theophanes 6289.471–472. On blinding as a punishment, see J. Ransohoff, "Sightless Eyes, Broken Bodies: Blinding, Punishment, and the Politics of Disability in the Byzantine World" (PhD diss., Harvard University, 2022).

39. Al-Tabari, *Hist.* 2.222, AH 182 (AD 798–799).

40. *Annales Laureshamenses* xxxiiii.801; Einhard, *VK* 15; Theophanes 6293–6294.475.

41. Theophanes 6290.473.

42. On the overthrow and death of Irene, see Theophanes 6295.476–480.

Chapter 37. The Medieval Roman State Takes Shape

1. Brubaker and Haldon, *Byzantium in the Iconoclast Era*, 582–584.

2. Brubaker and Haldon, *Byzantium in the Iconoclast Era*, 583–584.

3. Michael the Syrian 3.15; al-Tabari, *Hist.* 2.260.

4. Brubaker and Haldon, *Byzantium in the Iconoclast Era*, 601.

5. Theodore the Studite, *Laudatio Platonis*, I 5 (808A); Brubaker and Haldon, *Byzantium in the Iconoclast Era*, 602.

6. Ignatius of Nicaea, *Ep.* 17; Brubaker and Haldon, *Byzantium in the Iconoclast Era*, 576–577.

7. Theophanes 6298.482.

8. Theophanes 6302.487.

9. Theophanes 6300.483.

10. Theophanes 6302.486.

11. Theophanes 6302.486 states that the army was "outfitted by the inhabitants of the community, who also paid 18.5 solidi" per soldier.

12. Theophanes 6303.490.

13. Theophanes 6303.492.

14. J. Wortley, "Legends of the Byzantine Disaster of 811," *Byzantion* 50 (1980): 533–562.

15. Theophanes 6304.496.

16. Theophanes 6304.496.

17. Theophanes 6305.501. In part to prevent a repeat of this, Constantine's tomb was later destroyed.

18. Theophanes 6305.502–503.

19. Theophanes 6305.502.

20. *Scriptor Incertus de Leone Armenio* 349–355; Theosteriktos, *Life of Niketas of Medikion* 31. For discussion, see Kaldellis, *New Roman Empire*, 485.

21. For discussion, see Kaldellis, *New Roman Empire*, 486–487.

Chapter 38. The Roman System Abides

1. *Vita B* of Theodore the Studite 256C–260C; *Vita C* of Theodore the Studite 24, 269–271.

2. *Vita C* of Theodore the Studite 25, 271–272; cf. *Vita B* of Theodore the Studite 260C–261B.

3. Theodore the Studite, *Ep.* 128; *Vita of Nicholas the Studite* 884A, 888C–889A; cf. *Vita B* of Theodore the Studite 293C–296A, 301C.

4. Genesius 1.16; *Theophanes Continuatus* (*Theophanes Cont.* hereafter) 1.19.

5. *Scriptor Incertus* 346.

6. *Theophanes Cont.* 1.19.

7. Genesius 2.1.

8. Genesius 1.20. Other, often less dramatic, accounts are found in Nicetas, *Vita Ignatii* 493AB; *Theophanes Cont.* 1.25–26, 2.1.

9. Genesius 1.20.

10. Genesius 2.2–9.

11. Genesius 2.10–12; *Theophanes Cont.* 2.25. On the capture of Crete and its aftermath for the Romans living on the island, see M. Crum, "Unbecoming Romans" (PhD diss., University of California, San Diego, 2024), chap. 2.

12. *Theophanes Cont.* 2.27; Crum, "Unbecoming Romans," chap. 3.

13. *Theophanes Cont.* 2.27.

14. *Theophanes Cont.* 2.28.

15. *Theophanes Cont.* 3.9, 3.42.

16. *Theophanes Cont.* 3.3, 3.7.

17. *Theophanes Cont.* 3.3.

18. *Theophanes Cont.* 3.8; Kaldellis, *New Roman Empire*, 491.

19. Kaldellis, *New Roman Empire*, 493.

20. Genesius 3.3; cf. *Theophanes Cont.* 3.21. For discussion, see Kaldellis, *New Roman Empire*, 494. For the larger context, see Kaldellis, *Romanland*, 127–132.

21. Genesius 3.6; Genesius, *Genesios on the Reigns of the Emperors*, trans. A. Kaldellis (Leiden, 2017), 46.

22. *Theophanes Cont.* 1.5.

23. *Theophanes Cont.* 3.29.

24. Genesius 3.11.

25. *Theophanes Cont.* 3.34; Genesius 3.11.

26. *Theophanes Cont.* 3.29.

27. Genesius 3.7.

28. *Theophanes Cont.* 3.29.

29. *Theophanes Cont.* 3.13.

30. *Theophanes Cont.* 3.13–15.

31. For discussion, see W. Treadgold, "The Prophecies of Methodios," *Revue des études byzantines* 62 (2004): 231–232.

32. *Life of Euthymius* 13.39–41; *Life of Methodius*, PG 100.1252B–C; *Theophanes Cont.* 2.8. For discussion, see Treadgold, "Prophecies," 229–237.

33. *Theophanes Cont.* 3.24; Treadgold, "Prophecies," 235.

Chapter 39. The New Macedonian Dynasty

1. Kaldellis, *New Roman Empire*, 499–501.
2. Al-Tabari, *Hist.* 3:1417–1418; Kaldellis, *New Roman Empire*, 504.
3. Kaldellis, *New Roman Empire*, 504–506.
4. John Skylitzes, *Synopsis of History* (Skylitzes hereafter) 101–102. All translations follow *John Skylitzes: A Synopsis of Byzantine History*, trans. J. Wortley (Cambridge, 2010), with occasional adaptations for clarity.
5. Kaldellis, *New Roman Empire*, 532.
6. *Theophanes Cont.* 4.14–15; Kaldellis, *New Roman Empire*, 508–510.
7. Kaldellis, *New Roman Empire*, 520–521.
8. Nicetas, *Life of Ignatius* 28.
9. *Theophanes Cont.* 4.33. On Rus conversion, see Photius, *Ep.* 2.295–305. For more discussion, Kaldellis, *New Roman Empire*, 506.
10. Skylitzes 115–117; Genesius 4.24.
11. Genesius 4.26, 4.40; *Theophanes Cont.* 224–225, 230.
12. Genesius 4.28.
13. *Vita Basilii* (*Vit. Bas.* hereafter) 69.
14. *Vit. Bas.* 55, 65. For discussion, see Kaldellis, *New Roman Empire*, 522–523.
15. *Vit. Bas.* 41–43, 59–61; Genesius 4.37–38.
16. *Vit. Bas.* 43.
17. *Ecloga of Leo III and Constantine V*, proemium 36–40.
18. *Vit. Bas.* 33. For discussion, see Z. Chitwood, *Byzantine Legal Culture and the Roman Legal Tradition, 867–1056* (Cambridge, 2017), 25.
19. *Prochoion*, proemium, lines 63–76, abridged, following the translation of Chitwood, *Byzantine Legal Culture*, 27.
20. *Prochion*, proemium, lines 57–59; Chitwood, *Byzantine Legal Culture*, 25–29.
21. *Eisagoge*, proemium, lines 31–33, 33–36, following Chitwood, *Byzantine Legal Culture*, 30–31.
22. Simeon the Logothete 132.18.
23. Genesius 4.29.
24. Simeon the Logothete 132.26; S. Tougher, *The Reign of Leo VI (886–912): Politics and People* (Leiden, 1997), 35.
25. Genesius 4.29.
26. *Vit. Bas.* 101.4–6. The Greek here literally reads "the aforementioned thing," but the words of the parrot's call are given two lines above in the preceding sentence.
27. *Vit. Bas.* 101.10–14.
28. *Vit. Bas.* 101.18–21.
29. Simeon the Logothete 132.27.
30. *Sixty Books*, proemium, lines 28–31; Chitwood, *Byzantine Legal Culture*, 35–42.
31. E. H. Freshfield, *Roman Law in the Later Roman Empire* (Cambridge, 1932).
32. Tougher, *Reign of Leo*, 168–171.
33. For these strategies, see Chapters 18 and 19 of the *Taktika* as well as the discussion of Tougher in *Reign of Leo*, 190.
34. Al-Tabari, *Hist.* 38.193. For discussion, see Tougher, *Reign of Leo*, 191–192.
35. *Chronicle of the Logothete* 134.2–7; Skylitzes 193–196; P. Karlin-Hayter, "The Emperor Alexander's Bad Name," *Speculum* 44 (1969): 585–596.
36. *Life of Theophano* 6.6–24; *Life of Euthymius* 41.1–3; Tougher, *Reign of Leo*, 134–140.

37. Skylitzes 180; *Life of Euthymius* 45.33–35; Tougher, *Reign of Leo*, 140–141.

38. For them living together in the palace, see *Chronicle of the Logothete* 133.39.

39. Nicholas I, *Ep.* 32.52–54.

40. Nicholas I, *Ep.* 32.62–64; *Chronicle of the Logothete* 133.49–50.

41. *Chronicle of the Logothete* 134.4.

Chapter 40. The Age of Impotent Emperors

1. *Chronicle of the Logothete* 135.1–9.

2. *Chronicle of the Logothete* 135.11. For this interpretation of the episode, see Kaldellis, *New Roman Empire*, 541.

3. *Chronicle of the Logothete* 135.12–13.

4. Sear, *Byzantine Coins*, 1758.

5. *Chronicle of the Logothete* 135.21.

6. *Chronicle of the Logothete* 135.22.

7. *Chronicle of the Logothete* 135.24–27.

8. *Chronicle of the Logothete* 135.28–30.

9. Kaldellis, *Romanland*, 174–175.

10. Constantine VII Porphyrogenitus, *De Administrando Imperio* (*DAI* hereafter) 13.148–152.

11. *Chronicle of the Logothete* 136.3–18.

12. *Chronicle of the Logothete* 136.38.

13. *Chronicle of the Logothete* 136.81.

14. *Chronicle of the Logothete* 136.53.

15. *Chronicle of the Logothete* 136.47–50.

16. Skylitzes 234.

17. Skylitzes 236–237.

18. Skylitzes 237.

19. Skylitzes 241.

20. Patria Constantinopoleos, *Scriptores originum Constantinopolitanarum*, vol. 2, ed. T. Preger (Leipzig, 1901), 188; P. Magdalino, "The House of Basil the Parakoi-momenos," in *Le saint, le moine, et le paysan*, ed. O. Delouis, S. Métivier, and P. Pagès (Paris, 2016), 323–328.

21. Leo the Deacon 111.7.

22. *Theophanes Cont.* 445–447; Constantine VII Porphyrogenitus, *DAI* 1.6; D. Sullivan, *The Rise and Fall of Nikephoros II Phokas* (Leiden, 2018).

23. Skylitzes 237.

24. *Theophanes Cont.* 448.

25. Constantine VII Porphyrogenitus, *De Cer.* 1 preface 6.1–2.

26. Constantine VII Porphyrogenitus, *DAI* 1.1; Constantine VII Porphyrogenitus, *DAI*, proemium 26–28.

27. Skylitzes 248.

28. On the capture of Crete, see *Theophanes Cont.*, 473–477, 480; *Revised Chronicle of Symeon the Logothete* 18, 21; Skylitzes 249–250; Leo the Deacon 1.2–9, 2.4–8.

29. For discussion of the ethnic character, see Crum, "Unbecoming Romans," 13–53.

30. Leo the Deacon 2.8.

31. *Life of St. Nikon* 21.4–6, following Crum, "Unbecoming Roman," 38.

32. *Revised Chronicle of Symeon* 23.

33. Leo the Deacon 4.1–4.

34. Kaldellis, *New Roman Empire*, 566.
35. Leo the Deacon 4.6.
36. Skylitzes 274–277. On the fiscal situation, see P. Magdalino, "The Byzantine Army and the Land," in *To empolemo Buzantio (Byzantium at War, Ninth to the Twelfth Centuries)*, ed. N. Oikomides (Athens, 1997), 15–36.
37. Skylitzes 279–281; Leo the Deacon 5.6–9.
38. Leo the Deacon 6.1–4.
39. Kaldellis, *New Roman Empire*, 569–572.

Chapter 41. Basil II, the System, and the Peak of the Macedonian Dynasty

1. C. Holmes, "Political Elites in the Reign of Basil II," in *Byzantium in the Year 1000*, ed. P. Magdalino (Leiden, 2003), 35–71; C. Holmes, *Basil II and the Governance of Empire* (Cambridge, 2005), 461–475.
2. Skylitzes 316.
3. Skylitzes 314–317.
4. Skylitzes 317.
5. For a quick summary of this phase in the war, see Holmes, *Basil II*, 451–452.
6. Skylitzes 321. For Skleros's Armenian background, see *John Skylitzes*, trans. Wortley, 305n34.
7. Holmes, *Basil II*, 452.
8. Skylitzes 324.
9. On Georgian reinforcements, see Skylitzes 326; B. Martin-Hisard, "La vie de Jean et Euthyme et le statut du monastère des Ibères sur l'Athos," *Revue des études byzantines* 49 (1991): 89–91.
10. Skylitzes 327; Leo the Deacon 10.7.
11. Holmes, *Basil II*, 457.
12. *History of Yahya-ibn-Sa'id of Antioch* (*Yahya* hereafter); *Patrologia Orientalis* 23 (Paris, 1932), 417–418.
13. Leo the Deacon 10.8. See also Yahya 419.
14. Yahya 419–421.
15. For discussion, see Kaldellis, *New Roman Empire*, 577–578.
16. Yahya 423–424.
17. Yahya 426.
18. Holmes, "Political Elites," 56–61.
19. Holmes, "Political Elites," 58.
20. Holmes, "Political Elites," 57.
21. Skylitzes 332, 340.
22. Holmes, "Political Elites," 61.
23. Psellus, *Chronographica* (*Chron.* hereafter) 1.30.
24. Psellus, *Chron.* 1.20, 1.32.
25. Yahya 442.
26. Yahya 443; Holmes, *Basil II*, 475–477.
27. On the territory granted to David, see Stephen of Taron, *Armenisdhe Geschichte*, 141–142; Yahya 424, 429. For discussion, see Holmes, *Basil II*, 319–320.
28. Yahya 460.
29. P. Stephenson, *The Legend of Basil the Bulgar-Slayer* (Cambridge, 2003), 34–35.
30. Holmes, *Basil II*, 487–493; Stephenson, *Legend of Basil*, 16.

31. Skylitzes 341–342; Stephenson, *Legend of Basil*, 17.

32. Skylitzes 348; Yahya 461; P. Stephenson, *Byzantium's Balkan Frontier: A Political Study of the Northern Balkans, 900–1204* (Cambridge, 2000), 66–71.

33. Skylitzes 348–349; cf. Zonaras 3.564; Stephenson, *Byzantium's Balkan Frontier*, 71–77.

34. Stephenson, *Byzantium's Balkan Frontier*, 72–73; Stephenson, *Legend of Basil*, 33–34. Stephenson explains why the number of people blinded is likely overstated.

35. Yahya 3.217, quoted in Stephenson, *Byzantium's Balkan Frontier*, 77.

36. Stephenson, *Legend of Basil*, 36; Holmes, *Basil II*, 330–342.

37. Stephenson, *Legend of Basil*, 34.

38. Skylitzes 342–343, 357. For discussion, see Stephenson, *Legend of Basil*, 35.

39. Skylitzes 358.

40. Skylitzes 360.

41. Yahya 3.212, quoted in Stephenson, *Legend of Basil*, 36.

42. Kaldellis, *Romanland*, 244.

43. Kaldellis, *Romanland*, 247–250.

44. Kaldellis, *Romanland*, 256–257; Kaldellis, *New Roman Empire*, 578.

45. Kaldellis, *Romanland*, 233–268.

Chapter 42. From the Apogee to the Nadir

1. Psellus, *Chron.* 6.6; L. Garland, "The Eye of the Beholder: Byzantine Imperial Women and Their Public Image from Zoe Porphyrogenita to Euphrosyne Kamaterissa Doukaina (1028–1203)," *Byzantion* 64 (1994): 32–33.

2. Cedrenus 722.

3. Skylitzes 374.

4. Skylitzes 374.

5. Psellus, *Chron.* 3.5.

6. Skylitzes 390 (both poisons and Michael).

7. Skylitzes 391. For context, see A. Laiou, "Imperial Marriages and Their Critics in the Eleventh Century: The Case of Skylitzes," *Dumbarton Oaks Papers* 46 (1992): 170–172.

8. Skylitzes 392.

9. Skylitzes 395.

10. Skylitzes 408.

11. Skylitzes 403–404, 408.

12. Skylitzes 410, 415.

13. Skylitzes 416. See also Psellus, *Chron.* 5.4; Attaleiates, *History* (*Hist.* hereafter) 9 (oaths); Psellus, *Chron.* 5.12–13; Zonaras 3.607–608 (John's banishment).

14. Skylitzes 418.

15. Skylitzes 418.

16. Skylitzes 418.

17. Skylitzes 420–421.

18. Psellus, *Chron.* Book 6.

19. Skylitzes 422.

20. Skylitzes 427.

21. Zonaras 3.620.

22. Skylitzes 434.

23. Skylitzes 434.

24. Her death is mentioned by Skylitzes (478) as an aside when talking about the events of 1054 and by Attaleiates (*Hist.* 51), where he mentions that by the time Theodora took power in 1055, her sister had predeceased her. Psellus (*Chron.* 6.183) mentions her death as well, but primarily to note its effect on Constantine IX rather than to describe its impact on the state.

25. Psellus, *Chron.* 6.48.

26. On these techniques as they related to the Roman state, see Kaldellis, *New Roman Empire*, 611–613.

27. Attaleiates, *Hist.* 45–46. For discussion, see Kaldellis, *New Roman Empire*, 613–614.

28. Kaldellis, *New Roman Empire*, 615–617, offers a concise reconstruction of this complicated affair.

29. Skylitzes 476.

30. Skylitzes 462–464; Attaleiates, *Hist.* 46–47.

31. Attaleiates, *Hist.* 44. Note, too, the comment of A. Kaldellis and D. Krallis, *The History: Michael Attaleiates* (Cambridge, MA, 2012), 79n77.

32. Skylitzes 479.

33. Skylitzes 480.

34. For this revolt and Isaac's accession, see Skylitzes 483–500; Attaleiates, *Hist.* 52–59; Psellus, *Chron.* 7.4–43.

35. Attaleiates, *Hist.* 66–69 (Balkan campaign), 69 (illness and retirement).

36. Psellus, *Oratoria minora* 5.5–61, as quoted in Kaldellis, *New Roman Empire*, 621.

37. Attaleiates, *Hist.* 71–75.

38. Attaleiates, *Hist.* 79.

39. Attaleiates, *Hist.* 80–83.

40. Attaleiates, *Hist.* 93–102.

41. Kaldellis, *New Roman Empire*, 625.

42. Attaleiates, *Hist.* 95.

43. Attaleiates, *Hist.* 138.

44. Attaleiates, *Hist.* 149–151.

45. Attaleiates, *Hist.* 161–162.

46. Attaleiates, *Hist.* 163.

47. Attaleiates, *Hist.* 163.

48. Attaleiates, *Hist.* 164–167.

Chapter 43. Alexius I Comnenus and the Roman State's Last Great Revival

1. Bryennius 2.4, 2.14; Attaleiates, *Hist.* 183–193; Skylitzes Continuatus 160.

2. Attaleiates, *Hist.* 27.1–2.

3. *Alexiad* 1.6.

4. *Alexiad* 2.4.

5. *Alexiad* 2.4.

6. Kaldellis, *New Roman Empire*, 638.

7. Kaldellis, *New Roman Empire*, 645.

8. Zonaras 18.21–25, quoted in Kaldellis, *New Roman Empire*, 645.

9. Zonaras 18.29, quoted in Kaldellis, *New Roman Empire*, 662.

10. *Alexiad* 14.8.

11. *Alexiad* 2.49, following Stephenson, *Byzantium's Balkan Frontier*, 101.

12. Kaldellis, *New Roman Empire*, 644.

13. *Alexiad* 8.5.

14. William of Apulia 216, quoted in Stephenson, *Byzantium's Balkan Frontier*, 160.

15. Figures following Kaldellis, *New Roman Empire*, 639.

16. Stephenson, *Byzantium's Balkan Frontier*, 160–173; Kaldellis, *New Roman Empire*, 639–642.

17. Stephenson, *Byzantium's Balkan Frontier*, 168.

18. Stephenson, *Byzantium's Balkan Frontier*, 170n36.

19. *Alexiad* 6.5.

20. P. Gautier, "Diatribes de Jean l'Oxite contre Alexis Ier Comnène," *Revue des études byzantines* 28 (1970): 5–55, at 35.

21. P. Frankopan, "Co-operation Between Constantinople and Rome Before the First Crusade," *Crusades* 3 (2004): 1–13.

22. P. Frankopan, *The First Crusade* (Cambridge, MA, 2012), 92–95.

23. *Alexiad* 10.5.

24. Frankopan, *First Crusade*, 117–123.

25. *Gesta Francorum* 1.5.

26. *Alexiad* 10.8–9.

27. *Alexiad* 10.10–11.

28. *Alexiad* 14.2.

29. Kaldellis, *New Roman Empire*, 660.

30. *Alexiad* 14.5.

31. *Alexiad* 14.7.

32. *Alexiad* 14.5.

Chapter 44. The Stupidity of the Successors

1. Nicetas Choniates, *History* (*Hist.* hereafter) 5–6.

2. Choniates, *Hist.* 7–8.

3. Choniates, *Hist.* 9–10. On his military skills, see also John Kinnamos, *History* (*Hist.* hereafter) 1.2.5.

4. Choniates, *Hist.* 10.

5. Choniates, *Hist.* 11 (pardon for Anna), 12 (Irene).

6. Cicero, *De officiis* 1.17.53–58.

7. For discussion, see Kaldellis, *New Roman Empire*, 666.

8. Choniates, *Hist.* 42.

9. Choniates, *Hist.* 37.

10. Kinnamos, *Hist.* 6.10; P. Magdalino, *The Empire of Manuel I Komnenos, 1143–1180* (Cambridge, 2002), 35.

11. For the quote, see Choniates, *Hist.* 45. On the deaths, Choniates, *Hist.* 16, 38–41; Kinnamos, *Hist.* 1.10.

12. Kaldellis, *New Roman Empire*, 670–671; Choniates, *Hist.* 98.

13. Choniates, *Hist.* 209.

14. Choniates, *Hist.* 208–209.

15. Kinnamos *Hist.* 4.21.

16. Choniates, *Hist.* 110.

17. Kinnamos, *Hist.* 4.24.

18. Kinnamos, *Hist.* 5.3. For the treaty, see Magdalino, *Empire*, 76–78.

19. Kinnamos, *Hist.* 4.14.

20. Magdalino, *Empire*, 209–217.

21. Magdalino, *Empire*, 44.

22. Choniates, *Hist.* 61–62.

23. Choniates, *Hist.* 62.

24. Choniates, *Hist.* 65–66.

25. Kinnamos, *Hist.* 6.10.

26. Choniates, *Hist.* 223.

27. Kinnamos, *Hist.* 3.15.

28. Kinnamos, *Hist.* 3.17.

29. Kinnamos, *Hist.* 3.16–18; Choniates, *Hist.* 101, 104–106; Magdalino, *Empire*, 197–201.

30. Kinnamos, *Hist.* 5.11.

31. Kinnamos, *Hist.* 5.11.

32. Kinnamos, *Hist.* 6.1.

33. Kinnamos, *Hist.* 6.1.

34. Choniates, *Hist.* 226–227.

35. Choniates, *Hist.* 227–228.

36. Choniates, *Hist.* 246.

37. Choniates, *Hist.* 249.

38. Choniates, *Hist.* 250–251.

39. Choniates, *Hist.* 262.

40. Choniates, *Hist.* 258.

41. Choniates, *Hist.* 269 (garden), 270 (revolts in Nicaea and Prusa), 271–274 (Andronicus's promotion and the murder of Alexius), 275 (bride).

42. Choniates, *Hist.* 282 (mother), 283–285 (surrender).

43. Choniates, *Hist.* 288–289.

44. Choniates, *Hist.* 291.

45. Choniates, *Hist.* 297.

46. Kaldellis, *New Roman Empire*, 702.

47. Choniates, *Hist.* 342.

48. Choniates, *Hist.* 344.

49. Choniates, *Hist.* 345.

Chapter 45. Two Decades of Roman Collapse

1. Choniates, *Hist.* 347.

2. Choniates, *Hist.* 349.

3. Choniates, *Hist.* 349–351.

4. Choniates, *Hist.* 355–356.

5. Choniates, *Hist.* 357–361; Stephenson, *Byzantium's Balkan Frontier*, 284–288.

6. Choniates, *Hist.* 369–370.

7. Choniates, *Hist.* 368.

8. Choniates, *Hist.* 368–369; Stephenson, *Byzantium's Balkan Frontier*, 288–290.

9. Choniates, *Hist.* 374–388.

10. Choniates, *Hist.* 388.

11. Choniates, *Hist.* 392–393.

12. Choniates, *Hist.* 395.

13. Choniates, *Hist.* 399.

14. Choniates, *Hist.* 401.

15. Choniates, *Hist.* 411–412.

16. Choniates, *Hist.* 416 (death of Frederick), 418 (loss of Cyprus).

17. Choniates, *Hist.* 423 (feebleness), 441 (dwarves).

18. Choniates, *Hist.* 451–452.

19. Choniates, *Hist.* 454–455.

20. Choniates, *Hist.* 471.

21. Choniates, *Hist.* 475–476.

22. Choniates, *Hist.* 477.

23. Choniates, *Hist.* 478–480.

24. Choniates, *Hist.* 496.

25. Choniates, *Hist.* 498.

26. A. Andrea, *Contemporary Sources for the Fourth Crusade*, rev. ed. (Leiden, 2000), 33–34.

27. Geoffrey of Villehardouin, *La Conquête de Constantinople*, vol. 1 (Paris, 1961), chaps. 19–23.

28. The arrangements and the size of the shortfall are described by Villehardouin, *La Conquête*, 1:51, 1:56–61.

29. Robert de Clari xvi–xvii, in C. Hopf, *Chroniques gréco-romanes inédites ou peu connues* (Berlin, 1873), 11–12. See also Villehardouin, *La Conquête*, 1:62–63.

30. Robert de Clari 17, in Hopf, *Chroniques*, 11–12; Villehardouin, *La Conquête*, 1:70–74, 91–99.

31. *Register* 5:121 (122) of Innocent, dated November 16, 1202, in Andrea, *Contemporary Sources*, 35–37.

32. *Register* 6.48 of Innocent, April 21, 1203, in Andrea, *Contemporary Sources*, 51.

33. Choniates, *Hist.* 539–540.

34. Choniates, *Hist.* 541.

35. Villehardouin, *La Conquête*, 1:111–112; Choniates, *Hist.* 541.

36. Villehardouin, *La Conquête*, 1:123.

37. Villehardouin, *La Conquête*, 1:128.

38. Villehardouin, *La Conquête*, 1:146.

39. Villehardouin, *La Conquête*, 1:157.

40. Choniates, *Hist.* 543.

41. Choniates, *Hist.* 546–547.

42. Choniates, *Hist.* 550; cf. Villehardouin, *La Conquête*, 1:182.

Chapter 46. The Death of the Roman State

1. Choniates, *Hist.* 550; cf. Villehardouin, *La Conquête*, 1:189.

2. Choniates, *Hist.* 552.

3. Choniates, *Hist.* 552.

4. Choniates, *Hist.* 555.

5. Choniates, *Hist.* 556.

6. Choniates, *Hist.* 560.

7. Choniates, *Hist.* 558–559.

8. Villehardouin, *La Conquête*, 2:217–220 (quotation at 220).

9. Choniates, *Hist.* 561.

10. Choniates, *Hist.* 561–562.

11. Choniates, *Hist.* 562.

12. Choniates, *Hist.* 563.

13. Choniates, *Hist.* 563–564; Villehardouin, *La Conquête*, 2:222.

14. Villehardouin, *La Conquête*, 2:223.

15. He died of strangulation after surviving at least two attempts to poison him (Choniates, *Hist.* 564; Villehardouin, *La Conquête*, 2:223).

16. Choniates, *Hist.* 564.

17. Villehardouin, *La Conquête*, 2:224–225.

18. On the beams, see Choniates, *Hist.* 566.

19. Choniates, *Hist.* 567; Villehardouin, *La Conquête*, 2:226–228. On the banner and icon, see Villehardouin, *La Conquête*, 2:228.

20. Choniates, *Hist.* 570.

21. Choniates, *Hist.* 572.

22. Choniates, *Hist.* 586.

23. Robert of Clari, *La Conquête de Constantinople*, 81–82; D. M. Perry, *Sacred Plunder: Venice and the Aftermath of the Fourth Crusade* (University Park, PA, 2015); A. Andrea and P. Rachlin, "Holy War, Holy Relics, Holy Theft," *Historical Reflections* 18 (1992): 147–175.

24. Choniates, *Hist.* 595.

25. Choniates, *Hist.* 598.

26. Villehardouin, *La Conquête*, 2:270–271.

27. Villehardouin, *La Conquête*, 2:306–308.

28. Villhardouin, *La Conquête*, 309.

29. Choniates, *Hist.* 572.

30. Choniates, *Hist.* 603–604.

31. Choniates, *Hist.* 626.

32. On Chonai, see H. Magoulias, in *O City of Byzantium: Annals of Niketas Choniatēs* (Detroit, 1984), xi.

33. Michael Choniates, *Ep.* 44, 70.24–25.

34. For Nicetas Choniates's career, see Magoulias, *O City*, ix–xvi.

35. Michael Choniates, *Monodia* 350.4–9.

36. Michael Choniates, *Monodia* 350.22–24.

37. Choniates, *Hist.* 587.

38. Choniates, *Hist.* 587–589.

39. Choniates, *Hist.* 587–594.

40. Choniates, *Hist.* 594.

41. Choniates, *Hist.* 645.

Conclusion

1. Constantine VII Porphyrogenitus, *DAI* 13.61–65, 13.105–186.

2. N. Machiavelli, *Discorsi sopra la prima deca di Tito Livio*, "Proemio," in *Il principe e Discorsi sopra la prima deca di Tito Livio* (Milan, 1977), 125.

3. Merobaudes, *Panegyric* 1 fr. Ia 9–14.

4. E.g., T. Carlyle, *On Heroes, Hero-Worship, and the Heroic in History* (London, 1841).

INDEX

Katharine Calandra

Edward J. Watts is Distinguished Professor of History at the University of California, San Diego, where he holds the Alkiviadis Vassiliadis Chair in Byzantine Greek History and serves as codirector of the Center for Hellenic Studies. He is the author or editor of several prize-winning books, including *Mortal Republic*, and lives in Carlsbad, California.